Managing Country Risk i

Michel Henry Bouchet · Charles A. Fishkin
Amaury Goguel

Managing Country Risk in an Age of Globalization

A Practical Guide to Overcoming Challenges in a Complex World

Foreword by Tanya S. Beder
Afterword by Florencio de Silanes

palgrave
macmillan

Michel Henry Bouchet
Skema Business School
Paris-Sophia Antipolis-Suzhou-Raleigh, France

Amaury Goguel
Skema Business School
Paris-Sophia Antipolis-Suzhou-Raleigh, France

Charles A. Fishkin
Chappaqua, NY, USA

ISBN 978-3-319-89751-6 ISBN 978-3-319-89752-3 (eBook)
https://doi.org/10.1007/978-3-319-89752-3

Library of Congress Control Number: 2018939727

Cover illustration: Globe: © Delwar Hossain Missile: © Jackson Davis Compass: © Creaticca Creative Agency

Printed on acid-free paper

This Palgrave Macmillan imprint is published by the registered company Springer International Publishing AG, part of Springer Nature
The registered company address is: Gewerbestrasse 11, 6330 Cham, Switzerland

Foreword by Tanya S. Beder

Country Risk. You can't ignore it and you can't live without it. The good news, however, is whether you are a novice student or a seasoned executive, this book will help you analyze and manage it.

Simply stated, Country Risk has two broad elements associated with conducting business in today's global world: first, what can go wrong; and second, what can go well as a consequence of thoughtful assessment and management. Country Risk can impact you whether you yourself conduct business across borders or not. While you may operate primarily at home, your suppliers or competitors may not. Consequently, Country Risk matters irrespective of whether you are an international company, an international investor or creditor, a domestic company, a government, a university, a private economic participant, or if you play a multitude of other roles.

Country Risk does not discriminate. It affects you whether you are a multinational behemoth or a small firm working with a foreign supplier, competing with a foreign company, or hoping to expand activities abroad. It even affects you as an individual when you travel or if you have your own Airbnb.

As the authors observe, "in 2017, the total volume of financial assets reached four times the world GDP, that is, financial globalization is larger than global real economic wealth and well beyond the policy and regulatory reach of nation-states." In addition, the outcome of market alliances (the European Community, the North American Free Trade Zone, Asian, or other alliances) may be changing and place in question the definition of "home" market for country risk analysts. The timeliness of this book is without question—more than ever, you need to analyze, monitor, manage, and understand Country Risk.

My career, like those of the authors, spans the risk and return challenges of the emerging market crisis, the Mexican peso crisis, the Russian oil crisis, the Asian currency crisis, the (many) Argentine crises, the Global Financial Crisis, the European sovereign debt crisis, the Arab Spring crisis, the Brexit crisis, and numerous others. More crises—and lesser country risk challenges—preceded these and are yet to come. You will benefit from the history, wisdom, and insights set out by the authors. Examples abound of those who paid insufficient attention to Country Risk before, during, and after these crises. You will gain perspective from the many lessons learned and exemplified in this book. My hope for you is that this book will help you think about how to avoid the next mistake in the management of Country Risk.

Revising country risk measurement and management will be a substantial focus of the financial and fintech communities over the next decade. During the past four decades, we've experienced "once in 100-year" events far too often, exposing serious flaws in current techniques for identifying and managing risks. Further, the risk that a model's value may be different than that ultimately obtained in the market reared its head globally and without prejudice as to continent or type of firm, costing trillions during the Global Financial Crisis. Further, huge losses were sustained by those who assumed that engaging in multiple activities in multiple geographic markets would provide so-called natural diversification. Different financial markets and different types of financial services were found to be much more interconnected during times of stress than many risk measurement systems predicted.

This book adds focus to key dimensions of Country Risk such as financial risk, macroeconomic risk, sociopolitical risk, socio-economic risk, geopolitical risk, herding risk, spillover risk, and crisis contamination risk, among others. You will gain from the authors' acumen and experience regarding how quickly—and dramatically—business conditions can deteriorate in any country and spread. From country risk assessment during calm times to abrupt post-crisis downgrades and unexpected volatility, this book gives you, the reader, an up-to-date primer that covers common techniques.

And, for those in the fintech space—which is poised to advance the country risk field—this book sets out key dimensions and mitigation approaches that should be useful as we advance the analysis of Country Risk with important approaches such as big data analytics, machine learning, artificial intelligence, and others. This is sure to be an exciting area for new advances in country risk assessment, analysis, and management as the marketplace continues to expand technology-driven trading, investing, lending, and payment systems.

More than ever before, Country Risk has more complexity to analyze, estimate, and manage. You need to understand not only the current state of play, but also how this might change suddenly. And, while country risk specialists historically focused on emerging and frontier countries, this is no longer the case. Today, country risk specialists also focus on the most established countries.

This book—which sets out key data sources and methodologies for evaluating country risk, and shares a multitude of insightful stories and examples—could not be better timed. Whether you are new to Country Risk or a veteran in the topic, you will find this book a helpful resource. Enjoy!

Jackson Hole, Wyoming, USA

Tanya S. Beder
CEO, SBCC Group Inc.

Tanya S. Beder is Chairman and CEO of SBCC Group where she heads the global strategy, fintech, and asset management practices. She teaches the popular graduate course at Stanford University entitled "The Future of Finance," which focuses on the remarkable transformation of global finance since the Great Recession. She evaluates and identifies who is likely to thrive—and not survive—in the new global environment. Euromoney named Ms. Beder one of the top fifty women in finance around the world and The Hedgefund Journal named her one of the fifty leading women in hedge funds. Previously, Ms. Beder held senior positions as CEO of Tribeca Global Management LLC, a $3 billion multi-strategy fund with trading operations in New York, London, and Singapore and Managing Director of Caxton Associates LLC, a $10 billion asset management firm headquartered in New York.

Contents

List of Figures

List of Tables

Managing Country Risk in an Age of Globalization: Introduction

Over the last two decades, and remarkably since the Global Financial Crisis, there has been a spectacular increase in Country Risk in its multifaceted forms, that is, in trade, finance, social, and geopolitical dimensions. Today, Country Risk is everywhere, including at unexpected times and in places people do not expect it. No successful cross-border strategy can ignore Country Risk, and no lucrative domestic investment is possible without assessing the full range of risks stemming from a country's socio-economic, financial, and political environment—elements over which private agents have no bearing. The main objectives of country risk assessment can thus be summed up as ignoring the impossible while scrutinizing the possible in order to anticipate the inevitable.

More than ten years after the Global Financial Crisis, country risk analysts face an asymmetrical landscape. On one side, the global economy has recovered thanks to the actions of central banks and governments that have injected large amounts of liquidity fuelling debt-driven economic growth in developed countries. The jumpstart for this engine of growth has been a combination of ultra-low rates of interest and buoyant capital flows to emerging market countries in search of higher yield. On the other side, three large risks are looming. The first is simply the byproduct of the recovery's success—that is, the twin risks of inflation and private debt default that are often given insufficient attention by government officials and international agencies. The second stems from the very unequal distribution of the benefits of economic growth in both developed and developing countries. In contrast to what appeared as a broad societal preference for inclusive development and greater economic equality during the 1970s, wealth gaps have become larger both between and within countries, and this has created the potential for significant instability that could result from rising interest rates or from the perverse dialectics of political turmoil and repression. The third threat comes from geopolitical volatility whose spillover effects are accelerated and widened by globalization. The convergent signs of the US administration's retreat from multilateralism pave the way for the fragmentation of the post-World War II architecture of international relations and for a power vacuum that China, and to a lesser extent, Russia, appear ready to fill. The rising threats of trade protectionism make the world economy less safe and less conducive to positive sum games.

Faced with this complex environment, where self-congratulation for the resumption of growth would be sheer myopia, risk managers must decide which forces will stabilize or seriously damage countries' socio-economic systems over the next ten or twenty years (which is the horizon for many investors and creditors). At the same time, country risk assessment remains a formidable challenge for at least six reasons.

First, the globalization of the market economy and the mounting risk of crisis contamination have added a new dimension of complexity to country risk management. Globalization increases uncertainty through the integration of multiple economic and financial systems that breed volatility contagion. An exchange rate devaluation or a political crisis can quickly ignite a dangerous spillover process at regional and even global levels. Consequently, risk managers cannot assume that they have fully grasped the entire dimension of a country's multifaceted risks when dealing with only economic, financial, and sociopolitical variables. The globalized market system has added the spillover effects of regional crisis contamination to the equation, not to mention global and systemic risks such as global warming and terrorist threats. Demographic growth rates in Asia and Africa and fast-rising rates of urbanization certainly mean expanding market prospects for infrastructures and consumption, but these prospects also carry risks of increased social tensions.

Second, the very nature of Country Risk has changed. For too long, the definition of country risk analysis has been restricted to the assessment of a foreign entity's ability and willingness to meet its external obligations in full and on time. This narrow definition includes only foreign economic agents while excluding a wide range of risks such as advisory services, contractual obligations regarding suppliers, and real estate assets, as well as reputational, legal and regulatory, and cyber risks. We note in particular the complexity of managing cyber risks as this challenge evolves rapidly to take a global dimension.

Third, foreign investors and creditors do not hold the monopoly on Country Risk. Domestic residents of a risky country—including company managers, investors, and households—might feel "foreign" to their own government's arbitrary decisions that generate inflation, inconsistent growth cycles, and political instability. The irony is that managers whose strategy is to reduce the uncertainty of cross-border investment by refocusing on local markets face the turbulences of domestic Country Risk. Clearly, there is a new element of Country Risk for US corporations and American residents related to the Trump presidency. There are, moreover, other serious sources of Country Risk that are generated by volatile political leaders such as Erdogan, Duterte, Putin, Denis Sassou, Gnassingbé, Berdymoukhamedov, or Kim Jong-un. This political component has implications for those who live under their repressive rules, as well as for those living beyond their borders.

Fourth, the traditional divide between developed/emerging countries is at best obsolete, and at worst, a source of error in country risk assessment. Developing countries with weak sociopolitical institutions have lost the monopoly of political volatility. Country Risk is no longer rooted in the so-called Third World. Developed countries with mature and sophisticated legal, regulatory, and institutional frameworks are also subject to sociopolitical turbulence. This is caused by a combination of factors—limitations in the impact of domestic monetary policies, wealth gaps, large debt burdens, tax evasion, and more pervasively, a gradual dissatisfaction with established political leaders, including in deeply rooted democratic systems.

The fifth new dimension has to do with technological change and its impact on Country Risk. The fast emergence of Big Data technologies has already started transforming the world of financial risk management and this change also has an impact, albeit more indirect, on the field of country risk management. Big Data provides country risk managers with high-volume, high-velocity, and high-accuracy information inputs in the process of defining, assessing, and managing risks. The accessibility and accuracy of Big Data enhance transparency, hence reducing uncertainty and risk. In the field of Country Risk, where qualitative assessment is as important as quantitative measures, Big Data management imposes specific constraints to check the accuracy and quality of large stores of country economic and financial data whose format must be as standardized as possible. Country risk scenarios can be simulated in far greater detail by using the new technologies' computational power. The consequences of worsening liquidity and solvency indicators can be calculated with much better accuracy than before, including by integrating the situation of neighbor countries. The spillover of a national and regional crisis can also be modelized with more accuracy. Demographic data, purchasing power, financial ratios, and a number of macroeconomic data can be combined across time and across countries to provide a reliable picture of the scope of a market in a number of countries. However, the prerequisite for Big Data management, obviously, is the availability of the inputs. Practically, Big Data today is mainly the world of the OECD developed countries, though emerging market countries such as China and India devote a rising share of GDP in R&D.

The scope of information management technologies is not restricted to assessing financial and economic risks. In the field of political risk and foreign intelligence information, government agencies have made substantial efforts in managing large amounts of personal and social data, particularly to stem the risk of terrorism. Shortly after 9/11, the US Congress passed the USA Patriot Act which improved information sharing among federal agencies and expanded the FBI's authority to search phone numbers, emails, and financial records. Since 2008, the US government has been using Section 702 of the Foreign Intelligence Surveillance Act (FISA) to authorize the intelligence community to target the communications of non-US persons located outside the United States for foreign intelligence purposes while using vast amounts of data directly from the servers of major Internet companies like Microsoft, Google, and Facebook through the legal authority of the PRISM surveillance program. Private economic and political intelligence companies, though with much more reduced scope than national agencies, developed increasingly sophisticated technologies to gather and manage large volumes of data to assess and predict risk.

Sixth and last, country risk managers can no longer rely on traditional yardsticks of risk such as ratings and rankings. The quantitative assessment of Country Risk—including ratings and rankings—are at best partial tools and at worst recipes for a simplistic outlook. More nuanced approaches are now needed to address the fuzzier issues of volatility, spillover, herd instinct, and the complexity of the global financial system.

As a result of these new dimensions of Country Risk in the Age of Globalization, country risk analysis and forecasting remain a formidable challenge. Without a reliable compass and considering the limitations of quantitative risk ratings, country risk managers must be more agile than ever. Prudence, open-mindedness, and a good dose of modesty are essential. A consistent theme we stress throughout this book is that gathering information and enhancing the quality of economic intelligence are two key tools for mitigating uncertainty and improving risk management. Uncertainty stands at the heart of risk—this uncertainty is rooted in information deficits regarding the present and the future in a world that keeps changing in novel and sometimes unexpected ways.

We believe there is a compelling need for a concise and current overview of Country Risk that explores its relevance, changing dynamics, and practical implications. This is the reason we have written this book. We approach Country Risk from a practical, operational, and conceptual perspective. A proper understanding and careful assessment of Country Risk can have favorable outcomes. Organizations that understand the uncertainties they incur—including the various dimensions of Country Risk—are better managed, experience fewer surprises, and provide more desirable working environments for their people. Rather than fearing uncertainty, they embrace it. Such organizations have confidence in their strategies and their abilities to carry them out. Today more than ever, astute country risk management has become a competitive asset.

The book will tackle the various dimensions of the Country Risk in the following manner. Chapter 1 will introduce various crucial notions, such as "uncertainty"—an overarching term that refers to any condition whose particular outcome is not known; this is in comparison to "risk"—a special case of uncertainty where we know both the set of potential outcomes and the probabilities of such outcomes. Chapter 2 defines Country Risk and its multifaceted dimensions. It is a set of interdependent economic, financial, and sociopolitical factors, specific to a particular country in the global economy, which can negatively affect both domestic and foreign economic agents regarding savings, investment, and credit transactions. Country Risk, however, is more than just a source of loss and disarray. Risk can have outcomes which may be either positive or negative. Chapter 3 presents a thorough review of the scholarly community's literature regarding Country Risk. It shows that there is still little consensus among academics and practitioners regarding the definition of the term or its main components. Chapter 4 is a reminder that country risk analysis is as good as the quality of the information it is based on. Accurate information is the key behind timely decision-making, resulting in either good assessment or excess exposure with related losses. This chapter describes the main sources of information coming from official organizations. Chapter 5 explores the private sources of information and data coming from private agencies, such as rating agencies, financial organizations, and think tanks. Chapter 6 describes another important source that is provided by private organizations in the form of rating agencies, banks, investment funds, consulting firms, research services, and other establishments that play an important role in contributing to the understanding of Country Risk. Chapter 6 analyzes the macro-channels of crisis contamination, including the monetary policy of central banks, the exchange rate relationships between surplus and deficit countries, and role of the US Dollar as reserve currency versus the Yuan or the Euro. Chapter 7 explores the dependency links and contamination channels of the globalized economy. The focus is on integrated areas with pegged exchange rates or an irreversibly fixed exchange rate (single currency area) such as the Eurozone. It also examines why pegged exchange rates introduce new sources of vulnerability. Chapter 8 will remind the reader that external debt crises are rooted in balance of payments problems. Protracted imbalances between inflows and outflows translate sooner or later in, first, liquidity problems, and thereafter, in solvency tensions. This is because the balance of payments is the financial link between a country and the rest of the world. Chapter 9 defines the concept of political risk as well as its main consequences depending on the risk exposure of both foreign and domestic economic agents. Political risk involves the unexpected unfavorable consequences of the arbitrary exercise of power by a government and its domestic and foreign ramifications, as well as by non-governmental actors. Chapter 10 addresses the root causes of sociopolitical instability by exploring the various conditions behind inclusive economic growth and sustainable development—that is, the smooth transition of societies to meet the centrifugal forces generated by the globalization of the market economy and large and growing wealth gaps. This chapter analyzes the close correlation between corruption and unfavorable business conditions, as well as between corruption and income inequality that pave the way to social instability and political violence. Chapter 11 addresses the threat of secular stagnation in developed countries where slower growth reinforces the consequences of rising debt leverage. It discusses to what extent this threat affects country risk assessment. It discusses the challenge of OECD's central banks to maintain low-interest rates and boost long-term growth. And it also addresses the specific case of the Eurozone and the macroeconomic constraints of the Maastricht. Chapter 12 concludes that a debt crisis will emerge when a country faces constraints in meeting its external financing requirements and when the debt structure becomes vulnerable to external shocks, including higher rates of interest, shorter maturities, and shrinking access to capital markets. The astute risk analyst should closely watch the range of liquidity and solvency ratios as well as the spillover effects of regional developments, such as weaker trade markets, fluctuating commodity prices, foreign exchange and interest rate volatility, and rating agencies downgrading. Chapter 13 deals with the lack of reliability of most market price signals for Country Risk. It presents a number of main signals that help anticipate upcoming risk volatility and could be used independently or simultaneously. Chapter 14 deals with the useful insights which can be gained from the analysis of a country's capital flight. While it may sound appealing to watch multiple potential warning signs, these indicators, including bond yields, spreads, stock market indices, and credit-default swaps, do not consistently serve as reliable early warning signals. Country risk managers, therefore, have no better choice but to put themselves in the shoes of domestic residents of foreign countries. Finally, Chapter 15 concludes with a presentation of a number of country risk mitigation techniques. The reader will also find a Glossary of country risk concepts to help clarify various issues that are discussed in the book or elsewhere.

Country Risk Management in the Age of Globalization is a modest attempt by three country risk practitioners and analysts to share their experience, their convictions, and their doubts. They hope that this book will illuminate the fascinating and changing nature of Country Risk and that it will be useful, provocative, and enjoyable.

1

Assessing Risk in a Global Economy

1.1 Introduction

So here we are at the outset of our inquiry into Country Risk. We will explore a wide range of topics that are complicated, nuanced, and the subject of intense debate. This includes trade, treaties, political regime change, economic policy, and much more. Before we can delve into these topics, we initially need to ask two essential questions: "What is Risk?" and "What is Risk Management?"

1.2 What Is Risk?

1.2.1 A Multifaceted Concept

"Risk" is a multifaceted concept. Risk is about the future—what may occur this afternoon, tomorrow, next year, or further out in time. It is about outcomes that are unknown. It is a consequence of every meaningful action undertaken by an organization. It occurs in strategy setting, new product creation, employee hiring, model design, and so much more. Risk can create substantial financial gain or loss. It can also enhance or damage an organization's reputation.

The term "risk" is often used synonymously with the term "uncertainty," although it has no universal definition. It has been used in different ways for different purposes.

M. H. Bouchet et al., *Managing Country Risk in an Age of Globalization*,
https://doi.org/10.1007/978-3-319-89752-3_1

The term has assumed multiple meanings in "everyday" conversation.

- "I will take that risk."
- "This is a high risk strategy."
- "There are risks in proceeding."
- "I want to avoid this risk."
- "We may incur risk here."
- "We don't want any risk."
- "We run the risk of something we did not anticipate."
- "The program is at risk."
- "We can manage the risk."

We use this term, moreover, across the spectrum of business, government, and the non-profit sector—yet not always in a consistent manner. We work in departments of risk management staffed by risk analysts and led by chief risk officers. We engage in risk assessments, build risk models, and review risk statistics. We serve on risk committees, attend risk conferences, and read risk journals. We communicate with specialized terminology, referring to specific types of risk as—among others—credit risk, market risk, and operational risk. Yet, across this varied range of activity, we use multiple definitions, follow different policies, and engage in diverse practices relating to risk and risk management. We also encounter differences—some times significant—among organizations and working groups that have sought to promote common standards for risk management. (See Box 1.1, Definitions of Risk.)

So how can we improve our understanding risk and risk management? How can we have more constructive discussions about these essential concepts? How, ultimately, can we make better decisions about the future?

1.2.2 Risk, Uncertainty, and Ambiguity

A useful way to begin is to understand the nature and degree of uncertainty we confront in any particular decision. We need to ask how confident we are about the basis for our decisions. We further need to ask how much we know about the probabilities for outcomes associated with our choices. To answer these questions, we need additional definitions and a more specific meaning for the word risk itself. At the outset, three new definitions are important: Uncertainty, Risk, and Ambiguity.[1]

[1]Thanks to Richard Peter of the Department of Finance at the University of Iowa for his guidance on these concepts and for helping us distill key themes from a large body of academic literature on these topics.

They have their origins in the ideas of two influential economists (among others): John Maynard Keynes (1883–1946), the founder of modern macroeconomics,[2] and Frank Knight (1885–1972), a leader of the Chicago School of Economics at the University of Chicago. (See Box 1.2, Frank Knight's Legacy: Risk, Uncertainty, and Ambiguity.) These definitions are not, of course, the only valid ones for these concepts, but they serve as a useful starting point for our inquiry into the nature of Country Risk.[3]

For our purposes then, we define these terms as follows.

- "Uncertainty" is an overarching term that refers to any condition where the particular outcome is not known (i.e., the *set* of potential outcomes may or may not be known). As we have observed, this term is often used synonymously with the term risk in "everyday" discourse, but we can refine our terminology if we think of risk as a subset of uncertainty.
- "Risk" is a special case of uncertainty where we know both the *set* of potential outcomes and the probability of such outcomes. This has also been referred to as "measurable risk" or "Knightian" risk (in reference to Frank Knight's distinction between risk and uncertainty). Another complementary definition is "a situation in which there are well defined, unique and generally accepted objective probabilities" (Kelsey and Quiggin 1992, 134–135). (An often-used example of measurable risk is the "toss" of an evenly balanced coin. For each individual toss, there are only two unique outcomes, and for each such outcome there is a 50% probability that the coin will land on one side or the other side. One significant aspect of this definition of risk is the potential to insure against loses or negative outcomes. Familiar examples include individual insurance policies to cover health care, automobiles, homes, or a person's life. In such cases, insurance providers take into account extensive historical experience about potential outcomes, including average behaviors and measurable deviations from the average.)
- "Ambiguity" is a special case of uncertainty where we know the *set* of potential outcomes but do not know the probability of such outcomes.[4] A complementary definition is "uncertainty about probability, created by

[2]For one expression of Keynes' thinking on this topic, see his famous essay of 1937 in which he refers to situations for which "there is no scientific basis on which to form any calculable probability whatever. We simply do not know" (Keynes 1937, 214). See also Dequech (2000).

[3]For a thoughtful discussion of different conceptions of uncertainty, see Dequech (2011).

[4]The term ambiguity in connection with uncertainty was first introduced by Daniel Ellsberg in his now famous paper (Ellsberg 1961).

missing information that is relevant and could be known" (Camerer and Weber 1992, 330).

Another subset of uncertainty refers to the case where we do not even know the nature and extent of the possible outcomes. This is sometimes called Knightian uncertainty in reference to Frank Knight's framework. Another name for this, formulated by the economist David Dequech, is "fundamental uncertainty." This form of uncertainty can arise from a complex interplay of factors, including innovation and technological change as well as changes in cultural, social, and political conditions. Dequech writes: "The future cannot be anticipated by a fully reliable probabilistic estimate because *the future is yet to be created.*" He further observes: "… some relevant information *cannot be known, even in principle,* at the time of making important decisions" (Dequech 2000, 48).

Fundamental uncertainty also coexists with a related concept known as "procedural uncertainty." This form of uncertainty arises out of the computational and cognitive capabilities of individuals faced with decisions about the future. Procedural uncertainty comes in degrees and needs to be understood in relation to the complexity of a situation being assessed. Accordingly, it can result if either (i) there are limitations in computational or cognitive abilities of individuals in assessing their choices or (ii) a situation may be sufficiently complicated that it cannot be fully assessed even with the most robust computational and cognitive capabilities[5] (Dequech 2011, 627–629) (Fig. 1.1).

Exhibit 1.1 Types of Uncertainty

- Risk: Set of Outcomes Known; Probabilities Known (Insurable)
- Ambiguity: Set of Outcomes Known; Probabilities Not Known
- Fundamental Uncertainty ("Knightian"): Set of Outcomes Not Fully Known

These and other related definitions are also becoming a part of the vocabulary of risk practitioners. One such example is an informal discussion of risk and uncertainty by Edward Fishwick, the co-head of Risk and Quantitative Analysis at BlackRock, the global asset manager. Interviewed in 2013 about the Global Financial Crisis of 2008, he said: "There are just things we don't

[5]Thanks to David Dequech for his correspondence on these themes.

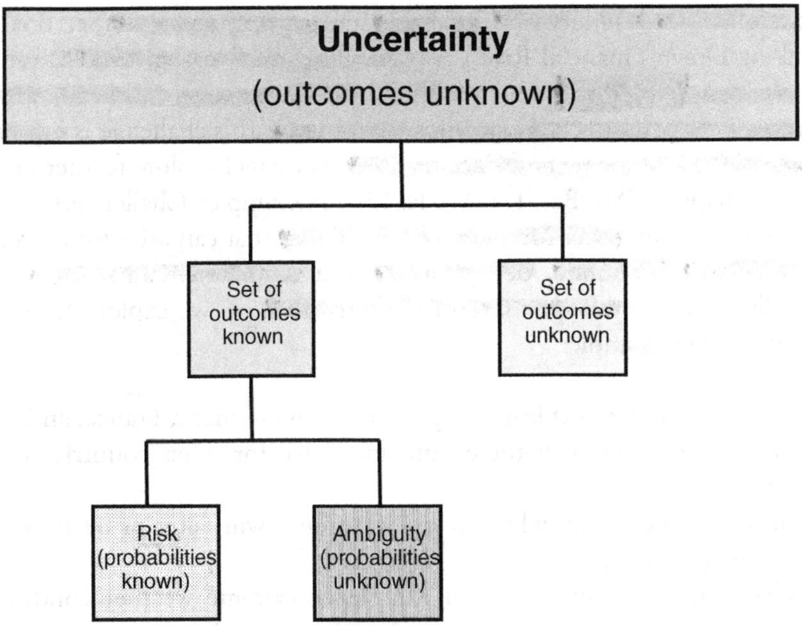

Fig. 1.1 Risk, uncertainty, and ambiguity: the relationship

know about. So sometimes I think of risk management as managing the things you understand and can quantify. Then uncertainty is the stuff you just don't know" (Fishwick 2013).

1.2.3 A Spectrum of Diverse Issues

Another way to think about uncertainty is to classify it into common types that we observe. As we look out across different countries and regions, there are numerous examples, especially in the financial and commodity markets. This is usually referred to as "market risk."

- Over the course of the next year, what will be the short-term interest rate in the United States, Canada, and Australia?
- In a month, what will be the rate at which a United States Dollar can be exchanged for a Euro?
- In six months, what will be price of a barrel of oil from Saudi Arabia?

In addition to market risk, we often find other types of uncertainty—that is, if we look carefully enough. These are commonly described as credit risk, operational risk, liquidity risk, legal risk, and reputational risk. (See Box 1.3, Breaking Down Financial Risk.) A particularly challenging subset of operational risk is model risk, which includes the design, use, and limitations of quantitative models to make or inform decisions. This challenge is especially relevant in the assessment of Country Risk, as we will explore further in subsequent chapters. (See Box 1.4, Model Risk: A Complex Challenge.)

There are many other instances of uncertainty that can arise from a country's political, economic, demographic, and cultural circumstances. They help illustrate the varied nature of Country Risk, as we explore further in Chapter 2. For example:

- Who will win the next leadership elections in Germany, France, and Italy? What implications will these outcomes have for other countries in the Euro zone?
- During the next year, which political regimes will falter or be subject to an attempted coup?
- What countries and cities will experience extreme weather conditions? What will be the impact on other countries and regions?
- Are there particular countries where the age of the population is changing faster than has been initially expected? If so, what are the consequences?
- What next technological innovation will fundamentally transform the way we work and live? In what country or countries will such innovation first emerge?

Box 1.1 Definitions of Risk

It is useful to examine how the term "risk" has been used overtime by risk managers, risks advisors, regulators, and other practitioners. In some cases, these definitions limit the scope of risk to negative outcomes. In other cases, risk is also a source of opportunity.

- International Organization for Standardization (ISO): Risk is "the effect of uncertainty on objectives" (International Organization for Standardization 2009).
- Committee of Sponsoring Organizations of the Treadway Commission (COSO):
  - Risk is "the possibility that events will occur and affect the achievement of strategy and business objectives."
  - Uncertainty is "the state of not knowing how potential events may or may not manifest" (Committee of Sponsoring Organizations of the Treadway Commission 2017).
- Government of Australia: Risk is "the effect of uncertainty on objectives" where "an effect is a deviation from the expected, positive or negative" (Australian Government 2014). An enterprise framework developed for the

US federal government uses a similar definition. See United States Chief Financial Officers Council and the Performance Improvement Council (2016).

- World Economic Forum: "A global risk is an uncertain event or condition that, if it occurs, can cause negative impact for several countries or industries within the next ten years" (World Economic Forum 2017).
- United States Department of Commerce, National Institute of Standards and Technology (NIST):
  - Risk is a "measure of the extent to which an entity is threatened by a potential circumstance or event, and typically a function of: (i) the adverse impacts that would arise if the circumstances or event occurs; and (ii) the likelihood of occurrence" (National Institute of Standards and Technology 2014).
  - Risk Management is the "process of identifying, assessing, and responding to risk."
- Financial Reporting Council (United Kingdom): "Principal Risk is a risk or combination of risks that can seriously affect the performance, future prospects or reputation of the entity. These should include those risks that would threaten its business model, future performance, solvency or liquidity" (Financial Reporting Council 2014).

Box 1.2 Frank Knight's Legacy: Risk, Uncertainty, and Ambiguity

Our understanding of risk and uncertainty continues to be influenced by the thinking of Frank H. Knight (1885–1972), a founding member of the Chicago School of Economics at the University of Chicago.

In 1921, Knight published *Risk, Uncertainty and Profit* (Knight 1921). He distinguished between risk and uncertainty, where risk was limited to measurable or known probabilities and uncertainty referred to a wide range of outcomes that could not be known in advance and accordingly not effectively measured. This distinction has important implications for the practice of risk management. It reminds us that there are different degrees of risk and uncertainty that should be managed in different ways. It further reminds us that even if we can measure some risks effectively, we must acknowledge the potential for surprises. We learned this from the Global Financial Crisis of 2008.

In addition to Knight's influence as a theorist, he played an influential role as a teacher of economics, serving on the faculty of the University of Chicago from 1927 to 1957. He was the Ph.D. thesis adviser to George Stigler, who won the Nobel Prize in Economics in 1982. Knight was also an influential mentor to Paul Samuelson during Samuelson's undergraduate years at the University of Chicago. Samuelson won the Nobel Prize in Economics in 1970, the first American to do so.

Knight was born on a farm in Illinois and obtained his undergraduate degree from the University of Tennessee. He received his Ph.D. from Cornell University in 1916. He was co-editor of the *Journal of Political Economy* (1929–1946), president of the American Economic Association (1950), and recipient of the prestigious Francis A. Walker Medal from the American Economic Association (1957). See Backhouse (2017), Dewey (1990), and Stigler (1973, 1985).

1.2.4 A Source of Loss and Gain

It is also necessary to think of uncertainty as having the potential to promote both favorable and unfavorable outcomes. We often associate the term uncertainty with the potential for harm or loss, but it also contemplates the potential for opportunity and gain. A useful example of this dual aspect of uncertainty is the development of a new mobile phone. In such an initiative, important questions can arise.

- Will the new features of the device be interesting enough to attract new customers?
- Will such features induce existing customers to replace their phones?
- Will the device appeal to buyers of all ages or will it sell better with certain age groups?
- Will the sales price be high enough to maintain profits and satisfy shareholders?
- Will the price be low enough to compete with other phone providers who may be willing to offer substantial discounts to maintain or grow their market share?

Different companies have assessed these and other instances of uncertainty in different ways. Some have thrived and gained loyal customers; others have failed to innovate or misjudged consumer demand. Compare the different outcomes for Apple, Samsung, Amazon, Ericsson, Motorola, Nokia, and Blackberry.

1.2.5 The Effect on Other Outcomes

Many instances of uncertainty are a consequence of other decisions. Some of these consequences can be anticipated, but others less so. Their impact can be significant. Consider two different examples:

- Although the Internet has increased the ease and speed at which goods and services can now be obtained, it has created huge amounts of personal data managed by governments, businesses, and non-profit organizations. Now there is greater potential that such information—which is quite valuable—may be illegally obtained.
- A country in an economic recession begins a stimulus program to modernize its roads, bridges, tunnels, and railways. As a result, the country's

public deficit rises, as does demand for construction labor and materials. Inflation also rises, as do long term interest rates. Bond prices fall while the profitability of the banking sector rises as a result of additional revenue from loans.

It is important, therefore, to contemplate the varied consequences that can result from a course of action.

1.2.6 A Function of Perspective

An important question about uncertainty is to ask "to whom?" The answer may vary depending on the type of uncertainty and the roles of the affected individuals or organizations. One person's gain may be another person's loss. Moreover, both persons may gain or lose at the same time, but in different degrees.

Suppose, for example, that interest rates increase following a period of sustained low levels. Higher rates benefit lenders who have extended loans with floating rates. Borrowers with excess cash can earn higher returns on their savings. In contrast, higher rates increase the cost of owning homes purchased with floating rate loans. Higher rates also reduce the value of bond portfolios and may also stimulate movement of assets from equity markets into bond markets. Furthermore, a loss by one entity can give rise to systemic effects that extend to numerous other individuals, organizations, and countries (as we observed during the Global Financial Crisis of 2008).

1.2.7 Inherent Versus Residual Risk

Another dimension of uncertainty is how well we can mitigate its unwanted effects. In this regard, risk managers use the terms "inherent risk" and "residual risk." Inherent risks are those fundamental exposures that are a consequence of an organization's mission. They are "part of doing business." Airlines, for example, are exposed to the fluctuations in the price of jet fuel that can reduce their profits. Residual risk, in contrast, is the level or extent of exposure that remains after an organization introduces controls or other steps to mitigate the inherent risk to a lower desired level. An airline may not want the exposure to potential increases in jet fuel prices, so it takes steps to reduce or "hedge" this inherent risk. It can do so by entering into certain derivatives transactions that require another party to make payments to the airline if fuel prices rise above a specified level. This reduces the inherent risk to a lower level, resulting in a lower residual risk. The inherent risk may be sizable but the residual risk may be tolerable.

> **Exhibit 1.2 Inherent Risk Versus Residual Risk**
>
> - Assess the Inherent Risk
> - Evaluate the effectiveness of existing controls or mitigation efforts
> - Determine the resulting Residual Risk
> - Evaluate the Residual Risk against the Risk Appetite
>
> Residual Risk = Inherent Risk offset by Controls or Mitigation

1.2.8 Risk Appetite

Yet another important concept related to uncertainty is referred to as risk appetite. This is the amount and type of exposure to uncertainty that an organization can effectively tolerate or believes it can manage effectively. Risk appetite may vary across an organization. Some organizations are willing to assume a relatively high level of exposure to new ventures but a low level of exposure in existing mature businesses. In certain cases, risk appetite can be expressed as an amount or an estimate. In other cases, risk appetite is a qualitative assessment.[6] Risk appetite may be based on the inherent risk or residual risk.

> **Box 1.3 Breaking Down Financial Risk**
>
> Below are examples of common categories of uncertainty that are especially relevant in financial services. These categories are usually referred to as risks.
>
> *Strategic Risk*
>
> Also referred to as business risk, strategic risk is the risk associated with pursuing a specific strategy or plan. It involves numerous choices that organizations must make: to specialize in a few activities or to diversify more broadly; to focus on certain market segments to the exclusion of others; to conduct operations in international markets or to concentrate or to limit activity to their domestic market.

[6] For an example of a qualitative approach to risk appetite in the public sector, see Office of the Comptroller of the Currency (2016).

Market Risk

Market risk is the risk associated with fluctuations in financial or commodity markets. It can involve increases or decreases in, for example, interest rates or equity prices. It can, moreover, involve the price of jet fuel, electricity, copper, or soybeans.

Credit Risk

Credit risk is the risk associated with the creditworthiness of a specific individual, company, industry sector, or region. Banks are obvious examples of organizations that incur credit risk, but other organizations do so as well, including corporations that buy commodities from other suppliers. Credit risk can include relationships with customers, suppliers, venture partners, or other parties.

Operational Risk

Operational risk is a broad term that includes inadequate or failed internal processes, people, systems, and exposure to external events. This includes such diverse issues as cyber attacks, labor strikes, compensation, incentives, governance, and internal controls. It has been a particularly challenging risk for financial services firms. It also includes the design and use of models (as we further explore in Box 1.4, Model Risk).

Liquidity Risk

Liquidity risk includes two major components: first, the ability of organizations to obtain funding and access to the capital markets when needed; second, the ability of organizations to sell or obtain prices for financial and other assets.

Reputational Risk

Reputational risk involves actions or outcomes that affect an organization's reputation. This potential area of exposure arises in all aspects of commerce, government, and elsewhere. It is arguably one of the most challenging issues an organization can encounter since it can arise from any course of action. An organization's reputation can be affected, for example, by sales practices, litigation, fraud, or treatment of employees. (See also Chapter 15, Reputational Risk: A Practitioner's Perspective.)

Regulatory Risk

Regulatory risk is the consequence of failing to comply with laws or regulation as well as the failure of an organization to maintain constructive working relationships with its regulators. Even organizations that are not subject to oversight by a particular regulatory agency are exposed to regulatory risk, including health and safety issues, employment practices, and pension requirements.

Legal Risk

Legal risk includes the ability of organizations to enforce rights under legal contracts, especially in the case of a bankruptcy proceeding. This can be a prominent concern when organizations enter into contracts with organizations in legal jurisdictions other than their own.

Box 1.4 Model Risk: A Complex Challenge

In Box 1.3, we explored different types of risk and uncertainty, including credit, market, and operational risk. A particularly challenging form of operational risk is model risk, which is especially relevant to the assessment of Country Risk.

A useful definition of model risk was set forth in 2011 by the United States Federal Reserve and the United States Comptroller of the Currency. They defined model risk as "the potential for adverse consequences from decisions based on incorrect or misused model outputs and reports" (Board of Governors of the Federal Reserve System and Office of the Comptroller of the Currency 2011).

They defined a model as "a quantitative method, system, or approach that applies statistical, economic, financial or mathematical theories, techniques and assumptions to process input data into quantitative estimates." They observed that a model consists of three components:

- an informational input component, which delivers assumptions and data to the model;
- a processing component, which transforms inputs into estimates; and
- a reporting component, which translates the estimates into useful business information.

They further observed that model risk occurs for two primary reasons. First, a model may have fundamental errors and may produce inaccurate outputs when viewed against the design objective and intended business uses. Second, a model may be used incorrectly or inappropriately.

Model risk can arise in multiple points in the process of designing and implementing a model. There may be flaws in the fundamental reasoning of a model or there may be operational risk in the overall system or process relating to the model, including the inputs and outputs. Such operational risks may include, for example, software bugs, computational errors, reporting errors, fraud, and incorrect data.

In the assessment of Country Risk, quantitative models may be used to estimate or forecast various outcomes, including currency exchange rates, interest rates, or commodity prices. They may also be used to assess performance of an investment fund or the quantification of risk within an investment portfolio.

The operational risks associated with models can be mitigated by rigorous controls, although this is a challenge for organizations to manage. An arguably more complicated challenge involves flaws or limitations in a model's fundamental design. Although any model can be improved, it will never be the "real thing," and it is inevitable that there will be some model risk associated with a model's design.

As has been well illustrated over the history of modern finance, it is essential to evaluate whether any particular model remains valid and plausible amid significant changes within financial markets and the global financial system. Changes over time can affect the usefulness of a model, including technological change, new product innovation, regulatory changes, or the size and growth of any sector of the financial markets.

It is essential to be aware of the potential for model risk. It must be considered in the making of any significant business decisions that use models.

1.3 What Is Risk Management?

1.3.1 A Way of Thinking

Risk management is an intentional effort to adapt to uncertainty in its various forms. Risk management means "looking over the hill and around the corner."[7] It is a way of thinking that, if applied, can inform the actions and responses of individuals, organizations, and countries. It helps provide that the future, while unknown, is not a surprise. Peter Bernstein (1919–2009), the author and portfolio manager, writes: "The essence of risk management lies in maximizing the areas where we have some control over the outcome while minimizing the areas where we have absolutely no control over the outcome and the linkage between effect and cause is hidden from us" (Bernstein 1998, 197).

In the most complete expression of its role, risk management is the capability to anticipate significant themes and issues that can impact the soundness of an organization. It involves an effort to understand potential outcomes that organizations should reasonably expect. It is an ongoing process that organizations use to identify, measure, monitor, and take actions relating to the wide range of issues they confront in carrying out their mandates and missions. (See Box 1.5, The Process of Risk Management and Box 1.6, Risk Management Frameworks.) It enables organizations to make thoughtful choices about priorities. Peter Bernstein observes: "The actions we dare to take, which depend on how free we are to make choices, are what the story of risk is all about" (Bernstein 1998, 8). When risk management is a priority, the results can be impressive. (See Case Study, BlackRock: The World's Largest Asset Manager; a Culture of Risk.)

1.3.2 What Risk Management Requires

Risk Management requires distinct conditions to achieve its aspirations. Among them are the following.

- First, organizations must continuously ask essential questions about their exposure to uncertainty:

[7]This was an expression used by William H. Donaldson when he served as chairman of the United States Securities and Exchange Commission from 2003 to 2005.

- What are our most significant sources of uncertainty?
- How well do we understand them?
- How well can we measure them?
- How well can we manage them?

- Second, they must ask questions that drive their organizations toward action:
  - What do we do next?
  - What have we learned from our progress or our mistakes?
  - What adjustments do we make to improve outcomes for our stakeholders?

  (See also Box 1.7, Asking Essential Questions.)
- Third, organizations must continuously adjust their risk management programs over time. They must enhance their approaches to uncertainty as they introduce new strategies, enter new markets and jurisdictions, develop and sell new products, and respond to new regulatory requirements. They must ask whether their existing risk programs are adequate for the scope and nature of their activity.
- Fourth, organizations must address their most significant issues and challenges. This includes strategy, culture, compensation, hiring, promotions, and governance. This means going beyond the important but conventional aspects of risk management (which include such initiatives as insurance, risk committees, risk assessment, and risk limits for easily identifiable risks).

Box 1.5 The Process of Risk Management

Risk management generally involves various steps. This suggests that risk management is a sequential and linear process. In practice, it usually is otherwise. Yet, to be successful, organizations need to devote meaningful effort to creating, maintaining, and enhancing their risk management programs. Here are among the key steps:

- Define key types of risks and other sources of uncertainty
- Set an appetite for such risk and uncertainty
- Identify specific risks and sources of uncertainty
- Measure risks, where possible
- Compare risk exposures to risk appetite
- Take action on risks and other forms of uncertainty
  - Reduce exposures (if such exposures exceed the risk appetite)
  - Keep exposures as is (if such exposures are deemed acceptable)
  - Increase exposures (if such exposures are below the risk appetite)
- Assess progress (and revisit risk types, risk appetite, and the process itself)

Box 1.6 Risk Management Frameworks

A number of organizations have created frameworks and approaches for risk management that explore the risk management process in further detail.

- International Organization for Standardization ("ISO"): International Standard 31000 [general framework]
- The Committee on Sponsoring Organizations of the Treadway Commission (COSO): COSO Enterprise Risk Management Framework [general framework]
- Australian Government: Commonwealth Risk Management Policy [public sector]
- United States Government acting through the United States Chief Financial Officers Council and the Performance Improvement Council: Playbook: Enterprise Risk Management for the U.S. Federal Government [public sector]
- United States Department of Commerce: Framework for Improving Critical Infrastructure Cybersecurity [cyber issues]
- Foreign Exchange Working Group: the FX Global Code [foreign exchange transactions]. (See Foreign Exchange Working Group (2017) and Chapter 15 herein.)

Box 1.7 Asking Essential Questions

Risk management involves asking essential questions.

Preventing Unwanted Uncertainty:

- Where is an organization vulnerable?
- What could damage an organization's reputation?
- What could cause an organization to sustain significant financial loss?
- What could cause an organization to become sufficiently weak that it would need to merge or be acquired to survive?
- What could cause an organization to fail?

Incurring the "Right" Uncertainty:

- Where are the opportunities that other organizations have not seen?
- What are the practices that can make an organization soar?
- What is the next successful product or service?
- How can an organization develop an approach, product, or process that fundamentally alters the course of daily life?

1.4 Conclusion

We began with two questions: "What is Risk?" and "What is Risk Management?" As may be evident, these are complex questions, indeed, and we have merely framed them rather than answer them. We will seek explore them in greater detail in the chapters that follow. Ultimately, our goal is inspire organizations to take action—to better understand their varied risks and sources of uncertainty and to manage them more effectively. Perhaps a useful way to express the importance of this goal is to pause and reflect on the signage outside the door of an organization, perhaps one that you work for now or would like to work for in the future. What strategy will enable the organization to continue to thrive amid change? What can keep the signage in place? Alternatively, what can cause the doors to be shuttered and the signage removed, as has been the outcome for numerous global financial firms? Well-managed organizations encourage employees at all levels to continuously ask and respond to these questions. Such organizations understand, as well as possible, their desired levels and types of uncertainty. They seek to anticipate the future rather than allowing circumstances to determine it. They are thoughtful and astute managers of change and recognize the responsibility to help maintain their organizations for the next generation of stakeholders.

Case Study

BlackRock: The World's Largest Asset Manager; a Culture of Risk

BlackRock is the largest asset management firm in the world. It is one of a very few global financial institutions that has emerged from the Global Financial Crisis of 2008 with an enhanced reputation and a stronger franchise.

The firm emphasizes a common approach to risk management, operations, and information technology. Its mantra is "One BlackRock." A related mantra is "one system, one database one process." The firm has developed a proprietary risk and portfolio management system called Aladdin. It describes Aladdin as its "central nervous system."

This mindset has arguably played a key role in the firm's growth and its relatively rapid rise as a global leader in asset management, especially "passive" investment strategies using index mutual funds, exchange traded funds (ETFs), and funds which employ a "rules-based" approach to investing.

The firm, which is publicly held, maintains its headquarters in New York City. It also has offices in over thirty countries. It has clients in over 100 countries, which include pension funds, foundations, endowments, insurance companies, and sovereign wealth funds.

As of March 31, 2018, its assets under management ("AUM") were approximately USD 6.317 trillion. Approximately 40% of the total AUM is managed for clients domiciled outside the United States.

As of December 31, 2017, the company had over 13,900 employees. Approximately 49% of the employees were located outside the United States.

The firm's annual revenue as of December 31, 2017 was USD 12.491 billion and it's net income was USD 4.970 billion

"Our global approach is central to our mission," wrote the firm's long time CEO Larry Fink in letter to shareholders for the 2016 Annual Report.

The firm began in 1988 in New York City. It was started by Fink and a small group of professionals from the First Boston Corporation, the New York investment banking and trading firm. Since the firm's inception, Fink has been the firm's only CEO. Among his prior roles was managing the mortgage-backed securities unit at First Boston.

The firm was initially part of the Blackstone Group and was named Blackstone Financial Management. In 1992—with AUM of USD 7 billion—the firm adopted the name BlackRock. In 1995, the firm became a subsidiary of PNC Financial in Pittsburgh. In 1999, the firm became publicly held under the ticker symbol BLK. It was then managing USD 165 billion of AUM.

The firm has grown significantly as a result of acquisitions of other firms, including State Street Research and Management (2005), Merrill Lynch Investment Managers (2006), and Barclays Global Investors (2009), which included the iShares brand of Exchange Traded Funds.

The firm's largest single shareholder is PNC, which owns 21.2% of the voting common stock.

The firm's Corporate Governance Guidelines set forth that the Board of Directors has "ultimate responsibility for overseeing the firm's risk oversight activities." The Board also maintains a Risk Management Committee. Its primary purpose, according to its charter, is to assist the Board with its oversight of the firm's "levels of risk, risk assessment and risk management."

The Risk Management Committee charter divides risk into two broad categories. "Enterprise Risk" addresses issues that relate to BlackRock, its shareholders, and various stakeholders. Enterprise Risk includes market risk, operational risk, technology risk, and reputational risk. "Fiduciary Risk" refers to those risks that relate to the investors in BlackRock's various investment products, including collective investment vehicles such as mutual funds, ETFs, and hedge funds. Fiduciary Risk includes investment risk, counterparty risk, and pricing and valuation risk.

The firm's Aladdin system enables it to identify and manage the investment and operational risks within and across its portfolios. It provides a single investment system and a common source of data within BlackRock. The system provides views of risks across various dimensions and attributes so that risk managers and portfolio managers can "analyze their exposures and risks across asset classes in accordance with their own internal risk management practices and policies, as part of each client's broader investment decision process," the company wrote in 2014.

The firm maintains a Risk and Quantitative Analysis unit that is co-led by the firm's Chief Risk Officer, Ben Golub, one of the founding members of the firm who also received a Ph.D. from the Massachusetts Institute of Technology.

The firm has repeatedly emphasized its commitment to risk management. "An integral part of BlackRock's fiduciary culture is our core belief that rigorous risk management is critical to the delivery of high-quality asset management services," the company wrote in 2016.

In March of 2017, the firm announced that it would be consolidating its actively managed equity mutual funds into other funds that rely on quantitative models and a "rules-based" approach to investing.

"The democratization of information has made it much harder for active management," said Fink in an interview with the *New York Times.* "We have to change the ecosystem – that means relying more on Big Data, artificial intelligence, factors, and models within quant and traditional investment strategies."

References

Australian Government, Department of Finance. 2014. Commonwealth Risk Management Policy, July 1.

Backhouse, Roger E. 2017. *Founder of Modern Economics: Paul A. Samuelson; Volume I: Becoming Paul Samuelson, 1915–1948*. New York: Oxford University Press.

Bernstein, Peter L. 1998. *Against the Gods: The Remarkable Story of Risk*. New York: Wiley.

Board of Governors of the Federal Reserve System and Office of the Comptroller of the Currency. 2011. Supervisory Guidance on Model Risk Management, April 4.

Camerer, Colin, and Martin Weber. 1992. "Recent Developments in Modeling Preferences: Uncertainty and Ambiguity." *Journal of Risk and Uncertainty* 5 (4): 325–370.

Committee of Sponsoring Organizations of the Treadway Commission (COSO). 2017. Enterprise Risk Management, Aligning Risk with Strategy and Performance.

Dequech, David. 2000. "Fundamental Uncertainty and Ambiguity." *Eastern Economic Journal* 26 (1): 41–60.

Dequech, David. 2011. "Uncertainty: A Typology and Refinements of Existing Concepts." *Journal of Economic Issues* 45 (3): 621–640.

Dewey, Donald. 1990. "Frank Knight Before Cornell: Some Light on the Dark Years." *Research in the History of Economic Thought and Methodology* 8: 1–38.

Ellsberg, Daniel. 1961. "Risk, Ambiguity, and The Savage Axioms." *The Quarterly Journal of Economics* 75 (4): 643–669.

Financial Reporting Council. 2014. Guidance on Risk Management, Internal Control and Related Financial Reporting.

Fishwick, Edward. 2013. "Interviews" by Alec Hogg, October 6. http://www.biznews.com/interviews/2013/10/06/2342.

Foreign Exchange Working Group. 2017. FX Global Code.

International Organization for Standardization (ISO). 2009. International Standard 31000, Risk Management—Principles and Guidelines.

National Institute of Standards and Technology, United States Department of Commerce. 2014. Framework for Improving Critical Infrastructure Cybersecurity.

Office of the Comptroller of the Currency. 2016. Enterprise Risk Appetite Statement.

Kelsey, David, and John Quiggin. 1992."Theories of Choice Under Ignorance and Uncertainty." *Journal of Economic Surveys* 5 (2): 133–153.

Keynes, J.M. 1937. "The General Theory of Employment." *The Quarterly Journal of Economics* 51 (2): 209–223.

Knight, Frank H. 1921. *Risk, Uncertainty and Profit*. Boston: Houghton Mifflin.

Stigler, George J. 1973. "Frank Knight as Teacher." *Journal of Political Economy* 81 (3): 518–520.
Stigler, George J. 1985. "Frank Hyneman Knight." Working Paper No. 37, Center for the Study of the Economy and the State, The University of Chicago.
United States Chief Financial Officers Council and the Performance Improvement Council. 2016. Playbook: Enterprise Risk Management for the U.S. Federal Government.
World Economic Forum. 2017. The Global Risks Report 2017, 12th Edition.

2

What Is Country Risk?

2.1 Introduction—The Discovery of Risk

Risk arises from uncertainty regarding current or future situations, where information about the situation's outcome is insufficient, lacking, or wrong. Uncertainty itself derives from a deficit of information, hence randomness of results. Information availability is in itself a crucial measure of risk. A country that is unable or unwilling to provide timely and reliable information regarding its economic and financial situation sends out risk signals. Balance of payments, debt, inflation, budget, and governance data transform uncertain future events into calculable and dependable scenarios that are useful for risk management. In return, information scarcity requires taking action that might produce negative and costly consequences, including investigation time, transaction costs, and delays.

Until the Middle Ages in Western Europe, the very idea of risk was ignored. Indeed, risk has to do with the concept of extending time in the future, hence the need to tackle forthcoming prospects. Risk requires being enlightened about the future. Time however, according to the Church's precepts in Europe until the fifteenth century, belongs to God. In the eyes of the medieval Church therefore, predicting the future and managing time would boil down to speculation, in other words, challenging God's intentions. Gradually, however, as the Renaissance began to emerge, the Church's conception of the wheel of time gave way to the merchant's idea of linear time. The ancient idea of the wheel of time, or circular time, arose from a connection with the permanent features of Mother Nature: life and death,

M. H. Bouchet et al., *Managing Country Risk in an Age of Globalization*,
https://doi.org/10.1007/978-3-319-89752-3_2

sunrise and sunset, the four seasons, planting, and harvesting. Modern or linear time, in contrast, enables merchants and farmers to plan ahead, to sell at trade fairs, to negotiate barter agreements, to assess crop yields and investment returns, and ultimately to hedge risk and protect profits. Economic and financial transactions require linearity to build prospective analyses. The emergence of European capitalism could not have taken place without the emancipation of time from the grasp of religion during the Renaissance in the fifteenth and sixteenth centuries, along with mechanical ways of measuring time, transatlantic discoveries, and technological breakthroughs. The secular emancipation of the notion of linear time coincided with the emergence of mathematical instruments to measure it rationally, accurately, and systematically. Clocks over municipal belfries started to challenge church bells, first in northern Europe in the twelfth century, and gradually all over the continent, though more slowly in Spain where the Inquisition kept a tight control over social and economic life almost until the eighteenth century.

2.2 The Emergence of Risk Assessment

The history of risk management has been a long journey in which highly expert professionals—among them mathematicians, physicists, statisticians, merchants, and economists—have tested various ways and means of reducing uncertainty to manage volatility and take reasonable risk. In the mid-seventeenth century, precisely in the summer of 1654, two scientists, mathematicians, and philosophers, Pascal and Fermat, developed probability and combination calculations using coins thrown into the air. Pascal's arithmetical triangle is a convenient tabular presentation that is commonly used in probability calculations, that is, for calculating probabilities of independent binomial events that are randomly sampled in sequence.[1] In 1765, Nicolas de Condorcet added probability distribution and a framework for statistics. Later, in 1827, Robert Brown, a Scottish botanist, established the foundation for analysis of randomness while examining grains of pollen suspended in water under a microscope; he observed minute particles being ejected from the pollen grains in a continuous jittery motion.

[1]Reportedly, Pascal was far from the first scientist to study the combination triangle. The Persian mathematician Al-Karaji had produced something very similar as early as the tenth century, and the Triangle is called Yang Hui's Triangle in China after the thirteenth century Chinese mathematician, and Tartaglia's Triangle in Italy after the eponymous sixteenth century Italian. See http://www.storyofmathematics.com/17th_pascal.html.

We call this "Brownian motion." This laboratory observation, which seems little to do with finance, nevertheless allowed Jules Regnault, a French economist, to lay the foundations for the random walk model of stock price variations in 1863, and thereby calculate the probable results of speculation. An important development occurred in 1900 with the young mathematician Louis Bachelier who concluded that stock price forecasting was impossible due to endless number of influences although he noted that it was possible to study the probability distribution of price variations (Bachelier 1912). However, Bachelier concluded that a continuous and normally distributed random process could be applied to the volatile path of approximate prices. Bachelier's sigma introduction became a key element for calculating volatility risk.

Two other important developments occurred in 1921 with the almost simultaneous publication of the seminal work of John Maynard Keynes and his *Treatise on Probability* (Keynes 1921), and Frank Knight's crucial delineation between risk and uncertainty. Keynes asserted that probability was the rational guide to life because the calculus of probability was supposed to be capable of reducing uncertainty. He added the destabilizing effect of the role of "animal spirits in volatility spill-over and herd behavior." Keynes emphasized the nonlinear nature of risks and the danger of expecting the future to be a simple projection of the past. Frank Knight asserted that risk stemmed from unknown outcomes that can be tackled with probability distributions while uncertainty must be restricted to cases of nonquantitative occurrences (Knight 1921). The manager's business environment shifts from uncertainty toward risk when the measurability of all possible outcomes, together with the probabilities of their occurrence, can be determined precisely. Unlike uncertainty, risk can be converted to near certainty through strategic planning and insurance. In Country Risk, insurance is provided by private and public, national, and multinational agencies. Export credit guarantee companies include COFACE in France, SACE in Italy, EDC in Canada, as well as Ex-Im Bank in the United States.

Alfred Cowles, whose motto was "Science is Measurement," continued Bachelier's work in the aftermath of the 1929 stock market crisis that erupted in the United States and whose spill-over effect contaminated all Western markets until World War II (Cowles 1960). Cowles initiated a dynamic research process aimed at combining economic models with statistical methods of risk measurement. In 1933, Cowles concluded that it was impossible to forecast stock market prices due to large gaps between actual stock prices and professional forecasting. Using a yardstick that was the beginning of market price indices, he concluded there was no evidence to support the forecaster's ability to predict the future of the market; he thus provided an early demonstration of the "random walk" in stock price movements. One way of reducing risk in a highly uncertain environment is to split one's assets into various risk categories, in other words, to avoid putting all one's eggs in the same basket. This common sense suggestion led Harry Markowitz to win the Nobel Prize in 1990. His pioneering research in modern portfolio theory focused on the effects of risk/return, correlation, and asset diversification. Since risk is measured by the probability of loss, risk managers can learn from the past trajectory of historical volatility in returns as measured by standard deviation or Beta. This risk assessment tool assumes that the future is in linear continuity of the past and that no major, exceptional, and systemic break in volatility will occur. It also assumes that the distribution of probabilities follows a Gaussian law or bell curve, and that exceptional events are marginal. The data is "normally distributed" around the mean; there is symmetry around the center, hence half the values are less than the mean and half are greater than the mean. Using the standard deviation as measure of the spread of values, 95% of values are around the average within two standard deviations of the mean. This type of data is more adapted for measuring blood pressure, people's height, daily travel time, or students' test grades than for measuring stock market prices or floating exchange rate variations.

Benoit Mandelbrot argued that it is insufficient to just take account of risk diversification and risk tolerance (Mandelbrot and Hudson 2004). He warned that normal distribution models are not appropriate when one expects a significant fraction of outliers, i.e., exceptional events that imply "fat tails," or in other words, values that lie many standard deviations away from the mean and least squares. In Mandelbrot's words, these events stem from wild risk where volatility is strong and erratic. His recommendation that is applicable for country risk managers is: "Do not add model risk to market risk" (Bouchet and Guilhon 2007) (see Box 2.1).

Box 2.1 Mandelbrot's contribution to (country) risk management

Benoit Mandelbrot (1924–2010), Sterling Professor of Mathematical Sciences at Yale University and the pioneer of "fractal geometry," used to say: "Don't add model risk to credit risk!" He was critical of the unrealistic risk management models which assumed price randomness, normal probability distributions, and stock prices that supposedly incorporate all relevant information. Mandelbrot gave mathematical form to Keynes' statement that markets can remain irrational longer than you can remain solvent (Sweeting 2010).

Mandelbrot stressed the broad scope of market turbulences and the consequent volatility that standard financial theories do not capture. The traditional measures of risk, so-called beta, include a wide range of gauges, such as standard deviation, the Sharpe ratio, variance, correlation, alpha, value at risk, and the Black-Scholes option pricing model. The problem with all these measures is that they are built upon the statistical model known as the bell curve that is used for mathematical convenience. Rare and unpredictably large deviations have a dramatic impact on long-term returns, though "risk" and "variance" disregard these.

Conventional financial theory suggests that price movements are random and unpredictable, independent of each other and distributed in a normal, bell-shaped curve. Yet, while it may be true that price moves are unpredictable, it is not true that they are mutually independent and randomly distributed; in Mandelbrot's words: volatility clusters. In the fractal theory of risk, "concentration and random jumps are not belated fudges but points of departure." Yet the common tools of finance were designed for random walks in which the market always moves in small steps. Despite increasing empirical evidence that random jumps provide a better picture of market reality, risk analysts still rely on the random walk and the bell curve when gauging risk or forecasting returns.

Another aspect of the real world tackled by fractal finance is that markets "store" the memory of past moves, particularly of volatile days, and act according to this memory. Volatility breeds volatility. Extreme positive or negative returns are much more likely under the assumption of fractal returns than under a normal distribution. Phenomena of scaling and long-term dependence make markets much riskier than conventional models assume. Prices often move discontinuously. Financial market moves tend to cluster, and a few big moves up or down are responsible for most gains and losses. Accordingly, bubbles are not exceptional events. If a price has gone from one to ten, it is equally probable that it will go from ten to one hundred. In the words of Mandelbrot, "financial prices scale." In bell-curve finance, the chance of big drops is tiny and is thus ignored. In power-law finance, big drops, while certainly less likely than small ones, remain a real and calculable possibility.

Risk analysts try to see patterns. However, markets are deceptive. Because of long-term price dependence, data may show that price changes occur in particular increments or directions. But these changes are merely products of chance. Reading "meaning" into them, as technical analysts do, is fatuous. Mandelbrot warns that value is not worth much in financial markets. Financial analysts like to think that companies, countries, or currencies have a basic economic value. They try to get at this value by examining assets, or cash flow, or national income accounts, or inflation, or other factors. Their modus operandi implies that some relationship among these factors determines the value to which rational buyers and sellers will inevitably assent. Such a value is elusive and extremely difficult to calculate (Mandelbrot 2001).

Overall, the level of uncertainty implied by fractal models means that it is important to avoid describing risk in terms of a single number or ratio. It is crucial to consider a range of information. This information should then be used to inform decisions. In country risk analysis, shrinking the whole economic and sociopolitical complexity of national systems into few numbers is not only extremely hard to do, it is also risky. Finance is fractal to the core.

Didier Sornette, of the Zürich-based Financial Crisis Observatory, and closely associated with Mandelbrot's and Nassim Taleb's views on the limitations of traditional risk modelization, explores the emergence of extreme risks such as epidemics, floods, volcanoes, traffic jams, wars, and financial crises that imply system changes. His research led him to conclude that outliers imply a deviation from power laws, hence what he calls "Dragon Kings," that is, extreme events that are both very large and born of unique origins and respond to amplifying mechanisms. These outliers are a class of their own. They are generated by specific mechanisms and triggers that make them predictable and perhaps controllable. Their volatility, totally nonlinear, is missed by standard risk management tools due to their endogenous origin. As Sornette observes: "It is often advanced that, because many phenomena in the physical, natural, environmental, economic and social sciences can be characterized in large part by power law statistics, large events are inherently unpredictable since they are undistinguishable from their smaller siblings and reflect the same underlying generating mechanism(s). In this view, major catastrophes are just events that started small but did not stop growing and are thus unpredictable, in the sense that the timing as well as final size of a future event cannot be forecasted in advance. If the 2008 financial crisis was a "black swan," nobody is responsible and we just have to prepare for the random occurrence of such unknown unknowns" (Sornette 2016). Contrary to the popular Black Swan concept that assumes that extreme events are unpredictable, Sornette and his Dragon Kings suggest that we identify the numerous early warning signals of abrupt crises and exponential nonlinear trajectories to obtain a degree of predictability. Self-reinforcing imitations, that is, herd instinct phenomena, are crucial triggers behind market crashes and financial crises (Focardi and Fabozzi 2009).

2.3 Risk, Uncertainty, and Volatility

Regarding Country Risk, the dynamics of a country's economic, financial, and sociopolitical phenomena, as well as interactions of these with the global economic system, are much too complex to be captured by mathematical formulae and econometric models—even though the latter give the reassuring but illusory comfort of being "hard science." Most risk managers are aware of the conceptual pitfalls of the underlying assumptions of models that become axioms, such as economic agents acting under the harmonizing influence of the "invisible hand," optimization process, or market efficiency.

Meanwhile, risk managers tend to continue using the simplified correlations based on incorrect axioms wrapped up in sophisticated equations. As Bouchaud, influenced by Mandelbrot, notes: "In reality, markets are not efficient, humans tend to be over-focused on the short-term and blind to the long-term: errors get amplified, ultimately leading to collective irrationality, panic and crashes. Free markets are wild markets" (Bouchaud 2008). Finally, Ulrich Beck developed an analysis of the global risk society at the turn of the millennium where current decisions and technological developments triggered long-term global impact, such as climate change, terrorism, pollution, and financial deregulation (Beck 1992).

As we shall see when discussing the various components of Country Risk, risk managers cannot assume that they grasp the full dimension of a country's multifaceted risks when dealing with economic, financial, and sociopolitical variables. The globalized market system has added the spill-over effects of regional crisis contamination to the mix, not to mention global and systemic risk such as global warming and terrorist threats.

A constant theme throughout the book is that gathering information and enhancing the quality of economic intelligence are two key tools for mitigation of uncertainty and risk management. Indeed, uncertainty is at the root of risk, that it is rooted in deficits of information regarding the present and the future, given that the world keeps on changing in novel ways. An example of uncertainty hurting business is Brexit. In the words of UK Chancellor Philip Hammond: "Large amounts of business investment are being postponed because of uncertainty over the future outcome of Brexit negotiations so Britain should seek clarity as early as possible over a transition arrangement" (Hammond 2017). According to Dequech's comprehensive survey of the varieties of uncertainty, different economists and different schools of economic thought have implicitly or explicitly dealt with a wide variety of uncertainty without agreeing on the definition, scope, and limits of the concept (Dequech 2011). Nevertheless, distinctions can be made among the different notions that Table 2.1 summarizes.

Regarding country risk management, globalization increases uncertainty due to the integration of a complex economic and financial system that breeds volatility contagion and crisis contamination. As noticed by Goldin and Kutarna (2017): "Growing complexity poses a severe challenge for risk management. The more complicated our interactions become, the harder it is for us to see relationships of cause and effect. We develop cognitive blind spots in our vision of the events around us. How can we make good decisions when we can't foresee the consequences? More complex systems also

Table 2.1 Tentative Distinctions between uncertainty, ambiguity, and complexity

Strong Uncertainty	Weak Uncertainty	Ambiguity	Complexity
1. Substantive uncertainty = Lack of all the information necessary to make decisions with certain outcomes 2. Fundamental uncertainty = List of possible events is not predetermined or knowable ex ante, as the future is yet to be created	Risk = Decision-makers use homogenous data for additive and fully reliable probability distributions to measure uncertainty	1. Unforeseen contingencies and " Judgmental uncertainty" = How specifying which of a set of distributions is appropriate in a given situation?	Individuals are exposed to the occurrence of unexpected events with wide range of ramifications and risk of spill-over effects
3. Procedural uncertainty = Lack of complete knowledge on the part of the economic agents about the very structure of the problem they face given the available information	Individuals can act on the basis of a probability that is objective (any reasonable person would agree on it) and known.	2. High ambiguity even with ample quantity of information due to conflicting opinion and evidence, or poor understanding of the causal process	

(Book Authors)

Table 2.2 Illustration of Country Risk examples of uncertainty, ambiguity, and complexity

Country risk event	Strong uncertainty	Weak and measurable uncertainty	Ambiguity	Complexity
Economic events	FDI decision in post-Brexit UK	Exchange rate depreciation	Inflation decrease; growth slowdown	Sharp fall in oil prices
Sociopolitical events	Revolution, strikes and coup d'état	New market-oriented and pro-business government	High rate of electoral abstention	Upcoming elections; mounting corruption
Financial events	Nationalization of banking system	Interest-rate increase	Overvaluation of tech companies	External debt default
Spill-over events	Regional crisis contamination	US economic recession	USD appreciation	Regional competitive devaluations

(Book Authors)

provide more scope for interdependent relationships, some of which may only become visible when it is too late. Where correlated risks rise, each individual element or economy in the system has a greater risk exposure, and this can magnify the impact of any economic or other risk if it materializes" (Table 2.2).

2.4 What Is Country Risk All About?

Country Risk is everywhere, including at times and in places people do not expect it. No successful cross-border strategy can ignore Country Risk, and no lucrative domestic investment is possible without assessing the full range of risks stemming from a country's socioeconomic, financial, and political environment, elements over which private agents have no bearing. Country Risk, however, still fails to be fully and formally recognized in risk management textbooks and seminars. For example, in a comprehensive criticism of why and how mainstream finance theory failed both to prevent or forecast the global market crash that resulted in large losses for investors, the CFA Institute provides a detailed list of risk components, while ignoring Country Risk altogether (Fabozzi et al. 2014). Managers discover Country Risk painfully if they are not prepared and well organized. Since the emergence of globalization during the 1980s, the globalized market economic system where competition and financial viability are all the rage has generated volatility and turbulence that are very costly. It is precisely the costly complexity of Country Risk that leads managers to reduce uncertainty by shifting their strategy back to the local markets. As 3M's chairman Inge Thulin declared in a 2017 interview: "Our strategy has changed. After a decade of producing at huge facilities around the world, and shipping to other countries, now we have a strategy of localization and regionalization. We think you should invest in your domestic market as much as you can" (Tett 2017). The strategy of production outsourcing to low-cost countries such as China, India, and Vietnam, hence building global value chains, has proved to be full of pitfalls. The reason is that lower labor costs do not compensate for political volatility, regulatory uncertainty, and logistics risks.

However, despite the current pervasiveness of Country Risk, academics and practitioners have so far failed to achieve consensus regarding its definition nor its main components. The terms "cross-border risk" or "sovereign risk" are often used as Country Risk to refer to the risk of investing abroad. As Bouchet, Clark and Groslambert observed (2003): "For a long time, Country Risk was considered an opaque unpleasant fact of life better left in the hands of the IMF and the export credit agencies." Country Risk, however, has been recognized as a key element of cross-border strategy since the mid-1970s, first at the time of the 1973 oil shock and later in 1978–1979 during the Islamic Revolution in Iran and the overthrow of the Pahlavi dynasty (that was supported by the United States and Europe), and its eventual replacement with an Islamic Republic under Ayatollah Khomeini. The Islamist government nationalized or otherwise took control of virtually all Western industrial and financial property in the country, resulting in substantial losses for American and European companies. But beyond the amount of sheer financial damage, the Islamic revolution created a worldwide shock due to the unexpected and abrupt conservative backlash against the Western alignment and the Shah's secularizing regime that had long been considered a stable strategic ally for the US government. Scholars, managers, and government officials in developed countries suddenly discovered the explosive combination of monarchy, wealth gap, and repression. Country risk assessment and management departments were born from the Iranian Revolution.

A combination of floating exchange rates, commodity price volatility, and sociopolitical turbulence led a growing number of multinational corporations to set up country risk analysis teams in the 1980s with a view to assessing, predicting, and mitigating the risk of cross-border investment. Foreign direct investment (FDI) and dynamic outsourcing production strategy in the 1990s focused country risk research on developing countries with low wages in Asia and Latin America or on countries with large commodity resources in Africa. More sophisticated and better equipped large country risk departments began to develop in international banks and insurance companies at the time of the first developing country debt crisis in the mid-1980s. The innovators in banking were BNP, CCF, and Indosuez in France; Citibank, Chemical Bank, JP Morgan, and Manufacturers Hanover in the US; Bank of Montreal and RBC in Canada; and Dai-Ichi Kangyo Bank and Bank of Tokyo in Japan. At the time of the Mexican default in the summer of 1982, many banks had accumulated a large exposure to developing country governments, mainly to Mexico, Argentina, Chile, Brazil, Ecuador, Venezuela, and the Philippines, with very little knowledge of the countries' economic and sociopolitical situation. Plenty of bank managers would have found it hard to locate the countries on a map or to assess their economic growth sustainability. A number of small and medium-sized banks had been attracted to cross-border lending by syndicated euro-credits that paid hefty fees. Sovereign debt often exceeded the capital base of international banks, hence threatening solvency crisis. Developed country governments feared that a chain reaction of defaults would lead to the collapse of the banking industry. By 1982, the nine largest US money-center banks held developing country debt amounting to three times their capital. A turning point occurred in the early 1980s with the creation of the Institute of International Finance (IIF) by a group of large commercial banks (IIF 2017).

Box 2.2 The IIF and the London Club of international banks

The Washington-based Institute of International Finance was set up in 1983 to enhance the quality of country risk assessment in international banks worldwide. It is the global association of the financial industry, with close to 500 members from seventy countries. Its mission is to support the financial industry in the prudent management of risks; to develop sound industry practices; and to advocate for regulatory, financial, and economic policies that are in the broad interests of its members. IIF members include commercial and investment banks, asset managers, insurance companies, sovereign wealth funds, hedge funds, central banks, and development banks. More than half of the membership comes from commercial banks, mainly in the United States, Europe, and Japan.

One of the key contributions of the IIF is country risk analysis. It offers an independent source of global economic, and financial research, including a comprehensive assessment of the global outlook with a focus on key emerging economies, timely analysis of capital flows to emerging markets and developments in international financial markets. IIF databases include annual macroeconomic and financial data for covered countries. Capital and portfolio flows databases cover annual, quarterly, and monthly frequencies.

The IIF is at the heart of the so-called London Club of international banks that includes Bank Advisory Committees and Economic sub-committees. The London Club has been active since the mid-1980s emerging market debt crisis, although its first meeting took place in 1976 in response to Zaire's debt payment problems. The IIF, on behalf of the London Club, meets regularly with the Paris Club of official creditors to assess global liquidity issues and country risk matters and to discuss debt restructuring negotiations.

2.5 The Evolution in the Nature and Scope of Country Risk

Country Risk is no longer what it used to be (Bouchet 2002). During the 1990s, there was a profound change in the nature and consequences of Country Risk. One can identify seven main new dimensions:

First, the traditional divide between developed/emerging countries is at best obsolete, and at worst, a source of errors in country risk assessment. This divide adds a conceptual myopia to the complexity of economic, financial, and sociopolitical risk assessment. Emerging market countries with large external debt and with little export diversification have been the traditional focus of country risk assessments. But liquidity and solvency challenges have shifted north-west, toward developed countries. On average, the solvency ratios (i.e., public debt to GDP) are near or well above 100% for the majority of Organization of Economic Cooperation and Development (OECD)

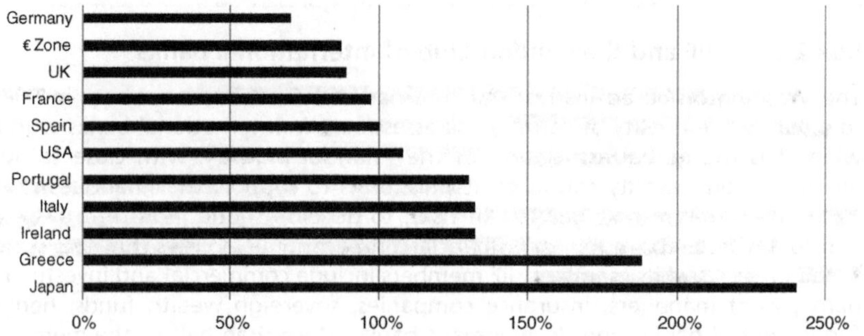

Fig. 2.1 Developed countries' public debt/GDP ratios (2018) (*Source* IMF and national authorities)

countries, while many emerging market countries have boasted substantial current account surplus since the late 1990s. Figure 2.1. illustrates the public debt to GDP ratios of several developed countries of the OECD. As discussed in Chapter 12, however, a much somber picture arises for both developed and developing countries when observing total debt ratios, which, combining private and public debt, reach well above 200%.

In recent years, such concerns have led rating agencies to shift the risk focus from emerging to developed markets, with a much larger number of downgrades concerning the latter. In addition, the categories used by investment funds and rating agencies such as emerging market countries versus "frontier nations" seem arbitrary. The MSCI Frontier Markets Index includes twenty-two developing countries. The MCI equity index considers a country such as Argentina as "frontier" due to its sociopolitical volatility, its five consecutive defaults over the last century (most recently in 2014), and the country's decade of financial isolation. However, Argentina still managed to issue USD 2.75 billion of century bonds with an effective yield of 8% in the Spring of 2017. Likewise, the Ivory Coast, structurally dependent on cocoa and coffee exports, and beset by military uprising and guerillas, still managed to issue sixteen-year bonds with a 6.25% yield a few weeks after a military uprising in the Spring of 2017. Both bond issues were heavily oversubscribed, not due to hedge funds' confidence in the future of these "frontier markets," but merely due to central banks' ultra-loose monetary policy, low real interest rates, and hence investors' frantic search for return. And Tunisia, though belonging to the "frontier market" category, managed to issue USD 1 billion of seven-year bonds since the 2011 Arab Spring, at a modest yield of around 2%, thanks to the guarantee of the US Treasury.

Second, since World War II, developing countries with weak sociopolitical institutions have held the monopoly of political volatility. Country Risk was rooted in the so-called Third World. This is no longer true. Developed countries with mature and sophisticated legal, regulatory, and institutional frameworks are not immune to sociopolitical turbulence. With this shift has come a rising concern for political risk in what were until recently seen to be the world's most politically stable regions. Drastic adjustment measures in advanced economies have contributed to sociopolitical turmoil, notably in the EU. Greece, Spain, Portugal, and to a lesser extent Italy, have witnessed the emergence of radical political parties as a response to the growing discredit of traditional channels of popular mobilization. The downgrading of developed countries' credit ratings since the inception of the Global Financial Crisis has in many cases been rooted in political risk. When S&P's lowered the US long-term sovereign rating to AA+from AAA in August of 2011, the agency put the spotlight on political uncertainty: "The downgrade reflects our view that the effectiveness, stability, and predictability of American policymaking and political institutions have weakened at a time of ongoing fiscal and economic challenges" (Standard & Poor's 2011). Global terrorism, in addition, targets developed countries' cities, hence creating a permanent threat for consumers and investors.

Third, country risk managers can no longer rely on traditional yardsticks of risk such as rating and rankings. Volatility, spill-over, herd instinct, and complexity make quantitative assessment of Country Risk, including ratings and rankings, at best partial tools and at worst recipes for simplistic outlooks. As discussed in Chapter 5, rating agencies almost systematically have been unable to predict crises or assess upcoming changes in Country Risk since the emergence of the globalized economic system in the 1980s, including the mid-1980s debt crisis, the 1994 Mexican or "Tequila" crisis, the 1997 Asian crisis, and the 2007 subprime crisis that paved the way for the Global Financial Crisis. Exchange rate depreciation, rising inflation, falling commodity export revenues, deteriorating creditworthiness, sociopolitical upheavals, and debt crisis have been followed rather than preceded by evolving rating signals. Rising risks without traditional warning signals thus require the risk analyst to be more agile, broad-minded, and innovative than in the past. Only an array of converging analytical approaches can lead to a more rigorous examination of the economic, institutional, and sociopolitical fabric that holds or distorts a country's development path. The latter should be tackled as economic growth, coupled with those conditions that make it sustainable. These conditions include a legitimate political power base, social mobilization, sound institutions, and robust infrastructures. Increasingly, country risk analysts focus on the close relationships between human capital, sound institutions, and sustainable socioeconomic development.

Fourth, Country Risk has become the by-product of complex intertwining between public and private sectors. The focus on excessive sovereign debts, hence the risk of financial crisis, has shifted toward all the adverse business consequences of the uncertainty surrounding a country's economic, banking, and sociopolitical situation. Banking sector weaknesses have become a new channel of Country Risk, not only in emerging markets, but also in more mature and supposedly more regulated markets such as Japan, the Eurozone, and the United States. As the International Monetary Fund (IMF) put it in the midst of the Global Financial Crisis: "Sovereign risks have been transformed in a number of important ways as a direct consequence of the crisis and major fault lines in the financial sector. As the public sector intervened to support financial institutions, distinctions between sovereign and non-sovereign and private liabilities have been blurred, and public exposure to private risks has increased" (International Monetary Fund 2011).

Fifth, for too long the definition of country risk analysis has been restricted to the assessment of a foreign entity's ability and willingness to meet its external obligations in full and on time (Bouchet 2017b). This narrow definition includes both economic and political uncertainty regarding the value of a cross-border investment, an export revenue, or a loan repayment. It concerns exclusively foreign economic agents. It excludes advisory services, contractual obligations regarding supplies, and real estate assets. This narrow concept excludes reputational, legal, and regulatory risks. More importantly, it also excludes domestic residents of a risky country. It follows that the very concept of Country Risk must be reassessed because its exclusive focus on a foreign country's uncertainty has proved elusive and in many ways risky. More than a decade prior to the Global Financial Crisis, Bouchet et al. (2003) restricted the scope of Country Risk to "all the additional risks induced by doing business abroad, as opposed to domestic transactions, ranging from political and social risks to macro- and microeconomic risks." But then how can we explain massive private capital outflows when residents of Venezuela strove to mitigate the risk of domestic inflation or exchange rate devaluation, and mounting political turmoil in 2017? How can we get across the so-called brain drain in Spain in the aftermath of the Global Financial Crisis of 2008, when thousands of young engineers, architects, and economists fled to work in Germany, Canada, or the United States to escape from massive unemployment and drying up job opportunities? How should we analyze cross-border financial investments from French banks in Switzerland and Luxembourg on the eve of a Socialist government being elected in 1981, helping residents to hedge against the risk of nationalization and heavy taxes? And finally, how should we interpret rising financial investment uncertainty in the US stock market during the tough election campaign of late 2016 between Clinton and Trump? A Clinton administration would have likely entailed rising budgetary deficits, higher taxes for corporations, and tighter regulations for banks. Meanwhile, the populist, trade protectionist and anti-globalization stance of Donald Trump has created considerable anxiety in US companies with large stakes in export markets such as Mexico. As noted by an investment bank's report to its clients: "Trump's election means that financial markets will have to digest additional monetary uncertainty. He has been saying for some time now that interest rates have been too low for too long" (Kempen Capital Management 2016). The appointment of a new chairman of the Federal Reserve, Jerome "Jay" Powell, a former investment banker, was the first time in forty years that a president did not ask an incumbent to stay on as head of the Fed. The new chairman is expected to continue the monetary policy that has come to define his predecessor Janet Yellen's term, while "reducing the cost of regulation without affecting safety and soundness." Regarding the tax bill approved by the US Senate and whose effects will materialize in 2018 and beyond, the economic trickle-down effects are supposed to produce an economic stimulus that would wipe out the substantial rise in debt this bill generates. The Republican tax overhaul bill leans heavily toward tax cuts for corporations and business owners, while eliminating personal exemptions as well as the deductibility of mortgage interest. The increase in the budget deficit, at least in the short term, and the wealth gap consequences of the corporate tax breaks, create uncertainty regarding their social impact.

In the United Kingdom, Brexit-related uncertainty will affect trade and financial relations with the EU in the long-run but also the domestic economic environment. Brexit's heightened volatility will weigh on investment, on jobs, and on inflation, hence hitting consumer purchasing power. Growth is expected to remain subdued. Similarly, Catalonia's drive toward independence in the fall of 2017 increased uncertainty and risk for the region's business community. The two major financial entities, Banco Sabadell and Caixabank, decided to shift their legal headquarters out of Barcelona to stem sharp falls in the groups' share prices and to protect depositors. Energy supplier Gas Natural Fenosa and Dogi International Fabrics, as well as a large number of Spanish and international companies, decided to move their legal bases from Catalonia's capital, Barcelona.

Each of these examples shares similarities in that Country Risk is not the monopoly of foreign creditors, exporters, importers, or investors. Domestic residents (households, investors, corporate sector) also face Country Risk from their own country's socioeconomic and political situation: a country's government can take arbitrary decisions that will affect the residents' economic and sociopolitical well-being. Private corporations, banks and insurance companies, and households all face the risk of rising uncertainty and destabilizing business environment that will affect profit, investment, and revenue opportunities. It follows that Country Risk is shared by both domestic residents who save, invest, and consume, and by global managers and international bankers who plan cross-country strategies and who must set up complex organizational structures and sophisticated quantitative econometric models to control uncertainty. The "man on the street" also faces Country Risk in times of threats of impeachment, of corruption, of volatile tax regulations, of heavy bureaucracies, and of rising domestic prices and negative real interest rates. As we shall see in the concluding Chapter 15, the commonly available range of risk mitigation tools is rather limited. Risk hedging policies for those whose real value of savings is at stake include cutting consumption, holding gold, and shifting liquid assets abroad. The country's government can take arbitrary decisions that will affect residents' socioeconomic situation. In addition, a country can be contaminated by negative regional or global forces and by the spill-over effect of crisis contagion. A deterioration in the risk perception by capital markets and rating agencies will also impact domestic residents' environment and well-being, taking into consideration that fund managers do not discriminate much and consider regional assets as one single class of risk (Bouchet 2017b).

Sixth, Country Risk cannot be restricted to the financial and macroeconomic dimensions of a country. There is a wide range of important risks such as legal and regulatory, reputational, and cross-cultural risks that can impact on business strategies and the scope for success and profits. The following concise examples summarize the main cross-cultural challenges that impacted the mergers between global companies such as Volvo and Renault Trucks as well as between Volvo and China's Geely.

Box 2.3 Cross-border mergers and cross-cultural management challenges

Country Risk has also a deeply-rooted cultural dimension. Merging two portfolios and combining two global business strategies might be easier than merging two different national and cultural backgrounds. The cases of Volvo Cars-Geely and Volvo Group- Renault Véhicule Industriels (RIV) mergers illustrate the challenge of cross-cultural management. Cultural differences involve a wide range of specific traditions, corporate culture, custom base, behaviors, and codes of conduct, such as way of working, languages, management styles, relationships with government agencies, decision-making process, bureaucracy/administration routines, delegation processes (manager decisions vs team consensus), decision levels (vertical organization vs low/flat structures), dress codes, titles, academic background, interactions with unions, and meeting culture (time management, agenda, length of meetings, participants, etc.)

Volvo Group-Renault Merger: On 18 July 2000, Volvo reached an agreement to acquire all of Renault's shares in RVI in exchange for a percentage of Volvo's share capital corresponding to 15% of the voting and capital thereof. Renault would have two representatives on the Volvo board. Volvo is registered in Sweden and is primarily active in the manufacture and sale of heavy and medium trucks, buses, construction equipment, marine and industrial engines, as well as aerospace components. RVI was then a wholly owned subsidiary of Renault S.A. of France, and was active in medium and heavy trucks, sold under the "Renault" brand name in Europe and under the "Mack" brand in the US. The Volvo Group made more or less the same mistakes as Mercedes/Daimler made with Chrysler in the merger of May of 1998. Renault-Trucks had to use the same engineering processes, always speak Swedish or English in meeting/emails, and implement a similar organization, while nearly all Volvo Group's top management positions were filled with Swedish staff. In addition, Renault had to use the Volvo drawing documentation system (i.e., implying that 45,000 drawings had to be changed for Renault). Nobody made a good/fair analysis of the cultural differences before the merger, which resulted in less synergies-of-scale than expected and a slower development of Renault-Trucks. As a listed company, Volvo had to apply the Swedish Corporate Governance Code. In October 2011, Volvo Group restructured its truck business and launched a large reorganization. Because the gross-margin increase that was promised at the time of the merger never materialized, both the Managing Director of Volvo Group and the Chairman of the Board had to leave.

Volvo Cars-Geely Merger: On August 2, 2010, China's Geely, a low-cost, low-end producer, completed its purchase of Ford Motor Company's Volvo unit, marking China's biggest acquisition of a foreign car maker and reflecting the nation's rapid rise in the global auto industry. Zhejiang Geely, parent of Hong Kong-listed Geely Automobile Holdings, paid USD 1.6 billion in cash and issued a USD 200 million note to Ford. Restoring Volvo to long-term profits was a key objective given that Volvo Cars posted revenue of USD 12.4 billion in 2009 by selling 334,000 cars, while recording a pretax loss of USD 653 million. Geely lacked the management skills to integrate a global company like Volvo and it did not try to reinvent the wheel. The Chinese management kept the Volvo's way of doing regarding development process, platform engineering, electronic architecture, safety research/testing, management organization, etc. in Gothenburg while only a few key-persons from Geely moved to Gothenburg. But the Chinese shareholders transferred much knowledge from Gothenburg to China regarding safety and platform engineering, while using a lot of common components between the brands. Further, they started production of some Volvo models in China, as the government decided that only locally produced cars were allowed to be used in the Government's public sector, hence opening large sales prospects for Volvo in China's market. Finally the take-over also gave Geely a large dealer/sales-network in Europe and North-America, for its future models. In retrospect, the merger can be deemed a success. In December 2017, Geely Holding Group that bought Volvo Cars in 2010 decided to acquire an 8% stake in AB Volvo, making Geely the truck maker's largest shareholder. *Source* Interview with M. Ake Nässlander, former Chief Project Manager, Product Development, Volvo Group.

Seventh and last, country risk managers are used to focusing on country-specific risk features, such as balance of payments deficits, inflation, exchange rate, indebtedness ratios, and political fragility. But the globalized market economy has added a new component of Country Risk, namely that of spill-over effect and crisis contamination. Indeed, the scope of the full range of risks faced by economic agents in the global economy is precisely that this economy is global. Strong, lasting, and inclusive global growth belongs to the past, given the many risks and vulnerabilities that spill-over creates and extends. Slower, more erratic growth might be the new reality. As the global economy becomes an "echo chamber" that propagates and accentuates imbalances, it is doomed to face volatility and crises. Investors and lenders worry about the reliability of corporate governance and accounting statements. The absence of institutional stabilization mechanisms, such as a lender of last resort fund, makes the global economy vulnerable to shocks as never before. Worldwide income inequalities within and among countries impede the conditions of stable, sustained growth. They feed social disorder, migrations, and political upheaval. Whereas economic planning has become increasingly refined and sophisticated, with the ideology of economic development as a vector of progress as the dominant paradigm, many investors and domestic residents are plagued by failed states, often in rich countries with poor people.

These changing conditions and spill-over effects in the globalized economic system mean that country risk managers have only done part of their job in analyzing the socioeconomic and political situation of a specific country. A number of destabilizing factors can come "from the outside" and harm a well-designed investment strategy. Box 2.4 illustrates eight of these external factors:

Box 2.4 The interplay between global variables and Country Risk

- **Capital flows volatility**: External capital inflows and outflows tend to precipitate crisis contagion, thereby affecting countries whose economic and sociopolitical outlook used to be predictable. Fund managers tend to look at developing countries as one single risk asset class, which can give rise to large, indiscriminate swings in portfolio management. In a first phase, countries that used to rely on short-term borrowing to finance large current account deficits are affected by sharp declines in capital flows. But those countries that attracted more stable financing vehicles such as FDI are also penalized given that inflows shrink while capital outflows by both MNCs and domestic economic agents increase, hence precipitating financial crises. Capital flow volatility hurt Eurozone countries in 2007–2010, contributing to liquidity market decrease and yield rises in the so-called PIGS countries, namely, Greece, Portugal, Italy, and Spain, despite their very different structural conditions. Capital outflows exert downward exchange rate pressure, hence forcing central banks to increase real interest rates that contribute to penalizing domestic investment, reducing growth, and stimulating further capital flight.

- **Global currencies' exchange rate depreciation**: Should a country's main trading partners decide to depreciate their exchange rates to enhance export competitiveness, they create the conditions for competitive devaluations and crisis contamination. This negative-sum game is what precipitated the Asian crisis in 1997/98 in the aftermath of the 45% devaluation of Thailand's Baht that led neighboring countries to follow suit, before the crisis extended to Latin America and East European countries. If all countries embark in nominal devaluation together, no one devalues in real terms.
- **Global interest rates hike**: A rise in the interest rates of global currencies, such as USD and Euro, exerts strong pressures for capital flight in emerging market countries. The expectation of a tightening of US monetary policy in 1994 led to large capital outflows from Asia and Latin America, destabilizing domestic economic policies and requiring capital controls. In China, a combination of tightening US monetary policy and strengthening of the US Dollar in 2014–2016 along with higher US yields in the wake of the election of Donald Trump in 2017, created a major challenge for Beijing that was already treading a thin policy line between supporting the Yuan's rate and boosting slowing growth. Consequently, the continued weakening of the Yuan forced the Chinese government to sell more Dollars, thereby straining domestic liquidity, contributing to higher interest rates, and rapidly eroding reserve assets. For most developing countries, tightening US monetary policy can generate a credit crunch, stimulate capital flight and increase corporate defaults. Private and public companies that borrow heavily in US Dollars but earn incomes in their local currency are particularly vulnerable to the prospect of a stronger Dollar and/or a stronger Euro.
- **IFIs**: in their own way, international financial institutions can also contribute to globally destabilizing country risk trends. First, in the 1980s, IFIs such as the IMF and the World Bank promoted balance of payments liberalization and financial globalization, under the assumption that it could help increase productivity and growth. The benefits that cross-border flows would bring to developing countries that tend to be relatively capital-poor were to include fostering development of the domestic financial sector and imposing discipline on macroeconomic policies. The surge in short-term financial flows, however, led to a number of currency and financial crises, particularly in Latin America and Asia in the late 1980s and 1990s. Second, the announcement of gloomy growth scope in specific countries, regions or in the global economy risks becoming a self-fulfilling prophecy. Numerous downward revisions of global growth by the IMF Research Department in 2013–2017 unsurprisingly failed to improve economic agents' confidence in the turnaround of the post-crisis global economy.
- **Global trade:** a major cause of the sharp decline in global GDP in 2009 has been an abrupt drop in trade. Since the 1980s, the global growth engine has been trade that grew twice as fast as the global economy (i.e., 7% versus 3.5%). Trade impetus, however, works both ways and the 12% fall in trade in 2009 pushed the global economy into recession with below trend growth rates until 2017. Countries with large trade openness ratios (trade to GDP), such as the Asian tigers, suffered the most and had to depreciate their

exchange rates, leading to competitive devaluations and beggar-thy-neighbor policies.

- **Global liquidity and market access**: Bond yields are as much a matter of country creditworthiness as of global market conditions, including liquidity, competition to raise financing, and financial regulations. A global credit crunch tightens bond yields and dries up market access for countries with lower credit ratings. The subprime crisis that erupted in the United States in 2007 and spread throughout the financial markets over the 2008–2015 period, led to a sharp fall in bond issues and banking credit. Tighter global liquidity affected a whole range of developed and developing countries, as investors' risk aversion did not discriminate between asset classes. Countries such as Greece, Portugal, Cyprus, and Spain faced refinancing constraints similar to those of Philippines, Peru, Indonesia, and Russia.
- **Country risk analysts' role in fostering crisis**: Mathematical portfolio and country risk-management models have been the academic backbone of the tremendous increase of cross-border transactions since the mid-1970s, in FDI, M&As, and financial investment. Country risk analysts rely on a range of thresholds, ratios, and rankings to gauge creditworthiness. Models aimed at defining trigger points beyond which a country's debt becomes unmanageable—supposedly a 60% debt to GDP ratio for developing countries and 90% debt to GDP ratios for more mature industrial countries. However, the search for thresholds, whatever the econometric sophistication of models, is akin to shooting a moving target given that debt crises have demonstrated a remarkable ability to mutate and develop in a manner previously unforeseen and where statistical data fall short of providing reliable inputs. The specific triggers for macroeconomic and financial imbalances to "go critical" have varied over time and across countries depending on the structure of external liabilities regarding maturity, creditors, exchange and interest rates, as well as the regional environment of the debtor countries (see Chapter 12). Overall, threshold values, though grounded in theory and historical analysis, have proved to be at best subjective yardsticks and illusive warning signals, and at worst, recipes for myopia.
- **Rating agencies:** Country risk managers must take into account the risk signals sent by rating agencies whose job is to assess the market price of debt issues. This is not due to the quality of risk assessment by rating agencies but merely because ratings still represent a market consensus, though a biased one. Rating agencies contribute to mercurial market sentiment and herd instinct. As discussed in Chapter 8, rating agencies have failed to predict banking, currency and debt crises in a large number of instances, including in Mexico (1994–1995), Asia (1997–1998), Russia (1998), Turkey (1994, 1998, and 2001), Brazil (1990, 1997, and 2002), South Africa (2001), Argentina (1990 and 2001), Greece (2010), and the subprime crisis of 2007. In addition, after ignoring or undermining the timing and extent of risk, rating agencies tend to overreact, thereby contributing to crisis contamination. A deterioration in the risk perception by rating agencies feeds back onto capital markets with negative consequences on investment and trade. Domestic residents protect their assets by shrinking domestic consumption and savings and by shifting their assets abroad.
- **Global terrorism**: There are very few spots on the world map that are immune from political upheaval and terrorist threats (AON 2017). Global terrorism is a threat for investors in almost every country, whether developed or develop-

ing, and can cost millions of USD in direct and indirect consequences, including kidnapping and ransom, confiscation, expenses for added security, shrinking revenues in the tourism sector, communication cuts, etc. Country risk managers must take terrorism into account when planning ahead, not only in Tunisia, Algeria, Nigeria, Malaysia, or the Philippines, but also in the EU.

- **Global GDP and systemic risk**: Country risk analysts must factor into a country projections the dynamics of the global economy and its influence on specific countries' growth trajectories. In the globalized market economy, a country cannot sail against the wind for too long. Weak global growth projections raise risk aversion, with consequences on investment, trade and capital flows, and bond yields. The below-par global GDP trend between 2007 and 2018, at roughly 3.3% versus more than 4% between 1973 and 2005, has had a bearing on both trade and capital flows, with negative consequences on socioeconomic development.

2.6 Defining Country Risk

Country Risk is a multifaceted concept. We define it as a set of interdependent macro-economic, financial, institutional, and sociopolitical factors, specific for a particular country in the global economy, which can negatively affect both domestic and foreign economic agents relating to savings, investment, and credit transactions. Country Risk, however, is never negative in itself, given that it can open positive opportunities if properly managed. The range of risks encompasses the uncertainty an economic agent is exposed to as a result of the unexpected turbulences in a country, given its institutional and socioeconomic weaknesses and the spill-over effect of regional and global volatility. This is surely a broad definition—intentionally so. Five main considerations must be taken into account by risk managers.

First, Country Risk can be further aggregated by geographical region though, as discussed earlier in this chapter, the globalized economic system introduces extensive porosity between geographical regions as well as between economic categories. The traditional divide between emerging and industrial countries is no longer appropriate and less advisable given the structural financial weaknesses of many OECD countries and the spread of global terrorism. Second, the spill-over effect of the Global Financial Crisis that emerged on the west coast of the United States is a clear example of systemic contamination rooted in the structural linkages of the financial system. Third, Country Risk is a far more encompassing concept than sovereign risk, which is the possibility that a country's government fails to fulfill its payment obligations fully and in due time. An organization can have country risk exposure even if it has no direct investment in another country or no contractual relationships with entities in another country.

Organizations may have exposure to Country Risk without realizing it. This is the case of crisis contamination and spill-over effect. This is also the case of domestic residents suffering from the uncertainty created by their government's decisions. The fallout from the UK decision to leave the EU has profound consequences for British investors, consumers, and workers, including rising inflation, a weaker Pound, slowing economic growth and investment, and a sharp cut in EU grants and contracts that affect university exchanges and research programs. Lastly, Country Risk fully depends on the specific exposure faced by those domestic and foreign economic agents. As we see later in this chapter, the size of risk, its timing, as well as cost and mitigation possibility, vastly differ from trade, financial, and investment transactions. Overall, risks can have an outcome which is either positive or negative. Taking risk, including Country Risk, can open fruitful opportunities for economic agents who know how to assess it and mitigate it.

2.7 The Main Components of Country Risk

The challenge faced by country risk managers is that uncertainty (often used interchangeably with "risk") is multifaceted. It is often complex as a result of the interdependence of its components and the "echo chamber" effect of the global economic system. Uncertainty varies greatly over time and across countries and can change abruptly, even in a national environment that appears stable and resilient. Uncertainty, even if planned for, can give rise to shocks that can have a wide and lasting impact due to almost immediate propagation in the global economy. Very few analysts predicted Brexit in the Spring of 2016. Likewise, many seasoned political analysts were amazed by the election of Donald Trump. In France, many were surprised by the rise and ultimate election of Emmanuel Macron—a political novice—in May of 2017 as well as the elimination of the traditional establishment that had held a de facto monopoly in the political landscape since World War II.

Country risk assessment seems akin to aiming at a moving target. To address its challenges and promote strategic decision-making, country risk managers must develop an analytical framework and actionable risk indicators and metrics that can be relied upon systematically over time. In portfolio management, expected volatility is arguably the best single metric for assessing the risk of an asset, although there are others. According to BlackRock: "Volatility can be measured in different ways, but most often it involves tracking the standard deviation of returns over some sample period and capturing the dispersion, or potential dispersion of returns, over time" (Fishwick and Sharma 2014). However, Country Risk can hide "sleeping volatility" to the extent that a seemingly stable economic or institutional environment can briskly capsize. Country Risk is one of the broadest and most diverse type of uncertainty and is therefore a challenge to manage effectively. Indeed, it is a distinct form of uncertainty but also a combination of other forms. It includes elements that are relatively easy to define and observe, but has other properties that are ambiguous, amorphous, and "out of plain sight." Some elements of Country Risk can be effectively measured; others, while plausible, are less frequently observed and cannot be quantified or effectively modeled. Moreover, some of its effects may be mitigated or lessened, but in other cases organizations must accept the consequences.

The main country risk components include economic risk, exchange rate risk, sociopolitical risk, sovereign and transfer risk, as well as regional contamination and systemic risks. There is also a range of risks that belong to portfolio management and that are not specific to Country Risk. One of these is concentration risk regarding asset classes or geographical distribution. Another is dependence risk regarding a borrower whose resources depend on a relatively small number of industries, commodities, or markets. The borrower can depend on a narrow range of markets for export revenues and also on a narrow range of key inputs to import for domestic production and export. Import-driven exports are discussed in Chapter 6. However, this risk will be tackled when the risk analyst will assess the sustainability of liquidity and solvency ratios that depend, among other variables, on the diversification of export products and markets. Figure 2.2 presents a classification of the main components of Country Risk.

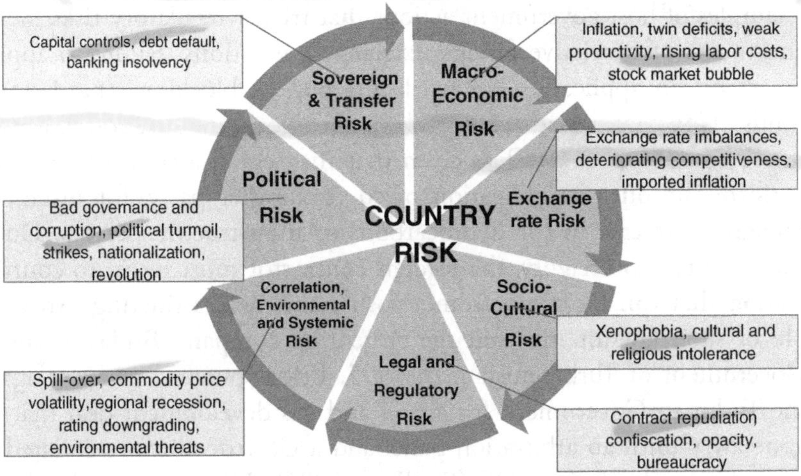

Fig. 2.2 A concise overview of the main components of Country Risk (Bouchet, Michel Henry, 2017a)

- **Macro-Economic risk**: This component of Country Risk is probably the easiest to understand and illustrate. It has do to with macroeconomic imbalances and their consequences on domestic and foreign economic agents' well-being, resulting from a government policy slippages or from regional and global contagion. Included among its many variables are over-heating and inflation, budget and balance of payments twin deficits, recession, weak productivity and rising labor costs, and high real rates of interest.
- **Exchange rate risk**: Exchange rate overvaluation has a negative impact on price competitiveness and foreign investment attractiveness. Conversely, exchange rate depreciation erodes the purchasing power of domestic economic agents and increases the price of imported goods and services, including inputs for exports. As discussed in Chapter 6, exchange rate depreciation stimulates a country's exports only under specific conditions, otherwise it generates a balance of payments "J-curve," hence increasing import costs without much positive impact on export stimulus.
- **Sovereign and transfer risk**: This risk is specific to cross-border transactions, that is, foreign direct investment, international banking credit, or bond issue. Investors and creditors literally depend on the "goodwill" of the sovereign borrower, whose legal and financial system, including the central bank, are out of range for foreign private economic agents. Capital controls, customs regulations, and the overall health of the banking system remain under the supremacy of the state.
- **Legal and regulatory risk**: This risk includes repudiation of contracts as well as inability to enforce them, but also indirect forms of risk such as bribes, regulatory opacity, or arbitrary changes in rules and regulations. Examples of host government actions that trigger regulatory risks include enactment of restrictive foreign exchange regulations, failure to approve or act on an application for hard currency, or blocking repatriation of funds. Contract repudiation and confiscation are probably the most severe cases of Country Risk given that they entail a country's refusal to perform the duty or obligation owed to another party, for instance, a foreign contractor in the hydrocarbons or infrastructure sectors. Due to the country's sovereignty, the foreign contractor must resort to court litigation that can be cumbersome, costly, and procrastinating. An example of such lawsuit involved the Argentine company Bridas versus the Government of Turkmenistan. In 1995, Bridas pursued recovery against the Turkmen Government for an oil and gas development deal that had gone awry until an arbitration panel and a US federal court declared the Government liable in 2006 (FindLaw 2006). Likewise, shareholders of the Russian oil company Yukos, including GML and BP, were awarded

USD 50 billion in the summer of 2017, after the Permanent Court of Arbitration in The Hague ruled that the energy giant had been illegally seized and sold to Rosneft by the Russian government in 2003. As discussed in Chapter 9, political risk insurance can protect against non-payment of invoices or non-honoring of contracts, as well as against cancelation of import or export permits, embargos, boycotts, sanctions, or decrees causing business interruption, payment defaults, or other losses.

- **Political risk**: This risk involves the quality or viability of the country's institutions and governance, including the independence of its executive, legislative, and judiciary branches. The resilience of national institutions transforms a country's economic growth into sustainable and inclusive development. Often failed states appear in rich countries with poor populations, notably in commodity-rich and hydrocarbons-dependent economies. National elites loot the country's resources and shift their wealth to offshore banking accounts. This will be discussed in detail in Chapters 9, 10 and 12. Political risk also includes the risk of national and regional fragmentation that is illustrated in Spain (Catalonia and Basque Country), France (Brittany and Corsica), Belgium (Flounders), United Kingdom (Scotland), or Italy (Veneto and Lombardy). Large regional economic discrepancies can trigger tax rebellion while feeding social frustration and secession demands.

A country may be able though not willing to honor its debt servicing obligations, fully and on time. This has often been the case of Latin American countries since independence in the early nineteenth century. A central bank can impose exchange controls and currency inconvertibility. A government can impose delays in debt repayments, or require refinancing, or unilaterally decide to default on its external indebtedness. The history of debt defaults provides useful lessons for risk managers given that history tends to repeat itself. The first suspensions of payments on sovereign bonds in Latin America spread internationally. Spanish American governments remained in default for decades. All in all, Argentina has defaulted on its international debt seven times and on its domestic bonds five times since its independence in 1816. The first sovereign default came only a decade after independence. In 1890 Argentina suffered a severe financial collapse leading to a banking collapse, a stock market crisis, and a debt default. Bolivia has defaulted five times since independence, Mexico eight times, as has Peru; Brazil nine times, like Chile and Costa Rica, and Ecuador ten times. Developing countries, however, do not hold the monopoly on debt defaults. Indeed, Germany defaulted four times since the nineteenth century, as many as Portugal. Russia and Greece defaulted five times, and Spain six times since the sixteenth century. Austria fell in external debt crisis seven times and remained in default during thirty six years (Reinhart 2010).

- **Sociocultural risk**: This risk entails the business consequences of a radical shift in a country's cultural, ideological, or religious values. This was clearly the case with the communist revolution in Cuba when the Castro-led guerillas ousted the authoritarian government of Batista on January 1, 1959, replacing it with a revolutionary socialist state; another example is the aftermath of the 1979 Islamic Revolution in Iran with the overthrow of the Pahlavi dynasty and the repressive leadership of Ayatollah Khomeini. However, there is no need for a full-fledged revolution to trigger sociocultural consequences on business and socioeconomic well-being. The election of the French socialist leader Mitterrand in May of 1981 led to a wide range of social reforms and nationalizations whose first impact was higher taxes, rising labor costs, and lower investment coupled with massive capital flight.
- **Exogenous and systemic risk**: This risk is associated with the echo chamber phenomenon in the globalized economic system that produces volatility and spill-over effect, hence crisis contamination. The contagion risk entails the potential consequence that a country's economic health is affected by volatility in a neighboring country or region, including rating downgrading, political turbulences, commodity price fluctuations, or trading partners' competitive devaluations. The systemic dimension of global risk produces global crisis, global warming, and terrorism.

2.8 How Does Country Risk Materialize?

Everything is about risk exposure. The extent to which an economic agent faces Country Risk depends fully on its specific exposure. An importer, an exporter, an investor, or an international bank do not face the same exposure to Country Risk, hence their mitigation strategy will not be the same. In addition, as discussed earlier in this chapter, Country Risk can exist in the absence of any explicit cross-border financial or commercial relationships. A key source of Country Risk is often referred to as correlated risk—one outcome gives rise to another that in turn gives rise to another. What happens in China or Russia or Citigroup or at the US Fed has repercussions throughout the global economic system. A few examples will shed light on that domestic dimension of Country Risk.

A first example is a chain of coffee shops in Chicago that purchases coffee through a local distributor, who obtains coffee beans from local growers. The coffee shop is influenced by the price of coffee and the trade policies of the country where the coffee is grown, as well as by global warming. Secondly, a coup d'état in the Ivory Coast, the largest Robusta producer in the world that produces 40% of coffee in the global market, will affect both prices and export volumes. Thirdly, Spain's local gas stations are affected by the price of oil, the exploration policies of countries where the oil is initially extracted and international fracking policies regarding shale oil. International banking regulations, central banks' monetary policy, tariffs and protectionist trade policy, cultural preferences, the weather, and the global interbank market—all these can create uncertainty and affect the volume and the price of goods and services. As another example, still in Spain, the Catalonia's sociopolitical upheaval in the Fall of 2017 had and will continue having deep and long consequences on the investment climate in the whole peninsula. In the wake of the Catalonia region's secession demands, around 3,000 companies shifted their headquarters outside Catalonia, and Spain became much less attractive to global investors. The stock market IBEX lost 2% and clients pulled almost USD 600 million from BlackRock's Spain-focused exchange traded fund in the month of October 2017 (*Financial Times* 2017) (Fig. 2.3).

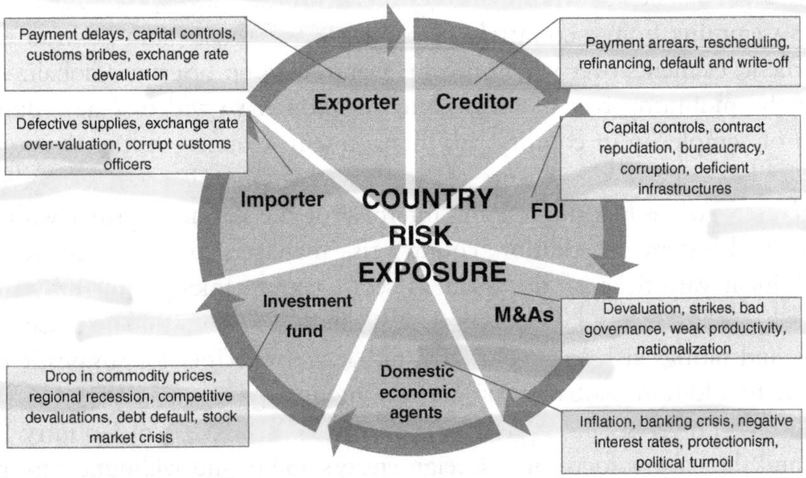

Fig. 2.3 Concise presentation of Country Risk exposure (Bouchet, Michel Henry, 2017a)

2.9 Is There an Optimal Institutional Organization for Country Risk Management?

Country risk management is a specialized though collaborative function. How an organization should be equipped to manage Country Risk depends on its specific exposure to risk. There are various steps to take. The organization should begin with a detailed exposure map regarding geographic exposure and categories of risks, as well as timing of the possible risks; it should then develop a common vocabulary to assess and manage Country Risk; integrate the concept of Country Risk into existing audit and risk programs, and then set up a comprehensive database of information and economic intelligence. Finally, it should identify an experienced individual to oversee and manage Country Risk with the right skill mix, including macroeconomics and geopolitics. One of the keys for optimum country risk management is creating a culture where employees at all levels can challenge assumptions relating to Country Risk.

2.10 Conclusion

Country Risk is everywhere, including at times and in places people do not expect it. No successful cross-border strategy can ignore Country Risk, and no lucrative domestic investment is possible without assessing the full range of risks stemming from a country's socioeconomic, financial, and political environment, elements over which private agents have no bearing. Globalization and the mounting risk of crisis contamination have added a new dimension of complexity in country risk management. Country risk analysts must assess the various components of a country's economic and sociopolitical weaknesses while focusing on the interplay of the national system with the globalized system. In addition, country risk managers can no longer rely on traditional yardsticks of risk such as scoring and ranking. Volatility, spillover, herd instinct, and complexity make quantitative assessment of Country Risk and ratings at best partial tools and at worst recipes for simplistic outlooks. In addition, globalization and the mounting threat of systemic banking crisis and terrorism require a reassessment of the scope of Country Risk beyond the narrow focus on a foreign entity's ability and willingness to meet its external obligations. Country Risk can affect trade flows, advisory services, contractual obligations regarding supplies, and real estate assets. And most importantly, foreign investors and creditors do not have the monopoly on Country Risk. Domestic residents face the negative consequences of the combination of uncertainty and turbulences in their home country that result from institutional deficiencies and a government's arbitrary decisions. Only an array of converging analytical approaches can lead to a more rigorous examination of the economic, institutional, and sociopolitical fabric that holds or distorts a country's development path. The latter should be tackled as economic growth coupled with those conditions that make it sustainable. These conditions include a legitimate political power base, social mobilization, sound institutions, and robust infrastructures.

Appendix 2.1: Four Examples of Country Risk Exposure

Example 1: Investment in Sovereign Debt

An endowment of a private US university seeks to earn a return on its investments to provide additional income for the school for scholarships, faculty salaries, and other expenses. In response to low interest rates in the United States, the endowment's investment team decides to buy the sovereign bonds of an emerging markets country, which are offering a higher yield than those available from domestic bonds. In purchasing the bonds, the investment team believes that the country will pay the periodic coupon payments on the bonds, plus the return of principal at maturity. In this case, the endowment can easily determine its particular exposure and can usually add to or decrease its exposure, assuming normal market liquidity conditions that permit the purchase and sale of the bonds.

The Country Risk here is relatively easy to identify. There is a well understood monetary transaction (i.e., the purchase of bonds); the location of the Country Risk is identifiable; there is a requirement for one or more parties to perform under a contract, usually under London or NY courts. The set of outcomes is identified as well as the risks (arrears, default); one can reasonably estimate the probabilities of the outcomes as well as measure the exposure (in net present value); the exposure exists for a finite, defined period; and the exposure can be adjusted to mitigate the risk through insurance contracts and hedging.

Example 2: Clothing Company with Off Shore Factories

A European manufacturer of popular and stylish clothing builds a factory in a Maghreb country. The company changes its merchandise throughout the year to attract buyers. To manufacture these different garments, the firm needs a large staff of skilled local workers who can cut and assemble fabrics into clothing. To remain competitive, labor, productivity, and manufacturing costs must be such that customers continue to adopt the combination of style and affordability. The company chooses a country that has a large supply of young workers with no requirement for local employers to provide costly health or retirement benefits. The company also chooses a country where it is relatively easy to hire or lay off workers. Although the company has been financially successful, it is criticized by prominent human rights organizations that its salaries are low, (well below the minimum wage) and it offers no health insurance and no retirement plans. The human rights organizations request that the company offer more extensive benefits and higher wages. Sensing a reputational concern, the company adjusts its compensation practices, but increases the prices of its clothing to offset some but not all the added costs. The company decides to maintain its manufacturing "offshore" despite the higher costs, but needs to boost productivity with new equipment and better management practices.

Example 3: A Manufacturing Firm Anticipates Global Growth

A publicly held US firm makes valves, gears, small engines, and industrial equipment. The firm does well when economies are expanding. The CEO, who is also the chairman, anticipates substantial growth in Latin America and the company significantly expands factories both in the US and in Latin America. In fact, the company makes significant "bet" that global demand will increase. To support its view of the opportunities in Latin America and Asia, the company relies on an analysis of a consulting firm which has a strong expertise in manufacturing and supply chain risk. The company does not have an internal staff of economists or risk managers, and the CEO has been given significant autonomy by the board of directors. The company buys raw materials in unprecedented amounts and adds workers and specialized industrial equipment to make its precision parts. The year after the expansion takes place, growth in Latin America slows down substantially. Global construction activity falls, as does demand for industrial parts and machinery. The company posts the largest loss in its history. The board of directors asks the CEO to step down and the job is divided between a Chairman of the Board and a CEO.

Example 4: A Coffee Shop

A coffee shop company in Boulder, Colorado is a business which is now run by the second generation of family owners. It has been buying coffee beans from the same suppliers for the last decade and has good relationships. It has four stores in the area. It is known for its service, eclectic interiors, and energetic young staff. It is also known for its varieties of coffee and tea, including its organic selections. It charges less for coffee than some of the national stores. It has considered expanding to adjoining states in Texas, New Mexico, and Wyoming. As a result of extreme climate conditions, the price of coffee beans substantially rises in the region where their coffee beans are grown, much more so than in other regions. The company fears that if it increases prices, it will lose some of its customers to other national coffee providers. It decides not to raise prices but now realizes that it needs to develop additional new relationships with coffee bean providers in other parts of the world. Diversification is an astute strategy though it will shift Country Risk to global producers in Africa, Asia, and Latin America.

References

AON. 2017. "Political Risk, Terrorism, and Political Violence Risk Map." http://www.aon.com/2017-political-risk-terrorism-and-political-violence-maps/index.html.

Bachelier, Louis. 1912. *Calcul des probabilités*. Paris: Gauthier-Villars.

Beck, Ulrich. 1992. *Risk Society: Towards a New Modernity*. London: Sage.

Bouchaud, Jean-Philippe. 2008. "Economics Needs a Scientific Revolution." *Nature* 455 (30): 1181, October.

Bouchet, Michel Henry. 2002. "Risque-Pays et Risque Politique." In *Comprendre et Gérer les Risques*. Moreau Franck Coordination. Paris: Editions d'Organisation.

Bouchet, Michel Henry. 2017a. "Country Risk Seminars and MOOC." Skema. https://www.developingfinance.org/.

Bouchet, Michel Henry. 2017b. "Country Risk in the Age of Trump and Globalization." *World Financial Review*, December.

Bouchet, Michel Henry, and Alice Guilhon. 2007. *Intelligence Economique et Gestion des Risques*. Paris: Pearson.

Bouchet, Michel Henry, Ephraïm Clark, and Bertrand Groslambert. 2003. *Country Risk Assessment: A Global Tool for Investment Strategy.* New York: Wiley.

Cowles, Alfred. 1960. "A Revision of Previous Conclusion Regarding Stock Market Behavior." *Econometrica* 28 (4): 909–915.

Dequech, David. 2011. "Uncertainty: A Typology and Refinements of Existing Concepts." *Journal of Economic Issues* 45 (3): 621–640.

Fabozzi, Frank, Sergio Focardi, and Caroline Jonas. 2014. "Investment Management, a Science to Teach or an Art to Learn?" New York, NY: CFA Research Institute Foundation.

Financial Times. 2017. "Spanish Retreat," November 10, p. 1.

Findlaw. 2006. "Bridas Versus Government of Turkmenistan." http://caselaw.findlaw.com/us-5th-circuit/1089023.html.

Fishwick, Edward, and Tara Sharma. 2014. "The Elements of Risk: Analyzing Changing Market Risk Conditions." New York, NY: BlackRock Investment Insights, March.

Focardi, Sergio M., and Frank J. Fabozzi. 2009. "Black Swans and White Eagles: On Mathematics and Finance." *Mathematical Methods of Operations Research* 69 (3): 379–394.

Goldin, Ian, and Chris Kutarna. 2017. "Risk and Complexity." *Finance and Development* 54 (3): 46–49.

Hammond, Philip. 2017. "Brexit Uncertainty Is Hurting Business Investment." *Reuters*, Top News, June 22. https://www.reuters.com/article/us-britain-eu-hammond/brexit-uncertainty-is-hurting-business-investment-finance-minister-hammond-idUSKBN19D0L4.

Institute of International Finance. 2017. https://www.iif.com/.

International Monetary Fund. 2011. "Definition and Measurement of Sovereign Risk Need to be Broadened." IMF Roundtable, Press Release No. 11/91, Public Affairs Department, Washington, DC, March 18.

Kempen Capital Management. 2016. "Turbulence with Trump." Special Report, November 9.

Keynes, John Maynard. (1921). 2004. *Treatise on Probability*. Macmillan & Co, Limited, St Martin's Street, London. Reprint, Mineola, New York: Dover Phoenix Edition.

Knight, Frank H. 1921. *Risk, Uncertainty and Profit*. Boston: Houghton Mifflin.

Mandelbrot, Benoît. 2001. Interview with the Authors. Financial Symposium, Ceram-Sophia Antipolis, July 3.

Mandelbrot, Benoît, and Richard Hudson. 2004. *The Misbehavior of Markets: A Fractal View of Risk, Ruin, and Reward*. New York: Basic Books.

Reinhart, Carmen. 2010. "This Time Is Different." NBER Working Paper 15815, March. http://www.nber.org/papers/w15815, http://www.nber.org/papers/w15815.pdf.

Sornette, Didier. 2016. *Why Stock Markets Crash: Critical Events in Complex Financial Systems*. Foreword. With a New Preface by the Author. August. Princeton: Princeton University Press. https://www.ethz.ch/content/dam/ethz/special-interest/mtec/chair-of-entrepreneurial-risks-dam/documents/Books/preface.pdf.

Standard & Poor's Global Rating. 2011. "Research Update: United States of America Long-Term Rating Lowered To 'AA+' On Political Risks and Rising Debt Burden; Outlook Negative." August 6. http://www.standardandpoors.com/en_AP/web/guest/article/-/view/sourceId/6802837.

Sweeting, Paul. 2010. "A Fractal View of Risk." *The Actuary*, December 1.

Tett, Gillian. 2017. "Executives Quietly Turn Away from Globalization." *Financial Times*, June 2, p. 9.

3

Country Risk in the Age of Globalization: Cycles and Dynamics. A Review of Literature

3.1 Introduction to the Main Approaches to Country Risk Analysis

3.1.1 The Analysis of Country Risk Has Continuously Evolved

Before the 1970s, country risk studies concentrated on the exposure of multinational corporations (MNCs) to political risk. This can be easily explained since many countries had just recovered their sovereignty from colonial powers and started "to question the benefits of having extremely powerful foreign firms in their backyard" (Bouchet et al. 2003). This question became particularly relevant when International Telephone and Telegraph (ITT) was involved in the *coup d'état* against Allende's socialist government in Chile in 1973.

The 1980s were marked by the advent of the international debt crisis in many developing countries. The focus was therefore on sovereign creditworthiness assessment and external debt servicing. The Mexican crisis in 1994 and the Asian meltdown in 1997 provided a new and decisive turning point in country risk analysis, with an emphasis on currency and banking crises. Kaminsky and Reinhart (1999) report 102 banking or currency crises from 1970 to 1995, among a sample of twenty industrialized and developing countries. Feldstein (2002) describes crises in emerging countries since the late 1990s as "more global and potentially more damaging to economic and political stability than

M. H. Bouchet et al., *Managing Country Risk in an Age of Globalization*,
https://doi.org/10.1007/978-3-319-89752-3_3

the crises of the past." He also observes that "the crises that hit Latin America in the 1980s were significantly different from those of the 1990s."

Moody's has one of the most historically complete databases on sovereign defaults. The agency notes: "Around a third of past sovereign defaults have been directly related to institutional and political weaknesses, ranging from political instability to weak budget management, governance problems, and political unwillingness to pay" (Tennant and Tracey 2015). As Toksöz (2014) observed: "Examples include the defaults by Mongolia in 1997 and Cameroon in 2004, due to weak budget management institutions and political uncertainty, Venezuela's 1998 default, due mostly to payment delays caused by administrative problems, and Ecuador's 2008 default which was simply political unwillingness to pay."

3.1.2 The Scope of Country Risk Has Continuously Evolved

A report from Fitch Rating (2013) provides a useful reminder: "The popular perception that sovereigns cannot default on debt denominated in their own currency because of their power to print money is a myth. They can and do. Examples in the last two decades include Venezuela (1998), Russia (1998), Ukraine (1998), Ecuador (1999), Argentina (2001), and Jamaica (2010 and 2013). Local currency (LC) defaults are less frequent than foreign currency (FC) defaults and are unlikely for countries with debt mainly denominated in local currency at long maturity."

The various debt crises have shifted attention from the current account to the capital account in what is known as the "second generation" of models (Dooley 2000). The purpose is to understand which policy options are available if there is a liquidity crisis resulting from capital flight. This may be caused by such events as raising interest rates or late devaluation to respond to a speculative attack on currency pegs.

In the aftermath of Bretton Woods' monetary system breakdown in the mid-1970s, central banks assumed greater independence to apply monetary policies to internal policy objectives. The International Monetary Fund (IMF) played a key role in promoting the constitutional and policy independence of the central monetary institutions. Examples range from Mexico to Brazil and Malaysia. As Mersch (2017) emphasizes: "First, there is sound economic evidence supporting the argument that an environment characterized by price stability is conducive to economic growth and high levels of employment which, in turn, positively contribute to the welfare of citizens. Second, in advanced economies, central bank independence and inflation traditionally show a significant negative correlation. And third, for independence to contribute to achieving the desired inflation target, it needs to be accompanied by a limited and clearly defined mandate for the central bank." From the year 2000, research studies flourished on the "stop and go" of massive cross-border of capital flows. Among the identified causes of capital flight and loss of market access were monetary policy considerations such as negative interest rates and abrupt turnarounds in the anticipations of investors.

3.1.3 Puzzling Over the Anatomy of Crises

The term "sudden stop crisis" was introduced in 1998 by Guillermo Calvo (2013), who produced econometric studies "puzzling over the anatomy of crises" suggesting that "about 50% of the variance of net capital flows in Latin America was due to the volatility of variables external to the region." Among those "external variables" were growth differences between developed and developing countries, low interest rates, and commodity prices, fueling a global credit boom that often precedes a financial crisis. Before the Global Financial Crisis, macroeconomists congratulated themselves for thinking they had learned how to manage volatility and economic cycles. Indeed, between 1985 and 2005, during the so-called "Great Moderation" period, volatility was much lower than it had been previously (Graph 3.1).

Former US Federal Reserve Chairman Ben Bernanke claimed that this "success" was above all due to the greater independence of central banks from political and financial influences, enabling them to follow macroeconomic stabilization. Paradoxically, after 2001, emerging markets improved substantially. Developing countries implemented more rigorous fiscal policies and controlled inflation, whereas developed countries adopted riskier policy measures, including very low interest rates. Toksöz (2014) notes: "Banking sectors had been restructured in previous crises and currencies were floating, thereby providing a cushion against external shocks. As a result, in the decade after 2001, there were no major defaults in emerging markets. Those that did occur were mostly home-grown crises in smaller economies: Belize (2006), Cameroon (2004) and the Dominican Republic (2005) for example."

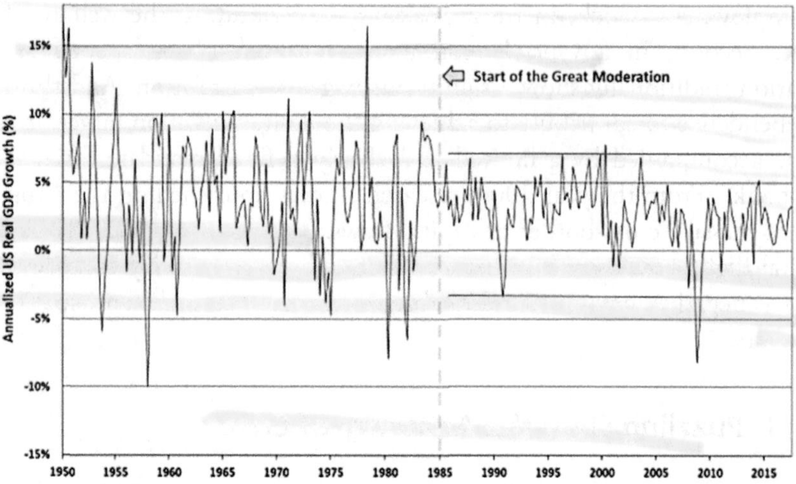

Graph 3.1 Lower volatility during the great moderation period (Federal Reserve Economic Data (FRED) database provided by Economic Research at the St. Louis Fed)

3.1.4 The Global Financial Crisis Has Changed the "Frame Analysis"

It is important to note that the Global Financial Crisis struck both developing and developed economies. Many studies, articles, and books have sought to explain the economic and financial vulnerabilities of OECD countries. Central banks have been heavily criticized, mainly because of their reliance on "Quantitative Easing" policies (or in more formal terms, "Large Scale Asset Purchases"), which blurred the line between fiscal policy and monetary policy (See also Chapter 11). This has resulted in a de facto "monetizing" of sovereign debt. Furthermore, rating agencies have been criticized for awarding investment grade ratings to subprime mortgage-backed products and failing to warn of the unsustainable buildup of the sovereign, or public, debt in the southern Eurozone economies (Langohr and Langohr 2009).

In the aftermath of the Global Financial Crisis, various signals of deglobalization emerged in the form of re-shoring and capital flow repatriation. Cross-border capital flows have fallen by around 60% from their 2007 peak as noted by Reinhart C. and V. (2008). In 2017, the Bank of International Settlement (BIS) published a significant report entitled "Financial Deglobalization in Banking?" (McCauley et al. 2017) One way of assessing the extent of any financial deglobalization is to look at home bias. One measure of home bias is the degree to which investment moves with the level of savings in the country. In countries that are not financially globalized, investment must be funded through savings by domestic individuals, companies, and the government (as further explained in Chapter 6). Home bias is greater if the correlation between domestic savings and investment is higher.

These new arrangements permitted a sharp rise in the leverage ratio of large US global banks toward thirty four on average (converted to an IFRS basis to be comparable to Europe). Table 3.1 shows the impact of this change on the leverage of US banks versus global banks in three other jurisdictions. Leverage of large EU global banks was always higher, and US leverage rose rapidly toward these levels, though it never became as large. The United Kingdom had the greatest acceleration, and Swiss leverage in two large banks was the highest of all. This quantum shift in leverage was a great enabling factor for banks to take advantage of the arbitrage possibilities in bank capital requirement and tax regulations. From 2004 there was a material acceleration in off-balance sheet mortgage securitization and the use of derivatives (particularly credit default swaps) to create synthetic bonds as key avenues to drive the revenue and the share price of banks.

Table 3.1 Deglobalization, investment home bias, and correlation with domestic savings (Forbes 2014. Referring to Lane and Milesi-Ferretti and IMF, WEO, Oct 2014)

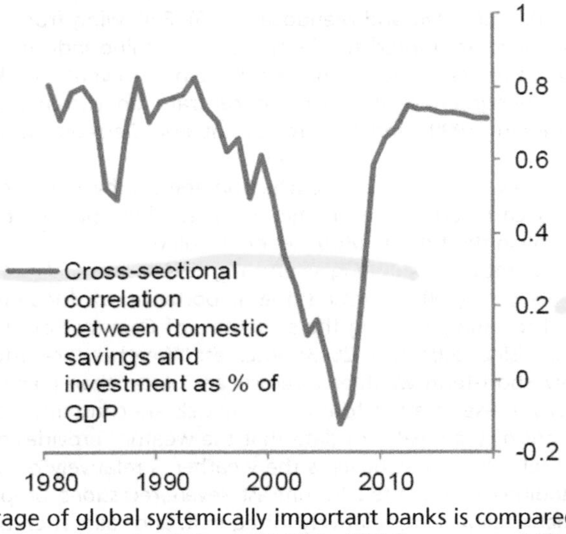

Notes The leverage of global systemically important banks is compared by converting the US banks and one Swiss bank from GAAP to IFRS for comparability. The ratios are total assets divided by core Tier-1 common equity

3.2 Is Country Risk Prediction Doomed to Failure in the Age of Globalization?

Modeling Country Risk is a challenge. There are not enough country defaults for proper model calibration. Also, as they happen in "waves," they are interrelated and lack of homogeneity for a "like-to-like" basis in the analysis.

Box 3.1: Are models useful for predicting future crisis?

Research in the field of Country Risk often follows an "event-driven" pattern, meaning that any new major crisis triggers a flurry of papers that seek to explain ex post the causes of the foregoing events. It also means that researchers may often "look through a finite lens" arising from changing diagnosis consensus, and specific context—namely "exchange rate crises" in the 1970s; "political crises" and their root causes in the 1960s and 1970s; "debt crises" and their explanations in the 1980s; "financial crises" and their sources in developing countries in the 1990s; and "Global Financial Crisis and contamination channels" in developed countries since 2000. It seems clear that the spectrum of analysis is never broad enough.

As stressed by Eichengreen and Rose (2000): "The success of future papers in explaining past crises does not mean that they will necessarily succeed in predicting future crises. This creates a real danger that the policy community if led to think otherwise, will be lulled into a false sense of complacency." In the same vein, Terrier (1999) wrote: "The New Risk is emerging."

The theoretical underpinnings of the articles about "financial crises" are rooted in the crisis models of Krugman (1979, 1998), Flood and Garber (1984), Obstfeld (1994), and Calvo and Mendoza (1996). Following from these papers, other authors have attempted to identify early warning indicators of crises in order to assess the risk of occurrence of this type of event. Frankel and Rose (1996) and Eichengreen et al. (1996) concentrate on currency crises. Hardy and Pazarbasioglu (1999) and Demirguc-Kunt and Detragiache (1998) tackle the banking crisis. Kaminsky (1999) and Goldstein et al. (2000) include these two types of crisis in a single approach. Nonetheless, by following an ad hoc approach after each series of economic collapses, these papers run the risk of "missing the call in the future" (Bouchet et al. 2003).

In an article entitled "Spotting a Banking Crisis Is Not Like Predicting the Weather," Calverley (2002) stressed the importance of fundamental analysis as opposed to simply tracking the symptoms of Country Risk such as declining reserves or rising debt. Kay (2013) observes: "Weather forecasters do rather well. Certainly, short-term weather forecasts are better than medium-term economic forecasts. These weather forecasting models are constantly calibrated and adjusted in light of the wealth of data that the weather provides hour by hour, and the physical system that governs the weather is relatively constant, even if our understanding of it is limited. In contrast, severe recessions, property bubbles, and abrupt bank failures are relatively infrequent, and calibration by economists has come to mean tweaking models to better explain the past rather than revising them to better predict the future - a particularly dangerous methodology when there are many reasons to think that the underlying structure of the economy is in a state of constant flux."

3.2.1 Quantitative Versus Qualitative Approach

In 1977, the Nobel economist Robert Solow wrote an influential article entitled "How Did Economics Get That Way and What Way Did it Get?" (Solow 1977). He defined economic modelers as "the overeducated in pursuit of the unknowable. But it sure beats the alternatives." One particularly challenging aspect of models is that they require an analyst to categorize and weigh risks. But it is hazardous to introduce hierarchy among the subsets of categories or indicators relevant to Country Risk. As Toksöz (2014) judiciously reminds us: "There may be a country, such as Russia, where sovereign risk is low because of low public debt and high FC reserves but jurisdiction risks are high because of the weakness of the rule of law."

The main shift in modeling Country Risk has been the emphasis on qualitative versus quantitative approaches. The early literature of the 1960s and 1970s clearly emphasized a qualitative approach to Country Risk, since the analysis was primarily concerned with political risk. With the sovereign defaults and financial crises that came later in the 1980s and 1990s, a more "quantitative approach" began to emerge. In 1978, Rummel and Heenan advocated an "integrated methodology" combining both quantitative and qualitative tools. Various economic crises have led researchers to question the quantitative perspectives of Gaddis (1992–1993) and Sionneau (2000). Gori (2002) observes that "social complexity is badly represented by neo-classical economics and rationalistic epistemology." A combined approach has emerged in response to progress in econometrics. "Logit" and "Probit" regression models have been useful when the explained variable is binary, thus aligned with the nature of default risk (default or non-default) that follows a normal distribution of probability.

More recent models have tried to capture indirect risks such as contagion and spillover. Kodres and Pritsker (2002) concluded that country risk analysis has moved from "normal statistical t-distribution stuff to extreme value theory… way out there." Gray and Jobst (2013) further state: "The suggested approach uses advanced contingent claims analysis (CCA) to generate aggregate estimates of the joint default risk of multiple institutions as a conditional tail expectation using multivariate extreme value theory (EVT). In addition, the framework also helps quantify the individual contributions to systemic risk and contingent liabilities of the financial sector during times of stress."

Another methodology for the assessment of Country Risk is CCA, which uses option pricing theory to value assets. In a manner similar to what is used in the valuation of financial derivatives, an asset's future value depends in turn on the future value of other assets. For instance, the Merton Model is an application of CCA for the valuation of corporate debt obligations.

Investors and analysts use the Merton Model to assess the ability of a company to meet its financial obligations and service its debt. It can also be used to assess sovereign risk.

The modeling of "contagion" has incorporated network and chaos theories, which do not rely on the traditional assumption of the normal distribution of risk (Toksöz 2014). These modern approaches to modeling are further discussed in Chapters 5 and 13, which explore ratings and private sources of insight into Country Risk. They are a significant improvement over previous approaches even if they are still sensitive to assumptions and cannot "stand alone" without human interpretation and analysis.

3.3 What About New Kind of Crises and New Related Indicators?

3.3.1 Push Versus Pull Factors

Indicators can never be analyzed in isolation, and the conclusions they lead to should not be accepted without further investigation. In defining and developing a range of indicators of Country Risk, analysts distinguish between two broad categories. First, there are "in-country structural fundamentals" (e.g., industrialization ratios, which were long seen as indicators of a country's ability to avoid payments crisis). Second, there are "external-to-country" destabilizing factors, which stem from a country's structural integration within the globalized market economy. These indicators are often correlated. New indicators are always being developed. A current area of emphasis is cyclical indicators and external "push factors" (global shocks in advanced economies that "push" other countries out of their comfort or safe zone, examples being abrupt changes in monetary or fiscal policies). These are in contrast to "pull factors" (country-specific determinants such as real divergences between emerging markets and advanced economies). A benchmark study by Fratzscher (2011) defined three periods associated with the Global Financial Crisis: the precrisis period (1 May 2005–7 August 2007); the crisis itself (8 August 2007–15 March 2009); and the postcrisis (16 March 2009–31 October 2010). The study analyzed the percentage share of portfolio flows to fifty countries, broken down into six regions. These flows were further broken down into push factors (common/global shocks to risk, liquidity, and asset prices) and pull factors (country-specific shocks, institutional quality, country risk rating, and macroeconomic fundamentals). Chapter 14 further tackles this question (Table 3.2).

Table 3.2 The role of push factors versus pull factors for global capital flows (Fratzscher 2011) (% of capital flows explained)

	Push factors			Pull factors		
	Precrisis	Crisis	Postcrisis	Precrisis	Crisis	Postcrisis
All countries	65.4	72.8	45.0	34.6	27.2	55.0
EM Asia	48.3	84.9	18.1	51.7	15.1	81.9
EM Europe	86.6	93.2	80.3	13.4	6.8	19.7
Latin America	48.8	150.0	36.9	51.2	−50.0	63.1
Africa/Middle East	109.3	104.4	54.8	−9.3	−4.4	45.2
Advanced Europe	90.8	23.2	84.2	9.2	76.8	15.8
Other advanced	76.1	80.5	58.8	23.9	19.5	41.2

Source Survey by authors: (1) Thomson Reuters; (2) Sources are proxy statements; (3) Majority shares owned by or stable and long-term management established by insiders, e.g., partners or family members; and (4) Includes banks where the board does not have a subcommittee primarily responsible for the company's risk policy

Negative figures in the table indicate that, other things being equal, a set of factors predicted capital inflows due to pull factors for some countries whereas these countries actually experienced net capital outflows due to the dominance of push factors.

In fact, on average, push factors turn out to be the main driver of net capital flows, except in the "postcrisis" period when country-specific pull factors dominate. It has also become clear that developing countries in Africa/Middle East and Latin America suffer heavily from "push factors."

Box 3.2: Categories of indicators to be monitored

- Type of exchange rate regime (more or less constraining)
- Regulatory and monitoring structures
- Microlevel transparency
- Country-level transparency
- Liberalization of Markets
- Independence and competency of asset rating companies
- Political situation
- Current account and fiscal deficits
- Level of inflation
- Level of public debt
- Currency and maturity mismatches in foreign borrowing
- Type of debt instruments
- Size of financial sector relative to real sector
- Size of banks
- Exposure to real shocks, such as commodity price spikes

Source http://www.economicsofcrisis.com

Currency and banking crises do appear to be key drivers of Country Risk. Reinhart and Rogoff (2009) studied early warning indicators for both banking and currency crises. It is increasingly recognized that changes in international investor sentiment are the main reason that led to a rapid shift in the direction of capital flows, providing a sudden excess of liquidity (risk of credit boom/bust) or a sudden shortage of liquidity (risk for countries and current account financing).

Arising from the collective body of thinking and research are a range of factors relating Country Risk. They include both obvious and non-obvious factors.

- Real exchange rates
- Real housing prices
- Short-term capital inflows/GDP
- Current account balance/investment
- Real stock price

More specifically for a currency crisis, the following are considered to be relevant factors.

- Real exchange rates
- Banking crisis
- Current account balance/GDP
- Real prices
- Exports
- M2/international reserves

Sovereign debt crises demonstrate similar cyclical patterns:

- Financial liberalization and credit boom
- Overvalued exchange rates
- Structural dependence of exports on a few commodity products
- Sudden stop and currency crises
- Devaluation and banking crisis
- Government bail-out of banks
- Sovereign debt default

In addition, the World Bank has provided a useful description of the key components of a banking crisis:

- Periods of high international capital mobility
- Preceding a period of sustained surges in capital inflows
- Preceding boom in real housing prices with a marked decline and
- Preceding expansion in the number of financial institutions

In a note entitled "How Many More 'Lehman Moments' to Come?" (2011), Agrawal summarized the main features of a banking crisis:

	Rogoff–Reinhart analysis	US economy since 2007
Housing	35% decline over 6 years	Declined by 23.8% between Dec-07 and Mar-11 Declined by 46.6% since peak reached in April of 2006

	Rogoff–Reinhart analysis	US economy since 2007
Equity markets	55% over 3.5 years	Declined by 53.7% in 1.5 years. Average decline since Oct-07 is around 27%
Unemployment	Rises to 7% over 4 years	9.1% in 3.5 years
GDP	9% decline over 2 years	4% decline over 2 years
Public debt	86% over 3 years	79% over 3 years

Banking crises have brought new rounds of thinking about modeling Country Risk, including the addition of more liquidity indicators. In 2000, the Institute of International Finance (IIF) noted that "robust methods exist for generating country risk ratings and incorporating (them) into the economic capital allocation process. Some banks have developed models to generate specific capital cushions for country risk using processes analogous to existing obligator credit risk models."

3.3.2 In the Long Run, We Are All Dead

In all cases, the main problem remains the unreliability of past data to explain future crises. As Keynes warned in 1924: "The long run is a misleading guide to current affairs. In the long run, we are all dead. Economists set themselves too easy, too useless a task if in the tempestuous seasons they can only tell us that when the storm is long past the ocean will be flat." From that cornerstone, the most "straightforward" and "second best" approach is the study of cycles that are part descriptive and predictive (short term) since they demonstrate some consistent and coincident features that are supposed to repeat. The predictive approach is supposed to track turning points in the economic variable cycle. Nevertheless, one must remember that history never repeats itself in exactly the same way.

3.4 The Cyclic Nature of Crises Is Increasingly at the Heart of Country Risk Analysis

Even if the literature before 2008 addressed the cyclical aspects of crises, the Global Financial Crisis reinforced the importance of using models for the investment cycle and the credit cycle, especially in the investigation of developed market financial and payments crises. The common features of credit cycles include the following phases: cumulative expansion, a peak, cumulative contraction, and a terminal stage. Niemira and Klein (1994) observe: "In all likelihood, the business cycles will continue to evolve. The role of the forecaster and analyst is to figure out what is enduring and to distinguish it from what is not and to understand how those enduring factors are evolving."

3.4.1 Sources of Cycles

One trigger factor of these cycles often comes from "global and international imbalances," like "push factors" driving overlending and cyclical indicators: "These capital flows cycles have taken over from policymakers as the key drivers of global cycles" (Suttle 2008). As discussed further in Chapters 6, 11, and 14, it is for this reason that it is important to monitor trends in global financial centers (US, UK, EU, China, and Japan). In addition, the following features may also help to assess global capital flows:

- International interest rates and interbank rates
- International cross-exchange rates relevant to the region
- Credit growth in systemically important economies
- Market volatility indicators (one example being the VIX)
- Rate of change of commodity prices and asset prices
- Electoral cycles
- Global leading indicators (OECD, IMF, Baltic Dry indexes)

3.4.2 Bunches of Defaults

Among the most comprehensive empirical studies of sovereign debt crises is the work by Tomz and Wright (2013). One striking feature of default crises is that they come in "bunches." Default crises almost always occur in "waves," as shown in Tables 3.3 and 3.4.

It is worth noticing that more than fifteen countries defaulted in the 1930s and 1940s, whereas less than five per annum defaulted during the period beginning in the 1950s up to 2010. Nevertheless, those figures must also consider the "serial defaulters" among Highly Indebted Poor Countries (HIPC). For instance, the Paris Club of developed country creditors has moved from providing time and money through rescheduling and refinancing to debt reduction, thereby providing debt relief and not only liquidity relief to low-income countries. But a combination of adverse terms of trade, weak export diversification, and bad governance has led debtor countries to seek debt relief agreements on a repeated basis. For instance, the Democratic Republic of Congo went through twenty rounds of debt restructuring between 1976 and 2010. Senegal met with the Paris Club fourteen times between 1981 and 2004.

Table 3.3 Default amounts, by debtor, till 2016 (CRAG, Bank of Canada, Database of Sovereign Defaults 2017)

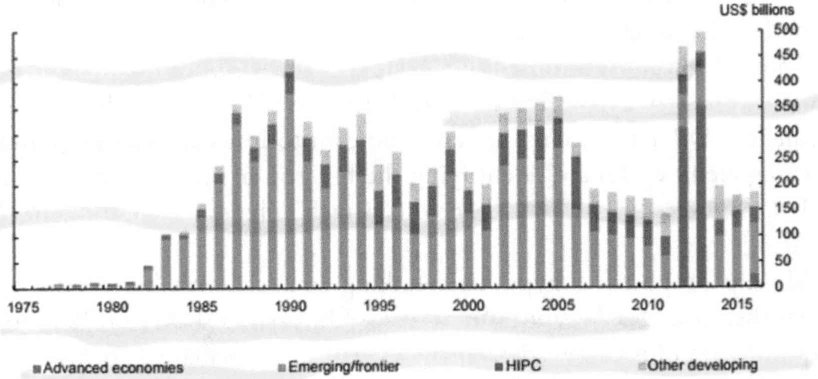

Table 3.4 Number of sovereign debtor countries in default/year (*Source* Standard and Poor's, Credit Agricole, SA). Reproduced with permission of Standard and Poor's Financial Services LLC

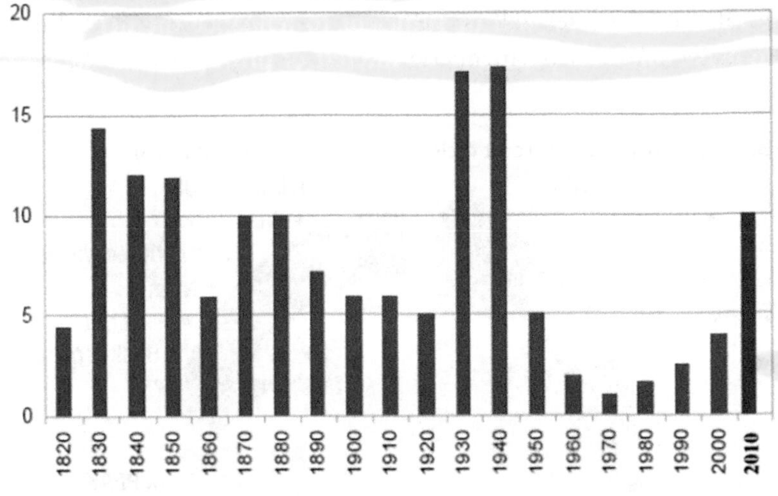

3.4.3 Amplifying Factors and Minsky Moment

Cyclical patterns are amplified by financial intermediation and the role of banks in the economy. Financial crises and banking crises often coincide. In many instances, especially in recent history, banking crises preceded financial crises. Reinhart and Reinhart (2008) confirmed this relationship in their study on capital flow "bonanzas." For 181 countries, they defined a capital flow "bonanza" as an episode in which there are larger-than-normal net inflows. Such episodes have become more frequent with the liberalization of capital flows since the 1980s.

Another common feature of financial crises is that they are often preceded by asset price and credit bubbles. In 2013, the BIS reported that the total-credit-to-GDP ratio seems to have some historical explanatory power in tracking credit cycles and identifying the buildup of credit bubbles (Toksöz 2014). The "credit cycle" and "credit crunch" phases can be described in Table 3.5.

Minsky proposed a hypothesis linking financial instability and credit cycles theories. He identified three types of borrowers that contribute to the accumulation of insolvent debt: hedge borrowers, speculative borrowers, and Ponzi borrowers. "The 'hedge borrower' can make debt payments (covering interest and principal) from current cash flows from investments. The 'speculative borrower' uses the cash flow from investments to service the debt, i.e., cover the interest due, but the borrower must regularly roll over, or re-borrow, the principal. The 'Ponzi borrower' (named after the Italian speculator turned crook) borrows based on the belief that the appreciation of the value of the asset will be sufficient to refinance the debt, but is not able to make sufficient payments on interest or principal with the cash flow

Table 3.5 Features of each credit cycle phase (Mehreen Khan 2015)

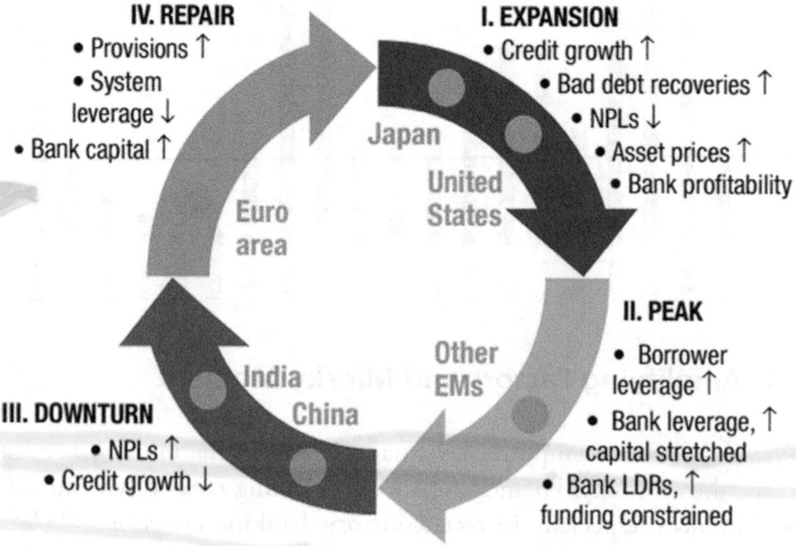

NB: NPL = Nonperforming Loans; Bank LDR = Loan-to-Deposit ratio

from investments. Only the appreciating asset value can keep the Ponzi borrower afloat" (Gottesman and Liebrok 2017). Usually, the "Ponzi scheme" refers to a pyramid scheme in which new investors' funds are used to pay the earlier backers. The "Ponzi scheme" was also used by Madoff in his classic example of fraud. Mr. Zhou, governor of the People's Bank of China, described China's heightened risks from excessive debt and speculative investment as a "Minsky moment," which is the turning point that occurs when investors start to realize that underlying asset prices are likely to move down (*Financial Times* 2017). Zhou advocated further financial liberalization reforms with enhanced regulation to deepen and stabilize China's financial system. In particular, the People's Bank in 2016–2017 pushed forward capital account opening, financial market reforms, and improvements to monetary and exchange rate policies, while paving the way for a gradual globalization of the Yuan. This was done to stem the risk of a "Minsky moment" (Islam 2014).

3.4.4 Recurrent Cyclic Patterns

Beyond credit cycles, some other patterns can be identified for bank runs and liquidity crises (Johnson 2002):

- Market participants become reluctant to do business with troubled banks, resulting in higher risk premiums for those banks, generally appearing two to three years in advance;
- Troubled financial news erupt, and consequently, the average maturity of deposits grows shorter;
- Retail depositors begin losing confidence in the banks, resulting in a noticeable decline in the "deposit surplus ratio";
- Liquid assets for sale are exhausted and the bank becomes insolvent.

An IMF report from Claessens and Kose (2003) indicates that the bursting of a financial bubble almost always follows an overexpansion of the money supply. Kaminsky and Reinhart (1999) observed that during numerous financial crises, "the M2/Reserves and M1 Excess Balances indicators rose prior to the crisis, dropping almost immediately after. Bank deposits also decreased post-crisis. Much of the money supply prior to the bursting of the bubble was on borrowed assets held by private citizens and public governments."

Another cyclic pattern arises from corporation valuation methods. A money supply increase results in lower interest rates, leading to lower discount rates. Based on discount dividends model (DDM) or other methods, lower discount rates increase a firm's valuation and equity market price. That market value becomes disconnected with a firm's "real value." Here, the cyclic pattern is caused by deficient model valuation or by investors bidding up the price beyond any real sustainable value.

Demographic issues can also impact financial cycles since an aging population will have higher savings, resulting in a greater supply of money (i.e., more bank deposits and increased capacity of financial institutions to lend) and hence lower interest rates. Other relevant factors may include the following:

- New societal aspirations
- Financial innovation to respond to those aspirations
- New risks due to financial innovation
- New regulations
- New efforts to bypass regulation

3.4.5 Vicious Spirals

As we have observed in numerous instances, an economy can go astray, trapped in a vicious spiral. A country's banking sector can take excessive risks to compete and gain market share. There is a well-established correlation between risk-taking and banking sector competition (as measured by the number of banks in a territory or through the Herfindahl-Hirschman index (HHI), which is a commonly accepted measure of market concentration). Another problem, as we saw in the subprime market in the Global Financial Crisis, is that lenders make lower credit quality loans and do not adequately take into account the additional risk in setting the interest rate on the loan, often extending credit at lower variable rates to enable the borrowers to qualify more easily. The downturn phase of the credit cycle is characterized by an increase of nonperforming loans (NPLs) due to asset bubble bursts, currency crisis, inaccurate ratings or credit risk measures, and abnormally complicated accounting practices and financial products.

Hoggarth et al. (2004) found that NPLs were between 17% and 33% of total loans at the beginning of the thirty-three banking crises studied from 1977 to 2002. Goodhart (2007) further states: "When housing prices go down, particularly at a time when effective interest rates are rising…the probability of default on the loans of the individuals in the pool ceases to be independent of each other; the correlations rise as well as the probability of default themselves." Then, the interbank liquidity dried up, and the TED spread (the difference between three-month interbank rates and government security rates) soared.

3.4.6 Distorted Incentives

A lack of regulation coupled with excessive or premature financial liberalization is often the cause of financial crisis both in developing and developed countries. The circumstances are often similar: financial markets usually decline faster than they rise and no tree grows to the sky! (Goodhart 2008). The "Washington Consensus," which emerged in 1989, refers to a framework of market-driven policy measures that aim to promote liberal financial reforms (Williamson 2000). (See Chapter 10 for a further discussion on Williamson's approach to deregulation and market liberalization.) It includes the following policy prescriptions:

1. Low government borrowing. Avoidance of large fiscal deficits relative to GDP;
2. Redirection of public spending from subsidies ("especially indiscriminate subsidies") toward broad-based provision of key pro-growth, pro-poor services like primary education, primary health care, and infrastructure investment;
3. Tax reform, broadening the tax base, and adopting moderate marginal tax rates;
4. Interest rates that are market determined and positive (but moderate) in real terms;
5. Competitive exchange rates;
6. Trade liberalization: liberalization of imports, with particular emphasis on eliminating quantitative restrictions (licensing, etc.); trade protection measures are limited to low and relatively uniform tariffs;
7. Liberalization of inward foreign direct investment (FDI);
8. Privatization of state enterprises;
9. Deregulation: removal of regulations that impede market entry or restrict competition, except for those justified on safety, environmental and consumer protection grounds, and prudential oversight of financial institutions; and
10. Legal protection of property rights.

The Washington Consensus has had an important impact on economic development in Latin America, South East Asia, and other regions. Nevertheless, a different interpretation of it has led some countries to over-loosen regulations, especially in financial markets. As we now realize, the challenge with deregulation is that it takes years to see its effects, and there are no reliable early warning signs.

3.5 Additional Sources of Cycles and Volatility

3.5.1 Prices and Exchange Rates

Prices and exchange rates are also cyclic. For instance, a rise in inflation may deter foreign investors. Hence, exchange rates tend to depreciate, increasing the value/price at which the country can purchase its imports. That "extra-cost" of imported goods is likely to be passed on to domestic prices of goods (since these incorporate imported intermediary goods), further stimulating the initial inflation. Additional inflation leads the currency to further depreciate and so on and so forth (Table 3.6).

Table 3.6 Dynamic instability of price level (Bouchet, Fishkin, Goguel)

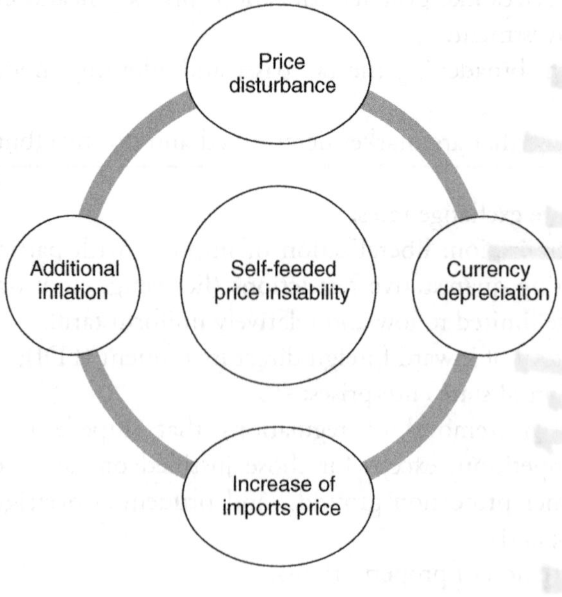

3.5.2 Risk Appetite and Market Sentiment

Beyond cyclic economic variables, the most powerful transmitter of financial contagion is the sharp reversal of international risk appetite driven by global events or what is known as "ro-ro" or risk-on/risk-off volatility. Market "feeling" is not always based on strictly rational thinking, often reflecting emotions that may be irrational. Behavioral finance has helped explain such changes in investor's mindset. In addition, investors use various indicators to measure market sentiment to determine which stocks to buy or sell. Some of these indicators include the Chicago Board Option Exchange (CBOE) Volatility Index (VIX), 52 weeks High/Low Sentiment Ratio, Bullish Percentage, and moving average calculations. Market sentiment is definitely not linear and it often overshoots. Among other factors, rating agencies' downgrades and upgrades can introduce sudden shifts in the investor's mindset and heighten pro-cyclicality. This may result in large adjustments ("cliff-edge effects") in ratings, triggering an overreaction in financial markets. Credit Rating Agencies (CRAs) are mostly criticized for lagging behind indicators.

3.5.3 Commodities are also "Super-Cyclical"

Graph 3.2 illustrates that various commodities (energy, food, metals) are highly cyclical.

Obviously, commodity cycles are a major concern for countries dependent on commodity exports. They suffer from terms of trade shocks when sharp fluctuations in the price of strategic exports or imports heavily impact on the country's international purchasing power and revenues. For instance, at the beginning of 2009, the countries of South Eastern Europe (including

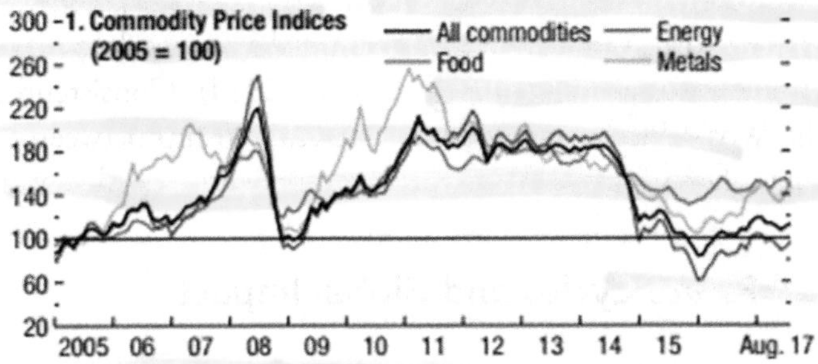

Graph 3.2 Volatility of commodity price indices (IMF, World Economic Outlook, Oct 2017)

Albania, Bosnia and Herzegovina, Bulgaria, Croatia, Greece, Former Yugoslav Republic (FYR) Macedonia, Montenegro, Romania, Serbia, and Kosovo) were simultaneously hit by three external shocks: an extended period of cold weather; disruption in the natural gas supply from the Russian Federation; and a financial crisis (Kovacevic 2009). Indeed, weather, natural disasters, and food prices increases are frequent sources of crises (Fan and Headey 2008). Their consequences can be significant. Egypt, for example, imports 40% of its food, like several Maghreb countries.

A wide range of academic research has attempted to identify which factors might have caused surges in food prices (Abbott et al. 2008; Baltzer et al. 2008; Schnepf 2008; Trostle 2008; von Braun 2008). Thus far, only one study has attempted to add explicit orders of magnitude to different factors.

As shown in Table 3.7, many factors may have a causal impact and they interplay to determine the magnitude of a commodity price shock. Erten and Ocampo (2012) write: "Decomposition of real commodity prices suggests four super-cycles during 1865–2009 ranging between thirty and forty years with amplitudes of 20–40% higher or lower than the long-run trend. Non-oil price super-cycles follow world GDP, indicating they are essentially demand-determined; causality runs in the opposite direction for oil prices."

One noticeable development is the reduced ability of the cartel of OPEC oil-producing countries to control the global market price of oil. Since the emergence of new non-OPEC producers, including Mexico, Russia, and Norway, OPEC members produce approximately 35% of the world's oil consumption, versus 80% when the cartel was created in 1960.

Commodity prices also depend widely on exchange rate regimes and fluctuations. "Commodity movements seem to have a possible inverse relationship to the strength or weakness of global currency regimes. When global currency regime weakens, uncertainty increases and commodity prices tend to rise as investors turn to physical assets such as gold. Conversely, a strong international monetary system corresponds to weaker commodity prices, boosting profitability and investment in manufacturing" (Toksöz 2014). Consistently, data collected by the World Bank suggest an inverse relationship between commodity prices and manufacturing that has existed over the past several centuries.

3.5.4 Real Estate Cycles and Global Impact

Another highly cyclical driver is housing construction and urbanization, both of which are demographically driven and linked to country's growth. Rural

Table 3.7 Explanations of the 2005–2008 global food crisis and their strengths and weaknesses (Fan and Headey 2008)

Explanation	Strengths	Weaknesses
Growth in demand from China and India	Partly explains rising oil prices, partly explains the demand for oilseeds	China and India are self-sufficient in most major grains but have not increased imports of any staple foods
Financial market speculation	Increased financial market activity coincides with a rise in prices	Higher prices induce speculation, so causality argument is weak; no clear evidence yet of a causal link
Hoarding: export restrictions	Price rises for rice were preceded by export restrictions by countries that account for 40% of global rice exports	Wheat, maize, and soybean price rises generally preceded restrictions; biggest players did not impose restrictions
Weather shocks	Australian wheat production 50–60% below trend growth rates in 2005 and 2006; there were also moderately poor harvests in the United States, Russia, and Ukraine	Only explains wheat prices; production shocks of this magnitude are common in international wheat markets, and in Australia over the last 15–20 years
Productivity slowdown	Production and yield growth of rice, wheat, and maize have slowed down over the last 20 years or so	Productivity slowed, but it is not clear that demand outpaced supply over this time period
Low interest rates	Low interest rates ought to increase demand for storable commodities, increase stocks, and shift investors from treasury bills to commodity contracts	Stocks/inventories of gold and oil are reasonably high, but stocks of staples are low; no clear evidence that futures markets are affecting spot prices (see above)
Depreciation of the USD	Real agricultural trade-weighted index for the United States depreciated 22% over 2002–2007; USD and commodity prices are a covariate	No critical weaknesses; Mitchell calculates that this factor probably increased Dollar-denominated prices by 20%
Rising oil prices	Have risen sharply and somewhat preceded food prices; a large component of production and transport costs, especially in wheat and corn production	No critical weaknesses, although some authors expect the effects of rising oil prices on food prices to be more delayed and to have a larger impact via biofuels demand
Biofuels demand	Has surged since 2003, and consumed 25% of US corn crop in 2007; two-thirds of global maize exports are from the United States	Strong for corn, less so for wheat, although substitution effects could account for rising in other products
Decline of stocks	Low stocks are traditionally associated with increased sensitivity to shocks; stocks of all major cereals declined prior to the price surge	Netting out China makes the decline in stocks less dramatic. Unless stock declines result from policies, declines only represent the effects of other factors

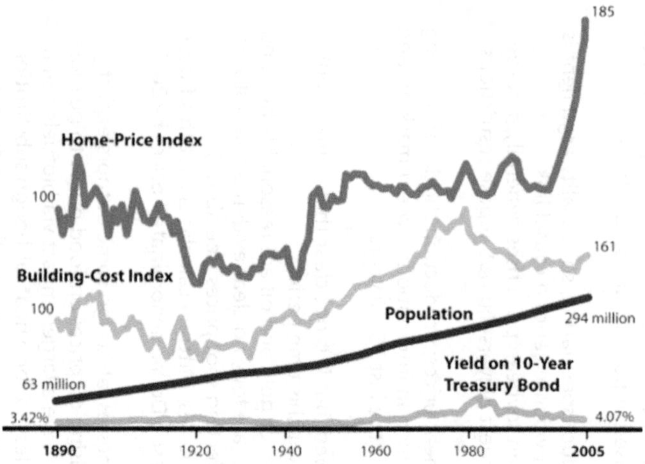

Graph 3.3 Inflation-adjusted US home prices compared with population growth, building cost index, and ten-year Treasury bonds for funding (Shiller 2000)

migrants move into cities to take advantage of economic opportunities, creating upward pressure on urban real estate prices. This problem is made worse in emerging markets, where there are fewer sources of long-term financing for home purchases. Housing price inflation may also reflect the weakness of local financial markets and the lack of other sources of investment.

Robert Shiller, the Nobel Prize winner who developed the S&P/Case-Shiller index, plotted US home prices, population, building costs, and bond yields. He shows that inflation-adjusted US home prices increased 0.4% per year from 1890 to 2004, and 0.7% per year from 1940 to 2004, whereas US census data from 1940 to 2004 shows that the self-assessed value increased 2% per year (Shiller 2000) (Graph 3.3).

An IMF study (Igan and Loungani 2012) observed the impact of globalization on domestic policies: "The findings suggest that long-run price dynamics are mostly driven by local fundamentals such as income and population growth. The effect of more globally connected factors such as interest rates appears to be less strong. Credit market conditions may cause short-run deviations from long-run equilibrium and, ultimately, when the correction starts, as it did in the most recent episode, financial stability and the overall economy bear important consequences in terms of credit institutions coming under stress and slowing real economic activity. The severity of the ultimate impact depends on various factors including structural characteristics of housing and mortgage markets."

Rising housing prices are accompanied by higher household consumption and firm investment that boost economic growth. However, excessive house price appreciation may distort capital allocation efficiency by crowding out investments in productive sectors, thus reducing long-term economic growth. Moreover, house price bubbles tend to burst sooner or later as shown by Bracke (2013).

3.6 Globalization and Country Vulnerabilities

3.6.1 Holistic Perspective and Interactions

In assessing any particular international investment, an analyst must study the particular features and terms of the transaction carefully. Yet, it is also necessary to adopt a holistic perspective, since different types of risk sources can interact with each other. Moreover, challenges in one country or region can affect others. For example, the Asian crisis of 1997/1998 started in Thailand with the devaluation of the Thai Baht, before spreading as far as Russia. But other economic and political factors contributed further, notably the imbalance of the current accounts and so-called "crony capitalism," an economic system in which personal relationships are rewarded more highly than risk-taking.

Payments crises and defaults can result from a range of factors including demographics, real estate conditions, financial markets, and political circumstances (as well as interactions among these). It is therefore important to track not just financial and credit cycles but the cycles of the real economy. Credit booms are not just a monetary phenomenon but a reflection of a complex mix of factors. As observed by Toksöz (2014): "Cycles could begin with a period of strong productivity-driven GDP growth, which is amplified by an increase in capital inflows in the context of liberalized capital markets." Another classic example is the significant portfolio of US treasury bonds accumulated by central banks of structural net exporter Asian countries. This is sometimes referred as the "global savings glut" because the size of savings exceeds the need for investments. Such purchases have helped keep US interest rates low (further stimulating a credit bubble even during the slowdown period of the US economy).

3.6.2 Vulnerability Factors Identified by Scholars

As emphasized in one of the latest articles on the subject, there have been changes over the years in the vulnerability or resilience of countries to payment crises. Pagliari and Hannan (2017) observe that "emerging and developing countries (EMDEs) tend to receive capital flows that, even in net terms, are large relative to their domestic economies and overall absorptive capacity in terms of the size and depth of their financial systems. Second, EMDEs are more vulnerable to shocks, partly because their economies are smaller and less diversified" (Table 3.8).

Most crises occur as a result of the complex interaction of several external and internal factors. Allen and Gale (1999) observe that specific causes tend to lead to deeper crises than others but most crises share several causes relating to market failure. Moreover, some factors are more likely to emerge than others.

3.6.3 Tolerance and Resilience Factors

The composition of capital inflows is a crucial component of a country's resilience to external shocks. Certain types of capital inflow are particularly favorable to funding current accounts in that they provide a better cushion against global shocks. These are "non-debt-creating capital inflows" such as FDI and portfolio capital inflows. FDI flows are good "shock absorbers" because they remain in place and investors have few other choices for redeploying their capital. FDI is a long-term strategic choice. This is in contrast to investments in bonds, which are among the most volatile sources of capital whereas equities are often considered as "longer-term" investments.

As observed in Chapter 11, the structure of debt also determines a country's debt tolerance level. Japan, for example, does not suffer from excessive market pressure even though its total debt amounts to 400% of GDP. Other countries can face solvency threats with a debt ratio of 50%. Over the past twenty years, emerging countries have progressively reduced their debt issuance in foreign currencies, which were originally targeted to attract international investors. This reduction is due to increased awareness of countries about market volatility and to the development of LC debt markets (even if these are still lacking in some countries).

3.6.4 "Communicating Vessels" Effect

A noteworthy feature of Country Risk is known as the "communicating vessels" effect. While countries have striven to reduce their exposure to credit and currency risk, low international interest rates since the Global Financial Crisis have pushed banks and other private sector entities to increase their foreign currency borrowing.

Table 3.8 Countries external and internal vulnerability factors

Internal/Policy vulnerabilities				
Savings imbalances	Economic structure	Policy accuracy	Financial sector imbalances	Institutional risk
Endemic fiscal deficit	GDP growth	Sovereign and fiscal stability indicators	Credit/GDP ratio	Domestic political stability
Low private or public savings	Volatility and structure	Contingent liabilities (variable rate debt)	Credit growth or loans/deposits ratio	Exposure to regional or geostrategic risks
High public and external debt/GDP ratio	Economic role of the state	Monetary stability (inflation)	Nonperforming loans rate/Interest rate spreads	Institutional structure
Portion of national holders of public debt	Competitiveness and productivity trends	Currency regime and currency status	Size of shadow banking sector	Governance & transparency
"Tax tolerance" from domestic citizen/ Recovery rate	Demographic trends	Economic policy risks	Financial sector structure, size relative to GDP	Infrastructure and business environment

External vulnerabilities			
Trade concentrations	Current account balance/GDP ratio	Savings and foreign payments imbalances	Access to capital markets and low share of FDI inflows
Exports and imports	Terms of trade	External debt and liquidity indicators	Exchange rate trends
Exchange rate imbalances	Concentrations in exports and imports	Foreign payments imbalances	External payments requirements/ foreign exchange reserves (liquidity ratios)

Source the economicsofcrisis.com

Case Study: How has the academic literature addressed the concept of risk exposure in investing? Downside risk versus total risk approach?

Adapted from Bouchet et al. (2003).

International investing gives rise to at least three different kinds of exposure: (1) FDI; (2) lending and other extensions of credit; and (3) foreign equities.

Country risk assessment is important for investors in different types of asset classes. In the case of corporate bonds, for example, an important consideration is the overall economic conditions of the borrower's country. In the case of sovereign bonds, moreover, the risk to the investor is the country itself and its ability to grow and repay the debt. Furthermore, investments in equities require an understanding of the overall macroeconomic environment as well as local conditions in the country.

Researchers started to extend portfolio theory to an international framework by applying the works of Markowitz (1952) to an international set of investment opportunities. Pioneering studies in this field are by Grubel (1968), Levy and Sarnat (1970), Lessard (1973), and Errunza (1977). In the same vein, after the seminal paper of Solnik (1974b), many articles such as those of Grauer et al. (1976), Sercu (1980), and Stulz (1984) derived the Capital Asset Pricing Model in an international context. For most of these researchers "capital markets are supposed to be perfect with free flows of capital between nations" (Solnik 1974a). However, as Solnik (1991) later observed: "The political risks of foreign investment might dampen the enthusiasm for international diversification. This political transfer risk might take the form of prohibition on repatriation of profits or capital investment from a foreign country." Jorion and Schwartz (1986) also mention "any other cost of doing investment business abroad" or "any other barrier linked to the country of origin of the security." Moreover, Adler and Dumas (1983) note that "financial economic theory does not deal easily with such imperfections which tend to segment international capital markets." Consequently, other research attempted to identify the specific features of international portfolio investment and establish a possible segmentation of these markets. Aliber (1973) explores the possible impact of "political risk" as a source of deviation from interest rate parity. Stehle (1977), Errunza and Losq (1985), Bekaert (1995), and Bekaert and Campbell (1995) aim to test the integration of international capital markets. Groslambert and Kassibrakis (1999) dispute the normal distribution hypothesis of some emerging stock market returns. Finally, some authors concentrate on the practical aspects of international portfolio management. Agmon (1973), Erb et al. (1995, 1996a, b), Rajan and Friedman (1997), and Madura et al. (1997) assess the influence of the country factor when explaining differences in portfolio performance. It is worth noticing that the literature on international portfolio investment addresses the issue of Country Risk in a risk/return framework, which is not always the case for other research streams, whose results, as Meldrum (1999) has noted, "would benefit greatly from additional research into the theoretical and quantitative relationships between risk and the returns earned in cross-border investments." As evidenced by March and Shapira (1987) and Baird and Thomas (1990), practitioners are more concerned about failing to achieve a given target performance than by the entire set of possible outcomes. Consequently, it is more appealing to follow a downside risk approach as opposed to a total risk perspective. Indeed, while investors try to minimize their downside risk exposure, they want to maximize their upside risk sensibility. Some, like Miller (1992), retain the concept of risk as performance variance because it "is widely used in finance, economics, and strategic management." Though the concept of downside risk was already mentioned in Markowitz (1959), the variance was favored as a measure of risk mainly because of computational difficulties in handling this type of model as well as the assumption of normally distributed returns. Nawrocki (1999) reviews the literature and presents the advantages of using a downside risk approach in lieu of a total risk stance. Even though Roy (1952) and Bawa and Lindenberg (1977) had already integrated the notion of downside risk into portfolio theory, it is only more recently that papers like those of Harlow and Roa (1989) have given this additional emphasis. If the returns were normally distributed (thus symmetric around the mean) both approaches would yield similar results. Harlow and Rao (1989), Sortino and van der Meer (1991), and Miller and Reuer (1996) explored this route. Estrada (2000) and Reuer and Leiblein (2000) have emphasized the usefulness of the downside risk approach for studying emerging markets and international joint ventures. Moreover, many studies such as those of Aggarwal et al. (1989), Harvey (1995) and Bekaert et al. (1998) have established the skewness of the return distribution at the international level, thus offering a further case for the downside risk line versus the increasingly challenged choice of variance.

3.7 Structural Vulnerabilities

3.7.1 Trade Vulnerabilities

Certain structural vulnerabilities are straightforward such as a country's strong dependency on certain commodity imports or an excessive reliance on some specific "demand-driven" revenues like tourism. Moreover, some countries are exporting products for which demand is more elastic (i.e., sensitive to changes in prices). German products are well known to be rather inelastic due to their perceived quality (the so-called "quality effect" being stronger than the "price effect"). It is also known that small economies are more open (high "Openness Index") and are more reliant on export-led growth than larger economies that often rely more on their domestic consumption (China is nevertheless a major exception). Contagion effects are likely to occur when export partners are not sufficiently diversified. A particularly noteworthy case is North Korea, which sends 95% of its exports to China. Another example is the depreciation of the Brazilian Real in the 1990s. This undermined the Argentina currency peg since Brazil was its first trade partner (in the wake of Mercosur trade agreements). Yet another example is the EU. An excessive trade surplus from one country (such as Germany) can be detrimental to another country within the trade area.

Trade partner diversification is crucial to stabilizing developing countries' growth path as noted by Önder and Yilmazkuday (2014): "Historical evidence based on threshold analyses shows that countries can use their trade networks to compensate for their low levels of financial depth, high levels of inflation, and low levels of human capital (…) Therefore, globalization of international trade is important as far as gaining access to better trade networks through multilateral free trade agreements is rather essential for developing countries."

When domestic companies seek to take over new markets, a key success factor is the reputation of the country in which the target firm is based. Some other structural vulnerabilities are much less obvious. For instance, if a country's growth is mainly driven by MNCs, heavy financial outflows (i.e., profit and dividend remittances abroad, worker's remittances, or interest payments on foreign debt) can cause a current account deficit which is "sticky." On the other hand, Toksöz recalls the case of Central American and Caribbean economies struggling over the US economic crisis since they were over-reliant on remittances from immigrant workers in the United States and revenue from American tourists.

3.7.2 A Mix of Structural Weaknesses and Growth Bottleneck

Each country may have its own mix of "structural weaknesses." In advanced economies, for example, there has been a recent rise in default risk among corporate borrowers. This is the result of weak structural growth ("secular stagnation"), high unemployment rates, and the threat of deflation. The latter is considered a more substantial danger than inflation since monetary policy seems powerless to fight it (nominal interest rates cannot go below zero). Counterintuitively, deflation undermines consumption since agents postpone their consumption, creating a self-fulfilling prophecy of endless price decreases. Deflation also reduces the value of most assets and increases the financial burden of incurred debt. Advanced economies are also likely to slow down innovation and technological progress with more stringent regulation ("precautionary principle"). All these factors make advanced economies over-reliant on monetary easing policies. (See Chapter 11 for a further discussion of the impact of monetary policy and regulation on advanced economies.)

3.8 Developing Countries: Geometrically Variable Models

3.8.1 Setting the Scene

One characteristic of developing countries is that they differ significantly from each other across the spectrum of economic activity. Stop and go economic cycles tend to characterize their growth trajectories. Emerging markets countries may grow quickly and then slow down, depending on a range of factors, including sociopolitical and economic characteristics and the degree to which they participate in the global economic system. Developing countries with volatile growth patterns include India, Brazil (with a recession of –35% of its GDP in 2017), South Africa, Turkey, and Indonesia. Moreover, some developing countries struggle with the high level of internal and external vulnerabilities (e.g., Argentina, Venezuela, Hungary, Ukraine, and Egypt). In contrast, other developing countries follow more prudent practices and policies regarding inflation, debt, and credit markets. A number of countries maintain credit market access; in yet others, such activity is highly constrained or limited to a narrow elite. If capital is not available within a country, borrowers seek foreign sources of capital, increasing external debt and exposure to currency fluctuations.

3.8.2 Inequalities and Wealth Gap

Another attribute of developing countries is a wide income and wealth gap. Such wide distribution obstructs sustainable growth and is associated with a higher occurrence of defaults. Rajan (2011) argues that credit can be made available to lower-income groups to support their consumption levels in response to rising income inequality. As discussed in Chapters 9 and 10, growing wealth gaps within and between countries are often root causes of sociopolitical destabilization. But wealth gaps are not a monopoly of developing countries, as illustrated by the research of Piketty (2013) and Coibion et al. (2014). They also explore this relationship in developed countries. In particular, they observed a positive correlation between income inequality in the United States and household debt relative to GDP, as further set forth in Table 3.9.

Table 3.9 Inequality and debt in the US (Coibion et al. 2014)

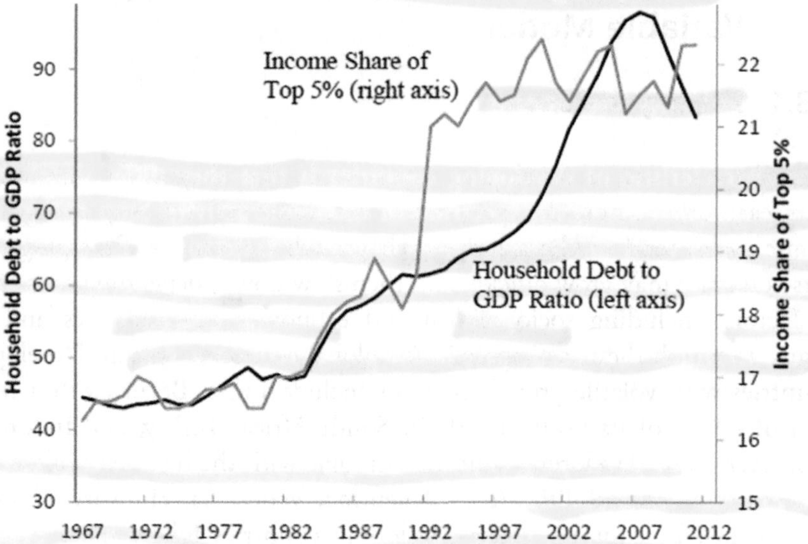

One way for developing countries to reduce their unequal distribution of wealth is to broaden and diversify the range of domestic production and exports of goods and services in order to sustain external shocks, such as price and capital flow volatility. They must also enhance the quality of institutional infrastructures (governance, legal systems, tax systems, and transparency) to promote sustainable growth. Rapid growth brings new societal aspirations. Even if the above challenges seem to be significant obstacles for many countries, some have experienced success (such as South Korea).

3.8.3 Institutions and Governance

Poor governance, opacity, and corruption are topics of great interest in the research on Country Risk. There is currently a large body of academic literature that explores the links between corruption and growth. One challenge associated with the assessment of a country's governance is the subjective nature of corruption and the subjective methodologies of measuring it. Examples of governance ratings include the International Country Risk Guide (ICRG) , Corruption Index from Political Risk Services (PRS) group, and the Corruption perception index (CPI) indicator of Transparency International. This theme is discussed further in Chapters 9 and 10.

According to Brunetti and Weder (1999), the development of a civil society is negatively correlated with corruption. Moreover, a lack of freedom

Table 3.10 Legal origin, institutions, and outcomes (La Porta et al. 2013)

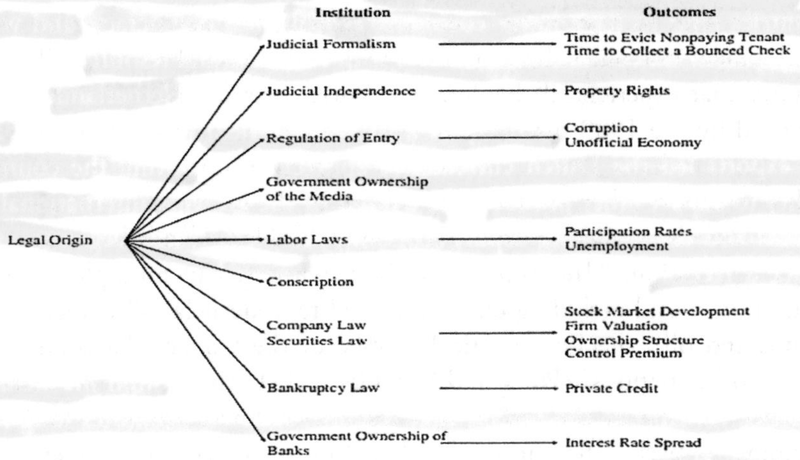

increases corruption (Ahrend 2002). Glaeser et al. (2004) address the question of whether institutions can influence growth. They conclude that corruption levels vary with the state of the economy and hence they are reactive rather than predictive.

Other research examines the themes of transparency, "disclosure by politicians," (Djankov et al. 2010), and government efficiency. Chong et al. (2014) conclude that governments are inefficient not so much because of corruption but because their leaders are not well organized. In light of that, an important factor is the extent and type of information disclosure by politicians (even if such disclosure is not necessarily made public). Another relevant factor relating to institutions is whether the country's legal system is common law or civil law (Table 3.10).

3.8.4 The Paradox of Plenty

Resource-based economies are often aware that they lack diversification. Many have attempted to diversify production and export revenues by encouraging FDI as well as domestic public investment and private investment. To do so, several countries established sovereign wealth funds that are government-owned investment vehicles that pursue long-term investment strategies. These funds can provide a cushion if commodity prices fall. They can also help sustain growth once commodity stocks deplete. Examples include Norway, Hong Kong, Chile, UAE, China, and Qatar. Countries dominated by a "resource-based" economy often, however, struggle to achieve greater diversity in their sources of revenue. An applicable term is "resource curse" or "paradox of plenty." Despite their vast wealth, these countries tend to have lower economic growth, less democracy, and worse development outcomes than countries with fewer natural resources. The first country that experienced the "resource curse" was the Netherlands. It was triggered by the 1959 discovery of a natural gas field in Groningen. Large gas exports led the Dutch currency to appreciate, impairing the country's ability to export other products. As a result of the growing international gas market and the shrinking export economy, the Netherlands began to experience a recession. "This process has been witnessed in multiple countries around the world including but not limited to Venezuela (oil), Angola (diamonds and oil), the Democratic Republic of the Congo (diamonds), and various other nations" (Ploeg and Venables 2011). They found inconclusive evidence to support the notion that resource richness promotes long-term economic growth. They also note that "approximately 40% of empirical papers finding a negative effect, 40% finding no effect, and 20% finding a positive effect."

It is noteworthy that a "resource-based" economy such as Russia, even with its skilled workers and advanced technology, has found it challenging to diversify. One particular challenge is what is known as the middle-income trap, a situation in which a country attains a certain income (due to given advantages) but cannot exceed that level. This can be explained by the so-called "rent-seeking behavior" that may push individuals to focus more on obtaining resource "rents" than developing successful innovative businesses (Acemoglu and Verdier 1998; Gelb 1988). Rent-seeking behavior is also more likely to generate civil wars or rebellions (Ross 2004). Another challenge is that significant dependence on natural resources in terms of exports is more likely to be associated with high corruption (Leite and Weidmann 1999).

The Russian economy is dependent on producing and exporting gas. An increase in the gas price, even a modest one, can impact the Russian GDP. Some economists have argued that oil price shocks may be narrowly linked to macroeconomic indicators. To do so, they have used Vector Autoregressive models (VAR) for multivariate time series. The structure of these econometric models is that each variable is a linear function of past lags of itself and past lags of the other variable. Actually, the impact of price shocks on an economy is not coincidental and a time lag of one or two years should be used for a better accuracy (Bouchet and Zelensky 2017). In addition to the time lag, some leakage effects must be considered. A portion of domestic petroleum revenues may be spent abroad through capital flight, which contributes to weakening the macroeconomic transmission vector.

Capital leakages can be measured from the Balance of Payment (BoP), the "net errors & omissions" rubric of the financial account, and by the non-bank private deposits in international banks (which is data maintained by the BIS). The focus must be on the "nonfinancial" rubric part to exclude "interbanking flows" and to consider only offshore private deposits. (For more detail, see the BIS website http://stats.bis.org, in particular, Global tables number A6.1 "by country (residence) of counterparty and instrument, sector and currency.") Scholars have duly established a strong link between export incomes and capital leakage (Bouchet and Zelensky 2017). More details on links between corruption, exports, and capital flight are provided in Chapter 14.

Considering the above analysis, there would appear to be a relationship between natural resources and poor governance. But similar behavior can be found in economies driven by completely different dependencies on natural resources. For instance, some countries may be highly dependent on a particular industry, or on resources driven by offshore financial centers and tax havens. In many of these economies, the key industry is often banking. The impact of such dependency should not be underestimated, as illustrated by the financial crises in Iceland (2008) and Cyprus (Chan et al. 2013). The graph shows that assets managed by Cypriot banks reached more than seven times the country's GDP, due to large speculative capital inflows attracted by an environment of minimal regulation (Table 3.11).

Table 3.11 Bank assets multiples of GDP in 2013 before the Cyprus crisis (Belgium Financial Sector Federation)

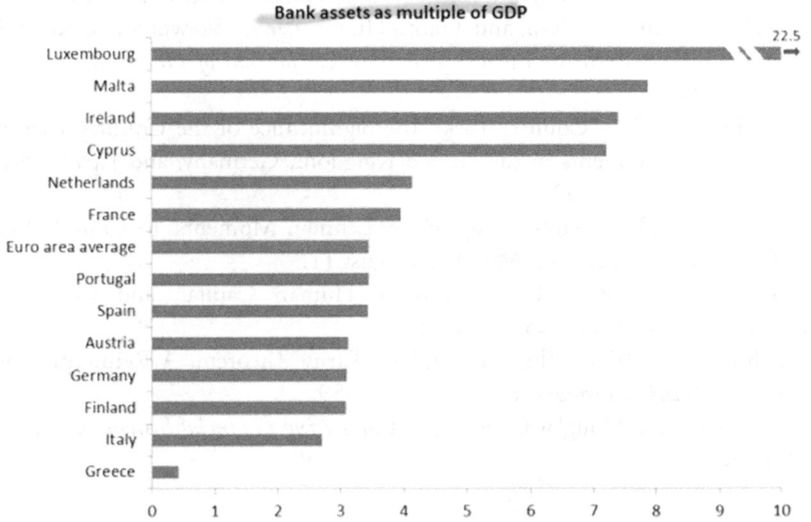

Even when banks try to downsize and deleverage, it often goes together with an offsetting increase in the nonbank and shadow banking activities. See Chapter 7, Case Study on China.

3.9 Concluding Remarks

Research on Country Risk has provided us with an abundance of knowledge regarding financial and sovereign crises. In the aftermath of the Global Financial Crisis, studies have focused increasingly on "push factors" and the cyclical nature of economic variables. The number of research papers is probably in proportion to what is at stake: nothing less than the wealth and stability of nations and individuals. However, if they are to be meaningful, these studies must rely on accurate data. Sources of information, both public and private, are discussed in next Chapters 4 and 5.

References

Abbott, P.C., Hurt, C., Tyner, W.E. 2008. What's driving food prices? Issue Report. Farm Foundation.

Acemoglu, Daron, and Thierry Verdier. 1998. "Property Rights, Corruption and the Allocation of Talent: A General Equilibrium Approach." *The Economic Journal* 108 (450): 1381–1403.

Adler, Michael, and Bernard Dumas. 1983. "International Portfolio Choice and Corporation Finance: A Synthesis." *Journal of Finance* 38 (3): 925–984.

Aggarwal, Raj, Ramesh P. Rao, and Takoto Hiraki. 1989. "Skewness and Kurtosis in Japanese Equity Returns: Empirical Evidence." *Journal of Financial Research* 12 (3): 253–260.

Agmon, Tamir. 1973. "Country Risk: The Significance of the Country Factor for Share-Price Movements in the United Kingdom, Germany, and Japan." *Journal of Business* 46 (1): 24–32.

Agrawal, Amol. 2011. "How Many More 'Lehman Moments' to Come?" Report STCI Primary Dealer Ltd., Mumbai, August 11.

Ahrend, Rudiger. 2002. "Press Freedom, Human Capital, and Corruption." DELTA Working Paper No. 2002–11.

Aliber, Robert Z. 1973. "The Interest Rate Parity Theorem: A Reinterpretation." *Journal of Political Economy* 81 (6): 1451–1459.

Allen, Franklin, and Douglas Gale. 1999. *Comparing Financial Systems.* Cambridge: MIT Press.

Baltzer, K., Hansen, H., Lind, K.M. 2008. A Note on the Causes and Consequences of the Rapidly Increasing International Food Prices. Research Report. Institute of Food and Resource Economics, University of Copenhagen.

Baird, Inga, and Howard Thomas. 1990. "What Is Risk Anyway? Using and Measuring Risk in Strategic Management." In *Risk Strategy and Management*, edited by Richard A. Bettis and Howard Thomas. Greenwich, CT: JAI Press.

Bawa, V.S., and E.B. Lindenberg. 1977. "Capital Market Equilibrium in a Mean-Lower Partial Moment Framework." *Journal of Financial Economics* 5 (2), 189–200.

Bekaert, Geert. 1995. "Market Integration and Investment Barriers in Emerging Equity Markets." *World Bank Economic Review* 9 (1): 75–107.

Bekaert, Geert, and Harvey R. Campbell. 1995. "Time-Varying World Market Integration." *Journal of Finance* 50 (2): 403–444.

Bekaert Geert, Claude B. Erb, Campbell R. Harvey, and Tadas E. Viskanta. 1998. "Distributional Characteristics of Emerging Market Returns and Asset Allocation." *Journal of Portfolio Management* 24 (2): 102–116.

Bouchet, Michel Henry, and Catherine Zelensky. 2017. "Russian Petroleum and Its Impact on the Domestic Economy." SKEMA MSc Thesis.

Bouchet, Michel Henry, Ephraim Clark, and Bertrand Groslambert. 2003. *Country Risk Assessment: A Guide to Global Investment Strategy*. New York: Wiley.

Bracke, Phillipe. 2013. "How Long Do Housing Cycles Last? A Duration Analysis for 19 OECD Countries." *Journal of Housing Economics* 22 (3): 213–230.

Brunetti, Amyo, and Beatrice Weder. 1999. "More Open Economies Have Better Governments." Economic Series No. 9905.

Calverley, John. 2002. *The Investor's Guide to Economic Fundamentals*. New York: Wiley.

Calvo, Guillermo. 2013. "Puzzling Over the Anatomy of Crises: Liquidity and the Veil of Finance." Discussion Paper No. 2013-E-9.

Calvo, Guillermo A., and Enrique G. Mendozo. 1996. "Petty Crime and Cruel Punishment: Lessons from the Mexican Debacle." *American Economic Review* 86 (2): 170–175.

Chan, Szu Ping, Denis Roland, and Andrew Trotman. 2013. "Cyprus Bail-Out: As It Happened." *Telegraph.co*, March 27.

Chong, Albert, Rafael La Porta, Florencio Lopez de Silanes, and Andrei Shleifer. 2014. "Letter Grading Government Efficiency." *Journal of the European Economic Association* 12 (2): 277–299.

Claessens, Stijn, and Ayhan Kose. 2003. "Financial Crises: Explanations, Types, and Implications." IMF Working Paper No. 13/28, CNAM, Sciences de Gestion.

Coibion, Oiver, Yuriy Gorodnichenko, Marianna Kudlyak, and John Mondragon. 2014. "Does Greater Inequality Lead to More Household Borrowing? New Evidence from Household Data." Federal Reserve Bank of Richmond, Working Paper No. 14–01.

CRAG. 2017. "Bank of Canada, Database of Sovereign Defaults." https://www.bankofcanada.ca/2014/02/technical-report-101.

Demirguc-Kunt, Asli, and Enrica Detragiache. 1998. "The Determinants of Banking Crises in Developing and Developed Countries." *International Monetary Fund Staff Papers* 45 (1): 81–109.

Djankov, Simeon, Rafael La Porta, Florencio Lopez de Silanes, and Andre Shleifer. 2010. "Disclosure by Politicians." *American Economic Journal: Applied Economics* (2): 179–209.

Dooley, Michael P. 2000. "A Model of Crises in Emerging Markets." *The Economic Journal* 110: 256–272.

Eichengreen, Barry, and Andrew Rose. 2000. *The Empirics of Currency and Banking Crises*. Cambridge: National Bureau of Economic Research.

Eichengreen, Barry, Andrew Rose, and Charles Wyplosz. 1996. "Contagious Currency Crises: First Tests." *Scandinavian Journal of Economics* 98 (4): 463–484.

Erb, Claude B., Campbell R. Harvey, and Tadas E. Viskanta. 1995. "Country Risk and Global Equity Selection." *Journal of Portfolio Management* 21 (2): 74–83.

Erb, Claude B., Campbell R. Harvey, and Tadas E. Viskanta. 1996a. "The Influence of Political, Economic and Financial Risk on Expected Fixed Income Returns." *Journal of Fixed Income* 6 (1): 7–31.

Erb, Claude B., Campbell R. Harvey, and Tadas E. Viskanta. 1996b. "Political Risk, Economic Risk, and Financial Risk." *Financial Analysts Journal* 52 (6): 28–46.

Errunza, Vihang R. 1977. "Gains from Portfolio Diversification into Less Developed Countries' Securities." *Journal of International Business Studies* 8 (2): 83–99.

Errunza, Vihang, and Etienne Losq. 1985. "International Asset Pricing Under Mild Segmentation: Theory and Test." *Journal of Finance* 40 (1): 105–124.

Erten, Bilge, and Jose Antonio Ocampo. 2012. "Super-Cycles of Commodity Prices Since the Mid-Nineteenth Century." United Nations Department of Economic and Social Affairs Working Paper No. 110.

Estrada, Javier. 2000. "The Cost of Equity in Emerging Markets: A Downside Risk Approach." *Emerging Markets Quarterly* 4 (3): 19–30.

Fan, S., and Headey, D. 2008. Anatomy of a Crisis: The Causes and Consequences of Surging Food Prices. IFPRI Discussion Paper 831, Table 2. Washington, DC: International Food Policy Research Institute. Reproduced with permission from the International Food Policy Research Institute www.ifpri.org. The full paper this table is from is available online at http://ebrary.ifpri.org/cdm/ref/collection/p15738coll2/id/16223.

Feldstein, Martin. 2002. *Economic and Financial Crises in Emerging Market Economies*. Cambridge: National Bureau of Economic Research.

Financial Times. 2017. "Zhou's Minsky Moment Seen as Reform Signal to Party Elites", October 22.

Fitch Rating. 2013. "Why Sovereigns Can Default on Local-Currency Debt: Printing Money Is No Panacea as High Inflation Is a Costly Policy Option." Special Report, May 10, 2013.

Flood, Robert, and Peter Garber. 1984. "Collapsing Exchange-Rate Regimes: Some Linear Examples." *Journal of International Economics* 17 (1–2): 1–13.

Forbes, Kristin. 2014. "Financial 'Deglobalization'?: Capital Flows, Banks, and the Beatles." Speech, Queen Mary University London, November 18, 2014. http://www.bankofengland.co.uk/publications/Documents/speeches/2014/speech777.pdf.

Frankel, Jeffrey A., and Andrew K. Rose. 1996. "Currency Crashes in Emerging Markets: An Empirical Treatment." *Journal of International Economics* 41 (3–4): 351–366.

Fratzscher, Marcel. 2011. "Capital Flows, Push Versus Pull Factors and the Global Financial Crisis." NBER Working Paper No. 17357.

Gaddis, John Lewis. 1992–1993. "International Relations Theory and the End of the Cold War." *International Security* 17 (3): 5–58.

Gelb, Alan. 1988. *Oil Windfalls: Blessing or Curse?* Oxford: A World Bank Research Publication.

Glaeser, Edward L., and Rafael La Porta. 2004. "Florencio Lopez de Silanes, and Andre Shleifer. Do Institutions Cause Growth?" NBER Working Paper No. 10568.

Goldstein, Morris, Graciela L. Kaminsky, and Carmen M. Reinhart. 2000. *Assessing Financial Vulnerability: An Early Warning System for Emerging Markets.* Washington, DC: Peterson Institute for International Economics.

Goodhart. 2008. The Background to the 2007 Financial Crisis. *International Economics and Economic Policy* 4 (4): 331–346.

Goodhart, Charles, and Boris Hofmann. 2007. *House Prices and the Macroeconomy: Implications for Banking & Price Stability.* Oxford: Oxford University Press.

Gori, S. 2002. "A Cognitive Approach to Political Risk Analysis." CERAM Working Paper, April 26.

Gottesman, Aron, and Michael Liebrok. 2017. *Understanding Systemic Risk in Global Financial Markets.* New York: Wiley.

Grauer, Frederick L., Robert H. Litzenberger, and Richard E. Stehe. 1976. "Sharing Rules and Equilibrium in an International Capital Market under Uncertainty." *Journal of Financial Economics* 3 (3): 233–256.

Gray, Dale F., and Andreas A. Jobst. 2013. "Systemic Contingent Claims Analysis—Estimating Market-Implied Systemic Risk." IMF Working Paper No. 13/54.

Groslambert, Bertrand, and Serge Kassibrakis. 1999. "The Alpha-Stable Hypothesis: An Alternative to the Distribution of Emerging Stock Market Returns." *Emerging Markets Quarterly* 3 (1): 22–38.

Grubel, Herbert G. 1968. "Internationally Diversified Portfolios: Welfare Gains and Capital Flows." *American Economic Review* 58 (5): 1299–1314.

Hardy, Daniel C., and Ceyla Pazarbasioglu. 1999. "Determinants and Leading Indicators of Banking Crises: Further Evidence." *International Monetary Fund Staff Papers* 46 (3): 247–258.

Harlow, William Van, and Ramesh K.S. Rao. 1989. "Asset Pricing in a Generalized Mean-Lower Partial Moment Framework: Theory and Evidence." *Journal of Financial and Quantitative Analysis* 24 (3): 285–311.

Harvey, Campbell R. 1995. "Predictable Risk and Return in Emerging Markets." *Review of Financial Studies* 8 (3): 773–816.

Hoggarth, Glenn, Jack Reidhill, and Peter Sinclair. 2004. "On the Resolution of Banking Crises: Theory and Evidence." Bank of England Working Paper No. 229.

Igan, Deniz, and Prakash Loungani. 2012. "Global Housing Cycles." IMF Report No. 12/217.

Islam, Jannatul. 2014. *Hyman P. Minsky Hypothesis to Evaluate Credit Crunch.* Dusseldorf: Lap Lambert Academic Publishing.

Johnson, Omotunde E.G. 2002. *Financial Risks, Stability, and Globalization.* Washington, DC: International Monetary Fund.

Jorion, Phillipe, and Eduardo Schwartz. 1986. "Integration vs. Segmentation in the Canadian Stock Market." *Journal of Finance* 41 (3): 603–614.

Kaminsky, Graciela L. 1999. "Currency and Banking Crises: The Early Warnings of Distress." International Monetary Fund Working Paper WP/99/178.

Kaminsky, Graciela L., and Carmen M. Reinhart. 1999. "The Twin Crises: The Causes of Banking and Balance-of-Payments Problems." *American Economic Review* 89 (3): 473–500.

Kay, John. 2013. "Spotting a Banking Crisis Is Not Like Predicting the Weather. Short-Term Weather Forecasts are Better than Medium-Term Economic Forecasts." *Financial Times,* August 13.

Keynes, J.M. 1924. "A Tract on Monetary Reform." *The Economic Journal* 34 (134): 227–235.

Khan, Mehreen. 2015. $3 trillion corporate credit crunch looms as debtors face day of reckoning, says IMF. The Telegraphe, 07 Oct 2015.

Kodres, Laura E., and Mathew A. Pritsker. 2002. "A Rational Expectations Model of Financial Contagion." *Journal of Finance* 57 (2): 769–799.

Kovacevic, Aleksandar. 2009. "The Impact of the Russia–Ukraine Gas Crisis in South Eastern Europe." Oxford Institute for Energy Studies NG 29.

Krugman, Paul. 1979. "A Model of Balance-of-Payments Crisis." *Journal of Money Credit and Banking* 11 (3): 311–325.

Krugman, Paul. 1998. *What Happened to Asia.* Massachusetts Institute of Technology, January. http://web.mit.edu/krugman/www/DISINTER.html.

La Porta, Rafael, Florencio Lopez de Silanes, and Andrei Shleifer. 2013. "Law and Finance After a Decade of Research." In *Handbook of the Economics of Finance,* vol. 2, edited by George M. Constantinides, Milton Harris, and Rene M. Stulz, Chapter 6, 425–491. Amsterdam: Elsevier.

Langohr, Herwig, and Patricia Langohr. 2009. *The Rating Agencies and Their Credit Ratings: What They Are, How They Work, and Why They Are Relevant.* New York: Wiley.

Leite, Carlos, and Jens Weidmann. 1999. "Does Mother Nature Corrupt? Natural Resources, Corruption, and Economic Growth." IMF Working Paper, International Monetary Fund.

Lessard, Donald R. 1973. "International Portfolio Diversification: A Multivariate Analysis for a Group of Latin American Countries." *Journal of Finance* 28 (3): 619–633.

Levy, Hyam, and Marshall Sarnat. 1970. "International Diversification of Investment Portfolios." *American Economic Review* 60 (4): 668–675.

Madura Jeff, Alan L. Tucker, and Marilyn Wiley. 1997. "Factors Affecting Returns Across Stock Markets." *Global Finance Journal* 8 (1): 1–14.

March, James G., and Zur Shapira. 1987. "Managerial Perspectives on Risk and Risk Taking." *Management Science* 33 (11): 1404–1418.

Markowitz, Harry. 1952. "Portfolio Selection." *The Journal of Finance* 7 (1): 77–91.
Markowitz, Harry. 1959. *Portfolio Selection*. New Haven: Yale University Press.
McCauley, Robert N., Benetrix Agustin, S., Patrick McGuire, and Goetz von Peter. 2017. "Financial Deglobalisation in Banking?" BIS Working Paper No. 650, June.
Meldrum, Duncan H. 1999. "Country Risk and a Quick Look at Latin America." *Business Economics* 34 (3): 30–37.
Mersch, Yves. 2017. Central Bank Independence Revisited. Key Note Address, "Symposium on Building the Financial System of the 21st Century: An Agenda for Europe and the United States," March 30.
Miller, Kent D. 1992. "A Framework for Integrated Risk Management in International Business." *Journal of International Business Studies* 23 (2): 311–331.
Miller, Kent D., and Jeffrey J. Reuer. 1996. "Measuring Organizational Downside Risk." *Strategic Management Journal* 17 (9): 671–691.
Nawrocki, David N. 1999. "A Brief History of Downside Risk Measures." *Journal of Investing* 8 (3): 9–25.
Niemira, Michael L., and Phillip A. Klein. 1994. *Forecasting Financial and Economic Cycles*. New York: Wiley.
Obstfeld, Maurice. 1994. "The Logic of Currency Crisis." *Cahiers Economiques et Monétaires* 43: 189–213.
Önder, Ali Sina, and Hakan Yilmazkuday. 2014. "Trade Partner Diversification and Growth: How Trade Links Matter." Globalization and Monetary Policy Institute Working Paper No. 192, Federal Reserve Bank of Dallas.
Pagliari, Maria Sole, and Swarnali Ahmed Hannan. 2017. "The Volatility of Capital Flows in Emerging Markets: Measures and Determinants." IMF Working Paper No. 17/41.
Piketty, Thomas. 2013. *Le Capital au XXIe siècle*. "Les Livres du nouveau monde." Paris: Le Seuil.
Ploeg, Frederick van der, and Anthony J. Venables. 2011. "Harnessing Windfall Revenues: Optimal Policies for Resource-Rich Developing Economies." *The Economic Journal* 121 (551): 1–30.
Rajan, Raghuram G. 2011. *Fault Lines: How Hidden Fractures Still Threaten the World Economy*. Princeton: Princeton University Press.
Rajan, Murli, and Joseph Friedman. 1997. "An Examination of the Impact of Country Risk on the International Portfolio Selection Decision." *Global Finance Journal* 8 (1): 55–70.
Reinhart, Carmen M., and Vincent Reinhart. 2008. "Capital Flow Bonanzas: An Encompassing View of the Past and Present." The National Bureau of Economic Research, NBER Working Paper No. 14321, September.
Reinhart, Carmen M., and Kenneth S. Rogoff. 2009. *This Time Is Different: Eight Centuries of Financial Folly*. Princeton: Princeton University Press.
Reuer, Jeffrey J., and Michael J. Leiblein. 2000. "Downside Risk Implications of Multinationality and International Joint Ventures." *Academy of Management Journal* 43 (2): 203–214.
Ross, Michael L. 2004. "What Do We Know About Natural Resources and Civil War?" *Journal of Peace Research* 41 (3): 337–356.

Roy, A. D. 1952. “Safety First and the Holding of Assets.” *Econometrica* 20 (3): 431–449.
Rummel, R.J., and David A. Heenan. 1978. “How Multinationals Analyze Political Risk.” *Harvard Business Review* 56 (January–February): 67–76.
Schnepf, Randy. 2008. High Agricultural Commodity Prices: What Are the Issues? CRS Report for Congress. Congressional Research Service, Washington.
Sercu, Piet. 1980. “A Generalization of the International Asset Pricing Model.” *Revue de l'Association Française de Finance* 1 (1): 91–135.
Shiller, Robert J. 2000. *Irrational Exuberance*. Princeton: Princeton University Press.
Sionneau, Bernard. 2000. “Risque-Pays et Prospective Internationale: Theorie et Application.” CNAM PhD Thesis.
Solnik, Bruno H. 1974a. “An Equilibrium Model of the International Capital Market.” *Journal of Economic Theory* 8 (4): 500–524.
Solnik, Bruno H. 1974b. “The International Pricing of Risk: An Empirical Investigation of the World Capital Market Structure.” *Journal of Finance* 29 (2): 365–378.
Solnik, Bruno H. 1991. *International Investments*, 2nd ed. Boston, MA: Addison-Wesley.
Solow, Robert M. 1977. “How Did Economics Get That Way and What Way Did It Get?” *Daedalus* 126 (1): 39–58.
Sortino, Frank A., and Robert van der Meer. 1991. “Downside Risk.” *The Journal of Portfolio Management* 17 (4): 27–31.
Stehle, Richard E. 1977. “An Empirical Test of the Alternative Hypotheses of National and International Pricing of Risky Assets.” *Journal of Finance* 32 (2) 493–502.
Stulz, Rene M. 1984. “Pricing Capital Assets in an International Setting: An Introduction.” *Journal of International Business Studies* 15 (3): 55–73.
Suttle, Phillip. 2008. “Global Capital Flow and the Global Business Cycle.” Special Briefing, Institute of International Finance.
Tennant, David F., and Marlon R. Tracey. 2015. *Sovereign Debt and Credit Rating Bias*. New York: Palgrave.
Terrier, J.L. 1999. “Assurance Credit Export: Le Risque Nouveau est Arrivé.” *Le MOCI*, September, 1405, 42.
Toksöz, Mina. 2014. *The Economist Guide to Country Risk*. London: Economist Books.
Tomz, Michael, and Mark L.J. Wright. 2013. “Empirical Research on Sovereign Debt and Default.” *Annual Review of Economics* 5: 247–272.
Trostle, R. 2008. Global Agricultural Supply and Demand: Factors Contributing to the Recent Increase in Food Commodity Prices. ERS Re-port WRS-0801. Economic Research Service, US Department of Agriculture (USDA).
Williamson, John. 2000. “What Should the World Bank Think About the Washington Consensus?” *The World Bank Research Observer* 15 (2): 251–264.
Valerie Mercer-Blackman, (2008) The Impact of Research and Development Tax Incentiveson Colombia's Manufacturing Sector: What Difference Do they Make? IMF Working Papers 08 (178): 1.
Von Braun, J. 2008. Rising Food Prices: What Should Be Done? IFPRI Policy Brief. International Food Policy Research Institute, Washington, DC.

4

Country Risk Assessment: The Key Role of Official Information Sources

4.1 Introduction: Assessing Uncertainty to Manage Risk

Relying on quality and timely information makes the difference between seizing great opportunities and missing them. There is a useful analogy between Quantum Mechanics and Country Risk in that both deal with uncertainty. It is impossible to attempt to measure both the exact position and the exact momentum of a particle at the same time. This relationship has important implications for such fundamental notions as causality and determining future behavior. Pinpointing risk involves influencing the risk momentum. Applying this analogy to Country Risk, a clear and abrupt warning of upcoming crisis announced by a rating agency, the IMF, or the US Fed will end up generating a self-fulfilling prophecy. Globalization of information can generate rising volatility of capital flows and crisis propagation. The wide availability and instant transmission of information combine to trigger a herd instinct that results in spillover effects and crisis contamination. A credit downgrading will create both spillover effects and regional contamination. The country risk analyst must, therefore, gather information from as wide a range of sources as possible, while bearing in mind their limitations and decoding the result into strategic decisions. As an example, should a rating agency abruptly declare a country's exchange rate to be substantially overvalued, devaluation and massive capital flight would follow. The IMF, for instance, is always cautious in assessing a country's exchange rate equilibrium, using wording such as "the real exchange rate was assessed

M. H. Bouchet et al., *Managing Country Risk in an Age of Globalization*,
https://doi.org/10.1007/978-3-319-89752-3_4

as broadly in line with fundamentals, erasing the moderate overvaluation at the start of the arrangement" (International Monetary Fund 2017a).

Country risk managers today suffer from a surplus of information sources rather than a deficit. Compared with the 1980s or even 1990s, today country risk analysts do not face a deficit of economic intelligence sources but, on the contrary, a surplus. Rating agencies, multilateral institutions, merchant banks, and think tanks produce sophisticated and comprehensive databases and rankings. Under pressure from the IMF and from rating agencies, countries compete to get market access via a regular flow of quality information. In turn, fund managers, investors, creditors, and bank depositors get flooded by a flow of information that requires careful discrimination and cross-checking. Information per se, however, is a necessary but not sufficient ingredient for a robust country risk assessment. As the CIA notes in the introduction of its World Factbook: "The Intelligence Cycle is the process by which information is acquired, converted into intelligence, and made available to policymakers. Information is raw data from any source, data that may be fragmentary, contradictory, unreliable, ambiguous, deceptive, or wrong. Intelligence is information that has been collected, integrated, evaluated, analyzed, and interpreted. Finished intelligence is the final product of the Intelligence Cycle ready to be delivered to the policymaker" (Central Intelligence Agency 2017). In the new global environment where Ulrich Beck regards risk as being the norm, there is an information paradox in that too much information and knowledge result in increasing uncertainty (Beck 2002). Measuring risk is thus closely related to how it is perceived. Since this perception varies across space and time, risk measurement is a volatile issue. A good measurement can only be made on the basis of clear perception and definition. Given that risk is made up of uncertainty, high-quality information is a key to accurate risk measurement.

In 1983, the deficit in reliable country risk intelligence precipitated the creation of the Washington-based Institute for International Finance that will be discussed in Chapter 5. The threat of systemic risk over the international banking system abated only in the late 1980s, after some progress had been made by debtor countries in restructuring and reforming their economies. All in all, the abruptness of the crisis, the ongoing uncertainties arising from overhanging debt, and the lack of robust country risk information resulted in commercial lenders' mounting reluctance to provide new funds to those countries, even on a concerted basis.

The root causes of financial crises, however, changed over the 1990s, illustrating the gap between the focus of country risk assessment—namely, balance of payments and liquidity indicators—and the diverse root causes of financial imbalances. Although the ultimate manifestation of a debt crisis is always protracted balance of payments tensions, the crises of the late 1990s and the early twenty-first century shifted the emphasis to microeconomic imbalances, where information is still a formidable challenge. In particular, the causes of banking crises are multifaceted, including lending booms, weak governance and "crony capitalism," destabilizing external factors, precipitous financial liberalization, inadequate prudential supervision, and weaknesses in the legal and institutional framework (Eichengreen and Arteta 2000). These are more complex causes of crises than a rising debt servicing ratio or a drop in official reserve assets.

As the global economy and its spillover effects compound the magnitude and abruptness of country risk crises, timely information has never been so crucial in risk assessment and prediction. Robert Dunn observes: "The herd-like behavior of lenders and investors in removing funds from many developing countries, after one encountered trouble, was based in part on the fact that the bankers lacked detailed and trustworthy knowledge about their economic and financial conditions. Operating with very limited knowledge, they flee at the first sign of trouble" (Dunn 2001, 56).

4.2 The Key Sources of Country Risk-Related Economic Intelligence

Country risk intelligence can come from both official and private sources including international organizations, central banks, and private risk assessment agencies as well as the academic community (Chart 4.1).

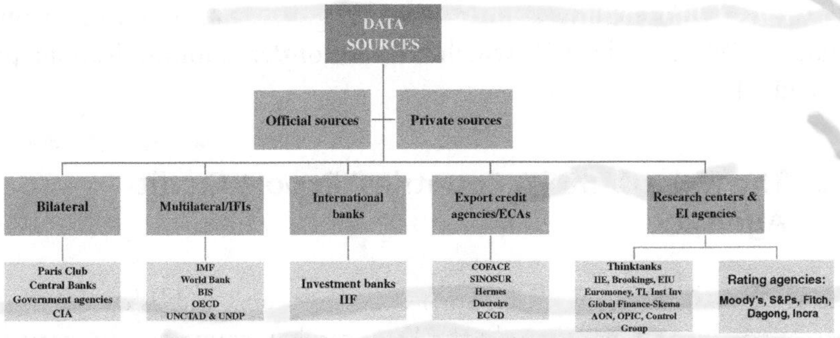

Chart 4.1 The breakdown of country risk information sources

4.3 Official Sources of Country Risk Information: The National Institutions

4.3.1 The Role of the Paris Club

The Paris Club is the forum of debt restructuring negotiations between twenty OECD developed countries and developing debtor countries. It dates back to 1956 when Argentina agreed to meet its public creditors in Paris. Since then, the Paris Club has reached 433 agreements with ninety different debtor countries. Overall, debt treated in the framework of Paris Club agreements amounts to nearly USD 600 billion up to 2017. Representatives of international financial institutions, such as the International Monetary Fund (IMF) and the World Bank, are often invited to attend the meetings as observers. In fact, since the late 1990s, the distinction between creditor groups and debtor groups has become blurred. Indeed, Russia and Brazil may find themselves being creditors of developing countries in Africa or Eastern Europe. In addition, the Global Financial Crisis has moved to OECD countries such as Greece and Cyprus. The IMF plays a key role in Paris Club debt negotiations given that the debtor country must first agree on macroeconomic adjustment policies to stabilize its financing requirements. In return, the IMF's staff will identify the financing gap to be filled by the Paris Club. The debt negotiations are made more efficient by a number of guidelines, including information sharing, consensus, case-by-case treatment, conditionality of IMF programs, and comparability of treatment.

For country risk analysts, the Paris Club provides three important sources of data: (1) debt restructuring conditions of the Paris Club, including debt servicing and debt stock reliefs; (2) detailed debt restructuring agreements between the Paris Club members and debtor countries; and (3) amounts due to Paris Club creditor countries by foreign sovereign and other public debtors. Website: http://www.clubdeparis.org/en/communications/page/paris-club-claims.

4.3.2 The Role of OECD Countries' Export Credit Agencies

National agencies in OECD countries produce and publish research and information on developed and emerging market countries. In particular, Export Credit Agencies (ECAs) provide investors and exporters with a combination of country risk analysis and insurance.

Table 4.1 Coface's assessment of Algeria's macroeconomic situation as of 2018

Major macroeconomic indicators	2014	2015	2016(f)	2017(f)
GDP growth (%)	3.8	3.8	4.2	1.4
Inflation (yearly average) (%)	2.9	4.8	5.9	5.5
Budget balance (% GDP)	−7.3	−16.1	−12.9	−9.3
Current account balance (% GDP)	−4.4	−16.4	−15.0	−13.7
Public debt (% GDP)	7.9	9.0	13.0	17.1

4.3.2.1 Compagnie Française D'Assurance et de Crédit à L'Exportation (Coface)

Paris-based Coface is France's leading private credit risk guarantee agency. The Coface Group is rated AA- by Fitch and A2 by Moody's, both with a stable outlook. Coface is a subsidiary of Natixis, the corporate, investment management, and financial services arm of BPCE, the second-largest banking institution in France. A risk rating is supported by a comprehensive database of economic and financial indicators, including a "risk outlook" that includes a concise evaluation of a country's economic and sociopolitical strengths and weaknesses. Coface provides freely available risk analysis for 160 developed and developing countries on the basis of macroeconomic, financial, and political criteria. The insurance company publishes a number of annual and quarterly reports, including a country risk assessment map, sectoral reports as well as regional payments surveys. The country risk assessments use an eight-level ranking range, from A1, A2, A3, A4, B, C, D to E (http://www.coface.com/Economic-Studies-and-Country-Risks).

Table 4.1 illustrates Coface's assessment of Algeria, with an overall assessment in Q1-2018.

4.3.2.2 US Export-Import Bank (EXIM)

The Export-Import Bank of the United States is the "official credit export agency of the United States." It was established in 1934 by an order of President Franklin D. Roosevelt. In 1945, it was made an independent agency of the executive branch pursuant to a charter adopted by the Congress. Under the terms of this charter, it must be reauthorized by Congress every four to five years. The Bank is located in Washington, DC and operates regional business development offices across the country. The Bank is self-sustaining for budget purposes.

The Bank's mission is to create and sustain jobs in the United States by promoting the exports of the country's goods and services. To support this mission, the Bank provides loans, guarantees, and insurance products. Its obligations are backed by the full faith and credit of the United States. It has exposure in over 160 countries. "Because it is backed by the full faith and credit of the United States, EXIM assumes credit and country risks that the private sector is unable or unwilling to accept," the Bank notes on its website (https://www.exim.gov).

The Bank defines its fee policy according to the guidelines established by the OECD that aim at providing level playing field for credit export agencies. Since the minimum exposure fee for a country is determined by the OECD country classification, EXIM Bank exposure fee levels are consistent with OECD country classifications. For markets which have not been classified by the OECD process, the EXIM Bank translates the US Government's Interagency Country Risk Assessment System (ICRAS) classification into a corresponding OECD exposure fee level. In addition, the US Export-Import Bank established a country limitation schedule for both private and public sector risk. As of 2018, a number of countries were excluded from the Bank's coverage policy, fully or above one-year, including the following: Afghanistan, Antigua, Bolivia, Burundi, Cambodia, CAR, Republic Democratic of Congo, Cuba, Greece, Haiti, Iran, North Korea, Libya, Mozambique, Somalia, Sudan, South Sudan, Syria, Tajikistan, Venezuela, and Yemen. For a few countries such as Bolivia, Cuba, Iran, North Korea, Sudan, and Syria, the Bank's export credit insurance program is prohibited by law (Export-Import Bank 2017a).

The Bank uses a risk matrix with a number of risk categories, under the form of different credit classification or "CC" levels, namely:

1. CC0 = exceptionally good credit quality (The likelihood of sovereign liquidity and solvency support is very high, both in relation to recovery prospects as well as default risk. This category is equivalent to that of a Triple A rating by risk rating agencies).
2. CC1 = very good rating quality (The risk of payment interruption is expected to be low or very low. The obligor has a very strong capacity for repayment and this capacity is not likely to be affected by foreseeable events).
3. CC2 = moderately good credit quality (The risk of payment interruption is expected to be low).
4. CC3 = moderate credit quality (There is a possibility of credit risk developing as the obligor faces major ongoing uncertainties or exposure to adverse business, financial, or economic conditions which could lead to inadequate capacity to meet timely payments).

5. CC4 = moderately weak credit quality (There is a possibility of credit risk developing as the obligor faces major ongoing uncertainties or exposure to adverse business, financial, or economic conditions which could lead to inadequate capacity to meet timely payments).
6. CC5 = weak credit quality (There is a likelihood of developing payment problems as the capacity for continued payment is contingent upon a sustained, favorable business and economic environment. Adverse business, financial, or economic conditions will likely impair capacity or willingness to repay).

Various materials on its website may be useful to the country risk analyst. These include:

- a detailed listing of the total exposure by country, as well as a breakdown of such exposure by type (i.e., loan, guarantee, or insurance)
- a discussion of trends in global finance and trade, including export credit volumes by country and composition of activity by credit rating
- a breakdown of its credit exposure by program, region, major industrial sector, and nature of borrower (private vs. public)
- country fact sheets when EXIM Bank amends its Country Limitation Schedule to open in a previously closed country. For instance, this was the case for Burma when President Obama signed an Executive Order terminating the US sanctions on Burma on October 7, 2016. Following the Executive Order, EXIM Bank opened its financing support program for short-term and medium-term transactions in Burma's public sector (Export-Import Bank 2017b).
- a discussion of the Bank's major risks, including repayment risk, market risk, operational risk, and a detailed discussion of the Bank's credit standards.

4.3.2.3 The Role of OECD Countries' Central Banks and Treasuries

Financial and currency crises in the 1990s were compounded by abrupt reversals of capital flows, both with regard to mounting capital flight and sharp cuts in foreign lending and direct investment. This "scissor effect" accentuated the impact of balance of payments deficits on liquidity ratios (e.g., short-term debt/reserves ratio). Hence, monitoring international bank exposure is a key component of country risk analysis, not only for close tracking of the confidence or nervousness of international banks in a particular country, but also for assessing the likelihood and extent of contagion effects.

In this regard, central banks in OECD countries have enhanced the quality and timeliness of national banking systems' cross-border risk exposure over the last twenty years, i.e., in the aftermath of the 1982 debt crisis.[1] Most of the OECD country central banks report bank claims on a regular basis, with a breakdown regarding borrowing country. This is the case, in particular, of national banking institutions in the US, UK, Canada, France, and Germany.

4.3.2.4 The Role of the Bank of Canada's Comprehensive Debt Database

The Bank of Canada's Credit Rating Assessment Group (CRAG) aims to fill an information gap regarding debt defaults. Its Sovereign Default Database tabulates data on debt owed to official and private creditors for all sovereign debtor countries' defaults between the years 1960 and 2016. For each year, the data are compiled by type of creditor on both a country-by-country and on a global aggregated basis. All country and global data on debt in default are expressed in nominal US Dollars. Sovereigns in default at any point during the year, together with the amounts of debt affected, are shown in the annual totals. http://www.bankofcanada.ca/wp-content/uploads/2016/06/r101-revised-june2017.pdf.

4.3.2.5 US Fed, US Treasury, Office of Financial Research, and FFIEC

US Federal Reserve System (FRB) The Federal Reserve System is the central bank of the United States. It consists of the Board of Governors of the Federal Reserve System (known as the Board), based in Washington, DC and twelve regional banks, each incorporated separately. The Board produces a wide range of financial statistics available on its website. This includes data on US bank assets and liabilities, bank structure, business finance, exchange rates, household finance, industrial activity, and money stock and reserve balances (https://federalreserve.gov). In addition, the Board produces research and other discussion papers that explore various topics in economics and finance, with a focus on the US economy and domestic financial

[1] The German Central Bank issues the Reihe 3 Quarterly report, while the Banque de France issues a Quarterly Bulletin as does the Bank of England.

markets. The Division of International Finance produces research on topics such as international macroeconomics, international trade, global finance, financial institutions, and international capital flows.

Each of the regional banks produces research and working papers in economics and finance. Of the twelve regional banks, the largest by asset size is the Federal Reserve Bank of New York. It is responsible for conducting open market operations—the buying and selling of United States Treasury securities to carry out US monetary policy. It also is responsible for buying and selling US Dollars to carry out US exchange rate policy.

US Department of Treasury The United States Department of the Treasury is a part of the executive branch of the US government. The Secretary of Treasury is appointed by the president and has usually been a visible figure in the discussion and shaping of economic policy. Among the department's roles is engaging in the borrowing of funds for operating the US government (https://www.treasury.gov).

The Treasury maintains a variety of financial and economic statistics, including:

- the Daily Treasury Statement, which sets forth the cash and debt positions of the US Government, including deposit and withdrawals as well as public debt transactions.
- the total amount of public debt, reported daily, including the total public debt outstanding and the debt held by the public and intragovernmental entities.
- the monthly Treasury Statement of Receipts and outlays of the US government.
- the monthly statement of public debt of the United States, including debt subject to the statutory debt limit.
- the gross external debt positions, which are the total amount of debt held by nonresidents.

In addition, the Treasury issues both regular and occasional publications relating to global economic developments, trade, and exchange rate developments. The Treasury staff also issues working papers of research findings relating to both domestic and international economic issues. Furthermore, the Treasury maintains a Monitoring List of "major trading partners that merit close attention to their currency practices." At present, this includes China, South Korea, Japan, Taiwan, Germany, and Switzerland.

Office of Financial Research Within the Treasury Department is a relatively new unit known as the Office of Financial Research (OFR). This is led by a Director who is also appointed by the president and confirmed by the Senate.

The OFR was established in response to the Global Financial Crisis and was created in 2010 following the Dodd Frank Wall Street Reform and Consumer Protection Act. The OFR "helps to promote financial stability by looking across the financial system to measure and analyze risks, perform essential research, and collect and standardize financial data" (https://www.financialresearch.gov).

"Our job is to shine a light in the dark corners of the financial system to see where risks are going, assess how much of a threat they might pose, and provide policy makers with financial analysis, information, and evaluation of policy tools to mitigate them."

A further mission for the OFR is to provide financial data, standards and analysis for the Financial Stability Oversight Council (FSOC), a body that is chaired by the Secretary of the Treasury and is composed of various federal financial regulators, selected state regulators, and an independent insurance expert appointed by the president.

The OFR maintains its own research staff, including experts with backgrounds in data standards, data collection, information technology, and other related fields. The staff produces publicly available working papers and research reports that have addressed a diverse set of issues relating to the United States and global economy, including the repo market, systemic risks, credit ratings, contagion in financial networks, hedge funds, and OTC derivatives. The staff also produces a financial stability monitor, which displays a "snapshot of weaknesses in the financial system based on five functional areas of risk: Macroeconomic, market, credit, funding and liquidity, and contagion."

Federal Financial Institutions Examination Council (FFIEC) The US government maintains an umbrella organization called the Federal Financial Institutions Examination Council. Established in 1979, it is an interagency body that is "empowered to prescribe uniform principles, standards, and report forms for the federal examination of financial institutions" operating in the United States. These include financial institutions that are regulated by the Board of Governors of the Federal Reserve System (FRB), the Federal Deposit Insurance Corporation (FDIC), the National Credit Union Administration (NCUNA), the Office of the Comptroller of the Currency (OCC), and the Consumer Financial Protection Bureau (CFPB). It is also empowered to make recommendations to promote uniformity in the supervision of financial institutions and to develop uniform reporting systems for such institutions.

The FFIEC produces and makes available data, reports, and other materials on its website. Some of the information is aggregated over all reporting banks in quarterly tables. The time lag is about one quarter. The reported data provide considerable detail on US bank claims on foreign countries, with itemization by individual country, maturity, and borrowing sector (https://www.ffiec.gov).

Among the available data are the following:

- total assets, liabilities, and net worth of US commercial banks, savings institutions, and credit unions as well as total income and expense data. The US FFIEC data provide a reliable creditor-reporting system of countries' external indebtedness with regard to both the public and private sectors. The agency's country exposure information report is a quarterly publication that provides data on US banks' claims and liabilities. The FFIEC publishes its E.16 Country Exposure Lending Survey and Country Exposure Information Report that includes US resident banks' country risk exposure above a certain concentration threshold (https://www.ffiec.gov/e16.htm#text).

In the case of Citicorp, Table 4.2 presents the bank's exposure survey with regard to a number of countries, including Australia, Brazil, Canada, and China in Q1-2017: (https://www.ffiec.gov/pdf/e16/009a_201703.pdf).

- aggregate financial exposure, by country, of foreign borrowers, including "off balance sheet" items such as cross-border commitments and guarantees, credit derivatives; and trade finance; and
- Reports of Condition and Income (Call Reports) for each regulated financial institution

4.3.2.6 The US Central Intelligence Agency

The Washington-based Central Intelligence Agency has produced the World Factbook since 1981 when this name was given to the annually produced publication. The first classified Factbook was published in August 1962, and the first unclassified version was published in June 1971. The 1975 Factbook was the first to be made available to the public. The Factbook was first made available on the Internet in June 1997. A total of 165 nations are covered,

Table 4.2 Citicorp's Country Exposure Survey

U.S. Dollar amounts in millions country	Amount of Cross-border claims outstanding after mandated adjustments for transfer of exposure (excluding derivative products)	Amount of foreign office claims on local residents (excluding derivative products)	Amount of gross claims outstanding from derivative products after mandated adjustments for transfer of exposure	Total of columns (1) Plus (2) Plus (3)	Gross foreign-office liabilities	Distribution of amounts in columns 1 and 2					
						By type of borrower			By maturity		
						Banks	Public	NBFIs	Other	One year and under	Over one year
Australia	6716	23,122	2134	31,972	19,697	5557	8271	4302	13,842	15,143	14,695
Brazil	13,485	17,054	1160	31,699	11,949	3967	12,289	1003	14,439	20,524	10,015
Canada	6173	9729	5436	21,338	5722	4914	4580	7474	4370	11,111	4791
Caymon Islands	53,003	1	4096	57,100	2	57	0	52,472	4570	36,841	16,163
China People Repub.	7591	20,316	975	28,882	20,006	4180	10,424	2435	11,844	17,003	10,905
France (Other)	38,712	2193	9197	50,102	710	16,426	5409	24,040	3228	38,839	2066
Germany	22,983	26,930	9693	59,606	1952	7622	40,423	4923	6638	39,973	9940
Hong Kong	3819	23,339	462	27,620	56,749	651	10,074	2568	14,326	16,738	10,420
India (Other)	12,472	22,425	1431	36,328	3386	5520	11,308	5393	14,108	24,570	10,328
Japan	17,755	32,189	2742	52,686	15,612	18,380	25,798	5395	3112	45,114	829

Table 4.3 Country economic data of the CIA's World Factbook

GDP (PPP) and GDP (official exchange rate)	GDP—real growth rate
GDP—composition, by end use and by sector	GDP—per capita (PPP)
Investment in fixed capital	Industrial production growth rate
Exports and Imports of goods and services	Labor force—by occupation and Unemployment rate
Population below poverty line	Gini index of income and wealth gap
Budget, Taxes and other revenues	Budget surplus (+) or deficit (–)
Public debt	Inflation rate (consumer prices)
Central bank discount rate	Commercial bank prime lending rate
Stock of narrow and broad money supply	Stock of domestic credit:
Market value of publicly traded shares	Trade flows (by commodities and by trading partners)
Trade and Current account balances	Reserves of foreign exchange and gold
Total external debt	Direct foreign investment—at home and abroad
Exchange rates	Macroeconomic overview

including both developed and developing countries, with a wide range of economic and social data, including the following economic indicators and data (Table 4.3).

4.4 Official Sources of Country Risk Information: The Multilateral Institutions

Solvency and liquidity risk always ends up in balance of payments and debt servicing difficulties in over-indebted countries. Typically, the debt overhang stems from a mismatch between financial obligations and revenues. This mismatch (in terms of volume, timing, currency, and interest rates) can stem from a combination of domestic and external problems. It can also be compounded by a gap between domestic savings and investment, structural domestic weaknesses, and exogenous shocks from the globalized system. However, most country risk analysts focus on the demand side of the debt overhang, i.e., over-indebtedness. The supply of capital available to emerging countries is not analyzed as fully as it should be. Financial turbulence, indeed, can be originated or accentuated and prolonged by capital volatility on the supply side. Tight credit, rising spreads, abrupt shortening of maturities, regional downgrading, and global credit contraction—are all factors that put pressure on emerging-markets' liquidity and solvency situation, whatever the soundness of a country's internal financial situation. OECD central banks' monetary policy swings have large consequences on emerging markets. An example is not only the actual reduction in the US Fed's quantitative easing (QE) policy in 2013 and 2014 but its sheer anticipation. Since its inception in 2008, the Fed's mortgage-backed securities purchase program was intended to lower interest rates and to boost the economic recovery process. The Fed's policy has been accompanied by a flow of funds into emerging-market economies in search of higher returns. However, the impact of "Fed tapering" on financial markets and capital flows in the more fragile economies has been large. As noticed by Rai and Suchanek (2014): "When Federal Reserve officials first mentioned an eventual slowdown and end of purchases under the central bank's QE program in May and June 2013, foreign investors started to withdraw some of these funds, leading to capital outflows, a drop in EME currencies and stock markets, and a rise in bond yields." Liquidity and solvency information must, accordingly, be assessed in close parallel with the global financial environment. This information is in the hands of multilateral financial organizations, such as the IMF and the World Bank, leaders in the field.

4.4.1 The Role of the International Monetary Fund

The International Monetary Fund (IMF) plays an important role as a provider of country risk data, including financial data regarding balance of payments, external indebtedness, macroeconomic adjustment programs, exceptional financing, and debt relief. For each member country, the IMF collects detailed statements of external current and capital accounts, including details on the capital flows relevant for measuring changes in external debt. This data is submitted by countries at least once a year. Many report on a quarterly basis and some on a monthly basis. The IMF is more focused on "flow data." The IMF's data are published on a monthly basis in the International Financial Statistics (IFS), combining balance of payments information on each of the 189 member countries.

The IMF has made a large effort regarding country risk information availability. This has involved timeliness, quality, and the standardization of economic and financial data. The IMF's work on data dissemination standards began in 1995 with the Fund's establishment of standards to guide member countries in the public circulation of their economic and financial data. These standards consist of two tiers: the General Data Dissemination System (GDDS) that applies to all Fund members, and the more demanding Special Standards for those countries having or seeking access to international capital markets. As a result, a growing number of countries can provide investors and creditors with comparable and timely financial and economic information. In addition, the IMF embarked on greater openness while expanding public access to its own operations and activities, including the release of Information Notices on the Fund's Article IV consultations with member nations. In particular, financing a country's public sector borrowing requirement (PSBR) appears in the evolution of the main monetary parameters, including the monetary base, domestic credit expansion, and the domestic money supply.

Since 2002, the IMF has performed a debt sustainability analysis for each of its member countries as tool to better detect, prevent, and resolve potential crises (International Monetary Fund 2017b). The framework consists of two complementary components, namely, sustainability of total public debt and that of total external debt, with a threefold objective:

1. Assess the current debt situation, its maturity structure, whether it has fixed or floating rates, whether it is indexed, and by whom it is held;
2. Identify vulnerabilities in the debt structure or the policy framework far enough in advance so that policy corrections can be introduced before payment difficulties arise; and
3. In cases where such difficulties have emerged, examine the impact of alternative debt-stabilizing policy paths.

On a yearly basis, IMF economists visit a member country to gather information and hold discussions with government and central bank officials. They often also meet with private investors, labor representatives, members of parliament, and civil society organizations. Upon its return, the mission submits a report to the IMF's Executive Board. These reports constitute a prime source of information and economic analysis for country risk assessment, mainly on emerging market countries (Table 4.4).

4.4.2 The Role of the World Bank Group

The World Bank and its sister institutions are prime sources of country risk information regarding macroeconomic fundamentals, external indebtedness, governance, institutions, and economic restructuring. Whereas the IMF focuses on debt flows in the balance of payments, the World Bank focuses on debt stocks. The Bank, as a major creditor, maintains a full record of the external debt of its 189 member countries. The World Bank's Debtor Reporting system was set up in 1951. Its main objective is monitoring long-term public or publicly guaranteed debt. In 1970, the system was extended to incorporate private, nonguaranteed long-term debt. The Bank has an internal system of cross-checks and it supplements reported data with

Table 4.4 Ivory Coast's balance of payments 2014–2020

	2014	2015	2016	2017		2018		2019	2020
		Est.	Est.	Prog.	Proj.	Prog.	Proj.	Proj.	Proj.
Current account	252	−119	−235	−574	−879	−636	−765	−815	−824
Current account excl. grants	−52	−401	−528	−917	−1222	−1033	−1161	−1267	−1303
Trade balance	1915	1874	1953	1843	1512	1948	1795	1957	2191
Exports, f.o.b.	6411	6938	6308	8021	6600	8885	7119	7787	8632
Of which: cocoa	2289	3031	2740	3027	2306	3067	2432	2462	2490
Of which: crude oil and refined oil products	1544	1121	785	1479	1068	1602	1030	1069	1129
Imports, f.o.b.	4496	5064	4355	6178	5088	6936	5324	5830	6441
Of which: crude oil and refined oil products	1676	1196	906	1607	1313	1796	1400	1473	1564
Services (net)	−1068	−1194	−1396	−1719	−1624	−1837	−1772	−1932	−2101
Primary Income (net)	−449	−596	−620	−661	−704	−726	−742	−809	−867
Of which: interest on public debt	94	152	177	210	206	229	253	241	308
Secondary Income (net)	−145	−204	−173	−38	−63	−21	−46	−31	−47
General Government	124	98	292	343	343	397	396	452	478
Other Sectors	−270	−302	−465	−381	−406	−418	−443	−483	−525
Capital and financial account	−212	157	1	801	935	904	721	927	991

(*Source* IMF, article IV report, September 2017)

information collected in country missions and by other organizations. The Bank requests information from member countries on all long-term debt, which consists of external liabilities with an original maturity of more than one year. The debt data, both aggregated and on a country specific basis, are published in the annual Global Development Finance report.

The World Bank's International Debt Statistics: The Bank's statistical data comprise a long-term debt breakdown of creditors (official bilateral and multilateral, banks, bonds, and private suppliers) as well as between debtors (public sector/private sector without public guarantee). The World Bank's International Debt Statistics release debt tables with an eighteen-month lag and are based on a Debtor Reporting System. Accordingly, these data are useful for academic research and are not considered sufficiently operational and timely for market-driven country risk assessment. World Bank data comprise major economic and debt ratios, as well as information on Paris and London Club restructuring agreements. In addition to a breakdown of external debt by maturity and by creditors, the World Bank calculates the present value of debt which is the sum of short-term external debt plus the discounted sum of total debt service payments due on public, publicly guaranteed, and private nonguaranteed long-term external debt over the life of existing loans (http://datatopics.worldbank.org/debt/ids/topic/1).

The previous table illustrates the World Bank's International Debt Statistics for Cote d'Ivoire (http://datatopics.worldbank.org/debt/ids/country/CIV) (Tables 4.5 and 4.6).

The World Bank's governance assessment data: Since the late 1990s, the World Bank has paid growing attention to governance issues in member countries. On August 18, 2001, World Bank President James Wolfensohn declared: "The biggest obstacle to the development of legal and judicial systems is a situation in which the economic elite uses the system in its own interests. Legal reform is not only a technical but also a political task" (World Bank 2005). The World Bank pioneered the efforts toward combating corruption in member countries in the early 1990s. (Klitgaard 1998; Gray 1998; Mauro 1998) The Bank set up an "Anticorruption Knowledge Center" as well as a Development Forum discussion on anticorruption strategies. The World Bank's increasing efforts to tackle governance and corruption have paved the way for a regular flow of information and data, including a composite Governance indicator that reflects the statistical compilation of perceptions of the quality of governance of many survey respondents in industrial and developing countries, as well as NGOs, risk agencies, and think tanks. The indicator uses six different underlying parameters, as follows:

Table 4.5 Cote d'Ivoire external debt data 2007–2015

$millions, unless otherwise indicated	2007	2008	2009	2010	2011	2012	2013	2014	2015
1. Summary external debt data									
External debt stocks	14,375.4	12,956.7	14,885.4	11,692.6	12,779.7	9502.2	9725.6	9607.6	10,028.1
Long-term external debt	12,238.5	11,366.2	13,563.7	10,420.2	11,217.7	7500.2	8307.7	8115.4	8519.8
Public and publicly guaranteed	11,647.7	10,628.7	12,715.7	9402.6	9885.7	5009.9	6240.8	6422.1	7150.2
Private nonguaranteed	590.8	737.5	848.0	1017.6	1332.0	2490.2	2066.9	1693.4	1369.6
Use of IMF credit	233.2	246.6	839.2	861.4	1090.4	1265.2	1417.9	1492.2	1508.3
Short-term external debt	1903.6	1343.9	482.4	410.9	471.5	736.8	0	0	0
of which Interest arrears on long-term	1522.6	1343.9	98.4	6.9	4.5	0.8	0	0	0
Official creditors	1133.0	920.5	71.7	6.6	4.1	0.5	0	0	0
Private creditors	389.6	423.4	26.7	0.4	0.4	0.4	0	0	0
Memo: Principal arrears on LDOD	2805.0	2526.5	181.3	6.0	4.8	2.2	10.7	15.4	19.3

Table 4.6 World Bank's governance assessment for Ivory Coast at the end of 2017

Indicator	Country	Year	Percentile Rank (0 to 100)
Voice and Accountability	Côte d'Ivoire	2015	
Political Stability and Absen..	Côte d'Ivoire	2015	
Government Effectiveness	Côte d'Ivoire	2015	
Regulatory Quality	Côte d'Ivoire	2015	
Rule of Law	Côte d'Ivoire	2015	
Control of Corruption	Côte d'Ivoire	2015	

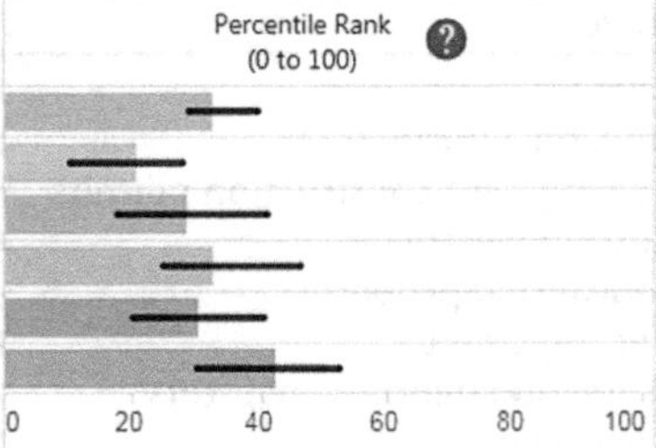

1. Voice and Accountability
2. Political Stability and Absence of Violence
3. Government Effectiveness
4. Regulatory Quality
5. Rule of Law
6. Control of Corruption

The World Bank's assessment of business conditions: The Bank's Ease of Doing Business Rank aims at evaluating the business conditions across time in around 190 developed and developing countries. A high ranking means the regulatory environment is more conducive to starting and operating a local firm. The rankings are determined by sorting the aggregate distance from frontier scores on ten topics, each consisting of several indicators, with equal weight to each topic. The Ease of Doing Business ranking compares economies with one another; the Distance to Frontier Rank benchmarks economies with respect to regulatory best practice, showing the absolute distance to the best performance on each Doing Business indicator (World Bank Group 2017). The chart illustrates the World Bank's assessment of the "doing business conditions" in Tunisia according to six key indicators. Tunisia exemplifies the sharp decline in the quality of business conditions in the midst of persistent uncertainty and sociopolitical turmoil in the wake of the Arab Spring revolution. The country's ranking improved after the ousting of Ben Ali, thereby improving its status from fifty-five to forty-six, given the new government's commitment to fighting opacity and corruption. In 2017, however, Tunisia's ranking fell to seventy-seven due to protracted sociopolitical volatility and unabated corruption (Table 4.7).

Table 4.7 Tunisia's doing business index 2017

Topics	DB 2017 rank	DB 2016 rank ⓘ	Change in rank
Overall	77	75	↓2
Starting a business	103	91	↓12
Dealing with construction permits	59	57	↓2
Getting electricity	40	38	↓2
Registering property	92	90	↓2
Getting credit	101	127	↑26
Protecting minority investors	118	112	↓6
Paying taxes	106	103	↓3
Trading across borders	92	91	↓1
Enforcing contracts	76	76	–
Resolving insolvency	58	55	↓3

Source World Bank-IFC

4.4.3 The Role of the BIS in Providing International Bank Claims and Liabilities Data

The Bank of International Settlements (BIS) is a key source of aggregate data on external sovereign liabilities and assets. The Basel-based institution provides debt stock and flow data collected by official monetary institutions on the international assets and liabilities of commercial banks. The BIS also gathers data on international bonds, Euronote issues, and certain derivative instruments. Much of this information is published in the BIS Quarterly Review on International Banking and Financial market developments.

International bank claims: The BIS consolidated banking statistics were launched in a comprehensive form following the onset of the Mexican debt crisis in 1982, with the purpose of monitoring international banks' exposure/claim on developing countries. The data cover contractual lending by the head office and all branches and subsidiaries on a worldwide-consolidated basis. The BIS data also contain breakdowns by maturity and by sector as well as information on unused credit commitments and facilities. Table 4.8 illustrates the international bank debt of Tunisia from the BIS' creditor-reporting system. The country's total liabilities vis à vis international banks amount to USD 3.7 billion in 2017, including USD 2.8 billion of loans. It can be seen that deposits in banks outside the country reached a higher amount than the country's bank debt. The BIS also provides a breakdown of claims and liabilities by maturity, debtor, and currency. One of the main contributions of the BIS data is to provide a focus on countries' short-term bank liabilities, due within one year. Calculating the actual short-term debt requires statistical calculations in order to exclude residual liabilities from the original debt falling due during the current year (Table 4.8).

Table 4.8 International banks' claims and liabilities on Tunisia (*Source* BIS)

Counterparties resident in Tunisia

Cross-border positions by instrument, sector of counterparty and currency, in millions of US dollars

Tunisia	Claims			Liabilities		
< Q1 2017	Adjusted changes USD mn		Outstanding USD mn	Adjusted changes USD mn		Outstanding USD mn
Level: 1 2 3 4 5	Q4 16	Q1 17	Q1 17	Q4 16	Q1 17	Q1 17
⊟ Cross-border positions	-262	303	3,661	-63	467	4,875
⊟ By instrument						
Loans and deposits	70	-78	2,779	-52	472	4,769
Debt securities	-1	32	241	0	19	36
Other instruments	-331	349	640	-18	1	10
Unallocated	-1	-0	1	7	-24	60
⊟ By sector of counterparty						
⊟ All instruments						
⊟ Banks	-356	359	1,813	-238	519	3,315

International bank liabilities: In a commercial bank balance sheet, bank claims are assets while deposits are liabilities. The BIS provides information regarding the breakdown of international banks' liabilities, distinguishing liabilities with regard to a country's government, its banking system, and also its nonfinancial private residents. The latter constitute a useful proxy for assessing the extent of a country's capital flight. In addition, the currency and maturity breakdown of loans and deposits can provide crucial information regarding the risk of mismatch between assets and liabilities. The overall Dollar amount of banking liabilities with regard to a country's nonfinancial private residents cannot be viewed as the mirror image of private expatriated capital outflows given that, for instance, they include "legal" and business-related deposits from private companies. Nevertheless, the change in private deposits (as well as its ratio to a country's macroeconomic accounts such as GDP, imports, or reserve assets) can be a useful indication of capital flight. For instance, the fact that nonbank private residents of Zimbabwe held nearly USD 1 billion of deposits in international banks at the beginning of 2017 should be related to the country's bad corruption and business conditions rankings, as well as to its unabated sociopolitical volatility.

The chart illustrates the sharp evolution in private deposits in international banks from Tunisia over the long term. It can be viewed as a summary of the country's turbulent sociopolitical evolution since the take-over of General Ben Ali in 1987 and his ousting at the beginning of the Arab Spring revolution in 2011. The BIS' cross-border positions reported by banking offices located in reporting countries is given in millions of US Dollars (*Source* http://stats.bis.org/statx/srs/table/A6.1?c=TN&p=) (Chart 4.2).

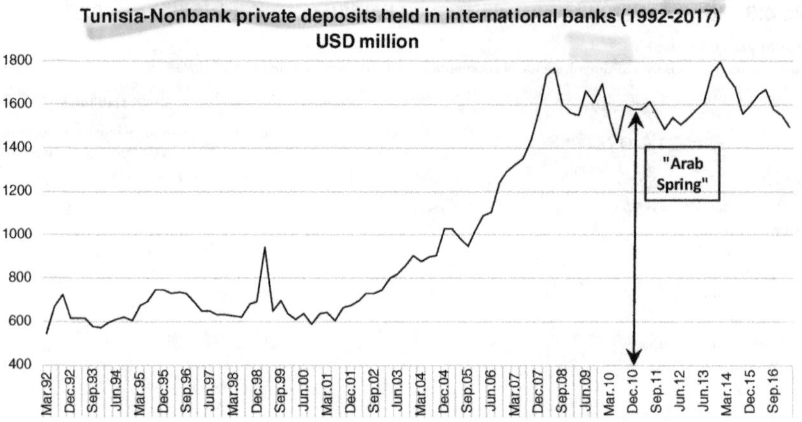

Chart 4.2 Evolution in Tunisia's private capital deposits in international banks (*Source* BIS data)

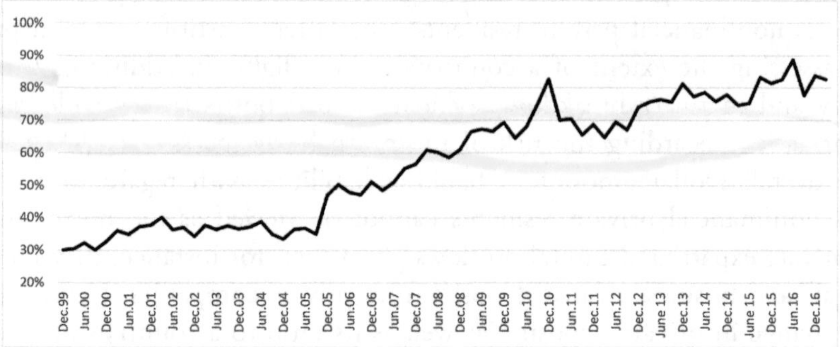

Chart 4.3 Tunisia-Ratio of expatriated private deposits/bank loans to private sector (*Source* BIS data)

Private nonbank deposits in foreign banks can also be compared with international bank loans to the given country and provide a useful measure of the distortion between a country's external bank debt and its private deposits held offshore. Chart 4.3 illustrates the sharp increase in Tunisia's ratio on the eve of the so-called Jasmin revolution in 2011. The ratio increased from 66% at the end of 2009 to more than 80% in 2011.

4.4.4 The Joint Aggregation Efforts of the BIS, the World Bank, the IMF, and the OECD

From a country risk perspective, assessing the full amount of a country's external debt is both crucial and puzzling. The level of external debt, its evolution, and its composition (that is, its structure of maturity, creditors, debtors, currency, interest rate, and securities vs. loans) are important elements in assessing a country's liquidity and solvency weaknesses, including for cross-country comparisons. However, country risk managers face two obstacles for a detailed and comprehensive picture of a country's external liabilities. The first has to do with the reliability of sources of debt data. A debtor country might underestimate the total amount of its external debt more than its creditors who tend to keep track of their claims methodically, at least since the debt crisis of the mid-1980s. A debtor country might exclude short-term liabilities, its debt to the IMF, or the debt incurred by state-owned companies with state guarantees. Overall, a creditor-reporting system of sovereign debt is more reliable. The Republic of Congo is a good example of the risks of understating a country's external indebtedness. In 2017, an IMF mission concluded that Congo's debt was higher than was reported to the international institution, as Congo authorities had not completed a full disclosure of the country's debt situation at the time of the March 2017 mission to discuss a possible program supported by the IMF (*Africa News* 2017). In addition, Congo was in a dispute with rating agencies over a default on the latest coupon payment of its USD 363 million Eurobond. Congo denied it was in default. The IMF encouraged Congo "to undertake all the necessary measures to put Congo's debt on a sustainable path." Reportedly, Congo's external debt should be revised from 77% of its GDP to 120%, the equivalent of twice the maximum debt burden that is authorized by the regulations of the Central African Economic and Monetary Union (CEMAC).

The second obstacle has to do with the wide range of information that comes from various categories of creditors, both private and public, bilateral and multilateral agencies. For too long, there has been no systematic effort to cross-check and gather debt data from various sources to provide a comprehensive measure of countries' external liabilities.

In 1984, recognizing the need for more intense dialogue to reconcile differences in debt compilation systems, the World Bank, the BIS, and the OECD joined the Berne Union to constitute the International Working Group on External Debt Statistics. In addition, since March 1999, the IMF joined the World Bank, the BIS, and the OECD in publishing joint external debt statistics in response to requests for dissemination of more timely debt and international reserves indicators. These organizations brought together for the first time the best international comparative data available on external debt stocks and flows. The new Inter-Agency Task force, chaired by the IMF, uses a creditor and market-based reporting system, with particular emphasis on short-term debt (International Monetary Fund 2008). A particular effort is made to cut the time lag before publication. The purpose of the joint series is to facilitate timely and frequent access on the joint website by a broad range of users to one data set that brings together data that are currently compiled and published by the contributing international agencies on components of countries' external debt.

The OECD provides debt stock and flows statistics that it receives through the Development Assistance Committee (DAC) creditor reporting system, including market sources (www.OECD.org/dac/debt). The OECD issues a comprehensive picture of a country's external liabilities including lending by multilateral institutions and non-OECD creditor countries, private export credits that are not officially guaranteed, and certain private sector borrowing. As the OECD recognizes, however, the two main gaps are understated intercompany claims and information on military debt, particularly for countries like Syria, Jordan, Libya, and Iraq.

Consequently, the Joint External Debt Hub (JEDH) is based on the BIS-IMF-OECD-World Bank statistics on external debt for disseminating comprehensive data on the external debt of developed, developing, and transition countries and territories, as well as statistics on selected foreign assets. The joint statistics—which include quarterly data obtained by creditor and market sources, as well as national sources—provide a breakdown by instrument and, importantly, show measures of short-term debt not easily available from other sources (BIS 2017). The table illustrates the external debt breakdown of Tunisia among various liability categories. Tunisia's total debt amounts to USD 22.6 billion at end of 2016, the equivalent of 53% of GDP (Table 4.9).

4.4.5 The Role of Regional Development Banks

In 2008, the African Development Bank (AfDB) launched its African Financial Market Initiative (AFMI). This program represents the commitment by the AfDB to contribute to domestic resource mobilization and capital market development on the continent. AfDB observes: "Developed

Table 4.9 External debt liabilities of Tunisia 2017 (in USD million)

Data are in millions	2016Q2	2016Q3	2016Q4	2017Q1	2017Q2
A1. Loans and other credits					
01_Cross-border loans, by BIS reporting banks	2726	2894	2830	..	..
02___o/w to nonbanks	1656	1862	1871	..	..
03___Official bilateral loans, total	..	..	..	..	..
04___o/w aid loans	..	..	..	..	..
05___o/w other	..	..	..	..	..
06__Multilateral loans, total	6772	6676	6860	6839	1902
07___o/w IMF	1721	1700	1620	1619	1902
08___o/w other institutions	5052	4976	5240	5221	..
09___Insured export credit, Berne union	2841	2686	2572	..	..
10___o/w short term	2137	2004	1914	..	..
11_SDR allocations	382	381	367	370	380
A2. Loans and other credits (Debt due within a year)					
12_Liabilities to BIS banks (cons.), short term	528	585	584	..	..
13_Multilateral loans, IMF, short term	149	231	328	448	531
B1. Debt securities (All maturities)					
14_Debt securities held by nonresidents	3458	..	..	..	..
B2. Debt securities (short term, original maturity)					
15_Debt securities held by nonresidents	24	..	..	..	..
C. Supplementary information on debt (liabilities)					
16_International debt securities, all maturities	4924	5459	5182	6246	..
17___o/w issued by nonbanks	4924	5459	5182	6246	..
18_International debt securities, short term	500	599	586	589	..
19___o/w issued by nonbanks	500	599	586	589	..
20_Paris club claims(ODA)	..	..	2608	..	..
21_Paris club claims (non ODA)	..	..	856	..	..
22_Liabilities to BIS banks, locational, total	3661	3767	3317	..	..

Source http://www.jedh.org/creditormarket.html

in Africa for Africa and focused on a cooperative approach with public and private sector partners, the AFMI is an integrated and tailored response to tackle some of the most important issues affecting the development of financial markets in the region. Through this initiative, the AfDB seeks to strengthen African economies by reducing their dependency on foreign currency denominated debt. It also seeks to increase the available financing options to the African corporate sector and "to act as a catalyst for regional market integration" (AFMI 2017). The African Financial Markets Database is a comprehensive database that provides well-needed updated information on African domestic bond markets by reconciling and standardizing data produced by several institutions, using different concepts and methods (https://www.africanbondmarkets.org/en/country-profiles/west-africa/cote-d%E2%80%99ivodire/).

Founded in 1958, the Luxembourg-based European Investment Bank is a major European Institution which aims to finance investment projects in Europe, Africa, Latin America, and some others in the frame of the UE development policy. Its lending operations reach around €75 billion annually. The EIB does not lend directly to corporations but operates through the intermediary of commercial banks. Each project selected must have dual financing: from the EIB and from a commercial bank, in order to leverage the amount of the loan (1€ granted by the EIB finance a 2€ project). Similar to the World Bank, the EIB issues bonds rated AAA in order to finance itself. The EIB is the biggest worldwide issuer of bonds, mainly Green bonds. It is at the forefront of attempts to lead that "green market" to maturity. Climate and environment is the first priority of projects' funding. Beyond its annual activity reports that focus on the Bank's project lending operations, the EIB's Economics Department provides a large number of specific thematic reports on a wide range of issues, including environment, banking sectors, policy reforms, energy, human capital, and innovation in both developed and developing countries. In addition, the EIB publishes surveys of interest for country risk analysts. The Central Eastern and South Eastern Europe (CESEE) Bank Lending Survey is a biannual survey covering around fifteen international banking groups and eighty-five local subsidiaries or independent local banks. Together these makeup more than 50% of banking assets in most countries. The survey is a unique instrument for monitoring banking sector trends and challenges in Central Europe. The annual EIB Survey on Investment and Investment Finance is an EU-wide survey that gathers qualitative and quantitative information on investment activities by 12,500 firms. The EIB survey provides a wealth of unique firm-level information about investment decisions and investment finance choices (EIB 2017).

Website: http://www.eib.org/projects/sectors/index.htm.

Alongside the EIB, the European Bank for Reconstruction and Development (EBRD) also plays an important role in financing projects (also with a new focus on energy efficiency). It provides loans, equity investments, and guarantees for private and public sector projects. The EBRD was established in 1991 in London with the initial aim of promoting transition to market-oriented economies in the countries of central and Eastern Europe and Central Asia. Beyond its core European member countries, the EBRD is active in more than thirty countries from Central Europe to Central Asia and the southern and eastern Mediterranean.

Regarding country risk-related economic intelligence, the EBRD publishes growth forecasts for its countries of operation three times per year together with its Regional Economic Prospects Update. It also monitors progress in transition and tracks structural reforms through a set of indicators, including privatization, governance, trade and foreign exchange systems, price liberalization, and competitiveness (http://www.ebrd.com/home).

4.4.6 UNDP and UNCTAD as Sources of Information Regarding Human Development, FDI, and International Trade

4.4.6.1 The United Nations Program for Development

UNDP provides an annual measure of countries' Human Development Index (HDI). This index is a summary measure of average achievement in key dimensions of human development for 188 countries, both developed and developing. It focuses on life expectancy, education, health, and standard of living. The HDI is the geometric mean of normalized indices for each of these dimensions. The health dimension is assessed by life expectancy at birth, the education dimension is measured by mean of years of schooling for adults aged twenty five years and more, and expected years of schooling for children of school entering age. The standard of living dimension is measured by gross national income per capita. The HDI uses the logarithm of income to reflect the diminishing importance of income with increasing GNI. The scores for the three HDI dimension indices are then aggregated into a composite index using geometric mean. GNI per capita (in 2011 Dollar in purchasing power parity) comes from the World Bank and the International Monetary Fund (Table 4.10). The HDI is also adjusted for inequalities (inequality-adjusted life expectancy index, inequality-adjusted education index, etc.).

Chart 4.4 illustrates the respective HDI trajectory of Morocco and Tunisia between 1990 and 2015. The UNDP's index underlines the higher score of Tunisia than Morocco, due to large differences in gender equality and education.

Table 4.10 Summarizes Tunisia's scores for the HDI in 2016

		Human development index (HDI)	Life expectancy at birth	Expected years of schooling		Mean years of schooling		Gross national income (GNI) per capita	GNI per capita rank minus HDI rank	HDI rank
HDI rank	Country	Value	(Years)	(Years)		(Years)		(2011 PPP $)		
		2015	2015	2015	a	2015	a	2015	2015	2014
97	Tunisia	0.725	75.0	14.6		7.1	c	10,249	3	97

Source UNDP

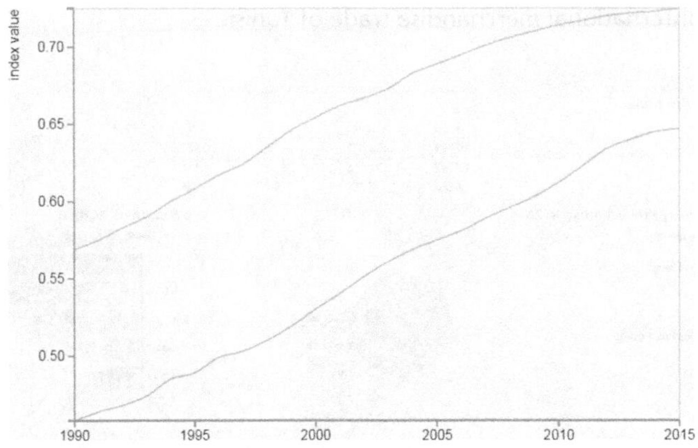

Chart 4.4 Morocco's and Tunisia's Human Development Index

4.4.6.2 The United Nations Conference for Trade and Development (UNCTAD)

UNCTAD is also a useful source of country risk information regarding trade flows and foreign direct investment.

Table 4.11 illustrates UNCTAD's data for Tunisia regarding the country's international trade structure by products and major trading partners. The agency also provides a cross-country comparison of the evolution of exports' purchasing power index, hence illustrating the competitiveness of exchange rates as well as the ratio of export prices to import prices.

UNCTAD has developed a recognized expertise regarding measuring and monitoring of foreign direct investment, both inward and outward flows and stocks. UNCTAD provides statistics of Foreign Direct Investment (FDI) and the operations of transnational corporations (TNCs) with a detailed data set on inward and outward FDI flows and stocks together with geographical and industry breakdown. It also presents a range of variables related to the activities of foreign affiliates in the country and foreign affiliates of home-based TNCs. The following chart illustrates the evolution in FDI capital inflows toward four northern African countries during the 1980–2016 period according to UNCTAD's database (Chart 4.5). (UNCTAD 2017)

UNCTAD also provides country risk analysts with cross-country assessment of the inward and outward flows of foreign direct investment, as well as their share of the countries' GDP. Table 4.12 casts light on Tunisia's FDI inflows and outflows at the end of 2016.

Table 4.11 International merchandise trade of Tunisia

Total merchandise trade
(millions of US$)

	2005	2010	2015	2016
Merchandise exports	10 494	16 427	14 073	13 572
Merchandise imports	13 177	22 215	20 221	19 462
Merchandise trade balance	-2 683	-5 789	-6 148	-5 890

-3.6 %
Merchandise exports growth rate in 2016

Export structure by product group in 2016
(as % of total exports)

Top 5 partners in 2016
(exports, millions of US$)

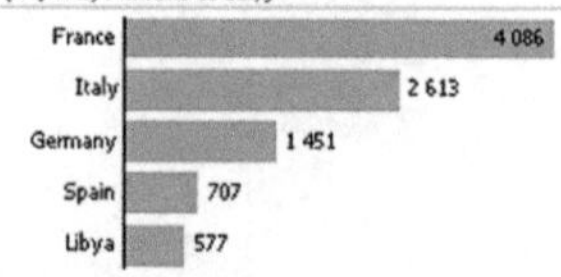

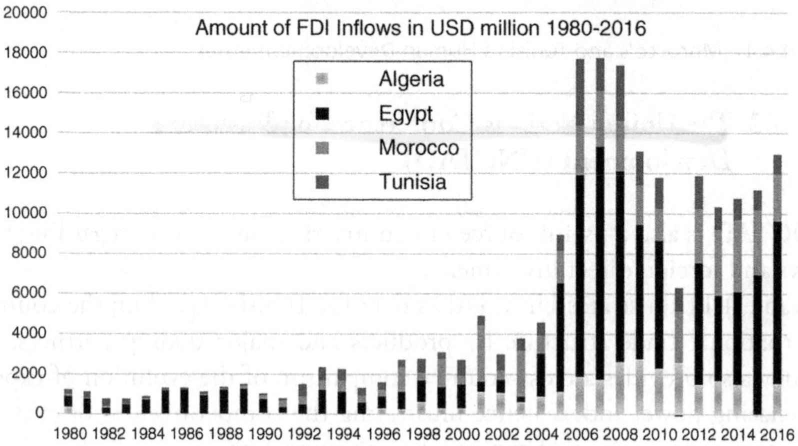

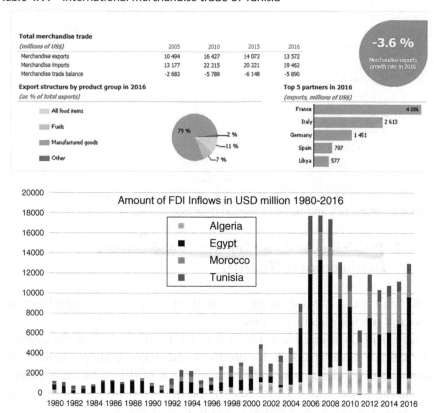

Chart 4.5 Cross-country comparison of FDI Inflows in North African countries (*Source* UNCTAD and authors' calculations)

Table 4.12 FDI and external financial resources of Tunisia

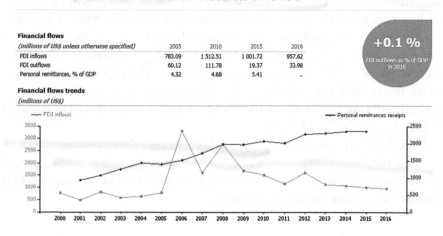

Financial flows
(millions of US$ unless otherwise specified)

	2005	2010	2015	2016
FDI inflows	783.09	1 512.51	1 001.72	957.62
FDI outflows	60.12	111.78	19.37	33.98
Personal remittances, % of GDP	4.32	4.68	5.41	..

+0.1 %
FDI outflows as % of GDP in 2016

Financial flows trends
(millions of US$)

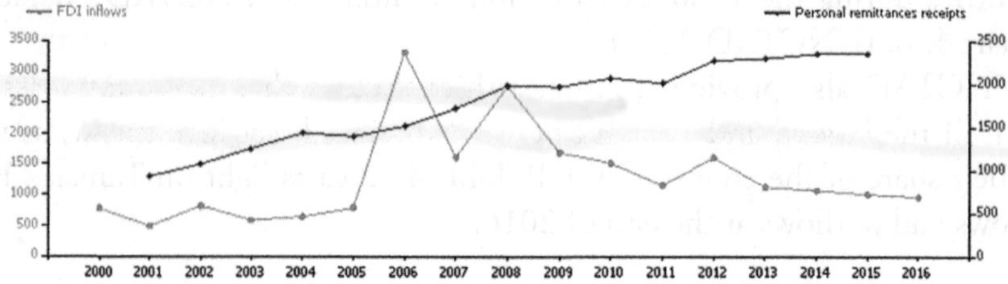

4.5 Databases from Scholars and Universities

Scholars and university databases constitute a prime source of data on country risk-related issues, including governance, institutions, and socioeconomic development. As a matter of illustration, one can mention the following databases:

- Caprio et al. (2005) produced the first detailed database on the issue of banking crisis.
- Two IMF economists, namely Laeven and Valencia (2008), provide a "new" database on the timing of systemic banking crises and policy responses to resolve them. The database covers the universe of systemic banking crises for the period 1970–2007, with detailed data on crisis containment and resolution policies for forty-two crisis episodes, and also includes data on the timing of currency crises and sovereign debt crises. The new database is the most complete and detailed database on banking crises to date, reportedly https://econpapers.repec.org/paper/imfimfwpa/08_2f224.htm.
- Dataset from Andrew K. Rose at University of California Berkeley: http://faculty.haas.berkeley.edu/arose/RecRes.htm#Software, and http://faculty.haas.berkeley.edu/arose/RecRes.htm#Attacks.
- World Bank's dataset of financial indicators: https://data.worldbank.org/data-catalog, and
- University of Gothenburg's database on governance and institutional quality: The QOG Basic dataset of The Quality of Government Institute, http://www.qog.pol.gu.se.

4.6 Conclusion

Country risk analysis is as good as the information it relies on. Compared with the 1980s or even 90s, country risk analysts do not currently face a deficit of economic intelligence sources—indeed the contrary is nearer the truth. Rating agencies, multilateral institutions, merchant banks, and think-tanks produce sophisticated and comprehensive databases and rankings. Under pressure from the IFIs and rating agencies, countries compete to get market access via a regular flow of quality information. In turn, fund managers, investors, creditors, and bank analysts are inundated by information flows that require careful discrimination and cross-checking. The quality of macroeconomic and financial information itself is a measure of Country Risk, and indeed an early warning signal. A country that is either unable or unwilling to provide timely and reliable information sends negative signals regarding the quality of its policymaking process and of its public and private administration, not to mention its transparency and governance.

References

Africa News. 2017. "Congo Republic Fights Ratings Downgrades as IMF Reports Hidden Debts," August 5, 2017.

AFMI. 2017. https://www.africanbondmarkets.org/en/.

Beck, Ulrich. 2002. *La Société du Risque: Sur la voie d'une nouvelle modernité*. Paris: Fayard.

BIS. 2017. Joint Statistics on External Debt. http://www.bis.org/publ/r_debt.htm?m=6%7C380%7C672.

Caprio, Gerard, Daniela Klingebiel, Luc Laeven, and Guillermo Noguera. 2005. "Appendix: Banking Crisis Database." In *Systemic Financial Crises: Containment and Resolution*, edited by Patrick Honohan and Luc Laeven. Cambridge: Cambridge University Press.

Central Intelligence Agency (CIA). 2017. Word FactBook Introduction. https://www.cia.gov/library/publications/the-world-factbook/docs/history.html.

Dunn, Robert Jr. 2001. "The Routes to Crisis Contagion." *Challenge* 44 (6): 45–58.

Eichengreen, Barry, and Carlos Arteta. 2000. "Banking Crises in Emerging Markets: Presumptions and Evidence." Working Paper No C00-115, Center for International Development Economics Research (CIDER), University of California at Berkeley.

European Investment Bank. 2017. http://www.eib.org/about/economic-research/surveys-data/investment-survey.htm.

Export-Import Bank. 2017a. "Country Limitation Schedule." https://www.exim.gov/sites/default/files/tools/countrylimitationschedule/CLSApril2017.pdf.

Export-Import Bank. 2017b. "Burma Fact Sheet." http://www.exim.gov/tools-for-exporters/country-limitation-schedule/burma-fact-sheet.

Gray, Cheryl, and Daniel Kaufman. 1998. "Corruption and Development." *Finance & Development* 35 (1): 7–10.

International Monetary Fund. 2008. "Twenty-First Meeting of the IMF Committee on Balance of Payments Statistics," Washington, DC, November 4–7.

International Monetary Fund. 2017a. "Debt Sustainability Analysis, Introduction." http://www.imf.org/external/pubs/ft/dsa/.

International Monetary Fund. 2017b. "IMF Executive Board Concludes the Ex-Post Evaluation of the Second Precautionary and Liquidity Line Arrangement for Morocco." Press Release 17/332, p. 14.

Klitgaard, Robert. 1998. "International Corruption Against Governance." *Finance & Development* 35 (1): 3–6.

Laeven, Luc, and Fabian Valencia. 2008. "Systemic Banking Crises: A New Database." IMF Working Paper, WP/08/224.

Mauro, Paolo. 1998. "Corruption: Causes, Consequences, and the Way Forward." *Finance & Development* 35 (1): 11–14.

OECD. www.oecd.org/dac/debt, and https://data.oecd.org/gga/general-government-debt.htm OECD—Development Assistance Committee, Development Finance Data, Country and Sectoral Data, Paris.

Rai, Vikram, and Suchanek Lena. 2014. "The Effect of the Federal Reserve's Tapering Announcements on Emerging Markets." Working Paper 2014–50, Bank of Canada.

UNCTAD. 2017. http://unctadstat.unctad.org/wds/TableViewer/tableView.aspx.

World Bank. 2005. "Corruption Bars Effective Legal Systems, August 13, 2001 Speech. Voice for the World's Poor. Selected Speeches and Writings of World Bank President James D. Wolfensohn, 1995–2005." Washington, DC.

World Bank Group. 2017. "Ease of Doing Business," 14th ed. http://www.doingbusiness.org/~/media/WBG/DoingBusiness/Documents/Annual-Reports/English/DB17-Report.pdf.

5

Country Risk Assessment: The Role of Private Sources of Market and Economic Intelligence

5.1 Introduction: Economic Intelligence, Ratings and Models: Underlying Assumptions, Limitations, and Best Practices

Despite the growing number of rating agencies worldwide, the quality of country ratings is still questionable. How can one explain this "halo of uncertainty" surrounding ratings quality? Econometric forecasting models—with their overreliance on complex mathematical correlations—have shown themselves to be no better at providing reliable risk signals. These models rely on "dynamic systems" that are highly sensitive to the initial hypotheses used by forecasters. Other models aim to quantify so-called black swan events—that is, abrupt shifts in trends, found in the fat tails of probability distributions. "Extreme events" or "extreme value" movements are essentially analyzed in the same way that insurers try to assess the likelihood of natural disasters such as floods or earthquakes, despite historical evidence that strongly suggests that such an approach is flawed.

In contrast, the potential for "conventional payment default" is often analyzed using the same methods and models that conventional finance theory uses to assess credit risk. This analysis is split between two factors: the country's ability to pay and its willingness to do so. The willingness is modeled through maximizing the so-called state's welfare. It takes into consideration how a country will weigh the cost and benefits of default and which of such trade-offs will maximize social welfare. Clearly, the country might face a short-

M. H. Bouchet et al., *Managing Country Risk in an Age of Globalization*,
https://doi.org/10.1007/978-3-319-89752-3_5

term benefit in defaulting but also incurs a long-term cost—being excluded from capital markets for many years or facing a higher cost of financing. How "long term" is the default cost, actually, depends on the country's reputation as a serial defaulter, its speed of creditworthiness recovery, investors' search for yield, and creditors' memory. Usually, the main types of costs from an international sovereign default include reputational costs, international trade exclusion costs, domestic economic costs with lower consumption and higher prices, banking system tensions due to worsening portfolio quality, the threat of a bank run and tighter access to interbank markets, and political costs to the authorities. Depending on the root causes of the default and on the subsequent debt restructuring process, the economic costs can be substantial but short-lived and market access recovery can be within a few years with gradual improvement in credit ratings and spreads. The reputational cost has been analyzed by Eaton and Gersovitz (1981) in a well-known article whose rhetoric assumes that a country faces an embargo on future loans by private lenders as a consequence of default. Default, thus, is costly and makes reentry into private capital markets difficult. Argentina's inability to access the global capital market for fifteen years in the wake of its 2001 default is a good illustration of markets' memory. As noticed by Pronina and Doff (2016): "As Argentina prepares amid much fanfare its first international bond sale since a record default 15 years ago, a little reminder of its less-than-stellar financial past crept into its sales pitch. On page 8 of the 266-page prospectus, a paragraph states that from time to time, the Republic carries out debt-restructuring transactions." Argentina has been a serial defaulter with eight debt defaults since the 1820s. Defaults occur in waves due to external shocks, tighter market liquidity, and cross-country contamination. Figure 5.1 shows the cycle of debt defaults with regard to each category of external creditors, both official and multilateral.

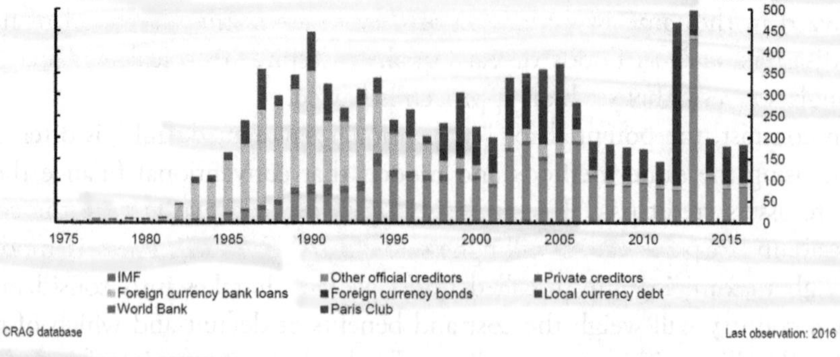

Fig. 5.1 Total sovereign debt in default, by creditor. USD billion (*Source* Bank of Canada, CRAG database)

Until the 1990s, country default modeling was subject to a relatively "small sample" size. A study by Bloomberg in 2013 estimated that only 251 sovereign defaults had occurred during the past 200 years, which is far from being enough to draw any meaningful inferences. This limitation has, however, been somewhat offset by new developments in Big Data and data mining, alongside the development of bond market data for emerging countries and financial data providers (e.g., Bloomberg, Reuters, and others). The choice of explanatory variables remains a challenging exercise due to the number of variables that are correlated between themselves. In addition, each crisis has its specific features, hence the choice of variables is an ad hoc process in itself. The unit of analysis is unavoidably the country, with its complex economic, sociopolitical, and institutional characteristics. Consequently, it is very difficult to identify exogenous variables. The interpretation of many results in the literature is clouded by the inclusion in the estimated relationships of many endogenous variables as explanatory variables (Eaton et al. 1986). A number of scholars have incorporated various aspects of chaos theory to explain the complexity and contagion risks in the global economy. Among fat-tail risks, geopolitical risk is probably the hardest to predict. The spread of terrorism across boundaries in the Middle East and well-beyond illustrates the complex influence of the rise of transnational agents that show growing impact on financial markets' valuation, the cost of insuring risks, and the methodology of rating agencies. Geopolitical volatility thus remains a difficult risk to assess and model for all these reasons, including the fact that its frequency, magnitude, and timing are so difficult to determine.

5.2 Model Deficiencies Justify Incorporating Economic and Human Intelligence

The limitations of using econometric and mathematical models to imply causality or predictability have led country risk managers to use a pragmatic approach, which is to assess Country Risk on a relative basis, incorporating elements of both quantitative models and qualitative analysis.

Clearly, it is wishful thinking to hope to predict the exact timing of debt crises. But useful signals can be identified from a wide array of changes in creditworthiness indicators and in countries' socio-institutional stability as discussed in Chapters 9 and 10. Risk assessment agencies seek to incorporate "collective intelligence" into their credit ratings and strive to map linkages between sovereign borrowers, global markets conditions, and investors' risk appetite. A number of risk signals, however, cannot be measured accurately nor quantified, including the role of institutions and the consequence of socio-political tensions on the country's debt servicing capacity and willingness. Nassim Taleb (among other scholars and practitioners) highlights the notion that one should stop focusing on the causality and instead emphasize uncertainty (Taleb 2005). Humans, indeed, have cognitive limitations. Risk analysts are not rational but rationalizing creatures. As Peter Bernstein already emphasized in Chapter 1: "Risk management is the process of maximizing the areas where we have some control over the outcome while minimizing the areas where we have absolutely no control over the outcome" (Bernstein 1998).[1]

5.3 The Growing Role of Quantitative Measures of Country Risk and the Limitations of Models

Quantitative risk analyses encompass six main features, none of which should be sidelined or given less emphasis:

1. *Indicator/variable screening*: The purpose is to define which variables will be explanatory, with the least feasible correlations between them to avoid statistical bias. In Country Risk, "one size does not fit all," and the screening must be targeted at the most salient variables. For instance, the public debt/GDP ratio is irrelevant for some countries that are not dependant on foreign capital. An extreme case is Japan with large current account surpluses, and accordingly no need for foreign currency financing. Japan can finance a public debt/GDP of up to 400% by capturing large domestic savings. A relatively low (though rising) share of private consumption in the country's GDP frees savings that are invested in domestic debt securities by an aging population.
2. *Indicator threshold setting*: To score risk levels and risk tolerance requires setting thresholds beyond which sovereign default looms. The risk profile can differ between the short and long run. In the short run, "push factors" can be excluded but high-frequency data of vulnerabilities can efficiently be used to shape early predictors. In the long run, institutional and structural factors must be considered as they evolve. Also important are exter-

[1] A useful discussion of these themes is set forth in the paper "Risk Assessment and Risk Management: Review of Recent Advances on their Foundation" (Aven 2016).

nal pull-factors and rising global threats that are discussed in Chapter 12. Thresholds may change over time. In the 1970s and 1980s, hyperinflation was frequent, with many economies sustaining inflation of over 20% for several years. But from the 1990s onward, a growing number of central banks became independent and their wish to build credibility resulted in a reduction in tolerance for inflation. Since the Global Financial Crisis, inflation has been subdued, however, and central banks have striven to increase domestic prices with little success between 2010 and 2017.

3. *Assigning relative weights to indicators*: Paolo Manasse and Nouriel Roubini compared the importance of fifty indicators in the two periods 1970–2002 and 1990–2002 (Manasse and Roubini 2009). They found that most of the top ten indicators were stable over time. These included total external debt/GDP and short-term debt/GDP, short-term debt to foreign-exchange reserves, and several variations of these. Other indicators—such as current account balance/GDP, terms-of-trade volatility, and openness—increased in importance when tested in the 1990–2000 period, reflecting the effect of increased liberalization and the global integration of financial markets compared with the earlier decades. Since the 2011 European debt crisis, many Credit Rating Agencies (CRAs) have decided to put more emphasis on GDP growth as one of the most efficient ways for countries to pay back their debt and improve solvency indicators. Another approach was to aim at stimulating inflation with loose monetary policy and "quantitative easing," despite its potentially negative long-term implications.
   Some indicators have a "double edge" impact, that is, too much inflation is detrimental for growth but not enough is detrimental for debt ratios. Lower inflation helps to absorb a share of nominal debt for private and public agents. Creditworthiness, however, also depends on the debt structure, including fixed or variable rates, maturity structure, and the currency match (or mismatch) between assets and liabilities. Overall, it is difficult to set a threshold reflecting the "maximum" debt level or the "optimal" level of inflation. The issue of debt/GDP threshold is further discussed in more detail in Chapter 8. Regarding inflation, European central banks target growth of prices "below but close to 2%" of the Harmonised Index of Consumer Prices (HICP) in the "medium run." If such a target demonstrates a fear of inflation, it also reflects a fear of deflation. The time horizon in the "medium run" is also blurred, in line with the "constructive ambiguity" used by central bankers. For the first time, on September 21, 2017, the US Federal Reserve Chair Janet Yellen acknowledged that "the fall in inflation was a bit of a mystery." To state the point concisely, assigning relative weight to indicators often turns out to be very challenging.

4. *Understanding the limits of models*: The ultra-well-known metaphor of the "streetlight effect" is often used to highlight economic observational bias:

> *A police officer sees a drunken man intently searching the ground near a lamppost and asks him what he is looking for. The drunk replies that he is looking for his car keys and the officer helps for a few minutes to no avail. The policeman then asks whether the man is certain that he dropped the keys near the lamppost. "No," is the reply, "I lost the keys somewhere across the street." "So why are you looking here?" asks the officer, surprised and irritated. The drunk retorts, "Because the light is much better here."*

Many economic indicators and ratios are shaped by the need to perform replicable measurements. Nevertheless, these measurements do not always accurately reflect the phenomenon that is being investigated. Moreover, many variables, are not always observable. For instance, even if the predominantly used Debt/GDP ratio is convenient and intuitive, it does not compare like with like. Which part of the country's annual revenue should be used to pay back the whole debt? Is annual national income growth enough (with the budgetary "primary surplus" generated) to face the outstanding debt burden? Debt is a stock whereas GDP is a sum of added value generated by annual production. GDP, thus, does not include a country's wealth and assets, nor do the production factors reflect the loss of value since GDP is a "gross" indicator. Pettis (2017) warns risk analysts not to read GDP growth as an indicator of countries' underlying economic performance, in particular, for emerging countries like China: "In China, bad debt is not written down and the government is not subject to hard budget constraints. (…) Reported GDP growth overstates the real increase in wealth by the failure to recognize the associated bad debt." Regarding solvency indicators, the term structure and maturity profile of debt may be far more important than the actual Debt/GDP ratio, whose denominator is of questionable value for the purpose it is being used. If a government has sufficient time to decide how to restructure its debt or establish measures to cut costs, it is significantly less likely to be forced into making a difficult default. The United Kingdom, for example, is able to engage in recovery and austerity efforts at least in part because it has a long-term debt that is carefully structured to promote economic and financial stability. The risk analyst should also take into account "who" holds the government's debt, that is, domestic or foreign investors. Less than 30% of the UK government debt is held by foreign investors versus 65% in the case of France. The rest of UK's debt is held by the UK private sector (pension funds, insurance companies, households, and other institutional investors) as well as by the Bank of England under the Asset Purchase Scheme that has been extended in August 2016. The higher the share of debt held in the global markets, the larger its yield and spread volatility.

5. *Avoiding overreliance on checklists or predetermined indicators*: Unless they are adjusted from time to time, checklists can miss new factors that can trigger different types of crisis. After the Global Financial Crisis of 2008, analysts began to realize that a focus on official interest rates set by central banks was not enough; they also needed to track asset prices. Consider the case of massive liquidity injections accomplished through large-scale asset purchase programs (LSAP). Such actions may not be reflected in the final prices of goods and services, but they may be reflected in asset prices. If such a transmission mechanism does not occur immediately, it may do so in the medium or long term. This time lag risk has been downplayed by OECD's central banks regarding the long-term inflation potential. Quantitative monetary policies seem to be "terra incognita" for most analysts and their effect cannot be deduced from previous crisis experiences.
   The relative importance of indicators, thus, may change over time. In a country like China, credit growth is increasingly channeled through the shadow financial system, which tends to reduce the impact of the central bank's monetary policy, hence making regulatory policy less efficient. An illustrative example of the historical evolution of Country Risk can be found in the various changes in the risk assessment methods of Coface, the French credit export agency, over recent decades. In the 1980s, Coface's analysis was mainly focused on external debt ratios. That narrow focus originated in the definition of Country Risk by scholars, including Nagy, one of the pioneers of country risk analysis: "Country risk is the exposure to a loss in cross-border lending, caused by events in a particular country which are, at least to some extent, under the control of the government" (Nagy 1979). It gradually began to include political factors after the Soviet Union breakup and the Gulf War of 1991. The Mexican financial crisis of 1994 forced rating agencies to consider financial instability as well. And, the 1997/98 Asian Crisis led rating agencies to incorporate governance and institutional factors (Bouchet et al. 2003).
6. *The incorporation of scenarios in prediction models*: Econometric models aim at simplifying the current reality to better predict the future. The objective is to avoid two interconnected phenomena: the cliff-edge effect

and markets overshooting. Granularity avoids these "cliff effects" (also known as "threshold effects"), reflecting the fact that variable interpretation is not "black or white" but rather "shades of grey." For instance, a central bank is never fully dependent or fully independent. The IMF has encouraged central bank independence, first in developed countries, and increasingly in developing countries based on the observation that central bank independence and inflation show a significant negative correlation. As noticed by Mersch, Member of the Executive Board of the ECB (2017): "Independence has been granted to central banks in order to shield them from short-term political influence when fulfilling their mandate of ensuring price stability. It is largely undisputed that an independent central bank with a clearly defined mandate is better able to keep inflation lower and more stable."
Granularity, that is, a well-defined purpose and scope, is particularly important for assessing qualitative indicators. For example, central bank independence can be scored qualitatively (scores ranging from very independent to not independent). The choice of proxy variables is crucial. For instance, is inflation a good proxy to measure a central bank's independence? Or should one try to spot any change in the money supply growth in pre-electoral cycles? Which criteria should one highlight to proxy a central bank's policy transparency? Should one rely on an average of criteria to get a "synthetic indicator"? In sum, modeling Country Risk is a complex adventure that can lead to diminishing returns, when the number of qualitative and quantitative variables increase to take into account a country's numerous characteristics.

5.4 The Pros and Cons of Country Risk Ratings

Since the late 1990s, the growing number and diversity of risk ratings have been spectacular. Almost every feature of a country's socioeconomic system has led to rating and scoring, including productivity, competitiveness, transparency, civil liberties, innovation, regulations, governance and corruption, and bribery. It is tempting for country risk analysts and managers to shrink a large number of underlying risk variables into one single number. Scoring, rating, and ranking make cross-country comparisons across time simple, if not simplistic. A sovereign credit rating is a quantitative assessment of a government's ability and willingness to service its foreign debt obligations in full and on time. As such, a rating is a forward-looking estimate of crisis probability and it is based on a large number of economic and social parameters. The appraisal is thus both quantitative and qualitative, even though the ultimate output is a grade or rank. As S&P observes: "The quantitative aspects of the analysis incorporate a number of measures of economic and financial performance and contingent liabilities, although judging the integrity of the data is a more qualitative matter. The analysis is also qualitative due to the importance of political and policy developments" (Standard & Poor's 2002).

Despite a history of ineffective prediction, country risk analysts keep relying on risk ratings that remains popular though disasters keep coming. One reason is that ratings make cross-country comparison easy. Another reason is precisely that ratings are widely used. To paraphrase Keynes on investors, an astute country risk manager stays clear of innovation and is only as right or wrong as the herd. A third reason is that ratings are influential. Should a country want access to international capital markets, a credit rating is a prerequisite. In the globalized markets, only a handful of countries shun credit ratings, including North Korea and Algeria. North Korea does not appear to have any interest in issuing sovereign bonds while Algeria's large, though declining, reserve assets and current account balance are supposed to maintain financial self-sufficiency. In the global markets, if you can't be measured, then effectively you don't exist, hence you can't borrow. The influential nature of ratings also comes from their wide use by sovereign wealth funds, pension funds, and other institutional investors to gauge the creditworthiness of countries. As such, ratings have a large impact on a country's bor-

Advantages/Pros	Shortcomings/Cons
Simple and easy to incorporate in graphs and country reports	Often simplistic and "black box" Assumptions, methodology, and weightings are not always transparent
Shrinks large number of variables into one single grade	Reductionist given the complexity of Country Risk
Cross-country comparisons	Risk of self-fulfilling prophecy
Comparison across time	Little predictive value
Useful tool for statistical and econometric analyses	Weighted average tends to bury salient trends and "fat tails"
Reliable for smooth risk evolution without abrupt worsening	Gives market consensus often made of herd instinct

Fig. 5.2 The Pros and Cons of Country Risk Ratings

rowing costs. In addition, country ratings put pressure on countries' policy efforts to improve scoring and to keep attracting investment flows.

Figure 5.2 summarizes the pros and cons of risk ratings.

5.4.1 Recurrent Pitfalls in the Methodology or Interpretation of Ratings

One can briefly consider several main shortcomings of country ratings.

1. Country ratings often create a risk of self-fulfilling prophecy. Country ratings might trigger herd instinct and spillover effect, hence transforming a national crisis into regional destabilization. As observed through several country risk crises, the rating agencies lag the market in that spreads and CDS prices react to worsening risk signals before agencies adjust their ratings. Downgrading is often abrupt and the rating's adjustment overshooting fuels investors' overreaction. S&P and Moody's, for instance, attach a negative, stable, or positive outlook to their ratings as a signal of another possible down/upgrade in the medium term. That is supposed to help to guide and anchor investors' expectations and to avoid excessive reactions. In practice, the change in outlook tends to have the effect of a self-fulfilling prophecy on investors' portfolio rebalancing strategies.
   When ratings incorporate a long-run horizon (e.g., more than two years), it is necessary to use scenario analysis with optimistic, neutral, or pessimistic views. Some preeminent indicators can be used as early signals of market change, including the money supply indicators (monetary base), the stock markets (which reflect investors' expectations), as well as lagging indicators such as inflation or employment rate that reflect economic cycles. Different kinds of indicators may be useful for different purposes and over different time horizons. Some may be useful in the short term (e.g., liquidity) but have less value in the longer term (whereas investment, growth, employment, and solvency are of higher importance). It may thus be useful to consider whether certain indicators may be subject to a greater margin of error with therefore less emphasis on the decision-making process. That an indicator is flawed does not mean per se it should not be used, rather it should be used in a different way and subjected to a higher level of scrutiny.
2. Country ratings often incorporate bullish or bearish biases. There is a well-documented "home bias," whereby rating agencies from the US and

China rate their respective domestic countries better than others. The US rating, for example, was long designated "AAA" by S&P and only "A" at most by Dagong Global Credit Rating (the Chinese agency discussed later in this chapter). Credit rating agencies may be tempted to replicate the political features of developed countries and may score the rest of the world on the basis of their own domestic values. This is the main argument of China's Dagong to differentiate itself from Western agencies.

3. Composite ratings incorporate a set of risk weights to encompass the effect of risk triggers such as economic, financial, sociopolitical, or external risk factors. Risk weightings, then, allow for cross-country comparisons across time. However, the stability of weightings across the countries and across time is crucial to obtain long series data while the stability of weights is highly questionable. Should one give a 25% political risk weight to both Cuba and Germany, or a 30% financial risk weight to both Singapore and Ivory Coast? Credit rating agencies as well as International Country Risk Guide, Euromoney, and Institutional Investor use risk categories whose weights are stable across countries of very different structures.
4. Rating agencies often ignore the historical similarity in crisis triggers. It is well documented that major forms of crisis repeat themselves. As former Federal Deposit Insurance Corporation (FDIC) Chairman Irving Sprague observed: "Unburdened with the experience of the past, each generation of bankers believes it knows best, and each new generation produces some who have to learn the hard way." This syndrome of "ignoring history" often coexists with the syndrome of "this time it is different." Investors should never forget that payment crises and defaults might have similar root causes though in specific socio-economic and institutional environments.
5. External debt is an important element of rating methodology. The "big three" rating agencies are first of all credit rating agencies. Country ratings focus on liquidity and solvency indicators though the specific structure of assets and liabilities is often ignored. The focus on the Debt/GDP ratio should not overlook the growth engines of the denominator while scrutinizing the maturity and creditor structure of the numerator. This point is further discussed in Chapter 8 that tackles a country's indebtedness. Analyzing the structure of the debt requires a focus on the long, medium, and short maturities of both public and private liabilities. In addition, the debt's structure by creditors is to be closely analyzed, focusing on public and private creditors, namely, official bilateral

and multilateral creditors, private banks, credit agencies, bond markets, and trade credits. Any robust debt analysis should include the following indicators:

Box 5.1 Main external debt indicators for debt sustainability analysis

- "Average terms of new commitments"—this provides information on the interest rate, maturity, and grace period of new commitments on public and publicly guaranteed external debt. The average is weighted by the amounts of the loan.
- "Fixed versus floating interest rate" as well as grace periods during which only the interest must be serviced and not the principal repayment.
- "Commitments of public and publicly guaranteed debt"—this represents the total amount of new long-term loans to public sector borrowers or agents with public sector guarantee.
- "Medium-term maturity structure" to cast light on the risk of bunching of maturities, hence the need to reschedule or to refinancing debt payments.
- "Contractual obligations on outstanding long-term external debt"—this is the anticipated debt service payments on long-term external debt contracted up to December 31st of the reporting year.
- "Concessional debt"—this is when the borrower receives aid from official lenders in the form of grants or subsidized loans.
- "Currency composition of public and publicly guaranteed debt"—this is the structure of outstanding and disbursed debt to measure the risk of currency mismatch between assets and liabilities.
- "Potential debt buyback"—when the debtor repurchases its own debt, either at a discount or at par value, depending on contractual clauses.

5.5 Bond Ratings Agencies

Despite their modest track record in assessing and predicting Country Risk, the three main rating agencies—S&P, Moody's, and Fitch—provide investors and analysts with web-based real-time credit ratings and research.

S&P is a premier source of weekly updated sovereign ratings regarding local and foreign currency debt, both for short-and long-term horizons. The analytical framework of sovereign ratings is based on ten categories that incorporate economic and political risk. In addition, S&P's financial and economic research includes a glossary of financial terms, as well as solvency and liquidity indicators, including estimates and forecasts for a limited number of developing countries. Moody's and Fitch provide similar research services.

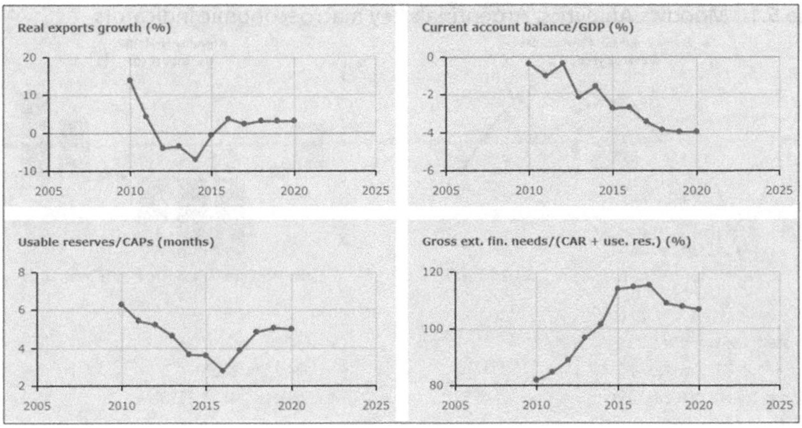

Fig. 5.3 Argentina: S&P's Current and Projected Macroeconomic Data of Argentina (2010–2020)

Standard & Poor's Emerging Markets Database covers fifty-four markets and more than 2,200 stocks. In addition, S&P launched an Emerging Bond Market Index (BMI) that captures all companies domiciled in the emerging markets within the S&P Global BMI with a float-adjusted market capitalization of at least USD 100 million (https://www.spglobal.com/ and https://us.spindices.com/indices/equity/sp-emerging-bmi-us-dollar).

Figure 5.3 illustrates the current and projected trajectory of Argentina's current account deficit, reserve assets, and external financing requirements between 2010 and 2020, based on S&P's Sovereign Risk Indicators (S&P 2017).

5.5.1 Moody's Sovereign Default Research

Moody's macroeconomic research provides a country risk analyst with the following analytical resources and forward-looking insights on the global economy:

1. Coverage by Moody's Analytics economists of fifty plus countries accounts for more than 90% of world GDP in purchasing power parity terms;
2. Consistent two-year macroeconomic forecasts for more than fifty countries, including national accounts, prices, and labor markets;
3. Data and analysis of 300 plus economic indicators from 150 public and private sources;

Table 5.1 Moody's Analytics: Argentina's key macroeconomic indicators

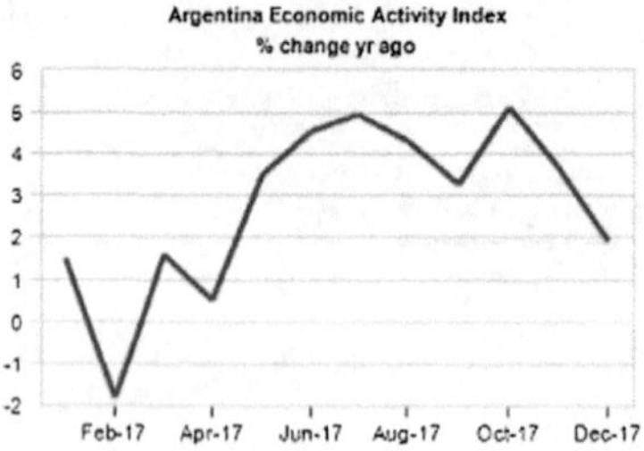

Economic Activity Indicator
Latest: 1.95% for Dec. 2017
Previous: 3.9% for Nov. 2017
Next Release: Mar 28, 2018

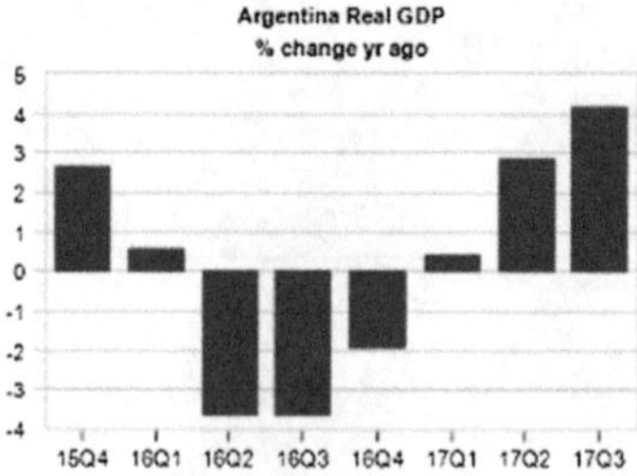

GDP
Latest: 4.2% for 2017Q3
Previous: 2.7% for 2017Q2
Next Release: Mar 21, 2018

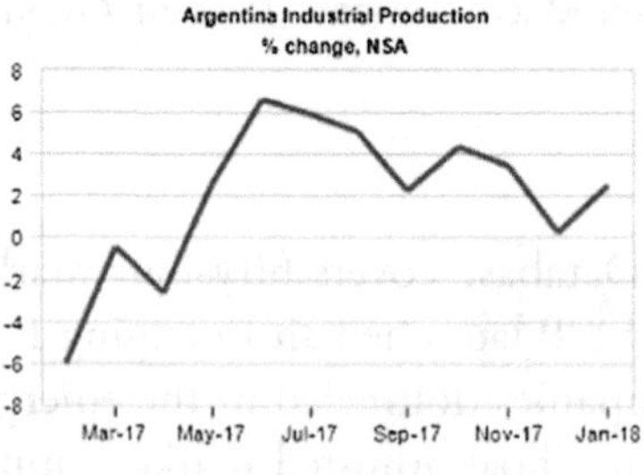

Industrial Production - Advance
Latest: 2.6% for Jan. 2018
Previous: 0.3% for Dec. 2017
Next Release: Mar 28, 2018

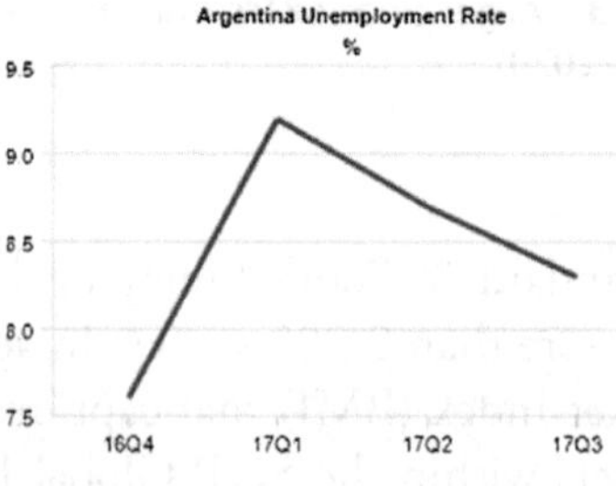

Employment Situation
Latest: 8.3% Unemployment for 2017Q3
Previous: 8.7% Unemployment for 2017Q2
Next Release: Mar 20, 2018

4. Real-time analysis of important economic events and regular, in-depth commentary on trends and specialized topics, such as central banks; and
5. Daily economic round-up newsletters regarding the day's key topics, with regular webinars on the global outlook. Table 5.1 from Moody's Analytics illustrates the evolution of Argentina's key macroeconomic indicators in 2016–2017: (Moody's 2017).

5.5.2 The Emergence of China's Rating Agency Dagong

Founded in 1994, Dagong Global Credit Rating is a rating agency that was established with the joint approval of China's People's Bank and the former State Economic and Trade Commission. Dagong is a globally oriented credit rating agency that presents itself as the first non-Western credit rating agency. Dagong published its first sovereign credit ratings in July 2010 and it offers surveillance ratings for seventy countries. To produce ratings and credit data in a standardized and systematic manner, Dagong created a customized data management system centered on a global credit search engine. Actually, despite Dagong's redesigning and enhancing its risk rating process in the interests of efficiency and transparency, its publicly available country risk data is limited to a one-page rating presentation with no background or detailed macroeconomic or financial data.

In the summer of 2011, Dagong Global Credit Rating Company decided to eliminate the AAA risk credit rating for the United States, ahead of S&P's decision to downgrade the credit rating of the US in August of the same year. In November 2011, Dagong lowered the United States to A+after the US Federal Reserve decided to continue loosening its monetary policy. It further downgraded the rating to A, indicating heightened doubts over Washington's long-term ability to repay its debts. In October 2013, Dagong again downgraded the United States to A- while maintaining a negative outlook on the sovereign's credit. The Chinese agency considered that, although a default had been averted by a last-minute agreement in Congress, there was no change in the fundamental situation of debt growth outpacing fiscal income and GDP. However, apart from the downgrades' symbolic significance, Dagong's rating changes are expected to have little effect on global markets and bond spreads. Website: http://en.dagongcredit.com.

5.5.3 A New Kid on the Credit Rating Block: INCRA?

The Global Financial Crisis of 2008 shed light on the governance and transparency deficit in credit agencies, particularly, in the "big three" CRAs that constitute a de facto oligopoly. The Global Financial Crisis also highlighted the need to improve early warning risk indicators. In 2015, this diagnosis led to a project named International Nonprofit Credit Rating Agency (INCRA) that was supported by the Bertelsmann Foundation, the North American arm of Bertelsmann Stiftung, a private foundation based in Germany. Its objective was to set up a new-rating agency supported by a sustainable endowment that would minimize the existing conflicts of interest in the sector and increase the participation of major stakeholders, such as governments and NGOs (INCRA 2012). INCRA would have the potential to merge the changing demands and interests of investors assessing sovereign risk and the desire of governments and the broader public for more transparency, legitimacy, and accountability. INCRA, with a nonprofit international network of offices, would provide a new legal framework, supported by an endowment to foster sustainability and security for the long term. Financially supported by a broad coalition of funding sources—from governments, private sector entities, NGOs, foundations, and private donors—it would thus be an independent entity. INCRA would be based on a sound governance model that would minimize and buffer potential conflicts of interest through a Stakeholder Council, which would separate the donors from the operational business. The initiative still seems in a very premature phase.

Though the aim is to develop forward-looking indicators that depart from the qualitative assessment of a country's institutional and sociopolitical status to assess the country's future capacity and willingness to service its debt, INCRA would still narrowly focus on a sovereign borrower's debt servicing capacity, hence restricting the domain of Country Risk to investors and creditors, and excluding exporters and importers, among others. INCRA emphasizes risk issues, such as transparency, accountability, and governance. It thus shares a territory already occupied by existing ratings, including those of Transparency International, IFC's Doing Business Conditions, and the UNDP's Human Development Index.

5.5.4 DBRS Rating Agency

Founded in 1976, the Canada-based DBRS is an independent, privately held, rating agency that is the world's fourth-largest rating institution. It strives to differentiate itself through in-depth research and an approach that is pragmatic rather than mechanistic. As the macroeconomic fundamentals and financial sophistication of emerging market countries have increased over recent decades, DBRS concluded that the basis for differentiating the risk between developed and developing countries debtors had diminished. In the case of investment grade emerging market sovereigns, larger reliance on local currency debt issuance and the frequent participation of international investors reduce the likelihood of selective defaults favoring local currency debtholders. While emerging markets with weak or deteriorating fundamentals may face serious foreign exchange constraints that increase the risk of a foreign currency default, local currency defaults have been at least as common among rated sovereigns in recent decades. To assess Country Risk, DBRS focuses on six main risk factors, each of which has a set of quantitative and qualitative underlying considerations: (1) Fiscal management and policy (2) Debt and liquidity (3) Economic structure and performance (4)

Monetary policy and financial stability (5) Balance of payments, and (6) Political environment. Website: http://www.dbrs.com/about.

5.6 Country Risk Indices of Magazines

5.6.1 Euromoney Country Risk (ECR)

ECR is an online community of economic and political experts who provide real-time scores in fifteen categories that relate to economic, structural, and political risk. ECR creates scores for 187 individual countries, both developed and developing. The overall score combines the assessment of ECR experts with other measures and viewpoints, including data from the IMF/World Bank on debt indicators, the results of a survey of debt syndicate managers at international banks on access to capital and Moody's/Fitch credit ratings. The ECR panel of around 250 leading economists in international financial institutions assesses a country's performance in the financial markets (taking into account factors, such as market access, bond issues, spreads, sell-down, terms, and maturity). Risk scoring ranges from 100 (excellent) to 0 (high risk). In addition, a panel of political analysts aims to measure the short-term risk of sociopolitical destabilization. In its rating process, ECR considers the different forms of country-related investment risk, including the risk of default on a bond, risk of losing direct investment, and risk to global business relations. The overall ECR rating is based on a combination of qualitative and quantitative variables. The qualitative expert opinions comprise 70% of the rating. This includes political risk (30% weighting), economic performance (30%), and structural assessment (10%). The quantitative values comprise 30% of the rating. This includes debt indicators (10%), credit ratings (10%), and access to bank finance/capital markets (10%). It is worth observing that the rating weights include the change in credit rating by agencies such as

Table 5.2 Euromoney's Country Risk Rating Weights

1.	Growth performance: 25% (GDP projection)
2.	Political risk: 25%
3.	External debt indicators: 10% (debt/GDP and debt/exports of goods and services)
4.	External payment default and rescheduling: 10%
5.	Credit rating Moody's or S&P: 10%
6.	Short-term credit market access: 5%
7.	Commercial bank medium-term credit: 5%
8.	Capital market access: 5%
9.	Spread over US Treasury bills: 5%

Moody's and S&P (thereby taking account of the spillover and contamination consequences of downgrading) (Table 5.2).

5.6.2 Institutional Investor Country Risk Scoring

Similar to *Euromoney*, *Institutional Investor* is a quarterly magazine for the global business community that provides a survey-driven country risk rating assessment. The underlying information comes from leading international banks. Bankers are asked to grade each of the countries on a scale from 0 to 100 (with 100 being the most creditworthy). The sample is updated every six months, ranging from seventy-five to one hundred banks, each of which provides its own ratings. The names of all participants in the survey are kept strictly confidential. Banks are not permitted to rate their home country. Individual responses are weighted using an Institutional Investor formula that gives more importance to responses from banks with greater worldwide exposure and more sophisticated country analysis systems. As of the end of 2017, Institutional Investor credit ranking includes 179 countries, ranging from Norway and Switzerland to North Korea and Somalia.

Figure 5.4 illustrates the evolution in the risk ratings of Ivory Coast, Greece, and Russia over the 1980–2016 period, with the abrupt deterioration in Ivory Coast' s credit risk between 2000 and 2011, and that of Greece starting in 2010.

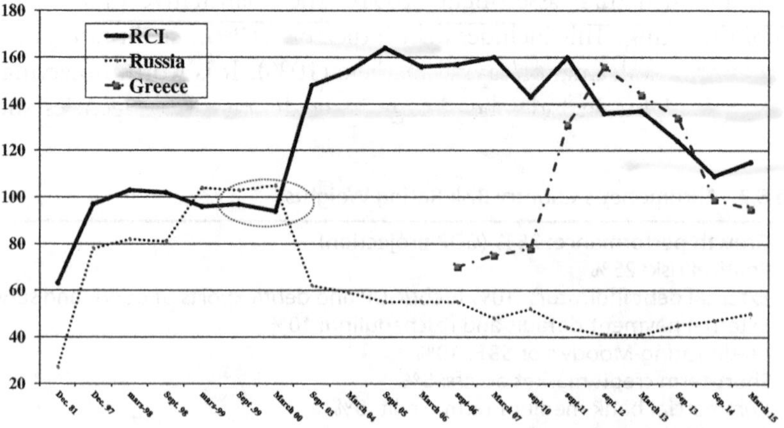

Fig. 5.4 Institutional investor risk rating 1981–2016 (*Source* Institutional Investor)

5.7 Ratings From Data Providers with Cross-Expertise: FTSE-Russell Indices, Beyond-Ratings, and Market Access

A number of information sources offer a unique perspective for long-term global investors striving to gather cross-expertise on ratings. One example is FTSE Russell that provides a wide range of market indices in both developed, emerging, and frontier market economies. For instance, the FTSE "Beyond BRICs Index" is designed to represent the performance of a diversified basket of ninety liquid companies in Emerging and Frontier markets. The index's market capitalization is weighted with 75% exposure to emerging and 25% to frontier markets. The FTSE "Emerging Index" provides investors with a comprehensive means of measuring the performance of the most liquid companies in the emerging markets (FTSE 2017).

Another example is "Beyond Ratings," a rating institution that mobilizes a wide network of experts in country risk from universities, research centers, foundations, and think tanks. Its purpose is to incorporate different types of expertise into a rating, as illustrated in Graph 5.1.

The objective is to bridge the gap between a "rigid frame" limited only to data and models and a "collective intelligence" process. This "augmented methodology" aims at "integrating more consistently all key drivers of a Nation's wealth: Human Capital, Natural Capital, Manufactured Capital and Financial Capital." The goal is not just to consider the static assets that

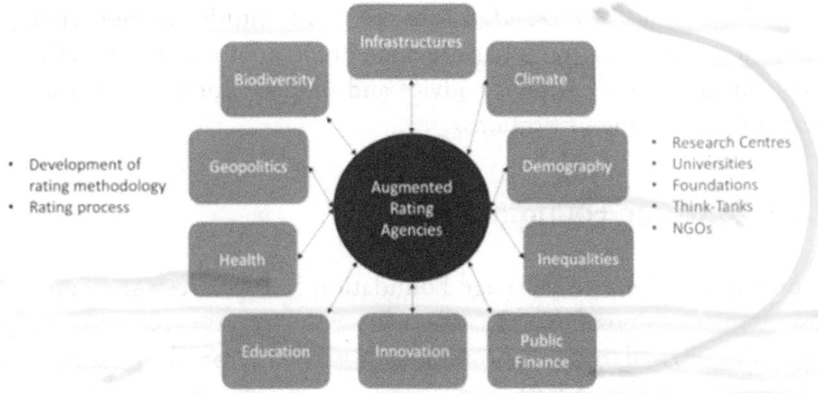

Graph 5.1 Cross-expertise and "augmented methodology" (*Source* http://www.beyond-ratings.com)

Table 5.3 Country risk dynamics with economic cycles (*Source* http://www.beyond-ratings.com)

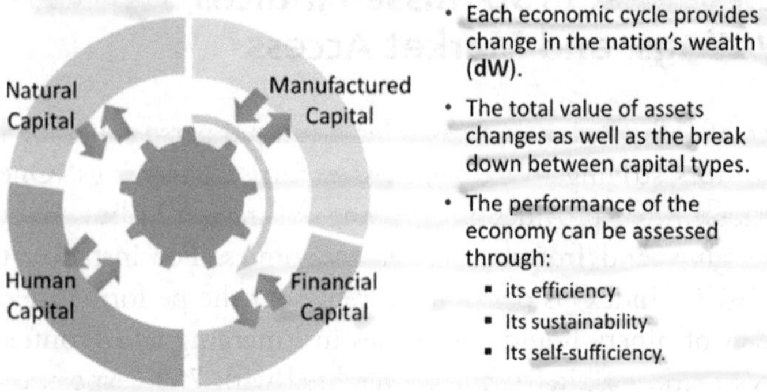
Natural Capital
Manufactured Capital
Human Capital
Financial Capital
• Each economic cycle provides change in the nation's wealth (dW).
• The total value of assets changes as well as the break down between capital types.
• The performance of the economy can be assessed through:
▪ its efficiency
▪ Its sustainability
▪ Its self-sufficiency.

contribute to a nation's wealth but also to assess how those assets will perform across different economic cycles (Table 5.3).

The "augmented methodology" also tries to consider the economy's resilience to external shocks (climate change, commodities international prices, geopolitics, and monetary policies) in order to complement the usual financial metrics (Debt/GDP vs. debt/total assets). Websites: http://www.beyond-ratings.com/new-rating-agency-project/#intelligence and https://www.marketaxess.com/data/marketdata.php.

5.8 Ratings from Think Tanks and Global Consultants

A number of think tanks and private research institutions devote significant efforts to researching country risk issues. Some offer assessments of government policies as well as policy advice and proposal for reforms. This is the case of the following institutions.

5.8.1 Heritage Foundation

Founded in 1973, the Heritage Foundation is a research and educational institute whose mission is to formulate and promote conservative public policies based on the principles of free enterprise. Its conservative ideological posture is firm and clear: encouraging market-oriented economic policies in the United States and beyond. This stance means that the Heritage Foundation prepares analyses, policy papers, and reports that promote privatization, sound macroeconomic adjustment, limited government, and individual freedom. As can be expected, Chile is praised more highly than Cuba. A subunit within the Foundation is the Center for International Trade and Economics (CITE), which provides research on the role of market-driven economic policies in fostering growth in countries around the world. CITE produces the annual Index of Economic Freedom. Website: http://www.heritage.org/about-heritage/mission.

5.8.2 The Cato Institute

The Cato Institute publishes regular reports evaluating government policies and offering proposals for reform. Cato is well known for its libertarian stance. Although the Cato Institute is not intended to focus upon macroeconomic and financial data, its policy papers on emerging market economies are based on a wide range of information sources that make its analyses highly valuable for the risk analyst. The Cato Institute produces a large body of policy analysis, research papers, and briefings on foreign and economic policy issues, white papers, and working papers on tax, budget, and security issues. From a country risk analysis standpoint, its two main annual publications are the Report on Economic Freedom in the World with the Fraser Institute and the Human Freedom Index that is based on a number of criteria including the following variables: Rule of law, security and safety, religion, association and civil society, size of government, legal system and property rights, access to sound money, freedom to trade internationally, as well as regulation of credit, labor, and business. The 2017 Economic Freedom Index ranks France 52 out of nearly 200 countries, well below Bulgaria, Peru, and Mongolia, due to the heavy weight of public expenditures in GDP (Cato 2017). Website: https://www.cato.org/human-freedom-index.

5.8.3 Brookings Institution

The Brookings Institution is a nonprofit public policy organization based in Washington, DC. Its predecessor organization, the Institute for Government Research, was founded in 1916. The Brookings' mission is "to conduct

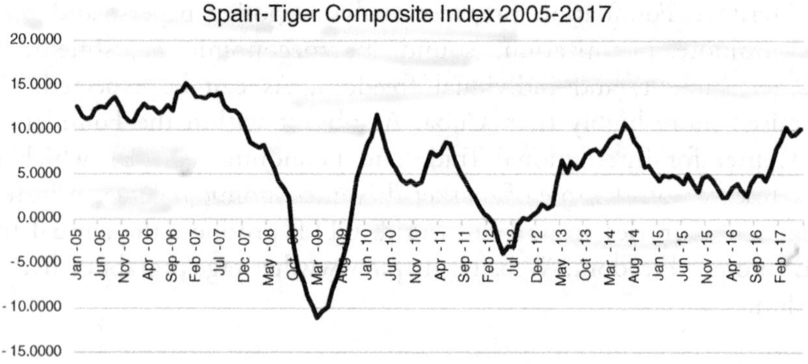

Chart 5.1 Spain: Brookings' Tiger Composite Index of economic recovery (*Source* Brookings, Foda and Prasad, October 2017)

in-depth research that leads to new ideas for solving problems facing society at the local, national and global level." The organization is affiliated with over 300 experts in government and academia around the world. It has a reputation for a center-liberal tilt toward public policy issues. Its research covers a diverse set of issues, including foreign policy, global development, and defense and security. Its initiatives in global development include developing economies, development financing, global health, global poverty, and multilateral development organizations. Its research covers countries in Asia-Pacific, Europe, Latin America-Caribbean, Middle East-North Africa, and North America.

In collaboration with the *Financial Times* (FT), a team of two economists of the Brookings provides the Tiger Index, a tracking index for the global economy (Prasad and Foda 2017). The index is based on a statistical procedure called Principal Component Analysis (PCA), used to extract indicators that capture common fluctuations among variables in large datasets. The dataset covers two dozen countries, including ten EMCs, and contains a set of key real, financial, and market variables, such as employment, trade flows, capacity utilization, credit growth, and bond spreads, as well as two confidence indicators, namely, business and consumer. The dataset also includes the Bloomberg-based Volatility index for national stock markets (usually named the VIX indicator). The economists generate country-specific indicators that cover all the variables for a given country and variable-specific indicators that cover all countries' data for a given variable. The previous chart illustrates the composite index for Spain, measuring real economic activity, financial system resilience, and consumer and business confidence between 2005 and 2017. The index evolution shows the consequence of the two sharp falls in GDP in 2009 and again in 2012, with rising unemployment, and a gradual and fragile process of economic recovery in 2017. Website: https://www.brookings.edu (Chart 5.1).

5.8.4 A. T. Kearney: The FDI Confidence Index

A. T. Kearney is a global private management consulting firm started in Chicago in 1926 by Andrew Thomas Kearney. It has offices in more than forty countries. Since 1998, the firm has been issuing the A. T. Kearney Foreign Direct Investment (FDI) Confidence Index. This is a qualitative ranking of countries perceived as the most favorable for long-term foreign direct investments. The ranking is based on the responses from senior executives and other senior regional and business unit leaders in companies that have revenues of USD 500 million or more. The executives surveyed represent companies located in thirty different countries, spanning a range of sectors. A.T. Kearney describes its methodology as follows: "The Index is calculated as a weighted average of the number of high, medium, and low responses to questions on the likelihood of making a direct investment in the market over the next three years."

In 2017, the United States was named the top country in the survey, followed by Germany, China, United Kingdom, Canada, France, India, Australia, Singapore, and Spain. The US has held the top rank for the fifth consecutive year. Among the most important considerations identified by the survey participants were the general security environment, efficiency of the legal and regulatory process, tax rates and ease of payments, and transparency of governmental regulations. Website: https://www.atkearney.com.

5.8.5 Marsh's Political Risk Analysis Service

To raise multinational organizations awareness of political and economic risks worldwide, Marsh annually shares the independent analysis of BMI Research, a leader in providing multinationals, governments, and financial institutions with forecasts, data, and analysis to guide critical strategic, tactical, and investment decisions. Starting in 2017, Marsh has partnered with BMI Research to provide an additional update on BMI Research's Country Risk Index (CRI) scores, which form the basis of Marsh's Political Risk Map to assess each country's economic, political, and operational environment.

BMI Research provides short- and long-term political and economic scores up to a maximum of 100, the higher scores denoting greater stability. The higher the index, the less political risk. It also looks at "operational" risks, which include measures related to labor markets, trade and investment, logistics, and crime and security (including terrorism). The index aims to provide an overall country risk score that considers the full spectrum of risk factors. Overall, though Marsh mainly focuses on the political risk assessment, it provides four separate risk indices, namely, country risk, political risk, operational risk, and economic risk. Each index provides cross-country comparisons on a global basis. Marsh also joined the World Economic Forum's team to provide an annual Global Risk Report that focuses on the evolution of global risks and the deep interconnections between them. In its 2017 release, the report highlighted the potential of persistent, long-term trends such as inequality and deepening social and political polarization to exacerbate risks associated with weak economic recovery and technological change (Marsh 2017). Website: https://www.marsh.com/.

5.8.6 IMD-Lausanne: World Competitiveness Index

At any moment in time, roughly 185 countries, both developed and emerging, compete to attract global capital flows as well as productive investment and human skills. Country attractiveness is closely related to competitiveness that is the extent to which a country is able to foster an environment in which enterprises can generate sustainable value.

The IMD World Competitiveness Yearbook (WCY), first published in 1989 by the Lausanne-based Institute of Management Development, is a comprehensive annual report on countries' competitiveness. It provides benchmarking and trends, as well as statistics and survey data based on extensive research. The report analyzes and ranks countries according to how they manage their competencies to achieve long-term value creation. The World Competitiveness Ranking of around sixty-three countries' economies is based on over 340 criteria resulting from comprehensive research using economic literature, international, national and regional sources and feedback from the business community, government agencies, and academics. Reportedly, the criteria are revised and updated on a regular basis as new theory, research, and data become available and as the global economy evolves. Two Asian countries, namely Singapore and Hong Kong, are within the top five most competitive countries, while the US, Switzerland, the Netherlands, and the Scandinavian countries are within the top 10. China is gradually catching

Table 5.4 IMD's Country Competitiveness Criteria

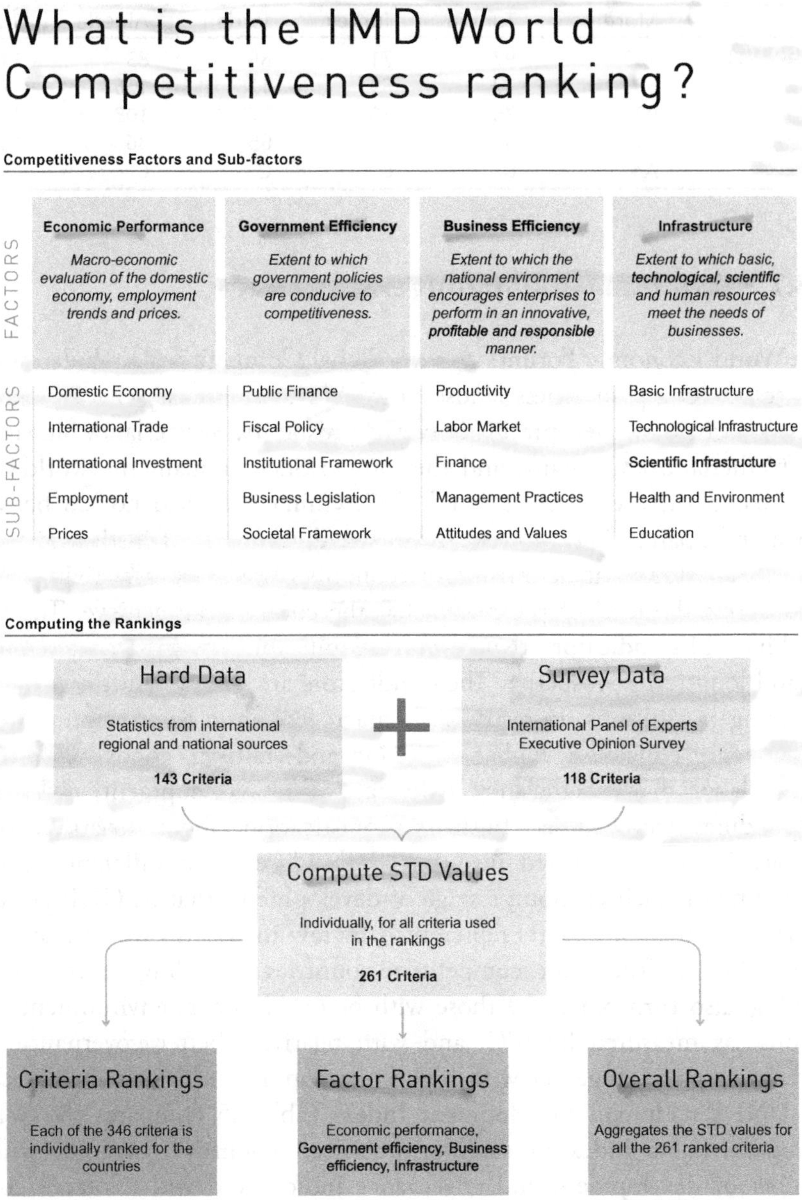
What is the IMD World Competitiveness ranking?
Competitiveness Factors and Sub-factors
FACTORS
Economic Performance
Macro-economic evaluation of the domestic economy, employment trends and prices.
Government Efficiency
Extent to which government policies are conducive to competitiveness.
Business Efficiency
Extent to which the national environment encourages enterprises to perform in an innovative, profitable and responsible manner.
Infrastructure
Extent to which basic, technological, scientific and human resources meet the needs of businesses.
SUB-FACTORS
Domestic Economy
International Trade
International Investment
Employment
Prices
Public Finance
Fiscal Policy
Institutional Framework
Business Legislation
Societal Framework
Productivity
Labor Market
Finance
Management Practices
Attitudes and Values
Basic Infrastructure
Technological Infrastructure
Scientific Infrastructure
Health and Environment
Education
Computing the Rankings
Hard Data
Statistics from international regional and national sources
143 Criteria
Survey Data
International Panel of Experts Executive Opinion Survey
118 Criteria
Compute STD Values
Individually, for all criteria used in the rankings
261 Criteria
Criteria Rankings
Each of the 346 criteria is individually ranked for the countries
Factor Rankings
Economic performance, Government efficiency, Business efficiency, Infrastructure
Overall Rankings
Aggregates the STD values for all the 261 ranked criteria

up, ranking no. 18 in 2017, well above Belgium, Japan, Korea, or France (IMD 2017a, b). Table 5.4 summarizes the key competitiveness criteria. Website: https://www.imd.org/wcc/world-competitiveness-center-rankings/competitiveness-2017-rankings-results/.

Table 5.5 Development, Governance, and Risk Indices

	Morocco	Tunisia	Turkey	Jordan	Algeria	Egypt
UNDP HDI	123	97	71	86	83	111
IFC	68	77	69	118	156	122
CPI	90	75	75	57	108	108
WEF	71	95	53	65	86	100
COFACE	A4	B	B	C	C	C

5.8.7 WEF Global Competitiveness Index

The World Economic Forum's annual Global Competitiveness Index (GCI) assesses the competitiveness landscape of 138 economies, providing insight into the drivers of their productivity and prosperity. Switzerland, Singapore, the Netherlands, Germany, and the United States remain the world's five most competitive economies as of 2017. China is ranked no. 28 between Korea and Spain. Competitiveness is defined as the set of institutions, policies, and factors that determine an economy's level of productivity, which in turn sets the level of prosperity that the country can achieve. The GCI combines 114 indicators that capture significant concepts for productivity and long-term prosperity. These indicators are grouped into twelve sets, including institutions, infrastructure, macroeconomic environment, health and primary education, higher education and training, goods market efficiency, labor market efficiency, financial market development, technological readiness, market size, business sophistication, and innovation. These sets are in turn organized into three subindexes with different weights, depending on each economy's stage of development, that is, GDP per capita and the share of exports represented by raw materials (World Economic Forum 2017). The most competitive countries according to the WEF's ranking, also turn out to be those with better "business environment conditions" as measured by IFC, and with relatively better governance and lower corruption, together with higher development scores as measured by the UNDP's Human Development Index. Table 5.5 compares the WEF's Competitiveness Index of six North African countries, together with a number of development and governance indices and with Coface's country risk assessment in 2017. Website: https://www.weforum.org/reports/the-global-competitiveness-report-2016-2017-1.

Table 5.6 Corruption Perception Index: The best and the worst rankings

Measuring corruption? Transparency International CPI				
1	New Zealand		162	Guinea-Bissau
2	Denmark		162	Kyrgyzstan
3	Singapore		162	Venezuela
3	Sweden	France = 22	168	Burundi
5	Switzerland	Brazil = 72	168	Equatorial Guinea
6	Finland	China = 80	168	Guinea
6	Netherlands	India = 94	168	Haiti
8	Australia	Russia = 133	168	Iran
8	Canada		168	Turkmenistan
8	Iceland		174	Uzbekistan
11	Norway		175	Chad
12	Hong Kong		176	Iraq
12	Luxembourg		176	Sudan
14	Germany		178	Myanmar
14	Ireland		179	Afghanistan
16	Austria		180	Somalia

5.8.8 Transparency International: The Corruption Perception Index

Transparency International is a German-based NGO, founded in 1993. Its global network is based on national chapters in more than seventy countries. It publishes an annual Corruption perception index (CPI) ranking of 180 countries as well as an Annual Bribe index. The CPI is a composite index, that is, a poll of polls conducted over a three-year period, drawing on thirteen surveys from eight independent organizations. Table 5.6 illustrates the ranking of country corruption in 2017 from least corrupt to most corrupt.

5.8.9 The Economic Complexity Index (ECI)

The Economic Complexity Index (ECI) is a holistic measure of the production characteristics of large economic systems, usually whole countries. Like most measurements used in complexity economics, this index aims to explain an economic system as a whole rather than the sum of its parts. The ECI seeks to explain the knowledge accumulated in a country's population (the networks that people form) and that expressed by the country's industrial fabric. To achieve this, the ECI combines metrics of countries' diversity and product ubiquity to create measures of the relative complexity of a country's exports. The ECI was developed by Cesar A. Hidalgo from the MIT Media Lab and Ricardo Hausmann from Harvard University's Kennedy School of Government. ECI data is available through The Observatory of Economic Complexity. Website: http://atlas.media.mit.edu/fr/resources.

5.8.10 The Economic Policy Uncertainty Index

The Economic Policy Uncertainty Index (EPUI) attempts to measure policy related to economic uncertainty. The index is based on the large amounts of data relating to US newspaper coverage of policy-related economic uncertainty and disagreement among economic forecasters as a proxy for uncertainty. The EPUI's team concludes that a significant dynamic relationship exists between the economic policy uncertainty index and real macroeconomic variables, i.e., increasing economic policy uncertainty as measured by the EPUI foreshadows a decline in economic growth and employment over the following months. The team of researchers from three US universities (Kellogg School of Management, Stanford University, and Chicago's Booth School of Business), summarizes their findings as follows: "As measured by our index, we find that current levels of economic policy uncertainty are at extremely elevated levels compared to recent history. Since 2008, economic policy uncertainty has averaged about twice the level of the previous twenty three years. A significant dynamic relationship exists between our economic policy uncertainty index and real macroeconomic variables. We find that the number of large movements in the S&P 500 index, defined as a daily change of 2.5% or more, has increased dramatically in recent years relative to the average since 1980" (Baker et al. 2015). Website: http://www.policyuncertainty.com.

5.8.11 The Fragile States Index (FSI)

The FSI, now in its thirteenth year, is an assessment of 178 countries based on twelve social, economic, and political indicators; it seeks to quantify the pressures countries experience and hence their susceptibility to instability. Since 2005, an annual assessment discussing these issues has been published by the US think tank Fund for Peace (FFP) and the magazine *Foreign Policy*. The list aims to assess states' vulnerability to conflict or collapse, ranking all sovereign states with membership in the United Nations where there is enough data available for analysis. The ranking is based on the sum of scores for twelve indicators. Each indicator is scored on a scale of zero to ten, with zero being the lowest intensity (most stable) and ten being the highest intensity (least stable), creating a scale from 0–120. The FSI produced by the FFP combines both qualitative and quantitative data sources for highlighting not only the normal pressures that all states experience, but also identifying when such pressures outweigh a state's capacity to manage them. By highlighting pertinent vulnerabilities which contribute to the risk of state fragility, the Index makes a political risk assessment and early warning of conflict accessible to policymakers and the public at large. The 2017 Fragility Index of the twenty most fragile countries includes fourteen African countries, including Somalia, Congo, Eritrea, Sudan, Chad, and Nigeria. The least fragile countries are found in Scandinavia, namely, Finland, Sweden, Norway, and Denmark, as well as Switzerland (Fund for Peace 2017). Website: http://fundforpeace.org/fsi/.

5.9 Commercial and Non-merchant Banks as Sources of Country Risk Intelligence

The quality of bank research is closely related to the scope and depth of international exposure of the banks in question. Indeed, research is not only made of quantitative data but also of a resilient network of contacts in the local private and public arenas. Several banking institutions have reduced their country risk staff in the wake of the Mexican, Asian, and Argentine crises. A growing number rely on the country risk reports of the Institute of International Finance. Other banks have maintained their country risk staffs, focusing on the specific purpose financing and client advisory services, viewing emerging markets as an important source of diversification and long-term profit potential.

5.9.1 The Institute of International Finance: The Global Banking Industry's Country Risk Think Tank

The Institute of International Finance (IIF) represents the private banking industry worldwide. A lack of macroeconomic data transparency was widely recognized as a problem after the 1995 Mexican crisis. However, in the aftermath of the Asian crisis, the IMF increased pressure on countries to provide better information on capital movements, bank deposits, holdings of securities, derivatives, and reserves. The IIF declared that "investors in emerging markets should have more timely and meaningful economic data to enable them to assess risks" (IIF 1998). The IIF covers 30–40 emerging and frontier markets, with a particular focus on economic and financing issues. Its reports feature topical analysis of macroeconomic fundamentals, policy developments, political economy dynamics, and downside risks. The Washington-based organization provides member banks with four main sources of data:

1. Country-specific data, with an emphasis on the balance of payments, exchange rates, and external debt indicators.
2. Specific and timely studies that seek to identify and assess underlying economic trends, creditworthiness, risks and the quality of policies, including monetary, foreign exchange, fiscal, and structural policies. Special reports are issued in case of debt crisis, default, political upheaval or exchange rate devaluation.
3. Global surveys of capital flow to emerging market economies.
4. Reports on the international financial system's architecture and regulatory issues.

Website: https://www.iif.com/.

5.9.2 Citibank

Citigroup is one of the world's largest financial institutions and has operated across the world's major markets and regions. The US bank is widely recognized as a significant participant in global finance and in steering committees of debt restructuring negotiations. To assist its clients in assessing global issues, Citigroup publishes a website called Global Perspectives and Solutions (GPS). Its team of writers and contributors includes experienced equity and fixed income research professionals, a global chief economist, and numerous other employees working in business units in different countries and regions. Moreover, a chief global political analyst contributes on themes relating geopolitical risk, socioeconomic risk, and other sources of uncertainty that are difficult to quantify. Among the themes discussed by the contributors are innovation, digitization, urbanization, and globalization. Website: https://www.citivelocity.com/citigps/.

5.9.3 Natixis and Credit Agricole

Natixis of BPCE Group and Credit Agricole (CA) are two French investment banks known for the quality of their economic research with a European focus. Natixis provides a regular flow of high-quality research papers that tackle global market and international economic issues in its "Flash Economics" reports (Natixis 2017). Credit Agricole follows developments in the economic policy of European and emerging market countries, also focusing on industry sectors and geographical regions. CA's Economic Research Department publishes a number of reports as follows:

1. Regional reports.
2. Sectoral reports (e.g., banking and insurance, industry, real estate, agriculture, and services).
3. Emerging Countries—Monthly News Digest that focuses on the key issues that could destabilize developing countries' economies.
4. Country reports.
5. World Macroeconomic scenarios that analyze key global variables, such as trade and capital flows, interest and exchange rates, deficits, and inflation.

Website: http://economic-research.credit-agricole.com/site/zones.php?racine=3&area_id=10#.

5.9.4 Blackrock Country Risk Index

The Blackrock Sovereign Risk Index (BSRI) breaks down risk data into four main categories that each counts toward a country's final BSRI score and ranking:

1. Fiscal Space (40%) represents the dynamics of a country to keep to a sustainable path, including its "distance from stability." This includes the following indicators: Debt/GDP; Per capita GDP; Proportion of domestically held Debt; Term structure of Debt; Demographic Profile; Growth and Inflation Volatility; Debt/Revenue; Depth of Funding capacity; Default history; Reserve Currency Status (to reflect the "exorbitant privilege" of some currencies perceived as "safe heavens" by investors); Interest Rate on Debt.
2. Willingness to pay (30%). This encompasses factors that gauge whether a country displays qualitative cultural and institutional traits that suggest

Table 5.7 Correlation between BSRI and 5 year CDS spread

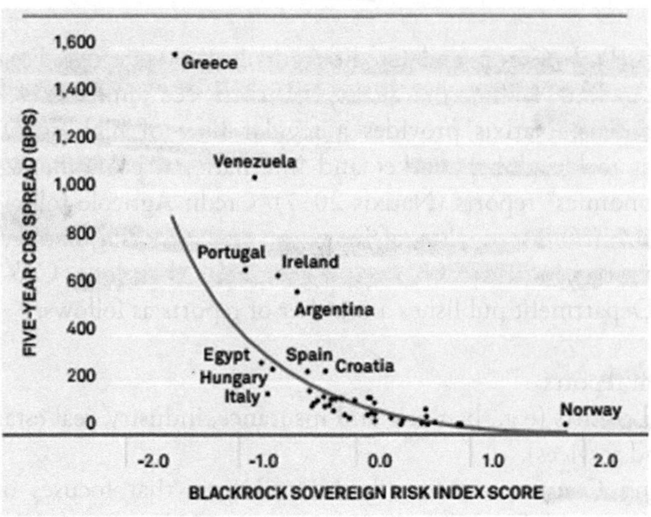

Sources: Bloomberg, BlackRock.

both the ability and willingness to pay off real debts. This is influenced primarily by political and institutional considerations.

3. External Finance Position (20%). This relates to how leveraged a country might be to macroeconomic trade and policy shocks outside of its control. Indicators include External Debt/GDP (Net of Foreign Exchange Reserves), and Current Account Position.
4. Financial Sector Health (10%). This relates to the degree to which a country's financial sector poses a threat to its creditworthiness in the event of nationalization. It includes indicators such as Credit Bubble Risk, Bank Credit Quality, and Size.

As the table above demonstrates, the BSRI is highly correlated with the five-year Credit Default Spread (CDS). Nevertheless, as we explore in subsequent chapters, CDS themselves are not always reliable signals of Country Risk (Table 5.7).

A detailed methodology is set forth in a research paper available on BlackRock's Website: https://www.blackrock.com/investing/literature/whitepaper/introducing-the-blackrock-sovereign-risk-index-us.pdf.

5.9.5 JP Morgan's EMBI Global (Emerging Markets Bond Index)

In 1999, JP Morgan introduced its Emerging Markets Bond Index. This index is weighted by the market capitalization of the underlying component bonds. It comprises twenty-seven countries and includes a wide range of financial instruments, such as Brady bonds, Eurobonds, traded loans, and local market debt issued by sovereign and quasi-sovereign entities. To be considered as "emerging," countries must have a low-or middle-income per capita income of less than USD 9,635 as reported by the World Bank. Countries must also have restructured their external or local outstanding debt. Bonds from Argentina, Brazil, and Mexico constitute more than half of the index.

The Emerging Markets Bond Index Plus (EMBI+) tracks total returns for traded external debt instruments (external meaning foreign currency denominated fixed income) in emerging markets. It covers USD-denominated Brady bonds, loans, and Eurobonds (which are bonds denominated in a currency other than the home currency of the country or market in which it is issued). To be included, instruments in the EMBI+ must meet liquidity criteria for secondary market trading and must have a minimum face value outstanding of USD 500 million. Website: http://www2.jpmorgan.com/MarketDataInd/EMBI/embi.html.

5.9.6 The MSCI's Standard Index

The MSCI Standard Index is designed to measure equity market performance in global emerging markets. It is a float-adjusted market capitalization index that consists of indices in twenty-three emerging economies. MSCI also produces research relating to factor investing, integrated risk management, real estate, and commodity markets. Website: https://www.msci.com/research and http://www.msci.com/equity/index.html.

5.9.7 VIX CBOE and Skew Volatility Index

- VIX CBOE Vol: VIX is the ticker symbol for the CBOE (Chicago Board Options Exchange) Volatility Index, which indicates the market's expectation of thirty-day volatility. It is built by deducing the implied volatilities from the price of a wide range of S&P 500 index options, both calls and puts. The index is considered to be the best known "investor fear gauge."

- Skew index: The SKEW is similar to the VIX, also being a measure of "market sentiment." It is also based on S&P 500 options but the focus is only on "tail risk." This is done by comparing several standard deviations from the mean in S&P 500 returns over a forward period of thirty days. SKEW values generally range from 100 to 150 where a higher rating suggests a higher perceived "tail risk" and the likelihood of a so-called black swan event (to use Nassim Taleb's terminology).

5.10 The Role of Specialized Country Risk Assessment Companies

5.10.1 TAC Economics

TAC Economics is a France-based provider of country risk analysis and macroeconomic reports. It focuses on country risk assessment and prospects, including currency, cyclical trends, cross-border payment, and political risks for more than 70 developing countries and emerging markets. TAC Economics also provides computation of cost of capital for individual developing and advanced economies, coupled with macroeconomic projections for major financial indicators in mature economies (e.g., growth, inflation, interest rates/yield curves, exchange rates) on both short- and long-term horizons. The risk assessment company also provides oil price analysis and projections for short-term to very long-term horizons. Its long-term macroeconomic scenario includes specific industry analysis, review of competition, and strategic recommendations for creditors, investors, and fund managers (www.taceconomics.com).

5.10.2 The Political Risk Services (PRS) and the International Country Risk Guide (ICRG)

The PRS Group Inc. was founded in 1979, the genesis of joint work between professors at the Maxwell School of Public Affairs (Syracuse University) and the US State Department. PRS later became the political risk arm of Frost & Sullivan, Inc. and was later acquired by the UK-based IBC Group. Acquired by Dr. Christopher McKee in 2010, PRS provides quantitatively based country risk analyses, ratings, and forecasts in the form of three main products: Political Risk Services (PRS), the International Country Risk Guide (ICRG), and CountryData Online (CDO). The PRS product line provides regime forecasts over an eighteen-month and five-year time horizon for 100 countries and examines the risk to foreign assets based on eleven types of government intervention. The country reports are produced monthly.

Since 1980, ICRG has furnished an international clientele with scores and ratings affecting political, economic, and financial risk for a set of 140 developed, emerging, and frontier markets. Forming the basis of an early warning system, over thirty metrics are used to assess these types of risk. ICRG's data series and forecasts extends to 1984 for most countries and is also updated monthly. Additionally, ICRG provides access to the dataset of Campbell R. Harvey (of Duke University's Fuqua School of Business) and includes monthly composite, political, economic, and financial risk ratings from the *International Country Risk Guide*.

The CDO product line combines all the data for both PRS and ICRG and produces nearly 100,000 original data points annually on political and country risk for all the countries covered by the firm. CDO is the gateway to the firm's historical data. PRS' data is used by institutional investors and sovereign wealth funds to position their portfolios and assign country exposure. Transnational firm uses the firm's data an analysis to assess their own country exposure and determine realistic hurdle rates. Research scientists and various multilateral agencies use the data to further their own academic needs and to explore new political and economic phenomena.

Quarterly revised country reports feature a concise analysis of potential political, financial, and economic risks to business investments and trade in a consistent format. Political risk analysis and forecast for 100 countries comes from the Coplin-O'Leary Rating Model that aims to measure and predict the likelihood of sociopolitical turmoil, including cross-border conflict, social unrest, ethnic tensions, civil war and disorder, terrorism, and war. A monthly political risk letter explores recent political and social developments, including discussions of government stability, party and coalition splits, corruption, civil unrest, democratic accountability, and criminal justice issues. It also offers a Political and Economic Forecast Table with estimates of the probability of turmoil. A composite risk rating incorporates political inputs with a 50% weighing as well as financial and economic inputs that contribute 25% each. Probabilities are assigned to three separate regime scenarios, covering an eighteen-month and five-year time horizon.

In 2018, PRS has unveiled a new website and related material that includes a new risk model with the academic support of a couple of business schools. PRS entered into a multiyear arrangement with Queen's University (Canada) and its Center for Computer Analytics to marry country risk data with various machine learning applications. The objective is improving the accuracy of a country risk predictive model that allows PRS to bring forward its ICRG composite scores by one year with a ninety percent accuracy (Website: www.prsgroup.com).

5.10.3 The Economic Intelligence Unit (EIU)

The Economist Intelligence Unit (EIU) is the research and analysis division of the Economist Group, one of the most well regarded and distinctive publishing brands. It also publishes *The Economist* magazine. The publications of the Economist units are known for their high-quality writing, distinctive editorial voice, and thoughtful analysis. The EIU, operating as a separate and independent division, provides regular and bespoke analysis of countries, regions industries, and economic and political trends. It also provides ratings for sovereign risk. Based in London, the EIU was created in 1946. It has a staff of 130 full-time analysts working in twenty-four countries. Although some of its work is provided through a subscription service, much is undertaken for clients on a bespoke and a confidential basis.

The methodology of the EIU is both quantitative and qualitative. It uses subsets of indicators to provide ratings for sovereign, currency, and banking-sector risks. Essentially, risks are categorized and then interconnected through human intelligence and qualitative analysis. Among its regular services are country reports for 199 countries, country forecasts for eighty-two countries, and country commerce reports for fifty-six countries. It also provides a wide variety of macroeconomic data (Website: www.eiu.com/site_info).

5.10.4 Eurasia Group

The Eurasia Group is a global consulting firm specializing in political risks. It was founded in 1998 by Ian Bremer, who holds a doctorate in political science from Stanford University. The firm is based in New York City and has seven offices on four continents. It has over 150 full-time employees, complemented by a network of approximately 500 experts in over ninety countries. The firm's motto is "Politics First." In 2006, Eurasia Group began issuing an annual list of the ten most significant global political risks. This list is announced in January and includes a general overview and brief commentary on each identified risk. The methodology for selecting these risks is primarily qualitative, reflecting the judgment of the Eurasia Group. In its overview of the 2017 risks, Eurasia observes: "This year marks the most volatile political risk environment in the postwar period, at least as important to global markets as the economic recession of 2008. It needn't develop into a geopolitical depression that triggers major interstate military conflict and/or the breakdown of major central governmental institutions. But such an outcome is now thinkable, a tail risk from the weakening of international security and economic architecture and deepening mistrust among the world's most powerful governments." Eurasia' Chairman Ian Bremmer went one step further in the agency's prediction for Country Risk in 2018: "In the 20 years since we started Eurasia Group, the global environment has had its ups and downs. But if we had to pick one year for a big unexpected crisis—the geopolitical equivalent of the 2008 financial meltdown—it feels like 2018" (Bremmer 2018). Website: https://www.eurasiagroup.net/issues/top-risks-2017.

5.11 Conclusion

As mentioned in the previous chapter, country risk assessment is as good as the information it depends on. A key element of analysis quality is relying on a broad range of public and private information sources while transforming informational raw material into economic intelligence that is conducive to robust decision-making. In this regard, diverse points of view and diverse methodologies and models are crucial to constructing a balanced and objective risk assessment. The private and nonprofit sectors provide rich sources of information and insight. It takes time and qualified professionals to absorb the vast amount of available information. Well organized, systematic, and dogged research efforts are the best path to cautious country risk management.

References

Aven, Terje. 2016. "Risk Assessment and Risk Management: Review of Recent Advances on Their Foundation." *European Journal of Operations Research* 253 (1): 1–13.

Baker, Scott, Tom Nichols, and Steven Davis. 2015. "Measuring Economic Policy Uncertainty." NBER Working Paper 2163, October. http://www.nber.org/papers/w2163.

Bernstein, Peter L. 1998. *Against the Gods: The Remarkable Story of Risk*. New York: Wiley.
BlackRock. 2011. Introducing the BlackRock Sovereign Risk Index.
Bouchet, Michel, Ephraim Clark, and Bertrand Groslambert. 2003. *Country Risk Assessment: A Guide to Investment Strategy*. New York: Wiley.
Bremmer, Ian. 2018. "Top Risks 2018: Overview". Eurrasia Group.
Brookings. 2017. "Global Economy and Development." https://c24215cec-6c97b637db6-9c0895f07c3474f6636f95b6bf3db172.ssl.cf1.rackcdn.com/interactives/2017/tiger/assets/2017-04/2017-04-tiger-spain.pdf.
Cato Institute. 2017. "Economic Freedom Index." https://object.cato.org/sites/cato.org/files/pubs/efw/efw2017/efw-2017-chapter-1.pdf.
Eaton, Jonathan, and Mark Gersovich. 1981. "Debt with Potential Repudiation: Theoretical and Empirical Analysis." *The Review of Economic Studies* 48 (2): 289–309.
Eaton, Jonathan, Mark Gersovich, and Joseph Stiglitz. 1986. "The Pure Theory of Country Risk." NBER Working Paper 1894, April.
FTSE Russell. 2017. http://www.ftserussell.com/.
Fund for Peace. 2017. https://www.fundforpeace.org/fsi/data.
IMD. 2017a. https://www.imd.org/globalassets/wcc/docs/methodology-and-principles-wee-2017.pdf.
IMD. 2017b. https://www.imd.org/globalassets/wcc/docs/release-2017/world_digital_competitiveness_yearbook_2017.pdf.
INCRA. 2012. http://www.bfna.org/sites/default/files/publications/INCRA%20Report.pdf.
Manasse, Paolo, and Nouriel Roubini. 2009. "'Rules of Thumb' for Sovereign Debt Crises." *Journal of International Economics* 78: 192–205.
Marsh. 2017. https://www.marsh.com/content/dam/marsh/Documents/PDF/US-en/The%20Global%20Risks%20Report%202017-01-2017.
Mersch, Yves. 2017. "Central Bank Independence Revisited." Keynote Address at the "Symposium on Building the Financial System of the 21st Century: An Agenda for Europe and the United States." ECB. Frankfurt am Main, 30 March.
Moody's. 2017. https://www.economy.com/dismal/countries/IARG.
Nagy, Pancras J. 1979. *Country Risk: How to Assess, Quantify, and Monitor It*. London: Euromoney.
Natixis. 2017. https://www.research.natixis.com/GlobalResearchWeb/External.
Pettis, Michael. 2017. "China's Growth Miracle Has Run Out of Steam." *Financial Times*, November 20.
Prasad, Eswar, and Karim Foda. 2017. *Update to Tiger: A Synchronized but Sluggish Recovery*. Washington, DC: The Brookings Institute.
Pronina, Lyubov, and Natasha Doff. 2016. "Argentina's Default-Riddled Past Flagged in Bond Sale Pitch." Bloomberg, April 11. https://www.bloomberg.com/news/articles/2016-04-11/argentina-s-default-riddled-past-flagged-in-bond-sale-pitch-imw7iy8c.

Standard & Poor's. 2002. "Sovereign Credit Ratings: A Primer," April 3.

Standard & Poor's. 2017. https://www.spratings.com/sri/.

Taleb, Nassim. 2005. *Fooled by Randomness: The Hidden Role of Chance in Life and in the Markets.* New York: Random House Trade Paperbacks.

World Economic Forum. 2017. http://www3.weforum.org/docs/GCR2016-2017/05FullReport/TheGlobalCompetitivenessReport2016-2017_FINAL.pdf.

6

Volatility, Spillovers, and Crisis Contamination: The New Dynamics of Country Risk Since the 1980s and 90s in the Globalized Market Economy

6.1 The Lack of Domestic Savings Can Lead to a Balance of Payment Crisis. How Do You Identify This Condition?

6.1.1 Relationship Between Savings and Investments

The best way to assess savings is to look at the components of gross domestic product (GDP) and gross national product (GNP). Indeed, the GDP is convenient in that it is both a quantitative indicator of production as well as a proxy of the national income and a country's total expenditures. The reason for this is intuitive: the amount of expenditure by buyers equals the amount of income for sellers. In accounting for a country's flows, everything that is produced is either consumed ("Consumption") or stored ("Investment"). In an open economy, a country's total expenditure is the sum of the following: Consumption (C) by private agents; Investments (I) by private agents; public expenditures, purchases, or investments (G); and the current account (CA), which is comprised of net expenditures by foreigners on domestic goods and services. A country's revenue, denoted Y, is equal to the entire amount of expenditures by domestic and foreign agents.

The amount of expenditure by buyers equals the amount of income for sellers, which equals the value of production. Accordingly, we have:

$$GDP = Y = C + I + G + CA$$

M. H. Bouchet et al., *Managing Country Risk in an Age of Globalization*,
https://doi.org/10.1007/978-3-319-89752-3_6

This identity illustrates that vulnerability can arise from a country's lack of savings.

Indeed, we deduce from the previous identity that the current account (exports–imports) equals:

$$CA = EX - IM = Y - (C + I + G)$$

This expression is particularly meaningful. When the production (Y) is lower than the entire amount of domestic expenditure ($C+I+G$), then the current account and the trade balance are in deficit. As the total production (Y) refers the country revenue (*GDP*), it implies that the country is living beyond its means and is dependent on foreign capital to finance its "extra-consumption" (that is, its "excess of expenditures" to be more precise). In other words, its "net foreign assets" position (net foreign wealth) is deteriorating. The "net" foreign assets (NFA) refers to the value of overseas assets owned by a nation (foreign assets holding), minus the value of its domestic assets that are owned by foreigners (foreign liabilities), adjusted for changes in valuation and exchange rates.

A nation's NFA position can also, therefore, be defined as the cumulative change in its current account over time (Graph 6.1).

Likewise, if a country runs a current account deficit of USD 50 billion, other things being equal, it has to borrow that amount from foreign sources

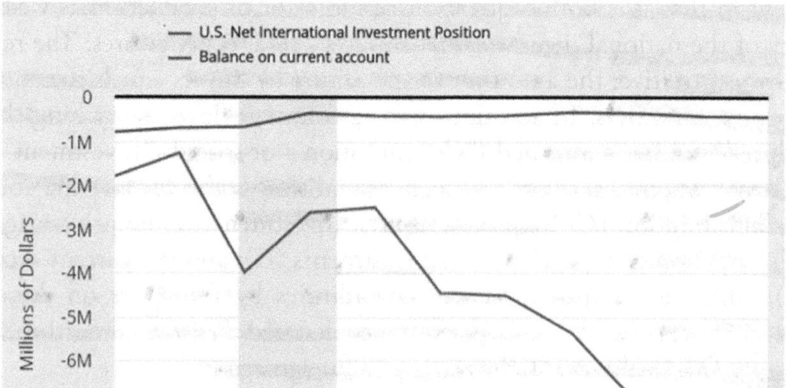

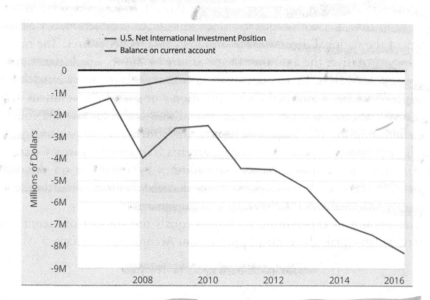

Graph 6.1 US Net International Position (IPP) and current account string of deficits (US Bureau of Economic Analysis. FRED Graph Series)

to finance the shortfall. In this case, a borrowing of USD 50 billion would increase its foreign liability and reduce its net foreign asset position by that amount. Any trade deficit must be funded either by net capital inflows or by selling of the central bank's foreign currency reserves.

If we observe that countries with structurally negative current account face a deterioration of their "net foreign assets" position, it is because those countries are incurring a shortage of savings. A structural lack of saving is a source of Country Risk.

A country's national saving (S) rate equals its national income (Y) that is not spent on consumption (C) or government purchases (G).

$$S = Y - C - G$$

We know that $CA = Y - (C + I + G)$.

We, therefore, deduce that:

$$CA = (Y - C - G) - I$$

$$CA = S - I$$

In a closed economy, there is no trade and $CA = 0$. The Savings are necessarily equal to the Investments ($S = I$). This is the main pitfall of poor countries that need investments to foster their future growth. But the savings required to "self-finance" their investments are precisely the outcome of the growth they wish to reach and what they lack before they grow. This is the "poverty trap" that besets less developed countries (sometimes referred to as the "Original sin").

In an open economy, a negative current account means that a country has a lack of savings ($S < I$). By contrast, a country with a positive current account will have a deficit of savings, higher than the domestic investments needs ($S > I$), leading to net outflows of capital abroad.

6.1.2 Consequences of Savings and Investments Misalignment

World exports equal world imports. They are two sides of the same trade. Therefore, the total volume of savings from countries with excess capital (capital outflows) equals the total volume of countries with a capital shortage (capital inflows), assuming they are globally aggregated.

In the long run, a country with a lack of savings is fully dependent on foreign capital inflows. Those inflows are never linear and can be erratic depending on changes in the mindset of investors.

Globalization has increased the size of international capital flows in absolute terms but also relative to the expansion of the trade in goods and services. In the meantime, those capital flows have also become subject to less regulatory constraint, creating difficulties for emerging economies that have struggled regularly with financial instability.

An inflow of capital from abroad may appear superficially attractive but it has consequences. It can increase domestic goods and asset prices. It can also shape, in a specific way, economic development and political opinion. The portfolio inflows can vanish even more quickly than they arrive.

For the first time, in 2012, the International Monetary Fund (IMF) changed its approach to the restriction to capital flows. This is particularly noteworthy since the IMF has been strongly attached to capital account liberalization since the 1990s. It finally acknowledged that direct control of capital flows may reduce volatility and international flows. The benefits of free capital circulation are clearly higher for mature economies than for well-developed financial markets. Capital inflows in countries with less than robust regulatory oversight may incite institutions to take excessive risks. Those risks give rise to a crisis when external capital leaves. Nevertheless, capital control is not a panacea and should be viewed as only a short-term solution. The IMF urges that "when an emerging market is facing a precipitate inflow of hot money, cutting the interest rate and tightening fiscal policy can be more effective than direct controls" (International Monetary Fund, February 2016, WP 16/25).

6.1.3 What Explains the Link Between a Country's Lack of Domestic Savings and Dependency on External Capital?

A country's saving rate can be categorized into the public saving rate (S^g) and the private one (S^p). None of them should be considered exclusively. Since a government deficit represents negative government savings, the current account equals:

$$CA = S^p + S^g - I$$

$$CA = S^p - \textit{government deficit} - I$$

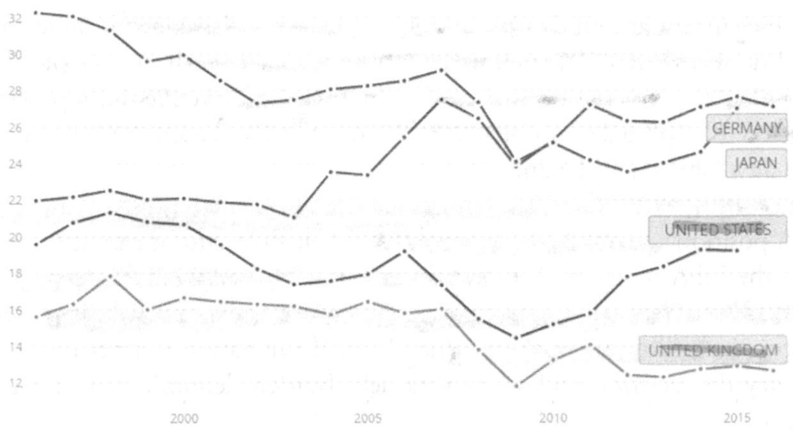

Graph 6.2 Gross saving rates (% of GDP) (data.worldbank.org)

Graph 6.3 Japan current account (JPY billion) (Tradingeconomics.com)

This identity further indicates that a public deficit reduces a country's saving rate and is likely, all else being equal, to generate a trade deficit. This is the theory of the "twin deficit," which jeopardizes the equilibrium of a balance of payment (BoP). A more dynamic view should also take into account what we call the "Ricardian equivalence," which posits that lower public savings (higher deficits) may lead private agents to increase their private savings (anticipating future tax increases), with an offsetting effect on the country's saving rate. When saving deficits come from both the public sector (all governmental and public entities) and the private sector (households and private companies), it will likely reflect through both trade and fiscal deficits (Graph 6.2).

Germany and Japan have structurally high saving rates and, consequently, surpluses in their current accounts (Graph 6.3).

These current account surpluses reflect the competitiveness of these countries but also their relatively low level of consumption. It creates problems and imbalances for trade partners. The US and UK have relatively poor saving rates (Graph 6.2) and structural trade deficits (Graph 6.4) relative to Germany, China, and Japan.

The saving rate affects a country's dependency on the rest of the world (NFA position), as do the exchange rates. Their fluctuations can also heavily affect the NFA position. A country's currency appreciation will decrease the value of both its foreign currency denominated assets and liabilities, while depreciation will increase their value. Thus, if the nation is a net debtor, its currency depreciation will worsen its debt burden denominated in foreign currency.

But in turn, the NFA position can itself influence exchange rates, since structural current account deficits can prove economic weakness and a lack of demand for the domestic product and domestic currency. In case of excessive NFA deficit, the currency may come under attack from speculators seeking to drive it lower.

NFA imbalances are reported in a document entitled "International Investment Position," which is published by the US Department of Commerce through its Bureau of Economic Analysis. For the EU, similar statistics are published by Eurostat (Tables 6.1 and 6.2).

As noted by Eurostat, the international investment position => **International Investment Position** is an indicator of an economy's external exposure in financial assets and liabilities to the rest of the world. This contributes effectively to monetary policy analysis and foreign exchange rate policies.

Before the Global Financial Crisis of 2008, the International Investment Positions were prepared by each country of the EU-28. For the purpose of financial stability analysis of the European Union and Member State, the EU authorities are required to compile them into a single document.

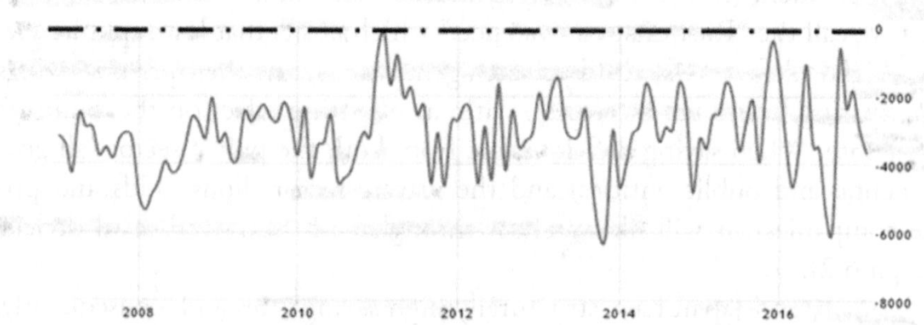

Graph 6.4 Great Britain current account (GBP billion) (Tradingeconomics.com)

Table 6.1 International investment position, components, EU-28 and EA-19, 2013–2015 (EUR 1000 million) (http://ec.europa.eu/eurostat/statistics-explained/ECB, IMF, and Eurostat)

	Assets	Liabilities	Net	Net (% GDP)
EU-28, total, excl. reserve assets	*24273.8*	*26831.2*	*−2557.4*	*−17.5*
Direct investment	8097.2	6506.2	1590.9	10.9
Portfolio investment	7560.4	11733.6	−4 173.3	−28.5
Financial derivatives and employee stock options	:	:	−24.8	−0.2
Other investment	5911.1	5861.3	49.8	0.3
EA-19, total	*24077.0*	*25042.7*	*−965.7*	*−9.3*
Direct investment	9747.6	7960.0	1787.6	17.2
Portfolio investment	7178.8	10282.5	−3103.6	−0.3
Equity	2569.7	1884.5	685.2	:
Investment fund shares	471.3	3274.2	−2803.0	:
Debt securities	4137.9	5123.8	−985.9	:
Financial derivatives and employee stock options	:	:	−28.3	−0.3
Other investment	4648.8	4914.3	−265.5	−2.6
Reserve assets	644.2	:	644.2	6.2

(:) not available
EU-28: Eurostat estimations
Source ECB, IMF, Eurostat

Table 6.2 Total net IIP with the rest of the world, EU-28 Member States (EUR 1000 million)/ECB and Eurostat (2015–16)

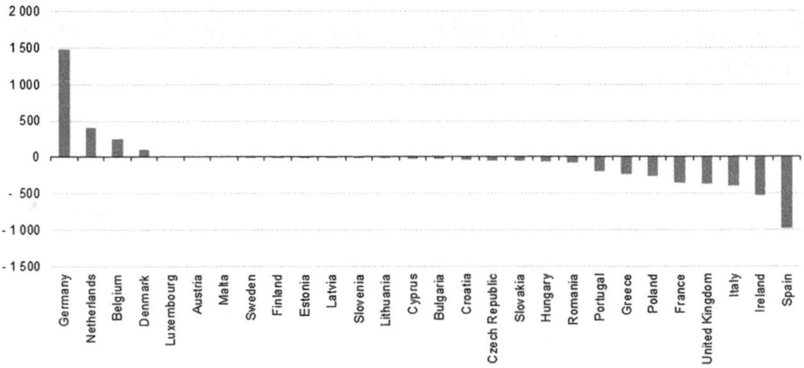

The applicable legal framework is "Regulation (EC) 184/2005" as amended in 2012 (Regulation 555/2012), which addresses statistics relating to balance of payments, international trade in services, and foreign direct investment.

The regulation requires that all members publicize to Eurostat their positions held outside the EU as well as their positions in reserve assets (as a component of the International Investment Positions). This is currently not occurring. Data requirements are often less demanding for the Member States not participating in the Monetary Union. Some improvements for other investment and financial derivatives components are expected by 2019.

6.1.4 To Keep in Mind

A country's net position and its dependency upon the rest of the word depend primarily on its current account position, which in turn depends on the country's rate of saving (both public and private). Monitoring this activity is important. Low saving rates can be due to decreasing productivity or low incomes. They can also reflect an underdeveloped or nonefficient banking sector. A lack of credit or an excessive cost of starting and doing business may hamper the growth of Small and Medium Enterprises (SMEs), having a direct impact on that country savings. In Ghana, for instance, SMEs contribute to 70% of its GDP and 92% of its businesses.

In developed countries, the saving rate may be more influenced by the consumption rate. The United States has a huge current account deficit, which is the result of US overconsumption (Graph 6.5).

In most developed countries, consumption is more than half of the GDP. Developing countries demonstrate high disparities as indicated in Graph 6.6.

Many variables potentially drive consumption rates. Among others, we can mention:

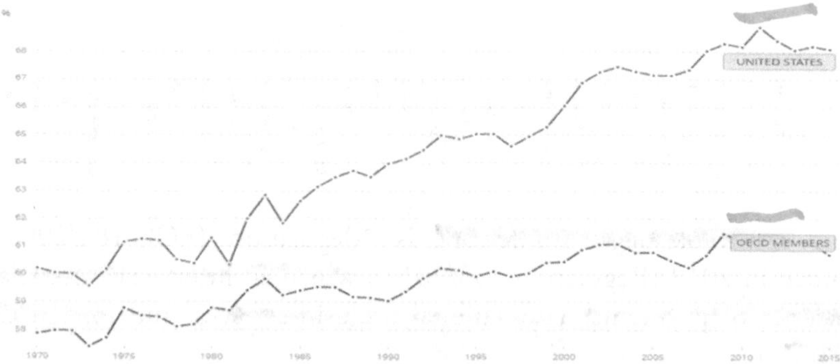

Graph 6.5 Household final consumption expenditure (% of GDP) (data.worldbank.org)

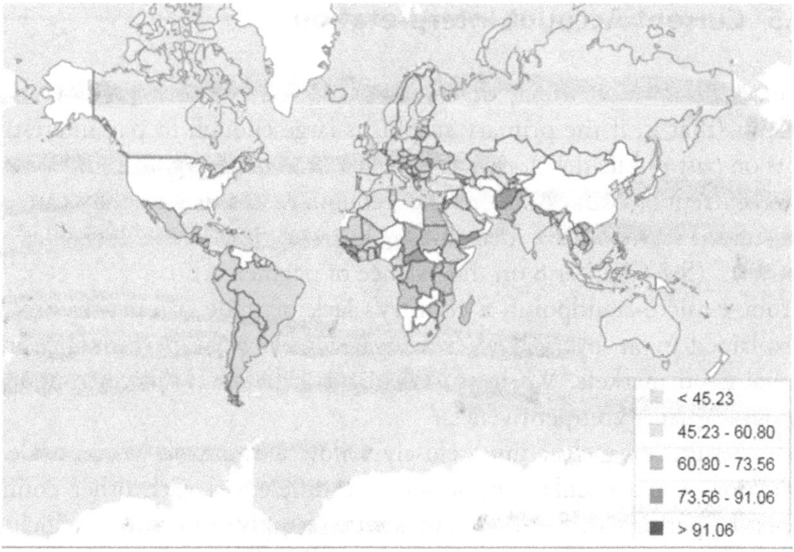

Graph 6.6 World countries rate of consumption, 2016 (data.worldbank.org)

- National revenue sharing between labor and capital
- The inflation rate that reduces savings
- The exchange rate (a price increase in the imported energy sector, for instance, may increase consumption and reduce savings)
- Real estate price and urban structures
- Fiscal policy
- The saving habits (public and private)
- Domestic interest rates
- Demographic trends

As mentioned in Chapter 3, demographic cycles are key drivers. According to Milton Friedman's permanent income hypothesis, young people spend more and start increasing their savings in middle age to prepare their retirement. Moreover, rural households also save more than urban ones. Accordingly, if a country faces both a strong urbanization trend and a young population, it can be expected to result in relatively low saving rates.

The consumption rate and the subsequent rate of savings may explain a current account deficit from a macro standpoint. When all domestic expenditures (private consumption, private investment, and public expenditures) are higher than 100% of the country's GDP, the current account is negative (participating negatively with the GDP).

6.1.5 Current Account Interpretation

If the current account widely deteriorates despite a budget balance with some surpluses (that is, if the primary surplus is large enough to pay interest payments on past public debt), then it clearly signals a loss of competitiveness.

The current account mirrors the economic weaknesses that can come from trade, services or other financial transactions like "invisibles" and "transfers." (See Chapter 8 on the balance of payments.)

From a micro-standpoint, a country's lack of trade competitiveness may be explained by an overvalued exchanged rate or weak performance in the external good markets. We usually distinguish between "price competitiveness" and "quality competitiveness."

As a result, an analyst must closely follow a country's global trade and production. Of particular importance are differences with other countries relating to performance drivers by exporter supply-side capacity, including product features and quality, scale (high/medium/low-end positioning), and geographical specialization.

The World Economic Report, for instance, is widely used by the international financial community. What makes it particularly valuable is that readers can make comparisons from year to year. It is important, nonetheless, to use this ranking or any other ranking as one of various factors that help assess Country Risk. Consider the following examples below of Switzerland, China, and Chile.

Box 6.1. Findings from the global competitiveness index 2015–2016

The World Economic Forum publishes an annual "global-competitiveness-report" (Schwab 2015) which contains extensive useful information for each country. Consider the following excerpts from Switzerland, China, and Chile.

Switzerland tops the GCI for the seventh consecutive year. Switzerland leads the innovation pillar, thanks to its world-class research institutions (1st), high spending on research and development (R&D) by companies (1st), and strong cooperation between the academic world and the private sector (3rd). But many other factors contribute to Switzerland's innovation ecosystem, including the level of business sophistication (1st) and the country's capacity to nurture and attract talent. Switzerland boasts an excellent education system at all levels and is a pioneer of the dual education system. The labor market is highly efficient (1st), with high levels of collaboration between labor and employers (1st) and balancing employee protection with flexibility and business needs. Swiss public institutions are among the most effective and transparent in the world (6th), and competitiveness is further buttressed by excellent infrastructure and connectivity (6th) and highly developed financial markets (10th). Last but not least, Switzerland's macroeconomic environment is among the most stable worldwide (6th) at a time when many developed countries continue to struggle in this area.

China ranks 28th—unchanged from last year. Its overall performance has barely budged in the past six years. Faced with rising production costs, an aging population, and diminishing returns on the massive capital investments of the past three decades, China must now evolve to a model where productivity gains are generated through innovation and demand through domestic consumption.

Chile remains the most competitive country in Latin America and the Caribbean, although dropping two places to 35th. Its strengths include solid institutions (32nd), a stable macroeconomic environment (29th), well-functioning financial markets (21st), high technological readiness (39th), and widespread uptake of ICTs (47th). The data suggest a downward trend in the efficiency of the goods market (40th, down 6 places) and labor market (63rd, down 13 places), with increasingly rigid hiring and firing practices (110th, down 44 places). Restrictive labor regulation is identified as the most problematic factor for doing business in Chile. In its transformation toward a more diversified and knowledge-based economy, Chile will also need to address long-standing issues such as its education system, specifically the overall quality of primary education (108th) and math and science education (107th). Higher education and training is in much better shape (33rd), but Chile must do more to improve its capacity to innovate (85th) in areas such as R&D (92nd) to diversify and foster robust growth.

6.1.6 The Role of Investments

What about "investment" (*I*) as a driver of growth and savings?

Investments mainly depend on a country's state of development: the initial takeoff implies a high rate of investment in that developing countries have historically invested more than they consumed. That is the opposite for developed countries. Investment is usually more volatile than consumption (that is, more dependent on domestic interest rates and financial markets). It impacts more medium and long-term potential growth. Investments are not homogenous: some of them impact growth faster than others. For instance, public infrastructure projects may have spillovers effect on the economy but they impact with a large time lag.

The country analyst must consider that an excess of investment has adverse effects. As a rule of thumb, rates higher than 45–50% for a sustained period are likely to be too much, potentially resulting in an "overinvestment" crisis. The capital-to-output ratio is one of the most common indicators used to assess the risk of "overinvestment."

This point is illustrated in the IMF working paper entitled "Is China Over-Investing and Does It Matter?" (2012):

> Now close to 50% of GDP, this paper assesses the appropriateness of China's current investment levels. It finds that China's capital-to-output ratio is within the range of other emerging markets, but its economic growth rates stand out, partly due to a surge in investment over the last decade. Moreover, its investment is significantly higher than suggested by cross-country panel estimation. This deviation has been accumulating over the last decade, and at nearly 10% of GDP is now larger and more persistent than experienced by other Asian economies leading up to the Asian crisis. However, because its investment is predominantly financed by domestic savings, a crisis appears unlikely when assessed against dependency on external funding. But this does not mean that the cost is absent. Rather, it is distributed to other sectors of the economy through a hidden transfer of resources, estimated at an average of 4% of GDP per year.

Developed countries have an investment rate lower than 30% (the average rate in EU is 20%, for instance). Among poor countries, polar cases can be found. The highest rates can reach 73% (for example, Mozambique) and the lowest rate reaches the ceiling of 6.5% for Swaziland (Table 6.3).

A "world investment report" is published each year by the United Nations Conference on Trade and Development (UNCTAD). It extensively discusses cross-border investments. The World Bank also tracks gross capital

Table 6.3 Countries with the highest investment-to-GDP ratios, 2017 (% of GDP) (data.worldbank.org)

Economic indicators: investment (% of GDP) 2017 Economic indicator listing in Year 2017	
Investment (% of GDP)	Value (%)
Mozambique	73.502
Suriname	62.616
Bhutan	55.891
Timor Leste (East Timor)	50.703
Algeria	47.131
Panama	44.000
Cape Verde	43.942
China	40.847
Niger	40.463
Vanuatu	39.489
Brunei Darussalam	38.012
Developing Asia	37.899
Mongolia	36.62
Belarus	36.041
Gabon	35.952
Ethiopia	35.833
Morocco	35.483
Indonesia	36.320

formation (which is defined as gross fixed capital formation as % of GDP). This is influenced by outlays on additions to fixed assets (plant, machinery, equipment, and buildings), plus the net change in inventories. In order to add capital stock for additional future growth, countries must generate enough savings and investments from households or public policies.

6.2 The Rate of Savings Determines a Country's Capital Inflows or Outflows. But What About Their Allocation?

International financial conditions following the Global Financial Crisis of 2008 have fuelled the growth of investments in transition and emerging economies. In fact, a large amount of liquidity that was injected into the financial system of developed countries has flowed to other countries that did not experience the immediate financial crisis. This was the case because these countries offered quite attractive investment opportunities.

Nevertheless, roughly half of the world's savings are invested in the United States because of their substantial trade deficit, mainly financed by China's surpluses. While true, this is quite counterintuitive. Worldwide savings should normally flow into countries with higher investment returns (i.e., countries with low rates of capital due to decreasing marginal return on capital). Countries with low reserves of capital are supposed to present more/better investments opportunities (known as the "Lucas puzzle").

Beyond a country's risk premium, the world savings allocation is influenced by interest rate differentials between countries. Floating exchange rates are also supposed to help the adjustment and the allocation. When capital flows into a country more attractive than others (with higher interest rates), the demand for its currency increases and its exchange rate appreciates, making it more expensive to invest in that country. The "exchange rate of equilibrium" is supposed to make the assets of concerned countries equally desirable in terms of real return (the exchange rate makes a capital "entry cost" to a foreign country high enough to offset any interest rate differential benefit). This phenomenon is known as the "Interest Rate Parity" theory (IRP). Similarly, if a country is exporting too much, the international demand for its currency will increase (to pay for those exported products) with an upward pressure on the exporting country currency. The subsequent appreciation makes the country's products less attractive (i.e., more expensive for foreigners with a relatively weaker currency). The exchange rate swings allow for "natural adjustment" and stabilization.

6.2.1 Implications of Imperfect Exchange Rate Adjustment?

What, then, are the practical implications for the country risk analyst? We must be careful to assess whether exchange rates are not performing such "natural adjustments". This may occur when exchange rates are not freely floating or when investors engage in what is known as the "carry-trade."

A carry-trade is "a leveraged cross-currency position." It is an investment strategy that attempts to take advantage of the apparent failure of the "Interest Rate Parity." The investor borrows low-interest rate currencies (the "funding currency") and exchanges them for higher rate currencies (the "target currency"). The purpose is to profit from the interest rate differential. The strategy is profitable if the gains from the interest rate differentials are not offset by exchange rate movements in the short to medium term. If the target currency depreciates, the result can be a sudden stop or reversal and unwind as investors seek to exit the carry position before the collapse. This can impair capital movement and further result in instability in emerging markets. The amount of carry-trade positions is difficult to determine based on available data. Depending on the circumstances, carry-trades can generate significant fragility and instability.

As we have discussed, problems in one part of the international economy can have global ramifications in both emerging and developed market economies. Such issues often disproportionately affect emerging economies as a result of the unwinding of carry-trade positions for which their currencies are frequently targeted. This is due to the fact that developing countries often have a higher inflation, less mature credit markets, and generally higher interest rates. The buildup of these carry-trade positions generally contributes to a steady strengthening of target currencies (associated with higher interest rates) and a weakening of funding currencies (associated with lower interest rates). However, in case of a change in interest rate expectations, there can be rapid unwinding of carry-trades positions. The outcome is a sharp depreciation for target currencies and sharp appreciation for funding currencies. (See IMF 1998; Béranger et al. 1999; Gagnon and Chaboud 2007.)

6.2.2 Investment Strategies with Self-Fulfilling Effects

Carry-trades amplify volatility and self-fulfilling effects. Imagine that a financial indicator suggests bad news for the US economy. Domestic investors will anticipate a strong rise of the Euro and will buy Euro forward transactions for hedging or speculative purposes. As a consequence, banking counterparts will take short positions in Euro forwards. Financial institutions then need to hedge themselves by immediately buying Euros (on spot market) and carrying them until the forward contract delivery date. This hedging process has self-fulfilling effects since it leads to an immediate upward pressure on Euro exchange rates. In addition, it increases US interest rates in the short turn since banks borrow Dollars to invest in Euros (as a result of the greater demand for US Dollars). It further decreases the EU interest rates since during the carrying period (before the forward delivery date), banks will lend or invest those Euros they have acquired (leading to higher supply in the EU money market). This is why, most of the time, the short-run interest rate of the "attacked" currency increases sharply and the short-run interest rate of the stronger currency remains low.

The carry-trade introduces additional vulnerabilities to countries with preexisting and specific economic features. A well-known example is the relationship between Japan and Australia.

During its so-called "lost decade" of the 1990s, Japan experienced ten years of weak growth and extremely low-interest rates. Investors were borrowing in Yen without any upward pressure on interest rates. Japanese monetary policy was facing a "liquidity trap," a situation in which prevailing interest rates are low and savings rates are high, making monetary policy ineffective. These low-interest rates affected the behavior of bondholders since they feared a decline in the value of their bonds.

The Yen was perceived as a weak currency (a funding currency) and was invested in the Australian Dollar (a target currency) since its economy was healthy and interest rates were higher. Among the financial instruments used for those investments were cross-currency swaps (along with spot transactions, forward transactions, and more advanced currency option transactions).

These circumstances at first seem to invalidate the IRP theory since it was more attractive to invest in Australian Dollar without apparent negative effects. For many years, the Australian Dollar was benefiting from large financial inflows and kept on appreciating (despite what was predicted by the IRP theory).

But when most investors started to become over-leveraged in 2008, a correction took effect. In addition to the international financial crisis leading to higher solvency and liquidity constraints, a catch-up phenomenon occurred. The Australian Dollar suddenly dropped, resulting in substantial losses for those who started to invest after 2005, jumping on the bandwagon too late (see Graph 6.7).

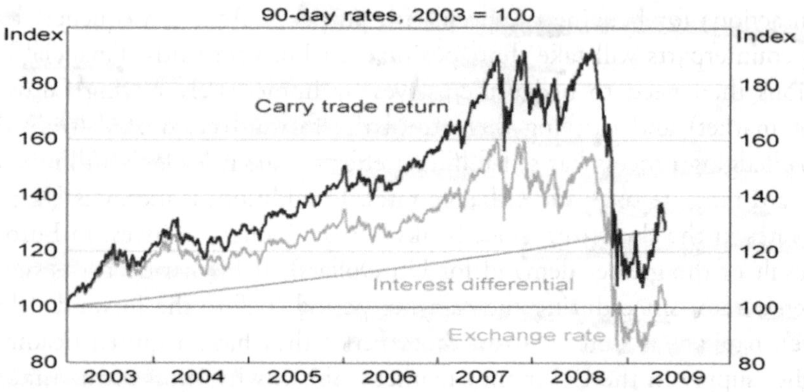

Graph 6.7 Cumulative return on AUD/JPY carry trade. 90-day rates, 2003 = 100 (Reserve Bank of Australia)

Another example is the sharp appreciation of the Yen against the US Dollar between the 6th and 8th of October 1998. This followed a prolonged period of depreciation. This was one of the most significant moves in major foreign exchange rates since 1974. Indeed, the one-month implied volatility reached 40% and bid-ask spreads widened remarkably.

Last but not least, a popular version of the carry-trade is a borrowing in US Dollars (buying T-bonds, for instance) and using the proceeds to buy Mexican Pesos or Brazilian Reals. If the USD/MXN or USD/BRL rate remains stable, investors can benefit from the difference between lower United States and higher Mexican or Brazilian yields alone. In retrospect, the significant reversal of carry-trade positions is likely to explain the huge spike in exchange rate move and volatility. The Bank of International Settlement (BIS) observed: "other episodes include the depreciation of the Icelandic Króna in February 2006 and volatility spikes mostly in emerging market currencies in December 2005 and May-June 2006" (Galati et al. 2007). All in all, carry-trade activities rely on the idea that most of the excess return, considering the IRP theory, is essentially a return for taking "crash-risk." Consistent with this intuition, Brunnermeier et al. (2009) concluded that the returns are characterized by negative skew and a larger than normal risk of extreme loss. Skewness is a term in statistics used to describe asymmetry from the normal distribution in a set of statistical data. We refer to "negative skewness" when returns present frequent small gains and few large losses (the tail on the left side of the probability density function is longer or fatter than the right side).

Jurek (2007) reached a similar conclusion by analyzing the cost of purchasing option protection against crash-risk. The price of out-of-the-money puts covers a proportion of the excess returns that seem to be generated by the carry-trade, implying that markets integrate the link between excess return and the likelihood of a sudden crash. Carry returns were also positive in smooth periods, in contrast with periods of crisis (as measured by elevated levels of the VIX index or SKEW index) with a negative return, skewed and fat-tailed (Hayward and Holscher 2016).

6.3 Which Instruments Can Be Used to Measure a Country's Vulnerability to Carry-Trade Activities?

The carry-to-risk ratio is a well-known measure of "ex ante" attractiveness of carry-trades. It adjusts the interest rate differential by the risk of future exchange rate movements, proxied by the expected volatility implied by foreign exchange options of the relevant currency pair. This ratio explains the success of carry-trade positions that were "short" in Yen and "long" in Australian Dollar or other target currencies from 2002 to 2005.

The BIS international banking statistics allow for the tracking of the flows of those targeted currencies. Nevertheless, precise tracking of carry-trade flows is difficult to determine since banks only report their on-balance sheet positions. These numbers track flows executed on the spot market (cash market) and secondary ripples in the spot markets caused by underlying activity in the derivatives markets. But most carry-trade positions are "off-balance sheet" (not recorded) since they use derivatives instruments (forward, swaps, or options transactions). Moreover, flows recorded on the spot market are not all linked to carry-trade activities but simply reflect basic corporate or interbank lending or borrowing.

The role of the bank in the transaction is an important factor. Banks can be intermediaries, providing loans in the funding currencies and taking deposits in the target currencies. They can also take carry-trade positions themselves for their own proprietary desks, leading to increase their assets in the target currency and their liabilities with the funding currency. They can be a counterparty using derivative instruments.

There is no clear tracking of carry-trade investments and we can only rely on a range of indicia. Data on hedge fund returns are another potential source of information. McGuire and Upper (2007) found that proxies for carry-trade returns are statistically significant determinants of hedge fund performance.

Graph 6.8 represents the global banking system as a network of interconnected countries and groups of countries, each representing a financial hub. The arrows and their thickness are proportional to the cumulative net bank flows between countries. It provides information about the direction and

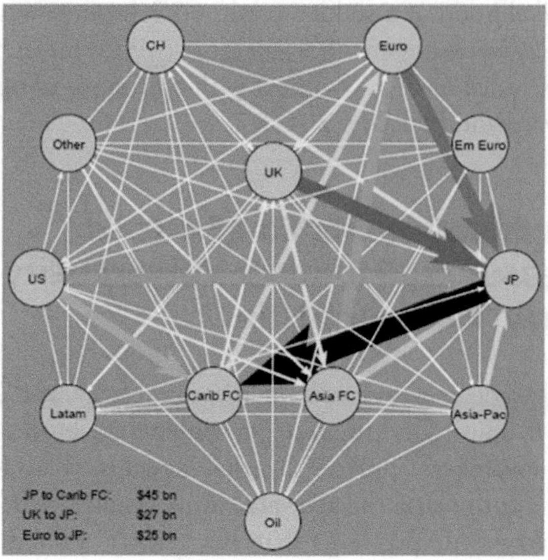

ASIA OSC = Hong Kong SAR, Macao and Singapore; ASIA PAC = China, India, Indonesia, Korea, Malaysia, Pakistan, the Philippines, Taiwan (China) and Thailand; CARIB = Aruba, the Bahamas, Bermuda, the Cayman Islands, the Netherlands Antilles and Panama; CH = Switzerland; EM EUROPE = Bulgaria, Croatia, Cyprus, the Czech Republic, Estonia, Hungary, Latvia, Lithuania, Malta, Poland, Romania, Slovakia, Slovenia, Turkey and Ukraine; EURO = euro area countries; JP = Japan; LAT = Argentina, Brazil, Chile, Colombia, Mexico and Peru; OIL = OPEC member states (excluding Indonesia) plus Russia; OTHER = Australia, Canada, Denmark, New Zealand, Norway and Sweden; UK = the United Kingdom plus the offshore centres Guernsey, the Isle of Man and Jersey; US = the United States.

Graph 6.8 Cumulative net flows of Japanese Yen through the banking system: 1998–2006 (BIS Quarterly Review: Tracking international bank flows)

size of the net flows of capital intermediated by banks. It helps portray market segments where carry-trade activity is likely to occur. Offshore financial centers, which host a significant number of hedge funds and other speculative traders, are an obvious place to look for activity related to carry-trades. Based on this graph, we can see that the Japanese Yen, as a funding currency, experiences significant outflows to the Caribbean.

6.4 Driving Forces of Current Instability and Global International Capital Flows

We observe first that the current move toward normalization of monetary policy in developed nations is causing a reversal in some international flows and may raise some concern about new financial crises in emerging countries.

The main international forces that have been identified as being potential triggers for such a reversal are the QE monetary policy, the international risk aversion, and the international liquidity. Cerutti et al. (2017) tried to answer three related questions: What drives global liquidity? Where does the global liquidity cycle originate? How can the recipient countries manage exposure to global liquidity?

6.4.1 What Drives Global Liquidity?

Following the Global Financial Crisis of 2008, the flow of capital to emerging countries has increased as a consequence of liquidity stoked by quantitative easing in most developed economies. The analysis of cross-border banking flows shows that global liquidity is affected by uncertainty and risk aversion. What must be stressed is that uncertainty and risk aversion are highly correlated across countries. Flight-to-Safety (FTS) describes capital flows toward main international financial centers and relatively safe assets. The FTS frequency is the object of many studies with no consensus across them. Quite counterintuitively, Baele et al. (2014) found that most of the events they analyzed over twenty-three countries are mainly "country-specific" and only 25% of the events are identified as "global." The FTS variables they selected are well-known global crises, including the October 1987 crash, the 1997 Asian crisis, the Russian crisis and LTCM debacle in 1998, the Lehman Brothers collapse, and several periods during the European sovereign debt crisis. They investigated the co-movement between the FTS variables and several types of "global stress" indicators. They examined implied volatility indices: the US S&P 500 (VIX), the UK FTSE 100 (VFTS), the German DAX (VDAX), and the Japanese Nikkei 225 (VXJ). They also integrated some confidence indices such as the Baker and Wurgler (2006) sentiment indicator (purged of business cycle fluctuations); the Michigan consumer sentiment index which measures sentiment in the United States; and the Ifo Business Climate indicator (which measures sentiment in Germany) and the (country-specific) OECD consumer confidence indicators (seasonally adjusted).

The VIX is an index of implied volatility on options from the S&P 500 index. It is commonly used as a measure of international risk aversion as it signals increased demand by fund managers for option protection of their equity portfolio. Similarly, the "TED spread" (Treasury Eurodollar spread) is used as a market measure of perceived credit risk of financial institutions. It records the difference between US Treasury Bills (T-bills) considered risk-free and the Eurodollar futures that are thought to reflect the credit ratings of corporate borrowers. Eurodollar bonds are USD-denominated debt securities issued by an overseas company and held outside both the United States and the issuer's home nation. Eurodollar bonds are a major source of capital fundings for multinational companies and foreign governments.

6.4.2 Where Does the Global Liquidity Cycle Originate?

Ahmed and Zlate (2014) also concluded that monetary policy and international risk interplay. To support those assertions, they studied gross and net capital flows before and after the financial crisis, showing that economic growth, interest rate differentials, and the level of global risk appetite are all important determinants of private capital flows to emerging markets: "in terms of their economic importance, the interest rate differential and risk aversion have been key determinants of total and portfolio net inflows, with the interest rate differential gaining a more prominent role in the post-crisis period. In contrast, the growth differential has always been a key determinant for the total, but not for the portfolio "net inflows."" They highlight that capital flows are not inherently more volatile but follow increases in interest rate differential postcrisis.

The slowing down of US quantitative monetary policy starting in 2018 will not necessarily lead to emerging markets capital outflow but may generate risk premium shocks, with higher returns required by investors, and a corresponding fall in asset prices. The consequence of US monetary policy may vary in a variety of ways depending on the country and the asset classes (see Chapter 11).

6.4.3 How Can the Recipient Countries Manage Exposure to Global Liquidity?

Noticeably, Mishra et al. (2014) indicate that exchange rates and bonds are less affected by international liquidity shocks than stock markets. They also observe that: "countries with stronger macroeconomic fundamentals, deeper financial markets, and a tighter macroprudential policy stance in the run-up to the tapering announcements experienced smaller currency depreciation and smaller increases in government bond yields. At the same time, there was less differentiation in the behavior of stock prices based on fundamentals."

To track those important features, twice a year (in October and April), the IMF publishes its well-known World Economic Outlook (WEO) report with a comprehensive analysis of international flows' structure and evolution (Table 6.4).

In the second half of 2015, capital flows to emerging market and developing economies reached their lowest level since the Global Financial Crisis. With capital outflows declining less than inflows, and with relatively little change in the aggregate current account balance, the change in reserves turned negative for those economies.

During good times (that is when funds flow globally), foreign capital inflows are channeled to assets that can act as a cushion against eventual negative shocks. As emphasized by Broner et al. (2013): "capital inflows intermediated by the banking system might prove particularly dangerous given the susceptibility of banks to runs. Flows into short-term debt might also generate fragility due to the rollover risk that countries face when their debt is about to mature and needs to be rolled over into new debt with new interest rates."

Table 6.4 Emerging market economies: capital flows (IMF, WEO report, October 2017)

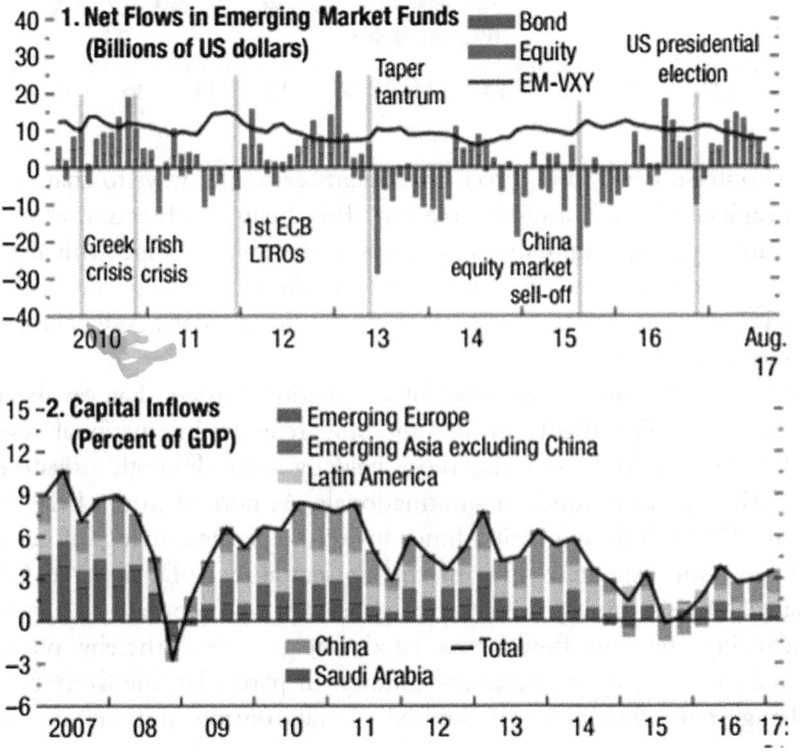

Table 6.4 (continued)

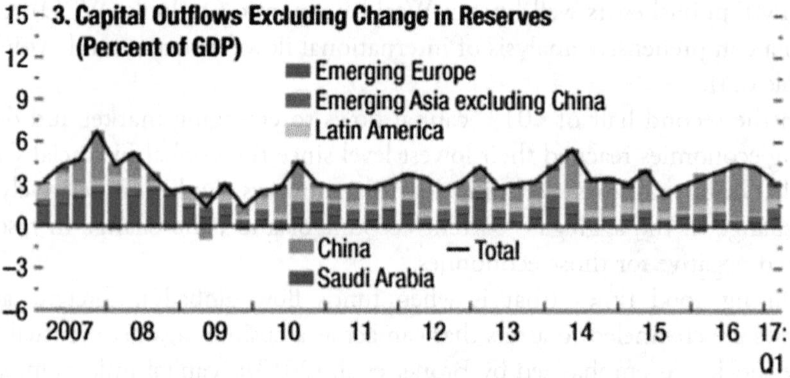

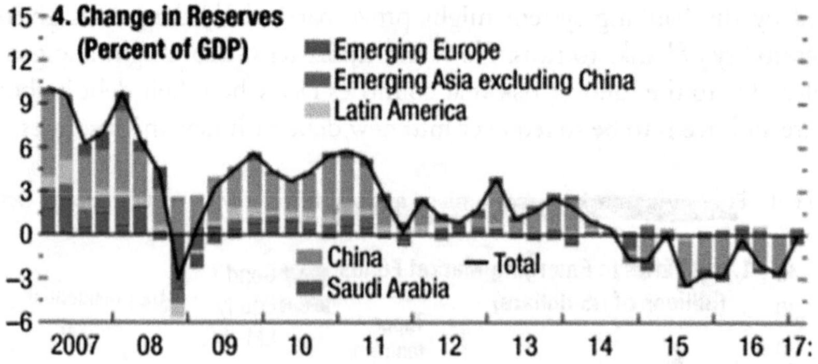

In contrast, equity and direct investment seem safer ways to channel foreign capital inflows in a sustainable way. This duality leads countries to keep accumulating large amounts of reserves to be able to cope with external shocks. It seems to be the strategy that middle-income countries have followed during the 2000s, which might explain their relative resilience during the global financial crisis.

When talking about "reserves" of international assets that can be used to "buffer" capital flight, we do not only refer to international reserves held by central banks but also those held by some domestic private entities such as pension funds or multinationals. As noticed in the IMF WEO report (2013): "Private pension funds invest the pension savings of Chileans and hold approximately 40% of their assets abroad. During the Global Financial Crisis, multiple incentives combined to encourage a significant rebalancing: pension funds repatriated foreign assets, thereby offsetting the reduction in foreign investors' inflows. In particular, the freely floating exchange rate combined with limited capital controls and well-developed financial markets, to quickly and efficiently encourage and facilitate financial adjustment that buffered volatile gross inflows."

6.4.4 To Keep in Mind

There is evidence that the international financial cycles are increasingly global. Since the 1990s, cross-border credit has become more correlated. As a result, credit and liquidity contractions in the United States, Eurozone, UK, and Japan affect the rest of the world (Cerutti et al. 2017). The concept of "global funding liquidity" helps explain international flows that affect financial conditions. Funding flows from the largest economies through the movement of cross-border credit. An excess of capital flows sometimes fuels an excess of liquidity and credit, with subsequent risk of inflation. By contrast, a sudden stop in capital flows amplifies the risk of deflation.

Box 6.2. Uncontrolled inflation or deflation are major dangers for countries

On September 21, 2017, Janet Yellen acknowledged that inflation rate during the prior month was "mysterious" for central banks.

To explain the "current threat" of expected future inflation, one can refer to the "toothpaste tube theory." It is based on the observation that when one squeezes the bottom of the toothpaste tube, toothpaste is inevitably extruded from the opening. Pressure built up in some finite bounded system needs to be released somewhere or the system will not function. For an economy, the release comes from the price increase if the monetary policy does not succeed to stimulate enough real aggregates such as real output, the real interest rate, and the subsequent real demand for money.

In short, if the money supply growth exceeds the real demand for money, the "release" goes through the price level, with a time lag and a magnitude that no one is able to know precisely. If the price level currently seems to stay flat despite the numerous quantitative easing programs, it is likely because we currently live in a world of absolute preference for money as described by Keynes many years ago. It is also because the money circulation speed likely slows down (trapped in savings and financial assets) due to various factors, structural and otherwise (including demographic changes and financial innovation).

It can also be mentioned that no monetary policy succeeds to control precisely monetary growth. Financial innovation always manages to develop new money substitutes (digital currencies are the latest example), which are not being tracked or regulated (Eggertsson 2017).

Long-term price evolution is hard to predict but important since it drives the economy long-run interest rate (the International Fisher Effect). The longer the time horizon, the less the central bank can impact market interest rates and the more they follow inflation path.

Consequently, price dynamic is important to assess but not so easy to do. In the short run, some leading indicators such as the Consumer Price Index (CPI) are informative. They include the Import/Export Price index and the Producer Price Index (PPI) that measures changes in prices the manufacturer and wholesalers pay for goods during various stages of production: "crude goods," "intermediate goods," and "finished goods." It helps to figure out how far in the production process inflation pressures have traveled and how close they are to emerging in the retail or consumer sector (Yamarone 2016).

The calculation for "core inflation" excludes food and energy prices, most notably oil and gas because food and energy prices fluctuate based on quick-changing emotions of commodity traders and speculators around the globe rather than the changes in economic supply and demand.

In the longer run, the bond market may be indicative since market participants routinely price bond securities based upon their inflation projections. For instance, the difference between the nominal ten-year Treasury rate and the inflation-adjusted Treasury Inflation Protected Securities (TIPS) rate implies the average inflation rate expected by bond market players over the next ten years in the United States. A market expectation for inflation can be deduced from the difference between yields on conventional government bonds and the yields on these indexed bonds. This is the so-called "break-even" inflation rate. "'Inflation-indexed' government bonds are now available in each major financial market. They were introduced in the UK in 1981 and since then they have been made available in Australia (1985), Canada (1991), Sweden (1994), the United States (1997) and Japan (2004), with government issues in the Eurozone from France (1998), Italy and Greece (2003), and Germany (2006). A number of emerging markets, including India, Brazil, Israel, and South Africa, have also made use of inflation-linked bonds" (Stanyer 2014).

Debt, deleveraging, and the threat of deflation

Current monetary policy must address the delicate balance between the risk of deflation and the risk of inflation. Both can influence Country Risk.

A debt crisis encourages countries to deleverage. But to do so, the nominal interest rate needs to be lower than the nominal growth rate. If this does not occur, then it sets up an environment where debt compounds at a rate faster than the economy can grow.

When public and private agents deleverage at the same time, it reduces the debt amount but it also generates some money destruction (if money creation comes from debt, the opposite is also true). In the meantime, the selling of assets participates to put a downward pressure on those asset prices. As a result, it increases the deflationary pressure that may paradoxically increase the debt financial burden. The future debt will have to be paid back with devalued money, requiring more units to honor past engagements. This is known as the "debt-deflation spiral."

Deflationary forces in the global economy represent a "headwind" to higher growth. As the spreads between overnight rates and sovereign bond yields continue to contract, this will challenge how effective monetary easing is going forward. Hence, it questions monetary policy effectiveness in the long run. It is of common wisdom that central banks have fewer tools to counter deflation than inflation (lending facilities can't have negative nominal rates to counter deflation but they can rise as much as needed to counter inflation). Also, a good metaphor to highlight the asymmetry between "counter inflation" versus "counter deflation" is the one of the "dog and his master." A leash can be useful to guide the dog and slow it down, but it cannot push it forward or make it go faster. Similarly, the monetary policy is the leash of the economy and has the same effects and limitations.

Alternatively, another relevant expression mentions that "you can lead a horse to water, but you can't make it drink (i.e., maintain adequate liquidity)." When an economy is stuck in a liquidity trap, no economic policy (fiscal or monetary) seems powerful enough to counter the economic stagnation and the associated Country Risks. This is why it appears preferable for central banks to undertake a "leaning against the wind" (countercyclical policy) rather than a "cleaning up afterward" (the latter case being expensive and ineffective most of the time). One should keep in mind that an economic policy cannot catch two birds with one stone and should stay cautious.

6.5 From Net to Gross Capital Flows

Country risk analysts have usually emphasized the behavior of net capital flows (capital inflows by foreigners minus capital outflows by domestic agents) that mirror the current account, though much less is known on gross capital flows.

Domestic and foreign investors have asymmetric behavior. Focusing on the gross capital flows may be more meaningful but also more "alarming" since they are "pro-cyclical." (Broner et al. 2013) During expansions, foreigners used to invest more heavily in domestic markets and domestic agents used to invest more abroad. During turbulent times there is a reduction in inflows by foreigners and larger outflows by domestic agents (often referred to as a "scissors effect"). The reduction in net capital inflows during crises is in fact substantially smaller than the reduction in gross capital flows. In periods of economic turmoil, domestic and foreign investors behave differently, partly due to asymmetric information or currency behavior. All currencies do not behave in the same way. For example, Canadian and Australian investors view foreign investments as less risky because their domestic currency is pro-cyclical, meaning that it tends to weaken when markets go down, and hence attenuate the decrease in foreign assets value. In contrast, the United States or Swiss investors have countercyclical or "safe haven" currencies, which tend to increase in value when markets plummet. They will be more eager to hedge their currency exposures or to unwind fast their foreign investments in case of financial distress.

Thus, during periods of distress, countries are less able not only to finance domestic investments with foreign savings but also to share domestic idiosyncratic risks with foreigners. Idiosyncratic risk is specific and endemic to a particular country or asset class (also referred to as "unsystematic risk").

A country risk analyst should definitely monitor the separate behavior of domestic and foreign investors.

6.6 The Asymmetric Monetary System Exacerbates Country Risk for the Most Fragile Countries

For most fragile countries, the "exorbitant privilege" of the US Dollar is undeniably one cornerstone of international system risk and instability.

There is no better way to describe the international monetary system today than the statement made in 1971 by US Treasury Secretary John Connally. He was speaking to his counterparts during a Rome G-10 meeting in November 1971, shortly after the Nixon administration ended the Dollar's convertibility into gold and shifted the international monetary system into a global floating exchange rate regime. He said: "The Dollar is our currency, but your problem." This statement is still relevant today. On several occasions Federal Reserve Chairpersons Ben Bernanke and Janet Yellen have reaffirmed that the Dollar is primarily a function of the US domestic policy, without necessarily taking into account its impact on other countries or regions.

Some analysts consider China's interventions to weaken the Renminbi versus the Dollar as a response to America's monetary policy. The accusation of "money manipulation" and fear of "currency war" is never ending story similar to the Ouroboros snake symbol. What is at stake is the lack of "alignment" between US interests and those of other countries.

The US Nobel Prize winner Robert Mundell even acknowledged that: "the United States would not talk about international monetary reform because a superpower never pushes international monetary reform unless it sees reform as a chance to break up a threat to its own hegemony." No other currency besides the US Dollar fully qualifies as a universal currency. Only the Euro could rival the Dollar since the Eurozone is the biggest world trade area (taken as a whole, the biggest exporter and biggest importer). But it would require creating a single market for sovereign debt (Eurobonds) along with budgetary transfers among countries, which seems unrealistic in short run (Table 6.5).

After the Global Financial Crisis, gold made a "comeback" into the international financial system. China and Russia significantly increased their gold reserves in order to reduce their dependency toward the United States. A system based on only the US Dollar inherently leads to undue exposure to one currency. It does not only impact foreign countries through their exchange

Table 6.5 Score Board of main international currencies: a review of their strength/weaknesses in order to participate in a more multipolar and balanced system (IMF Staff Discussion note. Internationalization of emerging market currencies, a balance between risks and rewards[a]) Maziad et al. (2011)

AE currencies	USD	Euro	Yen	Pound	SWF	AUD	CAD	NZD
Widely used as international reserves	●	●	●	●	◗	○	○	○
Widely used in capital and trade payments	●	●	◗	◗	○	○	○	○
Widely traded in FX markets	●	●	●	●	◗	◗	◗	◗
Economic size	●	●	●	●	◗	◗	◗	○
Trade network	●	●	●	●	◗	◗	◗	◗
Investability[b]	●	●	●	●	●	●	●	●
Capital account openness[c]	●	●	●	●	●	◗	●	●
Financial depth index[d]	●	●	●	●	◗	◗	◗	○
EM and NIE currencies	**HKD**	**Won**	**SGD**	**RMB**	**Real**	**Rupee**	**Ruble**	**Rand**
Widely used as international reserves	○	○	○	○	○	○	○	○
Widely used in capital and trade payments	○	○	○	○	○	○	○	○
Widely traded in FX markets	●	◗	◗	○	○	○	○	○
Economic size	○	◗	○	●	◗	◗	◗	◗
Trade network	◗	◗	◗	●	◗	◗	◗	◗
Investability[b]	●	●	●	●	◗	◗	◗	●
Capital account openness[c]	●	◗	●	○	◗	○	◗	○
Financial depth index[d]	◗	◗	◗	●	◗	◗	◗	◗

[a]"●" criteria fully met; "◗" partially met; "○" not met
[b]"●" Based on sovereign risk ratings "A" or above by Moody's and S&P
[c]Based on Chinn and Ito "Capital Account Openness Indicator, 2008"
[d]Country contributions to global financial depth, "●" for top five contributors

rate or their debt denominated in Dollars but also through the commodity prices. Gold, oil, and other commodities are negotiated in Dollars (benchmark pricing). When the value of the Dollar increases, it costs more for foreigners to buy commodities and producers might have to reduce prices.

Among the best ways to monitor the Dollar is to look at the price quotes of the Dollar index traded on the ICE Futures Exchange (InterContinental Exchange). These futures contracts value the Dollar against a basket of major currencies such as the British pound, Euro, and Yen, among others. In early March 2016, that Dollar index was trading around the 97 level—the Dollar had appreciated by around 23% over less than a two-year period (Kowalski 2017). Many commodity prices moved lower over this period. Those price fluctuations, which were due to the US currency, bring additional risks to commodity-dependent countries. Consider, for instance, the Australian economy for which agriculture and commodities represent 60% of

Australian exports. Gold is of high importance in Australian exports, leading to a strong positive correlation between gold and AUD. Since we know that USD has a negative correlation with gold, operators tend to be short AUD/USD when gold price decreases. Similarly, Canada is one of the biggest worldwide oil producers (hence a positive correlation between CAD and oil price). Since we know that USD has a negative correlation with oil, when oil prices increase, operators tend to be short USD/CAD. Those examples demonstrate that worldwide economies are dependent on the Dollar fluctuation, be they developed or developing economies.

When emerging markets faced sudden reversals in capital flows (such as those during summer of 2013), we cannot only ascribe such shifts to economic fundamentals. A major explanatory factor is a concern among investors about the direction of US monetary policy. The international economy relies overwhelmingly on the Dollar to manage international liquidity, trade, and investment. In 2013, the gross international investment position of the United States was twenty times bigger than Brazil's, fifty-one times bigger than India's and seventy-four times bigger than South Africa's (Mandeng 2013). Any movement into and out of US assets is sizeable relative to others and may translate into sharp asset price and exchange rate movements.

To conclude:
The relationship between the Dollar and the international importance of US assets implies that spillovers of US monetary policy are singularly influential. IMF resources are large enough to fend off only certain possible currency attacks and there are no international reserves sufficient enough to sustain foreign exchange interventions for long. At the same time, despite some improvements, not enough use is made of existing central bank reserves or multilateral cooperation such as central bank swap arrangements to signal forcefully that critical exchange market liquidity will be provided. In any event, the Global Financial Crisis has clearly revealed new dangerous feedback loops between savings, monetary policy, investment strategies, exchange rates, asset allocation, and international capital flows.

Case Study 6.1. How to spot central bank policy inconsistency with subsequent global risk?

Central bank activity and the relationship to country stability.

Since the Global Financial Crisis, the role of central banks in managing systemic risk has become predominant to such an extent that their mandates now incorporate financial stability objectives (statutory statements or extra-statutory guidance). This broader scope acknowledges that monetary or exchange rates objectives cannot be analyzed in isolation of their consequences in terms of financial stability.

The organization of a central bank defines its degree of independence from political authorities to set objectives and to define and implement policy. A central bank can be "operationally independent," "target independent," or a combination. Target independent means the central bank defines how inflation is computed, sets the target inflation level, and determines the horizon over which the target is to be achieved.

The Mexican and Chilean central banks, for instance, have been granted full independence whereas Brazil's central bank is still subordinated to the government despite some administrative autonomy and the promises of politicians of more independence in the near future.

Many studies demonstrate that central bank independence and low inflation are strongly linked (De Long and Summers 1992; Wynne 1993).

The degree of responsibility of a central bank is another feature that should be assessed by a country analyst. Does the central bank own financial instruments commensurate with all its objectives? Is the chairman required to justify his or her actions to a legislative branch or another body?

Another feature to examine is the transparency of the central bank's actions, as reflected in statement, meeting minutes, balance sheet disclosure, and regular speeches by the bank chairperson. Bank balance sheets are particularly important. As observed by Bindseil et al. (2004): "whenever a central bank transacts with the rest of the world, that is when it issues currency, conducts foreign exchange operations, invests its own funds, engages in emergency liquidity assistance, and, last but not least conducts monetary policy operations, all of these operations affect its balance sheet." (See Case Study 6.2. "Central Bank Balance Sheets.")

Confidence and "nudge theory," cornerstones to keep stability and to reduce Country Risk

Any breakdown of trust toward a central bank has had global economic consequences. It is crucial for a central bank to maintain its credibility. One major role of a central bank is to pursue a "forward guidance" policy, a trusted target that economic agents can monitor. A central bank must be in a position to provide a source of stability to the economy. To do that, different approaches may be used. One is to carefully examine the public statements from the bank's leader. Wim Duisenberg (the first governor of the European Central Bank) and Alan Greenspan (the longest-serving Federal Reserve head) were famous for the so-called "constructive ambiguity" of their remarks: "If I seem unduly clear to you, you must have misunderstood what I said." Consider another well-known example: "I know you think you understand what you thought I said but I'm not sure you realize that what you heard is not what I meant." Richard Thaler, the University of Chicago professor and winner of the 2017 Nobel Prize in Economics, has done research on so-called "Nudge Theory," which argues that indirect suggestion may have more impact on decision making than direct instructions. Certainly, such ideas have been put in practice carefully by central bankers.

Another way that central banks communicate with the marketplace is through their actions, as previously noted by Bindseil et al. (2004). Central bank market interventions in the foreign exchange market (in case of a "managed floating" exchange rate regime) are often said to be "open mouth open market" operations. Discrete interventions (so-called "shadow intervention") can also send a message, although one of a different kind.

Beyond these "rhetorical aspects," a key driver of central bank trust is the degree of coordination and cooperation that one central bank can have with other central banks. One common example of such a mutual relationship is for central banks to enter into bilateral derivatives transactions of various kinds, including currency swap transactions. These transactions, which may involve exchanges of currency, incur counterparty risk in that the other central bank may, depending on the type of transaction, have an obligation to make a currency payment at the maturity of the contract. The willingness of banks to assume counterparty risk is a meaningful expression of trust between them. It is a commonly held belief that the absence of cooperation between central banks is actually what allowed Gorge Soros to successfully short the British pound in 1992, benefiting from the crash (so-called "Black Wednesday"). Indeed, other EU central banks refused to cooperate with the Bank of England after their refusal to adhere to the Maastricht treaty and Euro currency.

If confidence in a central bank is crucial, excessive trust can also be a source of concern. The so-called "paradox of credibility" refers to the new dilemma posed to central bankers in their effort to conciliate monetary policy and banking regulation under inflation targeting regimes. When a central bank is "too successful" in reaching its inflation target, it may push investors to increase their risk-taking since their risk perception globally reduce. Too little volatility in prices (such as during the "great moderation" before 2007 in the United States), can paradoxically lead to future financial instability.

"Modern central banking" objectives: chickens and eggs? How is financial stability addressed?

Historically, central bank policies have been understood more in terms of their functions than their objectives. The objectives associated with the financial stability are typically much less well specified than the monetary policy objective.

Most central banks seek to promote price stability as a major objective. A number of jurisdictions, however, do not necessarily share this emphasis, including China, Hong Kong SAR, Indonesia, Russia, and South Africa. It is not always clear what is the "legally dominant objective." In Hong Kong SAR, for example, the primary objective is maintaining the exchange value of the currency (Archer 2009).

Central banks often have conflicting objectives. For example, the dual objective of domestic price stability and exchange rate stability can call for interest rate adjustments in opposite directions.

In addition to the previous "conventional objectives," many central banks operate under the presumption that they have responsibility for financial stability. That objective is crucial to reduce Country Risk.

In China, the People's Bank indicates that it "shall prevent and mitigate financial risks, and maintain financial stability." The language implies a more conditional degree of responsibility for outcomes, with the central bank being charged with promoting a safe, stable, and sound financial system. Examples include the central banks of Bermuda, Georgia, Hungary, Iceland, Mexico, Nigeria, Singapore, Slovenia, Turkey, and Zimbabwe (Archer 2009).

Apart from the "lender of last resort" actions, there have been to date no policy instruments that are uniquely suited to the task of safeguarding financial stability. More indirect supervision involves licensing, supervision, and formal or informal advisory role for financial stability (Archer 2009).

It is generally thought that central banks in emerging market economies tend to be allocated a wider range of roles than central banks in industrialized economies, including because they are a source of expertise for "immature financial systems" (Archer 2009). The question that arises is how many objectives assigned to a central bank is too much? To which extent a central bank accurately participates in financial stability and country risk reduction?

Case Study 6.2. "to go further": Central Bank Balance Sheets

The Global Financial Crisis clearly renewed the interest in central bank balance sheet analysis. Yet, if this is still largely underappreciated by many analysts. A first difficulty may be due to the time lag before receiving the balance sheet. The most common place for a central bank to publish its balance sheet is in its annual report. However, such reports by their very nature appear only on an annual basis and often with a significant lag. Hopefully, main central banks also publish their balance sheets on their websites at a higher frequency (Table 6.6).

A second difficulty is that all central bank balance sheets are not formulated the same way. Each may have different subcategories. Nevertheless, the main features can be easily understood. In many ways, the legal structure and the accounting principles are similar to a private sector entity. Balance sheets use a double-entry bookkeeping: each transaction enters the balance sheet twice. A purchase of any asset by the central bank will be paid for with currency or a check written from the central bank, both of which are denominated in domestic currency, and both of which increase the supply of money in circulation. The transaction leads to an equal increase in assets and liabilities.

A central bank stylised balance sheet can be represented in Table 6.7.

Central bank income and "net worth"

Central bank incomes are ultimately the difference between what is due on liabilities and what is earned on assets. While central banks aim to pursue policies that create socially optimal outcomes rather than maximizing their own profits, losses can impact their ability to operate in an efficient and independent manner.

Table 6.6 Publication of G20 central banks' balance sheets (Rule 2015)

Country	Frequency	Country	Frequency
Argentina	Weekly	Italy	Monthly
Australia	Weekly	Japan	Ten days
Brazil	Monthly	Mexico	Weekly
Canada	Weekly	Russia	Monthly
China	Monthly	Saudi Arabia	Monthly
European Union	Weekly	South Africa	Monthly
France	Monthly	South Korea	Monthly
Germany	Monthly	Turkey	Weekly
India	Weekly	United Kingdom	Weekly
Indonesia	Annual	United States	Weekly

Table 6.7 Hypothetical central bank balance sheet (assets/liabilities) (Barker et al. 2017)

Other assets	Equity
Lending collaterals (Repurchase agreements, etc.)	Other liabilities Central Bank Digital Currency? (projective)
Gold	Deposits from government
Other domestic reserves (government bonds)	Deposits from banks
Foreign reserves	Banknotes

Asset = liability + Net worth (equity capital)

Seigniorage is a source of income since it refers to the difference between the income earned from money's face value and the cost of producing it.

The cost of producing banknotes is relatively small compared to its face value but higher than a simple credit book entry on reserve accounts. Consequently, the amount of seigniorage income depends on the relative proportion of banknotes and reserves on the liabilities side. But the kind of operations a central bank is leading also heavily impacts its income. When a central bank wishes to counter an appreciation by trading foreign assets against domestic assets, it may support a cost (opportunity cost) if foreign assets bear lower interest rates than domestic ones.

Suppose the capital (equity) position worsens?

Studies such as Stella (2010) and Dziobek and Dalton (2005) have found at least a correlation between central bank losses and poor policy outcomes such as high inflation. Nevertheless, there is no restriction impeding a central bank to operate even with negative equity. (This was the case for many years with the central banks of Chile, the Czech Republic, and Israel.)

The central bank economic objectives will largely impact the structure and evolution of its balance sheet. This is the so-called "asset-driven" balance sheet evolution. For example, under inflation targeting, assuming the central bank allows the exchange rate to float freely and there is no monetization of government debt, then the central bank balance sheet will be characterized by monetary operations designed to control the short-term interest rate. If the central bank is successful in achieving low and stable inflation there should be little volatility in the balance sheet and the balance sheet should grow in line with the demand for central bank liabilities (money demand).

On the other hand, if the central bank is pursuing an exchange rate target, then the central bank may build up its holdings of foreign assets either to facilitate intervention or to counter a potential depreciation ("asset-driven" operations). The resulting increase in foreign assets can outstrip the natural demand for central bank liabilities for transactional purposes. In such cases, the liabilities of the central bank are characterized by free commercial bank reserves (in excess of those needed to fulfill reserve requirements).

More generally, it is widely accepted that there are conflicts between public policy objectives and the "financial profitability" of a central bank. For instance, maintaining price stability can reduce seigniorage income. Buying fixed-income assets during deflationary episodes when interest rates are very low may mean capital/value losses if the central bank succeeds to stimulate prices.

What matters is not the quantity of money issued but its quality. Hence, what matters is the quality of the collateral that the central bank is holding in connection with the money it is issuing. Each time the central bank buys an asset, be it domestic or foreign, it pays for it with domestic money, increasing the money available in the financial system (M_0). By contrast, each time the central bank is selling an asset, the buyer pays for it with domestic money that is extracted from the financial system (hence reducing the money supply).

The "monetary base" M_0 (sometimes called "Central Money") represents the commercial bank reserve account. This is the money physically held in the bank's vault and money circulating in the hands of the public (individuals and economic agents). That is the "most liquid" part of the money that can be immediately used. It also directly represents the liability side of the central bank balance sheet.

Broader money aggregates such as M_1, M_2, M_3 also give additional information for the analyst. They go "decrescendo" in terms of liquidity (since they include many saving products not always immediately liquid, such as saving deposits, time deposits or some short-run debt securities (certificates, repo agreements...). M_1, M_2, and M_3 represent the "monetary mass" (money supply) circulating in the economy.

On average, we estimate that coins and banknotes in circulation represent only 15% of M_1. To achieve their "final objective" of price stability, some central banks use to track M_1, M_2, or M_3 as "intermediary objectives."

M_2 is the monetary aggregate the most widely used as far as inflation is concerned since, in addition to cash, it includes liquid deposits. Although M_2 does not offer much insight into future spending growth, it is a key signal of inflation when it increases faster than the economic output.

M_3 and M_4 (including some treasury notes and commercial papers) are also interesting to track in order to spot any change in the saving support habits.

The exact breakdown of the different monetary aggregates differs between countries. Nevertheless, any global investor can follow those monetary aggregates on Bloomberg or Reuters. M_0 is maybe the most important since it proxies a central bank's balance sheet size (Table 6.8).

The Institute of International Finance (IIF) also provides an overview of the "monetary bases" of countries. Nevertheless, what matters most is not the size of the balance sheet but its composition.

Central banks do not lend to commercial banks in an unsecured way. The quality of the collateral is important. Collateral choice can have a significant impact on both the functioning of the central bank and the wider economy. It also affects the income and risk exposure of a central bank. For the economy, collateral choices have a portfolio impact and a liquidity impact.

Collateral choice also impacts the central bank's net worth. Like private institutions, equity (capital position) can be seen as a "buffer" to absorb losses. That capital "buffer" is linked to the "net worth" calculated as the difference between total assets and total liabilities. If the net worth becomes negative, the capital account position deteriorates.

Unlike private financial institutions, central banks are not subject to capital requirements depending on the size and riskiness of their assets and operations. Little regulation exists for central banks despite the effort of the Bank for International Settlements ("the bank for central banks") to establish international standards.

Table 6.8 Growth in the US, UK, and EU central banks' balance sheets (Rule 2015) (*Source* Bank of England, ECB and US Federal Reserve)

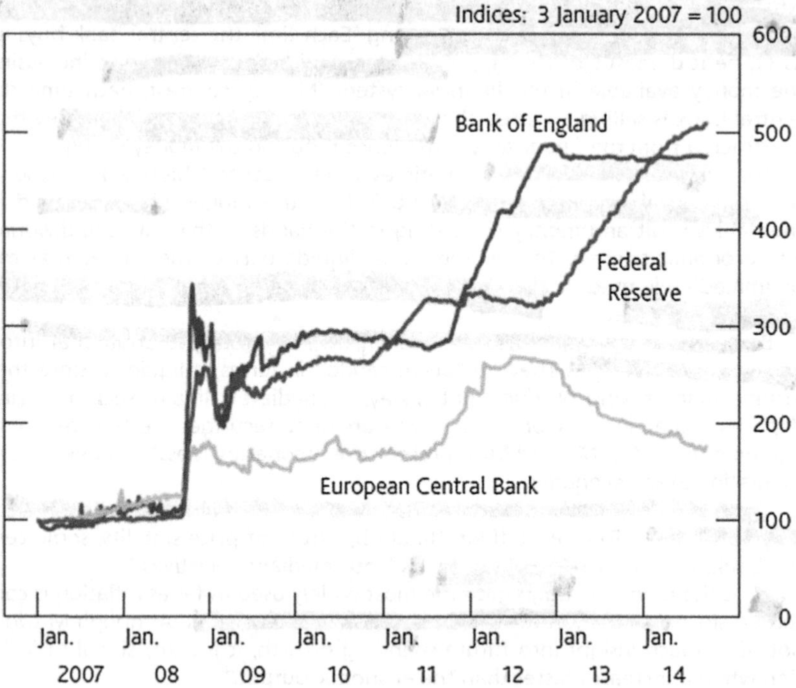

If a central bank wishes to raise additional funds without issuing money, it cannot rely on retained earnings like for another private institution. As central banks are owned by the government, any capital increase has fiscal implications and transfer implications if it comes to a single currency area. (This is discussed further in the next chapter.)

Along with the composition of the assets and their quality, the evolution of those components is the most meaningful. The evolution of a balance sheet may be "asset or liability driven" with fully different interpretation and impact on a country stability.

Liability drivers for balance sheet growth

A liability-driven central bank balance sheet grows through time as demand for central bank liabilities increases. As discussed above, such growth reflects an increase in nominal GDP (more trades, more transactions in the economy, more money demand). The central bank, to ensure payments are made and operational targets are met, must respond by supplying the required reserves through operations. Therefore, a liability-driven central bank balance sheet will be characterized by a majority of central bank operations on the asset side of the balance sheet. Such a situation is commonly referred to as a "shortage of liquidity" and lending operations.

A central bank can "soften" the liquidity constraint by decreasing the commercial bank's compulsory reserves. Those reserves have a compulsory and free part. For the first part, the reserve requirements are the minimum compulsory funds that a bank must have on hand each night. If the bank doesn't have enough on hand to meet its reserve, it borrows from other banks or borrows from the central bank (discount window in the United States or marginal lending facilities in the EU). The commercial bank's reserve account at the central bank must be balanced either at all time, at a specific point in time or on average over a period.

In the Eurozone, the reserve requirements are remunerated and have been decreased down to 1%. By contrast, the free reserve (deposit facilities) has a negative interest rate to discourage banks to keep an excess of savings instead of leading them to other banks or to the economy.

Those reserves are supposed to constrain the money multiplier impacting on the monetary mass (M_1/M_2/M_3). Commercial banks ultimately lend to the economy if it is profitable for them to do so, considering that market interest rates are just one element of the cost of funding/lending.

The traditional view is that forcing commercial banks to hold reserves that pay a return below the prevailing market rate creates a deadweight loss on commercial banks lending. To compensate, commercial banks will either raise lending rates or lower deposit rates (discouraging deposits and hence increasing bank funding costs).

In addition to maintaining balances for commercial banks, in many countries, the central bank may also act as banker for the government. Where government deposits funds at the central bank these appear as liabilities. There are similar to the reserve account but can be remunerated differently.

Asset drivers for balance sheet growth

An asset-driven balance will grow as a result of policy decisions made regarding the asset side of the balance sheet. Those operations may potentially lead to an increase in money supply that outstrips the demand for central bank liabilities. As a consequence, the liabilities of the central bank are then often characterized by the presence of excess free reserves. The two most common causes of a surplus of liquidity are growth in foreign assets and lending to the government (including monetization of public debt).

When there is a shortage of liquidity, commercial banks are forced to borrow from the central bank, potentially at penalty rates. By contrast, when there is a surplus of liquidity, the central bank, therefore, may be in a weaker position to dictate the terms on which it transacts with the market. Consequently, the central bank also has less control over the first step of the monetary transmission mechanism. The situation could turn out to be tricky for the country.

Last but not least, a central bank may also have some "off-balance sheet" items that worth being monitored.

Most central banks provide their balance sheet over a period of two years. For the Federal Reserve, the balance sheet breakdown and evolution is provided in Table 6.9.

Below are some interesting highlights:

- [1]The US Treasury securities and federal agency debt are recorded at their face value. The mortgage-backed securities are guaranteed by Fannie Mae and Freddie Mac. The current face value shown is the remaining principal balance of the securities.
- [2]The overnight securities lending are off-balance sheet transactions. There are indicated as a "memo" to indicate the portion of securities held out that have been lent through this program.
- [3]Unamortized premium or discount is the difference between the purchase price and the face value of securities that have not been amortized. Amortization is on an effective interest basis.
- [4]Lending to depository institutions includes primary, secondary and seasonal credit.
- [5]Central bank liquidity swaps are the Dollar value of the foreign currency held under these agreements valued at the exchange rate to be used when the foreign currency was acquired from the foreign central bank.
- [6]The net portfolio holdings of Maiden Lane LLC is the fair value that reflects an estimate of the price that would be received upon selling an asset if the transaction were to be conducted in an orderly market on the measurement date. They are updated quarterly. Maiden Lane Transactions refers to three limited liability companies created by the Federal Reserve Bank of New York in 2008 as a financial vehicle to facilitate transactions involving three entities: the former Bear Stearns, and the American International Group (AIG) in its lending division and former derivatives division.
- [7] Foreign currency assets are revalued daily at the current foreign currency exchange rate.
- [8]The reverse repurchase agreement is the cash value of agreements, collateralized by US debt securities or mortgage-backed securities.
- [9]Last but not least, other deposits include, for instance, deposits held at the Reserve Bank by international and multilateral organizations.

To conclude:

Balance sheets of central banks are important documents for the country risk analyst to review. They provide a picture of one country's economy from a global perspective and also provide insight into banks' operations and future policies. In the United States, the "summary of commentary on current economic conditions by Federal Reserve District"—more commonly known as the "Beige Book"—is published two weeks before each meeting of the Federal Open Market Committee (FOMC). It gathers "anecdotal information on current economic conditions in its District through reports from bank and branch directors and interviews with key business contacts, economists, market experts, and other sources." Despite its qualitative and "anecdotal" nature, it does provide forward-looking comments and is the only indicator that gives information by geographic region, rather than just by industry group or sector. Similarly, the "Tankan survey" in Japan is published by the Japanese central bank. There is much to be gained from the careful study of central bank balance sheets, reports and surveys, including central bank policies and their impact on the economy and the global stability.

Table 6.9 Federal Reserve balance sheet breakdown and evolution. Oct 2017 (Federal Reserve website)

Item	Current, October 25, 2017	Change from July 26, 2017	Change from October 26, 2016
Total assets	4461	−4	7
Selected assets			
Securities held outright	4243	1	25
US Treasury securities[1]	2466	1	2
Federal agency debt securities[1]	7	−1	−12
Mortgage-backed securities	1771	2	35
Memo: Overnight securities lending[2]	25	3	5
Memo: Net commitments to purchase mortgage-backed securities	18	−1	−21
Unamortized premiums on securities held outright[3]	162	−3	−15
Unamortized discounts on securities held outright[3]	−14	+*	1
Lending to depository institutions[4]	*	−*	+*
Central bank liquidity swaps[5]	*	−*	−4
Net portfolio holdings of Maiden Lane LLC[6]	2	+*	+*
Foreign currency denominated assets[7]	21	+*	+*
Total liabilities	4420	−5	6
Selected liabilities			
Federal Reserve notes in circulation	1537	22	105
Reverse repurchase agreements[8]	348	4	−37
Foreign official and international accounts[8]	236	−5	−7
Others[8]	112	9	−30
Term deposits held by depository institutions	14	14	−34

(continued)

Table 6.9 (continued)

Item	Current, October 25, 2017	Change from July 26, 2017	Change from October 26, 2016
Other deposits held by depository institutions	2242	−52	177
US Treasury, General Account	185	2	−235
Other deposits[9]	83	5	30
Total capital	41	+*	1

Arabic numbers appear superscript in this table refers in the Page 202 under the heading "Below are some interesting highlights"

References

Ahmed, Shaghil, and Andrei Zlate. 2014. "Capital Flows to Emerging Market Economies: A Brave New World?" *Journal of International Money and Finance* 48 (PB): 221–248.

Archer, David. 2009. "Chapter 2, Roles and Objectives of Modern Central Banks, the Governance of Central Banks: A Report from the Central Bank Governance Group, Bank for International Settlements." https://www.bis.org/publ/othp04_2.pdf.

Baele, Lieven, Geert Bekaert, Koen Inghelbrecht, and Min Wei. 2014. "Flights to Safety." Finance and Economics Discussion Series, 2014–46. Board of Governors of the Federal Reserve System.

Barker, James, David Bholat, and Ryland Thomas. 2017. "Central Banks Balance Sheets: Past, Present, and Future." Bank of England, July 3.

Béranger, Florence, Gabriel Galati, Kostas Tsatsaronis, and Karsten von Kleist. 1999. "The Yen Carry-Trade and Recent Foreign Exchange Market Volatility." BIS Quarterly Review, International Banking and Financial Markets Developments, Bank for International Settlements, March: 33–37. https://www.bis.org/publ/r_qt9902.pdf.

Bindseil, Ulrich, Andres Manzanares, and Benedict Weller. 2004. "The Role of Central Bank Capital Revisited." European Central Bank Working Paper No. 392.

Broner, Fernando, Tatiana Didier, Aitor Erce, and Sergio Schmukler. 2013. "Gross Capital Flows: Dynamics and Crises." *Journal of Monetary Economics* 60 (1): 113–133.

Brunnermeier, Markus K., Stefan Nagel, and Lasse H. Pedersen. 2009. "Carry Trades and Currency Crashes." NBER WP14473.

Cerutti, Eugenio, Stijn Claessens, and Andrew K. Rose. 2017. "How Important Is the Global Financial Cycle? Evidence from Capital Flows." IMF Working Paper WP 17/193, International Monetary Fund.

De Long, Bradford, and Lawrence H. Summers. 1992. "Macroeconomic Policy and Long-Run Growth." A Talk Delivered at Policies for Long-Term Growth, A Symposium Sponsored by Federal Reserve Bank of Kansas City, Jackson Hole, Wyoming, August 27–29.

Dziobek, Claudia H., and John W. Dalton. 2005. "Central Bank Losses and Experiences in Selected Countries." IMF Working Paper WP/05/ 72, International Monetary Fund.

Eggertsson, Gauti B. 2017. "Macroeconomic Policy in a Liquidity Trap," page 25. NBER, March 17 (1).

Fischer, Stanley. 1998. "The Asian Crisis: A View from the IMF." Address, Washington, DC, Midwinter Conference of the Bankers' Association for Foreign Trade, January 22.

Gagnon, Joseph E., and Alain P. Chaboud. 2007. "What Can the Data Tell Us about Carry-Trades in Japanese Yen?" International Finance Discussion Paper 899, Board of Governors of the Federal Reserve System, July.

Galati, Gabriele, Alexandra Heath, and Patrick McGuire. 2007. "Evidence of Carry-Trade Activity." BIS Quarterly Review, September.

Hayward, Rob, and Jens Holscher. 2016. "Carry Trade, Sudden Stops, and Instability in Emerging Markets." University of Brighton Business School.

Houng, Lee, Murtaza Syed, and Liu Xueyan. 2012. "Is China Over-Investing and Does it Matter?" IMF Working Paper WP/12/277, International Monetary Fund.

Jurek, Jakub, W. 2007. "Crash-Neutral Currency Carry Trades." Princeton University Bendheim Center for Finance.

Kowalski, Chuck. 2017. "How the Dollar Impacts Commodity Prices." *Thebalance.com*, May 15.

Mandeng, Ousmène. 2013. "Dollar-Based System is Inherently Unstable." *Bamboo Innovator.com*, October 2.

Maziad, Samar, Pascal Farahmand, Shengzu Wang, Stephanie Segal, and Faisal Ahmed. 2011. "Internationalization of Emerging Market Currencies: A Balance Between Risks and Rewards." IMF Staff Discussion Note SDN/ 11/17. International Monetary Fund, October 19.

Mcguire, Patrick, and Christian Upper. 2007. "Detecting FX Carry Trades." BIS Quarterly Review, March. https://www.bis.org/publ/qtrpdf/r_qt0703.pdf.

Mishra, Prachi, Kenji Moriyama, Papa N'Diaye, and Lam Nguyen. 2014. "Impact of Fed Tapering Announcements on Emerging Markets." IMF Working Paper WP/14/109, International Monetary Fund, June 1994.

Rule, Garreth. 2015. "Understanding the Central Bank Balance Sheet." Bank of England.

Schwab, Klaus. 2015. *The Global Competitiveness Report 2015–2016*, edited by Klaus Schwab. Cologny: World Economic Forum.

Stanyer, Peter. 2014. *The Economist Guide to Investment Strategy: How to Understand Markets, Risk, Rewards, and Behavior*, 3rd ed. London: The Economist.

Stella, Peter. 2010. "Minimising Monetary Policy." BIS Working Papers No. 330, Bank of International Settlements, November.

World Economic Outlook (WEO) Report. 2013. "Transitions and Tensions." International Monetary Fund, October.

Wynne, Mark, A. 1993. "Price Stability and Economic Growth." Southwest Money, Federal Reserve Bank of Dallas, May–June.
Yamarone, Richard. 2016. *The Economic Indicator Handbook: How to Evaluate Economic Trends to Maximize Profits and Minimize Losses.* Hoboken, NJ: Wiley.

7

Fragility and Vulnerability of Integrated Areas

7.1 Pegged Exchange Rates Introduce New Sources of Vulnerability

7.1.1 Many Exchange Rate Regimes Coexist

In its document named "Annual Report on Exchange Arrangements and Exchange Restriction" (AREAER) the IMF categorizes and analyses nothing less than ten different exchange rate regimes (Table 7.1).

"Floating exchange rates" are a minority practice in the current international monetary system. In fact, most currencies are "fixed" or "pegged" to another currency exchange rate (also known as the "target currency"). This is due to a complex interplay of considerations relating to trade, economic goals, historical practice, nationalism, public governance, and political ideology. To address these issues, countries support their currencies by intervening in foreign exchange markets. They do this primarily through their central banks.

In the case of a "purely floating" flexible regime, central banks generally do not intervene in foreign exchange markets, but instead generally use domestic money markets to implement domestic monetary policy (although they have used other asset markets in unusual circumstances).

A frequently adopted intermediate position is what we call a "managed floating" exchange rate regime, where central banks buy and sell assets from time to time, mainly in periods of volatility.

M. H. Bouchet et al., *Managing Country Risk in an Age of Globalization*,
https://doi.org/10.1007/978-3-319-89752-3_7

Table 7.1 Classification of exchange rate arrangements

Type	Categories				
Hard pegs	Exchange arrangement with no separate legal tender	Currency board arrangement			
Soft pegs	Conversional pegged arrangement	Pegged exchange rate within horizontal bands	Stabilized arrangement	Crawling peg	Crawl-like arrangement
Floating regimes (market-determined rates)	Floating	Free floating			
Residual	Other managed arrangements				

Source IMF 2016, Annual Report on Exchange Arrangements and Exchange Restrictions

7.1.2 Exchange Rate Operations Introduce Sources of Vulnerability

Exchange rate interventions may, however, contribute to new sources of vulnerability, generating contamination and spillover effects that spread from one country to another and from one region to another. The recent history of financial markets has provided us with numerous examples: the crises with regard to European exchange mechanism between 1992 and 1993; the Mexican crisis in 1994–1995; the Asian crisis triggered by the Bath crash in 1997, followed by the Russian crisis in summer 1998 with the collapse of the famous "LTCM" hedge fund, despite the fact that the fund's professionals included experienced traders and two Nobel Prizewinning economists, Myron Scholes and Robert Merton. Finally, the crisis moved overseas to Brazil in November 1998 and January 1999 spreading in 2001 to Turkey and Argentina. The "LTCM" failure and the Russian crisis also remind us that crises can occur even if the International Monetary Funds steps in—it provided funding of USD 22.6 billion to Russia. Despite this substantial financial support, the IMF was not being able to restore the confidence of investors and to avoid default.

To understand the challenges that can occur under rigid exchange rate regimes, we must first explain how central banks intervene in foreign exchange markets.

Central banks trade their own currencies, foreign government bonds, and other currencies that may serve as good substitutes in stable periods. This trading in both foreign currency deposits and foreign government bonds influences the exchange rate and affects the domestic money market and interest rates.

A country willing to counter the depreciation of its currency (e.g., to avoid further capital flight) will need to sell foreign assets to attempt to decrease the desirability of the foreign currency and enhance the value of its own currency (known as a "direct effect"). When a country sells foreign assets, another outcome can result (known as an "indirect effect"). This sale of foreign assets, usually executed by the central bank, will be paid for with currency or a transfer of funds to the central bank, both of which are denominated in domestic currency. The central bank maintains the amount in its vault or debits the deposit account of the commercial bank acquiring the asset. In all cases, this interplay reduces the money supply in the domestic money market and puts pressure on domestic interest rates to increase. It also pushes up the exchange rate, since higher interest rates attract more foreign funds.

This explains why central banks sell foreign assets and do not purchase domestic ones. Any purchase of assets would have a contradictory effect since a purchase is paid for with domestic currency (the only one the central bank is able to print or issue). The adverse effect would be an increase in the money supply and a drop in domestic interest rates, thus reducing the attractiveness of the currency to external investors (opposite effect to the initial objective of countering a depreciation and capital exit).

A country can fight against currency appreciation more easily than depreciation. To fight currency appreciation, the central bank purchases assets by issuing (printing) domestic money almost without limits (although there is a risk of inflation). In contrast, efforts to halt currency depreciation will require that the central bank sells foreign assets that must be previously held in its international reserves. These reserves clearly serve the role of a buffer to fight financial instability and currency crash (capital exit).

Exchange rate interventions present two main sources of Country Risk:

- The CB fights a natural tendency toward appreciation (this is typically the case of countries with high trade surpluses, one example being China). In such cases, interventions increase the money supply and a related risk of inflation, especially since a lower exchange rate will increase the price of imports.

- The country struggles with instability and seeks to fight the natural tendency toward depreciation. In such a case, its central bank sells foreign assets, thus depleting its international reserves. One way to track the evolution in international reserves is to examine the balance of official settlements—this is an important metric for assessing Country Risk. The official settlement account is used to monitor central bank's reserve asset transactions. It keeps track of transactions involving gold, foreign exchange reserves, bank deposits, and special drawing rights (SDRs) from the IMF. Essentially, the balance of official settlements is the sum of the current account and capital/financial account for its nonreserve part. Consequently, it indicates the evolution of the reserves. A negative official settlements balance implies that the country is depleting its official international reserve assets or may be incurring debts to foreign central banks.

7.1.3 Risk of Speculative Attack

A currency "attack" may be triggered well before the central bank starts running out of international reserves. The only escape for the affected country is to devaluate soon enough to exchange more domestic currency for a unit of foreign currency. Indeed, devaluation helps the central bank avoid depleting its international reserves excessively since each unit of foreign assets sold will reduce more domestic units of devalued currency. Therefore, the money supply is reduced even more drastically with a stronger upward pressure on interest rates to counter foreign capital flights. If successful, this process of devaluation will also allow the central bank to replenish its foreign assets by buying them back though at a devalued rate, and by printing domestic currency, increasing the money supply, reducing interest rates, reducing the value of domestic products, and thus stimulating exports. In summary, a successful devaluation in theory produces a rise in a country's output and official reserves. If the initial devaluation is not done soon enough, the country runs the risk of "walking a tightrope."

7.1.4 What Happens When Domestic and Foreign Assets Become Imperfect Substitutes?

To avoid the adverse effects of exchange rate intervention on the domestic money market and interest rates, a central bank may prefer to "sterilize" its intervention using an "offsetting effect." This process consists of selling foreign bonds and buying domestic government bonds, with the aim of keeping the amount of money in circulation unchanged.

Fixing the exchange rate implies that the central bank must trade foreign and domestic assets (mainly bonds and deposits) in the foreign exchange market until domestic interest rates equal foreign exchange rates (Interest Rate Parity). In other words, fixing the exchange rate implies adjusting the domestic money market (by buying or selling assets, as the case may be) until the domestic interest rate equals the foreign interest rate, given the level of average prices and real output. But in case of distress, domestic and foreign assets become imperfect substitutes and the domestic interest rates must rise to integrate a risk premium and keep the balance.

7.1.5 Risks and Constraints of Central Bank Intervention

The mechanism described above obliges the country to abandon any autonomy in its domestic monetary policy. This is highly constraining and may conflict with domestic political objectives. In order to anticipate a currency or balance of payment crisis, the country risk analyst should consider the consistency between the country's external objectives (exchange rate target and value) and its internal objectives (price level and growth). Consider an example. Suppose that the central bank has fixed the exchange rate at E^0 but the level of output (growth) is lower than expected (stagnation), thereby lowering the demand for domestic money. We would expect this situation to exert downward pressure on interest rates and on the value of the domestic currency exchange rate. To counteract this effect, the central bank should sell foreign assets, decreasing the domestic money supply, thereby increasing it back up to the desired interest rates in the short run.

The outcome is counterintuitive. An intervention is required to maintain expected exchange rate parity and alignment with domestic economic policy. But the intervention leads to higher interest rates despite the internal economy's stagnation. If the country is tempted to follow conflicting objectives (such as keeping a fixed exchange rate that is overvalued with respect to the state of its economy), investors may launch a speculative attack resulting in greater instability in its currency. In fact, a currency crisis occurs not when the central bank has fully depleted its international reserves, but as soon as investors have launched speculative attacks (which take the form of shorting the currency). These crises are usually triggered when the exchange rate is "overvalued" and diverges too far from the estimated state and fundamentals of the economy.

7.1.6 What Usually Causes Investors' Expectations to Change?

There are two principal factors that cause investors to change their expectations:

- The underlying health of the economy (in that shrinking demand for domestic products relative to foreign products usually reduces the value of the domestic currency).
- The ability and willingness of central banks to maintain the fixed exchange rate.

Expectations of a balance of payments crisis only worsen the crisis and hasten devaluation. In fact, expectations of devaluation can accelerate devaluation—a self-fulfilling crisis. Academic studies have integrated the role of expectations, financial markets, and the banking system, creating "second" and "third" generation of models for the balance of payments. In such theoretical frameworks, there is no single fundamental economic cause that explains a balance of payments crisis. There are rather "multiple equilibria" from different interactions between the country's government and markets. For instance, markets may consider whether (and in what way) a country is striking a balance between the long-run benefits of maintaining a fixed exchange rate and the short-run cost of high-interest rates. The outcome of this "balancing act" has the potential to create a self-fulfilling crisis as soon as investors expect a country to have no interest in maintaining its fixed exchange rate commitment in the short run. Moreover, investors consider both the country's current and long-term economic situation, including the possible macroeconomic options relating to the future debt burden. (This is referred to as an "intertemporal constraint.")

7.1.7 Inconsistent Policies

Generally, in order to prevent any risk of payments crisis, central banks do not simultaneously try to achieve the goals of low domestic interest rates (relative to foreign interest rates) and fixed exchange rates. When interest rates are too low, the currency starts depreciating and foreign reserves deplete quickly to maintain a fixed exchange rate. These constraints are summarized in what is known as the "Mundell triangle of incompatibility" (Table 7.2).

Table 7.2 Mundell "triangle of incompatibility" (Book Authors. Inspired by Beck and Prinz 2012)

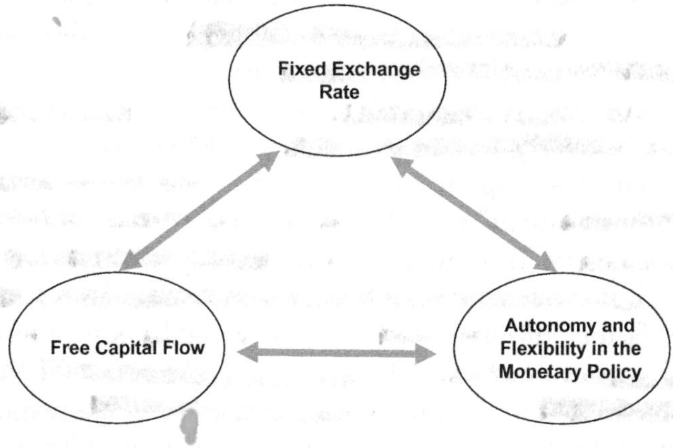

To reduce vulnerability, the country must drop at least one objective among the three on the sides of the triangle. If a country wants to have autonomy in its monetary policy, it must restrict capital movement or give up a fixed exchange rate policy (a free-floating system is necessary). If it wants to have fixed exchange rates, it must give up benefiting from foreign capital or having an independent monetary policy for domestic purposes. Monetary policy is ineffective under a fixed exchange rate regime in that domestic and foreign interest rates must remain in parallel. But a budgetary policy may be more effective than a floating exchange rate regime (in that it avoids the "crowding out effect" due to exchange appreciation following a budgetary stimulus or expansion).

7.1.8 Beyond "Conventional Wisdom"

Those elements constitute the "conventional wisdom." Yet, the assessment for the country risk manager is now more complex. Most developing countries have opted for intermediate solutions, blurring the distinction called for in the conventional thinking. What has been called the "middle ground convergence" is the introduction by many countries of "a portion" of liberalization, whereby there is "a degree" of capital control when needed over exchanges rates or the monetary policy. Introducing those "degrees" allows them to overcome the trilemma of policy incompatibilities and to maintain some flexibility. Aizenman and Ito (2012) found that: "the three dimensions of the trilemma configurations are converging towards a 'middle ground' among emerging market economies, managed exchange rate flexibility underpinned by sizable holdings of international reserves, intermediate levels of monetary independence, and controlled financial integration. Emerging market economies with more converged policy choices tended to experience smaller output volatility in the last two decades."

Although exchange rate vulnerability is caused by different factors, a key cause is inconsistent governmental policies. When investors have doubt about a central bank's capacity or willingness to maintain an exchange rate perceived as "inconsistent" with the domestic policy, they sell the assets they hold in that country. This results in a sharp change in foreign reserves triggered by a change in expectations about the future exchange rate. Among many other factors, this may occur when a central bank is purchasing large amounts of government bonds. This activity can be inferred from a central bank's balance sheet, which can provide significant insights into the goals that the central bank is attempting to achieve, be it an inflation target, an exchange rate target, or a response to a financial crisis. (Changes in a central bank's the balance sheet over time can also reveal how successful a central bank has been in achieving its goals and the sustainability of its current policy objectives. We explored these themes in the previous chapter.)

7.2 The Balance of Payment Distress Can also Be Rooted in a "Twin Crisis"

7.2.1 How to Identify a "Twin Crisis?"

A twin crisis refers to a situation in which there is both a banking and currency crisis. Problems in the banking sector typically trigger a currency crisis. The currency crisis, in turn, deepens the banking failure. Banking crises have been often preceded by periods of significant deregulation of the banking industry. Recent history suggests also that crises take place after a prolonged boom in economic activity incited by credit and capital inflows accompanied by an overvalued currency.

Very typically, these "new" crises do not spread randomly across countries, but are preceded by a "real exchange rate" appreciation and a lending boom, along with debts denominated in foreign currency. The "real exchange rate" is the most accurate indicator since it allows us to identify any nominal exchange rate misalignment (either because the country strives to peg its currency, or because market equilibrium is biased due to investors' specific strategy or mindset).

7.2.2 Which Exchange Rate Indicators May Be Informative?

The "real exchange rate" is defined as the ratio of the price level abroad over the domestic price level, where the foreign price level is converted into domestic currency units via the current nominal exchange rate. In other words, the "real exchange rate" tracks any price level difference between domestic and foreign goods and services, once converted in a single currency at the market (nominal) exchange rate. A persistent "real overvaluation" clearly indicates a loss of competitiveness since domestic prices increase faster than abroad, even considering nominal exchange rate potential adjustments.

A country can lose competitiveness either through nominal appreciation of its exchange rate or through real appreciation. If the country fixes its exchange rate, it loses competitiveness only through real appreciation since the nominal exchange rate does not adjust anymore. This lack of adjustment can give rise to a balance of payment crisis.

Unfortunately, it is difficult to measure whether an exchange rate is overvalued in nominal or real terms. Exchange rate measures are bilateral in nature. Overvaluation measures with respect to a single currency pair are not meaningful. Is a currency exchange rate high because of a strong base currency? A weak counter currency? Are they both strong or weak but in different ways? To get a better view of a change in a country's terms of trade (TOT), analysts should look at the Nominal Effective Exchange Rate (NEER) that measures the value of a currency against a weighted average of several foreign currencies. Then, the Real Effective Exchange Rate (REER) is derived by taking a country's NEER, adjusted by removing price or labor cost inflation.

Unfortunately, different deflating methods provide different results. Methods include deflating domestic prices by the average inflation of the trading partner or by the producer, wholesale or consumer price index and labor costs, among other factors.

Most of the time, price indexes are not designed the same way from country to country since they don't consider the same basket of goods or the same weighting between goods composing the referred basket. Another well-known estimate—"Purchasing Power Parity" (PPP)—relies on important assumptions such as low transaction and transportation costs or the absence of "hidden" trade barriers between countries.

An "overvalued" real exchange rate is certainly an important indicator but twin crises have occurred following specific paths, which are described below.

7.2.3 Which Are the Main Scenarios of Twin Crises?

A twin crisis usually involves three scenarios:

- A country experiences a credit boom in the private sector, growing unusually fast. This causes an appreciation of the real exchange rate due to an increase in the money supply and prices. That real appreciation leads to a loss of competitiveness and a deterioration of the balance of payments. When the depreciation occurs, often late, but sharply (due to capital flight), the banking system struggles. The failure is not caused by a bank run, but rather by a sharp deterioration in the quality of the loan portfolio of the bank. Generally, initial capital inflows from abroad are channeled into the country's economy through the domestic banking system. Since banks sometimes enjoy systemic bailout guarantees (implicit or explicit), they have incentives to adopt a higher risk exposure, which may take the form of holding of foreign-denominated currencies. This explains why higher economic growth may come at the cost of greater vulnerability to crises that are followed by long-lasting credit crunches.

  High economic growth, moreover, usually stimulates a "lending boom," which tends to inflate domestic prices. If a twin crisis occurs (i.e., both a banking and a balance of payment crises), a long-lasting credit crunch can also develop. This crunch will likely affect primarily small-and medium-sized firms or the non-tradable sector (mainly services that cannot be exported or imported) since they are more dependent on the domestic banking system (in that they have no direct access to international financial markets).
- As Kaminsky and Reinhart (1999) observed: "the opposite causal direction also sometimes occurs. Financial sector problems give rise to currency collapse." Under this scenario, central banks print additional money and banking regulators "bailout" troubled financial institutions. Accordingly, we return to the classic scenario of a currency crash prompted by excessive money creation.
- The initial shock may come from abroad. An external shock, such as an increase in foreign interest rates, coupled with a fixed parity commitment, will result in the loss of reserves. If the central bank's interventions (in the form of sales of foreign assets) are not sterilized (by the purchase of domestic bonds), then a credit crunch will occur, further increasing the likelihood of bankruptcies and financial crisis.

Kaminsky and Reinhart (1999) made an extensive study of indicators of crisis and found that most crises include multiple indicators.

Box 7.1 Toolbox of Twin Crisis Indicators

Among the tools for country risk analysts are indicators discussed in the Economics of Crisis website. These can be used to spot a potential twin crisis:

- Financial liberalization can be assessed through $M_1/M_2/M_3$ credit multiplier (of M_0), which can help determine whether commercial banks extend credit. Various ratios and measures can be used, including the ratio of domestic credit to nominal GDP, the real interest rate on deposits, and the ratio of lending-to-deposit interest rates. Last but not least, the loan-to-deposit ratio (LTD) is a commonly used statistic for assessing a bank's liquidity by dividing the bank's total loans by its total deposits.
- Other indicators of banking crisis risk include the ratio of M_2/foreign exchange reserves and the "excess real M_1 balances." This latter indicator refers to the M_1 aggregate, deflated by consumer prices less an estimated demand for money. The demand for real balances is determined by real GDP, domestic consumer price inflation, and a time trend.
- Indicators of both banking and payment crises include real exchange rates, terms of trade (the unit value of exports over the unit value of imports), real housing prices, price level, short-term capital inflows/GDP, current account balance/investment, real stock prices, real interest rate differential, and M_2/international reserves.

Of course, this is not an exhaustive list of potential indicators. In particular, political variables, such as the timing of an election, can also be linked to the timing of these crises.

7.3 Are Fully Integrated Monetary Areas More Vulnerable to a Balance of Payment Crisis?

Prior to the Eurozone debt crisis, the conventional wisdom was that fully integrated monetary areas (single currency areas) are not more vulnerable to a balance of payments crisis. The reason provided was that "payments imbalances among member nations can be financed in the short run through the financial markets, without the need for intervention by a monetary authority. Intracommunity payments become analogous to interregional payments within a single country" (Ingram 1973). That orthodoxy has been reasserted in the "One Market, One Money" Report of the European Commission (1990).

Garber (1998) disagreed. The precondition for an attack "must be skepticism that a strong currency national central bank will provide through Trans-European Automated Real-time Gross Settlement Express Transfer (TARGET) [as further discussed below] unlimited credit in Euros to the weak national central banks." He concluded that "as long as some doubt remains about the permanence of Stage III exchange rates (the Eurozone with one single currency), the existence of the currently proposed structure of the European Central Bank (ECB) and TARGET system does not create additional security against the possibility of an attack. Quite the contrary, it creates a perfect mechanism to make an explosive attack on the system."

7.3.1 Where Does the Risk Arise?

National Central Banks (NCBs) in the Eurozone have no control over the money supply and the exchange rate. This can lead to the same kind of vulnerability as that which occurs when developing countries are obliged to borrow abroad in a foreign currency. This is known in the academic literature as "original sin" since countries become vulnerable to (i) maturity mismatches as foreign capital is channeled into domestic investments which cannot easily be liquidated when capital flows reverse; and (ii) "twin" crises in balance of payments and the financial sector as current account deficits spillover into bank insolvencies, and vice versa.

From that perspective, the Euro is vulnerable to the same kind of interrelated weaknesses. The lack of control over the exchange rate and money supply directly hampers quick adjustments in current accounts. One example of

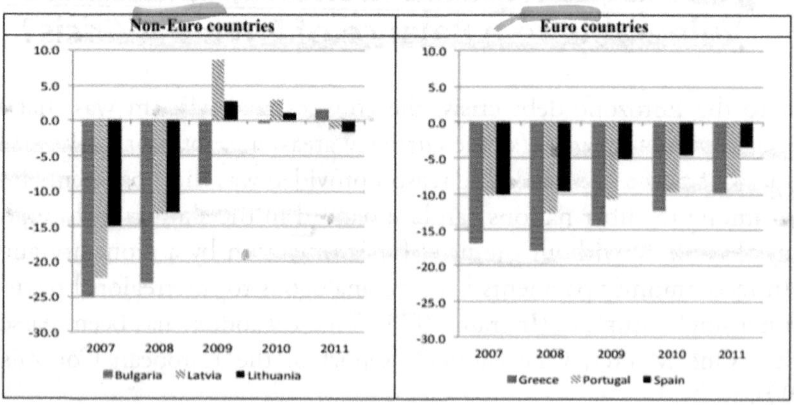

Graph 7.1 Current account adjustment/non-adjustment for Non-Euro and Euro countries (ECFIN Forecasts 2011 from Merler and Pisani-Ferry 2012a, b)

this situation is the sharp adjustment that took place after the 2009 crisis in EU non-Eurozone countries, contrasting with the "quasi-absence" of adjustments in Eurozone countries. (De Souza 2012) (Graph 7.1).

Of course, one should not look only at the current account, which is only relevant to the evolution of current account balances if they are a mirror image of net private capital flows (see Chapter 8). In a stand-alone country, this is largely the case except for foreign exchange interventions by the central bank or an International Monetary Fund programme. In such a case, CA (Current Account) = PCF (Private Capital Flows). This, however, is not the case for a monetary union in which several countries are integrated inside an open capital area. (The EU was constructed around four principles linking all member states: free circulation of capital, free circulation of goods and services, free circulation of labor, the free establishment of firms, plus the "mutual recognition" of norms and standards set by EU countries.)

7.3.2 How Do You Estimate the Risk of a Balance of Payment Crisis in Integrated Areas?

To be more comprehensive in our analysis, we now need to introduce new variables to estimate the risk of a balance of payment crisis. In a monetary area with a perfectly integrated capital area, the financial/capital account also includes "official capital flows." In the Eurozone, these are tracked through the so-called "TARGET2" system (Trans-European Automated Real-time Gross Settlement Express Transfer). TARGET2 is the Euro system's platform through which the national central banks of member states provide payment and settlement services for intra-Euro area transactions. The intra-Euro system claims arise from different types of transactions. These transactions may or may not have a "real" counterpart: they might be the result of transfers of goods that require a cross-border payment (i.e., imports) or the transfer of deposits to a different Euro area country. For example, when capital is transferred (e.g., a deposit is moved) from an Irish bank to a German bank via TARGET2, the transaction is settled between the Central Bank of Ireland and the Bundesbank, with the former incurring a liability to the latter. TARGET2 can be used for all credit transfers in Euros and it processes both interbank and customer payments. There are transactions for which TARGET2 must be used but for all the other payments—interbank and commercial payments in Euros—market participants are free to use TARGET2 or any other payment system of their choice. Banks prefer the TARGET2 system because most banks in Europe are accessible through it and payments are settled immediately and in central bank money (allowing credit institutions to transfer each other's money held in their accounts at the central bank).

With the European debt crisis, the number of claims from one EU central bank to another has increased. Investors feared the adoption of a regulation, under the impetus of Germany, to limit the size of TARGET imbalances, with a fixed cap threshold. But such an approach may underestimate both the importance of a smoothly functioning payment system in a currency union and the risk of speculative attacks that such limits would imply. The purpose of introducing a single currency is precisely to overcome the inherent weaknesses of fixed exchange regimes with implicit thresholds tracked by investors and speculators.

7.4 Dangerous Feedback Loops Between Sovereign and Private Economic Actors

Taking into account the TARGET2 system, the balance of payment breaks down as follows (without considering the balance of the capital account as well as "errors and omissions" detailed in the next chapter) (Merler and Pisani-Ferry 2012a):

$$\mathrm{CA} + \mathrm{PCF} + \mathrm{T2F} + \mathrm{PGM} + \mathrm{SMP} = 0$$

where:

- CA is the current account balance.
- PCF refers to private capital flows.
- T2F refers to Euro system financing through the TARGET2 system (change in net liability of NCBs vis-à-vis rest of Euro system).
- PGM means financing through official IMF and European assistance.
- SMP means the Securities Markets Programme for ECB purchases of government securities from residents.

The balance of payments crisis may occur in the case of a sudden constriction in financial inflows. Greece, Ireland, Italy, Portugal, and Spain experienced significant private capital inflows from 2002 to 2007, followed by sudden outflows (Merler and Pisani-Ferry 2012b). As a consequence, each country's TARGET2 net position started to diverge significantly.

7.5 Volatile Private Capital Outflows: How Do You Spot the Sudden Stop of Capital Flows in a Single Currency Area?

Of the five variables described in our previous balance of payment identity, four are recorded statistically. Only the SMP programme is unknown, making it hard to determine the exact amount of private capital outflows.

To approximate this number, we focus on the financial account balance that includes Net Foreign Direct Investment, Net Portfolio Investment, and Net Other Investment. The balance of payment data for Euro area countries is generally published monthly by central banks, which is convenient for processing/analyzing data.

A measure of private capital flows refers to the financial account net of changes in TARGET2 balances and of inflows associated with disbursements under the IMF/EU programs. Both these components are classified in balance of payments statistics under "Other investment." The ECB also publishes some details about its Securities Market Programmes (SMP). Unfortunately, there is no fully accurate way to account for the impact of the ECB's SMP.

First, the ECB only publishes an aggregate outstanding portfolio with no country breakdown of stock sales or purchases. There are estimates of the component parts, but these would not provide insight into the nationality of the agents selling the bonds to the ECB. For example, if the ECB bought Greek bonds from nonresident holders (as seems reasonable given the decline in nonresident bondholders), this would not immediately affect the Greek total financial account balance, as the bonds would only pass from one nonresident entity to another. But, at the same time, the capital inflows represented by the foreign ownership of those bonds would change from private to public.

Given the impossibility of making any assumption about activity in the SMP, the measure of private capital inflows is likely to somewhat overestimate the actual private capital inflows. Calvo et al. (2004) have developed a sophisticated method to estimate the likelihood of a sudden stop in capital flows. Bruegel, the Brussels-based think tank, also provides some estimates (as set forth in the Graph 7.2) of the breakdown of cumulative capital flows over the crisis period for Greece. It is apparent that public flows replaced private flows in 2008–11.

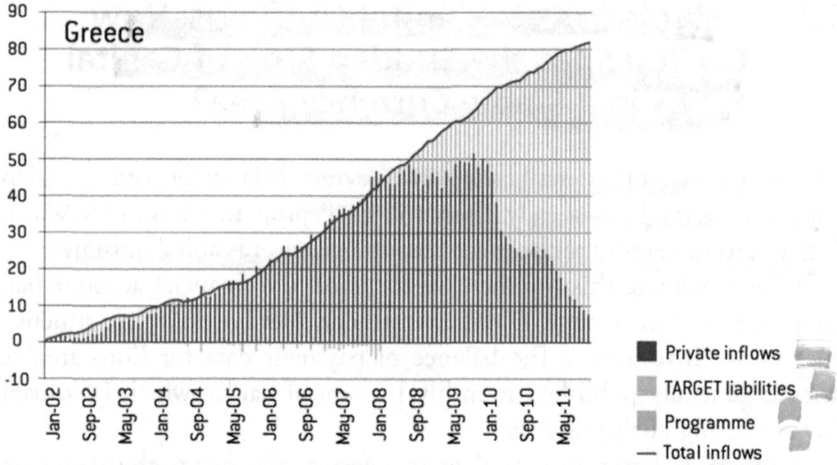

Graph 7.2 Breakdown of cumulative capital flows for Greece (Merler and Pisani-Ferry 2012b)

7.6 Does the Uneven Spread of Liquidity Within a Monetary Area Increase a Country's Risk?

It is useful to examine the TARGET2 balances of Euro area NCBs vis-à-vis the ECB that emerge from such cross-border interbank payment flow. These balances also reflect the decentralized distribution of central bank liquidity within the Euro system. Indeed, banking communities in some countries that face net payment outflows need more central bank liquidity than those in other countries where commercial bank money is flowing in. The differences in the distribution of central bank liquidity within the Euro system provide stability—it allows financially sound banks to cover their liquidity needs, thereby contributing to the effective transmission of the ECB's interest rate decisions to the wider Euro area economy (Table 7.3).

The conventional thinking is that there would not be a negative impact on banks from other countries as a result of TARGET2 liabilities that result from the provision of liquidity to financially distressed banks. This, again, is the prevailing conventional thinking, yet it does not appear to be the case for banks in countries where the NCB displays a positive TARGET2 balance. These banks tend to be recipients of cross-border payment flows from other countries, and there is currently no limit on the global liquidity supply.

Table 7.3 EU National Central Banks balance sheets with negative/neutral or positive TARGET2 balances (*Source* TARGET2 balances of national central banks in the Euro area. ECB Bulletin 2011)

NCB with a negative TARGET2 balance		NCB with a positive TARGET2 balance		NCB with a neutral TARGET2 balance	
Assets	Liabilities	Assets	Liabilities	Assets	Liabilities
Lending operations	Banknotes	Lending operations	Banknotes	Lending operations	Banknotes
Other (including financial assets)	CA and deposits	TARGET2 claim	CA and deposits	Other (including financial assets)	CA and deposits
	TARGET2 liability	Other (including financial assets)	Other		Other
	Other				

7.7 Monetary Area Fragility to External Shocks and the Risk of Contagion

7.7.1 Monetary Area Fragility

The *Financial Times* noted as follows: "The Eurozone was supposed to be an updated version of the classical gold standard. Countries in external deficit receive private financing from abroad. If such financing dries up, economic activity shrinks. Unemployment then drives down wages and prices, causing an "internal devaluation." However, in the Eurozone, much of this borrowing flows via banks. When the crisis comes, liquidity-starved banking sectors start to collapse. Almost all of the money in a contemporary economy consists of the liabilities of financial institutions. In the Eurozone, for example, currency in circulation is just 9% of the broad money (M_3)" (Wolf 2011).

When the ECB intervenes as the lender of last resort for distressed banks, it indirectly finances countries with external deficits. The current risk stems from the requirement that national central banks recapitalize the ECB should it became insolvent due to losses on its lending operations or assets portfolio. The statutes require national country central banks to contribute to this recapitalization in proportion to their country's relative weight in the Eurozone GDP.

In Germany's case, this would mean covering 27% of credit losses since it is the biggest Eurozone economy. If the Bundesbank does not have sufficient funds to cover these losses, it would need to be recapitalized by the German taxpayer. Nevertheless, there is no bilateral claim between National Central Banks but only toward the Euro system and the ECB. Hence, the risk is better spread.

Besides, the "one-size-fits-all" European monetary policy is only suitable when economies actually converge among countries within a currency area. If inflation rates diverged (due to different labor markets for instance) between Eurozone countries, real interest rates (nominal interest rate adjusted for inflation) would also diverge and the ECB monetary policy would be ineffective since the real interest rate is the one that impacts economic agents.

Furthermore, Kenen (1969) showed that monetary unions work smoothly when there is overlap in the industries in which the constituent economies specialize. This reduces the risk of asymmetric shock that is harder to adjust to without exchange rate autonomy. In most monetary unions, fiscal transfers play an important role in offsetting region-specific shocks. These transfers are large in the US but small in the EU. It is also harder to adjust to asymmetric demand shocks in case of wage rigidity and limited labor mobility between countries.

7.7.2 Risk of Asymmetric Shocks

We summarize here the factors decreasing the likelihood of asymmetric and adverse shock in single currency areas:

- There is a better outcome when there is more trade among countries and such countries have open trade policies. Traded good prices are set worldwide and do not depend on each country's exchange rate. For instance, a small economy is a price-taker, so the exchange rate does not affect competitiveness (wages and prices might adjust relatively quickly to a devaluation of the exchange rate).
- In a monetary area, a similar degree of centralization of wage bargaining across countries can also avoid wage and price divergence. It is known that centralizing wage bargaining gives no incentive to excessive wage claims (inflationary effects of wage increases are internalized).

All in all, the convergence of economies in a monetary area greatly reduces its vulnerability. There are different perspectives on this point. One, from the EU Commission, is more optimistic. Another, from Krugman, is more pessimistic. The optimistic view is that asymmetric shocks occur less frequently in a monetary union since integration leads to more intra-industry trade, thus converging specialization patterns. Integration also leads to more equal economic structures and fewer asymmetric shocks. The pessimistic view is that asymmetric shocks are more frequent in a monetary union since integration leads to more regional concentration of industrial activities; thus sector-specific shocks tend to become country-specific shocks. Arguably, the optimistic view is appealing in that national borders are less and less important for industrial clusters, with specialization occurring at the regional level.

Exchange rates cannot, in any case, cope with regional asymmetric shocks; accordingly, they reduce the cost of giving up exchange rate adjustments. In addition, nominal devaluations only lead to temporary real devaluations since the real exchange rate is not affected in the long-run (prices adjust and offset the nominal devaluation accordingly). This is why only structural economic reforms seem to matter in the long run. Devaluation can better be seen as a short-term support to facilitate reforms implementation. For instance, it is acknowledged that labor market reforms (liberalization) may at first have a negative impact before generating benefits in the medium/long run. Devaluation may help to soften initial adverse effects.

In addition, there are numerous advantages from a monetary area, including the elimination of financial transaction costs, higher price transparency, greater consumer choice, and stronger competition. These benefits are likely to increase with the degree of openness in that there are larger benefits from eliminating transaction costs and exchange rate risk. Similarly, costs are likely to decrease with the degree of openness in that asymmetric shock will be less frequent. Finally, the opportunity cost of devaluation increases with the degree of integration. In contrast, opportunity benefits of a single currency area increase with the degree of integration. Consequently, the country risk analyst must assess the degree of integration of the monetary area. The integration process is never linear and is often defined by the adage "one step forward and two steps back." Sometimes, the step back is a large and long one, including a country's exit from an integrated area.

Case Study 7.1 Beyond Brexit: Regional or Structural Ramifications? Managing Crisis in an Integrated Area

The outcome of the EU "Exit vote" marks the end of forty-three years of Britain's membership in the EEC (European Economic Community). This referendum has significant implications: roughly 50% of UK exports go to EU member states, and the UK accounts for roughly 15% of EU GDP (Forest 2016).

In an article in the *Financial Times* (Jenkins 2017), Paul Drechsler, president of the Confederation of British Industry, warned about the potential economic slowdown that could result from the Brexit: "40% of businesses had delayed or canceled investments due to Brexit uncertainty: Business can't wait. We need clarity right now."

The long-term risks of a more restricted access to the EU single market may force the United Kingdom to seek trade agreements with other players elsewhere, mainly by strengthening ties with emerging markets. Hence, the question: could Brexit have regional or structural ramifications?

"Estimating the impact on the economy of a vote to exit is difficult because no one knows what the alternative relationship with the EU and other countries would be" (Strauss 2016).

Different approaches have been used to measure the economic implications and opportunity cost of the UK leaving the EU (Minford 2010). The most commonly mentioned method is to evaluate the costs of membership in comparison to the benefits over the course of the trade relationship. A more global approach encompasses the UK's geopolitical plan for engaging trade with other global players, such as China.

It is clear that the BREXIT referendum has damaged the UK's relationship with its EU partners. A useful profile of UK's economic position on a global scale is expressed in the historical statistics related to UK's imports, exports, foreign direct investment (FDI), and financial instruments.

The Economic Complexity Index (ECI) measures the production capacity of large economies. It is an overall presentation of an economic system. The UK has an EC index of 1.60, which ranks it the 11th most complex country out of the 185 countries listed in the Observatory of Economic Complexity (OEC), a respected online resource for international trade data.

In 2011, the UK received more FDI than any other European country. Because the City of London has long been one of the major, if not the most important, financial capitals in Europe, it is not surprising that the UK has been used as a service export platform, giving non-European countries access to the rest of the Eurozone and the single market. Now that more trade barriers will be set up as a consequence of Brexit, the UK might very well receive fewer flows of foreign investments (unless negotiations lead to a completely new type of trade relationship).

FDI contributes to rising national productivity. Dhingra et al. (2016) note that the UK's financial services industry constitutes 45% of total FDI and represents 8% of the gross domestic product (GDP).

Banking regulation and freedom of travel will quite likely be among the highly prioritized aspects of the UK's renegotiation of trade laws with the EU, at least in the current regulatory environment. Norway, which is not an EU member state, has access to those privileges as part of the European Economic Area (EEA), but must nonetheless adhere to EU regulations. This is the kind of deal that could be put in place for Britain outside the union. A "hard Brexit" would mean that no deal is found and the UK would no longer access the single UE market.

Graph 7.3 is based on the data from the GPERC Policy Brief (Cozzi and McKinley 2016); it expresses predicted inbound capital flows to the UK as a percentage of GDP between the years 2015 and 2020 after Brexit.

We can observe that portfolio investments are predicted to decrease noticeably, due to the country and political risks associated with Brexit. This has caused geopolitical turmoil such that the very way the EU is governed has been questioned. Moreover, the unity of Ireland, Scotland, England, and Wales could now be compromised. Even if the financial status of the City of London still remains robust, the UK as a whole must find a way to keep its unity in order to preserve its political weight.

Countries like Ireland and Scotland are heavily affected by the exit. The irony for Scotland is that the main reason why voters decided to vote against

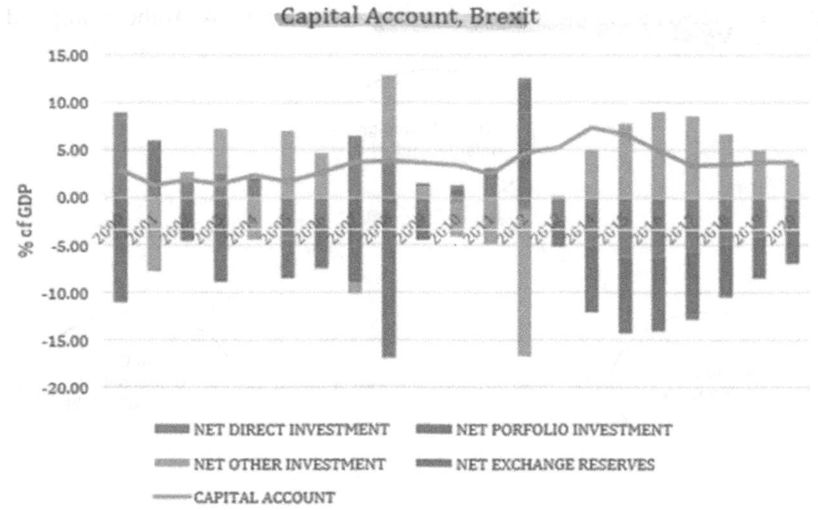

Graph 7.3 Capital inflows into the UK, Brexit scenario till 2020 (Cozzi and Mckinley 2016, GERP Policy Brief)

Scottish independence during the latest referendum was based on the promise that the UK would remain inside the EU. Another referendum for Scottish independence may return to the front stage. That independence option may be raised both for Ireland and Wales, with the aim of joining the EU as single entities, independent from the UK.

EU country exit mainly raises political and trade concerns with potential new regional ramifications. The nightmare scenario would be a Eurozone country exit. On top of previous concerns, it would bring huge financial implications. Capital markets in the Eurozone are heavily integrated (since exchange rates risk has disappeared as a result of the single currency) and an exit by one country would lead to massive financial transfers and wealth redistribution among the area countries.

The Brexit raises many new questions that will need to be examined closely by the country risk analyst.

7.8 Fragile Economic Design of Single Currency Area

7.8.1 The New Impossible Trinity

Pisani-Ferry (2012) has introduced what he calls the "new impossible trinity" or the "new trilemma." That concept is close to Mundell's "triangle of incompatibility" but is applied to single currency area such as the Eurozone (Table 7.4).

Table 7.4 Impossible Trinity for currency area (*Source* Book Authors. Inspired by Pisani-Ferry 2012)

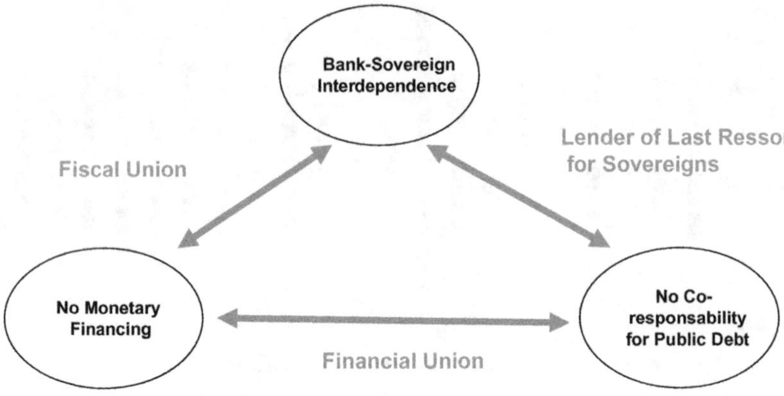

The fragility of the EU's institutional design comes from the conjoncture of the following three elements:

- No Co-Responsibility for Public Debt. Article 125 TFEU (Treaty on the Functioning of the European Union).
- Strict No-Monetary Financing. Article 123 TFUE.
- "Banks-Sovereign" Interdependence. The concept of "home bias" refers to the fact that domestic banks primarily purchase securities of their own country. This creates a two-way dependency since a country's public debt immediately impacts its domestic banking system; in a reciprocal relationship, any domestic bank distress impacts the state's funding.

In other words, any adverse shocks to sovereign solvency tend to interact negatively with adverse shocks regarding bank solvency. The central bank is constrained in its ability to provide liquidity to the sovereigns in order to stem self-fulfilling debt crises. Some remedies for this situation involve fiscal union, where joint responsibility for public debt is accepted; financial union, which would help break the bank-sovereign dependency; and a "lender of last resort" function for the ECB, which would relax provisions in the treaty covering non-monetary financing of debt.

"Strict no-monetary financing" rules cannot be touched without revising the Treaty. This excludes the third solution. "Breaking the bank-sovereign vicious circle" could be done in two different ways:

- First, "regulatory reforms" that would consist of "tightening supervision and inspection of European banks rather than placing fiscal authorities in a straightjacket" (Eichengreen and Wyplosz 1998). This objective is difficult because the financial systems of Euro area countries are mostly bank-based systems (rather than market-based systems) and banks consider a government bond as the ultimate safe asset. Diversification would merely distribute the risk more widely within the Euro area. No adjustments could make the default of a medium-sized Euro area member a minor financial event.
- Second, a "banking federation" that would move to the European level both the supervision of larger banks and the responsibility for rescuing them. But governments have consistently rejected any move that potentially implies mutualizing budgetary resources.

7.8.2 Specific Systemic Risk

There is a general consensus today among most economists that the EU system should rely much less on banks and more on financial markets. The EU and US approach to banks and capital markets diverge heavily. Overall, some 80% of corporate debt in Europe is in the form of bank lending, with just 20% coming from the corporate bond markets. This is almost the opposite of the US. It illustrates the relative differences in systemic risks between the US and the EU. Probably, the EU's banking system is providing a stronger transmission mechanism of monetary policy than in the US (i.e., a default of a systemic bank would have tremendous consequences on investment and on the real economy). Another difference is related to how banks use securitization techniques. US banks sell many of their loans into the much more developed institutional loan market, whereas in Europe most of the loans remain on bank balance sheets.

The European banking system is structured with a series of national "champion" banks that operate within their own borders, allied with a strong local network of regional banks. Hence, the EU system has a large deposit base without any clear-cut division between commercial and investments activities (the so-called universal banking model).

One positive development is an international initiative (G20) through the Financial Stability Board (FSB), based in Basel. It publishes a list of Global Systemically Important Banks (G-SIBs) and Domestic Systemically Important Banks (D-SIBs). These banks bear a high potential to create systemic risk if they fail. They are subject to additional layers of regulation. In addition to the Basel III Capital Adequacy Ratio requirements, they are subject to an FSB global standard for minimum amounts of Total Loss Absorbing Capacity ("TLAC") to be held by G-SIBs. All G-SIBs with headquarters in the US and Europe are required to submit an emergency Resolution Plan to their financial supervision authority each year. They are also subject to stringent annual stress testing by the Federal Reserve in the US and the ECB for the EU (single supervisor for each monetary area) (Table 7.5).

Despite the fact that many G-SIBs are European and the banking market is highly concentrated, there is no indication that EU countries are willing to accept a banking federation or co-responsibility for public debt—the latter case being inconsistent with principles enshrined in the treaty which created the monetary union.

Table 7.5 World G-SIBs Nov 2016. Most are EU banks

Additional capital buffer (%)	G-SIBs	Country
3.5		
2.5	Citigroup	USA
	JP Morgan Chase	USA
2.0	Bank of America	USA
	BNP Paribas	**FR (EU)**
	Deutsche Bank	**DE (EU)**
	HSBC	**UK (EU)**
1.5	**Barclays**	**UK (EU)**
	Credit Suisse	Switzerland
	Goldman Sachs	USA
	Industrial and Commercial Bank of China Limited	China
	Mitsubishi UFJ FG	Japan
	Wells Fargo	USA
1.0	Agricultural Bank of China	China
	Bank of China	China
	Bank of New York Mellon	USA
	China Construction Bank	China
	Groupe BPCE	**FR (EU)**
	Groupe Crédit Agricole	**FR (EU)**
	ING Bank	**NL (EU)**
	Mizuho FG	Japan
	Morgan Stanley	USA
	Nordea	**SE (EU)**
	Royal Bank of Scotland	**UK (EU)**
	Santander	**ES (EU)**
	Société Générale	**FR (EU)**
	Standard Chartered	**UK (EU)**
	State Street	USA
	Sumitomo Mitsui FG	Japan
	UBS	Switzerland
	Unicredit Group	**IT (EU)**

Source FSB and European Parliament

Another option that has been discussed is some form of fiscal union involving co-responsibility for public debt. One approach would be to introduce Eurobonds since indebted states could borrow new funds at better conditions given that they would be supported by different countries. Under such a plan, Eurobonds would be jointly issued in Euros by the Eurozone nations. This would decrease default risk and financing costs for indebted countries but increase financing costs for the carefully managed countries. The main criticism relates to the "moral hazard" it may generate for some countries. To overcome that pitfall, a "blue eurobond" project has been proposed: the senior "Blue tranche" of up to 60% of GDP would be pooled among participating countries and jointly guaranteed. The second part, the junior "Red tranche," would retain debt in excess of 60% of GDP as a purely national responsibility.

The following case study explores China, a country with "managed" exchange rates, market rigidities, and a highly centralized institutional design. The question arises: Could China give rise to global risks? In other words, could China be a source of Country Risk with global ramifications?

Case Study 7.2 Country Risk Analysis of China: A Genuine Growth Model

There are various challenges associated with the analysis of China's Country Risk. China has never experienced a major crisis. Even more, its large current account surplus demonstrates that China benefits from high saving rates, which constitute an important "buffer" to fight against both financial and monetary instability. Yet, China faces many challenges such as escaping from the middle-income trap, tackling its debt trap, maintaining under control its credit growth, a shadow banking that keeps on developing, the real estate and environmental pressures, and the existence of fraud. Those threats are all the more challenging since Chinese economic data suffer from opacity to such an extent that most analysts do not believe in official economic data, but use them anyway because there are no other alternatives. Some Chinese agencies are beginning to address this issue. For instance, the China Beige Book (CBB) is an independent agency that strives to gather data from the field. As one can read on their website:

"*Reliable data on China's economy are notoriously difficult to come by. Official Chinese government figures exist, but lack transparency and credibility, while the few private indicators that exist are far too limited in size and scope for strategic planning. We founded China Beige Book International in 2010 to help institutional investors and corporate CEOs navigate China's notoriously black box economy.*"

Nevertheless, some noticeable improvements should be mentioned. For instance, China's State Administration of Foreign Exchange (SAFE) has improved the quality of its external debt figures, more in compliance with the "Special Data Dissemination Standard" (SDDS). The coverage of financial instruments and the domestic debt held by nonresidents are now included. Importantly, intercompany lending now appears as such and not as a foreign direct investment (FDI) as it used to be. Using these new figures, the World Bank created a new historical series highlighting the difference in China's long-term debt assessment (Graph 7.4).

In addition to concerns about data, there is also a concern about the country's growth model itself. Michael Pettis has asked: "do measurements of the country's GDP even matter?" (Schiavenza 2013).

China's high growth rates during the last three decades are irrefutably a historical success. The question is how far in time and scope can that success continue. Some like Aldo and Lazzarini (2012) argue that China's hybrid form of capitalism can become a new growth model for the twenty-first century since it offers three very attractive features: less pronounced recessions, focus on long-term investing, and development of world-leading companies.

Other economists are much more pessimistic. For instance, Acemoglu and Robinson (2012) suggest that China's "extractive political institutions" are not compatible with long-run innovation and high growth. Consequently, it would stop as soon as China reaches the living standards of a middle-income country.

An analysis that best summarizes the different approaches is that of Wang (2014). Wang observed that "a political elite is able to extract surplus from the state sector and tax the private sector, but it also needs support from sufficiently many citizens to maintain the political power. "Divide-and-rule" strategy is implemented to guarantee such support: state workers receive high wages and become supporters of the elite, while wages of private workers are reduced due to the policy distortion. In the short run, the low wages in the private sector lead to rapid growth of the private firms and total output. However, long-run growth is harmed by capital market distortions favoring the state firms. The theory suggests that the economy develops along a three-stage transition: "rapid growth," "state capitalism," and two cases in the third stage: "middle-income trap" or "sustained growth," depending on whether democratization occurs endogenously."

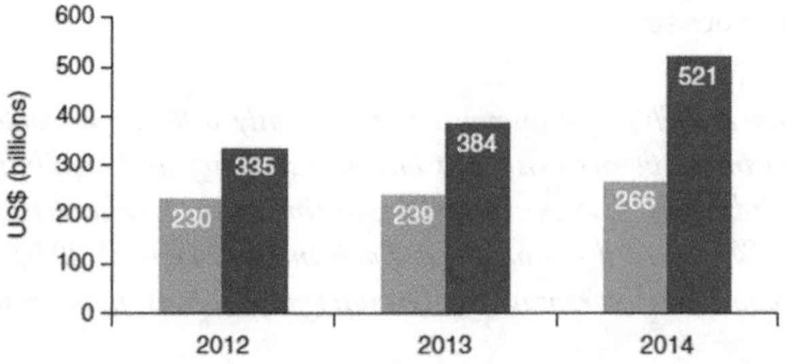

Graph 7.4 China long-term external debt (World Bank 2017, International Debt Statistic. Light gray: before SAFE revision/Dark gray: after the SAFE revision)

Is there another perspective to be considered? A more endogenous growth would imply a transformation from growth based on old drivers into a more inclusive/self-feed growth. Old drivers are mainly "exogenous" and "external" oriented, such as the import of foreign technology, export of low-end manufacturing products, and the use of "public" credit to fuel economic growth and employment. We previously considered that "old drivers" are normally time limited since a country cannot extend its market share of exports indefinitely. By contrast, "inclusive" or "endogenous" growth relies on more steady drivers that are "domestically" oriented. Domestic consumption mainly matters for inclusive growth but requires to increase wages, to keep prices low, which seems easier in a liberalized and decentralized economic system.

There is an argument that the Chinese economy is still relying mainly on manufacturing goods, real estate, and raw material ("old drivers") but not enough on services, transportation, and retails sales ("new drivers"). Most of the "old drivers" are "state-driven" such as manufacturing goods and real estate that are boosted by debt and infrastructure investment, themselves fueled by mortgage loans granted by state-owned banks and capacity investment undertaken by public companies. Of the state companies, 60% have increased their capital expenditures (much more than private companies).

Country risk analysts have to scrutinize whether the conversion to a more "inclusive growth" is likely or not to occur.

Case Study 7.3 China Risk Analysis: Unsustainable Credit Growth and Over-Indebtedness?

Anne Stepenson-Yang, co-founder and research director of J Capital, observes: "In China, the higher your level of government, the closer to heaven. The Big Four (the Postal Savings Bank is the ugly stepchild, founded as a mechanism for transferring money across regions and serving migrant populations) have all the advantages of national support. The commercial and rural banks (small size) have little autonomy. The joint stock banks (medium size) are in the interesting position of being free from direct government mandate but without the big, stable depositors that lend stability to the Big Five. Consequently, they need to take on a higher level of risk to capture funding and to extend loans…" (Keohane 2017).

Many Chinese companies have increased their leverage. (Wolf 2017) As a result, the banks (big four, medium or small size) and nonbank financial institutions (NBFIs) all face a substantial increase in their credit-to-deposit ratio. Another concern is the contribution of "shadow banking." It can be rather easily explained by the proverb "Nature hates vacuums." NBFIs fill that gap in a complex system (i) which is dominated by large state-controlled banks; (ii) subject to a variety of regulation as well as formal and informal guidance; (iii) has mandated low-interest rates on deposits; and (iv) restrictions on lending to certain industries. It is estimated that two-thirds of all lending in China by NBFIs are "bank loans in disguise." Elliott et al. (2015) from the Brookings Institute summarize the main pressures that fuel China's banking growth:

- Most NBFIs have lower capital and liquidity requirements.
- Shadow banks are not subject to bank limits on loan or deposit interest rates.
- There are caps on bank lending volumes imposed by the People's Bank of China (PBOC).

There is a limit on bank loans to deposits of 75%

- Shadow banking avoids costly PBOC reserve requirements.
- Regulators discourage lending to certain industries, creating a gap to fill.

It appears that "credit growth and old drivers" are clearly maintained to foster growth and employment. The unemployment rate is important to Chinese authorities and questions have been raised as to their reliability (consistently reported to be around 4% for the last ten years). But the choice of "short-term growth and employment," and "continued reliance on policy stimulus measures" do not allow for the rebalancing of growth and the absorption of macro-imbalances (rapid expansion of credit and slow progress in addressing corporate debt).

The IMF considers that an economy more oriented toward services could allow rising the part of labor revenues in GDP. But a redistributive budgetary policy would be necessary to lower subsequent wages inequality and to give more equal opportunities for urban and rural households. In a nutshell, it would imply to have more social transfers. This is the best option to lower the global rate of saving (mainly coming from profits and government reserves, not from households), enhancing internal domestic consumption smoothly before any potential "disruptive" adjustments.

Disruptive adjustments can be the result of, for instance, high Credit-to-GDP gap, which is the difference of the Credit-to-GDP ratio from its trend. Consequently, it reflects short-term tendencies that may not be sustainable if left unchecked in case of sudden economic distress. An "excessive" gap means that the private sector borrows at a level that is perhaps "not justified" by the current output-producing abilities of the economy. Banks may tend to experience abnormally high rates of loan defaults (NPL) that may lead to a banking crisis.

The "excessive reliance" on external growth drivers can also participate in global "over-indebtedness." When low-cost exports tend to decrease, authorities feel the need to unleash monetary and fiscal stimulus measures, causing the Chinese outstanding debt to reach almost 250% of its 2016 GDP (Graph 7.5).

From the graph, we observe that China nonfinancial debt to GDP ratio now roughly matches that of the US, the world's biggest debtor. The term "nonfinancial debt" is used to refer to the aggregate of debt owed by households, government agencies, nonprofit organizations, or any corporation that is not in the financial sector.

In China, a high part of the indebtedness is due to corporate debt and mainly state-owned companies that account for more than 50% of that debt, despite the fact that they account for only 20% of GDP. Local municipal debt is also an issue without full transparency, even if a debt-swap initiative has

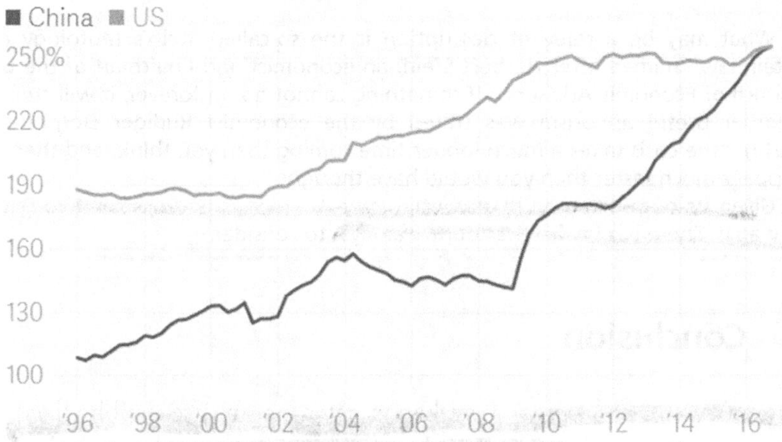

Graph 7.5 Nonfinancial debt-to-GDP ratio China vs. US (Huang 2017)

been launched a few years ago to extend the debt maturity through municipal bonds. In contrast, governmental authorities have a rather low indebtedness.

The corporate indebtedness raises various concerns. First, corporate debt likely reflects low industrial profits and poor returns on investment. The most indebted companies (with debt to equity ratio up to 120%) are those in heavy industry and building materials, which rely on real estate as market opportunities. Yet, real estate downturns are more and more frequent. The question arises whether China's foreign reserves could be large enough to fight nonperforming loans of state-owned enterprises (SOEs).

Some measure has been untaken by the authorities such as a debt-for-equity swap program. But beyond sporadic actions, China's growth is still highly dependent on fixed asset investments (infrastructures such as roads, railways, plants, and real estate) financed by state-owned banks.

There is a perception that authorities have used their control over banks to reduce the cost of capital, keeping benchmark interest rates low to boost domestic equity markets, direct spending, and reduction in the cost of debt. But when interest rates are too low, there is a risk of a liquidity trap, as had happened to Japan. More generally, economic-stimulus programs usually lose their effectiveness because of the inappropriate incentives they provide when money is costless (hazardous industrial projects, vanity infrastructure spending, etc.)

There may be some similarities between China's economic circumstances and Japan's situation thirty years ago, before the real estate and stock exchange bubble burst in Tokyo. Both economies have had bubbles in stocks and real estate (even if both were inflating at the same time in Japan, which is not the case in China); high nonfinancial corporate debt-to-GDP ratios; and most of all, a growth dynamic extremely reliant on external factors. Even if China strives to rebalance toward a more inclusive growth (for which Japan never did), the big question mark is when and will it be soon enough?

What may be a relevant description is the so-called Stein's tautology or "Stein law" named after Herbert Stein, an economist and Chairman of the US Council of Economic Advisers: "If something cannot go on forever, it will stop." Another useful aphorism was stated by the economist Rudiger Dornbusch (2012): "the crisis takes a much longer time coming than you think, and then it happens much faster than you would have thought."

Given its huge size and its potential impact, China is an important country to watch. There is a lot for the country analyst to consider.

7.9 Conclusion

Integrated areas with pegged exchange rates or an irreversibly fixed rate (single currency area) both introduce additional dependency links, with contamination channels that differ from "less constrained" economies. Consequently, country risk analysts must change their assessment process to integrate those specific weaknesses. Yet, when countries succeed to overcome some pitfalls inherent to the integrated areas, they can benefit. The next chapter will explore the balance of payment, liquidity, and solvency risk.

References

Acemoglu, Daron, and James A. Robinson. 2012. *Why Nations Fail: The Origins of Power, Prosperity, and Poverty*. New York: Crown Publishers.

Aizenman, Joshua, and Hiro Ito. 2012. "Trilemma Policy Convergence Patterns and Output Volatility." NBER Working Paper No. 17806.

Aldo, Musacchio, and Sergio G. Lazzarini. 2012. "Leviathan in Business: Varieties of State Capitalism and Their Implications for Economic Performance." Harvard Business School Working Paper No. 12-108, June.

Beck, Hanno, and Aloys Prinz. 2012. The Trilemma of a Monetary Union: Another Impossible Trinity. *Intereconomics* 47 (1): 39–43.

Calvo, Guillermo A., Alejandro Izquierdo, and Luis-Fernando Mejia. 2004. "On the Empirics of Sudden Stops: The Relevance of Balance-Sheet Effects." NBER Working Paper No. 10520.

Cozzi, Giovanni, and Terry Mckinley. 2016. "The United Kingdom's Brexit Vote Leads to a Major Economic Shock." Policy Brief 12-2016. Greenwich Political Economy Research Center.

De Souza, Eric. 2012. "European Macroeconomic Policy." Special Topics. College of Europe Lectures.

Dhingra, Swati, Gianmarco Ottaviano, Thomas Sampson, and John Van Reenen. 2016. "The Impact of Brexit on Foreign Investment in the UK." CEP Brexit Analysis No. 3. Centre for Economic Performance.

Dornbusch, Rudiger. 2012. United States Congress. Senate. Committee on the Budget. Concurrent Resolution on the Budget Fiscal Year 2013.

ECB Bulletin. 2011. TARGET2 Balances of National Central Banks in the Euro Area. *Economic and Monetary Developments*, October.

Eichengreen, Barry, and Charles Wyplosz. 1998. "Stability Pact: More Than a Minor Nuisance." *Economic Policy* 13 (26): 65–113.

Elliott, Douglas, Arthur Kroeber, and Yu Qiao. 2015. "Shadow Banking in China: A Primer." Economic Studies. The Brookings Institution.

European Commission. 1990. "One Market, One Money Report. An Evaluation of the Potential Benefits and Costs of Forming an Economic and Monetary Union." *European Economy*, No. 44, October.

European Parliament. 2017. Global Systemically Important Banks in Europe, Listed in November 16, 2016. Briefing, Economic Governance Support Unit.

Forest, Kieran. 2016. "Economic Implication of Brexit." MSc Thesis, Skema Business School.

Garber, Peter M. 1998. "Notes on the Role of TARGET in a Stage III Crisis." NBER Working Paper No. 6619.

Huang, Zheping. 2017. "260% of GDP: A Quick Look at the Debt Levels That Earned China a Rating Downgrade." *Quartz*, May 22.

IMF. 2016. "Annual Report on Exchange Arrangements and Exchange Restrictions (AREAER)." November 11.

Ingram, James, C. 1973. "The Case for European Monetary Integration." International Finance Section, Department of Economics, Princeton University, Essays in International Finance No. 98, April.

Jenkins, Patrick, 2017. "UK Businesses Want Answers on Brexit Deal." *Financial Times*, September 24.

Kaminsky, Graciela L., and Carmen M. Reinhart. 1999. "The Twin Crises: The Causes of Banking and Balance-of-Payments Problems." *The American Economic Review* 89 (3): 473–500.

Kenen, Peter. 1969. "The Theory of Optimum Currency Areas: An Eclectic View." In *Monetary Problems of the International Economy*, edited by Robert A. Mundell and Alexander K. Swoboda. Chicago: The University of Chicago Press.

Keohane, David. 2017. "Big Is Beautiful, China Banks." *Financial Times*, March 28.

Merler, Silvia, and Jean Pisani-Ferry. 2012a. "Sudden Stops in the Euro Area." *Review of Economics and Institutions* 3 (3): 1–23.

Merler, Silvia, and Jean Pisani-Ferry. 2012b. "Capital Flight in the Euro Area: From Bad to Worse." *Blog Post, Bruegel*, July 13.

Minford, Patrick. 2010. *Benefits and Costs of Forming an Economic and Monetary Union to the UK Economy*. Cardiff University, Cardiff Business School, Economics Section.

Pisani-Ferry, Jean. 2012. "The Euro Crisis and the New Impossible Trinity." Bruegel Policy Contribution.

Schiavenza, Matt. 2013. *Want to Understand How China Is Doing? Don't Look at GDP. Why the Classic Benchmark Statistic Is Unsuitable to Describing the World's Second-Largest Economy.* https://www.Theatlantic.com, October 4.

Strauss, Delphine. 2016. "CBI Chief Says Brexit Would Leave Economy Weaker 15 Years On." *Financial Times*, March 20.

Wang, Yikay. 2014. "Will China Escape the Middle-Income Trap? A Politico-Economic Theory of Growth and State Capitalism." Working Paper, University of Zurich.

Wolf, Martin. 2011. "Intolerable Choices for the Eurozone. At Stake Is Closer Union or Partial Dissolution." *Financial Times*, May 31.

Wolf, Martin. 2017. "China Faces a Tough Fight to Escape Its Debt Trap." *Financial Times*, April 11.

World Bank. 2017. "International Debt Statistics." External Debt.

8

At the Root of Country Risk: The Balance of Payments from Liquidity to Solvency Crisis

8.1 Introduction: The Challenge of Balance of Payments Data Availability

In country risk assessment, the balance of payment is not everything, but almost everything. Like an X-ray picture, it provides a clear and sometimes crude illustration of the strengths and weaknesses of countries with regard to the global economy. Countries' payments balances are the economic, financial, and even political converging points between the domestic economy and the global economic system. They give the astute country risk analyst a snapshot of a country's competitiveness, economic growth sustainability, liquidity, and solvency situation.

The crucial importance of the balance of payments in sovereign risk analysis is self-evident: Sovereign debt crisis, default payments, and exchange rate volatility are always rooted in excessive deficits and external borrowing requirements. This focus is not shared, however, by each and every investment manager, who sometimes advises clients to focus monitoring on GDP or inflation data. Thus, the American Association of Individual Investors (AAII) invite managers and risk analysts to scrutinize "ten of the most common and vital economic indicators" among which are residential construction, inflation, money supply, and S&P's 500 (American Association of Individual Investors 2016).

The risk analyst's challenge, however, is to get his or her hands on reliable and updated balance of payments data, an indispensable ingredient for risk analysis and risk forecasting. The balance of payments data are usually

M. H. Bouchet et al., *Managing Country Risk in an Age of Globalization*,
https://doi.org/10.1007/978-3-319-89752-3_8

provided by central banks of countries. In the United States, however, the balance of payments accounts are compiled by the Bureau of Economic Analysis (BEA), which belongs to the US Department of Commerce. In itself, the availability of reliable and comprehensive data is both a signal and a measure of Country Risk. A country that is unable or unwilling to provide timely data illustrates institutional weaknesses and/or bad will. This is the case of many countries, mostly in the developing world, which do not adhere to the standards of data of multilateral institutions and rating agencies. In the end of 2016, China's Director of the National Bureau of Statistics recognized that "local statistics are falsified in violation of laws and regulations," and this occurs despite harsher penalties for falsification (*Financial Times* 2016a). Underreporting of population data or overreporting of real GDP growth are mentioned most of the time. Lack of reliable data is a genuine problem for risk analysis regarding foreign debt in Cuba, the balance of payments in many African countries, reserve assets in Russia, or inflation figures in Argentina, Zimbabwe, or Venezuela. The availability of updated and reliable balance of payment data is in itself a key measure of a country's creditworthiness, institutional effectiveness, and transparency.

Regarding Zimbabwe, the protracted accumulation of payment arrears with the International Financial Institutions (IFIs) did not facilitate the gathering of reliable economic and financial data. Mounting payment arrears to official bilateral and multilateral creditors started in 2001. However, on October 20, 2016, Zimbabwe settled its long overdue financial obligations to the International Monetary Fund's (IMF) Poverty Reduction and Growth Trust program, hence paving the way to a gradual normalization of relationships with the Washington-based lender of last resort. Overdue financial obligations to the IMF usually have at least three negative consequences, namely, a declaration of noncooperation with the IMF that triggers a chain reaction with the World Bank and the Paris Club, the suspension of technical assistance, and the removal of the country from the list of eligible countries for balance of payments financing. In 2017, the reengagement process with the international community did not make much progress. In particular, the settlement of arrears with the World Bank and other multilateral institutions, as well as the resolution of arrears with Paris Club's bilateral creditors, remained pending. Consequently, the IMF's 2017 Article IV report on Zimbabwe did not include any balance of payment projections and it limited itself to prudent estimates for the previous year (International Monetary Fund 2017a). The November 2017 military take over and the ousting of President Mugabe might lead to sociopolitical liberalization, tighter control over corruption, and a resumption of relationships between the international community and this country that the IMF describes as "once among the most advanced economy in sub-Saharan Africa, that has become one of its most vulnerable" (International Monetary Fund 2017a).

Many countries in protracted arrears to the IMF, such as Iraq, Dominican Republic, Democratic Republic of Congo, Haiti, Bosnia, Central African Republic, Somalia, Sudan, Afghanistan, and Zimbabwe do not provide adequate and timely economic and financial data. But an Organization of Economic Co-operation and Development (OECD) and Eurozone member such as Greece has also illustrated opacity and misreporting of debt and current account data during the Global Financial Crisis. The IMF has taken steps to enhance member country transparency and openness, including setting voluntary standards for dissemination of economic and financial data since the mid-1990s. The idea behind this initiative is that opacity of country economic data increases rating agencies' and risk analysts' concerns, and that uncertainty translates into volatility. In short, capital markets and country risk analysts require a regular flow of reliable information. Regarding the all-important balance of payments data, the Special Data Dissemination Standards focus on four main variables, namely, External Current Account Balance, Exports and Imports of Goods and Services, Gross External Debt, and International Investment Position that measures external gross financial assets and liability positions vis-à-vis nonresidents. The quasi-overall membership of the IMF member countries participates in the framework for data improvement and for setting priorities. There are only eight IMF members remaining outside of the initiative (Equatorial Guinea, Eritrea, Lao Peoples Democratic Republic, Somalia, South Sudan, Turkmenistan, and Uzbekistan) (International Monetary Fund 2015a). In the case of Zimbabwe, the IMF requested the central bank to fully comply with the recommended reporting practices, e.g., improving timeliness from twelve months to nine months. Reliable balance of payments data, in standard international formats, can be found in the annual Article IV reports of the IMF with an in-depth analysis of external financing requirements coupled with a debt sustainability assessment.

The World Bank also publishes data on balance of payments, including current accounts since 1960, but based on the IMF Statistics Yearbook and in a less comprehensive format (World Bank 2017). In addition and contrary to IMF reports, the World Bank does not add any projections. The OECD publishes quarterly and annual balance of payments statistics with a three to six-month lag, for the thirty four member countries, with ten other large emerging market countries, including the five BRICS countries and Saudi Arabia (Organization for Economic Co-operation and Development 2017a).

Eurostat, which is the statistical agency of the EU-28 member states, also publishes balance of payments data that follow the IMF guidelines. Rating agencies such as Fitch, Moody's, and S&P also include balance of payments data in their economic analysis for clients, though in a less disaggregated format than the IMF. The Federal Reserve Bank of St. Louis (FRED) publishes balance of payments data of the United States, of course, but also often of countries or group of countries (i.e., Europe and Eurozone) (FRED 2017).

The only challenger to the IMF is the Institute of International Finance (IIF) in Washington DC. Following the eruption of the emerging country debt crisis in the summer of 1982, the confidential Ditchley Park's banking gathering led to the creation of the banking industry's own risk analysis initiative. Since then the IIF has become the global association of the financial industry, with close to 500 members from seventy countries. Its mission is to support the financial industry in the prudent management of risks; to develop sound industry practices; and to advocate for regulatory, financial, and economic policies that are in the interests of its members, hence working as the de facto syndicate of the international financial institutions. It has a broad and growing membership, including commercial and investment banks, asset managers, insurance companies, sovereign wealth funds, hedge funds, central banks, and development banks. Despite its inherent lobbying features, the IIF succeeds to provide an independent and comprehensive source of risk analysis and research with a focus on emerging markets (Institute of International Finance 2017). Regarding balance of payments analysis, the IIF's country risk economists follow approximately thirty countries and provide an in-depth coverage of inflows and outflows, as well as liquidity and solvency indicators. In addition to individual country research reports, its country risk department produces annual regional reports that provide cross-country analysis and explore topical themes and issues.

8.2 Interpreting the Balance of Payments

8.2.1 Current Account and Demand-Supply Imbalance

The balance of payments can be divided into two subaccounts, namely the current and capital accounts. The current account plays a role similar to a private company's income statement. It illustrates the country's economic performance vis-à-vis the rest of the world. A competitive country with prudent macroeconomic management will aim to balance its inflows of revenues and outflows of expenses, and it will stimulate its exports to increase its market share in those goods and services where it has a comparative advantage.

This objective requires a range of policy tools to prevent excessive absorption of domestic goods that would reduce the export potential and would end up in price increases, hence eroding external competitiveness. This is why a current account deficit is rooted in an imbalance between domestic savings and expenditures. Accordingly, it is not surprising that countries with strong imbalances between savings and spending show twin imbalances, that is, both external (current account) and internal (budget). In the aftermath of the Global Financial Crisis, the EU-28 members states have cut their budget deficits while increasing their overall current account surplus to roughly 2% of GDP in 2016–2017, with eighteen countries in surplus (mainly Germany, Netherlands, Denmark, Slovenia, Hungary, and Ireland) and ten countries in deficit (mainly UK, Romania, Finland, France, and Lithuania). One can observe that since the post-World War II (WWII) Bretton Woods agreement, a disproportionate pressure is placed on the imbalance of deficit countries that are seen "living beyond their means" whereas surplus countries are praised for their large domestic savings and competitive exports. Under the gold exchange standard, which pegged countries' currencies to the USD and the USD to gold, trade imbalances could not last long, due to the more or less automatic rebalancing mechanisms of gold transfers back and forth between importing countries (with tighter credit and shrinking money supply) and exporting countries (with larger gold holdings, hence expanding money supply). In practice, the IMF was set up to provide short-term balance of payments financing to deficit countries under the condition of tight macroeconomic adjustment policies, in short, by cutting expenses and boosting export revenues (Chart 8.1).

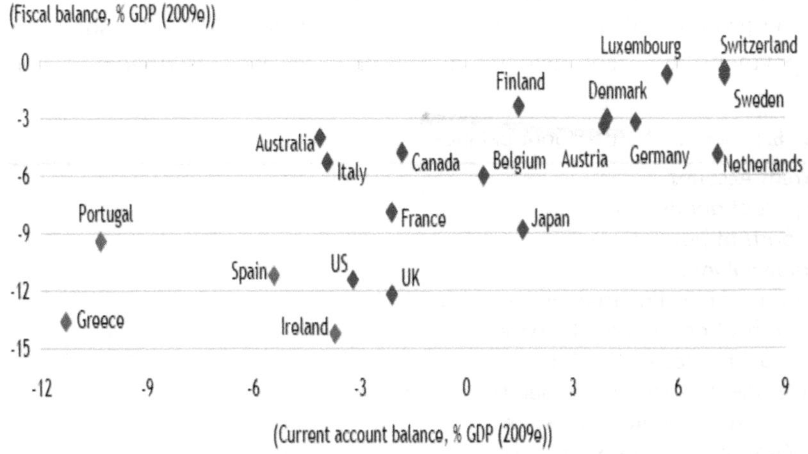

Chart 8.1 Twin imbalances in percent of country GDP (Riley and Coulton 2010) (*Source* Fitch)

The current account balance is made of three subaccounts: balance of goods, balance of services, and transfers, as shown in Table 8.1.

The various items in the current account are listed from the less liquid to the more liquid items, i.e., with regard to their relationship with the real economy. The trade balance includes goods and merchandises free on board; that is, without trade-related expenses such as shipping and insurance costs. In the United States, the balance on goods (i.e., merchandises) reached a stubborn deficit of around USD 750 billion in the 2005–2017 period, with a peak of USD 830 billion in 2006–2007, on the eve of the Global Financial Crisis. A trade deficit can be alleviated thanks to exports of services. The nonfinancial services comprise transport, insurance, and travel under the form of tourism revenues. For such countries as France, Tunisia, Morocco, Thailand, Vietnam, Italy, or Spain tourism receipts are substantial and can mitigate the consequences of a trade deficit. Investment income stems from the revenues that the country generates from its stock of past and current investment, including foreign direct investment (FDI) that earns dividends. More broadly, investment income is the return on holdings of financial assets and includes direct investment income, portfolio investment income, other investment income, and income on reserve asset (US Department of Commerce 2016).

The US balance on goods and services shows a slightly lower deficit than the trade balance thanks to large investment income receipts. It reached an annual deficit of roughly USD 500 billion in the 2003–2017 period, with a peak of USD 760 billion in 2006 and a short-lived reduction at USD 380 billion in 2009. In the US balance of payments, investment income annually reaches nearly USD 800 billion, of which 55% is from direct investment and 40% is from portfolio investment. Investment expenditures are the by-product of the accumulated external liabilities—in short, interest payments on debt held by nonresidents as well as dividends paid to

Table 8.1 The Current Account Balance

Current Account
+Export of goods f.o.b.
−Imports of goods f.o.b.
=Trade balance
+Exports of non-financial services
−Imports of non-financial services
+Investment income (credit)
−Investment expenditures (debit)
+(−)Private unrequited transfers
+(−)Official unrequited transfers
=Current account balance

foreign shareholders in national companies. In the US balance, primary income expenditures reach roughly USD 600 billion, of which 44% represents interest on US debt securities held by foreign holders. The balance on income in the United States, thus, is positive thanks to massive FDI revenue inflows in the global economy by US multinationals as well as interest on foreign countries' debt securities held by US residents. For most other countries, particularly emerging countries, interest payments are the largest negative item in the current account and can exacerbate the consequences of a trade imbalance, thereby expanding the current account deficit and the external financing requirements. Interest payments fluctuate according to the stock of outstanding debt as well as the average interest rate. The following chapter will cast light on a range of liquidity ratios to help the country risk manager gauge the sustainability of the interest payments burden.

The larger the expenditures with the rest of the world economy and the lower the export and investment revenues, the heavier the current account deficit. Economic overheating and excess spending generate external deficits. The current account balance, thus, reflects discrepancies between savings and domestic spending. A country that saves more than it invests at home sends its surplus abroad to purchase foreign assets. This is typically the case of Germany, Netherlands, Denmark, Japan, and Korea. A country that saves less than what it invests and spends, thus, needs to finance the shortfall by issuing liabilities to foreign investors, hence increasing external debt liabilities (or drawing on its official reserve assets). This is mainly the case of the United States, France, Mexico, Australia, Canada, Cyprus, and the United Kingdom. The accumulated history of current account surpluses or deficits, along with capital gains and losses on past investment, determines a country's net international investment position.

What is disposable income? The national income identity helps understand the relationship between the domestic economy and the balance of payments. Tables 8.2 and 8.3 summarize the relationships between the national income identity and the balance of payments.

A country's disposable income stands from the difference between gross income and expenditures such as imports and taxation, including the difference between capital inflows and capital outflows. Given that savings

Table 8.2 National Income and Balance of Payments

Y = National income	C = Domestic consumption
I = Investment	G = Government expenses
T = Taxes and government revenues	X = Export revenues
M = Imports	S = Domestic savings (= I > C)

Table 8.3 Disposible Income and Trade Balance

Y = National income
C = Domestic Consumption I = Investment
G = Government expenses
T = Taxes & Government revenues
X = Exports M = Imports
S = Domestic Savings (income > consumption)
KM = Capital Imports

What is disposable income?

Y = gross income - imports & taxation

$$Y = C + I + G + X - M - T + (KM - K\ outflows)$$

Savings = Y – C

(S – I)	+ (T – G) =	(X – M) +	(KM – K outflows)
Savings	Fiscal balance	Trade balance	Net capital inflows

are the difference or the residual between income and consumption, one observes that the savings–investment gap is equal to the trade balance. Any country that has a continuing deficit of savings while sustaining large investment—i.e., living "beyond its means"—will generate an absorption of domestic resources to the point that exports will fall and imports will rise, thereby creating a trade deficit. Conversely, a country with large savings will generate an export surplus in the trade balance.

The income identity shows that economic policy management is crucial to balance the trade account. Such variables as wages, budget, and monetary policies will impact on domestic consumption and investment, along with share buybacks, banking credit, and productivity. Similarly, export dynamism will depend on domestic competitiveness, inflation and the real exchange rate, and foreign markets' economic health. The following charts illustrate the relationship between the balance of payments and the savings–investment gap in the case of Thailand, particularly at the time of the 1997/98 crisis. Over the 1978–2017 period, the large savings surplus over investment is striking with the exception of the 1990–1996 period when a spending spree occurred on the back of large bank credits, thereby paving the way for mounting current account imbalances and for the abrupt baht devaluation of the summer of 1997 (Chart 8.2).

The root causes of the Asian crisis have been debated extensively by economists and risk analysts, mainly due to their inability to have predicted it. The crisis stemmed from a number of factors including domestic banking structural weaknesses, unproductive investment, and lack of financial sys-

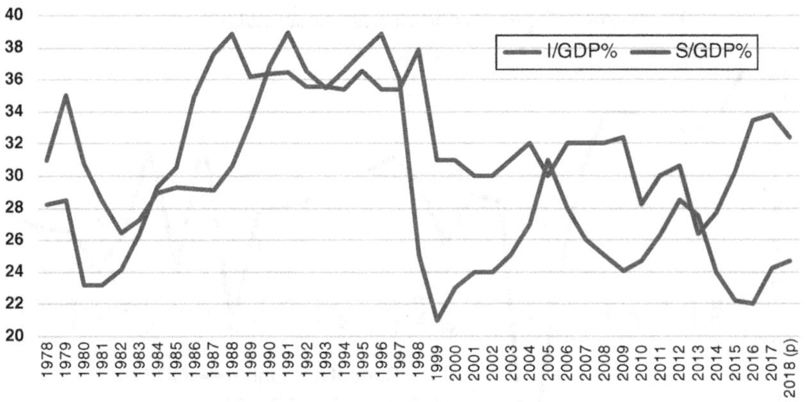

Chart 8.2 Thailand: Savings–investment gap 1978–2018 (*Source* IMF Art IV reports)

tem supervision coupled with premature financial liberalization and a fixed exchange rate that led to heavy intervention in the forward market and to depletion of international reserves. Speculation and bad governance, what Krugman (1998) called "crony capitalism," worsened the macroeconomic panorama. In Thailand, as with neighboring countries, the fixed exchange rate regimes gave borrowers a false sense of security, encouraging them to take on Dollar-denominated debt. The massive capital inflows, rising imports, and weakening exports were reflected in widening current account deficits. To make matters worse, a substantial portion of the capital inflows was in the form of short-term hard currency borrowing, leaving the countries vulnerable to external shocks. The crisis broke out in Thailand in July 1997 and led to a sharp devaluation of the domestic currency. A tough IMF program combined financial support and tight spending cuts. The austerity measures and the shock therapy created first more shock than therapy. The economic contraction was severe to the point that in 2000 nominal GDP was back to its level in 1995, i.e., less than Bhat 3 trillion (International Monetary Fund 2002b). In 1998, domestic consumption fell by 9.5% while investment contracted by 45%, resulting in a GDP recession of 10.8%. The one-off devaluation of the currency produced a 6.5% rise in exports while imports fell by 22%. The impressive shift in the current account balance in only two years was the result of a tight monetary policy that produced a sharp fall in domestic absorption, with shrinking imports, investment, and consumption (Chart 8.3).

Very few countries can achieve the current account readjustment that Thailand and other Asian countries implemented during the crisis of the late 1990s. The reason is that such a tight monetary policy in the wake of

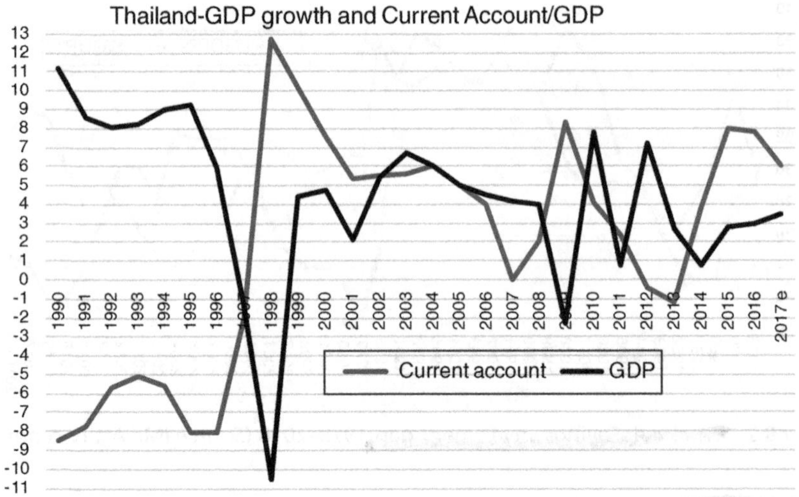

Chart 8.3 Thailand: The swing between domestic GDP and current account balance (1990–2017) (*Source* IMF data)

massive devaluation has economic, financial, and sociopolitical consequences. For boosting a devaluation-driven export drive, monetary policy requires a number of policy measures aimed at reducing domestic absorption and boosting income. The country risk analyst must look at the overall policy package that will make the deficit reduction a lasting success and not a quick fix. The societal distribution of the adjustment burden will make the rebalancing a success or a failure. In the aftermath of the Global Financial Crisis, household spending in Spain has shrunk abruptly due to a tight budget, monetary, and credit policy. In 2010, lowering wage bills became the key policy tool to make Spanish exports more competitive, not only with regard to other European countries, but also with regard to Portugal, Morocco, and Tunisia. A shift in labor rules giving companies more flexibility to cut salaries and change contract terms for employees has helped Spain pull itself back from the brink of default in 2010, paving the way to an export-led recovery. But the socioeconomic consequences have been large structural unemployment, soaring short-term contracts, brain drain, heavy private debt, and deepening poverty. In 2017, Spain's nominal GDP in USD was still below its precrisis level due to the abrupt contractions of 2009 and 2012.

8.2.2 Current Account and Domestic Policy Measures

One can cast light on four main policy tools that can be used to shrink an unsustainable current account deficit.

8.2.3 Exchange Rate Devaluation

The country risk analyst will expect a currency devaluation to shrink a country's trade deficit. The twin question is when and by how much. Indeed, the exchange rate measures the value of a currency in terms of another currency. A stronger exchange rate (overvaluation) might lead to lower exports, a decrease in current account surplus, and sooner or later a rising deficit. Exported goods would cost more for foreign partners, thus, decreasing demand for the good in the global markets. Conversely, a devaluation-driven weaker exchange rate will make domestic goods less expensive, hence more competitive, in the world economy, all this assuming price-elastic goods (i.e., sensitive to price changes). Other things equal, a devaluation leads to an expansion in the export sector since it reduces the costs of production measured in Dollars. In the real economy, other things are not equal. The success of a devaluation (which is a one-shot policy decision of the central bank) or an exchange rate depreciation (which is a gradual weakening of the currency's

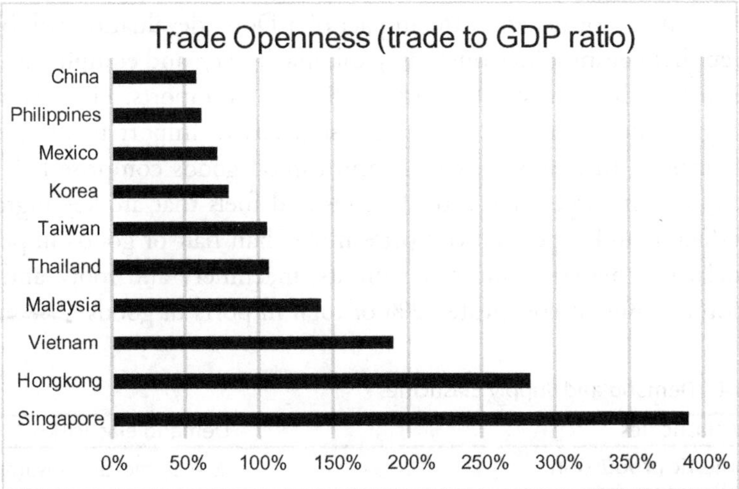

Chart 8.4 Ratios of Trade Openness (Exports + Imports/GDP) (*Source* Data from World Bank and UNCTAD)

value in the foreign exchange markets) is predicated on a number of conditions, both internal and external. One can stress three main conditions.

First of all, much depends on the country's trade openness ratio, which is the ratio of trade flows to GDP. The higher the ratio, the larger the trade response to the exchange rate variation. Typically, countries from Southeast Asia (such as Vietnam, Taiwan, Malaysia, Hong Kong, and Singapore) boast trade ratios well higher than GDP. Other emerging countries such as Thailand, Korea, Mexico, and Chile have ratios on the order of 50–75%. Overall, the larger the domestic market, the lower the trade openness. China's ratio is still around 55% though rising rapidly (Chart 8.4).

Second, the success of a devaluation will much depend on a dynamic foreign demand for the countries' goods and services. This is a necessary but not sufficient condition, given that there is still the prerequisite of a flexible supply to match the increasing demand. The supply-side conditions include production facilities, domestic and imported inputs, workers, infrastructures such as roads, harbors and transportation, and conducive institutions such as banking services, customs, and shipping. On the demand side, the success of a devaluation-driven export boost depends on trading partners' macroeconomic conditions and the foreign response to the price signal, as well as competing countries' exchange rate policy.

Last but not least, export competitiveness depends on the import content of the domestic production. Given that the devaluation will make imported inputs more expensive, any structural reliance on raw materials, oil, capital goods, and machinery will offset the exchange rate competitiveness. In the case of Vietnam, for instance, the impact of a Dong devaluation will be meager given that commodities (including oil, machinery, and equipment, as well as steel and leather) constitute nearly 50% of total imports. Like many other emerging market countries, Vietnam first needs to import to produce and then to export. In Morocco, energy and capital goods comprise half of the total imports. In Argentina, capital goods and fuels that are key ingredients for producing and exporting comprise more than half of goods imports. In Venezuela, raw materials and other inputs, machinery and tools, and transportation equipment constitute 72% of total imports of goods. These inputs

Table 8.4 Demand and Supply Elasticities

Supply elasticities	Demand elasticities
Δ + Domestic production	Δ – Domestic consumption
Δ + Foreign demand	Δ + Import prices
	Δ + Foreign demand
	Δ – Export prices

boil down to so-called incompressible imports whose costs will rise in the immediate aftermath of a devaluation, hence offsetting any export stimulus.

The risk analyst, thus, will welcome a currency devaluation with much caution and will first scrutinize the product structure of both imports and exports as well as the dynamism of foreign markets and the policy response of competing countries. On the supply side, an export stimulus is predicated on larger foreign demand to absorb larger domestic supply production. On the demand side, domestic consumption is to shrink in response to higher import prices, while the foreign demand is supposed to positively respond to lower export prices in foreign currencies. These conditions can be summarized in Table 8.4.

The relative dependency of domestic production's foreign inputs might generate a so-called J-curve in the trajectory of a trade deficit reduction. The exchange rate variation first will worsen the deficit given that the price response of imports will be quicker and larger than the enhanced competitiveness of exports whose inertia and time lag depend on many factors, often beyond the country's control. Figure 8.1 illustrates the worsening trajectory of a trade deficit after a one-off move in the exchange rate.

The second ingredient of a successful trade deficit reduction is tight monetary policy (i.e., an increase in interest rates and reserve requirements and a curb on banking credits, all aiming at reducing domestic consumption). This policy package has been illustrated in the case of Egypt at the end of 2016. According to the IMF report: "On November 3, 2016, the Central Bank liberalized the foreign exchange system and adopted a flexible market-determined exchange rate regime, to improve Egypt's external competitiveness, support exports, and tourism and attract foreign investment. This will also allow the Central Bank to rebuild its international reserves.

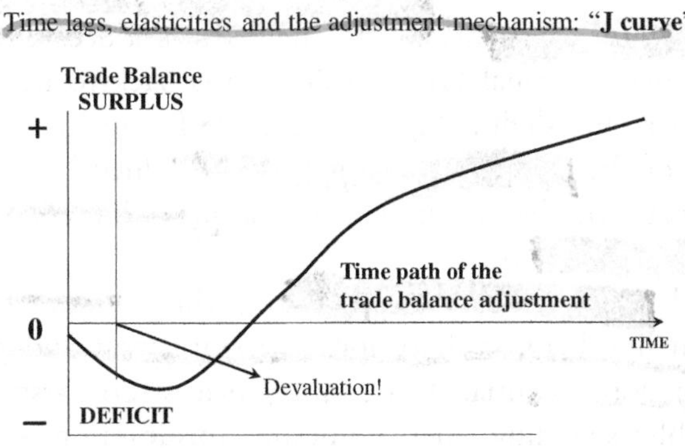

Fig. 8.1 The day after a devaluation: "J-curve" and time path of the trade deficit adjustment

Monetary policy will focus on containing inflation by controlling credit to government and banks" (International Monetary Fund 2016). The overall impact will be boosting FDI, capital inflows and export revenues, increasing domestic prices and reducing import growth. An income redistribution shift will occur with exporting companies winning and domestic consumers losing.

To quickly reduce a trade deficit, import controls often belong to the category of "wishful thinking" given that trade restrictions would trigger retaliation from foreign trading partners and would raise eyebrows at the IMF. Tariffs and quotas would also lead to strong objections at the World Trade Organization (WTO). The threat of import controls could be used as posturing and warning precisely to deter trade wars and competitive devaluations. This is what president-elect Trump used in the end of 2016 with regard to China in the aftermath of a campaign pledge to impose a punitive 35% tariff on US companies that import products from their factories abroad. The last resort for a tough trade policy stance would be to declare a balance of payments emergency and invoke a 1974 law that would allow the US administration to unilaterally impose tariffs or other restrictions on bilateral trade. If implemented, such a hostile stance on free trade would not only upset global supply chains and squeeze profits but would also push up the costs of inputs, leading to imported inflation (*Financial Times* 2016b, c).

Tight fiscal policy, along with higher taxes and spending cuts, also aims to "cool down" an overheated economy by reducing private consumption and shrinking public expenditures. The impact might be reducing domestic absorption and the deficit but at the price of restricting growth. This is this tough medicine that was imposed by the Troika (namely, the IMF, the European Central Bank, and the EU Commission) on Greece, Portugal, and Spain between 2009 and 2016, leading to a restoration of a balanced budget and balanced external accounts, but at the price of a deep cut in economic growth. In Greece, nominal GDP in 2017 was back to its 2003 level, to 2006 for Portugal, and slightly higher than 2008 for Spain. Due to the common currency of the Euro that could not be devalued by national central banks, deficit countries had to implement socially painful "real devaluation" by shrinking domestic costs.

A successful exchange rate depreciation, thus, requires policymakers to tread a thin line between boosting competitiveness and protecting the national production potential. If a country places too harsh a pressure on wages and public spending, then domestic consumption will backfire on domestic growth and on the export potential. Even if all the key ingredients are met, the country might still face the problem of belonging to a regional economic zone with low growth or a problem of competitive devaluations, further resulting in the erosion of the benefits of devaluation. Overshooting with tough austerity policies is a genuine risk. Lower nominal wage growth and spending cuts might lead to deflation, thereby suppressing domestic demand and increasing the real burden of debt. These effects could offset the beneficial effects of the depreciation on exports and worsen liquidity and solvency indicators, as will be discussed later in Chapter 12.

There are still two issues that can impact on a devaluation-driven deficit reduction policy. The first one is the real exchange rate depreciation, which is the difference between the nominal depreciation and the rate of inflation. A price competitive advantage in foreign markets stems from exporting goods and services cheaper than before (and cheaper than trading partners). It follows that the exchange rate depreciation must offset the price increase in the country; otherwise the country's competitiveness will not progress. More precisely, the depreciation must offset the price difference between the country and its major trading partners. The actual depreciation to monitor, thus, is that of the real effective exchange rate (REER), whose data are provided by a few international agencies such as the Bank for International Settlements (Bank for International Settlements 2017), the IMF and the OECD (Organization for Economic Co-operation and Development 2017b). REERs are calculated as geometric weighted averages of bilateral exchange rates adjusted by relative consumer prices. An increase in the index indicates an appreciation. The trade-weighted REER is a measure of price competitiveness given that it reflects the price difference between the goods produced at home and in other countries weighted by the share of the trading partners in the country's exports.

In Algeria, for example, Algeria's central bank strongly depreciated the Dinar/$ exchange rate, from 1 USD/D 60 in 2008 to 1 USD/D 110 at

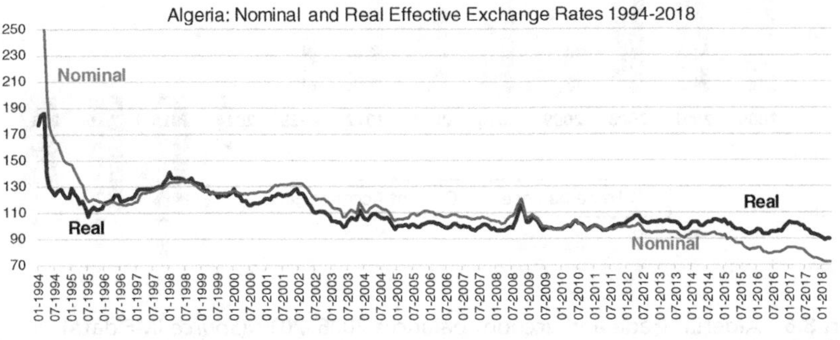

Chart 8.5 Algeria: The gap between nominal and real exchange rate depreciation (*Source* BIS)

the end of 2016. This was a weakening of 83%. In the same period, the dinar declined from 1€/D 80 to 1€/D 118. This was only a 47% weakening, though the Eurozone is the main regional trading partner of Algeria for both imports and exports. If one looks now at the nominal effective exchange rate and measures the dinar depreciation with regard to the country's major trading partners' currencies, then the dinar depreciated only by 25%. However, the country risk analyst should focus on the dinar's REER, measuring the actual price competitiveness of a dinar depreciation. As the previous chart illustrates, the dinar actually appreciated by around 2% during the period! (Chart 8.5).

The nominal depreciation of the Dinar by the central bank could not offset rapidly rising prices in Algeria, fully eroding the effect of the central bank policy. Worse, the nominal depreciation triggered an imported inflation given that the Algerian economy is structurally dependent on imported goods, ranging from foodstuff to pharmaceuticals, cars, and other manufactured products. On the other hand, the Dinar depreciation had no effect on hydrocarbon exports that comprise nearly 95% of total export revenues. The worsening trade deficit of Algeria, thus, could not be offset by an export boost given that Dollar-denominated hydrocarbon exports are not dinar-sensitive. The real depreciation, moreover, was not enough to stimulate export diversification. However, the nominal depreciation was such that it increased the cost of imported goods and services, thereby contributing to domestic inflation in the country. Goods imports rose from USD 21 billion

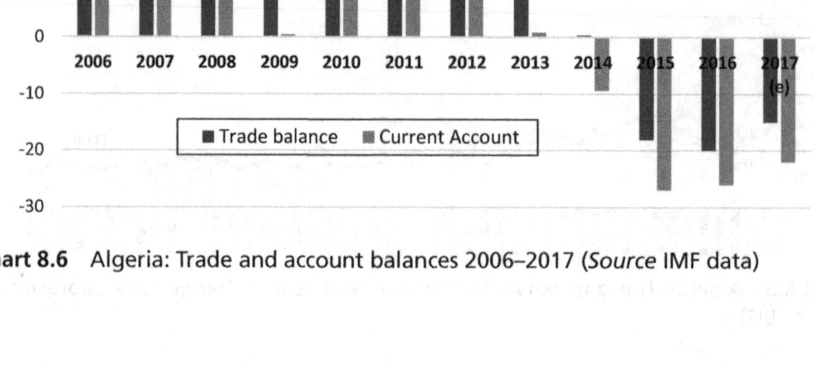

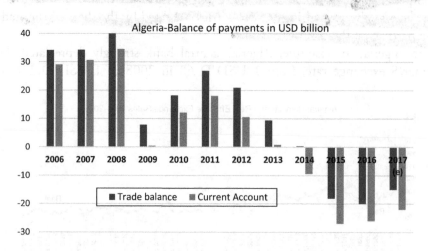

Chart 8.6 Algeria: Trade and account balances 2006–2017 (*Source* IMF data)

in 2006 to around USD 54 billion in the 2013–2017 period, hence substantial trade imbalances between 2015 and 2017 (Chart 8.6).

Second, certain countries cannot devalue or depreciate the exchange rate due to a regional common currency. This is the case of the fourteen African countries of the CFA Franc Zone, as well as the nineteen countries of the Eurozone. By definition, the benefits of exchange rate depreciation are possible only in countries with their own currency. Real or internal, not nominal, depreciation is then required through lower nominal wage growth—so-called, wage moderation—and lower inflation or higher productivity growth relative to trading partners. As the IMF observes: "In a currency union, such as the Euro area, a period of lower (productivity-adjusted) wage and price growth relative to trading partners is typically necessary to rebuild competitiveness" (International Monetary Fund 2015b). During the 2008–2016 Eurozone crisis, Greece, Portugal, and Spain took steps to address declining wage competitiveness relative to productivity. As a result, falling gross wage and salary indices in 2014 were still below their 2005 level (International Monetary 2014). In Greece, the problem was particularly challenging. Domestic consumption dropped by more than 30% between 2010 and 2014 while unit labor costs fell by 18% during the same period. A massive current account deficit of nearly 10% of GDP in 2011 gave rise to a surplus as early as 2013, a turnaround close to the performance of Asian countries back in 1998, albeit achieved through an "internal" devaluation and based on a fall in domestic consumption and imports. Economic growth could gradually be back to nearly 2% in 2017–2018.

A large and unsustainable current account deficit must be reduced with the right policy mix. As we have seen, however, the current account adjustment takes time. In the meantime, a country must finance its deficit by importing capital inflows. The financial account shows how the adjustment process is financed. It keeps record of sales of assets to foreigners and purchases of assets located abroad. Thus, the capital account measures changes in a country's net foreign asset position between residents and nonresidents. An implication of the double entry bookkeeping methodology is that the financial account is the mirror image of the current account. By definition, the balance of payments is balanced, thanks to capital inflows, reserve variation, exceptional financing, or arrears. Any change in the current account is reflected in an equivalent change in the country's financial account, measured by the difference between a country's purchases of assets from foreigners and its sales of assets. Liquidity difficulty then starts when a country's liquid assets and available domestic and external financing are insufficient to meet or rollover its maturing liabilities. A liquidity tension can arise due to adverse exogenous factors (including declining commodity prices, rising interest rates, shorter maturities, trading partners' competitive devaluations, bad weather and drought, shrinking export markets) and domestic factors (including high inflation, overvalued exchange rates, unsustainable domestic consumption, and rising imports). The IMF has developed a framework for analyzing a country's debt sustainability. Its definition of solvency, though conceptually impeccable in accounting terms, has little operational value for the country risk manager: "An entity is solvent if the present discounted value (PDV) of its current and future primary expenditure is no greater than the PDV of its current and future path of income, net of any initial indebtedness" (International Monetary Fund 2002a).

The risk analyst must focus on the six following issues to assess the sustainability of external financing requirements:

1. The growth of the current account deficit and of the Debt/GDP ratio compared to the GDP growth rate;
2. The volume of external financing requirements;
3. The liquidity conditions in the global capital markets;
4. The nature of financing sources (private/public);
5. The debt's short- and medium-term profiles, with a focus on the risk of bunching of maturities falling due; and
6. The sustainability of the financing (capital flow volatility, currency mismatch, floating/fixed rates, grace periods, and repayment conditions).

Similar to the current account, the various items in the financial account are listed in Table 8.5. According to their level of liquidity, from the less liq-

Table 8.5 The Financial Account of the Balance of Payments

Financial account
+/−Direct investment (non-debt creating flows)
+/−Portfolio investment (non-debt creating flows)
+/−Long-term private and public capital flows
+/−Short-term private and public capital flows
+/−Net errors & omissions
+/−Gold reserve revaluation
+/−Change in reserve assets
=Capital account balance
+Exceptional financing or arrears

Table 8.6 Table of uses and sources

Uses (outflows)	Sources (inflows)
Imports of goods	Exports of goods
Imports of services	Exports of services
Interest payments	Transfers and remittances
Principal debt payments	Dividends
ST capital outflows	FDI
Errors and omissions	ST and LT capital inflows
Reserve variation	Arrears or debt cancellation

uid to the more liquid financial assets. Direct investment and portfolio capital flows are real-economy related while private and public capital flows are purely financial, hence more liquid.

The basic balance draws the line under "Long-term private and public capital" to emphasize the role of economic performance and sustainable external financing. Another presentation is the Table of Uses & Sources that lists all the inflows and all the outflows between a country and the rest of the world, providing a useful snapshot of the country's strengths and weaknesses. Table 8.6 helps cast light on liquidity imbalances and on the risk of arrears buildup.

Financing a current account deficit depends on the sustainability of financing flows regarding volumes and financial conditions. The appropriate measure is not the nominal Dollar deficit but the ratio of deficit to GDP that helps to compare across time and across countries. This is why countries compete to attract long-term capital inflows, particularly foreign direct investments that do not create debt increases while boosting domestic jobs, technology transfers, and government tax revenues. Likewise, portfolio investment belongs to the non-debt creating flow category. The maturity structure—as well as the source of financing flows—has a direct impact on the country's liquidity and solvency situation. Short-term capital flows clearly are more volatile than FDI or long-term credits. Trade credits and working capital lines will expand or contract depending on economic, sociopolitical, or stock market signals. They will also be affected by regional developments, credit ratings, and spillover effects. Most investment funds consider emerging market countries as one single class of assets, and accordingly, they are subject to contagion and contamination. Likewise, rating agency downgrading of a specific country might affect neighbors. In addition, public versus private capital flows have consequences on the structure and the volatility of capital flows.

Table 8.7 Sources of external financing

Official (bilateral + multilateral)	Private (banks, capital markets, and corporate)
• Paris club (government credits) • Export insurance credit • IFIs (World Bank + IMF) • Regional development banks • Arrears and rescheduling • Debt cancellation	• Foreign direct investment • Portfolio investment • London club (bank loans) • Working capital lines • Short-term trade credits • Bonds and debt securities • Arrears and rescheduling

Table 8.7 distinguishes the main sources of external financing, each one with a specific impact on the future cost of debt servicing and the overall debt sustainability.

The final item in the financial account is errors and omissions. They represent statistical discrepancies as well as outflows that are not under the control of the central bank, namely capital flight that can stem from over-invoicing of imports or under-invoicing of export receipts. As the IMF observes: "The size and trends of discrepancy may help identify data problems, such as coverage, incomplete data sources, or misreporting. Patterns in net errors and omissions may provide useful information on data problems" (International Monetary Fund 2010). Errors and omissions of small magnitude and of opposite signs during a period of time are symptoms of inevitable statistical discrepancies. Protracted errors and omissions of large magnitude, with a negative sign reflecting outflows, and in a context of exchange rate volatility and/or political upheaval are signals of deep-seated problems. The magnitude itself must be assessed in relative terms, for instance as a share of GDP or as a share of official reserve assets. One can distinguish countries with large errors and omissions reflecting capital flight in relation to poor governance, wealth concentration, and weak institutions. Examples include Zimbabwe, Venezuela, Gabon, and many oil-producing developing countries.

One can distinguish countries with large capital flight in relation with sociopolitical volatility such as Greece in 2012–2013, Thailand in 2012 and 2015, Zimbabwe in 2015, and Tunisia in 2012–2015 in the wake of the Arab Spring turmoil. In the case of Zimbabwe, a rich country with poor people and a structurally corrupt political regime, errors, and omissions reached USD 200 million in 2015, the equivalent of 60% of gross international reserves. One can also distinguish large errors and omissions in the context of exchange rate volatility and the expectation of currency depreciation. The case of Russia is illuminating with considerable capital outflows in relation to exchange rate

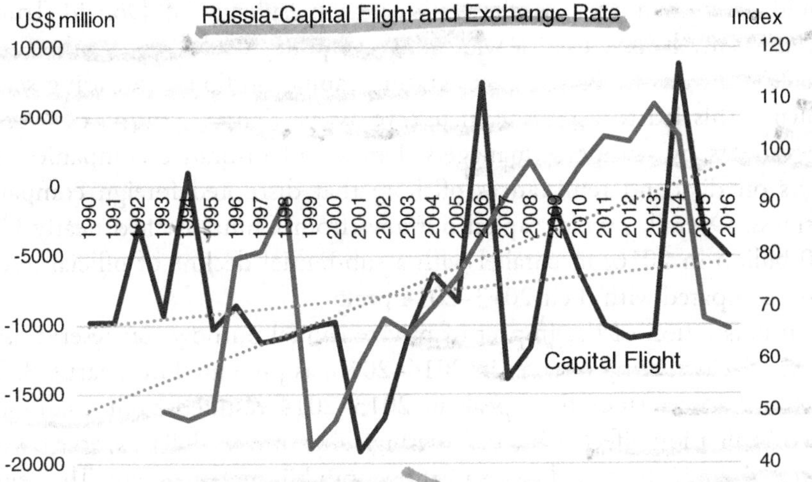

Chart 8.7 Russia: Ruble's real exchange rate and private bank deposits 1990–2016 (*Source* BIS data)

overvaluation in 2010, 2013, and 2015. Chart 8.7 depicts the close correlation between errors and omissions and the rubble's REER. A currency depreciation tends to lead to substantial outflows while a currency strengthening leads to capital flight repatriation (i.e., positive errors and omissions).

One last source of errors and omissions volatility stems from interest rate differential and actual or expected weakening exchange rate—that is, a combination of push and pull factors of capital flight. Residents of a country whose exchange rate is weakening will strive to shift their liquid assets abroad in international bank deposits. The root causes of exchange rate weakening might be related to a deterioration in the balance of payments, an interest rate differential, and a foreign currency appreciation. This is the situation that Chinese residents have faced between 2014 and 2017 (and similar to what they faced back in 1994). The weakening of the renminbi triggered an exodus of private capital out of the country since the summer of 2015. Concerns over the slowing economy, rising debt, and interest cuts by the People's Bank of China in 2015 reduced the appeal of holding renminbi assets for Chinese and foreign investors looking for yield. In the meantime, exchange rate depreciation hurt both importers who must squeeze margins as well as holders of Dollar-denominated debts. The latter faced a mounting cost of servicing Dollar-based debt, threatening midsize banks and investment funds as well as shadow banking institutions. The upside in the Dollar-renminbi rate was the by-product of the expectation that the US Federal Reserve would raise interest rates and that the Dollar would strengthen as a result of the new presidency of Donald Trump. China's central bank used a wide range of policy tools to stem the steady depreciation on the back of accelerating capital outflows, including selling Dollars. This led to a decline in reserve assets, tighter scrutiny of overseas investments by corporate managers, banks and insurance companies, and limits on dividend remittances offshore that disrupted foreign companies business. Overall, private capital outflows from China reached nearly USD 550 billion in 2016, in parallel with a substantial decline of official reserve assets compared with their 2013–2014 peak.

An illustration of the impact of private capital outflows on reserve assets is China's fluctuating reserves in 2014–2016, as presented in Chart 8.8. The drop in reserves since their peak in 2013–2014 resulted from a combination of valuation effects (due to lowering value of non-dollar reserve currencies) and the ineffective defense of the renminbi's exchange rate. The central bank's policy and regulatory measures to reduce capital outflows, coupled with the country's trade surplus, will probably restore the level of China's reserve assets.

In the national balance of payments, the sum of credit entries and the sum of debit entries is conceptually zero—that is, the accounts as a whole are in balance. The balance of payments gets always balanced, but the issue

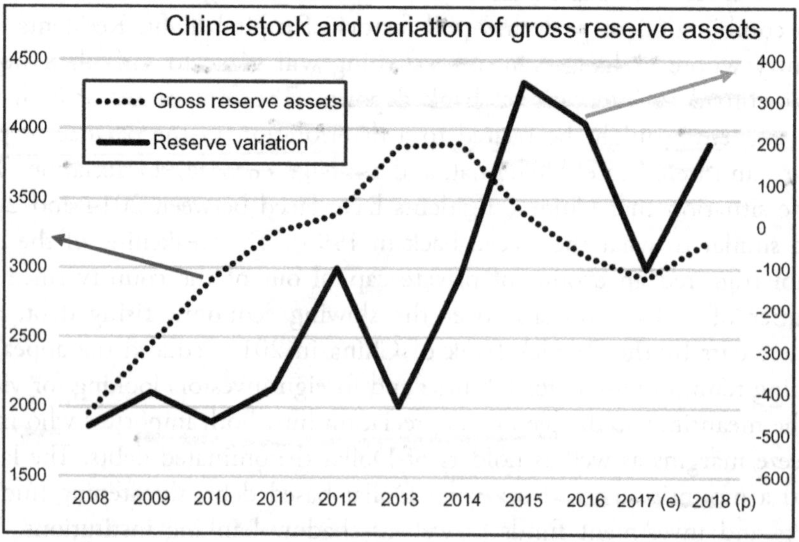

Chart 8.8 China: Overall official reserve assets and annual variation (USD million) (*Source* IMF data and authors' projections)

Table 8.8 China: Official Reserve Assets 2008–2017

USD million	2008	2009	2010	2011	2012	2013	2014	2015	2016	2017 (e)
Reserve variation	−479	−400	−471	−388	−100	−431	−117	346	250	150
Gross reserve assets	1953	2453	2914	3255	3388	3880	3900	3406	3100	2900

Source International Monetary Fund (2017b)

for the risk analyst is how the balancing gets performed. Once the financing sources have been exhausted, from long-term flows to short-term flows, the central bank must resort to its own hard currency reserves. The risk analyst must then watch for variations in the signs in the capital account. A positive sign means that the stock of reserve assets has fallen in order to finance the gap. A negative sign means that the financing is in surplus, hence the stock of reserve assets will increase. Table 8.8 illustrates the reserve variation in China's balance of payments in the 2008–2017 period, with a positive sign when reserves decline.

8.3 Conclusion

Overall, the balance of payments analysis is a prerequisite in country risk assessment. Balances give the expert analyst the means to assess the fragility of economic overheating as well as the unsustainability of rising external debt. However, country status and structural economic conditions matter in the balance of payments analysis. Most of the time, an industrialized country has access to wider capital markets than most developing countries, with the exception of crisis-stricken OECD countries like Cyprus, Greece, and Portugal. Market access makes financing a current account deficit easier both in terms of maturities and spread. In addition, a country whose currency has a global status will benefit from better liquidity conditions. This is the case in United Kingdom, Japan, the Eurozone, and the United States. In the case of the protracted and structural US deficit, the financing comes from surplus countries that are willing to accumulate Dollar balances—namely, Germany, Korea, and Japan. Dollar balances are then recycled in US Treasury securities, helping to finance the US budget deficit. Country risk analysts must focus not only on the volume and the root causes of the deficit but also on the sustainability of the financing that will have a direct consequence on the liquidity and solvency situation of the indebtedness process.

References

American Association of Individual Investors. 2016. http://www.aaii.com/investing-basics/article/the-top-10-economic-indicators-what-to-watch-and-why.

Bank for International Settlements. 2017. "Statistics." http://www.bis.org/statistics/eer.htm.

Federal Reserve Bank of St Louis. 2017. Economic Research. "Balance of Payments." https://fred.stlouisfed.org/categories/32951?t=europe&ob=pv&od=desc.
Financial Times. 2016a. "China's Statistics Chief Admits Some Economic Data Are False", December 7.
Financial Times. 2016b. "Trump Warns Business on Offshoring", December 5.
Financial Times. 2016c. "Strong Dollar Threatens Trade Deficit Plans", December 14.
International Monetary Fund. 2002a. "Assessing Sustainability." Policy Development and Review Department, May 28.
International Monetary Fund. 2002b. *Report*. Thailand: Statistical Appendix.
International Monetary Fund. 2010. Balance of Payments and International Investment Position Manual, 6th ed., Chapter 2. January.
International Monetary Fund. 2014. Country Report on Greece, No. 14/151, Table 1. June.
International Monetary Fund. 2015a. "Data Standard Initiatives in Retrospect", March. http://www.imf.org/external/np/pp/eng/2015/040615.pdf.
International Monetary Fund. 2015b. Wage Moderation in Crises: Policy Considerations and Applications to the Euro Area, November 17.
International Monetary Fund. 2016. IMF Executive Board Approves USD $12 Billion Extended Arrangement Under the Extended Fund Facility for Egypt, November 11.
International Monetary Fund. 2017a. Article IV Consultation Report on Zimbabwe. Country Report 17/196, July.
International Monetary Fund. 2017b. Article IV Consultation Report on the People's Republic of China. Country Report 17/247, August.
Institute of International Finance. 2017. https://www.iif.com/topics/global-macroeconomics.
Krugman Paul. 1998. "What Happened to Asia?" The Official Paul Krugman Webpage, January. http://web.mit.edu/krugman/www/DISINTER.html.
Organization for Economic Co-operation and Development. 2017a. "Balance of Payments." http://stats.oecd.org/index.aspx?datasetcode=MEI_BOP6.
Organization for Economic Co-operation and Development. 2017b. Economic Outlook no 101. Real Effective Exchange Rate Indices, June. http://stats.oecd.org/Index.aspx?QueryId=51626.
Riley, David, and Brian Coulton. 2010. FitchRatings. Special Report: "Sovereign Credit Crisis. Crisis Confidence in the Eurozone." Chart 18: The Emergence of Twin Deficits, June.
United States Department of Commerce, US Bureau of Economic Analysis. 2016. "U.S. International Transactions", September. http://www.bea.gov/newsreleases/international/transactions/transnewsrelease.htm.
World Bank. 2017. "Balance of Payments." http://data.worldbank.org/indicator/BN.CAB.XOKA.CD.

9

Root Causes and Consequences of Political Risk: Defining Political Risk and Its Various Dimensions

9.1 Introduction: The Rising Importance of Political Risk

In the aftermath of the end of the Cold War and of the fragmentation of the Soviet Union into a number of independent nation-states, political risk analysts might have thought that a new era of relatively peaceful international relations would emerge. The combination of global trade openness and large financing transfers by International Financial Organizations would pave the way for more dynamic and balanced economic growth ushering in a process of economic catching up within and between countries. Technology transfers coupled with MNCs' foreign direct investment (FDI) would accelerate the diffusion of technological progress in the world. The World Bank and the International Monetary Fund (IMF), coupled with a number of regional development agencies, would gradually widen the select club of developed countries. The globalization of the market economy would then become a driving force for social progress all over the world. The "End of History" would mark the termination of poverty and the dawn of sustainable and inclusive development. However, this optimism was short-lived. Commodity price volatility, terrorism, global warming, and mounting wealth gaps have shaken political risk analysts since the Global Financial Crisis. Political risk insurance and investment guarantees are becoming more than ever the name of the game.

Euromoney's 2017 Country Risk Survey underlines that currently rising risks include low oil prices, interstate conflict, and domestic political upheaval among the many factors affecting sovereign borrowers, with

M. H. Bouchet et al., *Managing Country Risk in an Age of Globalization*,
https://doi.org/10.1007/978-3-319-89752-3_9

political risk increasing in seventy-two countries, including the United States and other countries in the Americas—namely Barbados, Bolivia, Cuba, and Paraguay, as well as the UK and Zimbabwe (Euromoney 2017). The mere fact that post-Brexit UK, Catalonia, and several Eastern European countries are lumped together in the list of rising turmoil risk areas is a clear illustration of the end of political risk as the monopoly of developing countries. MIGA-EIU's annual political risk survey confirms that political risk is considered by managers of multinationals as the major constraint to foreign investment, almost on par with macroeconomic instability, in both developed and developing countries (MIGA 2013). Adverse regulatory changes and breach of contract are types of political risk of most concern to investors in developing economies. Political turbulence in the aftermath of the Arab Spring revolution and related to terrorist threats has been mounting. Consequently, political risk insurance (PRI) has continued to rise since the Global Financial Crisis, both from official agencies such as MIGA and export credit agencies, and private institutions, as discussed in Chapter 15. According to MIGA: "The important drivers of new issuance include ongoing instability in the Middle East and North Africa that have raised the spectre of unanticipated events in seemingly stable political regimes; high-profile expropriations and investor-state disputes in Latin America; contract renegotiations in resource-rich economies; and capital constraints and increased financial sector regulation, which make financing with PRI an attractive option" (MIGA 2014).

Political risk is as old as cross-border investments, commerce, and lending. In the words of a financial veteran: "The Florentine private bankers who lent to the princes of their day were entirely concerned with a political evaluation of their chances of recovering their money. They based their credit analysis on the principles of Machiavelli rather than Adam Smith" (Yassukovich 1976). During the Renaissance, as well as today, country risk managers faced borrowers' ability as well as their willingness to repay their obligations in full and on time. Bankers, investors, and merchants have often been reckless in ignoring or downplaying the political risk. Former Citicorp chairman Walter Wriston, the single most notorious global banker of his time, summarized the issue: "Countries don't go out of business... The infrastructure doesn't go away, the productivity of the people doesn't go away, the natural resources don't go away. And so their assets always exceed their liabilities" (Grant 1996). As a matter of fact, a number of sovereign crises in the twentieth century proved otherwise. Though nation-states don't go away, short-sighted bankers who ignore country risk management do. Although banks' shareholders paid a heavy price for their aloofness regarding political turbulence, the entities that were hurt the hardest were multinational corporations investing over the long haul in foreign countries through FDI. Indeed, regulatory and tax incentives helped banks to build up large loan-loss reserves while boosting their capitalization ratios and enhancing their margin of maneuver to get rid of risky assets in the secondary market of bank claims. Although the 1970s experienced the rise and proliferation of political risk analysis departments, the awakening tended to be reactive. As noted by a political risk analyst in 1980: "Over the past decade, American corporations have been discovering one supposedly rich foreign markets after another, only to have their hopes dashed or diminished by unexpected political changes or upheavals" (Kraar 1980, 86). After Fidel Castro's communist regime nationalized all foreign investment assets, a wave of foreign business expropriations in the 1970s and 1980s forced multinationals to reassess the magnitude of political risk. For many multinationals and banks, the Iranian revolution, as well as the overthrow of the Somoza regime in 1979 in Nicaragua, were a watershed and a wake-up call that political risk matters. Nevertheless, the rising tide of nationalism in developing countries has only slowly led to the use of geopolitical analysis with enhanced emphasis from internal research and intelligence departments. Risk insurance has often been a substitute for thinking. In addition, risk assessment models have overly simplified the complexity of the situation by reducing issues into seemingly comforting numbers and loss probability ratios.

We need to take two analytical biases into consideration. First, until the late 1990s, researchers, analysts, and risk managers tended to associate political destabilization with developing countries. There have been a few exceptions, including the First World War and the Russian revolution, the fascist era in both Germany and Italy, the 1936 military uprising and the subsequent civil war in Spain, and the numerous coups d'état in Greece (among them 1967 and 1973). All in all, sociopolitical violence, such as guerrilla warfare, revolutions, and dictatorships have been the trademarks of rapidly growing developing countries in an environment of repressive regimes and wealth concentration. There are notable exceptions, however, of emerging market countries with stable political environments and low corruption (based on the corruption perception index of Transparency International), such as Uruguay, Estonia, Mauritius, Bhutan, Botswana, Cap Verde, and Costa Rica.

Since the late 1990s, and particularly since the eruption of the Global Financial Crisis, social destabilization has spread to several developed countries of the Organization of Economic Co-operation and Development (OECD) together with the threat of terrorism. Political risk in developed countries stems from a number of factors, including regulatory change, rising wealth gaps and the prospect of eroding purchasing power, as well as the limits to social inclusiveness experienced by democratic systems. As the IMF notes: "Medium-term prospects are further clouded by rising inequality and, in advanced economies, sluggish median real wages, which can undermine the sustainability of growth. Over the longer term, weak income growth and increasing inequality can fuel discontent and affect the willingness to reform" (IMF 2017). Another form of political risk in developed countries is the cost of bribery in foreign countries, in terms both of the actual cost and of reputational damage. Indeed, the 1997 OECD Anti-Bribery Convention established binding standards to criminalize bribery of foreign public officials in international business transactions (OECD 1999). The Convention, which includes forty-one mostly developed countries, provides a broad definition of bribery and it permits countries to adopt national legislation making it a crime to bribe foreign public officials requiring countries to impose dissuasive sanctions. Likewise, the Inter-American Convention against Corruption, which was signed in 1996 in the Western Hemisphere, decided to promote international cooperation in fighting corruption while requiring members to criminalize transnational bribery.

Second, the political risk literature has tended to reduce the consequence of political risk to financial losses for foreign investors and, more recently, for cross-border finance. For instance, a Harvard Business School case study states: "Political risk refers to the possibility that political decisions or events in a particular country will cause foreign investors there either to lose money or fail to capture their expected returns" (Deringer et al. 1997). Kobrin at the Massachusetts Institute of Technology embarked on a meticulous review of the academic literature on political risk though with a narrow focus on the current and potential impacts of the political environment on the operations of the firm, that is, on investment cash flows (Kobrin 1979). This limited scope ignores the fate of importers and exporters, consultants, contractors, and NGOs, as well as domestic economic agents who are also exposed to political risk in their own country. In addition, the restricted focus of this definition reduces the consequences of political risk to financial losses only. However, other manifestations of political risk are bureaucracy, bad governance, abrupt regulatory changes, opacity, institutional deficiencies, or even crimes and kidnapping.

9.2 Defining Political Risk

Whereas political uncertainty refers to instability and threats in the sociopolitical system, political risk is the unexpected unfavorable consequences of the arbitrary exercise of power by a government or by nongovernmental actors (including its domestic and foreign ramifications). Overall, political uncertainty stems from a deficit of information and economic intelligence regarding a specific political risk. As discussed in Chapters 1 and 2, uncertainty is subjective as the assessment of the likelihood of a specific event depends on diverse perceptions as well as previous experience and risk exposure. Risk, in turn, represents a single outcome associated with a specific event. Exchange rate overvaluation triggers uncertainty whereas a central bank's devaluation triggers risk. The threat of a general strike generates uncertainty whereas roadblocks and urban guerrillas create risk. A careful information-based analysis will thus transform the assessment of uncertainty into the assessment of risk, thereby creating the basis for risk mitigation strategies, such as reduced exposure or insurance. Unexpected discontinuities that occur in the sociopolitical system can result in a wide range of consequences depending on the specific exposure of domestic versus foreign economic agents. A risk matrix is therefore required to link exposure, timing, and risk as precisely as possible. Contrary to the widespread idea of political risk in terms of government interference with foreign investment (i.e., confiscation) or international lending (default), the spectrum of sociopolitical risk has a far wider range, as it concerns both assets and flows, of both domestic and foreign agents. Overall business conditions and well-being can also be impacted by adverse political environment.

The risk analyst must tackle a number of questions such as: How resilient is the country's political system? Can the hazards of NGO action hurt the company's value? Is wealth concentration large and rising? Is there a tradition of peaceful transitions of power or are there struggles between conflicting groups? How robust are the institutional shock absorbers, such as political parties, unions, and associations that provide social buffers between citizens and governments? In most developed countries, the rising wealth gaps since the 1980s have reached their limits regarding the transformation of socioeconomic frustration into political polarization. In the United States, for instance, pre-income tax growth between 1980 and 2014 reached 600% for the top 0.001% whereas the bottom 50% of the population experienced no income growth at all (Piketty 2016, Ashkenas 2016)). The mere fact that wealth concentration is better documented and publicly available fuels discontent.

Table 9.1 Three main sources of political risk

Direct (hard risks)	• **Risk materialization directly hurts the company**: Nationalization, expropriation and confiscation, contract repudiation, sham contracting, bribery and corruption, blocked funds, kidnapping, crimes
Indirect (surrounding risks)	• **Risk materialization stems from the hostile environment**: Revolution and civil unrest, martial law, terrorism, war damage, ideological and cultural shifts. Capital and dividend remittance constraints, ineffective legal and regulatory systems, non-compliance, strikes, currency inconvertibility, regional crisis and volatility spill-over
Collateral (soft risks)	• **Risk materialization is the byproduct of unfavorable interactions between power groups**: Legal and ethical risks, reputational risk, protectionism, fiscal uncertainty, wealth gaps, bureaucracy and weak institutions, pressure groups and hostile NGOs, ethnic/linguistic fragmentation

Risk managers need to adopt a systematic analysis of political risk factors that are specific to their activities. In political risk as more generally in Country Risk, everything is a matter of exposure and intelligence. An oil company with a drilling project does not face the same political threats as a bank that holds sovereign bonds or a domestic resident who owns a shop. The challenge is to identify which threats are the most pressing, when, and how. A plan of risk mitigation strategy can then be defined and implemented. We can distinguish three key sources of political risk each with a range of consequences (Table 9.1).

9.3 Political Turbulence in the Age of Globalization

No country is immune to the complex ramifications of the global economic and geopolitical system. In the globalized economy, political risk can appear very suddenly and unexpectedly, including in regions that up to now seemed protected from sociopolitical turmoil. Until the late 1990s, political risk was largely confined to emerging markets as exemplified by political turmoil in Latin America in the 1970s and 1980s, the Asian crisis of late 1990s, ongoing geopolitical instability in the Middle East, and a long sequence of coups d'état in Africa. Usually, companies buy insurance to limit losses from adverse political developments. Risk mitigation tools are addressed in detail in Chapter 14. Political risk protection is usually restricted to specific, sudden hazards, such as nationalization, capital controls, confiscation, kidnapping, and terrorism.

Since the Global Financial Crisis, not only has sovereign risk increased but the political risk has returned to the policy agenda of MNCs and global economic agents, investors, and creditors. More importantly, political instability in such developed countries as Scotland, Greece, Turkey, Ukraine, and Spain has reaffirmed the idea that sociopolitical volatility is not the monopoly of developing countries. This is a timely reminder that political risk cannot simply be ignored in so-called modern societies. The looming withdrawal of the UK in the aftermath of Brexit has forced foreign investors in the City of London and in manufacturing to reassess their business strategy. Taken off guard, several banking entities have adopted plans to shift London-based activities to Ireland or to Continental Europe. Likewise, rising political volatility in Eastern Europe tempers strong profit prospects and robust economic fundamentals. Countries such as Romania, Poland, Hungary, Croatia, and the Czech Republic have attracted large flows of FDI and portfolio investment thanks to competitive wages, well-educated workforces, rising purchasing power, and dynamic consumer markets. Annual GDP growth rates of 3%–4% are impressive when compared with the otherwise anemic growth in the Eurozone since the Global Financial Crisis. However, populist governments in Central and Eastern Europe tend to adopt less friendly business policies, with unabated corruption, and looser corporate governance standards. More carefully calibrated investment decisions from American and Western European companies tend to open doors for Asian and Middle East investors (Bouchet 2010).

Most importantly, the globalization of the market economy has increased volatility and the spillover effect of local and regional contagion, making political risk more complex to analyze, predict, and manage. Regional contagion spreads in two directions. One is through increased instability and violence, as illustrated in the Arab Spring of 2011. The almost simultaneous overthrow of long-term autocrats in Tunisia, Libya, and Egypt had widespread repercussions in North Africa, including in Morocco, Algeria, and Syria, albeit with very different consequences. Another channel of contamination is through the herd instinct of investors who tend to consider emerging markets as one single asset class, hence rising spreads, shorter maturities, and stricter lending conditions. Rating agencies tend to exacerbate these ramifications by downgrading countries in a row. Aon, the political risk insurance agency, observed the following in the immediate aftermath of the Arab Spring: “The political upheaval across the Arab world continued to cause aftershocks in that region and beyond. Authoritarian governments in Africa and Asia took measures to protect themselves from similar challenges as civil unrest, property damage and localized protests continued in the Middle East and North Africa" (AON Risk Solutions 2012). As a result, thirty-seven countries were downgraded in the AON (2012) Terrorism and Political Violence Map, largely due to civil unrest.

Chart 9.1 summarizes the main types of political risk.

In addition, the risk of political turmoil does not affect only foreign investors and global creditors. Destabilization and uncertainty act as strong headwinds for domestic companies and private economic agents. During 2017, Brexit deeply affected both domestic and foreign business given that the UK hosts more than 250 foreign banks and that Britain's car industry is mostly foreign-owned. A KPMG survey showed that 90% of companies in the car industry considered that Brexit would hurt their business, while 75% concluded that an exit would negatively affect future investment. (Groom 2014, 10) In the United States, the perceived unpredictability of President Donald Trump generated economic, financial, and even legal volatility in the United States and in the global economy (Bouchet 2017). A number of companies decided to settle long-standing legal suits with the US Department of Justice, paying USD 20 billion in corporate settlements and penalties just ahead of the administration change (*Financial Times* 2017). Likewise, a number of American companies investing in China had to gauge the consequences of the Trump administration's harsh trade rhetoric as they braced themselves for painful repercussions if the President-elect was to follow through on his trade protectionist threats. The new US president ushered in a view of the global economy as essentially a zero-sum game, with jobs created in China coming directly at the expense of those in the United

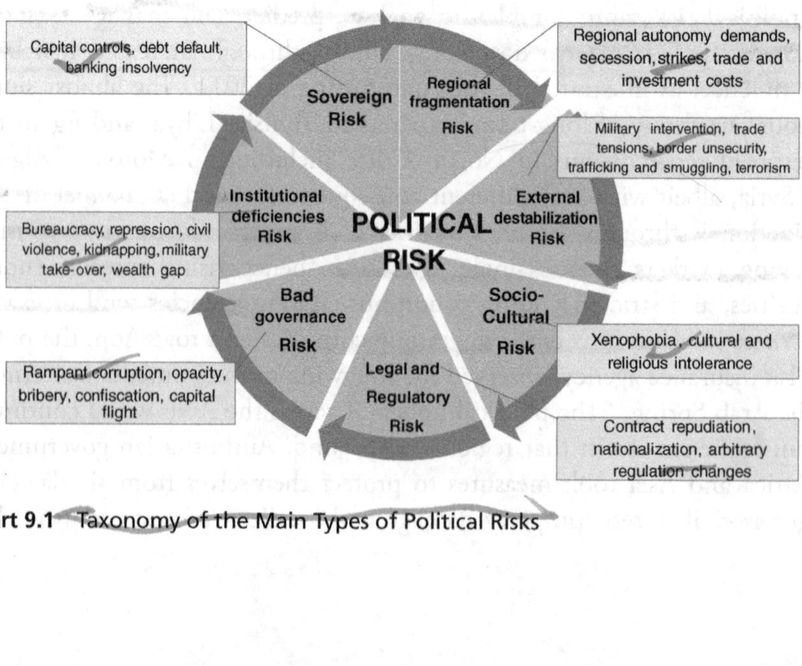

Chart 9.1 Taxonomy of the Main Types of Political Risks

States. As Lester Ross, chairman of the American Chamber of Commerce in Beijing's policy committee warned in early 2017: "China is threatening to, and is preparing to, take steps in retaliation" (Hornby 2017). Imposing high tariffs on Mexican or Chinese-made goods would destabilize global supply chains, thereby hurting the business strategy of American companies and raising consumer prices resulting in a double blow if US levies were followed by retaliation from Beijing. Regarding geopolitical risks and their domestic implications, the risks associated with the escalation in rhetoric and saber rattling between North Korea's leader Kim and US President Donald Trump in the summer of 2017 generated gold rally as well as exchange rate and stock market volatility hurting business in the trade and investment sectors.

The globalization of trade and financial transactions has clearly increased the risk of volatility spillover and crisis contamination. In 2017, the total volume of financial assets reached four times the world GDP, in other words, financial globalization is much greater than global real economic wealth and well beyond the policy and regulatory reach of nation-states. In the geopolitical arena, the end of post-World War II (WWII) US-dominated multilateralism generates uncertainty. Donald Trump's presidency is an additional destabilizing factor. The emergence of a bilateral deal diplomacy between four main blocs, namely China, Russia, the United States, and the EU, reduces the role of multilateral institutions, such as the United Nations, the IMF and the World Bank, and the WTO. But the globalization of information channels and of terrorist threats constitutes an even stronger destabilizing factor. As Thomas Wright of the Brookings Institute observes: "For over seventy years, the United States has led an international order organized around alliances, an open global economy, and multilateralism. This imperfect order had its fair share of mistakes, problems, and crises but it also produced the longest period of great power peace and relative prosperity in history (…). Today, the combination of Trump, Xi, and Putin makes the present situation so dangerous" (Wright 2017). Overall, the shrinking share of OECD countries' GDP, now less than 50% of global GDP, and the rising economic, financial, and geopolitical predominance of China, tends to reduce the effectiveness of "Pax Americana" while giving more influence to rogue states such as North Korea, and non-state actors, such as terrorist groups.

Chart 9.2 illustrates the rising uncertainty that has been generated by Donald Trump's November 2016 election to the White House from the standpoint of domestic, not foreign, economic agents. Domestic sources of Country Risk have been increasing since the turbulent election of Donald Trump. One can distinguish three main sources of Trump-driven volatility, namely, direct, indirect, and collateral sources of Country Risk (Bouchet 2017).

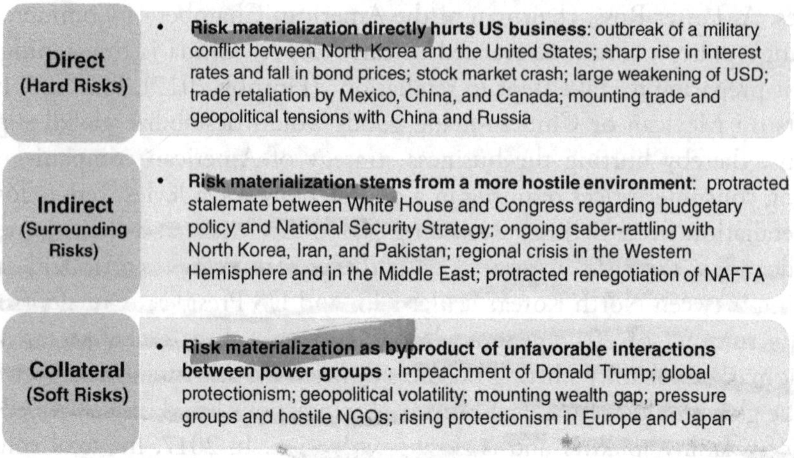
Direct
(Hard Risks)
• Risk materialization directly hurts US business: outbreak of a military conflict between North Korea and the United States; sharp rise in interest rates and fall in bond prices; stock market crash; large weakening of USD; trade retaliation by Mexico, China, and Canada; mounting trade and geopolitical tensions with China and Russia
Indirect
(Surrounding Risks)
• Risk materialization stems from a more hostile environment: protracted stalemate between White House and Congress regarding budgetary policy and National Security Strategy; ongoing saber-rattling with North Korea, Iran, and Pakistan; regional crisis in the Western Hemisphere and in the Middle East; protracted renegotiation of NAFTA
Collateral
(Soft Risks)
• Risk materialization as byproduct of unfavorable interactions between power groups : Impeachment of Donald Trump; global protectionism; geopolitical volatility; mounting wealth gap; pressure groups and hostile NGOs; rising protectionism in Europe and Japan

Chart 9.2 President Donald Trump-driven socio-political uncertainty

9.4 The Root Causes of Sociopolitical Instability

A number of academic scholars and scientists have pointed to the inherent instability of a worldwide market-based economic system. One example is Daniel Bell, one of the most influential cultural critics of the postwar era and a sociologist and professor emeritus at Harvard University, best known for his contributions to post-industrialism. In his two masterworks, *The Coming of Post-Industrial Society* (1999) and *The Cultural Contradictions of Capitalism* (1976), Bell analyses the post-industrial society that produces a dangerous polarization resulting in social tensions between the twin pressures of labor productivity and the hedonist drive of consumption. He concludes that capitalism is inherently unstable. Another example is Samuel Huntington, who approached the issue from a different perspective. According to Huntington, sociopolitical institutions are less and less efficient for mediating social demands in the process of modernization, as we shall see later in this chapter. Fred Hirsch also analyzed the "social limits to capitalist growth" given that the rising satisfaction of private goods consumption leads to new demands on the political system regarding income distribution, justice, education and knowledge, and social goods. The constraints set by social limits inexorably make society more dependent on collective provision and collective orientation or on a centralized and authoritarian decision-making process (Hirsch 1976). To sum up, there is an inherent contradiction between liberal democracy and a market-based economic system. Rising wealth gaps and wage stagnation lead to a social polarization that generates centrifugal forces that only an authoritarian regime might be able to stem. In the United States as in most developed countries, the polarization between wage earners and capital owners is widening. Since the early 1970s, the hourly inflation-adjusted wages have barely risen, growing only 0.2% per year. The benefits of dynamic growth are not equally distributed given that the primary way most people benefit from such growth has almost completely stalled (Shambaugh and Nunn 2017).

The globalization of the market economy since the 1980s has raised the issue of whether Democracy is still a shield against sociopolitical turbulence. In Western democracies where economic growth, social progress, and parliamentary elections proved to be a strong cohesion system after World War II, political risk has recently gained a systemic dimension. The resurgence of populist movements has always heralded a weakening of democracies. Such movements emerge when traditional political parties lose their legitimacy. They fill a political vacuum and are symptomatic of the crisis before becoming its cause. Although the crisis manifests itself differently from one country and type of regime to another, the chain reaction is similar across countries, starting from lower growth and unequal income distribution and leading to the emergence of populism and social turbulence, including centrifugal forces that challenge political power centralization, and with signs of regional fragmentation. This cycle has been occurring for nearly four decades as a result of the social imbalances born of globalization and technological progress. The spectrum of secular stagnation with expanding wealth gaps in most developed countries has generated feelings of mistrust vis à vis political elites that seem at best unable, or at worst unwilling, to offset the centrifugal forces of the globalized market economy. Political ineffectiveness in the age of globalization generates frustration and violence outside the traditional channels of social mobilization such as unions and political parties. Regional fragmentation and secession demands in several European countries (e.g., Catalonia, Corsica, Lombardy, Veneto, and Scotland) are symptoms of this frustration. Regional turmoil is a cause of costly Country Risk. In Catalonia, for instance, around 3,000 companies left Spain's eastern coastal region in the wake of the secessionist claims by year-end 2017. Regional economic growth declined with around half of the companies declaring they were suffering from a decline in sales, a loss of clients, and that they had implemented an investment freeze (*Les Echos* 2017).

In most OECD countries, Internet and the Global Financial Crisis of 2008 subsequently nurtured this frustration by enabling a heightened perception of socioeconomic imbalances. Tax evasion by global companies illustrates the limits of governments' policy influence to cement national unity and enforce solidarity. Finally, terrorism and nuclear proliferation have stoked fear, the final ingredient for a breakdown in political legitimacy (Bouchet 2004). In developed countries, this crisis of institutional legitimacy is exemplified with Podemos in Spain, Syriza in Greece, the Five Star Movement in Italy, Alternative for Germany, and the France Insoumise Party. The democratic systems in Europe and in North America seem less and less capable of stemming the rise of political extremism. In emerging market countries, the consequence of mounting social imbalances began to materialize with the Arab Spring and also in Latin American countries such as Mexico, Brazil, and Venezuela.

Democracy has always been experienced as a promise of equality with the challenge of fulfilling it. This is because that promise is always postponed. This paradox has become unbearable and perceptions of inequality and corruption have been multiplied by the Internet (Rosanvallon 2006). Indeed, democracy is a more unstable regime than proponents of democracy believe, as its legitimacy derives not only from a value system but also from a compromise of interests. Globalization and technological advances have led to larger and more visible socioeconomic divides between as well as within nations. It is the worldwide scale of this mix that has led to the manifestation of political risk in areas that were once felt to be stable and relatively "risk-free."

9.5 Where Does Social Turbulence Come from?

Samuel Huntington (1968) analyzed the consequence of distorted social behavior in rapidly growing economies. He considered that in nations evolving rapidly from gradual modernization to modernity, new exogenous demands on government cannot be adequately channeled through socio-political institutions. Traditional channels of social mediations are less and less efficient for mediating social demands, resulting in mounting tensions, upheaval, violence, and corruption. The latter is one measure of the absence of effective political institutionalization. Corruption, like violence, results when the absence of mobility opportunities, combined with a concentrated decision-making system and weak and inflexible political institutions, channels ambitions and frustrations into politically violent behavior. In that regard, the centralization of economic and political power coupled with repression can only postpone and exacerbate social tensions and lead to turmoil. As Nassim Taleb and Gregory Traverton observe: "On its face, centralization seems to make governments more stable. But that stability is an illusion. The best early warning signs of instability are found not in historical data but in underlying structural properties. Past experience is a bad bellwether of complex political and economic events, particularly so-called tail risks—events, such as coups and financial crises that are highly unlikely but enormously consequential" (Taleb and Traverton 2015). When economic power is concentrated into a few hands, the resulting wealth gap leads to political power concentration, particularly in commodity-dependent countries that rely on raw materials and hydrocarbon revenues. This is the case of a large number of countries in Africa, where one product accounts for more than half of total export receipts. The most commodity-dependent developing counties are also the most unstable and inherently corrupt. For instance, countries with the largest share of oil exports in total export revenues include Iraq, Libya, Algeria, Venezuela, Azerbaijan, Sudan, Nigeria, Oman, Kazakhstan, Russia, Colombia, Bolivia, Iran, Ecuador, Ghana, Indonesia, and Malaysia. Each of these has a high level of corruption according to the Transparency International ranking. A noticeable exception is Norway, where gas-driven tax revenues are invested in a wealth fund to protect the well-being of future generations, and, to a lesser extent, Brunei and Qatar. A key feature of these countries is that they have relatively stable governance, despite abundant hydrocarbon resources. Governance can be defined as "the traditions and institutions that determine how authority is exercised in a particular country" (Kaufmann et al. 2000). Collier has shown the inverse relationships between raw material endowments and economic development, given that coastal and resource-scarce countries in Africa performed much better than their resource-rich counterparts, whether landlocked or coastal. Most resource-rich states have unusually weak checks and balances and decentralized public spending, with few exceptions such as Botswana (Collier 2006). Figure 9.1 illustrates the strong relationship between oil-dependent revenues, weak institutions, and corruption.

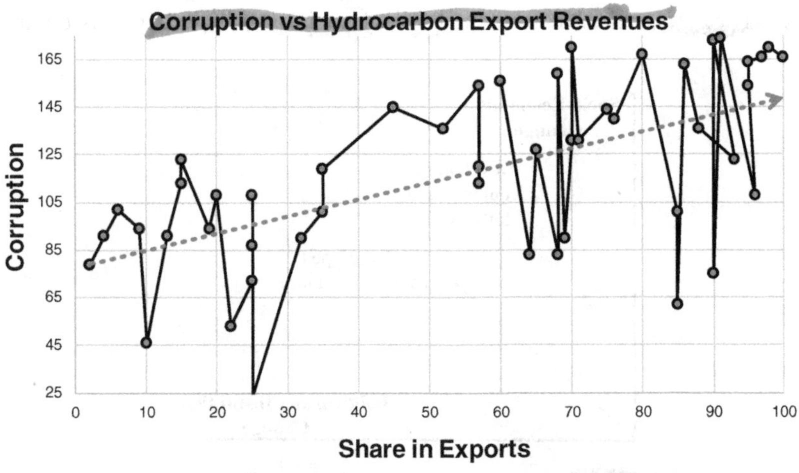

Fig. 9.1 Correlation between share of hydrocarbon revenues and corruption (*Source* authors' calculations, data from World Bank, WEF, and Transparency International)

In most rich countries with poor populations, the resulting concentration of policy and political decision-making creates patron–client relationships and marginalizes a significant portion of the population. Modernization that is not matched by institutional development and inclusiveness breeds political turmoil and corruption. In other words, fast economic change in emerging market countries is often not matched by the simultaneous development of socio-institutional channels to mediate and soften the emergence of new political demands. They take place in the sphere of immaterial goods and services, such as access to information, labor unions and working rights, political parties and associations, and democratic demands.

Economic growth extends political awareness and broadens social participation, consequently multiplying political demands. Any deficit in institution-building sooner or later leads to social upheaval. The resulting crisis of institutional mediation produces a sequence of frustration, tensions, repression, and violence. A case in point is Zimbabwe's four decades of autocratic rule with President Mugabe that ended in a military takeover in November of 2017. In sovereign credit ratings such as that of S&P, this risk is captured indirectly by the assessment of popular participation in political processes. Figure 9.2 depicts the rise in sociopolitical instability graphically, with the tension between the rapid social change that is at the heart of the modernization process, and a lag in the process of institutional change.

Political instability is thus the result of a weakness in the process of social mobilization in countries that experience fast socioeconomic change. Though dictatorship can enforce short-term stability through the resort to force and repression, this arbitrary use of force will be contested by citizens' collective action. A chain reaction will begin, increasing the necessary level of repression to maintain a given level of social stability. Citizens engage in

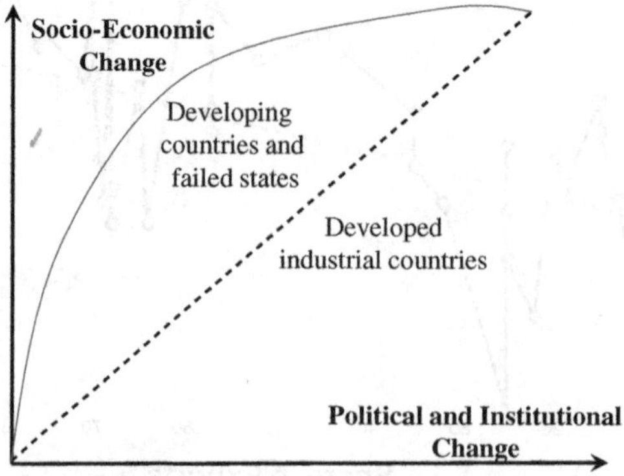

Fig. 9.2 Relationships between Socio-Economic and Politico-Institutional Changes

Country	Leader	Date	Years in power	Characteristics
Tunisia	Zine Ben Ali	1/2011	30	Popular uprising
Egypt	Hosni Mubarak	02/2011	30	Popular uprising
Egypt	Mohamed Morsi	07/2013	1	coup
Libya	Muammar Gaddafi	09/2011	42	Popular uprising
Burkina Faso	Blaise Campaoré	11/2015	27	Popular uprising
Angola	Jose Eduardo dos Santos	08/2017	38	coup
Angola Sonangol	*Isabel dos Santos*	11/2017	2	*dismissal*
Gambia	Yahya Jammeh	1/2017	23	coup
Ivory Coast	Laurent Gbagbo	04/2011	10	Civil war + French army
Niger	Mamadou Tandja	02/2010	11	coup
Guinea-Bissau	Carlos Gomes Junior	04/2012	8	coup
Mali	Amadou Touré	03/2012	10	coup
Central Afr. Rep.	François Bobizé	03/2013	14	coup
Zimbabwe	Robert Mugabe	11/2017	37	Popular uprising + coup
		Average years	20	

Fig. 9.3 Is Africa moving forward? Military coups 2010–2017

riots, demonstrations, strikes, and, in the limit, a revolution to remove the elite from power. Sooner or later, repression results in diminishing returns due to a combination of external and internal pressure, as exemplified by Spain and Portugal in the mid-1970s, China in the late 1980s, the Ivory Coast in 2010, Tunisia over the 2011–2018 period, and Venezuela, Burma, Zimbabwe, Iran, and Turkey in 2016–2017. Institution building is thus a prerequisite for channeling social mobilization with a view to preventing frustration, political upheaval, and corruption. Nye refers to the same challenge in different words when he concludes: "Political development refers to the recurring problem of relating governmental structures and processes to social change" (Nye 1967). Though the African continent does not hold the monopoly of political turmoil, the combination of rent-seeking based on raw materials, large wealth gaps, and corruption has generated a large number of military coups and popular uprising. Figure 9.3 illustrates a number of these events over the 2000–2017 period.

9.6 Conclusion

Since the Global Financial Crisis, political risk has increased in many regions of the world economic system. A combination of volatile capital flows, fluctuating commodity prices, terrorism, and mounting wealth gaps have kept political risk analysts on their toes. More than ever, political risk insurance and investment guarantees are the names of the game. Political risk involves the unexpected unfavorable consequences of the arbitrary exercise of power by a government and its domestic and foreign ramifications, as well as by non-governmental actors. Researchers, analysts, and risk managers have discovered that developing countries hold no monopoly over socio-political destabilization. Though socio-political violence, such as guerrilla warfare, revolutions, and dictatorships have been the trademarks of rapidly growing developing countries in an environment of repressive regimes, new forms of political risk have emerged, such as changes in regulatory frameworks, opacity, wealth gaps, and corruption. In developed countries, the nature of political risk is more subdued. Social stability prospects are clouded by rising inequality and sluggish real wages, which can undermine the sustainability of growth while fuelling discontent. In both developed and developing countries, the rise in sociopolitical instability is rooted in the tension between the rapid social change at the heart of the modernization process, and a parallel lag in the process of institutional change. Flexible institutions play a crucial role channeling social mediation as discussed in the following chapter.

Case Study: Tunisia and the 2011 Arab Spring's "Jasmin" Revolution (Bouchet 2018)

1. **A country with a Glorious History and an Uncertain Future:** Tunisia has long experienced waves of foreign political and cultural influence. This started in the eighth century BC with the Phoenicians who founded Cartago and dominated the entire Western Mediterranean basin until the second century BC. It was then the turn of the Roman Republic to impose its mark on the so-called Berber territory of Ifriqiya until the fourth century AD. In the seventh century, the Arab armies decisively defeated the Byzantine forces taking firm control of the new Muslim state, which it ruled from Damascus, despite continued stiff resistance from the Berbers. Ottoman imperial rule started in the mid-sixteenth century and resulted in the Bey's continuous taxation and financial transfers to the Turk capital Constantinople; this precluded any self-sustaining development of rural areas or of a modern society of merchants and entrepreneurs. The beginning of the French Protectorate in the late nineteenth century marked the end of Tunisia as an Ottoman province amid a situation of financial bankruptcy and civil unrest. French colonization led to numerous modernizing reforms in infrastructure, education, agriculture, and finance; nevertheless, it did nothing to diminish the social divide between urban and rural areas, nor in geographical terms between the developed coastal areas and the poorer western and southern territories.

   After World War II, the struggle for national independence intensified and led to the emergence of the Republic of Tunisia in 1956 under the leadership of Habib Bourguiba. The first President of Tunisia based his rule upon a combination of nationalism and cult of personality, a new constitution, and an ambitious socioeconomic reform program. Cronyism and deeply rooted corruption increased after Bourguiba's removal from power in November

1987 with a bloodless coup d'état by his prime minister, Zine Ben Ali. A subservient one-party system led Ben Ali to run for an unlimited number of five-year terms in an environment of human rights violations, wealth concentration, and money laundering. This lasted until widespread popular protest triggered the "Arab Spring," thereby forcing Ben Ali and his cronies to flee into exile in January 2011. The "Jasmin revolution" in Tunisia against Ben Ali's dictatorship proved deceptive, however. As summarized by the Carnegie Middle East Centre (Yahya 2016): "Tunisian society is in the transition from a repressive yet stable past to an open-ended future where all options seem possible. The path it takes depends on whether its political leadership is able to forge a vision inclusive of all Tunisian citizens; one that recognizes and addresses the grievances that prompted their momentous December 2010 uprising."

2. **The enduring blindness of IFIs and rating agencies**: When assessing political risk in Tunisia, risk managers and rating agencies used to justify their optimism on the country's repression-based sociopolitical stability. Between 1994 and 2000, Tunisia attracted roughly USD 500 million annually in net FDI flows as well as USD 1.5 billion in tourism revenues, the equivalent of 8% of GDP. Despite ongoing trade imbalances, the country managed to maintain an external debt to GDP ratio in the neighborhood of 50%. Yet, despite dynamic economic growth and large flows of FDI, a combination of structural unemployment, deep corruption, and unequal income distribution led to a spiral of intensive campaigns of civil resistance, street demonstrations, and repression, culminating in the ousting of President Ben Ali. Right up to the eve of the sociopolitical upheaval, in September 2010, the IMF continued to praise Tunisia's government: "Over the past two decades, the North African nation has undertaken wide-ranging structural reforms aimed at enhancing its business environment and improving the competitiveness of its economy. These reforms, accompanied by prudent macroeconomic management, have reduced the Tunisian economy's vulnerability to shocks—including the Global Financial Crisis—and provided more options for the authorities to respond to them" (IMF 2010). Despite mounting social tensions, the IMF's key policy advice was to implement "expenditure control, reform of the social security system, pension reforms, and containing subsidies for food and fuel products." Meanwhile, the UNDP kept improving the Human Development score of the country, amidst considerable income, regional and gender inequality. Since national independence, however, Tunisia has epitomized a country with dynamic growth and little development. Education and subsidies have never been enough to provide a gratifying future to a young and rapidly growing population.
   Figure 9.4 illustrates the sharp rise in the HDI level throughout the 1990s and the ongoing gradual improvement during Ben Ali's regime, according to the UNDP.
3. **The pitfalls of political and economic centralization:** Since the country gained independence from France in the mid-1950s and despite statewide advances in economic growth, political decision-making and policies in Tunisia remained strongly centralized. Social stability was built on a combination of subsidies and repression. Both Bourguiba and Ben Ali effectively controlled the country's capital and surrounding coastal zones.

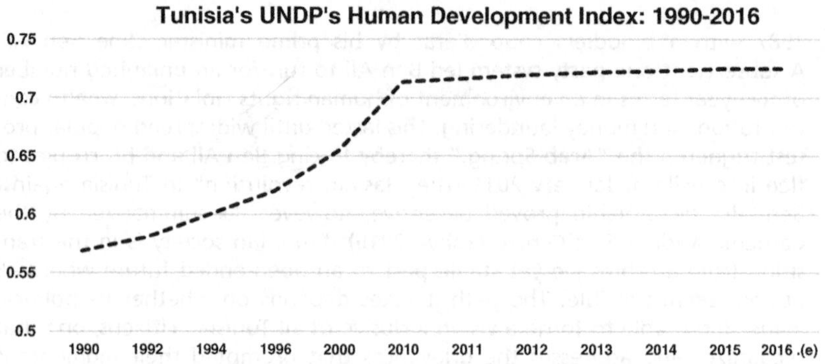

Fig. 9.4 Tunisia: Human Development Index 1990–2016

Unemployment remained stubbornly at 15% of total population and much higher for youth. Social peace was obtained through discretionary wage increases in the public sector and high recruitment, all contrary to the IMF's call for tougher market-based economic policies at a faster pace. The country's government could not adopt the IMF's recommendations of tight budgetary consolidation to tackle the "main budgetary rigidity of the wage bill" without giving rise to a social explosion. Consequently, though the Arab Spring was sparked by the self-immolation of a young street merchant on December 17, 2010, the roots of social upheaval in Tunisia go much deeper; they include corruption, lack of job opportunities for youth, poor living conditions except for the coastal areas, and repressed political freedom.

Rating agencies failed to take into account these structural and political constraints when analyzing the country's stability. Ratings improved continuously between 1994 and 2010, before abruptly worsening in the aftermath of the sociopolitical turmoil in 2011 (see Appendix 9.1). The inability of rating agencies to identify "Signal from Noise" contributed to the overreaction of investors in the wake of the shock effect of the political turmoil and abrupt downgrading.

Figure 9.5 shows the rise in the cost of insurance against a sovereign default after the ousting of Ben Ali, with no early warning signal provided.

4. **Country Risk in Tunisia: The explosive combination of social rebellion without a genuine revolution**. In the aftermath of the Arab Spring, a coalition between the Ennadah party, closely related to the Muslim Brotherhood, and politicians formerly associated with Ben Ali, ran the country's government. A new Constitution was enacted in January 2014, imposing Islam as the country's religion. The ongoing ambiguity between political and economic liberalization and continued adherence to religious principles in the sociopolitical arena has prevented Tunisia from regaining the confidence of global markets as well as that of the local population. A number of multinationals decided to transfer their activities to Morocco, Portugal or Spain, where they found better productivity and more stable sociopolitical environments. Corruption in Tunisia has continued unabated and the country is ranked no. 74 by Transparency International, worse than Bulgaria and Burkina Faso. Unemployment has remained a key obstacle to social peace,

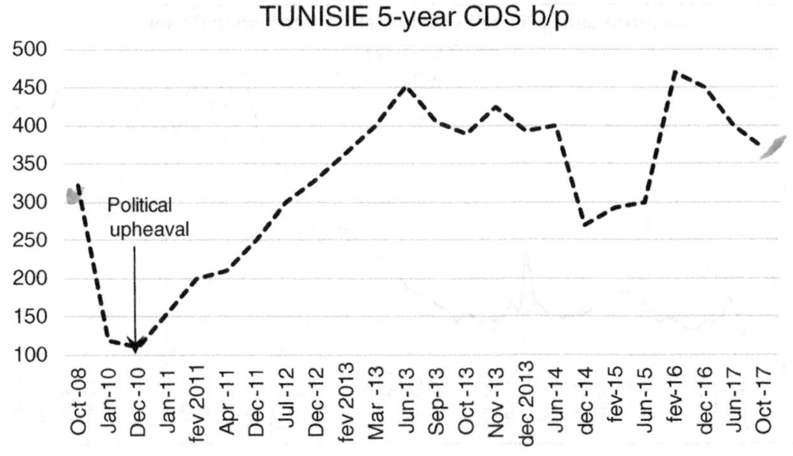

Fig. 9.5 Tunisia's 5-year CDS 2008–2017

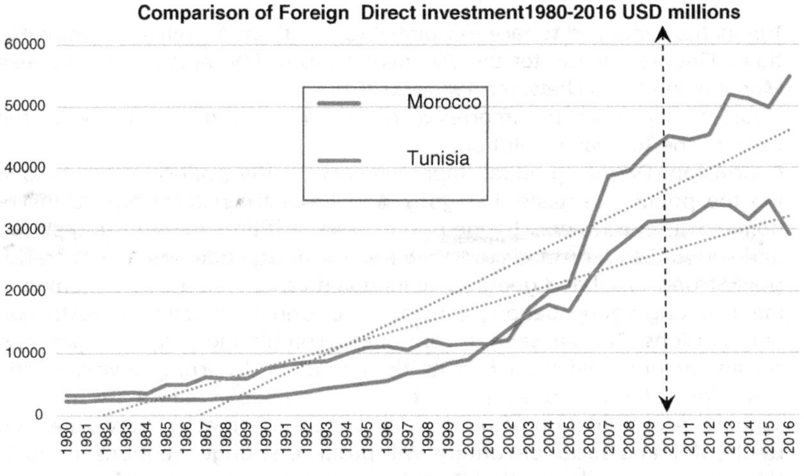

Fig. 9.6 Morocco and Tunisia: Foreign Direct Investment Capital Inflows 1980–2016 (*Source* IMF)

especially for youth. Since 2011, the country has faced a combination of anemic growth, high inflation (in the neighborhood of 8%), twin budgetary and current account deficits, and eroding external creditworthiness with a debt to GDP ratio that reached nearly 60% in 2017. Tourism revenues dropped from an average of USD 2.6 billion in the 2008–2010 period to only USD 1 billion in 2016–2017, slightly compensated by Russian, Libyan, and Algerian tourists. Overall, despite moderate improvements in sovereign ratings,

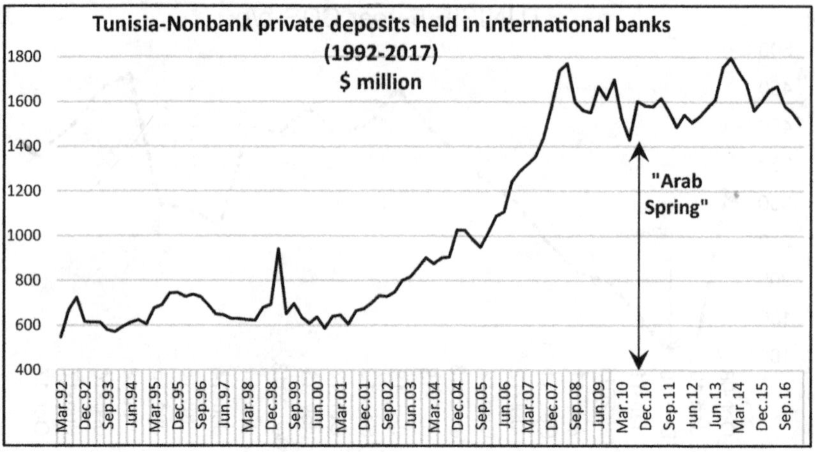

Fig. 9.7 Tunisia: Evolution in Offshore Private Banking Deposits (*Source* BIS data)

Tunisia has continued to face substantial capital flight as well as declining FDI flows. Figure 9.6 illustrates the divergent paths of FDI capital flows between Morocco and Tunisia between 1980 and 2016.

Figure 9.7 illustrates the impressive rise in private capital outflows in the wake of the Tunisian revolution.

5. **Conclusion:** Despite gradual improvements on the political front following the popular protests that got rid of Ben Ali's dictatorship, socioeconomic policies have not changed significantly since the pre-uprising period and Tunisia has remained stuck in what seems an endless phase of transition. Strong social and geographic inequalities, as well as high unemployment among young people, constitute continuing sources of frustration and tensions. Tunisia cannot continue accumulating large budget and current account deficits while its debt reaches disturbing levels. In the meantime, the Trump administration will probably reduce its financial support. A combination of tighter policy measures that are recommended by the IMF and social discontent will produce stronger tensions. In addition, a major challenge that Tunisia faces comes from ongoing security issues and, still more importantly, the ambiguity of the coalition government regarding freedom of speech, the path toward democracy, gender equality, and a clear stance against radical Islamism. The new Investment Code of September 2016 will fall short of restoring the attractiveness of the country in the absence of sociopolitical stability and an unambiguous commitment toward political openness. In the meantime, competition from Morocco and Southern Europe in attracting tourism as well as capital flows has become a genuine risk that Tunisia will be marginalized in the global arena.

Appendix 9.1: Ratings of Tunisia's Sovereign Risk 1994–2017

	R&I	Fitch	Moody's	S&Ps
1994	BBB+stable			
1995	BBB+stable	BBB– stable	Baa3 stable	
1996	BBB+stable	BBB– stable	Baa3 stable	
1997	BBB+stable	BBB– stable	Baa3 stable	BBB– stable
1998	BBB+stable	BBB– stable	Baa3 stable	BBB– stable
1999	BBB+stable	BBB– stable	Baa3 stable	BBB– stable
2000	BBB+stable	BBB– stable	Baa3 positive	BBB stable
2001	BBB+stable	BBB stable	Baa3 positive	BBB stable
2002	BBB+stable	BBB stable	Baa3 positive	BBB stable
2003	BBB+stable	BBB stable	Baa2 stable	BBB stable
2004	BBB+stable	BBB stable	Baa2 stable	BBB stable
2005	BBB+stable	BBB stable	Baa2 stable	BBB stable
2006	BBB+positive	BBB stable	Baa2 stable	BBB stable
2007	A– stable	BBB stable	Baa2 stable	BBB stable
2008	A– stable	BBB stable	Baa2 stable	BBB stable
2009	A– stable	BBB stable	Baa2 stable	BBB stable
2010	A– stable	BBB stable	Baa2 stable	BBB stable
2011	BBB–	BBB–	Baa3–	BBB–
2012	BBB– stable	BB+	Ba1 negative	BBB–
2013	BBB– negative	BB–	Ba2 negative	BB–
2014	BBB– negative	BB–	Ba2	n.a
2015	BB+negative	BB– stable	Ba3 stable	n.a
2016	BB+	BB– negative	Ba3 negative	n.a
2017	BB stable	B+stable	Ba3 negative	n.a

References

AON Risk Solutions. 2012. "Civil Unrest Leads Aon to Downgrade 37 Countries on Political Risk Map." *Insurance Journal*, April 25.

Ashkenas, Jeremy. 2016. "Nine new findings about inequality in the United States." *The New York Times*, December 16.

Bell, Daniel. 1976. *The Cultural Contradictions of Capitalism*. New York: Basic Books.

Bell, Daniel. 1999. *The Coming of Post-industrial Society*. New York: Basic Books.

Bouchet, Michel Henry. 2004. "The Impact of Geopolitical Turmoil on Country Risk and Global Investment Strategy." In *Terrorism and the International Business Environment, The Security-Business Nexus*, edited by Gabriel Suder. Northampton: Edward Elgar Publishing.

Bouchet, Michel Henry. 2010. "Economie de la Connaissance et Hyperfinance: De la Globalisation des Crises Aujourd'hui à la Régulation Globale Demain?" in *Management de l'Economie de la Connaissance,* edited by Dibiaggio, Ludovic and Pierre-Xavier Meschi. Paris: Pearson.

Bouchet, Michel Henry. 2010–2018. "Skema Business School. Country Risk Seminars and Country Risk MOOC." www.developingfinance.org.

Bouchet, Michel Henry. 2017. "The Changing Nature of Country Risk in the Age of Globalization and Donald Trump." *The World Financial Review,* November–December, vol. 217, pp. 34–37.

Collier, Paul. 2006. "Africa, Geography and Growth." Center for the Studies of African Economies, Department of Economics. Oxford University.

Deringer, Heidi, Jennifer Wang, and Debora Spar. 1997. "Note on Political Risk Analysis." *Harvard Business Review Case Study,* September 17.

Euromoney. 2017. *Country Risk Survey.* https://www.euromoney.com/article/b13rn-r3qdbyxj8/ecr-survey-results-q2-2017-russia-india-rest-of-asia-back-on-radar-portugal-most-improved.

Financial Times. 2017. "US Department of Justice." January 18.

Grant, James. 1996. "Too Big to Fail? Walter Wriston and Citibank." *Harvard Business Review,* July–August.

Groom, Brian. 2014. "Brexit—UK Could Find Itself Tied to EU Rules, But With No Say." *Financial Times,* September 29.

Hirsch, Fred. 1976. *Social Limits to Growth.* Cambridge: Harvard University Press.

Hornby, Lucy. 2017. "US Companies in China Sound Alarm on Trump Trade Stance." *Financial Times,* January 18.

Huntington, Samuel P. 1968. *Political Order in Changing Societies.* New Haven and London: Yale University Press.

IMF. 2010. "Tunisia: 2010 Article IV Consultation: Staff Report; Public Information Notice on the Executive Board Discussion; and Statement by the Executive Director for Tunisia." September 8.

IMF. 2010. *Survey: Tunisia Weathers Crisis Well, But Unemployment Persists.* September 10. https://www.imf.org/en/News/Articles/2015/09/28/04/53/socar091010a.

IMF. 2017. *Global Prospects and Policy Challenges. G-20 Leaders' Summit.* July 7–8. http://www.imf.org/external/np/g20/pdf/2017/070517.pdf.

Kaufmann, Daniel, Art Kraay, and Pablo Zoido-Lobatao. 2000. "Governance Matters: From Measurement to Action". *Finance & Development* 37 (2): 10–13.

Kobrin, Stephen J. 1979. "Political Risk: A Review and Reconsideration". *Journal of International Business Studies* 10 (1): 67–80.

Kraar, L. 1980. "The Multinationals Get Smarter About Political Risks." *Fortune,* March 24.

Les Echos. 2017. "Elections en Catalogne. Etude de ESADE." December 19, p. 5.

MIGA. 2013. "World Investment and Political Risk."

MIGA 2014. "World Investment and Political Risk."

Nye, Joseph S. 1967. Corruption and Political Development: A Cost-Benefit Analysis. *American Political Science Review* 61 (2): 417–427.

OECD. 1999. *Anti-Bribery Convention: Entry into Force of the Convention*, February 15. http://www.oecd.org/daf/anti-bribery/oecdanti-briberyconventionentryintoforceoftheconvention.htm.

Organisation of American States. 2008. *IMF Hails Tunisian Economic Policies*. November 21. http://www.oas.org/en/sla/dil/inter_american_treaties_B-58_against_Corruption.asp.

Piketty, Thomas, Emmanuel Saez, and Gabriel Zucman. 2016. "Distributional National Accounts: Methods and Estimates for the United States." Washington Center for Equitable Growth. Working Paper Series 120716, December. Washignton, D.C.

Rosanvallon, Pierre. 2006. *La Contre-Démocratie*. Paris: Le Seuil.

Ross, Lester. 2017. "US Companies in China Sound Alarm on Trump Trade Stance." *Financial Times*, January 18.

Shambaugh, Jay, and Ryann Nunn. 2017. "Why Wages Aren't Growing in America." *Harvard Business Review*, October 24.

Shambaugh, Jay, Ryann Nunn, Patrick Liu, and Greg Nantz. 2017. Thirteen Facts About Wage Growth. Figure B. Economic Facts, The Hamilton Project, The Brookings Institute, p. iii.

Taleb, Nassim Nicholas, and Gregory F. Treverton. 2015. "The Calm Before the Storm: Why Volatility Signals Stability, and Vice Versa." *Foreign Affairs*, January–February.

World Bank. 2007. *World Governance Indicators*. http://info.worldbank.org/governance/wgi/#reports.

Wright, Thomas. 2017. "Order from Chaos. Trump, Xi, Putin, and the Axis of Disorder." Brookings Institute, November 8.

Yahya, Maha. 2016. "Great Expectations in Tunisia." Carnegie Middle East Center, March.

Yassukovich, Stanislas Michael. 1976. "The Growing Political Threat to International Lending." *Euromoney*, April.

10

The Root Causes and Consequences of Political Risk: From Bad Governance to Wealth and Political Power Concentration and Social Instability

10.1 Introduction

Why do some countries seem to experience and enjoy a stable transition from one stage of economic development to another, despite the turbulence generated by the globalization of the market economy and the tensions produced by new technologies? Why are rating agencies and political risk analysts caught off guard by a sudden rise in sociopolitical volatility in both developed and developing countries? Why is the economic "catching-up process" still a remote dream while larger wealth gaps can be observed both within and between countries? And what are the ingredients of the delicate and crucial balance between economic change and institutional adjustment? Finally, why are corruption and opacity the two root causes of income inequality and sociopolitical turmoil in so many rich countries whose people are poor? These questions are addressed in this chapter after the previous one dealt with the main components of political risk.

10.2 The Role of Governance in Stimulating Inclusive Growth and Stabilizing Sociopolitical Systems

The question of "the roots of sociopolitical risk?" has been addressed since the 1970s and 1980s in many academic and policy circles, though mainly in the United States and, to a lesser extent in Western Europe. In many

M. H. Bouchet et al., *Managing Country Risk in an Age of Globalization*,
https://doi.org/10.1007/978-3-319-89752-3_10

countries of Latin America, Eastern Europe, Africa, and Asia, the economic change was not a smooth journey. A number of causes for sociopolitical turmoil have been discussed without no consensus: from the Dependency theory's structural constraints of the world capitalist system to the need to adopt market-based economic policies for the neoclassical school.

10.2.1 From economic growth to sustainable and inclusive development?

Where does socioeconomic development come from? The five main schools of thought regarding the key ingredients of socioeconomic growth can be summarized as follows: The traditional approach emphasizes the optimal combination of physical and human capital and the role of technological progress in accelerating the takeoff toward sustainable development. A second approach considers that the gap within and between rich and poor countries should disappear as countries progress through the stages of socioeconomic development that all societies eventually experience as they mature into industrialized modern societies. A third approach places geography as the key determinant of socioeconomic development due to the impact of climate, the endowment of natural resources, the burden of disease and transport costs on agricultural productivity, and the quality of human capital. Though geography is not completely down to fate, the conditions inherent to a location are the main driving forces behind successful economic takeoff. The fourth school of thought puts the emphasis on the role of trade openness as a driver of productivity change and competitive specialization in a typical Ricardian model. The fifth stream of academic research shows that large differences in income per capita and socioeconomic development can be explained by differences in institutions and property rights. According to Rodrik et al. (2004), countries with more flexible and resilient institutions tend to invest more in human capital. Accordingly, institutions provide social frameworks, incentives, and channels that formalize and organize socioeconomic and political interactions. As such, they are crucial elements in the process of transforming economic growth into sustainable and inclusive development (Acemoglu et al. 2015). This process requires the simultaneous emergence of robust institutions, social mobilization, and good governance—a triptych that International Financial Institutions (IFIs) have started to take seriously into consideration only since the late 1980s.

10.2.2 The crucial role of governance in transforming growth into development

What does "Good Governance" mean? Governance has become a platitude, a genuine "cliché" in discussions regarding the need to provide a long-term social horizon to private and public management in the globalized market economy, contrary to what Dominic Barton, Global Managing Director of McKinsey & Company, calls the "tyranny of short-termism" (2011). Though there have been several definitions that focus on the public or private dimensions of the concept, governance usually refers to sound public administration and service quality. According to a 1989 World Bank definition, "Governance means the exercise of political power to manage a nation's affairs" (World Bank 1989). The World Bank refined and expanded its definition of governance to stress the role of institutions: "Governance consists of the traditions and institutions by which authority in a country is exercised" (Kaufmann et al. 2000, World Bank 2017). The African Development Bank states: "Good governance speaks directly to the process by which authority is shared and exercised in the management of a country's economic and social resources" (African Development Bank 1998, 37). Overall, according to a former US Treasury official, governance includes transparency, government accountability in using public funds, and the rule of law and social inclusion (Summers 2000). Our own definition of governance is a slightly wider. Governance consists of a range of institutional channels of social mediation that ensure accountability, responsibility, and transparency in private and public affairs (Bouchet 2010).

One can summarize the required combination of economic dynamism, inclusive growth, and socio-institutional flexibility by concluding that development contains economic growth plus the conditions that make it self-sustaining. These conditions include democratic legitimacy, robust and stable institutions, and efficient public administrations (Bouchet 2010–2018). Efficient public sector institutions thus are at the heart of good governance. For the IFIs, institutional strengthening comprises the "second generation" of reforms that affect the relationship between the state, the market, and civil society. Second-generation reforms aim at strengthening so-called "social capital"—a concept that Fukuyama defines as group solidarity and trust in human communities. In the economic sphere, social capital reduces transaction costs while in the political sphere it constitutes the cultural component of modern societies that is necessary for the success of limited government, inclusive growth, and liberal democracy (Fukuyama 2000).

For both developed and developing countries, governance is a policy choice. It can thus be encouraged or discouraged by government officials, entrepreneurs, NGOs, foreign investors, and international institutions. At stake is the transformation of economic growth into long-term sustainable and inclusive development, hence the importance of policy choice and the respect of "public interest." What matters is the intersection of moral values and socioeconomic policy decisions. In that regard, economic policymaking inevitably affects the political and socioeconomic balance of power; it can thus lead to tensions between various groups of stakeholders, both public and private. Economic liberalization, trade openness, fiscal reforms, and dynamic growth have strong consequences on the balance between rural and urban areas, between the state and the private sector and between the need to regulate and the wish to stimulate risk-taking. At the heart of these balances is the sharing of the benefits of growth reflected in income distribution and wealth gaps. Krueger notes: "When an economic policy creates a new group of gainers or losers, or when it enhances the political influence of a group, that change affects the relative strength of different groups in the political process, which in turn changes the political equilibrium" (Krueger 1993).

10.3 The Centrifugal Forces of Market Globalization

The neoliberal agenda that is known as the "Washington consensus" has focused on two main objectives: the first aims at shrinking the role of the state through privatization and liberalization, constraining government through limits on the size of fiscal deficits and sovereign debt; the second aims at stimulating competition through deregulation, trade openness, and market liberalization. These are expressed in John Williamson's ten rules of market-based economic policies (Williamson 1990, 2004). The key objectives of structural reforms and fiscal consolidations are raising private sector confidence and maintaining market access by obtaining the rating agencies' blessing. In the medium term, market efficiency is supposed to generate positive growth effects through foreign and domestic investment and a more competitive legal and regulatory environment. Clear and conducive rules of the game, that is, property rights and the rule of law will help to transform economic expansion into sustainable and more inclusive growth.

From a political risk viewpoint, however, implementing the Washington consensus often requires macroeconomic adjustment with short-term negative economic and sociopolitical consequences. Recent academic research has explored the unequal distribution of the side-benefits of market liberalization. The International Monetary Fund (IMF) itself, after promoting economic liberalization for decades, reached a fairly disquieting conclusion: "The benefits in terms of increased growth seem fairly difficult to establish when looking at a broad group of countries. The costs in terms of increased inequality are prominent. Such costs epitomize the trade-off between the growth and equity effects of some aspects of the neoliberal agenda. Increased inequality in turn hurts the level and sustainability of growth" (Ostry et al. 2016).

In terms of structural reforms, accelerating the pace of economic liberalization can enhance income inequality with a negative impact on social cohesion. The distributional effects of competition and liberalization require supporting institutions to offset the social costs in both the short and medium term. Otherwise, the promise of faster growth and trickle down will quickly generate frustration and social turbulence. This has been the case in the European Union following the Global Financial Crisis, particularly in Portugal, Greece, and Spain. In terms of policy choice, a rapidly changing social system needs to adapt its values and norms to fully mobilize civil society toward public interest and sustainable development. This condition is illustrated by Chile's President Bachelet who emphasizes the links between strengthening democracy, economic growth, and social protection: "In Latin America, there are countries where people are uneasy about the process of economic liberalization, because structural economic reforms were not accompanied by the social policies that were necessary. The problem has not been with open economies per se but rather the lack of action in addressing poverty and social injustice" (Bachelet 2007). Likewise, China's Prime Minister Wen Jiabao warned in 2010: "Political reform is a necessary companion to economic modernization. Indeed, without the safeguard of political reform, the fruits of economic reform would be lost" (*The Telegraph* 2010).

10.4 The Relationship Between Corruption, Business Conditions, Income Distribution, and Sociopolitical Instability

The question is whether the combination of labor, capital, and technological progress are sufficient ingredients for stimulating economic growth and gradually bringing about the conditions for sustainable development. As discussed earlier, the latter can be defined as economic growth coupled with the specific conditions that make it sustainable: education, health, the requisite infrastructures, and an institutional system flexible and robust enough to provide adequate channels of social expression. There is a considerable corpus of academic research that tackles the relationship between economic growth and institutions, as summarized in Appendix 10.1. Policy-oriented research that focuses on the links between governance and socioeconomic development has emerged in international financial institutions, mainly at the World Bank and at the IMF, since the mid-1990s. As Abed and Gupta observe (2002): "Since the breakup of the former Soviet Union, and the consequent unwinding of regional conflicts, (…) sound macroeconomic policies, a healthy regulatory environment, more transparent and accountable public institutions, and protection of property and investor's rights became essential prerequisites for attracting foreign direct investment and for accessing financial markets at reasonable terms." Accordingly, academic research has focused increasingly on rent-seeking, the role of the state, regulations, and corruption, while bilateral and multilateral agencies have started to question government officials, regarding transparency and good governance. Since the mid-1990s, foreign aid is conditional not only on macroeconomic stabilization policies (in other words, reducing deficits) but also on transparency and social inclusiveness. The reason for such new conditionality is that bad governance runs counter to the transparency of the rules of the game, while opacity encourages rent-seeking behavior and privileges. At a certain point, external financing gets recycled through offshore banking accounts without any benefit for local populations. This is why Chapter 14 will address the issue of capital flight and expatriated private savings as a measure of Country Risk.

10.4.1 Corruption and Domestic Business Conditions

The first major consequence of bad governance and corruption is to distort the conditions for a level playing field. Corruption produces opacity that is obviously detrimental to risk-taking and entrepreneurial initiatives. High levels of corruption tend to decrease investment levels, contributing to weak infrastructures, and to loose regulatory frameworks, hence undermining the quality of institutions. The following table illustrates the close correlation between the quality of business conditions (that is, the legal and regulatory framework as well as labor market conditions) and the level of perceived corruption for eighty-five emerging market countries. The greater the amount of corruption, the worse the quality of business conditions (Table 10.1).

Table 10.1 Relationships between the Corruption Perception Index (Transparency International 2017) and the Doing Business Index (World Bank 2017). Authors' calculations

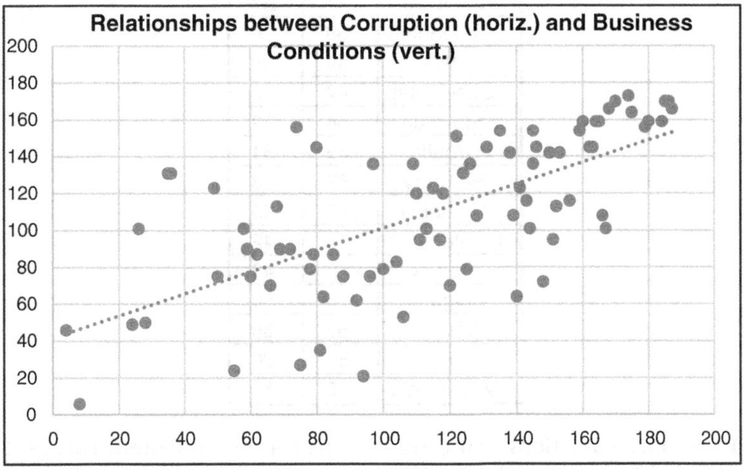

Nevertheless, as emphasized throughout this book, developing countries do not have a monopoly on the impact of corruption on the quality of business environment. In the group of thirty-five OECD developed countries, Spain, Korea, Italy, and Greece have worse corruption rankings than Cap Verde and Botswana. France repeatedly has a worse corruption ranking than Uruguay. In the case of Eastern European countries, abrupt market liberalization and privatization programs in the early 1990s have contributed to so-called "crony capitalism" (that is, privileges, information, asymmetry, and rent-seeking). Figure 10.1 summarizes the corruption and business conditions in sixteen Eastern European countries at the end of 2017 according to the Corruption Perception Index (CPI) of Transparency International and the business conditions (BUS) according to the International Finance Corporation (IFC), the private sector arm of the World Bank. One can observe a close convergence between corruption and the quality of "doing business" conditions, with the remarkable exception of Macedonia whose corruption index is one of the worst in the sample while its quality of business conditions is excellent, according to the IFC's annual rankings of 190 countries in 2018. The IFC measures the quality of business conditions with various quantitative indicators, such as the cost of construction permits, the length of procedures for getting electricity, labor costs, and flexibility in employment regulations. Little attention is paid to the quality of governance and transparency of contracts and transactions that are assessed by a

	CPI	BUS.
Estonia	22	12
Poland	29	27
Slovenia	31	37
Lithuania	38	16
Latvia	44	19
Czech Rep	47	30
Slovakia	54	39
Croatia	55	51
Hungary	57	48
Romania	57	45
Montenegro	64	42
Serbia	72	43
Bulgaria	75	50
Albania	83	65
Bosnia	83	86
Macedonia	90	11

Fig. 10.1 Business conditions and corruption perception in Eastern Europe (*Sources* World Bank and Transparency International)

separate department of the World Bank in a totally distinct exercise in the so-called Worldwide Governance Indicators. Overall, then, Macedonia gets a "corruption control" ranking almost half that of Estonia (47 vs. 85). One observes that the lower the corruption index, the better the quality of business conditions.

10.4.2 The Combination of Corruption, Income Inequality, and Political Risk

As discussed in Chapter 9, a measure of political risk can be found in the combined analysis of income distribution and wealth concentration, social programs cuts, and the distribution of fiscal pressure. In most developing countries, there is a correlation between the level of corruption and the level of income inequality. The Gini index, which takes the value of 0 with perfect income equality and 1 with extreme income concentration, can help focus on this dangerous relationship that is prone to generating social upheaval. Table 10.2 illustrates the close correlation between income inequality and corruption in eighty-five developing countries.

However, once again, developing countries have no monopoly on large and rising income gaps. The negative impact of fiscal adjustment on economic growth and wealth gaps is precisely what has happened since 2008 in

Table 10.2 Relationship between Corruption and Income distribution (*Source* Authors and data from Transparency International, the World Bank, and the CIA's World FactBook 2017)

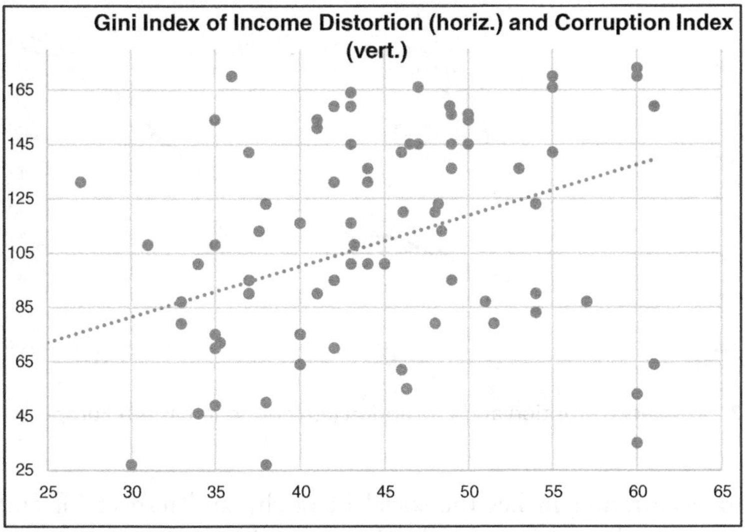

the OECD countries, specifically in the Eurozone. Income inequality levels have remained at historical highs. As such, the Gini coefficient of disposable income, a standard measure of income inequality, is a key variable for political risk analysis. According to the OECD, the Gini index reached 0.318 in 2014, the highest value on record since the 1980s (OECD 2016). The economic recovery in the OECD area between 2010 and 2017, exemplified by improvements in labor markets, has neither delivered inclusive growth nor reversed the trend toward mounting income inequality, a trend underlined by research at the OECD, the IMF, and in the scholarly community by authors such as Piketty (Piketty et al. 2016; World Wealth and Income Database 2017). Figure 10.2 illustrates the long-term distortion between labor compensation and productivity in the US economy, with a marked "scissor effect" since the mid-1980s (Shambaugh and Nunn 2017; Shambaugh et al. 2017).

Figure 10.3 summarizes the transmission process between corruption and sociopolitical tensions. In short, corruption discourages risk-taking and entrepreneurial initiatives, hence contributing to lower investment levels. Lack of transparency and rent-seeking contribute to tax evasion, the underground economy, and capital flight, increasing both income and wealth gaps. The corruption that emerges from economic and political

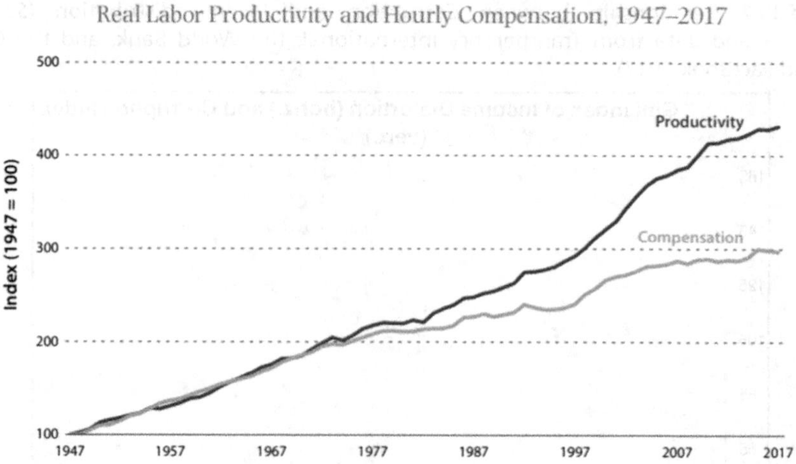

Fig. 10.2 Business corruption and Corruption perception in Eastern Europe

power concentration makes the social hierarchy and respect for authority less legitimate. It generates a disdain for political elites which are perceived as parasites of the system. Dissidence and discontent then increase. Mounting frustration, in turn, leads to social tensions and political repression, as witnessed by several countries during the "Arab Spring." In Iran, at the beginning of 2018, street riots witnessed the worse unrest since the 2009 pro-democracy revolt. Antigovernment protests in many towns and provinces, middle- and working-class strongholds, denounced not only economic hardships, including widespread youth unemployment and deteriorating purchasing power, but also unabated corruption, a wealth gap, and a repressive regime. In Venezuela, in the Philippines, in Zimbabwe, in Tunisia, and in many developing and more developed countries, corruption and wealth concentration are more than ever perceived as a glass ceiling between today's hardships and tomorrow's personal and social progress ambitions.

The links between inequality and insurgency were studied early on by Muller and Seligson (1987). They found that when income inequality was high, the probability of domestic political violence increased substantially, and could lead to uprisings. Sociopolitical upheaval, in turn, slows economic growth down in a perverse spiral of lower purchasing power, increasing income disparity, and mounting social frustration. Overall, the close observation of income distribution distortions, across time and countries, must be at the heart of political risk analysis.

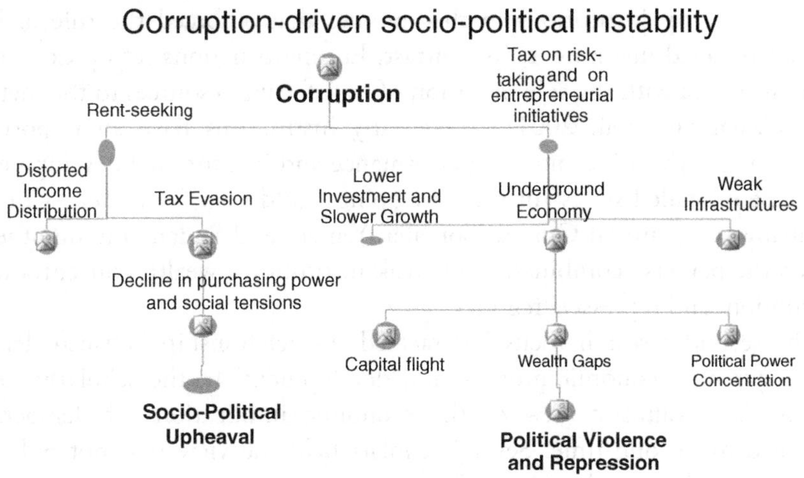

Fig. 10.3 Income inequality and Corruption perception in developing countries

10.5 The Role of Democratic, Legal, and Regulatory Systems

Political upheaval affects not only multinational corporations with cross-border transactions, but also international banks, hedge funds, and domestic economic agents in the country itself. There has been a renewed interest in how institutional development affects sociopolitical stability. Specifically, much of this research has focused in three directions. The first has tackled the relationship between political institutions and political risk in order to assess the links between democratic systems and economic liberalization in emerging markets. Jensen, for instance, has tested how domestic political institutions affect the premiums multinational corporations pay for coverage against political threats, such as government expropriations and contract disputes (Jensen 2008). The conclusion is that democratic regimes reduce risks for foreign direct investment, specifically through constraints and checks and balances on the executive. The superiority of the democratic environment regarding cross-border investment prospects stems from the limits of decision arbitrariness and the balance of power between the executive, the legislative, and the judiciary branches of government and the role of civil society. Overall, democratic regimes lead to lower levels of political risk. Academic research, however, has shown that history also matters, specifically, differences in colonial experience vis-à-vis Western powers. For instance, English based colonization (i.e., United States, Australia, and New

Zealand) set up institutions in the colonies that enforced the rule of law and encouraged investment. In contrast, European nations set up extractive states in Africa with the sole intention of transferring resources to the metropole (Acemoglu et al. 2001). These early institutions have an important effect on today's socioeconomic performance and institutional development. The case of "failed states" in the developing world (e.g., Venezuela, Congo, Zimbabwe, Equatorial Guinea, Somalia, Yemen, and Sudan, among others) shows the perverse combination of weak institutions, wealth concentration, corruption, and repressive regimes.

The second research focus has tackled the relationship between democratic systems, economic growth, and development. In the scholarly community, a pessimistic view of the economic implications of democracy prevailed for a long time. Several scholars held the view that not only do more political rights have no effect on economic growth, but also that a centrally controlled authoritarian political system can impose the critically important policies needed to promote modernization. This is for, instance, argued by Huntington, Gerring, Barro, and *New York Times* columnist Thomas Friedman. However, more recent research by Acemoglu et al. (2015) has shown that democracy has a robust impact on long-term and more inclusive economic growth. It increases GDP per capita by encouraging investment, increasing schooling, inducing economic reforms, improving public good provision, and reducing social unrest. A democratic sociopolitical system thus tends to promote social cohesion as well as trust in institutions, thereby contributing to creating the conditions conducive to entrepreneurship and risk-taking. In addition, Robinson's long-term observation of the cross-sectional relationship between the level of income per capita and the level of democracy illustrates a positive relationship between income per capita and democratization (Robinson 2006). In other words, economic growth also promotes democracy.

The third angle of analysis of the root sources of political risk is revealed by the Legal Origins Theory that focuses on investor protection, ownership rights, legal and regulatory rules, such as entry regulations, disclosure requirements and the range of procedural rules in litigation (La Porta et al. 2008). There is not much consensus in academic research, however, regarding the order of priorities between political stability and inclusive development. One school of thought gives priority to sociopolitical order as a prerequisite to igniting growth, while the other gives priority to robust institutions and good governance. One can summarize the polarized stances in the following Fig. 10.4.

How to move from Economic Growth to Sustainable and Inclusive Development?

Assumption no 1 **Buoyant economic growth first!**	Assumption no 2 **Robust institutions first!**
▸ Primacy of **human capital for both growth and democratization:** human and social capital shape both institutional and productive capacities of a society. ▸ Growth in **income and human capital** causes institutional improvement with better political institutions even with pro-market dictators. ▸ Policy choices matter, while institutional quality rises as a country grows richer. ▸ Economic growth and human capital accumulation promote institutional improvement, rather than the other way around	▸ **Democracy** and other checks on government are the **key mechanisms** for securing property rights and boosting growth ▸ **Good and stable institutions will enhance the pace and quality** of economic growth ▸ **Robust institutions and good governance matter for transforming** economic growth into sustainable social development ▸ Sustainable development and inclusive growth will shrink wealth gaps and ensure socio-political stability

Fig. 10.4 The polarized stances regarding the origins of development

History also matters regarding good governance and sociopolitical stability. Academic research shows that the laws of common law countries (originating in English law) are found to be more protective of outside investors than the laws of civil law (originating in Roman law) countries, particularly those of French civil law countries. The common law approach to social control of economic life performs better than the civil law approach. La Porta, Lopez de Silanes, Shleifer, and Vishny have shown that Britain managed to attract dynamic capital inflows through a conducive legal and regulatory framework (Glaeser et al. 2004; La Porta et al. 2008). Consequently, Britain always had a higher stock market capitalization to GDP ratio than France, often by a wide margin in the late nineteenth century as well as in the following century. Financial development is more widespread and deeper in common law countries than in civil law ones and has much better shareholder rights. In the mid-twentieth century, civil law countries relied heavily on state finance, bank nationalization, and state investment companies to promote economic growth and resolve crises, whereas common law countries relied more heavily on market-supporting regulations, such as securities laws, deposit insurance, and court-led improvements in the corporate law. All in all, thanks to legal and regulatory evolution, common law countries ended up with much better investor protection and their financial markets ran far ahead of those based on civil law. In civil law countries, heavy government intervention and regulation have led to bureaucracy and arbitrary decisions that are not conducive to entrepreneurship or private risk-taking and are more open to corruption when transplanted to developing countries.

Appendix 10.2 presents a concise survey of academic literature regarding the relationships between country risk stability, institutions, democracy, and socioeconomic development.

10.6 Assessing the Risks of Sociopolitical Destabilization? Hard Data Versus Subjective Analysis

Sociopolitical as well as geopolitical risks cannot be monitored and measured with precise metrics like exchange rate and stock market volatility. The risk analyst should aim at shedding light on the root causes of political turmoil in order to define and implement appropriate risk mitigation strategies. As we have seen, political risk assessment is not an "either/or" matter. A number of approaches can be used, including the so-called "grand tour approach." This consists of visiting the country "in-depth" with a wide range of meetings with government officials, union leaders, scholars, and NGOs. It is also useful to rely on a team of in-house experts, often including those who have previously held high positions in intelligence services or diplomacy. Further, econometric models can be used, although they are of doubtful credibility in the area of political risk assessment. The purchase of comprehensive intelligence analysis reports is the easiest and least demanding approach. However, nothing will ever replace a serious analysis of the sociopolitical turbulences that may emerge inside or outside of the country concerned.

10.6.1 The Prince Model

The Prince Model approach maps out a country's political power structure. This general political risk forecasting model is focused on a power analysis; it was developed in the 1970s by William D. Coplin and Michael K. O'Leary of the firm Political Risk Services (Coplin and O'leary 1972). They developed the acronym PRINCE, which stands for "Probe, Interact, Calculate, and Execute." The political risk analysis model is based on identifying the key players who can most directly affect a business strategy, including political luminaries, NGOs, lobbyists, unions, ethnic organizations, scholars, and even foreign governments and IFIs. The position of each player indicates its degree of positive or negative influence on the outcome being forecast. Reflecting the country's intricate sociopolitical ramifications, the model provides probability scores for the most likely regime, social upheaval, turmoil, and restrictions on trade and investment. The model outcome is, of course, as good as the quality of the expertise of the political specialists who supply information for the model and adjust the calculations generated by the model according to their own subjective knowledge about a given country. One of the limitations of the Prince Model is that it can quickly become outdated and must be refined and updated almost continuously. The power structure in Morocco in 2017, for instance, would present several power circles including King Mohammed VI and his inner circle of advisers and partners; the Justice and Development Party, a moderate, nonviolent and nonrevolutionary Islamist party that recognises the current political system of the monarchy; the Polisario front in the Sahara region that maintains unabated military tensions, tight diplomatic and economic relations with the EU, and the key US intelligence and military support for its oldest and closest allies in the Maghreb in the fight against global terrorism. A sketch of Algeria's power structure in 2018 could be summarized as shown in Fig. 10.5. Given that one-third of the roughly forty two million Algerians is less than sixteen years old and two-thirds are less than sixty five years old, the country's youth is in itself a formidable force of sociopolitical change, though today it is silenced by a combination of structural unemployment, social subsidies, and political control.

10.6.2 Macro-Political Economy Analysis

Of particular importance in political risk analysis is the risk of social disturbance resulting from economic policy choices, including in developed countries. A tension between market economic policies and social demands

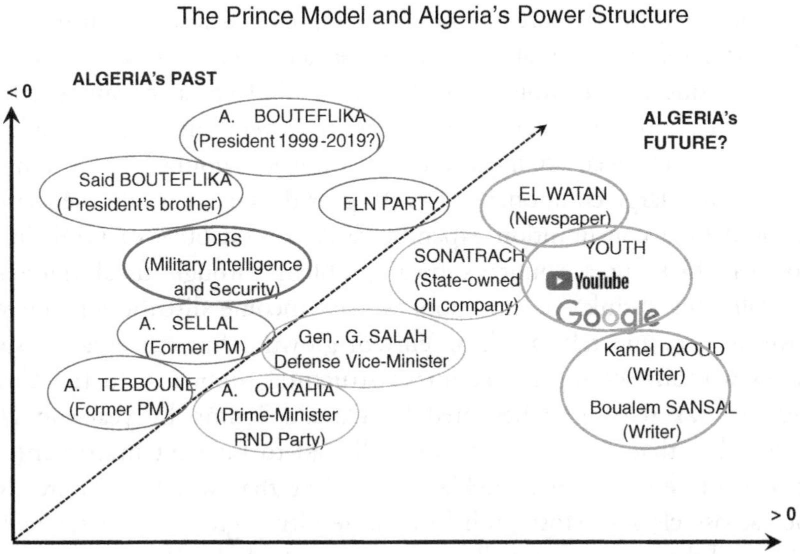

Fig. 10.5 Sketch of Algeria socio-political forces as of 2018

is a powerful trigger for a social disturbance. Depending on the country's institutional system, the eruption of sociopolitical strain will lead, at best, to marches and strikes or at worst, to a chain reaction of violence and repression. In OECD countries, and particularly in EU members, the eruption of the Global Financial Crisis has created mounting pressure on government budgets given that sovereign debt burdens have reached record highs. Today's sovereign debt accumulation boils down to postponed taxation, resulting in today's generations' claims on future generations that must be tackled by a combination of increased tax revenues and shrinking expenditure. Should one generation choose default regardless of the consequences for future generations, to maximize its current level of consumption? The key issue is that of the social and intertemporal redistribution of the fiscal retrenchment burden. Quite often these fiscal problems are due to market rigidities, entry barriers, and distortive tax systems. A program of reform must, therefore, include both fiscal consolidation and institutional reforms to enhance future growth.

Growth and the broader tax base that goes with it probably provide the best prospect for solving the fiscal challenge. The timing issue is that of the policy tradeoff between fiscal consolidation and institutional reform (Teulings 2012). In many European countries such as France, Spain, Portugal, Greece, and Italy, the two policy goals coexist under the pressure of the European Commission and the policy framework of the 1992 Maastricht Treaty. On the one hand, fiscal consolidation aims at protecting market access with low spreads and attracting capital inflows; on the other, institutional reform aims at expanding the tax base. Political risk is likely to increase due to a combination of postponed electoral promises, adjustment fatigue, and the reduction of the current generation's wealth and hence its consumption level. In most OECD countries, domestic consumption accounts for a large component of GDP growth, i.e., typically the share of household final consumption expenditure is around 60% of GDP in the Euro-area. Tackling a country's fiscal problem through fiscal tightening only, will thus shrink consumption, worsen income distribution, increase the wealth gap, and take a toll on current growth, thus exacerbating social tensions without solving the country's structural problems. In the United States, the tax reform orchestrated by Donald Trump by year-end 2017 is a risky bet that corporate tax cuts will lead to buoyant investment and employment resulting in a trickle-down effect that will boost purchasing power across classes. Most probably, the resulting growth impetus will be modest and the income gap will keep growing (Table 10.3).

Table 10.3 Illustrates and summarizes a number of socioeconomic indicators and indices that political risk analysts should take into account

Institution	Indicators	Focus	Web address
World Bank	World development indicators	National, regional and global estimates	http://data.worldbank.org/data-catalog/world-development-indicators
IFC	Doing Business Index	Legal and regulatory environment	http://www.doing-business.org/rankings
UNCTAD	Trade Openness Ratios	Investment, trade and sustainable development	http://unctad.org/en/Pages/statistics.aspx
OECD	Income Distribution Database	Gini coefficient	http://www.oecd.org/social/income-distribution-database.htm
UNDP	Human Development Index	Social and development indicators	http://hdr.undp.org/en/content/human-development-index-hdi
WID	Income inequality database	Cross-country income and wealth data	http://wid.world/
WEF	Global Competitiveness Ranking	Productivity and prosperity drivers	https://www.weforum.org/reports/

10.6.3 Rating Agencies

Three main agencies, namely Standard & Poor's (S&P), Moody's, and Fitch, hold a de facto monopoly of creditworthiness assessment, hardly challenged by Coface and China's agency Dagong. For the last four decades, credit rating agencies have shown a consistent track record of poor performance in sociopolitical analysis. Among their numerous shortcomings, we can underline an oversimplistic approach that reduces a large number of indicators to one single grade which has little predictive value and gives rise to a risk of self-fulfilling prophecy that encourages the herd instinct. Country ratings often lead to "follow the crowd" behavior by lenders and investors, thereby precipitating and expanding crises in fragile countries. An abrupt political risk downgrading in one country is likely to create ramifications in neighboring countries, thereby accelerating the crisis and contributing to capital flight and regional contamination. In addition, cross-country comparative assessment of risk levels relies on common criteria and on a more or less explicit methodology that is at times akin to black boxes. Despite the shortcomings of ratings and rankings, scholars have shown that perceptions of Country Risk are greatly influenced by the publication of annual risk ratings by a small number of financial publications and research institutions that produce a "market consensus"(Vijayakumar et al. 2009).

Despite this modest track record, rating and scoring still constitute the most popular form of political risk assessment, in parallel with in-house research teams. Rating agencies produce sovereign credit ratings that constitute a quantitative and qualitative assessment of each government's ability and willingness to service its debt in full and on time. According to S&P, "a rating is a forward-looking estimate of default probability." Sovereign ratings are not "country ratings" in that they only address the credit risk of national governments, but not the specific risk of other issuers (Standard & Poor's 2004). Although credit rating agencies, unlike more specialized institutions, do not focus on the risk of sociopolitical turbulence, they still incorporate a qualitative analysis to address the political and policy developments impacting future debt servicing prospects. The debt servicing capacity is ultimately based on the choices of economic policymaking, including fiscal and balance of payments policies. In this regard, political choices are crucial. A country can be significantly affected by the relationships with neighboring countries and the burden of military threats on fiscal policy. These factors can impact domestic investment, export revenues, and official reserve assets. In the case of S&P's credit ratings, political risk addresses the sovereign's willingness to repay debt through the following six subjective indicators among more than forty. Table 10.4 sums up the six political risk factors taken into account by S&P:

Table 10.4 Standard & Poor's sovereign credit ratings' political risk assessment

1	Stability and legitimacy of political institutions
2	Popular participation in political processes
3	Orderliness of leadership succession
4	Transparency in economic policy decisions and objectives
5	Public security
6	Geopolitical risk

A lack of attention to sociopolitical risk has been exemplified in many turbulence examples, including the 1982 EMCs crisis, the 1994 Mexican crisis, the 1997 Asian crisis, the 2000 Argentine crisis, the 2007 subprime mortgage meltdown, and the 2010 sovereign debt crisis in Southern Europe. As illustrated in the Arab Spring case study at the end of the previous chapter, the sociopolitical turbulence in Maghreb countries in 2011 was accompanied by widespread regional downgrading that hurt countries that had not been affected by the neighboring political turbulence, such as Morocco and Jordan. The 2011 spring revolutions in the Middle East and North Africa region witnessed a near complete lack of early warning signals. Political risk shortsightedness led to abrupt postcrisis downgrading, thereby contributing to deepening socioeconomic difficulties and encouraging costly spillover effects.

In March of 2010, less than one year before the political turmoil in the Maghreb countries, S&P upgraded Morocco's external debt to investment grade, i.e., to BBB- from BB+. The agency attributed the upgrade to the Kingdom's improved economic policy flexibility as well as its high sociopolitical stability. In the meantime, Moody's gave a Ba1 rating to both Egypt and Morocco coupled with a "stable outlook" and a Baa2 rating to Tunisia. Libya was then rated A—"stable" by S&P, ranked better than an OECD country such as Turkey. Moreover, the "big three" had no monopoly on mediocre country risk analysis. In its annual ranking of development in 2011, the United Nations Development Programme heaped praise on Libya, Tunisia, Saudi Arabia, Jordan, and Algeria for their "high level of human development." Rating agencies only began to react to the situation in April of 2011, while Moody's downgraded Tunisia to "Baa3 negative" from the prerevolutionary Baa2. S&P gave Libya a mere BB grade with a negative outlook. The range of credit ratings of Maghreb and other Arab countries in early 2011 in the wake of the Arab Spring shows the downgrading contamination of the entire region in Q1-2011 after the political turbulence in Tunisia and Egypt, given that the political unrest and its economic impact were hurting sovereign credit quality over the whole of the Middle East and North Africa. Table 10.5 shows a list of Maghreb's country ratings in the beginning of 2018.

The rating agencies' assessments appear to arise from the belief that authoritarian governments (such as the military dictatorship in Algeria, the authoritarian monarchy in Morocco, and the crony political system in Tunisia and Syria) were efficient deterrents against the centrifugal forces of wealth concentration and Islamic revolutionaries. In the Spring of 2009,

Table 10.5 Credit ratings Q1-2018

	Tunisia	Morocco	Algeria	Egypt	Jordan	Syria	South Africa
S&P's	BBB	BBB-		BB–	BB–		BBB+
Moody's	B1–	Ba1		Ba2–	Ba2–		Baa1
Fitch	B+	BBB–		BB–			BBB+
EIU	CCC	B	BB	CCC	CCC	CCC	BBB+
Coface	B	A4	A4	B–	B	C–	A3–
Capit. intelligence	BBB	BBB–	BBB	B	BB	BB–	
Dagong	BBB+	BBB+		BBB–			A
Euler-Hermes	B	B	C	C	B	D	BB
R&I-Japon	BBB-						A–

S&P confirmed its assessment of "stable outlook" for the Republic of Tunisia, adding that "the ratings on Tunisia remain constrained by a pace of political liberalization that is gradual compared to similarly rated countries, despite advances in recent years" (*CBonds* 2009). Rating agencies' confidence in the socio-economic stability of Tunisia reflected a decade of fast GDP growth, at around 4% per year. As late as in the end of 2008, the disreputable IMF's Managing Director, Strauss-Kahn, kept praising the "favourable prospects, the impressive progress and the significant gains of Tunisia's pragmatic approach to structural reforms," despite the sombre reality of deeply rooted corruption, a large gap in income distribution, structural unemployment, and a repressive regime (Middle East Online 2008). Four months before the start of political unrest in Tunisia, the IMF still commended Tunisia's macroeconomic management quality: "Over the last two decades, Tunisia has carried out a wide-ranging reform program based on improving the competitiveness of the economy, enhancing the business environment, and increasing trade openness" (IMF 2010). Contrary to Huntington's warning, an inadequate emphasis was given to the growing gap between the country's dynamic economic growth on one side and its lagging sociopolitical institutionalization on the other, resulting in the growing frustration of the youth and the urban bourgeoisie. Structural unemployment, wealth concentration, and repression were the three triggers of the upheaval in Egypt, Syria, Yemen, Morocco, and Tunisia.

10.6.4 Specialized Political Risk Ratings

Most banks, insurance agencies, and industrial companies use more specialized political risk ratings such as Euromoney, International Country Risk Guide (ICRG), Marsh, and Institutional Investor. Most of these ratings focus on the direct financial consequences of sociopolitical turmoil. Euromoney defines political risk primarily as the risk arising from nonpayment or non-servicing of payments for goods, services, trade-related finance, loans and dividends and the non-repatriation of capital. ICRG's model aims at predicting political risk based on twelve specific, weighted risk criteria. Table 10.6 lists ICRG's political risk indicators.

Table 10.6 Cross-country political risk measure by ICRG

Weights	ICRG's Political Risk Assessment Criteria
12	Government stability
12	Socio-economic conditions
12	Investment profile
12	Internal conflict
12	External conflict
6	Corruption
6	Military in politics
6	Religious tensions
6	L aw and order
6	Ethnic tensions
6	Democratic accountability
4	Bureaucratic quality
100	Total number of points for weighted influence

10.7 Conclusion

In the age of market globalization, sociopolitical risk has never been so ubiquitous. In emerging market countries, the process of modernization and social change has not been matched by the simultaneous emergence of robust institutions. Authoritarian regimes provide short-term stability at the price of growing repression. Rich countries often have poor populations when economic growth is based on commodity and hydrocarbon resources. In developed countries, the unequal distribution of the benefits of growth generates frustration and tensions that democratic systems can no longer absorb. Overall, risk analysts must look at the power structure of countries and identify the root causes of potential social upheaval. Ratings and rankings can never be substitutes for in-depth analysis backed by a wide range of information sources.

Appendix 10.2 Concise Survey of Academic Literature Regarding the Relationships Between Country Risk Stability, Institutions, Democracy, and Socioeconomic Development

Author	Topic	Relationships democracy, development, and country risk stability	References
Acemoglu, Daron and Robinson, James	Why nations fail	Openness of a society, its willingness to permit creative destruction, and the rule of law are decisive for economic development. Countries escape poverty only when they have appropriate economic institutions, especially private property and competition. In consensually strong states, politicians and political elites are weak, and citizens give them a "long leash" in the economy, consenting to high taxes, regulation, and involvement by the state, with the expectation that the politicians in power and the bureaucrats will work for the citizens' benefits	Crown Publishing Group, NY, 2012
Acemoglu Daron Johnson, Simon and James, Robinson	The colonial origins of comparative development	Differences in colonial experience could be a source of differences in institutional development. The feasibility of European settlement stemmed from differences in mortality rates. European colonization has led to institutions that enforced the rule of law and encouraged investment, or to extractive states and social systems that were detrimental to economic progress	NBER, Working Paper series no. 7771, June 2000
Acemoglu, Daron and James, Robinson	The role of institutions in growth and development	Institutions are collective choices that are the outcome of a political process. The economic institutions of a society depend on the nature of political institutions and the distribution of political power in society. The main determinants of differences in prosperity across countries are differences in economic institutions. Success and pitfalls of institutional reforms are keys to solve the problem of development and poverty	Commission on Growth and Development, Working Paper no. 10, The World Bank, 2008
Acemoglu, Daron, Suresh Naidu, Pascual Restrepo, and James Robinson	Democracy does cause growth	Democracy has a significant positive effect on GDP per capita: democratizations increase GDP per capita by about 20% in the long run by encouraging investment, increasing schooling, inducing economic reforms, improving public good provision, and reducing social unrest	NBER Working Paper no. 20004, March 2014, revised May 2015
Alesina, Alberto and Giuliano, Paola	Culture and institutions	Culture, including trust, family ties, individualism, and generalized morality, and institutions, including political and legal institutions, regulation, and the welfare state, interact and evolve in a complementary way, with mutual feedback effects on the speed of development and wealth	NBER Working Paper series no. 19750, December 2013

Author	Topic	Relationships democracy, development, and country risk stability	References
Barro, Robert J.	Democracy and growth	Favourable effects on growth include rule of law, free markets, small government consumption, and high human capital. But the *net* effect of democracy on growth performance cross-nationally is negative or null. Many countries have become rich under authoritarian auspices. Democracy enhances growth at low levels of political freedom	Journal of Economic Growth 1:1–27, March 1996
Depetris-Chauvin, Emilio	State history, contemporary conflict: evidence from sub-Saharan Africa	Regions with long histories of statehood are better equipped with mechanisms to establish and preserve order. They are less prone to experience conflict when hit by a negative economic shocks	Pontifical Catholic University of Chile. https://ssrn.com/abstract=2679594, October 2015
Diamond, Jared	A country's affluence depends partly on its institutions, on geographic and other historical factors	Institutions don't arise at random around the world but are outcomes of a long history shaped by geography, and they are linked inextricably with the origins of states. Countries with a long history of state societies have tended to enjoy high growth once they added advanced technology to their institutional advantages	"Economics: The wealth of nations", Nature 429: 616–617, June 2004
Chanda, Areendam and Louis, Putterman	Early starts, reversals and catch-up in the process of economic development	More rapid growth by early starters (China, India, Greece) than latercomers to agriculture and statehood has been the norm in economic history, and the "reversal of fortune" associated with the European overseas expansion that began around 1500 was both exceptional and temporary	LSU Working Paper series, 2005–2006
Feng, YI	Democracy, political stability and economic growth	Democracy has a positive indirect effect upon growth through its impacts on the probabilities of both regime change and constitutional government. Long-run economic growth tends to exert a positive effect upon democracy	British Journal of Political Sciences 27(3): 391–418, July 1997
Gorodnichenko, Yuriy, and Roland, Gerard	Culture, institutions, and the wealth of nations	Economic impacts of culture based on the frequency of specific genetic variables: Individualism or collectivism impact on innovation and growth. More individualist culture that emphasizes personal freedom and achievement leads to more innovation and to higher long-run growth	Review of Economics and Statistics 99: 402–416, July 2017

Author	Topic	Relationships democracy, development, and country risk stability	References
Gerring, John Bond, Philip Barndt, William And Moreno, Carola	Democracy and economic growth: A historical perspective	If Democracy matters for growth today, due to a country's regime history as well as its current status. The distant past may have contemporary effects. Democracy is thus best considered as a *stock*, rather than *level*, variable. Secular-historical experience of democracy and authoritarianism matters: long-term democracy leads to stronger economic performance	World Politics 57(3): 323–364, April 2005
Glaeser, Edward L., La Porta, Rafael, Lopez de Silanes, Florencio, and Andrei, Shleifer	Do institutions cause growth?	Existing research does not show that political institutions rather than human capital have a causal effect on economic growth. Much evidence points to the primacy of human capital for both growth and democratization. Poor countries get out of poverty through good policy choices, often pursued by dictators, to subsequently improve their political institutions	NBER Working Paper series no. 10568, June 2004. Journal of Economic Growth 9(3): 271–303, September 2004
La Porta, Rafael Lopez de Silanes, Florencio, and Andrei, Shleifer	The economic consequences of legal origins	Legal origins, i.e., highly persistent systems of social control of economic life, have significant consequences for the legal and regulatory framework of the society, as well as for economic outcomes. The policy-implementing focus of civil law versus the market-supporting focus of common law impacts on economic and social outcomes	Journal of Economic Literature 46(2): 285–332, June 2008
La Porta, Rafael Lopez de Silanes, Florencio Shleifer, Andrei and Robert, Vishny	The quality of government	Countries that are poor, close to the equator, ethnolinguistically heterogeneous, use French or socialist laws, have high proportions of Catholic or Muslims, exhibit inferior government performance. In Catholic countries, governments tend to be less efficient and more corrupt compared to Protestant and common law countries	Journal of Law, Economics and Organization 15(1): 222–279, March 1999
Kynge, James, McKinsey Global Institute	Data-centric approach to governance and economic growth	China's hybrid strain combines rigid political control, central planning and free-market flexibility. Data revolution and party-state lead to "techno-tatorship" to create new economic dynamics with sociopolitical stability. Digital technologies help resolve systemic inadequacies that stem from the corruption-driven centralized authority	*Financial Times*, October 28–29, 2017

Author	Topic	Relationships democracy, development, and country risk stability	References
Przeworski, Adam	Country-specific conditions shape institutions	Political regimes may have two effects on the rate of growth: a direct one on factor productivity, and an indirect one, via the growth of the labor force. Projects of institutional reform must take as their point of departure the actual conditions, not blueprints based on institutions that have been successful elsewhere	Government and Opposition, British Political Science Association, Blackwell Publishing, April 2004
Przeworski, Adam, et al.	Democracy and development, political institutions and well-being in the world,1950–1990	Economic development does not tend to generate democracies, but democracies are more likely to survive in wealthy societies. The type of political regime has no impact on the growth of national income, and political instability affects growth only in dictatorships. Per capita incomes rise more rapidly in democracies due to lower population increase. Political regimes have greater effects on demography than on economics	Cambridge University Press, 2000
Putterman Louis	Ripple effects of the Neolithic Revolution on modern development process	Differences among human societies with respect to the timing of the transition to agriculture led to differences in levels of technological development and social organization that persisted into the era of European expansion and colonization. Early reliance on agriculture at the time of the Neolithic Revolution is still impacting on today's income differences and levels of economic development across countries	Economica New Series 75(300): 729–748, November 2008
Muller, Edward and Mitchell A. Seligson	Inequality and insurgency	When income inequality is high, the probability of domestic political violence increases substantially, and can lead to uprisings and civil war, hence slowing economic growth	American Political Science Review 81(2): 425–450, 1987
Rodrik, Dani, Arvind Subramanian, and Francesco Trebbi	Institutions rule: The primacy of institutions over geography and integration in economic development	There are substantial, economic gains in improving institutions. Geography and History are not key determinants of development. If colonial experiences were the key determinant of income levels, how would one account for the income variations among countries that had never been colonized?	*Journal of Economic Growth* 131–165, November 2004

Author	Topic	Relationships democracy, development, and country risk stability	References
Robinson, James	Economic development and democracy	There is no evidence that economic development has a causal effect on democracy. Neither does it support the idea that economic development influences the probability of coups but not democratization. Economic development comes along with changes in the structure of the economy that are related to capital intensity. Countries with higher income per capita would be more capital intensive, hence generating an empirical relationship between income per capita and democracy but income has no causal effect on democracy	Annual Review of Political Science 9: 503–527, 2006
Sharma, Ruchir	Why economic forecasts fail	Straight-line extrapolations are almost always wrong. Institutions and demographics change too slowly to offer any clear indication of where an economy is headed. Though certain national cultures are good or bad for growth, the point is that culture can change quickly. Political cycles are as important to a nation's prospects as economic ones. To sustain rapid growth, leaders must balance a wide range of factors, and the list changes as a country grows richer	Foreign Affairs 52–56, January–February 2014
Sollogoub, Tania	Where the anger is coming from?	The resurgence of populist movements has always heralded a weakening of democracies. Such movements emerge when traditional political parties lose legitimacy. They fill a political vacuum and are a symptom of the crisis before becoming its cause. Wealth gaps and social imbalances born of globalization and technological progress feed frustration and social unrest	Credit Agricole Group, Economic Research, December 2016

References

Abed, George, and Sanjeev Gupta (eds.). 2002. *Governance, Corruption, & Economic Performance*. Washington, DC: International Monetary Fund.

Acemoglu, Daron, Simon Johnson, and James Robinson. 2001. "The Colonial Origins of Comparative Development: An Empirical Investigation." *American Economic Review* 91 (5): 1369–1401.

Acemoglu, Daron, Suresh Naidu, Pascual Restrepo, and James Robinson. 2015. "Democracy Does Cause Growth." NBER Working Paper No. 20004, March 2014. Revised May 2015.

African Development Bank. 1998. Annual Report: Governance and Economic Management.

Bachelet, Michele. 2007. "Promoting Growth and Social Progress. Interview: McKinsey Quarterly Special Edition." http://e-lecciones.net/archivos/loultimo/Bachalet.pdf.

Barton, Dominic. 2011. "Capitalism for the Long-Term." *Harvard Business Review*, March 2011.

Bouchet, Michel Henry. 2010. "Economie de la Connaissance et Hyperfinance: De la Globalisation des Crises Aujourd'hui à la Régulation Globale Demain?" In *Management de l'Economie de la Connaissance*, edited by Ludovic Dibiaggio and Pierre-Xavier Meschi. Paris: Pearson.

Bouchet, Michel Henry. 2010–2018. "Country Risk Seminars and Country Risk MOOC." Skema Business School. http://www.developingfinance.org.

CBonds. 2009. "Republic of Tunisia Foreign Currency Rating Affirmed At 'BBB'; Local Currency Rating Lowered to 'A–'; Outlooks Stable," April 6. http://cbonds.com/news/item/428938.

CIA. 2017. World FactBook. https://www.cia.gov/library/publications/the-world-factbook/.

Coplin, William, and Michael O'Leary. 1972. *Everyman's Prince: A Guide to Understanding Your Political Problems*. London: Duxbury Press.

Fukuyama, Francis. 2000. "Social Capital and Civil Society." IMF Working Paper WP/00/74, IMF Institute.

Glaeser, Edward L., Rafael La Porta, Florencio Lopez de Silanes and Andrei Shleifer. 2004. "Do Institutions Cause Growth?" NBER Working Paper No. 10568, June.

IMF. 2010. Tunisia: 2010 Article IV Consultation: Staff Report; Public Information Notice on the Executive Board Discussion; and Statement by the Executive Director for Tunisia, September 8.

Jensen, Nathan. 2008. "Political Risk, Democratic Institutions, and Foreign Direct Investment." *Journal of Politics* 70 (4): 1040–1052.

Kaufmann, Daniel, Art Kraay, and Pablo Zoido-Lobatao. 2000. "Governance Matters: From Measurement to Action." *Finance & Development* 37 (2): 10–13.

Krueger, Anne. 1993. "Virtuous and Vicious Circles in Economic Development." *American Economic Review Papers and Proceedings* 83: 351–355.

La Porta, Rafael, Florencio Lopez de Silanes, and Andrei Shleifer. 2008. "The Economic Consequences of Legal Origins." *Journal of Economic Literature* 46 (2): 285–332.

Middle East Online. 2008. "IMF Hails Tunisian Economic Policies." http://www.middle-east-online.com/english/?id=28865.

Muller, Edward, and Mitchell A. Seligson. 1987. "Inequality and Insurgency." *American Political Science Review* 81 (2): 425–450.

OECD. 2016. Income Inequality Remains High in the Face of Weak Recovery. *Center for Opportunity and Equality*, November, Paris: OECD Press. https://www.oecd.org/social/OECD2016-Income-Inequality-Update.pdf.

Ostry, Jonathan D., Prakash Loungani, and Davide Furceri. 2016. Neoliberalism: Oversold?" *Finance and Development* 53 (2): 38–41.

Piketty, Thomas, Emmanuel Saez, and Gabriel Zucman. 2016. "Distributional National Accounts: Methods and Estimates for the United States". Washignton Center for Equitable Growth Working Paper, December 6.

Robinson, James. 2006. "Economic Development and Democracy." *Annual Review of Political Science* 9: 503–527.

Rodrik, Dani, Arvind Subramanian, and Francesco Trebbi. 2004. "Institutions Rule: The Primacy of Institutions over Geography and Integration in Economic Development." *Journal of Economic Growth* 9 (November): 131–165.

Shambaugh, Jay, and Ryann Nunn. 2017. "Why Wages Aren't Growing in America." *Harvard Business Review*, October 24, 2017.

Shambaugh, Jay, Ryann Nunn, Patrick Liu, and Greg Nantz. 2017. Thirteen Facts About Wage Growth. Figure B. Page iii. Economic Facts. The Hamilton Project. The Brookings Institute.

Standard & Poor's. 2004. Sovereign Credit Ratings: A Primer, March 15.

Summers, Larry. 2000. Statement of Secretary of Treasury Lawrence H. Summers at the Development Committee of the World Bank and the International Monetary Fund. Prague, Czech Republic, September 25. https://www.imf.org/external/am/2000/dc/eng/usa.htm.

Teulings, Coen. 2012. "Fiscal Consolidation and Reforms: Substitutes, Not Complements." *VOX-CEPR's Policy Portal*, September 13. http://voxeu.org/article/fiscal-consolidation-and-reforms-substitutes-not-complements.

The Telegraph. 2010. "Wen Jiabao Promises Political Reform for China," October 4.

Vijayakumar, Jayaraman, Abdul A. Rasheed, and Rasul H. Tondkar. 2009. "Foreign Direct Investment and Evaluation of Country Risk: An Empirical Investigation." *Multinational Business Review* 17 (3): 184–204.

Williamson, John. 1990. "Latin American Adjustment: How Much has Happened?" Washignton, DC: Institute for International Economics.

Williamson, John. 2004. "The Washington Consensus as Policy Prescription for Development." Speech Delivered at the World Bank, January 13. https://piie.com/publications/papers/williamson0204.pdf.

World Bank. 1989. "Sustainable Growth with Equity: A Long-Term Perspective for Sub-Saharan Africa." Report No. 8014, Technical Department, Africa Region, August 15.

World Bank. 2007. "World Governance Indicators." http://info.worldbank.org/governance/wgi/#reports.

World Wealth and Income Database. 2017. "World Inequality Report 2018, World Inequality Database." http://wid.world/.

11

Why Emerging Markets Do Not Hold a Monopoly on Country Risk in the Twenty-First Century: An Analysis of Monetary and Systemic Risks in the OECD and in the Euro-Zone

The manner in which things exist and take place constitutes what is called the nature of things, and a careful observation of the nature of things is the sole foundation of all truth.

Jean Baptiste Say. A Treatise On Political Economy (1832).

11.1 Introduction

The words Country Risk at first convey the echo of a range of problems associated with doing business in emerging markets—among them larger default scope, corruption, political instability, lack of transparency in financial disclosure, and questions about the enforceability of contracts. Country Risk is something that one needs to worry about in faraway places. Or so we thought.

The nature of Country Risk has fundamentally changed as a result of the globalization of the market economy, spurred by intense competition for market share in every country and in every market. This is discussed in Chapters 1 and 2. Spillover effect and regional contamination are a permanent threat. The Global Financial Crisis, however, has added a new dimension, that of systemic risk, that contributes to blurring the frontiers between emerging and developed countries. Given that the share of developing countries in global GDP has now reached more than 50%, this group of countries alone contributes to systemic risk. In 2018, India became the fifth largest economy worldwide, ahead of France and the UK, while China's GDP has

M. H. Bouchet et al., *Managing Country Risk in an Age of Globalization*,
https://doi.org/10.1007/978-3-319-89752-3_11

overtaken the US in purchasing power parity terms. By the year 2030, four of the five largest economies will be in Asia, including China, India, Japan, and Indonesia, and the share of the OECD's GDP is anticipated to shrink to roughly 40%. Consequently, country risk managers must be alert to Country Risk in both developed and developing countries. In developed countries, they must assess a combination of potential pitfalls that can contribute to volatility, including excessive leverage in private and public sectors, weak governance, larger wealth gaps, and deregulation. In the age of globalization, the key is to remember that Country Risk is not the monopoly of one specific asset class or type of country.

More specifically, this chapter explores three main risks. First, it addresses the threat of secular stagnation in developed countries where slower growth reinforces the consequences of rising debt leverage. It discusses to what extent this threat affects country risk assessment. Second, it discusses the challenge to OECD central banks of maintaining low-interest rates and boosting long-term growth. And third, it discusses the specific case of the Eurozone and the macroeconomic constraints of the Maastricht Treaty. The chapter also includes two case studies—the root causes of the crisis in Greece, Ireland, Portugal, and Spain (so-called PIGS), and common risk factors arising out of the Global Financial Crisis, the first systemic crisis of the Age of Globalization.

11.2 Is the Threat of Secular Stagnation in the OECD Only an Academic Assumption?

The threat of secular stagnation was identified by Alvin Harvey Hansen (1887–1975), known as the "American Keynes." His conclusion came from his observation of long-term structural headwinds, including population growth decline, technological innovation, and productivity reduction, all leading to a growth slowdown. Hansen's solution was to boost public spending. The threat of long-term stagnation is an issue faced by developed countries. Gordon (2014) argues that slow potential real GDP growth is meaningful—both because of its direct impact on the standard of living and its indirect effect in reducing net investment, which in turn is expressed in slower productivity growth. Gordon identifies a number of underlying causes, including demography, education, and rising debt, while pointing out growing inequalities and slow productivity growth. Growth slowdown stems from the diminishing returns of the digital electronics revolution and a decline in the "dynamism" of the US economy as measured by the rate of creation of new firms. For Summers (2016), risk aversion and deflation due to low-interest rates, large savings, and weak demand are the main underlying forces for the long-term growth slowdown. The central cause of stagnation is the so-called "savings glut" given that the nature of macroeconomic behavior has changed dramatically since the Global Financial Crisis. Much of the concern arises from the long-run effects of short-run developments and the inability of monetary policy to accomplish much more when interest rates have already reached their lowest bound. Figure 11.1 illustrates the long-term trend in developed countries' GDP growth over the 1950–2018 period.

Krugman (2014a, b) shares most of Summers' analysis while focusing on the limitations of a monetary policy that cannot, alone, boost demand and jobs because of the liquidity trap, while generates risks of financial volatility and speculative bubbles. He also highlights the lack of aggregate demand growth and the high savings rates in countries such as Germany, Japan, and China. An indication of this demand weakness is the persistence of financial and savings surpluses (excesses of income over spending) in the private sectors of these high-income economies, despite ultra-low interest rates. Another underlying structural cause of the threat of secular stagnation is the larger share of the aging population in both developed and developing countries. This includes China, Germany, Japan, and Russia, as well as Spain, Thailand, and Tunisia. Long-run demographic trends lead Hudecz (2017) to consider several hypotheses that could explain the decline of long-term neutral interest rates, such as slower population growth and rise in life expectancy, higher dependency ratio, social inequality, and high debt levels in developed countries. Table 11.1 summarizes several hypotheses behind the long-run trend in low real interest rates in developed countries.

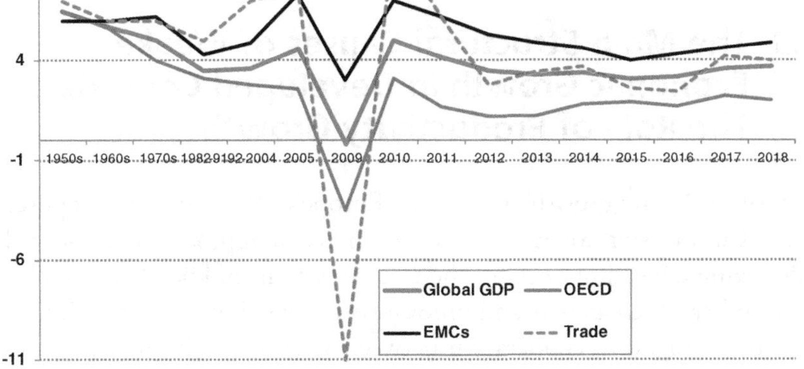

Fig. 11.1 Post-World War II Trends in Trade and GDP growth (*Source* IMF data and SKEMA 2017)

Table 11.1 Alternative hypotheses explaining a decline in real interest rates

Hypothesis	Predicted effect			
	Savings	Investment	Interest rates	Permanent/temporary
Demographics				
-slower population growth		↓	↓	Permanent
-rise in longevity	↑		↓	Temporary
-higher dependency ratio	↓		↑	Permanent
Cheaper capital goods		↓	↓	Permanent
Inequality	↑	↓	↓	?
Greater risk aversion/ increased regulation	↑	↓	↓	?
Increase in demand for state assets			↓	?
-savings glut (emerging markets central banks)	↑		↓	Temporary
-precautionary (emerging markets private)	↑		↓	?
Financial deepening in emerging markets		↑	↑	Permanent
Disinflation				
-impact on pre-/after-tax interest rates			↓	?
-inflation expectations			↓	?
Debt levels in advanced economies			↑	Temporary
Deleveraging				
-public sector (tight fiscal policy)	↑		↓	Temporary
-private sector	↑		↓	Temporary

Source Hudecz (2017)

11.3 The Main Structural Causes of Weaker Economic Growth in Developed Countries: The Role of Productivity Growth

The goal of "smart growth" set out in Europe's 2020 Strategy proposed by the EU Commission focuses on a wide variety of approaches. These include modernizing education systems, the free movement of knowledge (including the flexibility of researchers and innovators to cross borders), simplifying EU innovation programs, cooperation between science and business, improving access to capital for investment, and affordable intellectual property rights. These goals also include smart regulation and targets, European innovation partnerships: pooling expertise and resources, open access to research and development programs, and a common approach to protecting EU interests. In an environment of intense global economic competition, clearly, those countries that will attract a larger share of investment flows will be those that are more receptive to innovation and commerce.

One of the challenges facing the EU is productivity, which is one of the main drivers of medium-long term growth (another being investment). Since the 1990s, capital productivity has fallen sharply in all developed countries. The New Technologies of Information and Telecommunication (NTIC) revolution, which began in the late 1990s, was expected to increase productivity. Yet this did not happen. Solow's productivity paradox seems relevant here—one readily observes the effects of the proliferation of computers except in productivity statistics. While productivity has slowed all over the OECD, it has slowed even more in Europe. After World War II and until 1970 or so, there was a convergence of labor productivity levels among the United States, Western Europe, and Japan. Since the mid-1990s or so, this convergence has stopped and reversed. Van Ark et al. (2008) have shown that labor productivity growth in Europe has significantly slowed since that period compared to the three decades of 1960–1980. In contrast, labor productivity growth (measured as GDP per hour worked) accelerated in the US, leading to a larger productivity gap whose development is attributable to the slower emergence of the knowledge economy in Europe and to the smaller role of market service sectors in Europe. The US invests more in knowledge and technology than Europe. In the US, the share of R&D relative to total GDP is about 3% versus 2% in Europe. This is the case despite the productivity-boosting objectives of the 2000 Lisbon Summit. In addition, US firms have a higher propensity to invest in R&D while they also show a higher capacity to translate R&D investment into productivity gains (Castellani et al. 2015).

Regarding the role of labor, Drew-Becker and Gordon (2008) found anegative correlation between employment per capita and labor productivitygrowth. They observed that employment increases alongside less employment protection, fewer unemployment benefits, less product market regulation and lower average tax rates. This increase in employment occurred at the expense of productivity which partly or totally offset the total effect on GDP per capita. In the EU, when capital/labor substitution slowed down, productivity growth also decreased. Enlarging the EU to less developed countries and EU labor market reform (as in Directive 96/71/EC for example) made it possible to hire less skilled workers and this in turn has resulted in a productivity slowdown. Graph 11.1 illustrates the multifactor productivity growth rates over the 1990–2016 period between the United States, Germany, and France. The total-factor productivity (or multifactor productivity) is calculated by dividing output by the weighted average of labor and capital input. If all inputs are accounted for, then total factor productivity can be taken as a measure of an economy's long-term technological change or technological dynamism. Academic research suggests that Total Factor Productivity may account for up to 60% of growth within economies even if labor and investment are important contributors (Easterly and Levine 2001). Graph 11.1 shows that on average US multifactor productivity growth is higher than in the two European countries, while exhibiting less abrupt decline during the 2008–2009 global recession.

Graph 11.2 compares labor productivity across a range of developed OECD countries. It shows that productivity rates have slowed down in all countries in the 2004–2014 period compared with the earlier 1996–2004 period. It also suggests that the Global Financial Crisis was not the only underlying cause of the productivity decline, despite the fact that the crisis gave rise to a cut in corporate and public investment. Other more structural forces are at work.

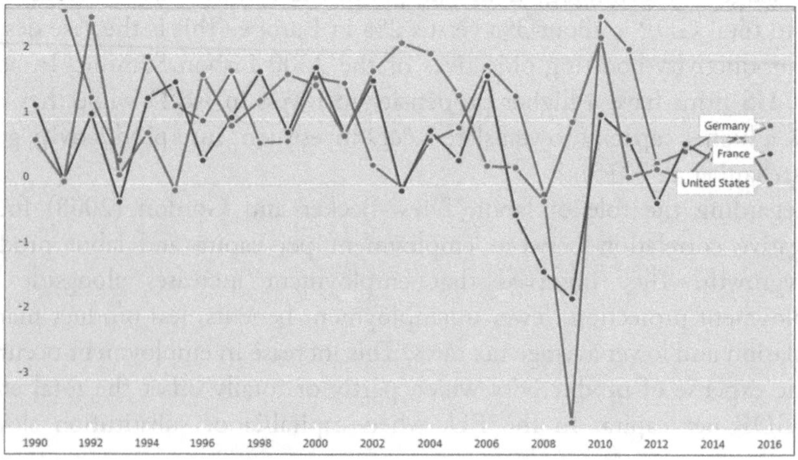

Graph 11.1 Multifactor productivity growth rates 1990–2016 (OECD)

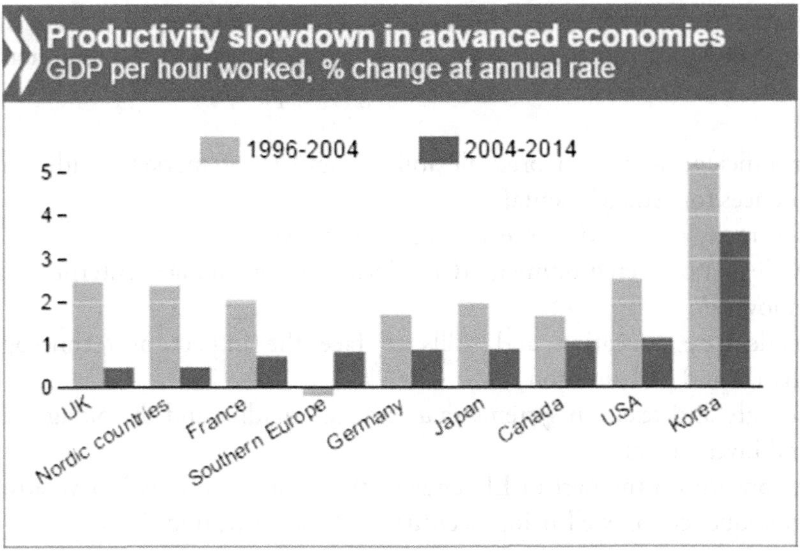

Graph 11.2 Productivity slowdown in advanced economies (thirty five OECD countries) (OECD, Compendium of Productivity Indicators, 2016)

11.4 The Consequence of Weaker Economic Growth on Country Risk

Before Brexit and the election of President Trump in the US, a global consensus seemed to prevail regarding the importance of a global, interdependent economic system. There was a shift away from tariffs, subsidies, and other forms of trade protection. This trade openness has benefited the EU, with its strong manufacturing base that provides high added value and the bulk of export revenues. Since then, however, rising protectionist threats and mounting geopolitical risks have tended to signal the emergence of a weaker multilateral framework for crisis resolution and a subdued role for international financial organizations. This changing environment is likely to affect long-term growth.

A weak potential for growth is a significant source of enhanced Country Risk. When wages or prices increase faster than productivity, a country risk analyst can justifiably raise concerns about a country's loss of competitiveness. Tension on prices can come from excessive wage increases (resulting, for instance, from unions' influence) or also from "excessive growth" (caused by an excess of budgetary expansion) beyond an economy's "potential" or "natural" output level. A "potential output level" is the level that occurs when all a country's resources (labor and capital) are being used to their full and sustainable capacity. To push growth further would put pressure on the cost of those resources, with a subsequent cost-pull inflation. Micossi (2016) summarizes six of the main reasons for relatively weak growth performance in the EU.

1. Insufficient wage and price flexibility; rigid labor markets, with consequences for "sticky" capital
2. Too many protected markets (notably services)
3. A regulatory environment that does not encourage enterprise and innovation
4. Inadequate education and skills to face the impact of technological change and globalization
5. Welfare and taxation systems that enhance rigidity and discourage effort and investments
6. A concern on the part of EU citizens that globalization will have adverse consequences on well-being, security, and cherished traditions.

11.5 To What Extent Does the EU's Maastricht Treaty Create a Socioeconomic Policy Straightjacket?

The institutional design of an economic area is crucial for Country Risk. The EU is a typical example. New EU treaty provisions on the monitoring of economic policies have been made legally binding through six legislative decisions (named the "Six-Pack"). In addition, the "European Semester"—introduced in 2010—constitutes a policy framework for the coordination of economic policies across the European Union. It provides guidelines for organizing the discussion of economic and budget plans and for monitoring progress at specific times throughout the year. This framework requires member states to align their decisions on economic policies according to the decisions of the European Council. Those common guidelines, with legally binding rules, have to be detailed in the "national stability, convergence and structural reform" programs that all member states have to submit each year to the Commission (European Commission 2017).

The substance of this new economic governance entails a number of common principles for a new integrated economic policy cycle covering:

1. Fiscal stability that takes into account the new stability initiatives
2. Stability and Growth Pact (SGP), with new operational criteria for debt reduction

3. Prevention of "excessive" economic imbalances, achieved through structural reforms, more flexible labor markets, better alignment of wages to productivity, and investment in human capital and new technologies.

The European Semester implements a de facto subordination framework between member countries and the centralized Commission. It requires that the European Council provides guidance to member states on implementing their economic, employment, and budgetary policies. Countries need to do so before taking key decisions on national budgets for subsequent years. The Commission monitors the progress on implementation of the guidelines in each member state. A member state's failure to act upon the policy guidelines may result in (a) further recommendations to take specific measures; (b) a warning by the Commission under Article 121(4) of the treaty on the functioning of the European Union (TFEU); and (c) corrective measures. Implementation of measures is subject to Commission's reinforced monitoring that may include surveillance missions. Growth and any potential revenue windfalls should be allocated to debt reduction.

The surveillance mechanism also includes both preventive and corrective components. The preventive component establishes a public expenditure benchmark: expenditure growth must not exceed a reference medium-term rate of GDP. It also sets a new operational criterion to evaluate the public debt and the excessive deficit that takes account of "all" relevant factors, such as private sector debt, (pension) implicit liabilities, and aging population. The Commission has declared a new principle of the independence of national statistical authorities, along with EU budgetary coordination of public accounting systems.

In the corrective component, EU regulations introduce sanctions in case of significant deviation from the medium-term structural budgetary objectives (Micossi 2011). Eurostat auditing powers and professional independence are to be strengthened. For member states, this process implies setting minimum standards for statistics, forecasting practices, a medium-term budgetary framework, and adopting multiannual fiscal planning to ensure that the medium-term objectives are met. Preventing macroeconomic imbalance is fostered through a number of macroeconomic indicators and scoreboards. This includes current account balance, net international investment position, export market shares, nominal unit labor costs, real effective exchange rates, the evolution of unemployment, private sector debt, private sector credit flow, house prices, and government sector debt (Eurostat 2016).

These indicators play a similar role as those defined by the International Monetary Fund for developing countries since 1996. Indeed, the IMF has defined specific guidelines to enhance member country transparency and openness with voluntary standards for the dissemination of economic and financial information that are discussed in Chapter 5: the Special Data Dissemination Standards. In the EU, these data standards set by the Commission can be particularly useful for the assessment of Country Risk. Indeed, the Commission evaluates member states' economies and the risks of "excessive" imbalances in its reports to the European Council. In case of excessive economic imbalances, the member state concerned will be required to adopt detailed corrective action within a specified timeframe. The Commission will be able to act autonomously to signal emerging deviations from budgetary objectives (early warning) and macroeconomic imbalances ("in-depth" review), without any need of Council authorization.

The Commission has several main areas of focus for countries: keeping wages developments in-line with productivity; implementing labor market reforms (flex-security; decreasing undeclared work; increasing labor participation; lowering taxes on labor); sustainability of public finances, sustainability of pensions, health care and social benefits; and reform of financial stability (supervision and regulation of the financial sector). The Kok Report (named for the chairman of the initiative, Wim Kok) recommends that member states take responsibility for implementing reform goals and processes through National Reform Programmes (NRP). The report also encourages peer pressure and benchmarking at EU level, notably by stronger reliance on public "naming and shaming" through public leagues on member states' performance (High-Level Group 2004).

11.6 Could Europe's Debt and Budget Ratio Targets Become Sources of Country Risk?

The Maastricht Treaty imposes constraints on public debt management given its focus on a 60% debt-to-GDP ratio target that EU countries should not exceed (see Appendix 11.1). The question arises as to the appropriateness of comparing a country's GDP (i.e., the sum of all income produced during a given period of time) with its stock of debt. Since the "Maastricht debt" is valued at its nominal value (when the debt was issued), it is hardly related to the amount of income needed to pay back the debt (at the maturity date). For instance, the "Maastricht debt" is not suited to inflation-indexed debt (bonds), since each yearly capitalized inflation is not reflected in the recorded nominal value of the debt. To soften their reported financial burden, most states have increased the issuing of inflation-indexed debt securities. In Great Britain, more than 25% of the debt is made up of inflation-indexed securities (sometimes with a maturity date of up to fifty years). In that regard, European countries have adopted similar borrowing strategies as several developing countries, such as Brazil. The Brazilian debt has a part indexed to LIBOR plus a specific risk related spread. Depending on the inflation breakeven rate, it can easily double or triple the nominal value of the debt by the time it arrives at maturity. An equivalent reasoning can be made with zero-coupon bonds issued by Italy for instance. When the zero-coupon bonds mature, states will have to pay a lump sum equal to the initial investment plus the imputed and capitalized interest. These new debt instrument strategies tend to invalidate the usual measuring tools—such as the "Maastricht debt to GDP ratio"—that are too rigid to encompass the debt structure of a country. Often, these instruments undervalue the real financial burden of the debt and tend to increase the implicit exposure to inflation (which has to be linked with monetary policy developments discussed below). In periods of financial distress, countries tend to modify their debt structure, resulting in greater divergence among them. For instance, currency-linked bonds have their coupon and/or redemption value linked to the movement in an exchange rate. There is a divergence between the market debt value and the nominal debt value. As always, an excessive debt ratio reduces the debt's market value. For instance, in December 2012, Greece did manage to repurchase 30 billion Euros of its nominal debt as a result of a European loan of 10 billion Euros. A new source of Country Risk in the EU arises out of accounting techniques and financial transactions used to circumvent the stricter regulations (see Case Study 11.1, The Root Causes of the Crisis in Greece, Ireland, Portugal, and Spain). As such, these techniques and transactions should be carefully analyzed by the country risk analyst.

11.7 Shrinking Growth Rates and Rising Debt Levels: The Trap Risk

Many developed countries—most notably the EU members—are facing a new macroeconomic environment of "slow growth." This is the case, despite positive signs of debt-driven economic stimulus in the United States, coupled with the short-term drive of corporate tax cuts. To address this challenge, a number of economists favor the promotion of a combination of "smart growth" (a knowledge and innovation-based economy), sustainable growth (a resource efficient, green and competitive economy), and more inclusive growth (a high-employment economy delivering social and territorial cohesion).

To stimulate consumption and investment—the two main drivers of GDP expansion—OECD countries have implemented an expansionary monetary policy that is characterized by very low rates of interest along with substantial bond-buying programs. The expected result has been an abrupt increase in the Public Debt to GDP ratios that reach roughly 100%. Graph 11.3 describes these high ratios for a number of developed countries while comparing with three emerging market countries, China, India, and Korea (although the latter is a member of the OECD). Chapter 12 presents a still more dramatic picture of developed countries' total debt ratios, including private liabilities.

Many observers have expressed the view that the Global Financial Crisis was partly caused by the belief that financial market discipline—that is, the scrutiny of investors and analysts—would itself induce countries to monitor leverage ratios and to balance their budgets. In the Eurozone, the problem is made more complex by the separation of monetary and fiscal policy. As such, a self-fulfilling prophecy could occur when monetary policy becomes the major policy tool to stem a contagion. In the EU, this situation was close to occurring when Greece was on the verge of default in 2010, leading to a crisis of confidence in the overall EU's stability, with a widening of bond yield spreads and rising prices of credit default swaps.

In principle, the diagnosis of debt sustainability and the debt restructuring depends, not on the market, but on the Commission's analysis of the underlying causes of the imbalances. If the public debt is considered sustain-

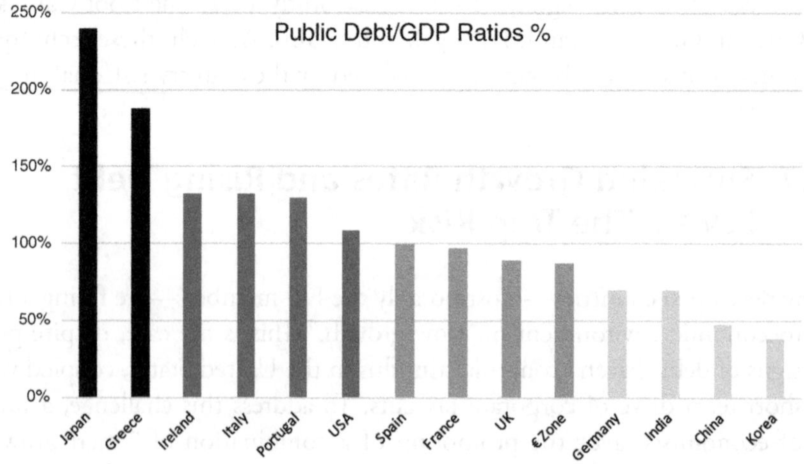

Graph 11.3 Public Debt to GDP ratios 2017 (*Source* IMF data)

able, then the concerned member states should take initiatives to encourage private investors to maintain their exposures. If the public debt is considered unsustainable, then the member state should be required to engage in active negotiations in good faith with its creditors to secure their direct involvement in restoring debt sustainability. As observed by Micossi (2011): "De facto, so far, this has not been a functioning procedure, everything is up for political negotiations, which is highly destabilizing for markets." The European Stability Mechanism, established in September of 2012, may help serve as a permanent "firewall" for the Eurozone "to safeguard and provide instant access to financial assistance programmes for member states of the Eurozone in financial difficulty, with a maximum lending capacity of €500 billion."

11.8 The Consequences of Quantitative Easing Programs on Country Risk in Developed Countries and in the Global Economy

Quantitative easing programs can also be seen as a source of Country Risk if they are not implemented in a careful and cautious manner, including their onset and the wind-down. Indeed, such unconventional monetary policies affect not only countries that undertake them, but the economies of entire regions and possibly the entire global financial system. There is an argument that they can actually increase the frequency and magnitude of financial events with global impact. Large liquidity injections by central banks can generate asset price bubbles in the stock and bond markets while low-interest rates lead investors to search higher yields in more risky assets, including in developing countries with weaker institutional and regulatory frameworks. A second round of risks can start when central banks decide to reduce bond buying and scale back quantitative easing. The withdrawal of monetary stimulus can trigger substantial capital outflows from developing countries while rising rates will hurt debtors' solvency. The ECB initiated the process to unwind five years of unconventional monetary policy at the beginning of 2018, by deciding to halve its bond-buying programs to smooth the return to normality.

The Federal Reserve first started to use unconventional monetary policy at the end of 2008. Then, the Federal Open Market Committee (FOMC) decided to set up its first Large Scale Asset Purchases (LSAP) program, better known as the "quantitative easing program" or QE. The Bank of England

(BOE) started to implement unconventional monetary policy in March 2009 through the launch of a £75 billion Asset Purchase program (APF). This first LSAP consisted of purchasing public sector assets with between five and twenty-five years' maturity, financed through the expansion of the money supply by the central bank. Because of the intrinsic characteristics of the Eurozone governance and some reserves expressed by European countries (especially Germany), the European Central Bank (ECB) was the last major central bank to launch its own asset purchase program, beginning in March 2015.

The Bank of Japan experimented its own quantitative easing programs between 2001 and 2006 and again in 2011. This was done in connection with the so-called "Abenomics" policy and was intended to address the two main Japanese macroeconomics issues: deflation and economic downturn. Japan is highly dependent on exports because of its relatively modest share of private consumption in GDP (roughly 50%) and its lack of natural resources. The country must attract foreign reserves to finance its economy and manage an aging population. As a result, the central bank must be particularly careful in developing and implementing monetary policy. It recognizes this, and carefully monitors business conditions and expected capital expenditures to evaluate domestic output and exports. It also conducts the "Tankan Survey," which asks a number of "qualitative questions" to gain further insights into general business economic and trade activity. Moreover, it closely monitors the employment outlook and overall job dynamic through the participation ratio combined with the unemployment ratio.

The Japanese economy has been subject to the liquidity trap since the 1990s and the so-called "lost growth decade." Facing an economic trough, the country increased the money supply at a zero interest rate, but this had no effect on output or prices since it did not change expectations about future interest rates. What is relevant is a remark by former Fed Chairman Bernanke: "QE works in practice but not in theory" (Eggertsson 2011 and 2017). The objective of changing investors' expectations is the main focus of Krugman's suggestions for the Bank of Japan that, given exceptional circumstances, it needed to take exceptional policy measures to the point to "commit to being irresponsible" (Eggertsson 2006; Eggertsson and Krugman 2012).

The US, EU, and Japanese central banks have not been alone in implementing quantitative easing programs to bring costless financing of unsustainable budget and balance of payments deficits. On average, central banks of OECD countries are holding between 10% and 40% of their domestic public debt. That monetization of public debt reached around 20% in the US, 30% in Great Britain, and 40% for Japan. Considering that the

Japanese public debt reached 240% of its GDP in 2017, it implies that the central bank is holding the equivalent of 100% of its GDP. This has been possible as a result of the deflationary environment in Japan. History suggests that this kind of policy has the potential to result in hyperinflation (as occurred in Argentina or Venezuela, though in very different economic and institutional environments). In the case of Venezuela, Sempledec (2017) has summarized the situation as follows: "In a country ravaged by inflation, this boils down to a race for survival." In 2017, the inflation rate reached close to 1,000% and the IMF forecasts prices to soar more than 2,300% in 2018.

Beyond the risk of hyperinflation, another major source of uncertainty is that quantitative easing programs of central banks can have diverse and unpredictable consequences. Among the most direct effects is an upward pressure on asset prices. Quantitative easing differs from conventional policy in that it does not only steer interest rates and the cost of money but also impacts the level and quality of the money supply. At first impression, it would seem to be a pragmatic solution to provide costless financing of large deficits. But there are direct and indirect implications and feedback mechanisms that can affect a country's overall stability. Indeed, the assets purchased are used to influence macroeconomic aggregates. More precisely, a quantitative easing program tends to make short and longer-term interest rates decrease, an effect which reduces the cost of borrowing for both households and companies, inciting them to consume and invest. (Of course, in moderation this can be positive, but excessive money creation gives rise to significant challenges with lagged effects difficult to predict and manage.)

The assets purchased in a QE program consist primarily of bonds. As a result, the subsequent additional demand for bonds puts upward pressure on their price with an inverse effect on returns. Consequently, most investors prefer other assets, which results in an overall increase in the price of global assets. This "wealth effect" is likely to redistribute the "well-being" of some individuals (mainly towards capital owners) and to increase the volatility and magnitude of financial price movements. In short, QE tends to significantly increase the sovereign financial risk for most countries, be they developed or developing. In fact, the cost of unconventional monetary policy does not only affect countries that undertake these policies; it also affects the global economy as a whole.

The global risk consequences can be illustrated by the frequency and magnitude of financial events with a high market impact. For instance, during summer 2015, market analysts observed large capital outflows from numerous emerging countries, along with a 10–30% depreciation of their currency. The cause of such capital flow volatility came from investors' worries about exchange rate stability and growth prospects. According to economists Artus and Virard (2016), capital outflows during the summer of 2015 reached between USD 300 and 400 billion—that is, roughly ten times more than during the 1994 crisis. The Shanghai composite index lost 37% over three months, despite the injection of more than 1500 billion Yuan by some of the largest Chinese banks and brokerage firms. Some weeks after this capital flight in developing countries, stock exchanges in OECD countries were, in turn, receiving capital back. Most economists believe that the glut of liquidity drastically increased capital transfers, thus affecting Country Risk for both developing and developed countries. The crisis spread quickly, limiting the alternatives for investors. The "flight to quality" phenomenon is no longer a "safe heaven" strategy, as Warren Buffet observed: "it's only when the tide goes out that you learn who has been swimming naked." The liquidity glut biased the perception of risk, shrinking the spread between risky and non-risky assets.

In developed countries, the risk of a liquidity trap stems from the consequence of low rates of interest on investors and consumers' behavior. When prevailing interest rates are low and savings rates are high, the authorities fear that most consumers and investors will prefer to keep their cash savings and will be reluctant to acquire bonds or assets. Actually, in such a context of "liquidity preference," the common belief is that bond values will decrease since interest rates are likely to rise sooner or later since they have reached the "zero lower bound." In that case, conventional monetary policies become ineffective and direct purchasing of assets appears to be the only possible remedy.

When financial institutions start selling their bonds and credit instruments to central banks, they receive cash in return. The objective of central banks' unconventional monetary policy is first to temper surging debt costs and stimulate bank lending to households and business. However, the recycling of central bank liquidity in the "real economy" is subject to the willingness of banks. Increasing bank credit to the private sector has been weaker than expected in Japan and in the EU. The ECB's program of so-called targeted long-term refinancing operations (TLTROs), i.e., cheap loans from the ECB to commercial banks, did not manage to stimulate bank lending. As noticed by Credit Suisse (2015), commercial banks in Northern Europe had little interest in the program because they could borrow almost as cheaply in the market. Conversely, the weakness in demand for corporate credit in the Eurozone "periphery" limited these countries' banks' need for the ECB loans. Bouchet and Isaak (2015) have shown that the decline of bank credit to the real economy and SMEs in the EU has led to declining investments, fewer jobs, and weaker economic growth. Figure 11.2 shows the scissor effect in Spain between higher unemployment and shrinking

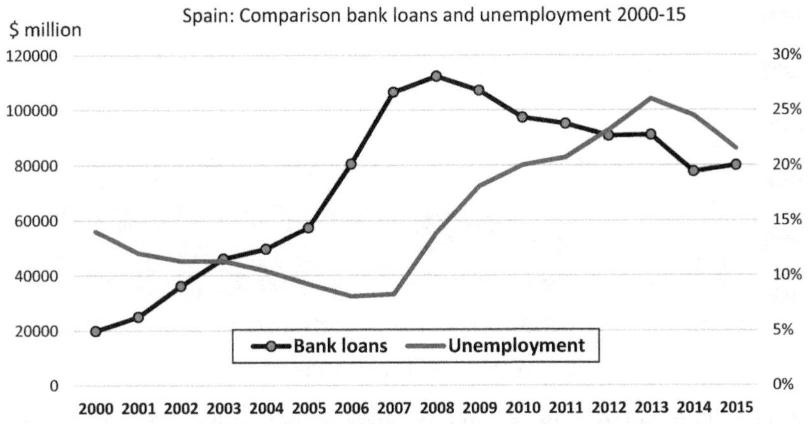

Fig. 11.2 Spain: comparison bank loans and unemployment 2000–2015 (*Source* Authors and OECD, compendium of productivity indicators 2016)

bank loans, despite the ECB's ambitious unconventional monetary policy and very low rates of interest (BIS data and authors' calculations).

In addition, in order to rebalance their portfolio, commercial banks purchase other assets such as stocks or real estate, resulting in price inflation of those asset classes. The "wealth effect" (wealth increase for capital owners) following the subsequent rise of asset prices differs according to the country. It seems to be more effective in the US, UK, and Japan than in the Euro-zone. This is quite possibly due to the quasi-absence of pension funds invested in the Euro-zone. Monetary policies, moreover, that are not undertaken alongside budgetary policies are relatively ineffective. To some extent, stock exchanges have become indirect tools of monetary policy to stimulate a "wealth effect." To illustrate this situation, Graph 11.4. describes the correlation between the monetary bases (directly linked to the policies of central banks) and the evolution of stock exchange indices in Japan and in the US.

Between 2010 and 2015, the Nikkei index (Japan) grew by more than 90% in five years. In the US, there was a 72% increase of the S&P 500 between September 2010 and September 2015, closely related to the sharp increase in the country's monetary base, a direct consequence of the Fed's monetary policy expansion.

Rogers et al. (2014) have described the relationship between unconventional monetary policy and financial markets. Remarkably, the "pass-through" from bonds to other asset prices such as stocks, can be observed in the four main geographic areas where QE was implemented, while this

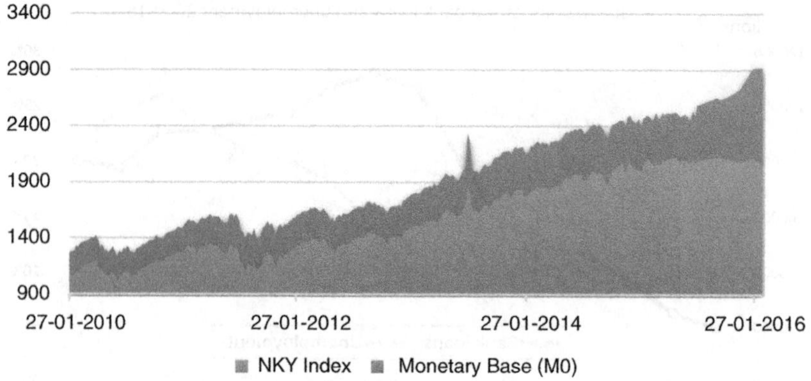

Graph 11.4 Correlation between the Japanese monetary base M_0 and the Nikkei Stock Index (NKI Index) from 2010 to 2016

relationship is strongest in the US. Joyce et al. (2011) first explained the different ways through which Large-Scale Asset Purchase (LSAP) influences the entire asset price channel. They defined four different channels: the signaling effect, the market liquidity channel, the scarcity effect, and the portfolio rebalancing effect.

Stock exchange fluctuations have become an indicator for assessing the dynamic prospects of countries as well as the risks of "market overheating." It has been argued that the expansionary policy of former Federal Reserve Chairman Alan Greenspan pushed up US equity market indexes (the so-called Greenspan "put"). Each time these indexes threatened to become bearish, the Federal Reserve injected liquidity, effectively boosting asset prices. The term "put" refers to the fact that losses were limited due to Federal Reserve intervention, but the gains were unlimited (the same outcome that might be achieved by owning a Put financial option). Monetary policy stimulus was carried out each time the US economy faced domestic or international challenges, including the Asian crisis spillovers in 1997, the Russian crisis in 1998, the LTCM hedge fund bankruptcy of 1998, the Internet bubble in 2000, and the "World Trade Center" attacks on September 11, 2011. In the beginning of 2018, the impact of ten years of monetary stimulus has resulted in a dynamic economic recovery, coupled with signs of increasing wages and rising median income, and record levels in the stock market. The sustainability of this recovery and of the bullish stock market may be questionable.

11.9 Country Risk and the "Liquidity Glut" Challenge

There are several causal links between a systemic crisis and a liquidity glut. First, an excess of money in circulation reduces the cost of financing for risky projects. This results in the development of inefficient projects, asset price distortions, and eventually global savings misallocation. The excess of money in circulation reduces potential long-term growth. It also creates incentives for investors to take more risks in a context of generalized "moral hazard," enhancing the risk of a global crisis. Low-interest rates tend to modify the business models of banks and insurance companies, reduce savers' incomes, weaken the solvency of pension schemes, raise asset prices, and increase inequality between capital holders and wage earners. Low-interest rates also decrease the cost of borrowing and shift income from creditors to debtors.

The bigger the monetary base in circulation, the faster and more volatile capital movements are from one country to another and from one asset to another. An example of the predominance of monetary policy occurred on October 7, 2016. Surprisingly, the Private Non-Farm Payroll, one of the most important US indicators for employment, was very positive (nearly full employment) though the S&P 500 index reacted negatively. This scissor effect was not because investors anticipated a better employment rate but because those figures were "too good" and could incentivize the Federal Reserve to push interest rates up. These circumstances illustrate that market participants focus more on monetary policy than on "real economy" indicators. There is more consensus on the long-run than on the short-run neutrality of monetary policy. QE alone cannot sustain economic growth for the long-term when growth is impaired by structural weaknesses. Examples usually given of such weakness are as follows: Labor market rigidity in the French economy; the lack of professional training in France, Spain, and Italy; the relative weakness of research and development in the Euro-zone (compared to US or Japan); the price/cost sensitivity of Chinese products; unequal revenue sharing in Japan (to the detriment of labor); energy sector dependency in the US; the lack of robust infrastructures in most developing countries (except China); excessive private and public debt in Europe (except Germany and the Netherlands); and lack of confidence and associated under-investment in many countries. One or several structural weaknesses of this kind can prevent monetary policy from being fully effective.

There is growing acceptance of the belief that monetary policy cannot be the single answer to remedy financial and macroeconomic imbalances. Furthermore, monetary policy, if not effectively implemented, can also contribute to subsequent crises. The practices and policies of a country's central bank are thus an important topic for country risk analysts.

11.10 The Mix of Consequences of Expansionary Monetary Policy on Growth Prospects

In the aftermath of the Global Financial Crisis, accommodative monetary policy in the OECD has reduced the risk of economic recession, as well as the risk of contamination in the global economy. However, ten years of unconventional monetary policy have created challenges, including how to exit the program without fueling asset bubbles and future inflation. Providing more liquidity would lead to diminishing returns while tightening interest rates in a non-incremental way would generate a corporate, household, student, and public debt crisis. Excessively prolonged quantitative easing has the consequence of reducing market pressure on governments that would otherwise face higher borrowing costs, hence the need to deal responsibly with their public finances. The combination of large budget deficits and growing current account deficits in the US has increased the country's public debt to record levels. Chapter 12 discusses the close relationship between the rising US current account deficit since the mid-1980s and the unabated increase in the US public debt to GDP ratio.

More precisely, the impact of the LSAP can be observed on the US Fed balance sheet. Figure 11.3 illustrates the sharp growth in the US Federal Reserve's balance sheet whose assets rose from around USD 900 billion in September 2008 to USD 4,452 billion at end of 2017.

Though the US negative net foreign wealth (foreign debt) still remains below 20% of the country's GDP, the absolute value is so large that any exchange rate fluctuation would massively impact the US as well as the wealth distribution globally. For instance, a 10% appreciation of the US Dollar would have no impact on US foreign liabilities since 100% of them are denominated in Dollars (US treasury bonds are all issued in Dollars). However, roughly 70% of foreign assets held by the US are denominated in foreign currencies and these would be adversely affected by an appreciation of the Dollar. A large Dollar appreciation would also lead to sharp capital flow volatility and to asset value fluctuation in central banks' reserves worldwide.

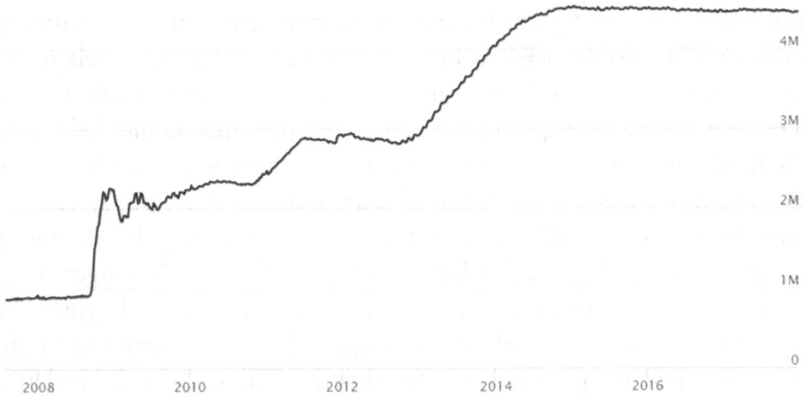

Fig. 11.3 The surging balance sheet of the US Federal Reserve: Total assets in USD trillion (*Source* US Federal Reserve 2018)

Brunnermeier and Schnabel (2016) conducted an extensive study of all historical financial bubbles. In each case, the bubble inflation is always preceded by strong monetary expansion and a debt ratio increase due to financial innovations or deregulation. Particularly interesting is that whatever the assets associated with the bubbles, the most significant feature is the way they have been financed and the associated leverage ratios. In the US, the Federal Reserve has launched the exit of quantitative easing with the gradual tightening of interest rates throughout the second half of 2017. The Fed unanimously decided it would start normalizing its balance sheet in the last quarter of that year, after having more than quadrupled the size of its balance sheet by purchasing Treasury bonds and mortgage-backed securities. In the EU, England, and Japan central banks have also decided to wind down their asset purchase schemes in response to more robust growth in their respective economic zones despite little signs of inflation increase.

11.11 Conclusion: The Stubborn Challenge of Identifying Crisis Signals in Developed Countries

Most policymakers in developed counties have inherited a challenging task in the aftermath of the Global Financial Crisis. The dilemma is encouraging further "re-flation" ("return of inflation") by maintaining unconventional monetary policies or generating a risk of triggering a new debt crisis if central banks move to tighter increase in interest rates. OECD country governments will probably need to broaden the range of policy tools to stimulate a return to sustainable economic growth with a combination of fiscal policy, debt restructuring, and structural reforms that could help central banks to deliver the more vigorous economic growth the world economy needs to restore a more stable financial environment. These policy challenges confirm that Country Risk is less than ever the monopoly of emerging countries. Developed countries face a number of other challenges, including a wealth gap and distorted income distribution, financial fragilities, savings misallocation, low growth and demographic trends, large indebtedness ratios, twin deficits, productivity slowdowns, and structural bottlenecks. Clearly, these challenges greatly exceed the impact of the monetary policy of any country. To assess the potential for adverse outcomes, country risk managers will need to scrutinize private and public leverage as well as the sustainability of domestic and external borrowing requirements. This will help anticipate abrupt volatility in bond spreads and exchange rates (and ultimately debt default).

Since the outbreak of the Global Financial Crisis, there have been significant improvements in micro-regulation (including higher capital requirements for "pure equity," protocols to unwind failing banks, approaches to limit "moral hazard," stronger controls to avoid conflict of interest within investment banks, additional requirements for trading functions, and greater regulation of derivatives products and shadow banking). The Dodd-Frank Act in the US has established and empowered the Financial Services Oversight Council (FSOC) and the Office of Financial Research (OFR). The EU countries have also adopted a new architecture for financial supervision that strengthens reciprocal links between micro and macro levels. Current concerns lie more on macro-imbalances that have not been fully assessed. Indeed, the US economy still faces considerable twin deficits (budget and current account), real exchange rates are often misaligned, private and public debt ratios are rising, and the "Global Liquidity Glut" remains a genuine challenge.

For country risk analyst and managers, the crucial question is how to identify the early warning signals of the next crisis. This is further discussed in Chapters 13 and 14. Even if all major global financial crises have some common features, it remains challenging to spot the specific early warning signs of another crisis. No single model or set of indicators provides the answer. Reinhart and Rogoff (2009) have studied the history of financial crises covering sixty-five countries across five continents while showing that, each time, economists and policy-makers claimed "this time is different"—that is, declaring that long established concepts of prudent risk-taking no longer apply and that the current financial situation exemplifies little similarity to past disasters. These two economists proved them wrong. Financial fallouts occur in clusters and strike with surprisingly consistent frequency, duration, and sharpness, an observation confirmed by Mandelbrot, as discussed in Chapter 2. Some striking similarities are evident, particular weaknesses in economic fundamentals, as illustrated by currency crashes, hyperinflation, and sovereign defaults on international and domestic debts—as well as the cycles in housing and equity prices, capital flow volatility, unemployment, and government revenues.

Further illuminating this theme, Rose and Siegal (2009) sought to identify the early warning signs of the Global Financial Crisis. They acknowledge that it was much easier to identify which countries were affected than why. "Despite the fact that we use a wide number of possible causes in a flexible statistical framework, we are unable to link most of the commonly-cited causes of the crisis to its incidence across countries. This negative finding in the cross-section makes us skeptical of the accuracy of "early warning systems" of potential crises, which must also predict their timing." Accordingly, the key behaviors needed are agility, alertness, constant vigilance and the ability to question conventional thinking. Policymakers and market participants must realize that they must be vigilant in protecting against weak macroeconomic fundamentals, such as profligate international and domestic borrowing, rising budget and current account deficits, distorted income distribution, lack of transparency, and weak governance. They must not forget that, amid an environment of weak fundamentals, an upcoming financial crisis is "just around the corner."

Case Study 11.1 Some underlying causes of the crisis in Portugal, Italy, Greece, and Spain (PIGS)

In July 2015, at the heart of the EU debt crisis, Greek sovereign bonds had reached rates of +50% and +25% for two and ten years respectively, versus −0.2% and +0.80% for German debt. Greek bond interest rates were higher for short-term than longer-term time horizons—that is, an "inverted yield curve" in which long-term debt instruments have a lower yield than short-term debt instruments of the same credit quality. This type of yield curve is considered to be a predictor of economic recession (based only on empirical correlation with no theoretical foundations).

Greek and German bonds were obviously denominated in the same Euro-currency but the perceived "credit quality" explains the difference in rates. For Germany, the two year borrowing rates were even negative. How can we explain such a striking difference in the same monetary zone?

The EU sovereign debt crisis started in 2009 when the newly elected Greek Prime Minister confessed that his country's debt figures had been largely underestimated. Some of the problems have been attributed to certain OTC derivatives transactions that had the effect of reclassifying its debt (a complicated situation which is beyond the scope of our inquiry).

While the rating agencies decided to downgrade the Greek debt quite sharply (from A+down to CCC between 2008 and 2012), its risk premium drastically increased. Investors' fears started to spread over other EU countries such as Ireland in 2010 and Portugal in 2011. The threat spread to larger countries (Spain and Italy) with a systemic impact over the entire Eurozone. The macroeconomic imbalances in each of the countries shared some similarities but also striking differences.

In Portugal, even if its private debt (241% of GDP) and external debt (104% of GDP) had reached a high level, the public debt seemed under control (with a 3.6% deficit and 72% of debt to GDP). Spain was in a similar situation with 220% of the private debt (very high), 10% of the current deficit but a limited public debt of 40% to GDP. In Ireland, the public debt was relatively low (44% against 70% average in the Eurozone) but private debt reached almost 300% of its GDP. On the contrary, in Italy, the public debt (106%) was the only imbalance. However, Greece had accumulated all the imbalances.

Interest rates were relatively low within the Eurozone, with the lowest rates being in Germany. These low-interest rates fueled excess demand for credit, causing an increase in private and commercial debt. At the same time, however, the Eurozone was experiencing high growth, low unemployment, and increasing purchasing power.

In a single country, rising inflation might have been a useful indicator expanding credit. However, such an indicator is not as useful in a single market such as the EU market, where price differences among different countries are more moderate than otherwise a result of the free circulation of goods, labor, capital, and services (Graph 11.5).

The convergence/divergence phenomenon appears clearly. The crisis hit the Eurozone even more strongly since EU countries had (excessively) strong links between their public accounts and their domestic banks (with implicit guaran-

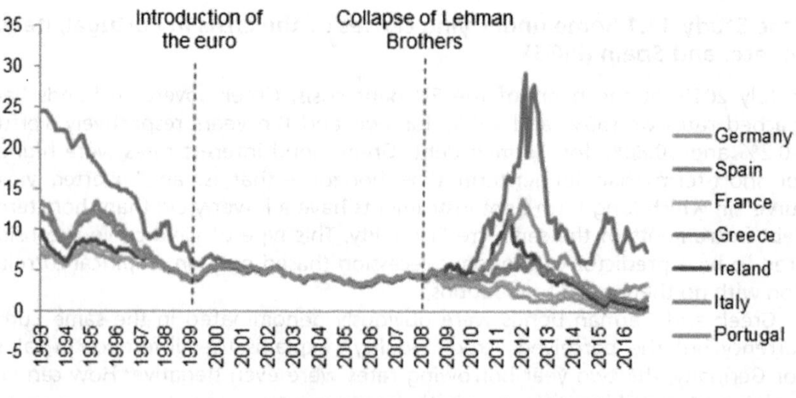

Graph 11.5 Interest rates on ten years' government bonds (%) (ECB Long-term interest rate statistics for convergence purposes)

tees of a bailout). To help banks get rid of some "bad loans" from their balance sheets, countries started to guarantee risky assets, and to isolate or to redeem those assets/loans. Ireland, for example, established the NAMA (National Asset Management Company). Its mission was to redeem risky assets at a price higher than the market price in exchange for bonds issued by the NAMA and guaranteed by the Irish State. This is a classic way (a so-called "bad bank" program) to transfer risk from banks to governments. This "sovereign state-domestic banks" loop contributed to the crisis. Ireland had to bail out various banks that were on the brink of default. Its public debt suddenly jumped from 44% in 2007 to 96% by the end of 2010.

Spain was burdened by real estate debt that fueled a rise in real estate prices. Households found it difficult to pay back their loans, especially since most of these had variable rates. Credit increased with low "nominal interest rates." The additional credit increased the money supply (the monetary base) and generated inflation (after a time lag). That expected inflation again lowered the expected real interest rate on which the long-term credit demand for real estate was based. Moreover, real estate crises have usually been deeper and have lasted longer than other asset bubbles. This is the case because real estate investment usually coincides with relatively high amounts of long-term financial debt for households and private agents.

Looking back at the EU crisis, several risk factors are apparent. Regulations were not adequate to address the risks in the economic and financial system. There were weaknesses in economic sectors that were underestimated, particularly in banking and real estate. Off-balance sheet exposures of countries were not adequately identified. Since the crisis, however, various steps have been taken by governments and the Eurozone to address these issues. Ten years after the outbreak of the crisis, it is worth remembering Hyman Minsky's warning of the combined risk of myopia and euphoria in prosperous times when deregulation takes place in a context of larger corporate and sovereign debts, while interest rates start rising. Continued vigilance, therefore, remains essential.

Case Study 11.2 2008 financial crisis: Common features between crises and early warnings

What can we learn from prior crises? Are there important factors we can identify that can help anticipate the next crisis? These are ambitious questions, and we will not be able to fully answer them, but at least we can begin to frame the line of enquiry as we look more closely at the Global Financial Crisis.

This crisis may at first seem to be unique in the history of finance given its magnitude, scope, and complexity. Yet if we look more closely at its origins, we can identify some similarities to prior crises. As former FDIC Chairman Irving Sprague observed: "Unburdened with the experience of the past, each generation of bankers believes it knows best, and each new generation produces some who have to learn the hard way."

Let's consider some of the commonly discussed factors that led to the crisis. (Maxfield 2015) Among the micro-factors, one can identify the following issues:

- Securitization of loans

Banks repackage and sell off assets that they formerly kept on their balance sheets. Securitization is useful to the extent that it enables them to convert less liquid assets, which they can redeploy into cash. Yet they no longer have to "live with" with assets they originated. Hence, it expands the bank's capacity to extend credit. But the drawback is that securitization can, if improperly used, reduce the incentive for banks to closely monitor the quality of underwriting standards.

- Off-balance-sheet treatment

To engage in the "securitization process," banks set up special purposes subsidiaries to hold assets. Although these assets were moved from one entity to another, they did not leave the financial system. They were financed by issuing debt securities named "CDO's" (Collateralized Debt Obligation). These CDOs raised funds for the special purpose issuer and allowed the investors to receive monthly payments made from multiple mortgages (the collateral held by the special purpose issuer), with junior (sub-prime) and more senior tranches of loans.

As a result of this process, illiquid and riskier credits were no longer reflected on the balance sheets of financial institutions. They were spread out into financial markets in the form of other securities, preventing investors from fully understanding the underlying financial risks. For example, in a financial instrument known as a "CDO2," the underlying assets were composed of other CDOs. This process was further repeated with "CDO3" composed of tranches including "CDO2". In such complex transactions, the risks become difficult to discern.

- Credit Default Swaps (CDS)

CDS transactions were initially developed by banks to create a market in credit risk and promote efficient transfer of risks. They aimed to promote efficient risk transfer from those who wanted to shed credit risk to other entities who had the capacity and willingness to assume more credit risk. A challenge is that these transactions give rise to counterparty risk that must also be carefully monitored. For example, American International Group (AIG) accumulated far more liabilities than the company was able to withstand.

- Rating agency issues

The financial system depends on the risk assessments of credit rating agencies. In the US, the issuance of ratings continues to be done by only three primary organizations. Yet they have consistently missed major signals of danger or have acted far too slowly to give investors the opportunity to take action. Credit agencies can also cause markets to overshoot. In 2007 sub-prime instruments and CDOs were rated as "investment grade" (AAA) by Standard & Poor's, Fitch, and Moody's. Rating agencies also have the potential for significant conflicts of interest in that the issuers pay the agencies to be rated.

- Mark-to-market accounting

The Financial Accounting Standards Board (FASB) has required publicly held companies to value their assets at market value rather than at historical cost. In many situations, this is useful in that the valuations more accurately reflect their real values. But in a period of significant volatility, the values of the companies can swing widely even if their business model remains unchanged.

Particularly large swings can cause firms to become insolvent. In a period of turmoil, this can have a strong "pro-cyclical" effect.

- Fraud

Fraud, sooner or later, drives crises. In advance of the Global Financial Crisis, many financial institutions sold mortgage assets without fully disclosing the risks and the true nature of the assets. The sellers of these assets incurred large regulatory fines and legal fees to resolve claims of fraud.

- Model misuse and overly simplified economic assumptions

In 2007, central banks put the emphasis on the price levels of goods and services. They did not address sufficiently the prices of real estate and other real assets. Moreover, many models made the assumption that home prices would not fall on a nationwide basis but rather would only sustain losses in certain regions. This led many investors in home mortgages and mortgage-backed securities to believe erroneously that they would be protected if they had mortgages of geographically diverse homes.

- Complex Regulatory Framework

The US has a complex system of multiple regulators for banks, savings and loan institutions, insurance companies, broker-dealers, and asset managers. This includes the Federal Deposit Insurance Corporation, the Office of the Comptroller of the Currency, the Federal Reserve, the Securities and Exchange Commission, and the Commodities Futures Trading Commission. This complex system has evolved over time but has surely been a source of challenge. Changes have been made to enable regulators to consider risks across the financial system, but this will be an ongoing challenge as markets, products and organizations evolve.

- Moral hazard

Market participants relied on the so-called "Greenspan Put." The injection of liquidity after each major financial shock created a belief that markets would remain liquid and operate in an orderly manner. Market participants became dependent on low-interest rates and believed the adage that "profits will be privatized but losses will be mutualized."

- Belief in ever-rising prices

The higher the oil prices, the more oil-producing countries accumulated reserves of so-called "petrodollars" that were recycled back into the US financial system. Such funds were used to purchase US securities such as Treasury Bills. This maintained liquidity in financial markets, kept interest rates relatively low, and promoted non-inflationary growth. Yet all this had adverse effects by generating incentives for economic agents to take on additional risk, hence creating the risk of asset bubbles.

Various other factors have been suggested as contributing to the Global Financial Crisis. Among them are inadequate risk management programs at financial institutions, inadequate capital requirements for banks, lack of technical expertise on the part of regulators, an overemphasis on deregulation, and the existence of an unregulated shadow banking system (mainly in China). A clear deficit in reliable country risk assessment has also been a major cause of the costly globalized financial and economic turmoil.

Perhaps one of the most important factors has been inadequate financial incentives. Alessandri and Haldane (2011) have studied the impact of "distorted incentives" on the returns of financial agents. They found that increased returns are mainly due to increasing leverage (more funds available on cheaper

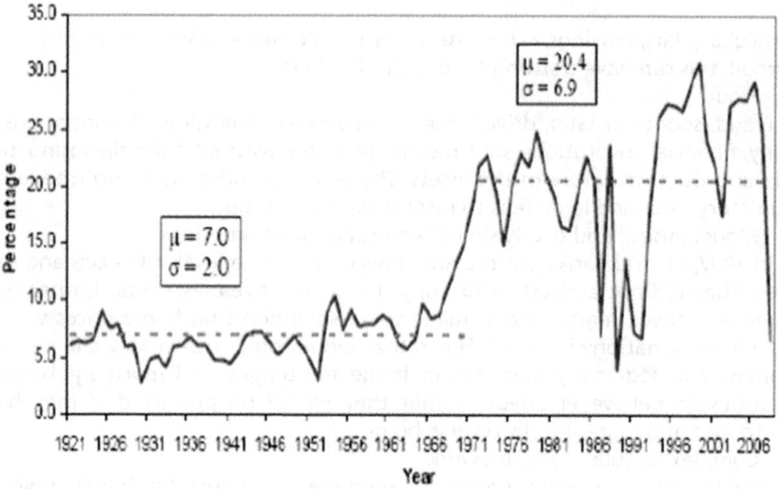

Graph 11.6 Return on equity for UK banks 1921–2007. μ = mean of returns; σ = standard deviation, a proxy for volatility and risk (*Source* Alessandri and Haldane 2011)

financial conditions), proprietary trading, and use of lower quality assets, which resulted in increasing return on equity sensitivity to global aggregate risk (also called "market risk"). This created the illusion that financial institutions improved their own return whereas their return drivers relied on an increased correlation to the market risk since all institutions are following similar strategies. This situation can be observed in the aggregate return on equity (ROE) with a time series approach (Graph 11.6).

Risk managers should continue to study the causes of the Global Financial Crisis. We have much to learn. Many changes have been introduced in countries, regions and throughout the global financial system. Yet more scrutiny will be needed as markets and financial innovation continue to evolve. Everything we have learned so far reminds us that the future will not be what it used to be. (Graph 11.6).

Appendix 11.1 The Maastricht Treaty's Convergence Criteria in the Euro-Zone

- Inflation rates: No more than 1.5% higher than the average of the three best performing (lowest inflation) EU member states.
- Annual government deficit: The ratio of the annual government deficit to the gross domestic product (GDP) must not exceed 3% at the end of the preceding fiscal year. If not, it is at least required to reach a level close to

3%. Only exceptional and temporary excesses can be granted for exceptional cases.

- The ratio of gross government debt to GDP must not exceed 60% at the end of the preceding fiscal year. Even if this target cannot be achieved due to specific conditions, the ratio must have sufficiently diminished and must be approaching the reference value at a satisfactory pace. As of mid-2018, of the countries in the Eurozone, only Estonia, Latvia, Lithuania, Slovakia, Luxembourg, Netherlands, and Malta still met this target.
- Exchange rate: Applicant countries should have joined the exchange-rate mechanism (ERM II) under the European Monetary System (EMS) for two consecutive years and should not have devalued their currency during that period.
- Long-term interest rates: The nominal long-term interest rate must not be more than 2 percentage points higher than in the three lowest inflation member states.

References

Alessandri, P., and A.G. Haldane. 2011. Banking on the state. In *The International Financial Crisis: Have the Rules of Finance Changed?* vol. 14, edited by A. Demirgüç-Kunt, D. Evanoff, and G. Kaufman. *World Scientific Studies in International Economics*, University of Chicago.

Artus, Patrick, and Marie-Paule Virard. 2016. *La Folie des Banques Centrales: Pourquoi la Prochaine Crise Sera Pire.* Paris: Fayard.

Bouchet, Michel Henry, and Robert Isaak. 2015. "From Hyperfinance to Secular Stagnation and Mass Unemployment: Analyzing the Impact of Shrinking Bank Lending on SMEs in the Aftermath of the Global Financial Crisis." *The World Financial Review*, December.

Brunnermeier, Markus K., and Isabel Schnabel. 2016. *Bubbles and Central Banks. Historical Perspectives. Central Banks at a Crossroads: What Can We Learn from History?* Cambridge, UK: Cambridge University Press.

Castellani, Davide, Piva Mariacristina, Schubert Torben, and Vivarelli Marco. 2015. "R&D and Productivity: The US/EU Productivity Gap Before and After the Crisis." http://dipartimenti.unicatt.it/dises-Innovation_Vivarelli_151113.pdf.

Credit Suisse. 2015. Quantitative Easing Improves Prospects for the Eurozone.

Dew-Becker, Ian, and Robert J. Gordon. 2008. "The Role of Labor Market Changes in the Slowdown of European Productivity Growth." NBER Working Paper 13840.

Easterly, William, and Ross Levine. 2001. "It's Not Factor Accumulation: Stylized Facts and Growth Models." *The World Bank Economic Review* 15 (2): 177–219.

Eggertsson, Gauti. 2006. "The Deflation Bias and Committing to Being Irresponsible." *Journal of Money, Credit, and Banking* 38 (2): 283–321.

Eggertsson, Gauti. 2011. "What Fiscal Policy Is Effective at Zero Interest Rates?" In *NBER Macroeconomics Annual 2010, Volume 25*, edited by Daron Acemoglu and Michael Woodford, 59–112. Chicago, IL: University of Chicago Press.

Eggertsson, Gauti B. 2017. "Macroeconomic Policy in a Liquidity Trap." NBER Reporter 2017 Number 1: Research Summary.

Eggertsson, Gauti, and Paul Krugman. 2012. "Debt, Deleveraging, and the Liquidity Trap: A Fisher-Minsky-Koo Approach." *The Quarterly Journal of Economics* 127 (3): 1469–1513.

European Commission. 2017. "The European Semester: Why and How." https://ec.europa.eu/info/business-economy-euro/economic-and-fiscal-policy-coordination/eu-economic-governance-monitoring-prevention-correction/european-semester/framework/european-semester-why-and-how_en.

Eurostat. 2016. "Macroeconomic Imbalance Procedure Scoreboard: A Broad Set of Indicators for Early Detection of Macroeconomic Imbalances." News Release 226/2016, November 16, 2016.

Gordon, Robert J. 2014. "The Turtle's Progress: Secular Stagnation Meets the Headwinds." VOX CEPR's Policy Portal, August 15.

High-Level Group. 2004. "Facing the Challenge: The Lisbon Strategy for Growth and Employment." Report from The High-Level Group Chaired by Wim Kok. European Community, November.

Hudecz, Gergely. 2017. "Secular Stagnation: What the Debate Is About?" *Society and Economy* 39 (1): 125–140.

Joyce, Michael A., Anna Lasaosa, Ibrahim Stevens, and Matthew Tong. 2011. "The Financial Market Impact of Quantitative Easing." *International Journal of Central Banking* 7 (3): 113–161.

Krugman, Paul. 2014a. "Four Observations on Secular Stagnation." In *Secular Stagnation: Facts, Causes, and Cures,* edited by Coen Teulings and Richard Baldwin. London: CEPR Press.

Krugman, Paul. 2014b. "What Secular Stagnation Isn't." *The New York Times,* October 27.

Maxfield, John. 2015. "Twenty-Five Major Factors That Caused or Contributed to the Financial Crisis." *The Motley Fool,* February 28.

Micossi, Stefano. 2011. "The New Economic Governance of Europe After the Crisis." Luiss School of Government, Rome, Italy, May 23.

Micossi, Stefano. 2016. "Thirty Years of the Single European Market." 15th European Economy Lecture. Bruges, Belgium, October 19.

Reinhart, Carmen, and Kenneth Rogoff. 2009. *This Time Is Different.* Princeton: Princeton University Press.

Rogers, John H., Chiara Scotti, and Jonathan H. Wright. 2014. "Evaluating Asset Markets Effects of Unconventional Monetary Policy: A Cross-Country Comparison." International Finance Discussion Papers Number 1101, Board of Governors of the Federal Reserve System.

Rose, Andrew K., and Mark M. Spiegel. 2009. "Cross-Country Causes and Consequences of the 2008 Crisis: Early Warning." NBER Working Paper No. 15357.

Sempledec, Kirk. 2017. "In a Venezuela Ravaged by Inflation, a Race for Survival." *The New York Times,* December 2.

SKEMA Business School. 2017. "Globalization Seminars." Michel Henry Bouchet. www.developingfinance.org.

Summers, Larry. 2016. "The Age of Secular Stagnation: What It Is and What to Do About It." *Foreign Affairs*, March/April.

US Federal Reserve. 2018. "Recent Balance Sheet Trends." https://www.federalreserve.gov/monetarypolicy/bst_recenttrends.htm.

Van Ark, Bart, Mary O'Mahoney, and Marcel P. Timmer. 2008. "The Productivity Gap between Europe and the United States: Trends and Causes." *Journal of Economic Perspectives* 22 (1): 25–44.

12

Country Risk and External Debt Sustainability

12.1 Introduction. Living Beyond One's Means with a Current Account Deficit: How Much Is Too Much?

Risk is a multifaceted challenge. Reducing risk to a single, abrupt shock such as default, coup d'état, or contract repudiation misses the subtle and gradual forms of risk that can emerge in cross-border investment. Although the most visible element of emerging market crises is debt servicing suspension or, at worst, sheer defaulting, the root causes of debt crises are still complex and subject to endless academic debates. Policymakers and risk analysts focus primarily on such fundamental questions as: What are the relationships between external debt and domestic growth? Is external indebtedness a transitory but necessary ingredient behind sustaining long-term development? Beyond what threshold level does debt impair economic growth and generate liquidity and solvency imbalances? Should creditors provide debtor countries with debt relief in order to improve solvency ratios, hence repayment prospects? They also ask whether official and private debt reduction workouts are key to restoring growth and market access.

Country risk analysts and fund managers, as well as economists at international organizations, have devoted much time to the question "how much is too much," in other words, when does the debt overhang become too large and precipitates a financial crisis, often coupled with socio-economic and political turmoil. The truth is that external debt often carries with it a subordination relationship with external creditors and it limits the room for maneuver of the

M. H. Bouchet et al., *Managing Country Risk in an Age of Globalization*,
https://doi.org/10.1007/978-3-319-89752-3_12

indebted country. In the nineteen century, foreign creditors did not hesitate to send troops and to seize assets to get their money back (Bouchet 1987). However, a country in default also imposes a subordination relationship with regard to its private and public creditors. Russia's default in 1917 led to heavy losses for many private European bondholders. Indebtedness, thus, means first of all forced solidarity between debtors and creditors, and the balance of power can shift on either side depending on many financial and even political variables, including the sheer size of the debt (Bouchet 2004).

As we observed in Chapter 8, sooner or later, the balance of payments difficulties will beset countries that face a large and protracted gap between savings and investment. The clock starts ticking when rising external financing requirements cannot be met, and the crisis will stem from higher debt cost, shorter maturities, shrinking market access, or a combination of the three. Costly refinancing or debt rescheduling will alleviate the country's liquidity constraints, with both time and money. But solvency constraints will require full-scale debt relief. From a country risk analyst's viewpoint, it is crucial to observe the intricate relationships between the flow accounts in the balance of payments and the stock variation of debt liabilities and official reserve assets (Bouchet et al. 2007) (Table 12.1).

Any current account deficit will lead to external capital inflows, fluctuating official reserve assets, or payments arrears. As discussed earlier, external capital flows will not necessarily lead to an increase in debt liabilities. Non-debt creating flows such as foreign direct investment (FDI) and portfolio capital flows will finance the deficit without increasing the country's external debt. FDI will lead to dividend payments in the future, but in a timely manner when investment produces economic growth, jobs, tax revenues, and corporate profits. The intensity and success of FDI attractiveness can be measured by the ratio of FDI to country GDP. The most successful countries are not always the largest recipients. According to the International Monetary Fund (IMF), Singapore boasts a ratio of 10%, while Chile, Vietnam, and Mauritius receive FDI and portfolio inflows of about 7% of GDP. Myanmar receives the equivalent of 6% of GDP, and Morocco, Sri Lanka, and Poland the equivalent of only 3% of GDP. The relationship between flows and stocks is depicted in (Table 12.2).

The relationship between payment flows and stock variations of reserve assets and external liabilities means that a country's debt is the mirror image of its accumulated current account deficit. Charts 12.1 and 12.2 illustrate the sharp increase in the US current account deficit since the mid-1990s up to an annual USD 500 billion in 2016–2017—the equivalent of 5% of GDP.

Table 12.1 The accounting relationships between inflows and outflows

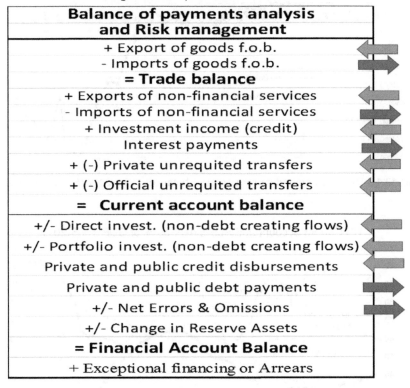

Balance of payments analysis and Risk management
+ Export of goods f.o.b.
- Imports of goods f.o.b.
= Trade balance
+ Exports of non-financial services
- Imports of non-financial services
+ Investment income (credit)
Interest payments
+ (-) Private unrequited transfers
+ (-) Official unrequited transfers
= Current account balance
+/- Direct invest. (non-debt creating flows)
+/- Portfolio invest. (non-debt creating flows)
Private and public credit disbursements
Private and public debt payments
+/- Net Errors & Omissions
+/- Change in Reserve Assets
= Financial Account Balance
+ Exceptional financing or Arrears

Table 12.2 The relationships between current account and external indebtedness

Balance of Payments and External Debt

Balance of payments = Flow variation	**External debt and reserves = Change in stocks**
• Receipts = capital inflows (exports of goods and services, transfers, dividends, credit disbursements, capital flight repatriation)	**Δ+ Reserve assets** **Δ- External debt obligations**
• Debits = capital outflows (imports of goods and services, interest payments, debt repayments, capital flight)	**Δ- Reserve assets** **Δ + External debt liabilities**

The Chart 12.2 thereafter sheds light on the close correlation between the deepening deficit in the 1995–2006 period and the sharp rise of the debt/GDP ratio from 50% to over 100% in 2017 (IMF data).

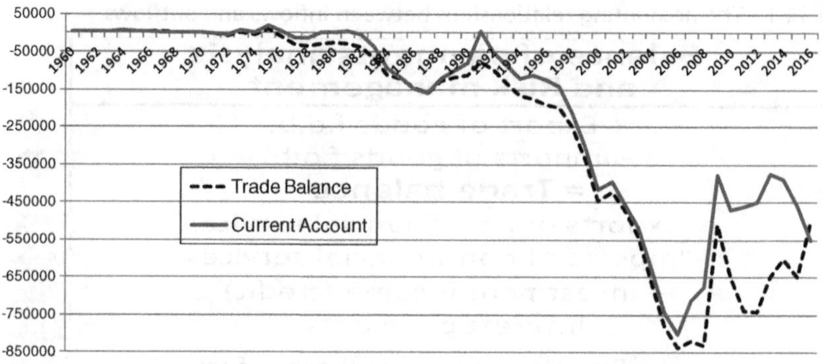

Chart 12.1 The US trade and current account balances 1960–2017 (*Source* IMF data)

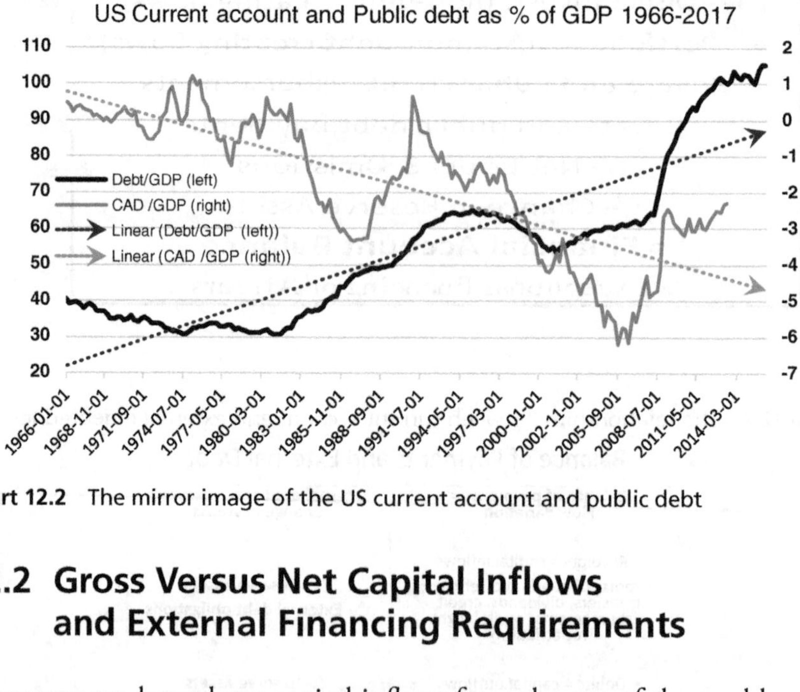

Chart 12.2 The mirror image of the US current account and public debt

12.2 Gross Versus Net Capital Inflows and External Financing Requirements

A country can boast large capital inflows from the rest of the world economy while experiencing a rising structural deficit as long as its economy's competitiveness is not in doubt. This has been the case of the US economy since the mid-1990s as well as several Euro-zone countries such as France and Spain. The key issue for deficit countries is to ensure sustainable external financing. That means convincing foreign investors and creditors that capital inflows are invested in the domestic economy in such a way as producing positive returns and promising economic prospects in the future. According to the US Bureau of Economic Analysis, the financial account consists of transactions between residents and nonresidents for direct investment, portfolio investment, other investment, reserves, and financial derivatives other than reserves (Bach 2010). A country thus receives direct investment as well as portfolio investment transactions that consist of cross-border transactions involving equity and investment fund shares and debt securities. In addition, should the country still face a deficit, it can rely on long- and short-term capital flows. All these flows are gross. What stays in the country's economy, however, are net flows—that is, gross inflows minus debt repayments and capital flight. A bundling of debt payments will reduce the financing impact of capital inflows to the point of turning into negative net flows. In addition, the country must service its annual interest payments bill, and the net flows will lead to net transfers. A sharp increase in the average interest rate or an increase in the total debt outstanding in a given year will produce a rising interest cost that might wipe out all gross capital inflows. This was the case in Mexico in 2012 when a sharp rise in disinvestment coupled with an investment of Mexican MNCs abroad, more than offset USD 21 billion FDI inflows into the country, resulting in a negative net flow. Capital flight reflected in errors and omissions can also substantially reduce the benefits of large capital inflows from the global economy. In the case of Mexico, errors and omissions of around USD 20 billion annually between 2012 and 2014 inflated the country's external financing requirements to match its large current account deficit. Table 12.3 illustrates the difference between gross and net capital flows.

Table 12.3 Gross and net capital inflows

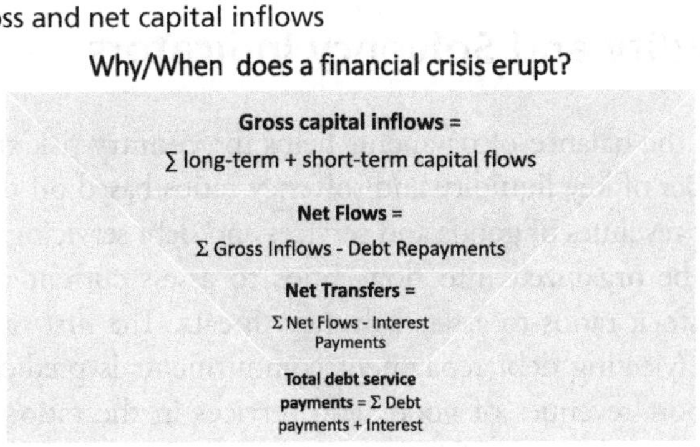

Why/When does a financial crisis erupt?
Gross capital inflows =
Σ long-term + short-term capital flows
Net Flows =
Σ Gross Inflows - Debt Repayments
Net Transfers =
Σ Net Flows - Interest Payments
Total debt service payments = Σ Debt payments + Interest

12.3 Sources of Reliable Data Regarding Flows and Debt Indicators

As discussed in more depth in Chapters 2, 4 and 5, country risk analysis is only as reliable as the quality and timeliness of the underlying data. Five main institutions specialize in providing debt data: central banks, IMF, the World Bank, the Bank for International Settlements (BIS), and the Institute of International Finance (IIF), which is the Washington-based global banking industry's risk analysis agency. The IMF and the IIF publish comprehensive analyses on the "quality" of the growth-cum-debt process that focuses on the sustainability of the indebtedness. Both organizations tackle the relationships between the volume and root causes of the country's borrowing requirements, as well as the country's market access and the lasting impact of the outstanding debt on the balance of payments and the debt indicators. The IMF is a robust source of quality information on the debt situation in emerging and developed countries. Country governments' Letters of Intent to the IMF's managing director include useful information on annual external debt ceilings as well as on the maturity composition of new money flows. In addition, the annual Article IV consultation reports provide information and analysis on the country's overall external debt strategy. The BIS gathers debt data from the IMF, the World Bank and the Organization for Economic Co-operation and Development (OECD) to publish comprehensive annual and quarterly data while the IMF provides disaggregated data on the balance of payments. The Joint BIS-IMF-OECD-World Bank Statistics on External Debt provide data on the external debt of developed, developing, and transition countries and territories, as well as statistics on selected foreign assets, such as official reserve assets (BIS 2017). Additional historical information on sovereign defaults can be found in Beers and Nadeau (2014), Beers and Mavalwalla (2017) and Reinhard and Rogoff (2013).

12.4 Liquidity and Solvency Indicators

The analysis of the balance of payments helps the country risk analyst to build a limited number of key liquidity and solvency ratios based on the relationship between export revenues of goods and services and debt servicing cost. The debt indicators can be organized into flow ratios to assess current and upcoming constraints or stock ratios to assess solvency threats. The first ratio is the debt servicing ratio. Meeting debt repayment commitments is predicated on stable or growing export revenues of goods and services in the ratio's denominator. On the numerator, the sum of interest and principal payments due provides a gauge of debt servicing sustainability. The interest ratio is the ratio of annual interest payments to export revenues, thereby assuming that debt repayments falling due will be refinanced thanks to capital market access. Given a current account in balance, the necessary condition for stabilizing the interest ratio at a given level requires the growth rate of export revenues to be at least equal to the average interest rate on total indebtedness. Indeed, interest payments grow every year at the interest rate times overall debt. The growth rate of export must, therefore, match the interest rate to generate a stable interest/exports ratio. In addition, a broad liquidity ratio includes all inflows in the numerator (exports revenues, transfers, investment, and disbursements) compared with all outflows that the country faces in a given year (imports of goods and services, interest and debt repayments as well as capital flight). Solvency ratios compare the country's stock of economic wealth (i.e., GDP) and the country's debt outstanding, as well as the relationship between debt and official reserve assets. Every year, assuming that debt repayments are refinanced, the country's debt will grow at the rate of interest minus the primary budget balance. The country's GDP will grow at the average growth rate of the economy. The relationship between debt and GDP can be presented in the following equations, where r is the average rate of interest and g the annual GDP rate of growth (Fig. 12.1):

It follows that reducing the country's indebtedness requires a reduction in "r" (beyond the country's reach), or an increase in "g" (depending on the country's structural economic flexibility and its degree of globalization), or a boost to its primary budget and balance of payments surplus (depending on taxes and exports dynamism). More precisely, regarding sovereign indebtedness, everything else being equal (including official reserve assets), external liabilities will grow each year depending on the current account deficit. It follows that stabilizing the Debt/GDP ratio means reducing the current account/GDP ratio below the GDP growth rate (see Appendix 12.1).

- DEBT t= DEBT t-1 * (1+r) – Primary Budget Balance
- GDP t = GDP t-1 * (1 + g)
- $\frac{\text{DEBT t}}{\text{GDP}} = \frac{\text{DEBT t-1} * (1+r)}{\text{GDP t-1} * (1+g)} - \frac{\text{Primary Budget Balance}}{\text{GDP}}$

$$\frac{\text{DEBT}}{\text{GDP t}} = \frac{\text{DEBT}}{\text{GDP t-1}} \cdot \frac{1+r}{1+g} - \frac{\text{Primary Budget Balance}}{\text{GDP}}$$

Fig. 12.1 The accounting relationships between debt, budget, and GDP

Table 12.4 The key risk ratios of liquidity and solvency

External debt analysis: The dual face of Country Risk	
Liquidity risk	Solvency risk
• Debt service ratio: (P+I/X)	• Debt/export ratio • Debt/GDP ratio
• Interest ratio (I/X)	• Debt/reserves
• Current account/GDP	• ST debt/total debt
• Growth rate of exports/ Average interest rate	• ST debt/reserves • Reserve/import ratio

Bouchet /Skema © 2018

Another way to look at stabilizing the external debt to GDP ratio is that the country must run a primary surplus in its current account balance. That means a surplus in the country's non-interest current account (which includes the trade balance coupled with workers' remittances and private and public transfers). In fact, stabilizing the country's debt ratios results from a race between two variables: the GDP growth rate; and the external rate of interest, which is exogenous. The primary balance must be at least equal to the debt/GDP ratio times the differential between the real interest rate paid on the debt and the economy's growth rate. Otherwise, the debt ratio will increase faster than the growth rate of the country's economy. Comparing the economic growth rate and the debt burden, the annual current account deficit must be lower than: Debt/GDP × GDP growth rate. A numerical example will illustrate this relationship. If the economy's growth rate is 2% and the Debt/GDP ratio is to be set at a maximum of 85%, then the deficit must be lower than 1.7% of GDP. Otherwise, the solvency ratio will deteriorate. The previous table illustrates the main range of solvency and liquidity indicators that the country risk analyst is to scrutinize in debt sustainability assessment reports (Table 12.4).

As we shall see later in this chapter, country risk analysts and fund managers, however, must keep in mind not to focus on debt ratios that could have been used for previous "traditional" crises but that do not grasp the changing nature of the financial crisis in the age of globalization.

12.5 The Debt Crisis Threshold Issue: Is There Life Beyond 90% Debt/GDP?

Risk analysts need to be able to detect when a country's debt reaches the point beyond which debt default becomes inevitable. Despite considerable academic research and debates on the topic, there is no reliable threshold or

Table 12.5 Wanted: Debt default yardsticks?

Liquidity and solvency risk thresholds	
Flow variables	Stock variables
• Debt servicing ratio < 33% of exports of goods & services	Debt/GDP < 90%
	Debt/Exports < 150%
(Σ Interest + debt repayments/exports revenues)	Reserves/imports > 6 months
• Interest ratio < 25% of Exports	Short-term debt/Total debt < 15%

yardstick that can be used to predict an upcoming debt default. Table 12.5 illustrates the questionable consensus regarding solvency and liquidity thresholds. Clearly, the thresholds of debt default will depend on a broad range of global and domestic economic variables, including commodity prices, export markets, debt structure, rating agencies, and interest rates. Given that a country is not expected to repay its debt with its GDP resources (since that would lead to both a national crisis and the creditors' bankruptcy), country risk analysts focus on external liquidity ratios. One example is DBRS' measure of the amount of financing sources in foreign exchange immediately available to meet a country's external financing needs, as follows: the sources of foreign exchange (official reserve assets, exports of goods, services and income, and net transfers) are divided by foreign exchange needs (imports of goods, services and income, amortizations, and short-term public and private debt). A ratio of more than 100% suggests adequate liquidity. This concept is less relevant in countries with highly liquid currencies (DBRS 2016) (Table 12.5).

Box 12.1. The crisis threshold issue: Is there life beyond the 90% debt/GDP level?

Are debt levels weak or strong predictors of growth outcomes? Risk analysts have debated whether there is a threshold in the level of government debt to GDP above which a nation's medium-term economic growth prospects are dramatically compromised. C. Reinhart and Rogoff (2010) and C. Reinhart et al. (2012) argue that there is a threshold effect: when debt in advanced economies exceeds 90% of GDP, there is an associated dramatic worsening of growth outcomes. For developing countries, the threshold is closer to 60% due to structural weaknesses and little production and export diversification. For a wide range of countries, GDP growth averages about 2% in countries with debt below 90% and tumbles to about—2% in countries whose debt ratio rises above that level.

Others dispute the threshold notion. They suggest that it is weak growth that causes high debt rather than high debt that causes weak growth (Panizza and Presbitero 2012; Herndon et al. 2014). A recession will raise the debt-to-GDP ratio because the denominator (GDP) decreases. Other economists (Pescatori et al. 2014) focus on the medium-to-long-term relationship between today's stock of debt to GDP and subsequent GDP growth rather than on just the short-term relationship to reflect the fact that debt reduction is typically a long, drawn-out process. They find that the trajectory of debt is an important predictor of subsequent growth, buttressing the idea that the level of debt alone cannot explain the growth potential of an economy. Much depends on the debt structure, the regional and global macroeconomic situation, and whether countries have dealt with their budget and current account deficits, hence a stabilizing or declining debt level. IMF economists conclude that policymakers should not focus on a specific debt threshold while keeping greater flexibility when considering the best path toward an ultimate objective of declining debt ratios.

Graph 12.1 shows a range of Debt/GDP ratios for both developed and developing countries in 2017. It includes countries in debt crisis (i.e., Greece and Ireland) and countries with high debt ratios (i.e., Japan, US, and to a lesser extent Spain, Portugal, and France) that can refinance debt payments with local currency borrowing. However, each of these countries, particularly in Europe, remains vulnerable should interest rates continue rising, which is a plausible scenario, given what appears to be a tighter monetary policy at the Federal Reserve in 2018 and beyond. Other central banks in the UK, the Euro-zone, and Japan followed suit in 2018, gradually tightening monetary policy.

12.6 Measuring the "Real" Debt Burden on Economic Growth

Krugman (1989) and Sachs (1989) have shown the following relationship: if a government implements tight austerity policies with a shift towards export-led economic growth, then the balance of payments might adjust, the current account might turn to surplus, and reserve assets might well accrue

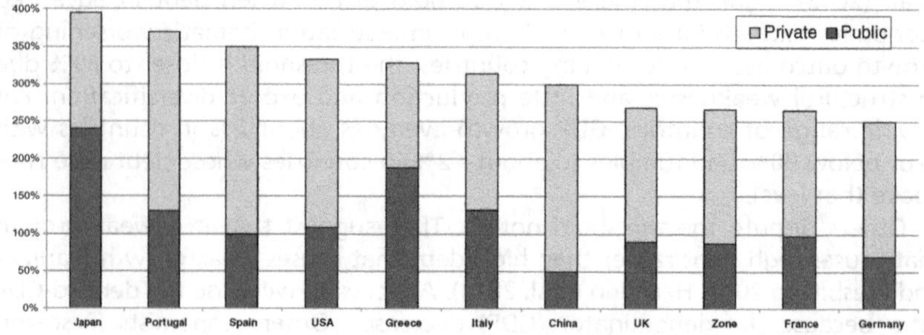

Graph 12.1 Public and total indebtedness (IMF and national authorities' data)

to foreign creditors. In sum, a heavy debt burden acts like a high marginal tax rate on economic adjustment. This situation supports the efficiency case for debt relief so that the debtor country and foreign creditors will share the benefits of economic growth recovery and rising export revenues, hence improving creditworthiness (Sachs 1989). Should creditors demand full repayment, the country might fall in full default, hence no payment at all. The debt overhang is illustrated by a debt "Laffer curve" which posits that larger amounts of debts tend to lead to lower probabilities of debt repayment and shrinking market value of bank claims, hence hindering growth. Capital flight and low domestic investment then result from the implicit "tax" creditors exert on the country's resources to service the external debt.

The nonlinear effects of debt on economic growth have been examined in an IMF study of nearly 100 developing countries over a thirty-year period (Pattillo et al. 2002). The cross-country debt analysis concludes that the overall contribution of debt to growth turns negative beyond a critical point. Likewise, in an effort to promote US aid flows with strong conditionality attached, the compound annual GDP per capita growth of countries that received substantial US official development aid between 1980 and 2000 was close to zero (Schaefer 2002). As an example, the Philippines, received more than USD 4 billion during the period, in constant 1999 Dollars, while per capita GDP level remained stubbornly flat at USD 1,170. Boyce (1992) showed a typical case of "revolving door" in the Philippines with substantial linkages between capital flight and external debt disbursements. This point will be discussed further in Chapters 13 and 14 that deal with early warning signals, capital flight and debt sustainability. In many developing countries, capital inflows get recycled into foreign bank accounts or external assets accumulation, without much productive impact on the country's socio-economic prospects. Similarly, Alesina and Tabellini (1988) provided an explanation of the simultaneous occurrence of a large accumulation of external debt and relatively low domestic capital formation in developing countries by focusing on private capital outflows. As we shall see in Chapter 14, private capital flight results from a number of variables, including exchange rate mismanagement, inflationary expectations coupled with negative interest rates, distrust of government's economic policies, insurance search against the risk of future taxation and capital controls, and widespread corruption. At a certain point of systemic corruption, all the money that can leave a country crosses the border by whatever means, both from corrupt elites and from those private residents who are discouraged by endemic corruption, hence paving the way for the financial crisis. In that environment, large capital inflows, from both foreign direct investment and M&As, portfolio capital, bonds, and international bank loans fuel a perverse system of recycling into foreign tax havens.

12.7 Analyzing the Various Triggers of a Country's Debt Crisis

Country risk analysts and rating agencies tend to conclude that the combination of weak economic fundamentals and rising indebtedness leads to debt overhang, deteriorating creditworthiness, and ultimately, default. Much depends, however, on overall market liquidity and the so-called herd instinct that leads investors to increase or shrink their risk exposure. This view was challenged by Williamson during the 2002 Argentine and Brazilian crises (Williamson 2002). He argues that a heavy debt burden is not sufficient to trigger a debt crisis when a country's fundamentals are strong enough to service the debt taking into account the market's psychology. Otherwise, the negative perception by the market will generate a self-fulfilling prophecy leading to the crisis. The markets' choice between focusing on the good versus the bad debt equilibrium is influenced by a range of variables including the political situation, policymakers' credibility, the independent status of the central bank, IFIs' support, and rating agencies, inter alia.

In order for risk analysts to assess the growth-maximizing level of debt beyond which a crisis becomes likely, they must first "measure" external indebtedness and the extent of debt overhang. This is more difficult than simply looking at the nominal amount of accumulated debt. The sheer amount of debt is not so easy to grasp, given the diversity of sources and the unequal quality of debtor and creditor reporting systems. Risk analysts by experience know that they better trust creditors than debtors, given the traditional amnesia of debtors regarding calculating liabilities. The uncertainty regarding the debt data reliability was at the root of the creation of the Institute for International Finance during the eruption of the emerging market debt crisis in 1982. In fact, the global banking industry was not aware of the specific volume and conditions of sovereign borrowers' outstanding debt. Hundreds of small banks, attracted by the fees, acquired lending exposure through syndicated Euro-currency loans. Yet, many of these lenders had minimal familiarities with the borrowers.

Clearly, a country's ability to sustain any particular debt ratio depends on a large number of internal and external factors including the outlook for exports (markets, demand/supply conditions, and prices), import requirements, exchange rate competitiveness, deteriorating terms of trade, interest rate developments, and the flexibility to adjust policies and economic structures. The first priority in debt analysis is to measure the external debt relative to macroeconomic indicators such as GDP, exports, and official reserve assets so as to obtain solvency indicators. This is not a trivial exercise. These ratios have also some limitations (Sebastian 2015). One important limitation is that, according to Roubini and Setser (2004), it is not easy to determine the "capacity to make payments." Should the debt threshold be the same for all countries, both developed and developing? Does the ratio change through time depending on the degree of trade and financial globalization of the debtor countries? Another limitation is that calculating the ratio of debt to GDP can be a complex exercise. The basic problem is that this implies comparing a number expressed in foreign currency, usually in USD (foreign debt), to a number expressed in domestic currency (GDP). In most cases, the current exchange rate is used to convert GDP in domestic currency into GDP in foreign currency. However, there is a problem with this approach. After a large devaluation—say from 1 Peso equal to 1 Dollar to 3 Pesos equal to 1 Dollar—GDP denominated in Dollars shrinks to one-third of the value it had immediately prior to the currency event. There are several possible ways of dealing with these issues. For example, calculating the country's domestic GDP in purchasing power parity terms (PPP) will provide cross-country comparisons based on the purchasing power of the USD in various counties. The PPP-adjusted national incomes aim to measure the relative living standards between two or more countries given that prices are not equal at current exchange rates (assuming similar consumption baskets and similar GDP calculations!). A number of international agencies such as the IMF, the World Bank, the OECD, and the United Nations Development Programme calculate PPP-based GDP for both developed and developing countries. This is a significantly more stable figure than GDP converted using spot exchange rates. Another alternative is to use an estimate of the long run "equilibrium" real exchange rate to make the GDP conversion (not mentioning the Big Mac Index published by The Economist since 1986).

Solvency ratios illustrate stock/stock relationships, linking the country's debt obligations with its overall assets and its hard currency reserves. However, solvency indicators alone are not sufficient to assess a country's financial weaknesses. This is primarily because it is necessary to compare stock indicators with flow relationships as well to tackle the debt composition. In the aftermath of the Second World War, both Britain and the US had a debt to GDP ratio larger than 200%. Japan—faced with the threat of protracted deflation—had a solvency ratio close to 240% between 2011 and 2018. In addition, nonfinancial corporate debt reaches 130% of GDP while household debt reaches a similar level of disposable income. However, Japan, the most indebted country in the world, has strong domestic savings and its central bank keeps interest rates low while purchasing government bonds. Its debt, moreover, is denominated in local currency and held mostly by domestic investors.

The second priority is to measure the "real" weight of the debt through its net present value—a measure that takes into account the fact that a significant part of the external debt has been contracted at below-market interest rates. This methodology is being used by the World Bank to calculate eligibility criteria for the Highly Indebted Poor Country's Debt Reduction Initiative (known as HIPC's Initiative). The real debt burden should comprise forward foreign exchange transactions as well as key contingent liabilities. The intertemporal solvency condition requires that the discounted value of trade balances be at least as large as the initial stock of the country's foreign debt. Otherwise, the country will be unable to repay its debt fully and in due time, and thus will require debt relief.

The third priority is to focus on debt flows vs. debt stocks, i.e., on debt servicing payments relative to export receipts as scaling factors to obtain a range of liquidity indicators. The latter combine financial relationships between flows of obligations and current export earnings. Sachs (1989) pointed out that stabilizing the debt-to-export ratio depends on nominal interest rates remaining below the growth rate of Dollar exports or real interest rates remaining below the growth rate of real exports. Several approaches have been suggested for managing the level of external liabilities, such as limiting the total debt service ratio to a specific number, around 33%. Federal Reserve Chairman Alan Greenspan (1999) suggested adopting a "liquidity-at-risk" standard whereby countries should be expected to hold sufficient liquid reserves to ensure they can avoid new borrowing for one year with a certain ex-ante probability, such as 95% of the time. In other words, usable foreign exchange reserves should exceed scheduled amortizations of foreign currency debts (assuming no rollovers) during the following year. Greenspan called for strengthening this rule to meet the additional test that the average maturity of a country's external liabilities should exceed a certain threshold, such as three years. The constraint on the average maturity ensures a degree of private sector "burden sharing" in times of crisis since the market value of longer maturities would doubtless fall sharply. Short-term foreign creditors, on the other hand, are able to exit without loss when their instruments mature. If the preponderance of a country's liabilities is short term, the entire burden of a crisis would fall on the emerging market economy in the form of a run on reserves.

The fourth priority is to analyze the volume and stability of net flows and net transfers, i.e., the amount of financing that is actually available in the country's economy to finance key imports, infrastructure investment, and debt repayments. As discussed above, net flows are equal to gross capital inflows from all creditors minus debt repayments, while net transfers are equal to net flows minus interest payments. The Institute of International of Finance shed light on the meager net flows from bilateral and multilateral official creditors to emerging market economies in the aftermath of the Global Financial Crisis, and particularly between 2012 and 2015. The Institute's flagship report provides a comprehensive assessment and forecasts of flows for twenty five emerging markets (Institute of International Finance 2017). The bulk of external financing comes from direct investment, portfolio investment, and bonds. Still worse, for many emerging market countries, depending on current interest rates and the size and conditions of the "inherited" debt, net transfers often turn negative. Principal and interest payments are larger than capital inflows. Reserves then fall while interest rate volatility and the share of debt at floating rates can precipitate a balance of payments crisis. As the debt crisis emerges, the net outflow is exacerbated as short-term debts are not rolled over or as maturing term debts cannot be replaced with new credits. Countries suddenly find themselves facing a liquidity "swing" from financial surplus to a payments gap.

Finally, the risk analyst should understand the debt's structure in order to assess the impact of the financial conditions of capital flows upon the debt servicing capacity. An analysis of the debt composition (regarding creditors, debtors, floating/fixed rate, currency, maturity) will illustrate the "quality" and sustainability of the country's market access. Indeed, whereas identifying sovereign debt outstanding can be relatively easy, thanks to the statistical frameworks imposed by the IFIs, private debt, both from corporate and household debtors, can be a genuine puzzle that requires combining various databases.

12.8 Debt Structures, Risk of Mismatch, and Solvency

To shed light on a shortsighted threshold analysis that rating agencies and risk analysts often use, consider two countries that have the same Debt/GDP ratio, namely, 100%. At that level, any private company would be bankrupt given that liabilities are larger than corporate assets. Walter Wriston, Citicorp Chairman in the mid-1980s, famously declared that, contrary to private corporations, "countries don't go out of business." It seems he forgot that commercial banks do fail if they blindly lend to sovereign borrowers without careful analysis of the relevant Country Risk. Indeed, during the 1970s, international banks recycled billions of petro-Dollars to the developing countries at floating interest rates. Between 1979 and 1982, interest rates more than doubled worldwide, dramatically raising the cost of loans, while the price of commodities slumped because of the recession brought about by tighter monetary policies. A chain reaction of defaults forced banks to refinance and reschedule emerging market countries' debts, through a combination of London and Paris Club debt restructurings under the auspices of the IMF. Now to return to our example: two countries, Solvencia and Liquidia, have similar solvency ratios but quite different economic and financial structures that the risk analyst carefully takes into account. Solvencia has a diversified export base while its debt is held by bilateral and multilateral official creditors, hence long maturities and fixed interest rates. Liquidia, on the other hand, suffers from a currency mismatch between export revenues and debt payments, while facing a bunching of short-term debt servicing obligations and the threat of floating interest rates. Any increase in international interest rates such as LIBOR, or any decline in export prices or rising import prices—hence deteriorating terms of trade—will trigger liquidity tensions (Table 12.6).

Comparing two Maghreb countries such as Morocco and Tunisia can be illuminating. At first glance, Morocco's financial indicators for both solvency and liquidity ratios seem more favorable than Tunisia's, although the two countries have similar trade openness ratios of exports/GDP of roughly 32%. Morocco boasts a better rating than Tunisia while enjoying a much healthier Debt/Reserves ratio. Tunisia has been severely hit by the turmoil of the Arab Spring and the need to defend its weakening currency. Table 12.7 summarizes a range of debt indicators.

Table 12.6 Two external debt trajectories

Solvencia	Liquidia
Debt/GDP = 100%	Debt/GDP = 100%
1. Diversified export base	1. Main export: hydrocarbons
2. Diversified export markets	2. One main export destination: EU
3. Mainly official creditors	3. Currency mismatch = Exports revenues in €/$ debt servicing
4. Long-term maturities = 10 years	4. Average debt maturity = 3 years
5. Fixed rate = 80% of debt	5. 66% of debt on floating rates
6. Similar currency structure: (Export revenues/Debt liabilities)	

Table 12.7 The tale of two neighbors' external indebtedness (2017 data)

Country risk indicators	Morocco	Tunisia
Debt/GDP	34%	80%
Debt/Exports	103%	180%
Exports/GDP	32%	32%
Debt/Reserves	128%	360%
Debt Servicing ratio	7%	17%
Reserves in months of imports	6	3
Current account deficit %	−4.5%	−7%
Coface Rating 2018	A4	C

However, the structure of external debt in each country is telling. Morocco's external debt depends largely on capital markets and on private creditors—that is, bonds, banks, and exports credits, whose share amounts to nearly 2/3 versus roughly 1/3 for Tunisia, making the latter's debt less vulnerable to shortening of maturities and higher market rates of interest. The high commitment of official creditors vis à vis Tunisia helped the country to retain market access in the wake of the Arab Spring turmoil of 2011. In June of 2016, Tunisia signed a loan guarantee agreement with the United States to access up to USD 500 million in affordable financing from international capital markets (USAID 2016). That was the third US loan guarantee to Tunisia. The earlier guarantees for USD 485 million in 2012 and USD 500 million in 2014 were successful in facilitating Tunisian access to global capital markets. Since 2011, the United States has provided more than USD 750 million in other types of foreign assistance to Tunisia. Likewise, the French export guarantee agency Coface has provided Tunisia with official guarantees to facilitate dynamic trade flows with Western European countries. The debt structure of the two countries is presented in graphs (Graphs 12.2, 12.3).

12.9 The Challenge of External Debt Sustainability Analysis

Overall, given the lack of "one size fits all" solvency and liquidity thresholds, the country risk analyst should examine not only the level and trajectories of debt ratios but also the structure of both revenues/assets and payments/liabilities. The country's revenues are subject to volatility regarding export volumes and prices. The central bank's reserve assets are subject to variations in exchange rate valuation. The country's debt payments depend on the maturity structure of the debt as well as its contractual clauses, including grace

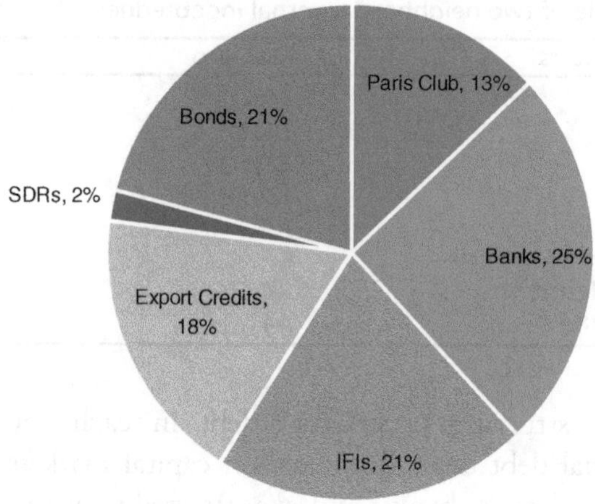

Graph 12.2 Structure of Morocco's external debt obligations (*Sources* IMF, central banks, and BIS)

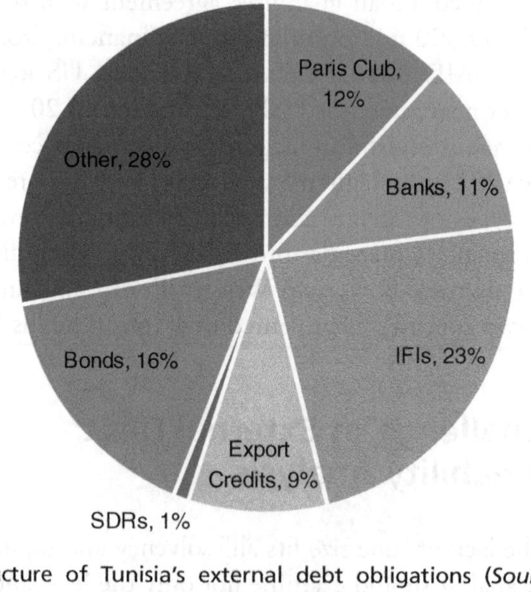

Graph 12.3 Structure of Tunisia's external debt obligations (*Sources* IMF, central banks, and BIS)

periods and fixed or floating interest rates. The stock of external liabilities depends on the currency structure of the debt. A currency mismatch will expose the debtor country to the rising cost of external liabilities, despite no external borrowing during the current year. During the 2015–2017 period,

Table 12.8 A broad range of toolkits for assessing sovereign debt

External debt sustainability analysis	
Capital flows	Debt stocks
• Balance of payments analysis • Gross and net flows	• Structure of debt by creditors, maturity: short term/long-term, currency and interest rates (fixed/floating)
• Net transfers	
• Floating –rate interest payments • Liquidity profile: Short-term/ long-term flows	• Structure of debt by debtors (sovereign/ corporate/household)
• Volatility	• Risk of mismatch assets/liabilities (interest rate, maturity)
• Capital flight and E&Os • Sustainability of debt strategy (refinancing, market access, rescheduling, restructuring)	• Solvency ratios • Secondary market debt discount, spread, yield and CDS

the large pile of foreign debt owed by Chinese companies, from state-owned banks to airlines, has given added impetus to Beijing's efforts to keep the Yuan from falling too steeply against the rallying Dollar, as the Dollar hit a fourteen-year high against sixteen currencies in the end of 2016. The faster-than-expected depreciation resulted in more businesses and individuals escaping from the weaker yuan, further pressuring the currency. The risk analyst thus must carefully examine the currency structure of a country's assets and liabilities to detect any potential costly mismatch. The previous table illustrates the main parameters of an in-depth debt analysis (Table 12.8).

12.10 The Relationship Between External Indebtedness and Economic Growth

12.10.1 Capacity Versus Willingness to Meet Debt Payment Obligations

Economic theory suggests that external debt is a temporary phenomenon that supplements domestic savings, bridges the resources-investment gap, and speeds up the growth process towards the "take off" stage of sustaining development (Bouchet 1987). The conventional approach stipulates that as long as borrowing countries invest capital inflows in productive investments with high return rates and without sizable adverse shocks, growth should increase and generate the proceeds for timely debt repayments. The key condition is that the investment project yields a return that is above the international cost of capital when the project's costs and returns are measured at appropriate shadow prices (i.e., taking into account the distortions in incentives in the borrowing country's economy).

The reality, however, shows that countries do not grow smoothly out of external indebtedness. Two different theoretical approaches underlie attempts to predict the risk of default. One approach regards default as arising out of an unintended deterioration in the borrowing country's capacity to service its debt. The other, in contrast, views the rescheduling of (or default on) a country's external debt as a rational choice made by the borrower based on an assessment of the costs and benefits of rescheduling or defaulting. This is why there is a large number of rich countries with poor people whose governments have the capacity but not the willingness to meet their external borrowing obligations. Much of these countries belong to the hydrocarbon and minerals producer and exporter categories where wealth concentration is large, coupled with high corruption and large capital flight, as discussed in Chapter 14.

In the debt-service-capacity approach, the probability of default is a function of the unsustainability of a given level of external debt, either as a result of short-term illiquidity or of long-term insolvency reflected in an abrupt worsening of liquidity problems. It is assumed that the debtor's budget constraint is breached, either (i) because of short-term economic mismanagement, long-term structural problems, domestic policy, or domestic shocks such as harvest failures; or (ii) because of external shocks such as an increase in international interest rates, deterioration in a country's terms of trade, and slowing growth in main trading partners. With this approach, a number of key economic variables could serve as indicators of future liquidity and solvency problems, including export growth rates, current account balance, real exchange rate, as well as the various liquidity and solvency indicators that have been discussed above. Table 12.9 illustrates a number of potential internal and external sources of debt crisis.

The probability of default will increase for at least five reasons. First, economic mismanagement will lead to real exchange rates significantly overvalued, seriously hurting exports' competitiveness. Second, domestic saving will remain flat due to low real rates of interest, hence investment levels inconsistent with sustainable rapid growth. Third, as noticed by analysts of the "Lost Decade" in Japan, a large proportion of the capital inflows will be used to finance consumption or investment projects of doubtful quality (Radelet and Sachs 1998; Sebastian 2000). In emerging markets countries, including in China and Brazil, most of these funds will be intermediated by banks that are subject to minimal supervision, which can quickly become

Table 12.9 The main triggers of an external debt crisis

	Trade flows	Capital flows	Interest rates	Exchange rates	Volatility and turmoil
Internal	Falling export production	Capital controls	Negative real rates	Overvalued rates	Socio-political crisis
	Rising costs and input prices	Tighter regulations	Inflation	Capital Flight	Debt repudiation
	Infrastructure bottlenecks		Weak banking system	A/L currency mismatch	Nationalization
External	Shrinking export markets	Shrinking FDI and	Risign interest rate	USD appreciation	Export market turbulences
	Falling commodity prices	Portfolio flows	differential	Higher debt servicing cost	Regional crisis contagion
	Rising import costs	Regional downgrading	Capital flight		
Interactive	Trade protectionism	Decline in working	Rising global interest rates	Competitive devaluations	Rating downgrading
	Non-trade barriers	Capital lines	Shorter maturities		Stock market crises
	Global recession	Global risk aversion	Flight to quality		Systemic crisis

the Achilles' heel of a sustainable growth trajectory. As a result, the debt will not be invested as it should, but instead will be used to finance current consumption spending and/or the black hole of the government budget deficit, or the debt will be recycled in international bank accounts via capital flight. Fourth, the debt composition, in terms of maturity, currency or interest rates is such that the borrowing country will become highly vulnerable to external shocks and to imported crises via a contraction of capital availability for refinancing or via more severe financial conditions linked to floating interest rates or higher spreads. Many scholars highlighted the importance of the role of global shocks for both the 1982 debt crisis and the 1997 Asian financial crisis. (During the 1980s, developing countries, particularly in Latin America, experienced brutal and repeated external shocks. Tight monetary policies in the developed countries of the OECD caused a protracted slowdown in the industrial world, which generated a negative spill-over effect on export prices and terms of trade.)

Fifth and finally, the debtor countries can be subject to "debt overhang" in that the accumulated debt is larger than the country's repayment capacity. Increasing debt servicing obligations will discourage domestic investors and exporters, as well as foreign creditors. If the discounted sum of current and future trade balances is less than the current debt, the country can never service the debt out of its own resources, and it will have to borrow forever, in an amount growing at the real interest rate. However, there could be an additional shock, namely, the drying of global capital markets resulting in tougher rollover transactions for external debt repayments. This point has been highlighted by Radelet and Sachs (1998) in the case of the Latin American and Asian debt crises of the 1980s and 1990s. Debt payment difficulties included elements of self-fulfilling crises in which capital withdrawals by creditors cascaded into a financial panic and resulted in an unnecessarily deep capital contraction. To put things in another way, foreign creditors and the IMF precipitated a worsening of the balance of payment problems of the developing countries. The "one size" fits all therapy of the IMF contributed to transforming national payment crises into regional crises, which led to a global systemic crisis in the emerging markets.

12.10.2 Providing Liquidity or Solvency Relief?

Unsustainable debt servicing requires debt ratios to be reduced in various ways that depend on the diagnosis of the debt overhang, namely challenges relating to liquidity (providing time and fresh financing) or solvency (providing debt relief). But the solution is predicated on the diagnosis of the root causes of the debt problems. Is the country unable or unwilling to meet its contractual obligations? There are many rich countries with poor people, weak institutions, and bad governance, where much of the debt has been recycled in bank accounts in offshore centers. The lack of any permanent multilateral forum of debt restructuring negotiation, despite the London and Paris Club frameworks, requires an ad hoc and case by case approach to sovereign debt relief (see Appendix 12.1). Box 12.2 offers a concise summary of Venezuela's methodic march toward default between 2000 and 2017 (see also Case Study 12.1).

Box 12.2 Venezuela's steps toward debt default: A toxic combination of oil dependence, corruption, Chavista revolution, and economic recession

Venezuela best illustrates the case of willingness versus capacity to pay. The country is a case in point with a combination of low oil prices since mid-2014, economic mismanagement, corruption coupled with capital flight, and international sanctions that precipitated payment arrears and default. The IMF closed its offices in Caracas in 2006, and in May 2018 the IMF issued a declaration of censure against Venezuela.

1. 2005–2014: Large and rising oil revenues, excess liquidity, and regional influence: Venezuela has been loosening its ties to the IMF and the World Bank since Chávez took office in 1999. Venezuela repaid its debts to the World Bank five years ahead of schedule, while accumulating reserves of more than USD 34 billion and making generous loans to Latin American neighbors. China started to lend large financing resources to Venezuela mainly for government infrastructure projects, with repayment in oil.
2. 2014–2016: A combination of falling oil prices, declining government revenues, hyperinflation, and deepening recession, led to shrinking reserve assets and worsening debt ratios.
3. 2016–2017: The country's liquidity crisis deepened in a context of low oil prices and falling export and government revenues. In a controversial operation, in May 2017, Goldman Sachs bought USD 2.8 billion worth of PDVSA bonds maturing in 2022, at a 70% discount to the market price. A few months later, Goldman's asset management arm reportedly sold at least USD 300 million of the bonds to a hedge fund.
4. November 2017: Russia has provided liquidity relief for Venezuela's struggling regime between 2014 and 2016 through sovereign debt purchases. In addition, the state-owned company Rosneft provided about USD 6 billion in cash advances to PDVSA guaranteed by oil supplies and a 49.9% stake in CITGO, the oil company's US subsidiary. Russia agreed on a ten-year rescheduling of USD 3.15 billion of bilateral debt payments, including a favorable six-year grace period.
5. November 2017: Caracas missed a deadline to pay USD 200 million in interest on two government bonds, prompting S&P to declare it in default, in the wake of USD 420 million of overdue interest on sovereign bonds, as well as payments on debt issued by PDVSA. Markets reacted with a steep discount

on debt trading, reaching market prices in the range of twenty five cents on the Dollar. In addition, five-year credit-default swap spreads stood at almost 17,000 basis points, compared with 600 for its closest peer, at the time of the default announcement.

Indebted countries that face short-term liquidity problem have to tackle a flow mismatch between payments and revenues. The solution can be a combination of economic and export growth, or inflation, and a mix of additional time relief and fresh money (that is, debt refinancing and/or debt rescheduling). A solvency problem requires a combination of debt relief and economic restructuring to contain the risk of defaulting. In an in-depth analysis of debt crises in both developing and developed countries, Tang and Upper (2010) of the BIS noted that debt reduction has always been a combination of factors, including inflation and GDP growth recovery, which exert a downward pressure on debt ratios. The exceptions were Colombia and Mexico in the 1990s, where the decline in debt ratios was almost entirely driven by inflation. In the United States, the ratio of household debt to GDP peaked in the middle of 2006 in the wake of higher interest rates and slowing economic activity. In European countries, household debt continued to go up at rates outstripping GDP growth for another couple of years. Debt ratio reduction came in full force between 2009 and 2012 in a number of countries, most notably in Greece, Ireland, Spain, and Portugal.

12.11 No Silver Bullets for Debt Restructuring Workouts: Rescheduling, Refinancing, Debt Conversion, or Debt Reduction?

The default is as old as indebtedness itself. Sovereign debt defaults are a recurring feature of public finance since the nineteenth century. The sequence of over-indebtedness, financial crisis, and austerity policy measures has given rise to the questioning of the legitimacy of debt contracts between the State and foreign creditors. Since its emergence in the early twentieth century, the "odious debt" concept seeks to provide a moral and legal foundation for severing the continuity of legal obligations where the debt in question was contracted by a prior "odious" regime and was used in ways that were not beneficial to the interests of the population (see Appendix 12.2). As early as the 1820s, a large number of Latin American countries defaulted on their debt obligations vis à vis European bondholders, including Ecuador, Venezuela, Costa Rica, Chile, Nicaragua, Guatemala, Brazil, and Argentina. But in Europe itself, Greece already defaulted four times on its debt obligations at the beginning of the nineteenth century (1826, 1843, 1860, and 1894). The combined length of the period under which Greece was in default during the modern era totaled ninety years, or approximately 50% of the total period that the country has been independent (*Forbes* 2011). The first rise of "modern" defaults started in 1982 due to debt overhang in emerging market countries, spill-over effect, and interest rate increases. On the front line were international banks, the so-called London Club, which had lent at floating rates of interest, based on LIBOR (the inter-bank refinancing cost in the London market). Developing countries' over-indebtedness was treated by a combination of debt reduction, rescheduling, and refinancing within the framework of the "Brady Plan," named after Nicholas Brady, the US Secretary of the US Treasury between 1988 and 1993.

In total, seventeen Brady debt restructuring deals were implemented on a country-by-country basis, starting with Mexico in September 1989 and ending with the last Brady type agreements in Côte d'Ivoire and Vietnam in 1997. Most Brady countries were in Latin America, namely Argentina, Bolivia, Brazil, Costa Rica, Dominican Republic, Ecuador, Mexico, Panama, Peru, Uruguay, and Venezuela. The other seven countries were Bulgaria, Côte d'Ivoire, Jordan, Nigeria, Philippines, Poland, and Vietnam. A menu of debt restructuring options was used to match the diverse strategic and regulatory incentives of commercial banks. Substantial debt relief was obtained through the restructuring of bank loans into thirty-year discounted bonds, with a principal guarantee backed up by zero-coupon bonds and a rolling interest guarantee.

A second wave of defaults started in 1998, due to a combination of currency mismatch and short-term bank borrowing in Asian countries, worsening global economic conditions, as well as an increase in the share of speculative-grade sovereign bond issuers in the mid-1990s. Actually, the so-called Asian crisis did not generate any sovereign default, contrary to Russia, Pakistan, Ukraine, Venezuela, and Ecuador. The largest default of 1998 was that of Russia as the country suffered a currency, banking, and fiscal crisis as a result of external shocks in the form of weak oil and nonferrous metals prices, unfavorable market sentiment after the Asian crisis, and unsustainable government budget policies.

A third wave of defaults emerged during the 2000–2006 period—with seven additional defaults, led by Argentina's USD 82 billion default in 2001, which spilled over to Uruguay two years later (Moody's 2009).

A more recent wave of defaults coincided with the Global Financial Crisis of 2008, and took place in the developed group of countries of the OECD, including Greece in 2012. Ukraine, a European country that is primarily middle-income, defaulted in 2015 and obtained a 20% debt relief, backed up by a substantial financing rescue program from the EU and from the IMF. In addition, Puerto Rico defaulted on its municipal bonds in 2016, and Venezuela in end-year 2017. Although defaults have typically involved low-income and emerging-market economies, Greece's default in 2012 inaugurated a new chapter in creditor losses in advanced economy sovereigns. Five of the Eurozone countries—Greece, Portugal, Ireland, Italy, and Spain—have, to varying degrees, failed to generate enough economic growth to balance the rise in their external financial obligations to pay back bondholders and to reduce their debt ratios to sustainable levels. Slower growth and rising debt ratios led to a perverse circle of demand for higher yields, hence higher borrowing costs, leading to further fiscal strain, prompting investors to demand even tighter yield conditions, coupled with a general loss of investor confidence and with cross-country contamination.

Table 12.10 summarizes the main debt defaults between 1998 and 2017.

Many developed countries will face challenges in the years ahead as a result of several key factors—uncertainty in economic growth in the Eurozone, economic decoupling between the US and European growth trajectories, and rising interest rates. France, for instance, pays roughly €45 billion per year of interest payments, equal to 2% of GDP, for a public debt that reaches €2200 billion, or close to 100% of GDP. A 100 basis point rise in interest rates would cost France an additional €2 billion interest bill the first year, rising to €4.6 billion the second year, and close to €12 billion the sixth year (FIPECO 2016). In several Eurozone countries, rising rates are not the only threat given an environment of political volatility that prompted a number of elections. In France, for instance, international investors, particularly in Japan, have sold French government debt in the first half of 2017 due to mounting political risk in the run-up to the two-round elections in the Spring of 2017. Many investors have shunned French sovereign debt and have shifted to short-dated German debt as a hedge against political risk in the Eurozone, sending the yield down to a record of minus 1% in Q1-2017. To state the matter concisely, the socio-political risk is no longer a monopoly of emerging market counties. As observed by Didier Saint-Georges, managing director of the investment fund Carmignac: "Political risk in Europe is no paranoid fantasy" (Moore 2017).

Table 12.10 Sovereign debt defaults and creditor loss level

Main Debt Defaults & Restructuring 1991–2017						
COUNTRY	Restructuring	Haircut/ loss level	USD billion	Restructuring	Debt relief	USD billion
	Bonds & London Club				Paris Club	
Argentina	1989–2001–2005	77%	61	2001–2014		
Belize	2006		0.2			
Cyprus		banking crisis			n.a	
Ecuador	2009	68%	6.7	1999–2003		1
Ethiopia	1996–2004	92%	0.2	1996–2004	85%	1.5
Dominican Rep	2004–2005	11%	1.3	2005	37%	0.2
Greece	2011–2012	53%	107	2012–2016		
Guyana	1998–2004	91%		1996–2004	90%	0.1
Honduras	1998–2004	82%		2005	71%	0.2
Iceland	2008–2013	banking crisis			n.a	
Iraq	2005	89%	18	2004–2006	30%	11.6
Ivory Coast	2010	55%	2.9	1998–2012	80%	4.7
Kenya	1998–2004	45%		1998–2004	69%	0.2
Nicaragua	1995–2003	92%	1.1	1995–2004	96%	1.6
Nigeria	1991	40%	5.9	2005	60%	18
Pakistan	1999	15%	1.4	2001	0%	14
Peru	1997–2000	64%	10.6	1996		6.7
Philippines	1992	25%	4.5	1991–1994		1.6
Poland	1994	49%	13.5	1990–1991		30
Puerto Rico	2015–2017	municipal bonds	70			
Russia	1997–2000	51%	32	1999–2006		68
Serbia	2004	62%	2.7	2001–2006	51%	4.3
Seychelles	2010	56%	0.3	2009–2015		0.02
Tanzania	2004	88%		2002	90%	0.7
Ukraine	1998–2000	20%	2.2	2001		0.6
Uruguay	2003	10%	3.1	2003	20%	1
Venezuela	1998–2017–2018	to be confirmed				
Vietnam	1997	52%	0.8	1993	50%	0.5
Yemen	2001	97%	0.6	2001	67%	0.4

Source Rating agencies, IIF, authors, and IMF

12.12 Where Will the Next Crisis Come From?

The country risk analyst and the fund manager must keep in mind not to focus on ratios that could have been used for previous "traditional" crises but that do not grasp the changing nature of financial crisis in the age of globalization. Rising debt servicing ratios and rising banks' non-performing loans in an environment of weak regulatory frameworks are textbook signals of mounting risks that might appear too late. Actually, country risk managers must add five new features in their toolkit: first, declining savings and rising private debt from both corporate and household borrowers; second, financial disintermediation with rising financing from unregulated "shadow" financial entities; third, increasing domestic currency security issues in emerging markets with financing from global investors in search of higher yield and whose behavior can be very volatile; fourth, opportunistic Dollar-denominated loans and bonds at floating rates in emerging market countries to benefit from short-lived low-interest rates; and fifth, debt stress that is not driven by immediate sovereign default threats but by the negative impact of rising private debt servicing ratios on consumption and investment, resulting in a perverse feedback on growth, profits, and the quality of banking portfolios.

These signals are important to take into account in order to broaden the outlook of risk managers, although this is not enough. One must add three important nuances to assess the likelihoods of financial crises and so-called "Minsky moments" of unsustainable bubbles. The first one is that "countries" do not build up debts. There are specific institutions in each country, with distinct leverage levels, unequal resilience to liquidity shocks, and particular risks of balance sheet distress, accounting frameworks, creditworthiness, management guidelines, and governance. A micro-analysis of the debt build-up process is required to identify signals of sectoral weaknesses. Granular information is necessary to assess the risks of scissor effects between higher corporate and households leverage and shrinking revenues. The second is that the transmission mechanisms of debt crises are also crucial to assess the likelihood of contagion. Herd instinct and the "echo chamber effect" of globalized markets can precipitate crises with abrupt contamination consequences. McKibbin and Stoeckel (2009) analyzed the impact of the global reappraisal of risk on the large contraction in output and trade in 2007–2010. They noted: "When there is a reappraisal of risk everywhere including China, investment falls sharply – in a sense, there is nowhere for the capital to go in a global crisis of confidence. The implication is that if markets, forecasters, and policymakers misunderstand the effects of the crisis and mechanisms at work, they can inadvertently fuel fears of a 'meltdown' and make matters far worse." The third is summarized by the General Manager of the Bank for International Settlements (Caruana 2014): "Improving risk management systems is very important, but even with state-of-the-art systems some risks can't be measured and internalized. As in any complex system, the behavior of the whole financial system is dependent not only on the parts but also on the linkages. Dynamics can easily become non-linear; small causes can produce large effects." To sum up, technological innovation increases complexity and uncertainty, hence increasing the risk of fat tails.

12.13 Summing Up and Conclusion

Over-indebtedness, so-called "debt overhang," liquidity and solvency problems are at the root of Country Risk for many investors and creditors, both public and private. Nevertheless, Country Risk can take a wide range of forms from sheer default to payment arrears. Three main issues should inform the assessment of debt repayment difficulties. First, debt crises are always rooted in balance of payment problems, though for sovereign debtors only. A micro-analysis of the debt build-up process is required to observe signals of sectoral weaknesses. Granular information is necessary to assess the risks of scissor effects between high corporate and households leverage and shrinking revenues. To assess sovereign debt risk, careful analysis should focus on the structure of the liabilities of public and private debtors, before analyzing the sustainability of current account deficits. Terms of trade deterioration can hurt export competitiveness while overvalued exchange rate can worsen the trade deficit. In addition, the relationship between deficits and debt crisis stems from the financing of the deficit, depending on the intertemporal transformation of capital inflows into debt repayments. Second, Country risk advisers and managers should use liquidity and solvency threshold ratios with caution. Countries with similar external debt indicators can hide different levels of fragility depending on the structure of the debt, including maturity (short-term vs long-term), creditors (private vs official, banks vs institutional investors, bilateral vs multilateral), financial instruments (loans vs securities), debt purpose (project financing vs trade credit or balance of payments financing), and interest rates (floating vs fixed). Third, ultimately, the debtor country repays its external debt with its export revenues and its external capital inflows. The country risk analyst thus must assess the likelihood of shrinking hard currency revenues, depending on commodity prices, terms of trade, overvalued exchange rate, and economic contraction in trade partners. Contagion from adverse regional and global economic developments must be always factored in the risk analysis.

Overall, borrowers and creditors are linked by forced solidarity, hence the need for rolling forward the loans and for maintaining capital and trade market access. Consider the remarks of David O. Beim, former head of investment banking at Bankers Trust, made well before the cycle of debt crises of the 1980s and 1990s: "It is entirely a game of confidence. In banking, as in military matters, the ideal is strength sufficiently great that no one would feel the need to test it" (Beim 1977, 723).

Case Study 12.1: Venezuela's PVDSA bond swap transaction of October 2016

Following the sharp drop in international oil prices in the summer of 2014, the combination of declining output and shrinking hard currency export revenues have left Venezuela's national oil group PDVSA struggling to find enough cash to make payments and import basic necessities. In March 2016, Moody's changed its outlook on Venezuela's rating from stable to negative. In the aftermath of the downgrading, the six months' CDS reached 7000 bps estimating that the government has a 90% chance to default shortly. In September of 2016, Venezuela's indebted national oil group had to ask bondholders to swap its debt maturing in April and November 2017 for new notes due in 2020. The oil company faced a bunching of debt repayments, reaching USD 1bn on October 28, USD 2.2 bn on November 2, and USD 7.1 bn worth of bonds maturing in April and November 2017. In addition, the company and Venezuela faced USD 15 bn of debt payments for the end of 2017. PDVSA asked if the payments could be done in local currency. Fitch Ratings announced that if payment were to be made in local currency it would be considered a distressed debt exchange and would amount to a default.

To avoid default on its large 2017 payments, PDVSA decided to negotiate a swap for around USD 5.325 bn worth of bonds against long-dated bonds maturing in 2020. Venezuela had to pawn half of its most attractive assets—Citgo Petroleum Corp., the US unit of PDVSA—to convince investors to accept the deal. Despite using CITGO, the US refining subsidiary of Petroleum de Venezuela as collateral, the company had to extend the subscribing period three times to be able to fulfill the offer and to persuade investors that the collateral was a genuine guarantee. Reluctant creditors forced PDVSA to improve the terms. Instead of a par exchange, Venezuela offered bondholders as much as 1.22 times the principal they held, while also lowering the size of the bond tender. That provided the creditors who agreed to the swap with a potentially larger stake in Citgo.

By exchanging the old notes due in 2017 for new debt with annual payments through 2020, the state-owned oil company managed to reduce bond outlays that would have totaled USD 3.05 bn by more than USD 900 million. PDVSA still faced USD 6.1 bn of principal payments by the end of 2017. After protracted negotiations, 39.4% of the bondholders, holding USD 2.8 bn, agreed to swap their holdings for USD 3.4 bn of new bonds maturing in 2020. The swap deal was far short of the USD 5.325 billion that PDVSA had been seeking to exchange.

In conclusion, PDVSA's swap transaction provided well-needed liquidity relief to the cash-strapped oil company as it battles lower prices, falling production and tight market access. However, it added nearly USD 1 bn of debt to its payments over the 2018–2020 period. With international reserves falling to record-low levels, conflicting relations with the IMF and with most IFIs, and oil output declining, the prospects of a default still loomed large as Venezuela has no buffers to avoid a sovereign debt default in a context of rising sociopolitical turmoil.

Appendix 12.1: The Relationship Between GDP Growth Rate and the Debt/GDP Ratio

See Fig. 12A.1

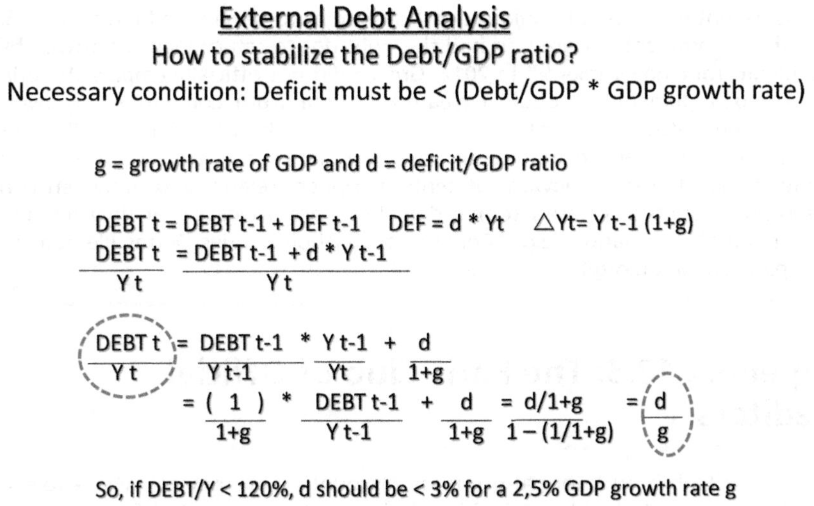
External Debt Analysis
How to stabilize the Debt/GDP ratio?
Necessary condition: Deficit must be < (Debt/GDP * GDP growth rate)
g = growth rate of GDP and d = deficit/GDP ratio
DEBT t = DEBT t-1 + DEF t-1   DEF = d * Yt   ΔYt= Y t-1 (1+g)
DEBT t / Y t = DEBT t-1 + d * Y t-1 / Y t
DEBT t / Y t = DEBT t-1 / Y t-1 * Y t-1 / Yt + d / 1+g
= (1 / 1+g) * DEBT t-1 / Y t-1 + d / 1+g = d/1+g / 1 − (1/1+g) = d / g
So, if DEBT/Y < 120%, d should be < 3% for a 2,5% GDP growth rate g

Fig. 12A.1 The relationship between the Debt/GDP ratio and economic growth

Appendix 12.2: The "Odious Debt" Concept

Debt crisis, debt repudiation and "odious debt"

In the early seventeenth century, Grotius claimed that contracts made by the sovereigns that are of no advantage and harmful to the State should not be honored, in particular where public money has been pledged for purposes that are not for the public good. In the nineteenth century, the doctrine of odious debt emerged after the Spanish-American war when the United States argued that neither it nor Cuba should be held responsible for the debt the colonial ruler had incurred without the consent of the people nor for their benefit. The modern concept of odious debts was first articulated in the post-WW I context, by the jurist Alexander Sack, a Russian legal theorist, in his 1927 book *The Effects of State Transformations on their Public Debts*. Odious debts are contracted and spent against the interests of the population of a State, without its consent, and with full awareness of the creditor. Then, according to Sack, the debt is not an obligation for the nation; it is a "regime's debt", hence a personal debt of the power that has incurred it. Consequently, it disappears with it.

The odious debt concept seeks to provide a moral and legal foundation for partly or entirely severing the continuity of legal obligations where the debt in question was contracted by a prior "odious" regime and was used in ways that were not beneficial or were harmful to the interests of the population (Howse 2007). The repudiated "odious" debts, therefore, are supposed to be unenforceable against the successor regime. Since the 1960s, the concept has been invoked with little effect in several instances with regard to the financing of a dictatorship and in the context of military aggression, including in Nicaragua, Haiti, Iraq, Iran, South Africa, and low-income African countries. One of the most recent examples of "odious debt" strategy was Ukraine in March of 2015, as the government declared "it had the right not to return loans borrowed by a kleptocratic government." In 2012, Greece did not officially employ the odious debt argument, although it created a "Debt Truth Committee" to investigate the status of its debts. See also Kremer and Jayachandran (2002). Most of the people referring to "odious debt cancellation requests" wrap them up within the Marxist framework of center-periphery relationships between rich and poor countries where external debt flows are a weapon of financial and geopolitical domination (e.g. "Comité pour l'Abolition des Dettes Illégitimes" http://www.cadtm.org/).

Appendix 12.3: The Paris Club of Official Creditors

The Paris Club is an informal group of 21 country governments whose role is to find coordinated and sustainable solutions to the payment difficulties experienced by developing debtor countries. Though the vast majority of countries belongs to the OECD, Russia and Brazil have joined the Paris Club.

Since its beginning in 1956, when Argentina agreed to meet its public creditors in Paris, the Club has remained strictly informal in a kind of "non-institution" framework. Monthly sessions are prepared by a Secretariat General that is run by senior officials from the French Treasury. A few rules and principles are accepted by all members, including solidarity, consensus, information sharing, case by case, conditionality, and comparability of treatment.

The Paris Club of official creditors provides debt restructuring only to debtor countries that need debt relief and that are committed to implementing the reforms necessary to restore their economic and financial situation. In practice, the country must have a current program with the IMF supported by a conditional arrangement. Liquidity or solvency relief is provided through flow or stock treatment. Flow treatments aim to close the debtor country's financing gap identified by the IMF. Paris Club agreements usually coincide with the period of time covered by the IMF program, which demonstrates a financing gap that can only be covered by debt rescheduling during a so-called "consolidation period."

Only maturities owed to Paris Club creditors and falling due during this period are treated. In some cases, accumulated arrears are also renegotiated. However, since the 1990s, some Paris Club treatments tackle the entire stock of debt to provide a debtor country with a so-called "exit treatment." Such agreements are used in two cases. (1) Under the Highly Indebted Poor Country initiative, Paris Club creditors propose a once and for all debt stock reduction granted at completion point. And (2) debt stock reduction from 33 to 80% may be granted, on a case-by-case basis, for countries that have a satisfactory track record with both the Paris Club and the IMF and where there is sufficient confidence in the debtor country's ability to meet its future obligations.

References

Alesina, Alberto, and Guido Tabellini. 1988. "External Debt, Capital Flight, and Political Risk." NBER Working Paper No. 2610. http://www.nber.org/papers/w2610.pdf.

Bach, Christopher. 2010. "A guide to the US Financial Transactions accounts", US Bureau of Economic Analysis, http://www.bea.gov/scb/pdf/2010/02%20February/0210_guide.pdf, February.

Beers, David T., and Jean-Sébastien Nadeau. 2014. "Introducing a New Database of Sovereign Defaults," February 28. https://papers.ssrn.com/sol3/papers.cfm?abstract_id=2609162.

Beers, David, and Jamshid Mavalwalla. 2017. "Database of Sovereign Defaults, 2017." Bank of Canada Technical Report 101, June.

Beim, O. David. 1977. "Rescuing the LDCs." *Foreign Affairs*, July.

BIS. 2017. "Joint BIS-IMF-OECD-World Bank Statistics on External Debt." http://www.bis.org/publ/r_debt.htm?m=6%7C34.

Bouchet, Michel Henry. 1987. *The Political Economy of International Debt*. Greenwood, IL: Quorum Books.

Bouchet, Michel Henry. 2004. *La Deuda de la Naciones*. Colombia: FELABAN-Federación Latinoamericana de Bancos.

Bouchet, Michel Henry, Sarmiento Aleida, and José Lumbreras. 2007. *Riesgo-País: Un Enfoque Latino-Americano*. Peru: ESAN Publicaciones.

Boyce, James K. 1992. "The Revolving Door? External Debt and Capital Flight: A Philippine Case Study." *World Development* 20 (3): 335–349.

Caruana, Jaime. 2014. "Financial Regulation, Complexity, and Innovation." Speech for the Promontory Annual Lecture, London, June 4. https://www.bis.org/speeches/sp140604.htm.

DBRS. 2016. Methodology. Rating Sovereign Governments, October. http://www.dbrs.com/research/300639/rating-sovereign-governments.pdf.

FIPECO. 2016. La charge d'intérêt de la dette publique, July 10.

Forbes. 2011. "Debt Defaults Have Greek History." September 28.

Greenspan, Alan. 1999. Remarks Before the World Bank Conference on Recent Trends in Reserve Management. Washington, DC, April 29.

Herndon, Thomas, Michael Ash, and Robert Pollin. 2014. "Does High Public Debt Consistently Stifle Economic Growth: A Critique of Reinhart and Rogoff." *Cambridge Journal of Economics* 38 (2): 257–279.

Howse, Robert. 2007. "The Concept of Odious Debt in Public Law." UNCTAD Report No. 185, July.

Institute of International Finance. 2017. Capital Flows to Emerging Markets Report. https://www.iif.com/publications/capital-flows-emerging-markets-report.

Kremer, Michael, and Seema Jayachandran. 2002. "Odious Debt." *Finance & Development* 39 (2), http://www.imf.org/external/pubs/ft/fandd/2002/06/kremer.htm, June.

Krugman, Paul. 1989. "Private Capital Flows to Problem Debtors." In *Developing Country Debt and the World Economy*, edited by Jeffrey D Sachs. Chicago: University of Chicago Press.

McKibbin, Warwick J., and Andrew Stoeckel. 2009. "The Global Financial Crisis: Causes and Consequences." Australian National University, September.

Moody's. 2009. Sovereign Defaults and Recovery Rates, 1983–2008. Special Comment. Moody's Global Credit Policy, March. https://www.moodys.com/sites/products/DefaultResearch/2007400000587968.pdf.

Moore, Elaine. 2017. "Investors Look to Gauge Scale of Draghi's Optimism." *Financial Times*, March 8.

Panizza, Ugo, and Andrea Presbitero. 2012. "Public Debt and Economic Growth: Is there a Causal Effect?" *Journal of Macroeconomics* 41 (C): 21–41.

Pattillo, Catherine, Hélène Pourson, and Ricci Luca. 2002. "External Debt and Growth." *Finance & Development* 39 (2), June.

Pescatori, Andrea, Damiano Sandri, and John Simon. 2014. "No Magic Threshold." *Finance & Development* 51 (2): 39–42.

Radelet, Steven, and Jeffrey Sachs. 1998. "The East Asian Financial Crisis: Diagnosis, Remedies, Prospects." Brookings Papers on Economic Activity, No. 1.

Reinhart, Carmen M., and Kenneth S. Rogoff. 2010. "Growth in a Time of Debt." *American Economic Review* 100 (2): 573–578.

Reinhart, Carmen M., Vincent R. Reinhart, and Kenneth S. Rogoff. 2012. "Public Debt Overhangs: Advanced-Economy Episodes since 1800." *Journal of Economic Perspectives* 26 (3): 69–86.

Reinhart, Carmen M., and Kenneth S. Rogoff. 2013. "Financial and Sovereign Debt Crises: Some Lessons Learned and Those Forgotten." IMF Working Paper WP/13/266, December.

Roubini, Nouriel, and Brad Setser. 2004. *Bailouts or Bail-Ins? Responding to Financial Crises in Emerging Economies.* Washington, DC: Peterson Institute Press.

Sachs, Jeffrey D. 1989. "Introduction." In *Developing Country Debt and the World Economy*, edited by Jeffrey D. Sachs. Chicago: University of Chicago Press.

Schaefer, Brett. 2002. "The Millenium Challenge Account: An Opportunity to Advance Development in Poor Nations." The Heritage Foundation, July 12.

Sebastian, Edwards. 2000. Chapter 7, "Capital Flows, Real Exchange Rates, and Capital Controls: Some Latin American Experiences." In *Capital Flows and the Emerging Economies: Theory, Evidence, and Controversies*, edited by Sebastian Edwards. Chicago: University of Chicago Press.

Sebastian, Edwards. 2015. "Sovereign Default, Debt Restructuring, and Recovery Rates: Was the Argentinean "Haircut" Excessive?" NBER. Working Paper 20964. http://www.nber.org/papers/w20964.

Tang, Garry, and Christian Upper. 2010. "Debt Reduction after Crises." *BIS Quarterly Review*, September.

USAID. 2016. Press Release. Tunisia Signs 500 Million Loan Guarantee with the United States, June 3. https://www.2012-2017.usaid.gov/tunisia/press-releases/jun-3-2016-tunisia-signs-500-million-loan-guarantee-agreement-united-states.

Williamson, John. 2002. "Is Brazil Next? International Economics Policy Briefs." Number PB 02-07, Peterson Institute for International Economics, August.

13

In Search of Early Warning Signals of Country Risk: Focusing on Market Price Signals

13.1 Introduction: Looking for a Range of Warning Indicators of Upcoming Country Crisis for Predicting the Uncertain

Conventional wisdom in assessing financial risk is to consider credit, operational, and market risk (and in the case of investment portfolios, investment risk). This thinking is reflected in a 2017 report that presents the stance adopted by the Mutual Fund Directors Forum, which focuses on this three-pronged dimension of risk (Mutual Fund Directors Forum 2017). Assessing these three risks is useful but not sufficient in that it does not formally recognize an important and complex form of uncertainty—namely Country Risk in its broadest sense. Even a company located in a particular country and doing essentially all its business in that country will have an exposure that can be affected negatively due to its own government's economic and financial policy measures—in addition to the risk of domestic sociopolitical turmoil. This has been discussed in Chapter 2. Accordingly, domestic Country Risk can also be material, substantial, and costly.

One main objective of a risk manager is to measure risk in order to build defensive strategy scenarios and contingency plans. As we have seen in Chapters 5 and 11, ratings and rankings fall short of meeting their (costly) promises of announcing an increase in Country Risk. Not only were rating agencies unable to predict crises in most EMCs in 1982, in 1994 in Mexico, and in 1997 in Asia—not to mention the Global Financial Crisis of 2008—but they have also tended to overshoot ex-post, transforming national turbulences

M. H. Bouchet et al., *Managing Country Risk in an Age of Globalization*,
https://doi.org/10.1007/978-3-319-89752-3_13

into regional crises through the spillover effect of downgrading whole asset classes. Country risk analysts who rely on sophisticated econometric models also introduce a model risk by incorporating unrealistic hypotheses of risk probabilities. According to a warning by Mandelbrot and Taleb (2006): "Such measures of future uncertainty satisfy our ingrained desire to 'simplify' by squeezing into one single number matters that are too rich to be described by it." So-called mild uncertainty can be tackled by using probability distributions under a symmetrical format incorporating the so-called Gaussian Bell Curve. However, in the words of Mandelbrot and Taleb, the Bell Curve has "thin tails" in that large events are considered possible but far too rare to be consequential. Country Risk, clearly, is a world of "fat tails" where a higher probability of extreme values can have a significant impact on the total distribution. This is, for instance, the case of sharp jumps in stock market prices, volatility of spreads and yields, currency depreciation, market returns, short-term interest rates, labor strikes, and abrupt events such as military coups. Spreads and yields, however, have much to do with overall market liquidity, herd instinct, and regional contamination, hence little predictive value for abrupt turbulence risk in a specific country.

For example, consider the nationalization of Spanish-Argentine venture Repsol YPF and Brazil's Petrobras' facilities in Bolivia in May of 2006 when President Evo Morales ordered the military to occupy Bolivia's gas fields, giving foreign investors a six-month deadline to comply with demands or leave. Foreign companies had invested around USD 4 billion since Bolivia opened up its energy sector in the late 1990s, while Repsol YPF alone had invested more than USD 1.2 billion in Bolivia's energy industry and Petrobras had USD 1 billion at stake in Bolivia's natural-gas industry. Nationalization was not the by-product of a military coup or a revolution. Morales, a former coca farmer and socialist union leader, won a resounding victory at the end of 2005 elections. Though the nationalization was not quite a surprise, it was difficult to anticipate the timing or the process. Neither rating agencies nor bond yields conveyed any warning of the impending risk. In the case of Brazil, the country's economic deterioration started in 2014, yet Credit Default Swap (CDS) prices remained at roughly 200 basis points between September 2011 and January 2015, before shooting up to more than 500 basis points in September of the same year. (We discuss CDS in greater detail in this chapter and in Case Study 13.1.)

Another example of an abrupt surge in Country Risk is the June 2016 UK referendum to leave the European Union. The 52% Brexit majority was a surprise indeed, given that most polls had not anticipated the turnaround. Perceptions of Country Risk were manifested in a 15% fall of the Pound against the Dollar and a 10% decline against the Euro, with the unintended result of providing a boost to the UK stock market, including a rise in the dividend yield offered by the UK equity market. Uncertainty and the weakness in the British Pound triggered opportunistic takeover bids. All this change brought both positive and negative effects, which country risk analysts are still seeking to assess. Depending on the complexity of the Brexit negotiations, a key objective of their analysis is to measure the medium and long-term impact on domestic consumption, investment, inflation, and exchange and interest rates.

The freefall devaluation of the Argentine Peso in January of 2014 and that of Venezuela's currency in 2017 are additional examples of volatility that elude the predictive ability of quantitative models. Moreover, in Argentina, the Dollar exchange rate soared vis-à-vis the parallel exchange rate—the so-called "blue dollar"—breaking new records and surprising most traders and risk managers.

Regarding the saga of the autonomy demand by Spain's Catalonia region in the last quarter of 2017, financial markets did not anticipate, nor did they take seriously the Catalan secession crisis. Credit Default Spread prices on Spanish bonds rose and then decreased, while the IBEX stock market index in Madrid was highly volatile during only a few weeks in October of 2017 before the announcement of the snap elections for the region on December 21, 2017. But the increasingly vocal demands of the secessionist party were not incorporated in any significant market price signal volatility.

13.2 Looking for the Canary in the Coal Mine

The challenge for risk analysts is to forecast turmoil and destabilization before discovering the impact of a devaluation in exchange rates or a political crisis on the front page of newspapers. Risk analysts, however, will never match the volume and quality of information and economic intelligence of local residents. The former scrutinize second-hand reports, while the latter have a close connection to the sociopolitical, cultural, and economic risk factors that must be understood. The former is only a few people; the latter are numerous and thus represent the so-called "wisdom of crowds." Ideally, country risk analysts and fund managers should identify a risk yardstick similar to that used by country residents to assess and anticipate turmoil.

Seven main signals are candidates for anticipating upcoming risk volatility and could be used independently or simultaneously. We assess their strengths and weaknesses, concluding that even the most seemingly promising signals have significant limitations. One is the credit rating. A second is the country's stock market that could act like a barometer of turbulent times ahead. A third is a sharp rise in the current account to GDP and debt/GDP ratios, hence deteriorating liquidity and worsening solvency. The fourth is a bunching of debt payments in the current year, with a rise of the debt servicing ratio and a drop in reserve assets. The fifth possible warning comes from rising bond yields and their spread over the "risk-free rate"—that is, a threshold that exceeds the borrowing rate of the United States Treasury bills or that of Germany bunds. The sixth is a rising cost of CDS of the debtor country. And finally, in mature and liquid markets, a high-volatility environment can signal rising uncertainty, with a higher VIX index. In practice, while it may sound appealing to watch multiple potential warning signs, these indicators do not consistently serve as reliable early warning signals. We further explore this next.

13.2.1 Expecting Risk Signals from Credit Rating Agencies

As already noticed in Chapters 9 and 10, a lack of attention to the underlying institutional causes of Country Risk was exemplified in the turbulence of many countries, with no prediction from rating agencies, including the 1982 Emerging Market Countries' crisis (Mexico and Latin America), the 1994 Mexican or "tequila" crisis, the 1997 Asian crisis, the 1998 Russian crisis, the 2000 Argentine crisis, the 2007 subprime mortgage meltdown, the 2010 sovereign debt crisis in Southern Europe, and the 2011 "Arab Spring" turmoil. Despite being popular, credit ratings provided weak early warning signals. In the case of Argentina's default by missing an interest payment on January 3, 2002, Moody's downgraded the long-term foreign and local-currency credit rating to Ca on December 20, 2001, whereas financial stress had kept mounting during the previous year. South Korea, for example, was rated similarly to Italy and Sweden until October 1997, but was then abruptly downgraded to junk bond status. On the eve of the South East Asian financial crisis, S&P's credit rating for South Korea stood at AA with a stable outlook. Moody's credit rating for South Korea was set at Aa2 with a stable outlook. Fitch's credit rating for South Korea was reported at AA– with a stable outlook (*Trading Economics* 2017). The rating agency Fitch recognized the shortsightedness of these ratings on the eve of the abrupt crisis: "There were no early warnings about Korea from us or, to the best of our knowledge, from other market participants, and our customers should expect a better job from us" (Fitch IBCA 1998). Beyond macroeconomic and financial weaknesses, two main problems explain the abruptness and severity of the Asian crisis: first, the limited availability of data and lack of transparency, both of which hindered market participants from taking a realistic view of economic fundamentals; and second, problems of governance and political uncertainties, which worsened the crisis of confidence (International Monetary Fund 1998).

Similarly, looking at the corporate sector, Enron's collapse in December 2001 was no better predicted by rating agencies than were the emerging market debt crises. The credit agencies were still rating the energy firm as an investment-grade credit four days before it filed for bankruptcy protection on December 2, 2001. Moody's and S&P finally downgraded Enron to junk status on November 28, 2001. US Senator Joe Lieberman summarized the situation in abrupt terms: "There is a real crisis of confidence in the markets today. (...) The credit raters – despite their unique position to obtain information unavailable to other analysts – were no more astute and no quicker to act than others. (...) In the Enron case, the credit raters were no more knowledgeable about the company's problems than anyone else who was following its fortunes, including those who were following it in the newspapers" (US Senate 2002).

Despite being popular and widely used, however, credit ratings have not proven to send timely warning calls to risk managers. Furthermore, abrupt downgrading provoked spillover effects. No clear evidence has been found regarding the ability of rating agencies to forecast country risk crises. Furthermore, rating agencies have often been accused of having a pro-market-performance behavior, which influences a country's economy dramatically in different ways. First, when rating agencies downgrade a country, the borrowing cost of that country increases, undermining the ability of the state to borrow and to repay the debt. Second, countries with a similar macroeconomic environment of the downgraded Country Risk suffer a contagion effect, both regionally and non-regionally. This is a point raised by Flores (2010) who shows that rating changes are often anticipated by the markets. Rating agencies wake up late, but when they do, they tend to overreact and their downgrading has been expected such that stock prices and bond spreads begin to move in the expected direction before the announcement is actually made.

Overall, Table 13.1 summarizes eight main pitfalls of rating agencies.

Actually, rating agencies do not assess the full scope of Country Risk but rather the narrower threat of credit default. They zero in on the debt servicing capacity and willingness of a sovereign borrower. Ratings give a synthetic valuation on the credit merit of the counterparty. S&P, Moody's, and Fitch provide ratings describing the creditworthiness of sovereign bonds. The best

Table 13.1 The pitfalls of risk rating agencies

1	Power without accountability
2	Potential conflict of interest
3	Conformity bias and herd behavior
4	Sociocultural bias
5	Punishment of disobedient firms/countries that do not request a rating
6	Procyclical bias, hence following the majority opinion of market participants without reliable early warning signals nor predictability track record
7	Rating agencies tend to exacerbate crises, upgrading countries in good times and downgrading them in bad times
8	Spillover effect with risk of regional crisis contamination

rating is AAA, which means that the probability of default is almost zero. An example of a AAA bond offering is the issuance by the European Investment Bank, which offer the lowest yields to investors. Similarly, as of 2018, a small and exclusive club of eleven countries still enjoyed a AAA rating by S&P, including Germany, Norway, Singapore, Australia, Canada, Denmark, Luxembourg, Netherlands, Sweden, Switzerland, and Liechtenstein. The share of investment-grade sovereign issuers (i.e., Baa category and above) declined to 50% by year-end 2016, while all rated issuers in 1983 were investment grade, due to the growing number of emerging market countries that gained market access. For Moody's at year-end 2017, only twelve or 9% of sovereign issuers boasted a Triple A rating, compared with 77% in 1985 and 14% in 2000 (Moody's 2017). For S&P, a bond is considered in the prime category of "investment grade" if its credit rating is BBB− or higher. Bonds rated BB+ and below are considered to be risky, that is, in the "speculative grade" category, sometimes also referred to as "junk" bond. Overall, when a rating is attributed to a country, various inputs are used to assess the bond issuer's creditworthiness. The higher the credit rating, the lower the risk profile of the country, and hence the lower the default probability. Figure 13.1 summarizes the rating categories of the three main agencies.

Regarding the regional distribution of Moody's-Rated Sovereign Issuers, at year-end 2016, 23% of issuers were from the Americas and 35% from Europe. The share of developing and emerging market countries reaches about 72%, including 18% from Asia and 14% from Latin America (Moody's 2017). According to Moody's, sovereign default rates have been, on average, modestly lower than those for their corporate counterparts over the 1983–2016 period, that is, 18% for speculative-grade sovereign issuers, compared with 31% for speculative-grade corporate issuers. However, on a value-weighted basis, recovery rates on defaulted sovereign bonds—as measured by trading prices at

Credit Ratings*

		Moody's	S&P's	Fitch
Investment Grade	Strongest	Aaa	AAA	AAA
		Aa	AA	AA
		A	A	A
		Baa	BBB	BBB
Non Investment Grade		Ba	BB	BB
		B	B	B
		Caa	CCC	CCC
		Ca	CC	CC
		C	C	C
	Weakest	D	D	D

**These credit ratings are reflective of obligations with long-term maturities.*
Source: investingbonds.com

Fig. 13.1 Main country credit ratings

the time of default—have averaged only 30%, compared with 33% for senior unsecured corporate bonds (Moody's 2017). Rating agencies use a default frequency time series for each class of rating in order to identify a frequency approach of the probability that an entity with a given risk profile can default. Moreover, frequencies tables also make it possible to monitor the probability that a country will be upgraded or downgraded. As noticed by Glasserman (2000): "CreditMetrics (and similar methodologies) attempt to measure the risk resulting from rating transition. An essential element of this approach is a rating transition matrix giving the probabilities of rating changes over a period of, e.g., one year." This so-called migration risk and the instrument used to measure this risk is the transaction matrix.

There is no evidence of the predictive power of the rating agencies in detecting country crises, neither from the traditional three main agencies, nor from more specialized country risk assessment agencies, such as Euromoney and Institutional Investor. Table 13.2 shows Euromoney's risk rankings of South-East Asia countries before, during, and after the 1997 crisis. The higher the score, the larger the risk. Country risk analysts acted too slowly and then hammered the countries with abrupt downgrading. Thirteen years after the 1997 downgrading, South Korea, the Philippines, and Thailand were hardly back to their pre-crisis ranking.

Table 13.2 Euromoney's country risk rankings in the midst of the Asian Crisis

	1996	1997	1998	1999	2000	2005	2009	2010
Korea	28	**30**	**42**	44	29	28	40	25
Thailand	45	**51**	54	49	65	49	60	45
Philippines	55	**57**	55	53	78	75	77	58
Malaysia	33	**35**	**56**	46	46	46	45	60
Indonesia	45	**49**	**91**	98	107	81	76	61

Bold represents Inception of the "Asian Crisis"

13.2.2 Expecting Risk Signals from Stock Market Prices

A country's stock market is a reflection of domestic and international investors' confidence in the country's corporate and macroeconomic perspectives. The drivers of a stock market index are numerous, including general country risk variables, corporate earnings growth, investment, consumer spending trends, inflation and interest rates, and the regional and global environment. The number of influential variables is such that the stock market alone cannot be a reliable country risk indicator. It is instructive to consider Venezuela's financial and sociopolitical crisis in 2017. One can observe the paradox of a combination of buoyant stock market and large domestic savings in the midst of an economic recession, falling government revenues, and high inflation. Due to hyperinflation and the freefall of the country's currency, the Caracas' stock market became a shield against melting purchasing power. Accordingly, despite PDVSA's oil output downward slide since 2002 and the 2017 fears of imminent default, the state-owned oil giant's stock price volatility remained relatively muted. In the second half of 2017, the Caracas stock market index IBVC rose sharply in September and still more abruptly in November, in a speculative frenzy that was fueled by domestic investors as well as by speculative institutional investors who looked to emerging markets for higher returns, while Country Risk kept mounting.

Another example is the US stock market performance from 2008 to 2017. The sharp rise in the Dow, the Nasdaq, and the S&P 500 indices did not owe much to buoyant private consumption and investment or to wage increases. The main driver of the dynamic stock market was the Federal Reserve's accommodative monetary policy. Despite signs of overheating, including high PE ratios by historical standards and repeated warnings of irrational exuberance by Shiller that the stock market had become prone to bubbles, the US market continued climbing in 2016–2017 to record highs, confirming Shiller's definition of a bubble—namely, a social epidemic where feedback from price increases leads to further price increases (Shiller 2014). Chart 13.1 illustrates the close correlation between the S&P 500 index and the three main central banks' quantitative easing program between 2008 and 2017.

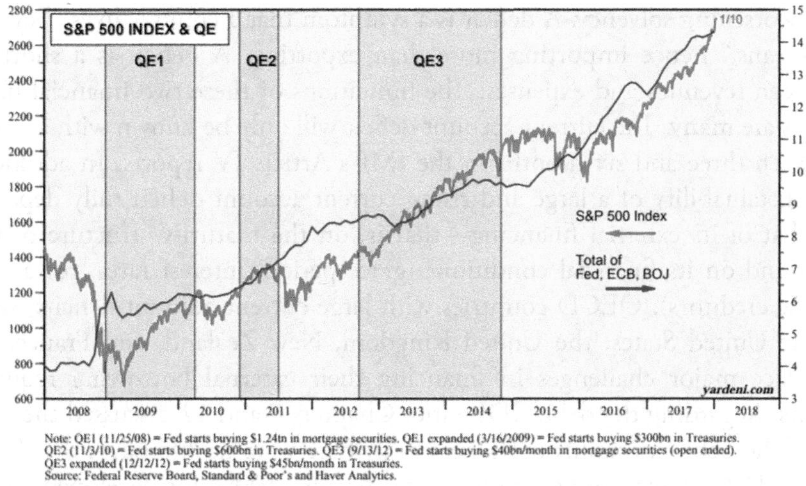

Chart 13.1 Relationships between US Stock Market and OECD Central Banks' Monetary Policy (*Source* Yardeni and Quintana 2017, 4)

In China—despite converging signals of a three-pronged bubble of real estate, the stock market, and rising private credit—the Shanghai stock market crash did not erupt before the summer of 2015 for three reasons. First, domestic credit growth remained unusually high, mostly from nonbank financial intermediaries, reaching a record 33% annual rise in 2010, hence stimulating debt-driven stock market speculative investment. Second, the central bank maintained monetary policy stimulus with low bank reserve requirements and low rates of interest. Third, the government's commitment to substantial spending on new roads, ports, and other infrastructure contributed to driving up consumption of commodities such as iron ore, copper, and nickel. China's investment spending surge added upward pressure on stock market shares, not only in Shanghai but also in commodity-producing countries such as Brazil, where Vale and Petrobras benefitted from China's dynamic demand.

A similar decoupling between stock market performances and underlying economic and financial risk sources can be found in many countries, including in the Eurozone, where the ECB maintained ultra-low interest rates coupled with its bond-buying program between 2010 and 2018, pushing the region's stock markets to exceptionally high levels despite underlying anemic growth and rising levels of indebtedness.

13.2.3 Balance of Payments and Debt Ratios

A third candidate for warning signals is a sharp rise in the current account to GDP and debt/GDP ratios, which would suggest deteriorating liquidity and worsening solvency. A deficit is a symptom that a country lives "beyond its means," hence importing more than exporting. A deficit is a shortfall between revenues and expenses. The limitations of these two financial indicators are many. The current account deficit will only be known with a lag of between three and six months in the IMF's Article IV reports. In addition, the sustainability of a large and rising current account deficit fully depends on that of its external financing—that is, on the maturity structure of the debt and on its financial conditions (grace period, interest rates, private or public creditors). OECD countries with large current account deficits, such as the United States, the United Kingdom, New Zealand, and France, do not face major challenges in financing their external borrowing requirements. Regarding the debt/GDP ratio, Chapters 8 and 12 discussed the limits of the debt thresholds usefulness as if there were no life beyond 66% of debt/GDP for developing countries and beyond 100% for developed countries. In practice, no one has ever expected a country to repay its external debt out of its GDP resources. Overall, countries with a similar high current account deficit/GDP ratios might face very different financial outcomes as illustrated by the cases of the United Kingdom, Canada, Argentina, and Colombia in the end of 2017, each with a similar deficit/GDP ratio of around 3 to 4%. The sustainability of the financing of the deficit is the key to measure the prospects of a liquidity or a solvency crisis.

13.2.4 Country's Debt Structure

Fourth, the maturity structure of the debt and a bunching of short-term payments should clearly be a signal of the upcoming risk of debt default and, at least, of liquidity tensions. An increase in debt payments falling due can be observed in the balance of payments of the country that is monitored by the IMF and also in the short-term debt that can be observed in the BIS statistical tables with a six-month lag. This is too late to warn a risk analyst about an upcoming debt servicing problem. In addition, the issue is not the gross payment outflows but rather the net payments—that is, taking into account the debt refinancing. Similarly, the issue at stake is not monitoring the gross capital inflows in the capital account of the balance of payments, but the net transfers—that is, gross inflows minus debt repayments and interest payment. A mismatch between debt repayments and capital inflows will exert pressure on the central bank's reserve assets and the exchange rate.

13.2.5 Capital Markets' Yield Volatility

Fifth, the spread and the bond yield that the country pays above the so-called risk-free rate is a function of the country's creditworthiness but also of the overall market liquidity as well as regional and global spillover effects. The management of wide asset classes in portfolios tends to encourage herd instinct that results in regional contamination. Consequently, spreads and yields are of minimal predictive value in assessing abrupt turbulence in a specific country. Bond yields in emerging market countries are also influenced by US monetary policy and by the Dollar exchange rate trends. In 2017, emerging bonds—which offered an average yield of nearly 6%—attracted record capital inflows due to the search for higher yield by global investors. In addition, the ultra-low interest rate environment generated interest in emerging market debt denominated in local currencies, with still higher average yields, roughly four percentage points above the ten-year US Treasury bond. Consequently, emerging markets had no difficulty in financing government and balance of payments deficits despite economic, financial, and institutional weaknesses. Large liquidity inflows also resulted from the lack of risk differentiation of credit quality between emerging and non-emerging markets.

Bond yields are also influenced by rating agencies' decisions and their impact on portfolio management. Should an agency demote a country's bonds to "junk status"—that is, out of the investment grade category—its bonds would be forced out of major indices, including Citi's popular World Government Bond Index, a move that would cause USD billions of forced selling out of the country's debt, hence increasing yields mechanically.

In the case of Latin American countries, Aronovich (1999) shows that the behavior of the country risk premium for Argentina, Brazil, and Mexico during the spillover effect of the Asian crisis in the late 1990s was determined by several factors. These included the US Dollar bond market structure, restrictions on the acquisition of emerging market bonds imposed by foreign regulators, and the country credit rating. The conclusion is that country risk yield spreads overreacted to changes in the US Dollar interest rates. IMF research also shows that overall liquidity conditions influence short-term sovereign spreads, particularly through the effect of the global volatility index. It is in the long run that fundamentals are determinants of emerging market sovereign bond spreads, including political instability, macroeconomic variables, corruption, and asymmetry of information (Bellas et al. 2010).

Chart 13.2 illustrates the sharp rise in bond yields of emerging market countries in early 1998—that is, well after the beginning of the Asian crisis and its global spillover effect, as well as another sharp rise at the end of 2008—that is, well after the inception of the Global Financial Crisis. In both cases, bond yields shot up for all countries, without discrimination, confirming that investors look at the roughly 160 EMCs as one single asset class in fund portfolios.

The regional spillover effect of the Asian crisis was markedly strong for Latin American countries, with a lag of six months. In addition, a sharp rise in yields occurred between the end of 2001 and 2004 for the entire Western Hemisphere, as a consequence of Argentina's economic recession coupled with its debt crisis. The Argentine financial crisis led to 6,000 basis point spreads between US Treasury bonds and Argentine government bonds. It also resulted in a bank run. Many developing countries were contaminated by rising risk aversion of investors.

In the case of Greece, the sharp decrease in the bond yield since mid-2014 is as much the by-product of the country's austerity policy measures as it is of the European Central Bank's vigorous accommodative monetary policy. The ultra-low rates of interest in the 2014–2017 period and investors' search for yield explain the abrupt (and probably premature) fall in the country's bond yield. Athens returned to capital markets with much fanfare as early as July 2017 with its first bond issue in three years, selling €3 billion in five-year government bonds, while demand for the debt exceeded €6.5 billion. The debt was priced with a modest yield of 4.625%, for a country whose debt/GDP ratio still reached 180% (and while the IMF refuses to anticipate sustainable growth prospects without a major debt restructuring). Indeed, on July 20, 2017, the IMF Executive Board approved in principle

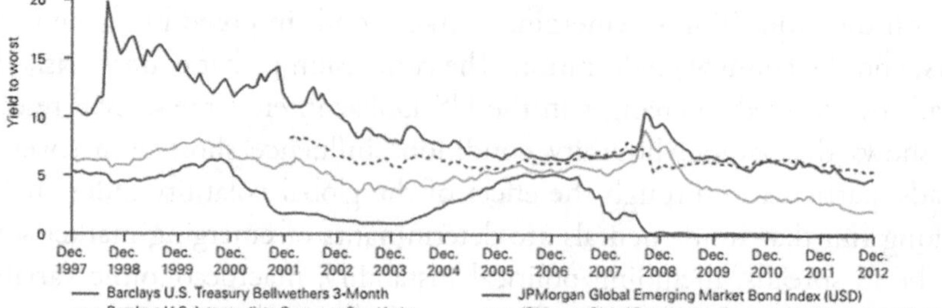

Chart 13.2 Emerging market bond yields 1997–2012 (*Source* Vanguard 2013, with data from Barclays and JP Morgan)

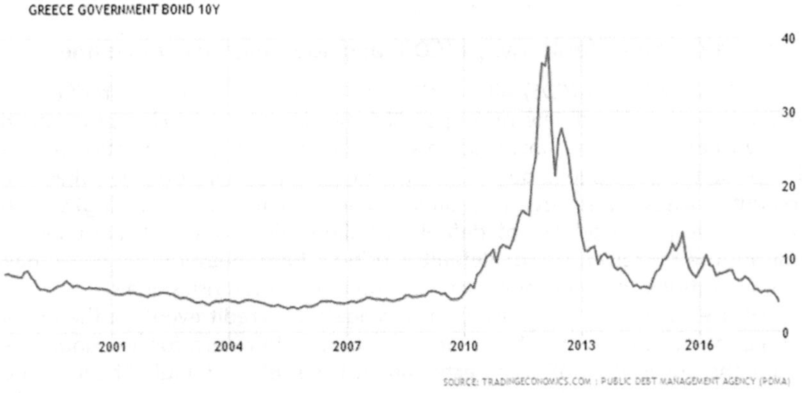

Fig. 13.2 Yield on Greece's debt in percentage points 2000–2018 (*Source* https://tradingeconomics.com/greece/government-bond-yield)

a new Stand-By Arrangement for Greece, though conditional on receiving specific and credible assurances on debt relief from Greece's European partners, thereby applying a similar debt restructuring conditionality that the IMF historically demanded African or Latin American over-indebted countries (International Monetary Fund 2017). Figure 13.2 shows the abrupt rise in Greece's ten-year bond yield in 2011 and 2012, which has been followed by a similarly abrupt decline in 2013 and 2014, to reach less than 4% in the beginning of 2018.

13.2.6 What About Country Risk Signals from CDS?

Sixth, CDS provides insurance against the borrower's failure to repay debt obligations. Accordingly, a CDS measures the riskiness of lending to a country and the willingness of creditors to purchase a guarantee. CDS spreads, thus, are one way the markets assess country creditworthiness. Volatility in CDS rates makes possible calculations of the implied probability of debt default.[1] CDS spreads have been a useful alternative to credit ratings for measuring sovereign risk, with tighter (smaller) spreads indicating a lower risk of sovereign default, and widening (larger) spreads suggesting a higher event-risk. Box 13.1 provides a concise presentation of CDS as a measure of Country Risk while Case Study 13.1 illustrates the limitations of CDS prices as early warning signals of mounting Country Risk.

[1]A CDS spread of 400 bp for five-year Italian debt means that default insurance for a notional amount of EUR 1 million costs EUR 40,000 per annum; this premium is paid quarterly.

Box 13.1 Credit Default Swaps (CDS) and sovereign risk assessment?

Credit Default Swaps (CDS) allow sellers to assume, or buyers to reduce, the default risk on a bond. The pricing of CDS measures how much a buyer needs to pay to purchase, and how much a seller demands to sell, protection against the default of an issuer's debt. CDS spreads should, therefore, be taken into account in assessing sovereign creditworthiness. Falling (or narrowing) spreads indicate the perceived risk of default is falling. Rising (or widening) spreads indicate the perceived risk of default is rising. These measures, however, have their limitations and they might send wrong or distorted risk signals.

CDS are essentially insurance contracts against a credit event on the underlying debt, typically with a five-year time horizon. In return for an annual premium, the buyer of a CDS is protected against the risk of default. The insurance premium is the annual insurance payment relative to the amount of debt. For example, a spread of 1,000 basis points implies that the buyer pays an insurance premium of 10% per year of the value of the securities. The seller of the credit default swap receives the premiums and pays out if a credit event happens, i.e., a substantial and identifiable loss related to default. The buyer will receive from the seller the face value of the debt.

CDS spreads can be interpreted as a measure of the perceived risk that a government will restructure or default on its debt. CDS on sovereign bonds, however, have been used as speculative instruments similar to short selling stocks (i.e., the sale of a security that the seller does not own, with the intention of buying back an identical security at a later point in time in order to be able to deliver the security). The European Commission proposed to restrict CDS transactions for up to three months in distressed markets to stop "negative price spirals" in government bonds stemming from CDS trading, notably in the case of Greece and Ireland. On July 5, 2012, European regulators announced a ban on so-called "naked" sovereign CDS that can destabilize the sovereign debt markets in a similar way to short selling (European Commission 2011). The ban is aimed at the bonds of the twenty seven members of the EU. Two years later, market analysts observed a marked decline in CDS trading volume for the majority of EU Member States on which there was credit default swap trading (Deventer 2015).

In the wake of the Global Financial Crisis of 2008 and the introduction of tighter financial regulations, it became clearer that CDS were subject to inefficiencies and herding behavior. As a result, they may be limited as effective measures of sovereign risk. In particular, new EU legislation introduced in November of 2012 stipulated that market participants and traders can only purchase a sovereign CDS contract if they simultaneously own the underlying bond or another asset, hence banning short selling and "naked" CDS trading. As observed by Weltman (2012) regarding the influence of regulatory changes on the CDS market: "The new legislation was preceded by a rational market response – a collapse in market volume before the ban, as well as increased demand for alternative instruments, government bond futures for instance, where short (or long) positions can still be adopted. The drop in liquidity was accompanied by a tightening of spreads." Tighter regulations of the CDS market have been criticized due to their negative impact on the market's liquidity. However, Salomao (2017) argues that a CDS contract enhances the lenders' bargaining power during debt renegotiation, increasing the share repaid by the country in renegotiation for all debt levels. This leads to higher equilibrium debt levels and lowers debt financing cost. Consequently, the liquidity of the CDS market and the level of the CDS coverage were affected by 2012 EU Regulation 236 that banned uncovered positions where investors do not have exposure to the underlying bond.

A striking example of CDS inertia relating to worsening Country Risk is Venezuela's liquidity crisis that erupted in the last quarter of 2017. The country's reserve assets fell to USD ten billion, near twenty-year lows. Imports dropped while the black market exchange rate soared in an environment of unabated money printing, hyperinflation, and capital flight. However, five-year CDS prices stubbornly remained around 3,000 basis points until July 2017. Nathan Crooks, writing in *Bloomberg*, observes: "The implied probability of the country missing a payment over the next 12 months rose to 56 percent in June, according to CDS. That's the highest level since December. The odds of a credit event over the next five years increased to 91 percent last month" (Crooks 2017). The combination of debt default and debt restructuring request of November 2017 sent five-year CDS prices to exceptionally high levels though the protracted crisis was rooted in falling reserves, economic recession, and falling government and export revenues as early as 2014, that is, three years before the inevitable solvency crisis.

Exogenous factors, too, have powerful effects. On November 3, 2016, Mexico's CDS prices abruptly shot up from 100 to 200 basis points. At that time, the rating agencies S&P and Fitch maintained a BBB+ rating with "Stable Outlook" for the Latin American country. The debt/GDP ratio has not worsened suddenly nor the deficit/GDP ratio, and there was no rumor of any military coup in the country south of the Rio Grande. The rise in Mexico's CDS was the by-product of Donald Trump's election in early November and the harsh rhetoric of the new president to stem immigration and resort to trade protectionist measures. This is illustrated in Fig. 13.3.

Overall, CDS levels stem from a combination of creditworthiness, market liquidity, regional contamination, the country's ability to refinance its debt as it comes due, and the global environment. Grossman and Hensen of Fitch Ratings caution against using CDS for deriving estimates of a company's default risk (2010): "It is important to note that CDS pricing can be

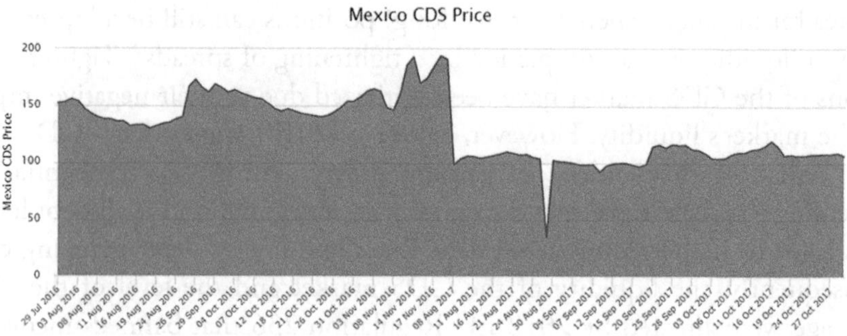

Fig. 13.3 The volatility of Mexico's 5-year CDS 2016–2017 (*Source* https://www.assetmacro.com/mexico/credit-default-swaps-cds/mexico-cds/)

driven by a number of factors not directly related to an entity's fundamental creditworthiness, such as the leverage inherent in CDS trading, liquidity conditions, counterparty risk, and the risk aversion of market participants." As Table 13.3 illustrates, there is a minimal correlation between CDS levels, bond yields, and spreads, as well as sovereign debt and current account ratios. The United Kingdom is rated AA with a current account deficit as large as 5% of GDP while Russia is rated BB+ with a 3% surplus.

13.2.7 Is the VIX a Reliable Signal of Risk Increase?

Seventh, and finally, the average daily moves of the VIX index—a measure of short-term expected turbulence nicknamed the "fear gauge"—could also be an indicator of upcoming rise in risk in a liquid and mature stock market such as in the United States. The Chicago Board Options Exchange (CBOE) Volatility Index (VIX) is a key measure of market expectations of near-term volatility conveyed by S&P 500 stock index option prices. Since its introduction in 1993, the VIX Index has become a gauge of investor sentiment and market volatility. Since 2004–2006, VIX futures and options allow global investors to take positions regarding the market's expectation of future volatility with a view to diversifying portfolios in times of market stress. VIX is calculated using the prices of S&P 500 puts and calls that mature in one month. If investors expect S&P 500 fluctuations to average 1% a day for the next month, then the VIX level is about twenty—roughly its long-run average—while a level of fourty implies 2% moves (Wigglesworth 2017). However, rising volatility that should signal higher risk has turned itself into an alternative and complex asset class for hedge fund managers and traders. The market hit an all-time high level of sixty at the time of Lehman Brothers

Table 13.3 The weak correlation between CDS, deficits, bond yields, and debt levels

	USA	UK	Germany	France	Spain	Mexico	Turkey	Russia	Portugal	Greece	Egypt	China
Debt/GDP (%)*	106	90	65	96	100	40	55	51	130	185	25	60
CDS*	29	32	23	38	78	160	280	180	280	862	453	138
Bond yield (%)***	2.35	1.32	0.25	0.80	1.53	7.70	11.00	8.40	4.04	6.7	17.70	3.20
Spread in bp (%)*	2.10	1.07	0	0.55	1.28	7.40	10.70	8	3.79	6.48	17	3
S&P Rating	AA+	AA	AAA	AA	BBB+	BBB+	BB	BB+	BB+	B–	B–	AA–
Current account (%)**	–2.50	–4.5	8	–0.50	2	–3	–3.50	4	–0.50	0	–5.50	2.20

*as of 2017
**current account/GDP % (*Source* IMF 2017)
***ten-year bond yield

collapse in October of 2008. Later it reached a short-term peak of fourty three in September 2011 at the time of the terrorist attack in the US. Since then, expansionary monetary policy by the Federal Reserve has maintained a situation of "repressed volatility," keeping the index at more modest levels. In addition, stock buybacks and investment strategies that focus on passive investment vehicles like index-tracking funds and exchange-traded funds (ETFs) have become powerful forces subduing individual stock volatility. A low-interest rate environment and the large liquidity brought about by central banks since the Global Financial Crisis of 2008 have created a disconnect between markets and risk signals. Together, there are both endogenous and exogenous factors that combine together to influence volatility, including geopolitical turmoil, trade protectionism, rising short-term rates, and the emergence of populist leaders in both developed and emerging market countries.

Overall, credit ratings, bond yields, spreads, CDS, debt ratios, and the VIX index do not adequately capture rising risk, nor do they capture volatility. Alternative measures of risk indicators are being investigated by financial institutions, rating agencies, and the academic community to develop new gauges to measure risk and uncertainty in a constantly changing environment. One example is Bank of America Merrill Lynch's Global Financial Stress Index that seeks to detect significant market turning points. Another example is the academic work done by Menachem Brenner of New York University's Stern School to pinpoint heightened levels of ambiguity. The new index focuses on uncertainty rather than the CBOE's sheer volatility to tackle the so-called "unknown unknowns," where the probabilities themselves are a mystery (Eisen 2017). However, Country Risk remains much more complex than stock market risk given that it includes market risk coupled with sociopolitical and institutional volatility.

13.3 Conclusion

In the assessment of Country Risk, our tendency is to look for indicators that will tell us in advance when a country will be subject to a financial, economic, or sociopolitical crisis. Country risk advisers and managers scrutinize the financial markets in search for early warning risk signals. Sophisticated econometric models are designed to transform discrete noise signals into converging warning indicators, using relationships and correlations. Yet despite the best efforts, and despite costly modeling, risk signals fall short of providing reliable country risk warning. We now realize, after years of research and practice, that one of the most important components of country risk assessment is local intelligence. As we shall see in the following chapter, another key component is following domestic residents' arbitrage behavior, that is, capital flight.

Case Study 13.1 Are CDS prices reliable early warning signals of Country Risk?[2]

The following case study focuses on five examples of CDS premium volatility related to abrupt country risk worsening to illustrate whether CDS prices react to signals of risk increase. It concentrates on the 2012–2017 period when the EU-based CDS regulation prohibited the short selling or the holding of "naked CDS," with an impact on the overall volatility and liquidity of the CDS market. The case study looks at two default events in Argentina and Greece, the financial and macroeconomic crisis in Portugal in 2012, and the political upheaval in Venezuela and in Lebanon in the second half of 2017.

1. Argentina: Since its independence in 1816, this Latin American country has defaulted on its sovereign debt obligations seven times and on its domestic debt five times. This serial defaulter stopped bond payments in January 2002, illustrating the twin components of Country Risk—namely, willingness and capacity to pay. The country had been downgraded by Moody's a few days before, at the end of December 2001. In July 2014, Argentina defaulted again on USD 29 billion worth of bonds, after failing to make a USD 540 million interest payment. The default was triggered when US hedge funds, also known as "hold-outs" which bought debt cheaply on the secondary market of EMCs debt, demanded full payments on their claims. For a sovereign debtor, the *pari passu* clause in bond contracts stipulates that all holders be treated as equal. Hence paying a minority of "holdouts" would have triggered payments to the majority of Argentina's creditors who accepted a large 70% "haircut" on their bonds when the debt was restructured in 2005 and again in 2010.

Figure 13.4 shows how prices of CDS evolved in the twelve-month period before the default date. The CDS price was on average 2,183 basis points (bp) over the period before the default month. The stability of the CDS contrasts with the combination of macroeconomic, political, and financial upheaval, including hyperinflation, rising current account deficit, large debt payments falling due, and the tensions surrounding threats of legal action by "vulture" funds. The month of default the CDS price picked up to 3,066 bp, an increase of 67% of the price the month before. Furthermore, one year and six months before the credit event, the CDS had generated false signals of default, which did not materialize. We calculated the implied probability of default by assuming a recovery rate of 40%. Despite various flaws in using fixed recovery rate instead of a stochastic one, it is still useful for casting light on false signals. The average implied probability of the overall period was around 35%. One month before the credit event, the implied probability was 30%, which is lower than the average of the year. During the month of default, the probability

[2]The case study is a summary of the MSc FMI's Research Thesis of Antonino Conforto and Pietro Veronesi, under guidance from Michel H. Bouchet. Skema Business School. December 2017.

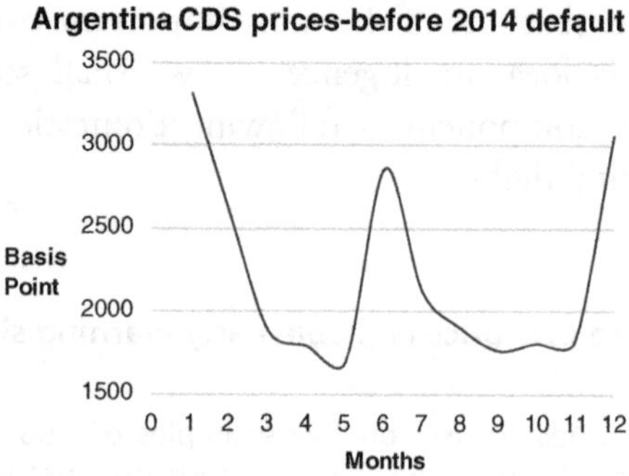

Fig. 13.4 Argentina's CDS prices before debt default

reached 51%. From the implied probability point of view, the CDS price underestimated the actual risk. Figure 13.4 shows the CDS price evolution during the twelve-month period preceding the default (with data from Bloomberg).

2. Greece: On June 30, 2015, Greece defaulted on its payment of USD 1.8 billion to the IMF and it became the first developed country to fall into arrears on payments to the international institution. Though the IMF did not formally declare Greece in default, and decided to apply a four-week grace period before calling a state of default, not paying the Fund is an exceptional event left to countries such as Zimbabwe, Somalia, and Sudan, which triggers a chain reaction that cuts a country off from private and public market access. The average price during the eleven months before the default was 1,354 bp. The CDS price rose from 2,775 bp the month before the default to 7,639 bp in June 2015, an increase of 142% in one month. CDS prices did not show any marked reaction until Greece actually defaulted on the loan toward the IMF. Calculating the implied probability of default of the CDS illustrates how the market changed its perception of Greece's financial distress. The average implied probability over the eleven months, without including the month of default, was 22%. One year before the default event, the implied probability of default was around 7.58%, and then it sharply increased up to 13% after six months. The month before the credit event, the implied probability was still only 46%. The month of default the implied probability rose to more than 100%. Figure 13.5 shows the modest rise in the CDS price until the actual missed payment to the Fund.

3. Venezuela: Venezuela's economic, financial, and sociopolitical situation abruptly worsened with the fall in oil prices in the summer of 2014, although mismanagement and corruption had occurred previously during the Chavez administration, thereby generating a deep recession and an inflationary spiral coupled with an exchange rate fall, culminating in a humanitarian crisis. Figure 13.6 shows the CDS price from 2014 to 2017 on a monthly basis (with data from Bloomberg). We can observe from the chart that several false signals appeared over the crisis period. First, over the three years, price volatility measured by the standard deviation of the CDS reaches 25% on a monthly basis though Venezuela had not yet defaulted on its debt. Indeed, on January 30, 2015, Venezuela CDS prices rose to 7,106 basis points. Essentially, the mar-

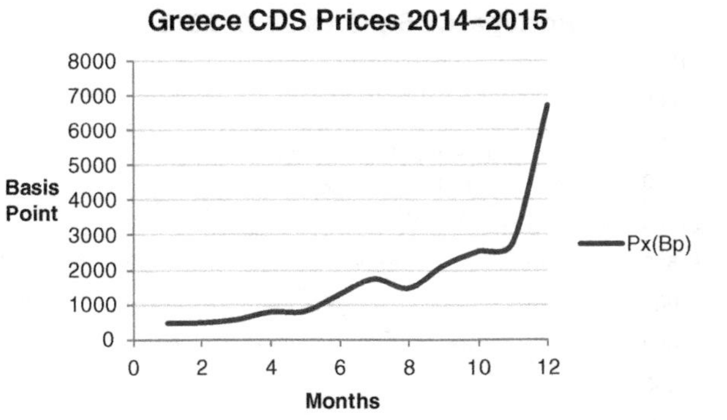

Fig. 13.5 Greece's CDS prices before IMF debt payment arrears

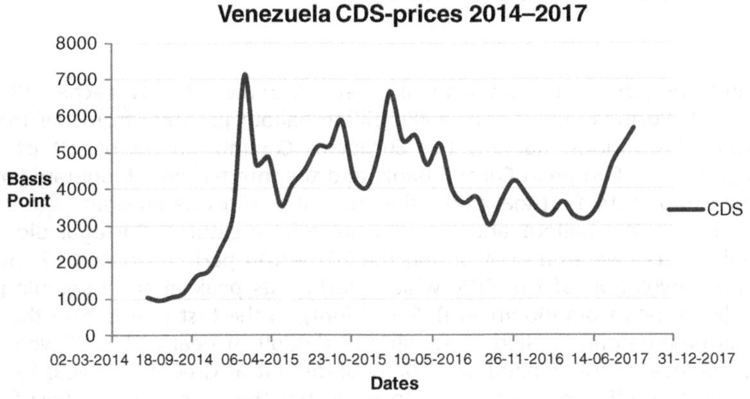

Fig. 13.6 Venezuela's CDS prices 2013–2017

ket was pricing Venezuela as being in default. The average implied probability of default over the three years was 65%, over the same period the CDS market shows that a credit event is likely though the country was declared in default on mid-November 2017 by S&P Global Ratings after a thirty-day grace period expired.

4. Portugal: Portugal provides another example of a false signal from the CDS market. Portugal suffered a substantial recession from 2010 to 2014. The crisis stemmed from an excessive public and private sector leverage as well as the domestic consequences of the bursting of a credit-driven real estate market bubble. After the financial crisis of 2008, Portugal's banks suffered from rising non-performing loans (NPLs) on the order of 15% and large losses, which undermined the country's market credibility. In November 2009, market speculation focused on Portugal's large budget deficit and unsustainable debt burden—approximately 130% of GDP. Consequently, risk premiums on Portuguese bonds hit record levels as investors and creditors worried that the country might default, hence triggering systemic consequences for the Eurozone and

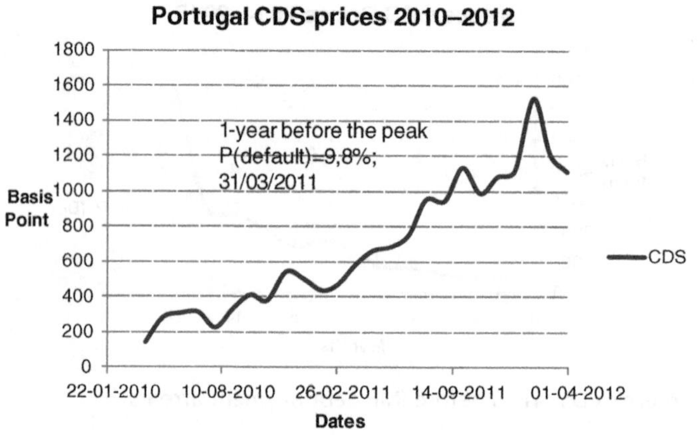

Fig. 13.7 Portugal's CDS prices 2010–2012

beyond. The yield on the country's ten-year government bonds reached 7%. In May 2011, Portugal applied for a €80 billion bailout program from the Troika of three institutions, namely, the European Commission on behalf of the Eurogroup, the European Central Bank, and the International Monetary Fund. At the end of 2014, Portugal exited the international rescue program.

Thanks to the bailout and to tight austerity measures, Portugal did not default on its sovereign debt during the 2010–2014 period. Figure 13.7 shows the price evolution of the CDS, which reached its peak at the beginning of 2012 (with data from Bloomberg). Surprisingly, in the first year before the crisis, Portugal had an implied probability of default of nearly 10%. If we compare this level to the implied probability of default of Greece, one year before it missed the IMF repayment, we can note that the probability of Portugal's default was even higher than that of Greece, which had a default probability of around 7%. There are, of course, limitations associated with attempts to compare Portugal and Greece, given that the subsequent change in European regulation in 2012 has had an impact on the liquidity of the CDS market.

5. Lebanon: Lebanon has experienced deep political and social instability not only due to the dramatic spillover effect caused by the Syrian war but also to the challenging relations between Iran and Saudi Arabia. Lebanon has historically been a battleground between Saudi Sunnis and Iranian Shiites. Though the unrest in Syria started at the time of the 2011 Arab Spring, it escalated when Russia and Iran-backed Hezbollah brought massive military support to the Syrian regime, while a coalition of NATO countries began launching airstrikes again the Islamic State in 2014. During this convulsive period, Saad Al-Hariri was prime minister of Lebanon from November 2009 to June 2011 and again in December 2016, before abruptly announcing his resignation on 4 November 2017 on the Saudi state TV, plunging the country into deeper political uncertainty. Observing CDS prices from 2014 to 2017, one can notice the CDS price on the ten-year government bond did not react to the spillover effect of the Syrian civil war during 2014 and 2015. CDS prices remained remarkably stable at roughly 400 basis points before surging to 550 basis points

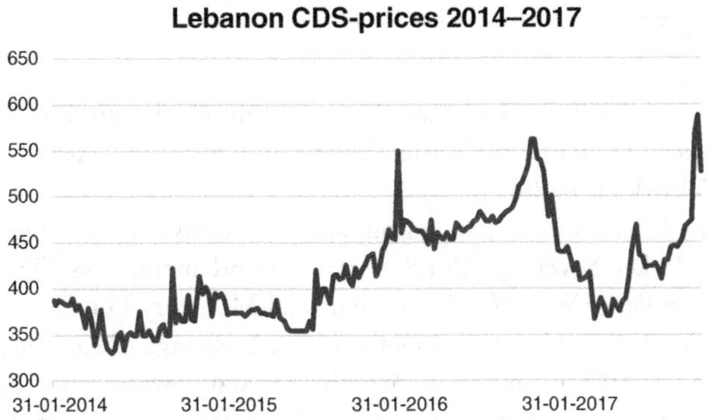

Fig. 13.8 Lebanon's CDS prices 2014–2017

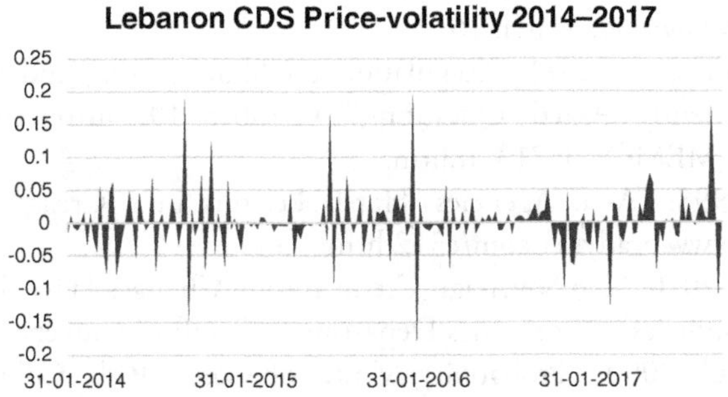

Fig. 13.9 Lebanon's CDS price volatility 2014–2017

in early 2016, due to the combination of the coming of Syrian refugees and to the domestic political deadlock until the election of a new president, at the end of 2016. The CDS prices dramatically increased only in the aftermath of Prime Minister Hariri's resignation announcement under Saudi influence and Hezbollah threats. Though CDS price levels cannot be considered as reliable country risk signals, the volatility in CDS prices provides more reactive signals of turmoil. Figure 13.8 illustrates Lebanon CDS prices while Fig. 13.9 shows Lebanon CDS volatility between 2014 and the end of 2017 (with data from Bloomberg)

Figure 13.9 clearly shows that behind the evolution in CDS prices, one can observe four periods of intense volatility, namely, in October 2014, in August 2015, in February 2016, and in October–November 2017 each corresponding to a crucial moment in the spillover effect of the Syrian civil war, and to the end of 2017 resignation announcement of Prime Minister Hariri, via the Saudi-funded news channel Al-Arabiya in Riyadh, while accusing Iran and its Lebanese ally, Hezbollah, of destabilizing Lebanon and the whole region.

References

Aronovich, Selmo. 1999. "Country Risk Premium: Theoretical Determinants and Emperical Evidence for Latin American Countries." *Revista Brasileira de Economia* 53 (4): 463–498.

Bellas, Dimitri, Michael G. Papaioannou, and Iva Petrova. 2010. "Determinants of Emerging Market Sovereign Bond Spreads: Fundamentals vs Financial Stress." IMF Working Paper WP10/281. International Monetary Fund.

Crooks, Nathan. 2017. "Venezuela's Default Risk Is Rising." *Bloomberg*, July 5.

Deventer, John. 2015. "Sovereign Credit Default Swaps and the European Commission Short Sale Ban, 2010–2014." Blog, January 9. https://seekingalpha.com/instablog/420043-donald-van-deventer/3626475-sovereign-credit-default-swaps-and-the-european-commission-short-sale-ban-2010minus-2014.

Eisen, Ben. 2017. "Wall Street's Volatility Pioneer Searches for Latest Fear Trade." *The Wall Street Journal*, March 10.

European Commission. 2011. "Regulation on Short Selling and Credit Default Swaps—Frequently Asked Questions," October 19. http://europa.eu/rapid/press-release_MEMO-11-713_fr.htm.

Fitch IBCA. 1998. "Asia: Agencies' Harsh Lessons in a Crisis." Press Release, January 13. www.bradynet.com/e312.html. January 14.

Flores, Esteban. 2010. "Do Sovereign Credit Rating Changes Have Spillover Effects on Other Countries?" Economics Department, Stanford University, May 9.

Glasserman, Paul. 2000. "Probability Model of Credit Risk. Columbia Business School." https://www0.gsb.columbia.edu/faculty/pglasserman/B6014/Prob_Credit.pdf.

Grossman, Robert J., and Martin Hensen. 2010. "CDS Spreads and Default Risk: Interpreting the Signals." Fitch Ratings Special Report, October 12.

International Monetary Fund. 1998. "The Asian Crisis: Causes and Cures." *Finance and Development* 35 (2). http://www.imf.org/external/pubs/ft/fandd/1998/06/imfstaff.htm.

International Monetary Fund. 2017. "Key Questions on Approval in Principle and Greece," July 20.

Mandelbrot, Benoit, and Nassim Taleb. 2006. "A Focus on the Exceptions That Prove the Rule." *Financial Times*, March 23.

Moody's Investors Services. 2017. "Sovereign Default and Recovery Rates, 1983–2016." Data Report, June 30.

Mutual Fund Directors Forum. 2017. "The Role of the Mutual Fund Director in the Oversight of the Risk Management Function." http://www.mfdf.org/images/Newsroom/Risk_Publication_2017.pdf.

Salomao, Juliana. 2017. "Sovereign Debt Renegotiation and Credit Default Swaps." *Journal of Monetary Economics* 90 (C): 50–63.

Shiller, Robert. 2014. "Robert Shiller Says Markets Have Become More Prone to Bubbles." Interview with Robert Stowe England. *Institutional Investor*, February 27.

Trading Economics. 2017. https://tradingeconomics.com/south-korea/rating.

US Senate. 2002. "Hearing, 107th Congress," Washington, DC, February 5. https://Fr.Scribd.Com/Document/341381004/Senate-Hearing-107th-Congress-Retirement-Insecurity-401-K-Crisis-At-Enron; see also US Senate Hearing March 20, 2002. https://www.gpo.gov/fdsys/pkg/CHRG-107shrg79888/pdf/CHRG-107shrg79888.pdf.

Vanguard. 2013. "Vanguard Research. Emerging Market Bonds-Beyond the Headlines," May. http://www.vanguard.com/pdf/s710.pdf.

Veronesi, Pietro, and Antonino Conforto. 2017. "Country Risk: In Search of Early Warning Signals." SKEMA Master of Science-Financial Markets and Investments. Research Thesis Under the Direction Michel Henry Bouchet.

Weltman, Jeremy. 2012. "Country Risk: Is This the End for CDS Spreads as a Useful Measure of Sovereign Risk?" *Euromoney*, November 16.

Wigglesworth, Robin. 2017. "The Fearless Market Ignores Perils Ahead." *Financial Times*, April 18.

Yardeni, Edward, and Mali Quintana. 2017. "Global Economic Briefing: Central Bank Balance Sheets." Yardeni Research, Inc., December 8.

14

In Search of Early Warning Signals of Country Risk: Focusing on Capital Flight

14.1 Introduction: Observing Domestic Residents' Risk Hedging Strategy

The major challenge and frustration that country risk analysts face are to gauge uncertainty while being "outsiders." Whatever the quality of data sources, risk assessment models, and economic intelligence, they will never match the information and signals that domestic residents receive and accumulate daily, given that the latter are embedded into an endless flow of sociopolitical, cultural, economic, and financial information inputs. Country risk assessment, as we have seen throughout this book, stems from a wide number of observations, reports, ratings, cross-country data, models, and ratios. All these tools, however, fall short of representing the true picture and complexity of a sovereign country with its complex legal, economic, institutional, and cultural characteristics.

Ideally, country risk managers should put themselves into "the shoes of foreign residents" to absorb all the available information coming from private and public economic agents in the country, including unionized workers, local media, the unemployed, retired workers, university scholars and students, investors and bankers, civil servants, and government officials. Local "intelligence" is the key to detecting risks and opportunities. However, publicly available information (such as local newspapers, research reports, and databases) may be difficult to gather and costly to process. Inversely, public information might be easy to obtain and relatively cheap, though of doubtful quality, such as outdated information from central banks and

M. H. Bouchet et al., *Managing Country Risk in an Age of Globalization*,
https://doi.org/10.1007/978-3-319-89752-3_14

finance ministries. This is often the case in African countries. Debt, official reserve assets, and balance of payments data are sometimes outdated, partial, or wrong. For instance, at year-end 2017, the Central Bank of Tunisia provides statistics for the debt/GDP ratio of the country as of end-2014 (Central Bank of Tunisia 2017). Worse, the Reserve Bank of Zimbabwe published balance of payments estimates for 2014 and projections for 2015 at year-end 2017 whereas timely external financing data are made available by the African Bank of Development's Statistical Yearbook (Reserve Bank of Zimbabwe 2017, and https://www.afdb.org/fileadmin/uploads/afdb/Documents/Publications/African_Statistical_Yearbook_2017.pdf).

Risk managers thus face an uncertain environment that is depicted by the efficient markets hypothesis, popularly known as the Random Walk Theory. This states that current stock prices fully reflect all available information about the value of a firm at any given point in time. Consequently, investors and financial advisers must spend a significant amount of time and resources to gather information and to detect "mispriced" stocks and investment opportunities despite often confusing risk signals. However, Country Risk is far more complex than predicting security prices. It stems from the interplay of domestic and international economic, financial, institutional, and sociopolitical variables that only well-trained analysts can put together into a forward-looking strategy. Country Risk, in its traditional and narrow meaning, encompasses both the capacity and the willingness of a foreign entity to meet its obligations fully and in time. Even sophisticated global banks and investment funds as well as multilateral agencies do not always comprehend the full complexities of Country Risk. Questions such as the timing of political turmoil, social upheaval, and revolutions are genuine challenges given that they emerge out of the fertile but obscure ground of institutional weaknesses. Questions such as the impact of exchange rate depreciation on current account balances and external debt ratios are also hard to assess. When "much becomes too much," the country's external debt situation requires an in-depth assessment of the sustainability of the external borrowing requirements. Moreover, there are often puzzling questions regarding the risk of regional contamination of tighter market liquidity, as well as of declining export prices and deteriorating terms of trade.

14.2 So What Should We Do?

An important area to examine is how domestic residents managed their savings, in short, capital flight. When attempting to understand the complexities of Country Risk, it is perhaps most useful to turn to those who are embedded in a country's matrix of social, political, and economic forces. We can best understand these forces from the perspective of a country's residents, which can enable us to arrive at a new and often very different understanding of risk levels in countries. A crucial component of such assessment is expatriated private savings—that is, capital flight. When citizens consistently over time and *en masse* transfer their money abroad—a process that incurs both costs and risks—country risk managers should "pay attention." When citizens suddenly shift their savings in offshore accounts, such arbitrage requires the analyst's attention. In short, capital flight matters.

Yet, the issue of capital outflows has attracted less attention than that of external capital inflows in emerging market countries (Bouchet et al. 2005). In particular, capital flight kept a low profile in policy and academic circles until the late 1990s. The reason for this limited attention stems from the scarcity of reliable data. By definition, capital flight uses informal (and sometimes illegal) channels. Academics and risk managers have considered the issue from several perspectives. Capital flight widens the gap between domestic savings and investment. It is a symptom of distrust in the country's macroeconomic and sociopolitical environment. Consequently, the larger the amount of capital flight, the greater the need to rely on heavier taxation and on external indebtedness to finance national development objectives. As such, capital flight is a manifestation of misguided economic policies, including mismanagement of interest and exchange rates, excessive tax burden, inflation, budget deficits, and an excessive public sector borrowing requirement resulting in crowding out the private sector's access to financing. Until the mid-1990s, the main focus of the root causes of capital flight was restricted to macroeconomic mismanagement, including the risk of losses in the real value of domestic assets resulting from inflation or exchange rate devaluations. Consequently, sound macroeconomic policies complemented with appropriate structural reforms were expected to be key elements in stemming or reversing capital flight since only those policies could decrease the risks associated with holding domestic assets (Rojas-Suarez 1990).

Throughout the 1990s, it became more and more evident that bad governance was also a major ingredient in triggering private capital outflows, thereby contributing to financial crises. Though developing countries have no monopoly on capital flight, it makes financial crises more severe in these countries due to a higher volatility of capital flows and more limited market access. Finally, capital flight raises doubt about the usefulness of official development aid flows. Bilateral and multilateral agencies have expressed growing concern about the recycling of a large portion of official development aid that flows right back out in the form of capital flight. As Roubini and Setser note (2004, 16): "A country that is not running a current account deficit and has little maturing external debt—and thus little need to borrow from abroad—can still get in trouble if its citizens want to shift their savings abroad. Depositors in the banking system can decide to pull their funds out of the local banks and deposit them abroad. The depositors need foreign currency to purchase foreign assets. Consequently, the shift from domestic to foreign assets places enormous pressure on the country's reserves under a fixed exchange rate, on its exchange rate under a float, or if the country has a managed float, on both reserves and the exchange rate."

Which countries, then, would fall in the category "current account surplus" and "capital flight" given that current account surplus countries usually exemplify a combination of competitive exchange rates and dynamic exports? In the last few months of 2016, the governments of Germany, the Netherlands, and Denmark paid large sums to buy leaked data allegedly implicating hundreds of their citizens in the so-called Panama Papers, which revealed massive offshore tax evasion, hence capital flight. But a better example, as we shall discuss later in more detail, is the case of Russia. This gas-producing country managed to boast current account surpluses on the order of 3% of GDP, with around USD 400 billion of official reserve assets, while experiencing large errors and omissions coupled with substantial private deposits held in international banks.

14.3 The Renewed Interest in Private Capital Outflows

Measuring capital flight clearly depends on the adopted definition of the phenomenon. Capital flight remains an elusive phenomenon, both conceptually and empirically. The key challenge is differentiating between normal and legal capital outflows on one side, and illegal and volatile flows, on the other. The economic literature on capital flight focuses on several alternative measures (Bouchet and Groslambert 2006). The two starting points were an important article in Morgan Guaranty Trust Company's World Financial Markets Review (Morgan Guaranty Trust Company 1986) and a conference organized under the auspices of the Institute for International Economics, gathering academics and policymakers (Lessard and Williamson 1987). Since then, a number of academic studies have tackled the complex issue of measuring capital flight, starting with the pioneering work by Cuddington (1986, 1987), Luke (1986), Dooley (1988), Dooley and Kletzer (1994), Khan and Ul Haque (1985), Rodriguez (1987), Rojas-Suarez (1990), Sheets (1995), and more recently, Boyce and Ndikumana (2001, 2002, 2003), Schneider (2003), Ndikumana and Boyce (2008), and Kharrat and Bouchet (2017).

Economists have assessed the magnitude of capital flight with a number of methodologies, including the following five ones: (1) the hot money approach through errors and omissions in the balance of payments; (2) the World Bank Residual model that focuses on the gap between a country's source of funds (inflows of capital) against its recorded use (outflows and/or capital expenditures); (3) trade misinvoicing that generates illicit capital accumulation overseas through export over-invoicing and import under-invoicing; (4) nonbank private deposits held in international banks, as reported by the BIS; and (5) there is a fifth definition and measure of capital flight when it takes the form of dollarization of private residents' savings, as has been the case in Peru, Russia, Ecuador, Cambodia, North Korea, and Zimbabwe (Quispe-Agnoli 2002, Mwase and Kumah 2015, and Mecagni and Maino 2015). In these countries, private savers have sought to protect their assets by shifting to Dollar holdings. This has been motivated by political instability, immature capital markets, and macroeconomic turbulences with high inflation and devaluation expectations, coupled with few investment opportunities. Table 14.1 provides a concise summary of each method.

Capital flight has attracted renewed interest since the late 1990s for several reasons. First, the combination of financial liberalization and market

Table 14.1 Summary of main measures of private capital outflow

Definition	Methodology and measure	Authors
1. Hot money: short-term volatile outflows	Balance of payments: Errors and omissions	IMF
2. "Narrow definition": short-term speculative and volatile capital flight	Balance of payments: net short-term capital outflows of the nonbank private sector + errors and omissions	Cudddington, J.
3. "Residual" measure: private residents' accumulation of foreign assets	Balance of payments identity = (Change in gross external debt + FDI flows) – (current account deficit + change in official reserve assets)	World Bank, Cline, W., Guaranty, M., Lessard, D., and Dooley, M.
4. Offshore bank deposits of nonbank residents	Nonbank private deposits held in international banks, as reported by the BIS banking statistics	Bouchet, M.H., Kharrat, O., Khan and Ul Haque, Bank of England
5. Partial and unofficial dollarization of private assets	Share of foreign currency in the money supply M1 and in bank deposits	Quispe-Agnoli, M., Mecagni, M., Maino, R., Mwase, N., and Kumah, F.

Source Authors

volatility in developing countries increased the scope for capital flight in response to global risk signals. Economic agents, from both industrialized and emerging market countries, can obtain access to instantaneous and inexpensive information while their range of choices widens. This stronger focus emerged when it became clear that capital outflows played a catalytic role in financial crises, such as the Mexican crisis of 1994, the Asian crisis of 1997–1998, the Russian crisis of 1998, and the Argentine crisis of 2001. Capital flight also accelerated and deepened Greece's crisis in 2012, as well as the liquidity crisis in EMCs in 2014–2016 in relation with the expected tempering of quantitative monetary easing in the United States.

Second, government agencies, as well as taxpayers, raise concerns when capital flight occurs in a context of generous development aid flows and heavy borrowing in international capital markets. Debt and capital flight show a large correlation in many Latin American countries. Pioneering statistical analyses of capital flight in the mid-1980s shed light on the size of the phenomenon in relation to capital inflows (Institute of International Economics 1986).

Third, corruption and capital flight have become an embarrassing issue for official aid agencies who face growing pressure to give top priority to productive investment and social projects. At the 1995 Annual Meeting, World Bank President James Wolfensohn declared that "there is nothing more important than the issue of corruption" while denouncing "the cancer of corruption" and its devastating effect on development (Wolfensohn 1996). Increasingly, large-scale debt reduction follows scrutiny of the domestic use of the debt servicing relief proceeds, so that the alleviation of liquidity constraints benefits high priority social projects, and not international bank accounts. The magnitude of the problem is such that it led to a special UN Convention against corruption and capital flight, signed by forty three countries in Mexico (United Nations 2003).[1]

Fourth, endemic corruption delays the implementation of anti-money-laundering standards, along with the necessary legal and law-enforcement systems (Platt 2005). The relation between corruption, money laundering, and terrorist financing received a new emphasis with the Financial Action Task Force, the OECD-based global watchdog on money laundering. The Stolen Asset Recovery Initiative (STAR) estimates up to USD 40 billion is

[1]Other official initiatives to fight corruption include the UN Global Compact in 1999, the Extractive Industries Transparency Initiative that constitutes a voluntary cooperation framework between governments and companies, the World Bank/OECD Global Corporate Governance Forum, and the OECD Principles of Corporate Governance.

lost each year to developing countries through corruption and capital flight, and most are never found nor returned (O'Murchu 2014, 5).

One additional reason for the renewed impetus of the research focus on capital flight is the increasingly blurred line between emerging and developed market countries since the Global Financial Crisis. In the Spring of 2016, leaked documents, known as the Panama Papers, showed that a Panamanian law firm had helped 14,000 clients worldwide create offshore accounts to conceal assets or dodge taxes. The vast majority of these offshore accounts were not from emerging market countries' high-net worth residents, but from the United States, the United Kingdom, and the Eurozone—that is, in the OECD. People who were suspected of involvement in money-laundering schemes were being investigated and fined. In the United States alone, unpaid taxes on foreign accounts are estimated at roughly USD 50 billion a year. Alstadsaeter et al. (2017) have made country-by-country estimates of tax haven wealth holdings. They conclude that wealth worth about 10% of global GDP is held offshore, roughly USD 5.6 trillion. That number rises to nearly 15% for continental Europe, confirming that developing countries have no monopoly on tax evasion.

In the Eurozone, Greece's case of tax avoidance and capital flight is striking. At the peak of the financial crisis, in 2011–2012, Greece reportedly had €66 billion in unpaid taxes due to tax avoidance and lack of compliance, the equivalent to around 25% of Greek gross domestic product (Reuters 2011). The figure rose to around €76 billion by 2014. This country illustrates two push and pull forces of capital flight. Large official and private capital flows in the Greek economy have been recycled in international bank deposits and in real assets overseas. In addition, during the financial crisis, private capital flight was the by-product of a bank run and tax evasion. Reportedly, in 2014–2015, roughly 64 billion Euros in private money have left the country—the equivalent of more than a third of Greece's annual economic output (Whitehouse 2015). If one focuses exclusively on nonbank private deposits in international banks, Greek deposits have surged from USD 12.3 billion at year-end 2010 to USD 32 billion in 2017, a 160% increase (Bank for International Settlements 2017).

14.4 Private Capital Outflows and Corruption: Unsuspected Bedfellows?

There is extensive research on the relationship between governance, corruption, political instability, and economic development, including research performed by Bardhan (1997), Tanzi (1998), Murphy et al. (1991, 1993),

Shleifer and Vishny (1993), Mauro (1995), Ades and Di Tella (1997), Tanzi and Davoodi (1997), and Leite and Weidmann (1999), as well as Glaeser et al. (2004) and Le and Zak (2006). As discussed in Chapter 9, there is a growing consensus that strong and stable institutions as well as robust governance are crucial inputs in the process of transforming economic growth into sustainable development. There is also a large flow of research on the links between corruption and capital inflows, including by Mauro (2004), Wei (2000, 2001), Wei and Wu (2002), Alesina and Weder (2002), and Groslambert and Bouchet (2006).

There has been an impressive cohort of research papers that investigates the relationships between capital inflows, indebtedness, institutions, and corruption; however, less work has been done on the relationships between corruption and private capital outflows. The Commission for Africa assumes a likely link between corruption and capital flight and it suggests measures to enhance laws and practices in both developing and developed countries (Ndikumana 2017). Moreover, Collier et al. (1999, 2001, 2004) analysed capital flight from forty-three emerging market countries throughout the 1980s, concluding that corruption is positively related to capital flight. At the IMF, Cerra et al. (2005) have tested whether weak institutions and corruption lead to capital flight as well as the revolving door hypothesis that links debt accumulation and capital flight. Le and Meenakshi's econometric analysis (2006) shows that, holding other determinants of capital flight constant, corruption does have a significant impact on capital flight. Yet there are good reasons why the relationship between capital outflows and corruption deserves a deeper research focus for assessment of Country Risk. We briefly examine four reasons for a closer look at the relationships between corruption, capital flight, and socioeconomic development.

First, there is growing evidence that in countries with weak institutions, private capital outflows and dollarization are the by-product of a political and regulatory environment that is not conducive to private investment and savings mobilization. The lack of a favorable economic policy climate and deeply embedded corruption are detrimental to dynamic domestic savings, along with other factors such as exchange rate overvaluation, negative real rates of interest, and macroeconomic mismanagement (Bouchet 2013). Capital flight is bound to rise when government officials loot the country's assets, particularly in two situations: (i) when savers do not trust the legal, banking, and regulatory frameworks; and (ii) when the political and economic system is so volatile that investors fear their assets might be confiscated or subject to arbitrary decisions.

Second, and as mentioned above, capital flight is not the monopoly of developing countries with poor institutions as wide-scale tax avoidance in the OECD has been illustrated by the Panama Papers in 2015–2016. A powerful force for private capital outflows is also a fragile banking system, with doubts regarding the management quality and the robustness of capitalization ratios. A crisis of confidence in the financial sector might be found in sub-Saharan countries, but also within Eurozone countries, such as in Greece, Cyprus, Portugal, and Spain. In addition, the fall in the Russian currency in the second half of 2014 precipitated a financial and banking crisis that led the central bank to implement a massive bailout program to recapitalize or nationalize several banks. Overall, the majority of Russia's wealth at the top of the social structure is held outside the national borders, and about 13% of the country's GDP is estimated to be parked in offshore tax havens, excluding assets such as art collections, gold, yachts, and real estate holdings. In a report that assesses the causes and consequences of capital flight in Russia, two analysts of the IMF note: "Large capital outflows from Russia are a symptom, one highly visible manifestation of the deeper and wider problems of the country's investment climate. What lies behind this symptom is a syndrome of country-specific historical afflictions that provide the backdrop for Russia's deep and decade-long confidence crisis and the resulting low level of trust in the rules of the game, policies, and institutions" (Loungani and Mauro 2000). According to the EBRD, a crucial factor contributing to this situation is the continued low level of confidence of savers and investors in the banking/financial sector (Buiter and Szegvari 2002). Russia's financial sector crisis has been exacerbated by the fall in the real exchange rate of the ruble, hence the combination of two "push forces" for capital flight: a strategy of protecting private assets from the risk of a bank run and of banking insolvency; and a strategy of expatriating private assets to benefit from the exchange rate differential with the US Dollar and the Euro. Figure 14.1 illustrates the close correlation between the real exchange rate evolution of the ruble and Russian deposits in international banks.

Figure 14.2 shows a similar relationship though based on a narrower measure of capital flight—that is, nonbank private deposits in offshore banking accounts, as reported by the BIS.

In addition, still looking at the case of Russia, it is clear that the country's economic growth trajectory is driven by hydrocarbon prices and revenues. The sharp drop in oil prices since the summer of 2014 has caused a severe slowdown in Russia's GDP growth, and a de facto recession in 2014 and 2015. It is not surprising then that one can observe a close correlation

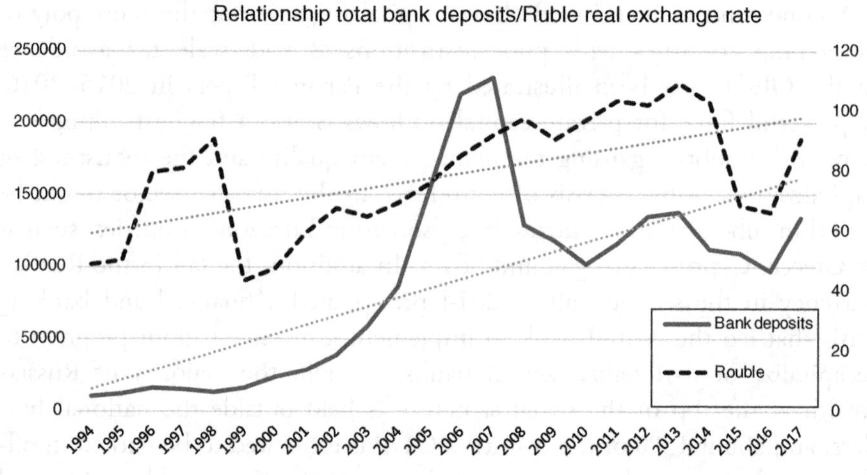

Fig. 14.1 Relationships between Russia's ruble exchange rate and offshore banking deposits (*Source* Data from the Bank for International Settlements 2017)

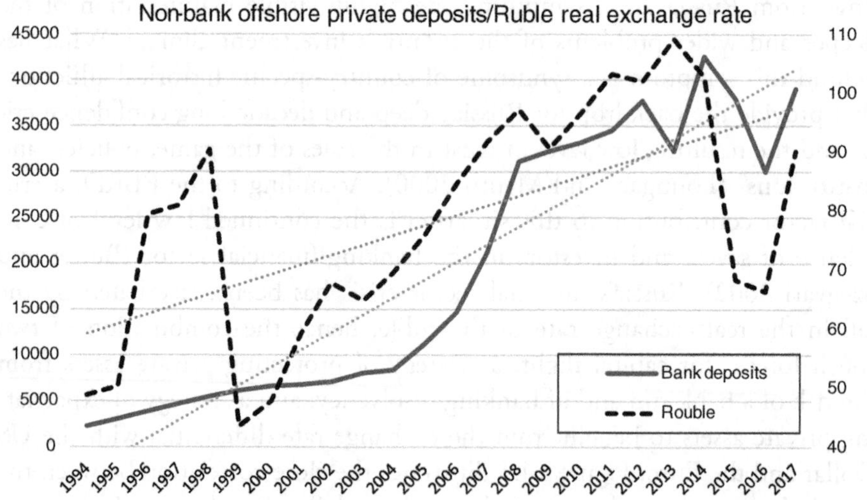

Fig. 14.2 Relationships between Russia's ruble exchange rate and offshore private banking deposits (Dollar millions)

between oil prices and Russia's private deposits held in international banks, as illustrated in Fig. 14.3. USD-denominated oil prices are on the vertical axis while private deposits are listed on the horizontal axis in millions of USD.

Third, the causes of capital outflow stem from a combination of "push and pull forces." Centrifugal forces thus work both ways regarding the

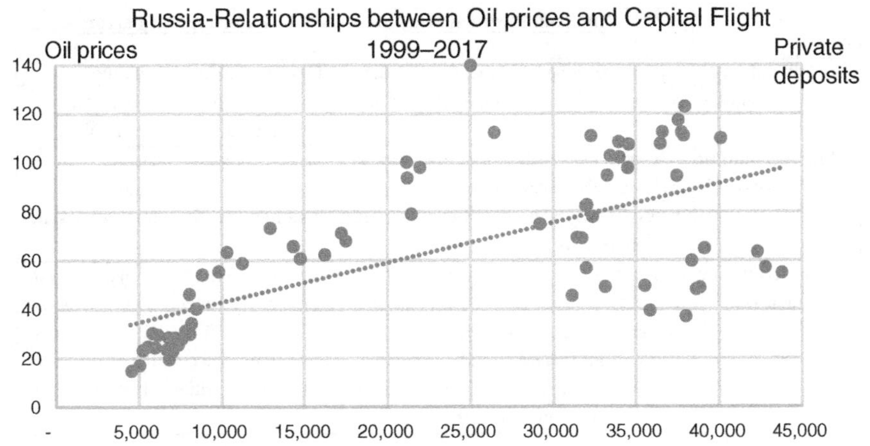

Fig. 14.3 Russia: Relationship between oil prices and capital flight (*Source* Authors and Bank of International Settlements banking data 2017)

impact of corruption on capital leakages. One can identify two sets of "push forces." First, corruption generates an income flow that is illegal, hence those who benefit from corrupt practices expatriate their assets. Second, corruption is a "push factor" since it works like a tax on private savings. Legitimate private savings, which run the risk of getting confiscated or whose purchasing power might be eroded by policy mismanagement, will be held overseas in hard currencies. Private agents export their assets to safer places because they do not trust corporate and official practices due to corruption and bad governance. In addition, one can identify external "pull forces" that attract private savings outside a country's boundaries. Expatriation of private financial assets outside the national authorities' grips is encouraged by investment opportunities in foreign markets, including positive real rates of interest, strong exchange rates, loose regulatory frameworks, tax incentives, and deeper financial markets. The so-called Panama Papers in the summer of 2016 shed light on global attempts by high-net worth individuals who had created offshore accounts to conceal assets and evade taxes. Hence geography matters in capital flight stimulation. According to the NBER, the emerging tax havens of Asia have been powerful magnets for Asia's private wealth, while Caribbean havens have attracted wealth from the Americas, and Switzerland (and Luxembourg) has attracted wealth from Europe and the Middle East (Alstadsaeter et al. 2017). Figure 14.4 summarizes the push and pull forces behind private capital outflows (Bouchet 2015).

	Internal Push Factors	External Pull Factors
Political and institutional factors	Political upheaval; social instability, corruption, bribery, money laundering	Opacity and loose banking regulations; monetary policy and accommodative financial policies
Macroeconomic factors	Negative real interest rates, overvalued exchange rates, inflationary pressure; capital account liberalization; solvency crisis, rising tax rates	High real interest rates, undervalued exchange rates, dynamic stock and real-estate markets abroad
Microeconomic factors	Banking undercapitalization, liquidity crisis, institutional weaknesses; rise in corporate income taxes, inefficient and immature financial system with few portfolio diversification instruments	Strong asset management competitive advantage; dynamic offshore financial systems; attractive tax havens, and inadequate due diligence on customers

Fig. 14.4 The centrifugal forces of private capital outflows

Fourth, the real challenge is as much to measure capital flight as understanding what type of socioeconomic structures stimulates expatriated private savings. There are close links between corruption, private capital outflows, and oil-driven growth, as hydrocarbon-based revenues are more likely to coincide with wealth and political power concentration, feeding private capital expatriation. Oil windfalls encourage rent-seeking behavior at the opposite of good governance. Arezki and Brückner of the IMF (2009) find that oil rents significantly increase corruption and are detrimental to political rights. The correlation between oil revenues, corruption, and capital outflows is also illustrated by Boyce and Ndikumana's research (2013) as well as by Kharrat and Bouchet (2017). They show that revenues from the extraction of natural resources can be a major source of flight capital, what can be called a "black gold faucet." Chapter 9 tackles this relationship between oil-based growth and corruption as measured by the Corruption Perception Index (CPI). Regarding oil revenues that country officials have transferred overseas in personal banking accounts, a 2002 IMF report on Angola found that more than USD 900 million in oil revenues was missing from state coffers in 2001—roughly three times the total value of humanitarian aid to Angola—and that USD 4 billion had gone missing over the previous five years (Boyce 2004). A substantial share of developing countries' oil revenues remains outside the state budget and is confiscated by corrupt intermediaries, with little positive socioeconomic impact on the national population (Talahite 2000).

14.5 Focus on Analysis and Data Sources

14.5.1 Defining the Dependent Variable

What follows is an overview of the results of our own cross-country research regarding the determinants of capital flight. The econometric analysis suggests that ongoing capital flight is a symptom of underlying bad governance and a "warning light" which signals that underlying country and political risk levels are higher than is commonly realized. We apply this research to a large sample of developing countries, including those in Southeast Asia, Latin America, and Africa. Estimates of the scale of capital outflow vary with the type of definition employed. The literature that tackles the magnitude of private capital outflow, though large and ever expanding, does not provide any clear-cut conclusion regarding a coherent definition.

The main weakness of the models presented in Table 14.1, whatever their econometric sophistication, is that they rely on estimates. Private capital leakages comprise all forms of capital accumulation invested abroad where it cannot be reported, seized, or taxed by the local government. Expatriated savings can be invested in both real and financial assets. In order to adopt a narrow but reliable focus, our approach to private capital outflow is based on the accumulation of deposits in international banks by the domestic nonbanking private sector. The stock of private deposits held in international banks by nonbank citizens outside their countries of origin is reported by the Bank of International Settlements (BIS). The BIS publishes both quarterly amounts outstanding as well as exchange rate adjusted changes in stocks. This creditor-reporting method thus adopts a stock approach to private capital outflows (Bouchet 1986). This measure is both larger and narrower than capital flight per se. These statistics omit mutual funds, private trusts, custodian accounts, and money market funds that hold assets in international banks. They also exclude other types of investments such as real estate, art, antiques, bonds, jewels, cash outside the banking system, and foreign business ventures—all difficult to trace. Yet they provide a reliable measure of the centrifugal forces that react to sociopolitical and economic volatility in the home country. A study by Global Financial Integrity (2017), the Washington, DC-based anticorruption group, estimates around 75% of illicit flows are deposited in banks in developed countries.

The working hypothesis is that a significant increase in the rate of private capital outflows will be reflected in the accumulation of private external assets held in international banks. The case study presents the key parameters of the econometric model that analyzes the underlying causes of private expatriated savings while highlighting the relationship between corruption, oil revenues, and private capital outflows in forty-three developing countries over the 1984–2014 period. In addition, Case Study 14.1 presents four countries where market-based economic policy and relatively good governance have contributed to capital flight repatriation, namely two in Latin America (Chile and Mexico) and two in East Asia (Indonesia and Philippines). Case Study 14.2 focuses on capital flight in Tunisia before and after the Arab Spring of 2011, thereby illustrating how the combination of dictatorship and corruption is a powerful force for discouraging the domestic investment of private savings.

14.5.2 The Key Explanatory Variables for Stimulating Capital Flight

- **Institutional variable (ICRG).** The corruption index captures the extent to which "high government officials are likely to demand special payments" and the extent to which "illegal payments are generally expected in the form of bribes connected with import and export licenses, exchange controls, tax assessments, police protection, or loans."
- **Oil revenues** in relation to GDP reflect the structural dependence of national governments' revenues on natural resources, including hydrocarbon products. The underlying assumption is that a large reliance on hydrocarbon revenues tends to concentrate political and economic power in a few hands, with little power checks, and with bad governance. Data are provided by the World Bank's World Development Indicators.
- **The dependent control variables** include five macroeconomic indicators, as follows:

  1. Inflation: Other things being equal, a high inflation rate will reduce the real rate of return on liquid assets. Inflation, an indicator of market distortions, is expected to be positively related to capital outflow.
  2. Exchange rate: Other things being equal, a depreciated exchange rate will lead domestic residents to expatriate their private savings overseas in order to protect the real value of their assets.
  3. GDP: anaemic economic growth tends to discourage both domestic investment and private savings in the domestic economy, hence "push forces." Higher economic growth rates in foreign countries work as "pull forces," stimulating private capital outflows.

4. Foreign debt: The increase in external borrowing stimulates capital outflow if residents fear the likelihood of an unsustainable burden of debt service, and therefore a future liquidity crisis, as observed by Bouchet and Seto (2011).
5. Trade openness: The ratio of total trade flows to GDP, is a measure of economic liberalization. Trade might become a channel for capital flight, based on over- and under-invoicing of trade transactions.

14.6 Where Does Capital Flight Come from?

The model presented in Appendix 14.1 has substantial explanatory power. We found statistical significance in a variety of factors, including the level of corruption, the oil rent, the inflation, the exchange rate, GDP growth, trade openness, and bilateral external debt. The coefficient of determination R^2 shows that 61% of the variability in the level of capital outflow is explained by institutional indicator taken alone (model 1), while 69% of the variability is explained by the institutional and oil-driven revenues factors (model 2), and around 71% by all variables, including ICRG, the oil rent and macroeconomic factors (model 3) (Table 14.2).

Table 14.2 Summary of regression results with expatriated private savings as dependent variable

	Model 1	Model 2	Model 3
Constant	−0.766068***	−1.110331*	−2.195448***
	(−11.06906)	(−9.306815)	(5.820252)
ICRG	0.067221***	0.167374***	0.099565***
	(2.368707)	(4.918486)	(2.771766)
INF			0.134821***
			(5.756451)
EXCH			−0.035521***
			(−3.145220)
GDP			−0.012810**
			(−2.164105)
DEBT			0.041693***
			(3.322873)
TRADE			0.300747***
			(3.431728)
OIL		0.106086***	0.068947*
		(2.779647)	(1.815599)
R^2	61.07%	69.15%	70.76%
Adjusted R^2	59.68%	67.96%	69.33%
Prob (F-statistic)	0.000000	0.000000	0.000000

Econometric research illustrates that private capital outflows stem from a combination of push and pull forces as well as both domestic and global influences. On the domestic front, one observes the influence of the inflation rate and the exchange rate as well as the strong correlation between capital flight with both trade openness and the oil rent. The inflation coefficient is positively and significantly correlated with capital flight, confirming the hypothesis that a decline in real interest rates at home, coupled with overvalued exchange rate, leads to "push forces" of private capital outflows. Capital flight increases when residents anticipate inflation-driven taxation of domestic deposits. In a context of inflationary expectations, exchange rate depreciation results in declining purchasing power of domestic assets, hence an incentive for expatriated private savings. Regarding trade, a high level of economic openness provides greater ability to manipulate export and import prices to shift capital overseas. Capital flight is stimulated by under and over-invoicing transactions. Regarding economic growth, there is a significant and negative impact of GDP growth on capital flight. Dynamic growth is associated with dynamic buoyant investment, hence reducing the scope of capital flight. Finally, the analysis confirms the relationship between external debt and expatriated savings, hence larger foreign debt leads to larger private capital outflows that illustrate the revolving door hypothesis.

14.7 Conclusion

In the assessment of Country Risk, we conclude that it is crucial to look for indicators that will tell us in advance when a country will be subject to a financial or political crisis. Yet despite the best efforts of some our finest minds, we haven't been able to accomplish that objective. We now realize, after years of research and practice, that one of the most important components of country risk assessment is combining external and local intelligence. Another key component is observing the management of private expatriated savings, that is, capital flight. Our analysis of a large sample of forty-three emerging market countries over the 1984–2014 period confirms the large impact of institutions and macroeconomic policies as well as oil rent on private capital outflows. Clearly, weak institutions and poor governance stimulate capital flight, even taking into account the macroeconomic policy framework. Overall, good macroeconomic policy alone cannot offset the centrifugal forces of bad governance that will push private capital outside the national economy. The study also casts light on the role of oil-driven export revenues on capital outflows. Hydrocarbon-based economic growth tends to generate wealth concentration, impacting the political and governance process. Economies where natural resources occupy a dominant role usually suffer from several shortcomings, including income inequality and high budget and export revenues volatility, coupled with deeply rooted corruption and high level of private expatriated savings.

Private capital outflow, measured by external private bank deposits, rises in countries with high corruption and weak governance. Overall, private capital outflow is the result of both internal "push" and external "pull" factors that are shared by all countries, both developed and developing. Monitoring the stock of private deposits in international banks as well as the exchange rate adjusted changes, as reported by the BIS, can contribute to an in-depth and forward-looking assessment of Country Risk.

Case Study 14.1 Looking at capital flight repatriation in four emerging market countries (Source Kharrat and Bouchet 2017)

Capital inflows to developing countries have increased sharply since the 1980s from both private and official sources. Official creditors provided development aid as well as guaranteed trade credits. Private financing took the form of international bank loans until the late 1980s and, increasingly, bond issues in global markets as well as local currency-denominated securities. Since the Global Financial Crisis, private capital inflows increased due to the search for yield by global investors. A combination of improved economic prospects in emerging market countries, low international interest rates, and a slowdown of economic activity in the capital exporting countries, has led to large amounts of external financing at good financial conditions. External financing could be used to supplement official reserve assets to finance budget deficits and to boost investment, but also to recycle funds in offshore accounts. A few countries, however, managed to stimulate the return of capital flight with a combination of tax incentives, high real rates of interest, stable exchange rates, and encouraging investment prospects. Following Corbo and Hernandez (1998), one can consider six categories of market-based economic policies that are conducive to capital flight repatriation: (1) moves toward a more flexible exchange rate; (2) fiscal restraint; (3) sterilization by means of open market operations that offset capital inflows to stem inflationary risks; (4) restrictions on short-term capital inflows; (5) liberalization of the current account; and (6) selective liberalization of the capital account to reduce speculative capital outflows.

To test this positive combination, we analyze four countries that have received large capital inflows since the early 1980, both with foreign direct investment and portfolio flows: two in Latin America (Chile and Mexico) and two in East Asia (Indonesia and Philippines). We examine how the extent of financial liberalization and structural reforms has encouraged capital flows while limiting or even reversing capital flight in these after a period of economic, financial, and political crisis. Figure 14.5 provides a measure of expatriated private bank deposits in percentage of each country's GDP. The right axis shows Chile's moderate amounts of capital outflows that remained at roughly 0.2% of GDP between 1990 and 2014, after a sharp decline in 1986–1989. The striking increase in capital flight in Indonesia during the 1997–1998 crisis was followed by a gradual decline. Mexico shows two clear increases in capital flight. The first rise took place during the debt crisis of mid-1980s that led to a successful debt reduction. The second took place during the so-called "tequila crisis" of 1994 that led to a sharp depreciation of the currency, as discussed later. Finally, in the case of the Philippines, Fig. 14.5 shows relatively moderate capital flight at the equivalent of 1% of GDP, after large outflows in the 1970s and mid-1980s.

Table 14.3 summarizes the main policy measures adopted by each of the four countries to stem capital outflows.

1. **Chile**: In a turbulent region, Chile has distinguished itself by the robustness of its economy with responsible monetary and fiscal policies and a well-developed financial system. Inflation started to decline and GDP growth to become more sustainable in the mid-1990s. This combination enabled Chilean economy to resist a series of external shocks including Mexico's crisis of 1994–1995, the Argentina crisis contagion in 2001–2002, as well as the Brazilian financial markets turbulence at the end of 2002. Gradual capital account liberalization has been combined with exchange rate arrangements to allow for greater flexibility. Chile has adopted a crawling peg policy since the middle of the 1980s. Initially pegging to the Dollar and within a narrow band, Chile adjusted its exchange rate policy to accommodate a moderate real appreciation of the exchange rate that started in 2003 with a wider band around the central parity, and shifting the peg from the Dollar to a basket of currencies. With inflation under control, the current account deficit could be financed by net Foreign direct investment (FDI) flows of around 3% of GDP. Figure 14.6 illustrates the differences in exchange rate manage-

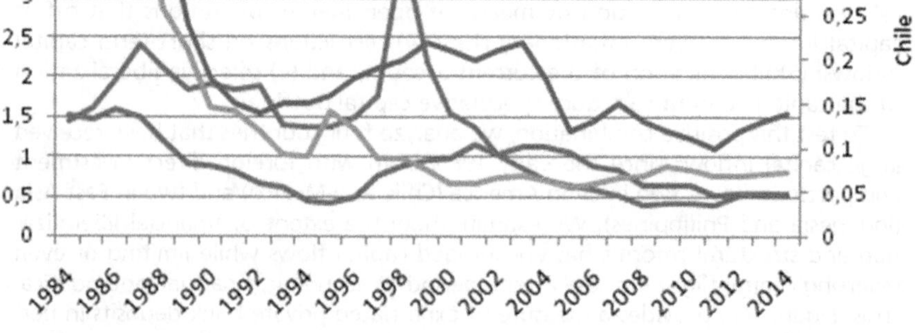

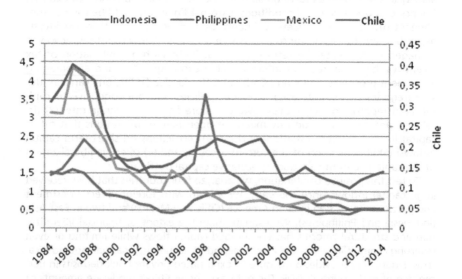

Fig. 14.5 The ups and downs of capital flight (in % of GDP) 1984–2014 (*Sources* Bank for International Settlements 2017 and World Bank 2017)

Table 14.3 Policies adoped to stem capital outflows

Country	Moves toward a more flexible exchange rate	Fiscal restraint	Sterilization by open market operations	Restrictions on capital inflows	Liberalizing the current account	Selective liberalization of the capital account
Chile	x		x	x	x	x
Mexico	x	x	x	x	x	
Indonesia	x	x	x	x	x	
Philippines		x	x	x	x	x

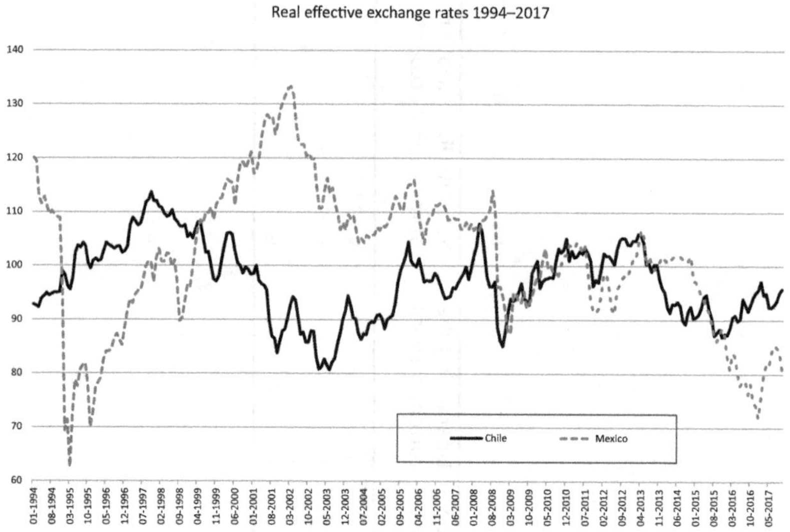

Fig. 14.6 Evolution in Chile's and Mexico's real effective exchange rates (*Source* Authors' calculations from BIS data)

ment policy between Chile and Mexico over the 1994–2017 period. Clearly, Chile's central bank managed to stabilize the Peso's real effective exchange rate in the aftermath of the sharp depreciation of the Peso between 1997 and 2003, due to the spillover effect of the Asian crisis.

2. **Mexico**: In the early 1980s, Mexico used fiscal adjustment to counteract the effects of capital inflows in expanding expenditure and causing the real exchange rate to appreciate. In the end of 1994, the so-called "tequila crisis" reflected the strength of capital flight. In an effort to boost the country's competitiveness and to offset the damaging effect of inflation and capital flight, the peso was devalued and the exchange rate was allowed to float. To stem ongoing capital outflows, the Mexican treasury issued short-term peso securities with the backup of guaranteed repayment in US Dollars, attracting foreign investors while the central bank maintained the peso's US Dollar peg by issuing Dollar-denominated public debt. The peso's appreciation between 1995 and 2001 fueled a trade deficit, unabated inflation, and more capital flight. Net FDI flows reached roughly the equivalent of 2% of GDP, or USD 25 billion per year, though with large volatility.
3. **Indonesia:** This Southeast Asia country was strongly affected by the 1997–1998 crisis that resulted in a 13% drop in GDP. The abrupt devaluation of the rupee was followed by tight monetary policy, resulting in a stabilization of the real effective exchange rate. Macroeconomic adjustment aimed at boosting direct investment inflows with the elimination of barriers to trade and the liberalization of restrictions on payments and current transfers. To offset the liquidity associated with the foreign reserve accumulation, the Bank of Indonesia increased its interest rate on domestic certificates to make them more attractive to domestic financial institutions.
   Gradual liberalization of direct investment inflows resulted in financing a current account deficit of around 2% of GDP, while increasing official

reserve assets, and contributing to buoyant gross domestic investment that reached 25–30% of GDP. External debt was stabilized at around 30% of GDP. The Indonesian authorities liberalized the inflows of portfolio investment by eliminating the quantitative limits on bank borrowing by nonresidents. Foreigners were allowed to invest on the stock market and to acquire more than 49% of the shares on their behalf. Restrictions on direct investment inflows were also relaxed, in particular by allowing non-residents to sell currencies directly to commercial banks instead of through the central bank. Figure 14.7 shows the steep fall in the rupee's real exchange rate in 1997 followed by a quasi-stabilization between 2003 and 2017.

4. **Philippines:** Excessive and premature financial liberalization in the Philippines provides a textbook case of capital flow volatility. The country liberalized its trade, current, and capital accounts during the 1980s and 1990s, resulting in large though volatile capital inflows. The country suffered from the regional contamination of the 1997 Asian crisis, with capital flight, drop in investment, and a deep economic recession. International reserves started to increase only since 2000 and the current account surplus reached roughly 5% of GDP between 2007 and 2011 to decline to around 3% between 2012 and 2015. Net FDI flows remained very volatile as well as errors and omissions. Contrary to Indonesia, FDI flows in the Philippines have remained subdued at around USD 1.5 billion annually. The experience of Philippines is instructive in the field of asset recovery given that large sums of money transferred overseas have been recovered. Looking at Fig. 14.7, one can observe that the Philippines exchange rate policy fueled a deep depreciation of the peso between 1997 and 2004 followed by ongoing appreciation until 2017, hence eroding competitiveness and generating centrifugal forces for capital flows.

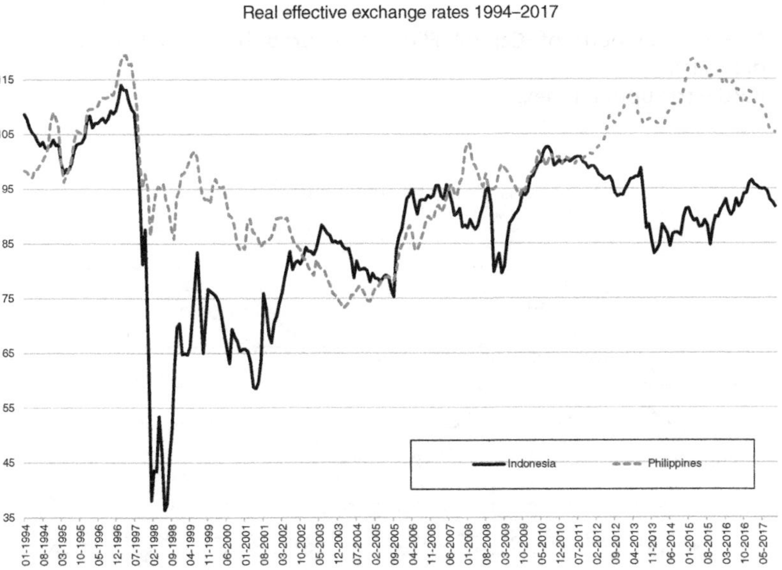

Fig. 14.7 Evolution in Indonesia's and the Philippines' real effective exchange rates (*Source* Authors' calculations from BIS data)

Case Study 14.2 Capital Flight in Tunisia Before and After the Arab Spring (see Fig. 14.8) (Source Kharrat et al. 2015)

In Tunisia, capital flight has been a severe problem causing heavy losses in government revenues, foregone investment, and lost output. The total amount of private capital outflow from Tunisia reached over $54 billion during the 1984–2014 period. The annual average capital flight was about USD 1.8 billion during the regime of Ben Ali (1987–2010) (see Fig. 14.8), compared with roughly USD 1 billion during the Bourguiba's regime (1977–1987).

Ben Ali and his supporters exemplify a case of crony capitalism with a strong hold on assets in many profit-generating activities, including in industry, services, and trade. The amount of annual outflow consistently grew between 1984 and 1987, followed by a slight decline until 1994. The total amount of capital outflow grew from USD 1 billion in 1994 to more than USD 2 billion in 2014. The largest amount of capital outflow occurred in 2004 (more than USD 3 billion, or the equivalent of 10% of GDP and 72% of loans from international banks). After the 2011 Arab Spring revolution, capital flight continued unabated, with USD 2.13 billion leaving annually, according to BIS data.

The analysis of the "push and pull forces" of capital flight in Tunisia is based on the following econometric model:

$$CF_t = \alpha + \beta_1 ICRG_t + \beta_2 POLITY_t + \beta_3 OIL_t + \beta_4 DOM_t + \beta_5 DEBT_t + \beta_6 MARK_t + \beta_7 DIFINT_t + \beta_8 EXCH_t + \varepsilon_t$$

where, $t = 1,2, \ldots, T$: the time index, and ε_{it}: a random error term,

- CF = total amount of Capital Flight measured by the BIS (private bank deposits).
- ICRG = corruption index.

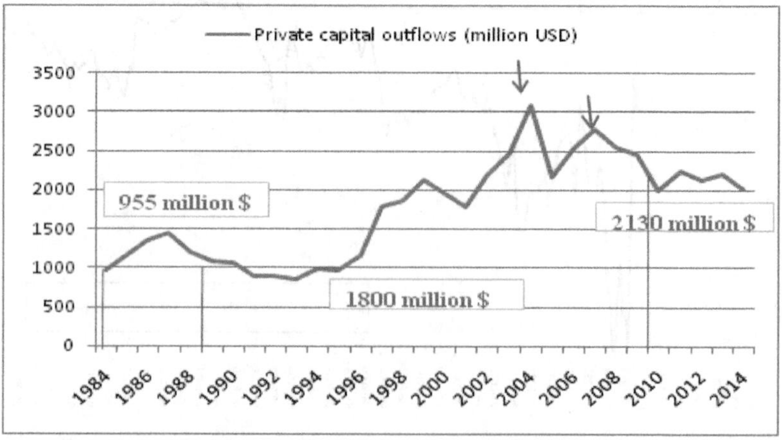

Fig. 14.8 Estimates of capital flight from Tunisia (BIS, 1984–2014)

- Political stability (POLITY): polity score, proxy of governance.
- Oil rent (OIL): measured as total oil rent divided by GDP.
- Domestic credit (DOM): measured as domestic credit allocated to the private sector divided by GDP.
- External Debt (DEBT): measured as change in external debt divided by GDP.
- Exchange rate (EXCH): yearly average of exchange rate USD/Tunisian Dinar.
- Differential Interest Rate (DIFINT) between foreign and domestic interest rates.
- Stock market quotation (MARK): Market capitalization of the Tunisian stock market.

Determinants of capital flight are investigated with both ordinary least squares and an Error Correction model for mutual relationship between these variables. The Error Correction model is introduced by Engle and Granger (1987) for examining co-integration for long-run relationship between variables.

The two major "push forces" of capital outflows in Tunisia during the 1984–2014 period have been corruption and political volatility, exacerbated by significant exchange rates overvaluation, and rising external debt. Seven main variables shed light on the sources of capital flight in Tunisia:

1. Capital flight has been ongoing in Tunisia since the mid-1980s during the repressive regimes of Presidents Bourguiba and Ben Ali. Corruption under the Ben Ali regime was widely known within and outside the country, resulting in rising frustration for Tunisian entrepreneurs and households, further discouraging both private savings and investment, and reducing public budget revenues. However, private capital outflows continued and even increased in the postrevolution period due to unabated corruption and opacity. The results of estimating the long-term equation (Table 14.4) reveal that the "ICRG" and "POLITY" variables are significant and highly correlated to capital flight (+0.254 and −0.037, respectively). This relationship between institutional variables and capital flight shows that private capital outflows are strongly affected by bad governance and strong corruption in Tunisia. Since the uprising on January 14, 2011, Tunisia has experienced political

Table 14.4 Least square estimation results

Variable	Coefficient	Std. error	*t*-statistic	Probability
Constant	−1.111	0.835	−1.330	0.1969
ICRG	0.254	0.111	2.284	0.0324
POLITY	−0.037	0.018	−2.008	0.0570
OIL	0.041	0.009	4.188	0.0004
DOM	−0.823	0.745	−1.105	0.2809
DEBT	1.640	0.386	4.242	0.0003
MARK	−0.011	0.006	−1.844	0.0793
DIFINT	−0.050	0.015	−3.488	0.0021
EXCH	0.700	0.291	2.401	0.02252
R^2	0.89			
Adjusted R^2	0.85			
Prob (Fisher)	0.0000			
D-W test	1.34			

instability, losing fourteen points in the Corruption Perceptions Index (CPI) ranking in the aftermath of the revolution, dropping from 59th in 2010 to 73th in 2011, and up to 75th in 2015–2016. Sociopolitical turbulences has continued feeding private capital outflows, with negative impact on both investment, savings, and economic growth.

2. The "oil rent" variable is positively and significantly correlated with capital flight, with a level of correlation of respectively 41% and 29%. These results confirm that the natural resource extraction revenues are also strong forces behind capital flight. Despite that Tunisia has modest oil resources compared to its neighbors (Libya and Algeria), this sector has an important role in the economy. Large corruption and minimal transparency have led to the development of alternative distribution channels and the loss of control on the borders with neighboring countries.
3. The analysis confirms the relationship between exchange rate overvaluation and capital flight (0.7). All things being equal, ongoing currency depreciation will stimulate shifting private savings abroad to protect the real value of assets. However, the exchange rate depreciation indicator of competitiveness is not statistically significant in the short run.
4. The interest rate differential between Tunisia and the United States has a negative and significant impact on capital flight in Tunisia, in the short and long term with a level of correlation of −0.060 and −0.050, respectively. Interest rate differential is a powerful "pull force" of capital flight between Tunisia and global financial markets (Table 14.5).
5. Domestic banking credit in Tunisia has little impact on the phenomenon of capital flight. This result is not surprising, considering the extent of corruption within this sector. In fact, Tunisian banks have suffered from weak corporate governance. Under the Ben Ali's regime, their lending decisions and their ownership structures were subject to political interference. Board members lacked independence and their appointment was more influenced

Table 14.5 Cointegrating error correction model

Variable	Coefficient	Std. error	*t*-statistic	Probability
Constant	−0.038	0.122	−0.317	0.7544
D(ICRG)	0.009	0.045	0.212	0.8342
D(POLITY)	−0.003	0.004	−0.749	0.4625
D(OIL)	0.029	0.014	2.010	0.0581
D(MARK)	−0.019	0.006	−3.154	0.0050
D(DEBT)	1.940	0.488	3.973	0.0007
D(DOM)	−0.575	0.504	−1.140	0.2674
D(DIFINT)	−0.060	0.018	−3.421	0.0027
D(EXCH)	0.328	0.2770	1.186	0.2494
RESIDU(−1)	−0.859	0.267	−3.205	0.0044
R^2	0.617			
Adjusted R^2	0.435			
Prob (Fisher)	0.0118			
D-W test	1.79			

(CF/GDP) is the dependent variable; (.) = Student t; (***, **, *) = Significance at the 1, 5, and 10% level, respectively by their political position than their competence. Tunisia is considered to have limited financial freedom with a small and fragmented banking system, which penalizes access to domestic credit and increases the cost of credit for both companies and households.

6. The econometric results of the two models in the long and short run show a significant and positive correlation between the ratio of external debt to GDP and capital flight in Tunisia (1.640 in the short run) and (1.940 in the long-run). In fact, when Tunisia increases external borrowing, much of this debt is diverted. Debt inflows end up deposited in foreign banks, hence fueling capital flight in a debt recycling process.
7. The variation of stock market prices in Tunisia is an additional "push force" of capital flight. The negative and significant coefficient for this variable in both models are (−0.011) in the long run and (−0.019) in the short run. These results confirm the theoretical assumptions of Boyce and Ndikumana (2003, 2011) who found that financial development can reduce capital flight if it is accompanied by an expansion of opportunities for diversification of domestic portfolio.

Overall, these results appear to be significant and are consistent with prior studies such as Murphy et al. (1991, 1993), Shleifer and Vishny (1993), Mauro (1995), Blanchard et al. (2010), and El Mesbahi (2013). These studies demonstrate that corruption and political events have a negative impact on economic development. For the country risk analyst, capital flight is not only associated with weak governance and economic imbalances, but it can also serve as useful early warning signal of upcoming turbulence.

Appendix 14.1: Empirical Analysis of the Relationship Between Corruption and Overseas Private Bank Deposits

The econometric model uses panel data. It is performed in three stages.

First, the study focuses on the relationship between capital flight and the explanatory variable Corruption (named "ICRG"). Equation (14.1) of the model will therefore be as follows:

$$\mathrm{CF}_{it} = \alpha_i + \beta_1 \cdot \mathrm{ICRG}_{it} + \varepsilon_{it} \tag{14.1}$$

where ε_{it} is a random error term;

$t = 1, 2, \ldots, T$ is the time index;

$i = 1, 2, \ldots, N$ is the country index.

Second, to highlight the link between oil resources and the level of flight capital, the model introduces a new variable that measures the intensity of hydrocarbon production in a country's economic growth path, namely the ratio oil rent/GDP.

$$\mathrm{CF}_{it} = \alpha_i + \beta_1 \cdot \mathrm{ICRG}_{it} + \beta_2 \cdot \mathrm{OIL}_{it} + \varepsilon_{it} \tag{14.2}$$

where ε_{it} is a random error term;

$t = 1, 2, \ldots, T$ is the time index;

$i = 1, 2, \ldots, N$ is the country index.

Third, in order to test the robustness of the model, it incorporates several macroeconomic control variables to cast light on "pull" and "push" factors of capital flight. Equation (14.3) of the model is as follows:

$$\begin{aligned}\mathrm{CF}_{it} = \alpha_i + \beta_1 \cdot \mathrm{ICRG}_{it} + \beta_2 \cdot \mathrm{OIL}_{it} + \beta_3 \cdot \mathrm{INFL}_{it} + \beta_4 \cdot \mathrm{EXCH}_{it} \\ + \beta_5 \cdot \mathrm{TRADE}_{it} + \beta_6 \cdot \mathrm{DEBT}_{it} + \beta_7 \cdot \mathrm{GDP}_{it} + \varepsilon_{it}\end{aligned} \tag{14.3}$$

where ε_{it} is a random error term;

$t = 1, 2, \ldots, T$ is the time index;

$i = 1, 2, \ldots, N$ is the country index.

References

Ades, Alberto, and Rafael Di Tella. 1997. "The New Economics of Corruption: A Survey and Some New Results." *Political Studies* XLV: 496–515.

Alesina, Aberto, and Beatrice Weder. 2002. "Do Corrupt Governments Receive Less Foreign Aid?" *American Economic Review* 92 (4): 1126–1137.

Alstadsaeter, Annette, Niels Johannesen, and Gabriel Zucman. (2017) "Who Owns the Wealth in Tax Heavens? Macro Evidence and Implications for Global Inequality." NBER Working Paper No. 23805.

Arezki, Rabah, and Markus Brückner. 2009. "Oil Rents, Corruption, and State Stability: Evidence from Panel Data Regressions." IMF Working Paper WP/09/267.

Bank for International Settlements. 2017. http://stats.bis.org/statx/srs/table/A6.1?c=GR&p=.

Bardhan, Pranab. 1997. "Corruption and Development: A Review of Issues." *Journal of Economic Literature* 35 (3): 1320–1346.

Blanchard, Olivier, Giovanni Dell'Ariccia, and Paolo Mauro. 2010. "Rethinking Macroeconomic Policy." *Journal of Money, Credit and Banking* 42 (S1): 199–215.

Bouchet, Michel. 1986. *Capital Flight in Latin America.* Washington, DC: Internal Memorandum, Institute of International Finance, March 21.

Bouchet, Michel. 2013. "Capital Flight and Global Crisis: In Search of a Barometer of Country Risk." *The World Financial Review*, July 13. http://www.worldfinancialreview.com/?p=700.

Bouchet, Michel. 2015. "Capital Flight as Early Warning Signal." Chapter 7. In *Country and Political Risk*, edited by Sam Walkin, 2nd ed. London: Risk Books.

Bouchet, Michel, and Bertrand Groslambert. 2005. "Country Risk and Governance: Strange Bedfellows?" In *Governance and Risk in Emerging and Global Markets*, edited by Sima Motamen-Samadian, 69–88. Basingstoke: Palgrave Macmillan.

Bouchet, Michel, and Bertrand Groslambert. 2006. "An Empirical Study of the Relationships Between Corruption, Capital Leakages and Country Risk." *ESAN Cuadernos de Investigacion* 11 (20): 10–23.

Bouchet, Michel, and Haro Seto. 2011. "Governance and the Root Causes of EMCs' Expatriated Private Savings." In *6th International Finance Conference: Crise Financière, Economie et Finances Internationales: Nouveaux Défis*, Sousse, Tunisia, Février 22–24.

Boyce, James K. 2004. "Aid, Conditionality, and War Economies." Economics Department Working Paper Series 72, University of University of Massachusetts, Amherst.

Boyce, James K., and Léonce Ndikumana. 2001. "Is Africa a Net Creditor? New Estimates of Capital Flight from Severely Indebted Sub-Saharan African Countries, 1970–96." *The Journal of Development Studies* 38 (2): 27–56.

Boyce, James K., and Léonce Ndikumana. 2002. "Public Debts and Private Assets: Explaining Capital Flight from Sub-Saharan African Countries." Economics Department Working Paper Series 91, University of Massachusetts, Amherst.

Boyce, James K., and Léonce Ndikumana. 2003. "Public Debts and Private Assets: Explaining Capital Flight from Sub-Saharan African Countries." *World Development* 31 (1): 107–130.

Boyce, James K., and Léonce Ndikumana. 2011. "Capital Flight from Sub-Saharan African Countries: Linkages with External Borrowing and Policy Options." *International Review of Applied Economics* 25 (2): 149–170.

Boyce, James K., and Léonce Ndikumana. 2013. *La Dette Odieuse de l'AFRIQUE: Comment l'Endettement et la Fuite des Capitaux ont Saigné un Continent*. Dakar: Amalion.

Buiter, Willem H., and Ivan Szegvari. 2002. "Capital Flight and Capital Outflows from Russia: Symptom, Cause and Cure." EBRD Working Paper No. 73, June.

Central Bank of Tunisia. 2017. Main Parameters of External Debt, December. https://www.bct.gov.tn/bct/siteprod/tableau_statistique_a.jsp?params=PL130040&la=an.

Cerra Valerie, Sweta Saxema, and Rishi Meenakshi. 2005. "Robbing the Riches: Capital Flight, Institutions, and Instability." IMF Working Paper WP/05/199. International Monetary Fund.

Collier, Paul, Hanke Hoeffler, and Catherine Pattillo. 1999. "Flight Capital as a Portfolio Choice." IMF Working Paper WP/99/171.

Collier, Paul, Hanke Hoeffler, and Catherine Pattillo. 2001. "Flight Capital as a Portfolio Choice." *World Bank Economic Review* 15 (1): 55–80.

Collier, Paul, Hanke Hoeffler, and Catherine Pattillo. 2004. "Africa's Exodus: Capital Flight and the Brain Drain as Portfolio Decisions." *Journal of African Economies* 13(Suppl. 2): ii15–ii54.

Corbo, Vittorio, and Lonardo Hernandez. 1998. "Private Capital Inflows and the Role of Economic Fundamentals." Banco Central de Chile.

Cuddington, John T. 1986. "Capital Flight: Estimates, Issues, and Explanations." Princeton Studies in International Finance, No. 58, Department of Economics, International Finance Section, Princeton University.

Cuddington, John T. 1987. "The Economic Determinants of Capital Flight: An Econometric Investigation." Washington, DC: Georgetown University, Economics Department.

Dooley, Michael. 1988. "Capital Flight: A Response to Differences in Financial Risks." *IMF Staff Papers* 35 (3): 422–436.

Dooley, Michael, and Kenneth M. Kletzer. 1994. "Capital Flight, External Debt and Domestic Policies." NBER Working Paper No. 4793.

El Mebashi, Kamal. 2013."La Prévention de la Corruption au Maroc, entre Discours et Réalité." *Pouvoir* 145 (2): 83–97.

Engle, Robert F., and C.W.J. Granger. 1987. "Co-integration and Error Correction: Representation, Estimation, and Testing." *Econometrica* 55 (2): 251–276.

Glaeser, Edward L., Rafael La Porta, Florencio Lopez de Silanes, and Andrei Shleifer. 2004. "Do Institutions Cause Growth." *Journal of Economic Growth* 9 (3): 271–303.

Global Financial Integrity. 2017. "Illicit Financial Flows." http://www.gfintegrity.org/issue/illicit-financial-flows/.

Groslambert, Bertrand, and Michel Bouchet. 2006. "The Persistence of Corruption and International Capital Flows." CERAM Working Paper, January.

Institute of International Economics. 1986. "Conference on Capital Flight and Third World Debt." Washington, DC, October 2–3.

Khan, Moshin S., and Nadeem Ul Haque. 1985. "Capital Flight from Developing Countries." *Finance & Development* 24 (1): 2–5.

Kharrat, Olfa, and Michel Bouchet. 2017. "Foreign Debts and Private Assets: Explaining Capital Flight from Tunisia." Submitted Paper. *The Journal of International Trade & Economic Development.*

Kharrat, Olfa, Michel Bouchet, and Rochdi Feki. 2015. "The Root Causes of Expatriated Private Savings: Governance, Oil Rent, and Macroeconomic Variables." ESC Sfax Working Paper, March.

Le, Quan Vu, and Paul J. Zak. 2006. "Political Risk and Capital Flight." *Journal of International Money and Finance* 25 (2): 308–329.

Le, Quan Vu, and Rishi Meenakshi. 2006. "Corruption and Capital Flight: An Empirical Assessment." *International Economic Journal* 20 (4): 523–540.

Leite, Carlos, and Jens Weidmann. 1999. "Does Mother Nature Corrupt: Natural Resources, Corruption and Economic Growth." IMF Working Paper, WP/99/85. International Monetary Fund.

Lessard, Donald R., and John Williamson (eds.). 1987. *Capital Flight and Third World Debt.* Washington, DC: Institute for International Economics.

Loungani, Prakash, and Paolo Mauro. 2000. "Capital Flight From Russia." Research Department, IMF Policy Discussion Paper PDP/00/6.

Luke, Paul. 1986. "Capital Flight from Latin America: 1981 to 1984." International Division, International Monetary Fund, March.

Mauro, Paolo. 1995. "Corruption and Growth." *Quarterly Journal of Economics* 110 (3): 681–712.

Mauro, Paolo. 2004. "The Persistence of Corruption and Slow Economic Growth." *International Monetary Fund Staff Papers* 51 (1): 1–18.

Mecagni, Mauro, and Rodolfo Maino. 2015. "Report on Dollarization in Sub-Saharan Africa." IMF Africa Department.

Morgan Guaranty Trust Company. 1986. "LDC Capital Flight." *World Financial Markets*, March.

Murphy, Kevin M., Andrei Shleifer, and Robert W. Vishny. 1991. "The Allocation of Talent: Implication for Growth." *The Quarterly Journal of Economics* 106 (3): 503–530.

Murphy, Kevin M., Andrei Shleifer, and Robert W. Vishny. 1993. "Why Is Rent-Seeking So Costly to Growth?" *American Economic Review* 83 (2): 409–414.

Mwase, Nkunde, and Francis Y. Kumah. 2015. "Revisiting the Concept of Dollarization: The Global Financial Crisis and Dollarization in Low-Income Countries." IMF Working Paper 15/12, January.

Ndikumana, Léonce. 2017. "Curtailing Capital Flight from Africa". Friedrich Ebert Stiftung. *International PolicyAnalysis.* Berlin.

Ndikumana, Léonce, and James K. Boyce. 2008. "New Estimates of Capital Flight from Sub-Saharan African Countries: Linkages with External Borrowing and Policy Options." Political Economy Research Institute, Working Paper 166.

O'Murchu, Cynthia. 2014. "Asset Tracing: Follow the Money." *Financial Times*, August 13.

Platt, Gordon. 2005. "Hung Out to Dry; Focus, Money Laundering." *Global Finance* 19 (11): 14–15.

Quispe-Agnoli, Myriam. 2002. "Costs and Benefits of Dollarization." Federal Reserve Bank of Atlanta, Research Department, Working Paper, March 4.

Reserve Bank of Zimbabwe. 2017. "External Statistics." December. http://www.rbz.co.zw/tablet/external-statistics.html?devicelock=tablet.

Reuters. 2011. "Greece Has 60 Billion Euros in Unpaid Taxes: EU Report." November 17.

Rodriguez, Miguel A. 1987. "Consequences of Capital Flight for Latin American Countries." In *Capital Flight and Third World Debt*, edited by Donald R. Lessard and John Williamson. Washington, DC: Institute for International Economics.

Rojas-Suarez, Liliana. 1990. "Risk and Capital Flight in Developing Countries." IMF Research Department, Working Paper WP/90/64, July.

Roubini, Nouriel, and Brad Setser. 2004. *Bailouts or Bail-ins? Responding to Financial Crises in Emerging Economies*. Washington, DC: Peterson Institute Press.
Schneider, Benu. 2003. "Measuring Capital Flight: Estimates and Interpretations." Working Paper 194, Overseas Development Institute.
Sheets, Nathan. 1995. "Capital Flight from the Countries in Transition: Some Theory and Empirical Evidence." International Finance Discussion Papers 514, Board of Governors of the Federal Reserve System, Washington, DC.
Shleifer, Andrei, and Robert W. Vishny. 1993. "Corruption." *The Quarterly Journal of Economics* 108 (3): 599–617.
Talahite, Fatiha. 2000. "Economie Administrée, Corruption et Engrenage de la Violence en Algérie." *Revue Tiers-Monde* 41 (161): 49–74.
Tanzi, Vito. 1998. "Corruption Around the World: Causes, Consequences, Scope, and Cures." *IMF Staff Papers* 45 (4): 559–594.
Tanzi, Vito, and Hamid Davoodi. 1997. "Corruption, Public Investment and Growth." IMF Working Paper WP/97/139. International Monetary Fund.
United Nations. 2003. "Resolution Adopted by the General Assembly-58/4." United Nations Convention against Corruption Fifty-Eighth Session, October 31.
Wei, Shang-Jin. 2000. "How Taxing Is Corruption on International Investors?" *Review of Economics and Statistics* 82 (1): 1–11.
Wei, Shang-Jin. 2001. "Domestic Crony Capitalism and International Fickle Capital: Is There a Connection?" *International Finance* 4 (1): 15–45.
Wei, Shang-Jin, and Yi Wu. 2002. "Negative Alchemy? Corruption, Composition of Capital Flows, and Currency Crises." In *Preventing Currency Crises in Emerging Markets*, edited by Sebastian Edwards and Jeffrey A. Frankel. Chicago: University of Chicago Press.
Whitehouse, Mark. 2015. "The Greek Damage, in One Chart." *Bloomberg*, June 29.
Wolfensohn, James D. 1996. "Address to the Board of Governors at the Annual Meetings of the World Bank and the International Monetary Fund." October 1. https://openknowledge.worldbank.org/bitstream/handle/10986/7304/343620PAPER0Vo101OFFICIAL0USE0ONLY1.pdf;sequence=1.
World Bank. 2017. "Combatting Corruption." *The World Bank Group*, September 26. http://www.worldbank.org/en/topic/governance/brief/anti-corruption.

15

Country Risk Mitigation Strategies

15.1 Introduction

The mitigation of Country Risk begins with essential questions. Which countries and regions are sources of Country Risk? Can these exposures be identified, compared, and measured? What are the available options to mitigate the risk? What are the costs of the mitigation in relation to the benefits? Will the mitigation strategies be effective? Can an opportunistic partnership with an official agency, be it national or multilateral, provide enough "umbrella" to reduce the risk exposure in a foreign country? Finally, what is the range of guarantees and risk protection devices that is provided by the market and by private and public institutions? These and other related questions are continuously being asked by organizations that think about Country Risk. Posing these questions, exploring the answers, and making adjustments—these are essential aspects of managing Country Risk.

15.2 Identifying Country Risk Exposure

How does an organization develop a strategy to mitigate Country Risk? First, it must identify the various sources of exposure across all products and services and across all subsidiaries and affiliates. This is not easy and can be a particular challenge for large global entities that maintain different IT systems for different businesses. After this step, an organization must aggregate the individual exposures to develop a comprehensive profile of

M. H. Bouchet et al., *Managing Country Risk in an Age of Globalization*,
https://doi.org/10.1007/978-3-319-89752-3_15

Country Risk, including the countries and regions where it resides. In so doing, an organization may also rank such exposures, taking into account the frequency and severity of potential problems (as not all components of Country Risk pose similar threats).

In assessing exposures to Country Risk, organizations must also seek to identify the less obvious or indirect exposures. When a bank makes a loan to a company incorporated in an emerging market country, the maximum potential for loss is known—this is the amount of the loan, plus any legal or administrative costs that may be required to pursue a claim in the event the borrower defaults on the loan. There may, however, be other exposures to Country Risk that are more difficult to identify. Suppose, for example, that a bank provides a loan to a company and, subsequently, the bank learns that the company sold equipment to terrorist groups. Here the harm can involve damage to an organization's reputation, which could further attract the attention of regulators and cause clients to seek services from other banks. One example is the case of the Franco-Swiss cement giant LafargeHolcim in the second half of 2017, after being accused of financial links to jihadist groups in Syria in 2013 and 2014. In a clear statement, the company acknowledged money transfers to armed groups in Syria, including the Islamic State, to keep operations up and running at its Jalabiya cement works in northern Syria. It said, "It appears from the investigation that the local company provided funds to third parties to work out arrangements with a number of these armed groups, including sanctioned parties, in order to maintain operations and ensure a safe passage of employees and supplies to and from the plant" (LafargeHolcim 2017). In this case, risk mitigation took the form of several press releases, legal and public relations advisory services, a thorough internal review, and the decision of the board of directors to create a new Ethics, Integrity, and Risk Committee, supervised by a member of the Executive Committee.

Mitigation of reputation risk can also be illustrated by the lawsuit against Chevron and the French oil company Total with regard to oil and gas exploration projects in Burma. In 2002, Myanmar refugees filed a lawsuit against Total and his senior executives in Brussels Magistrates' Tribunal, pursuant to a 1993 Belgian law of universal jurisdiction, to hear cases for certain serious crimes, even those committed outside Belgium. The plaintiffs alleged that Total had been complicit in crimes of forced labor committed by the Myanmar military junta in the course of the construction and operation of the Yadana Gas Pipeline. The plaintiffs alleged that Total provided moral and financial support to the Myanmar military government with full knowledge that its support resulted in human rights abuses by the military.

The Belgian authorities declared the "case closed" in March 2008, dropping the case against Total (Business and Human Rights Resource Center 2014). Total's risk mitigation strategy led to a combination of denials, declarations, and compensations. When the company learned of forced-labor cases involving the Burmese pipeline, "Total paid compensation immediately, on humanitarian grounds" (Walt 2010). Regarding the UN accusations of Burma's government of ethnic cleansing in oil and gas-rich Rakhine Basin, and after years of pressure from activist investors, Chevron declared in 2017 that "it would work for a business environment that respects human rights while continuing to work with other US companies and the government to promote the value of US investment in Myanmar and the need to foster a business environment that respects human rights" (Masud 2017). Chevron adopted a Human Rights Policy in 2009 and it set up a Global Issues Committee to adhere to the United Nations Guiding Principles on Business and Human Rights and to conduct business in a socially and environmentally responsible manner, respecting the law and universal human rights to benefit the communities where it works. In 2016, Chevron reported on the corporate responsibility efforts it had undertaken in Myanmar in accordance with the US Department of State's Responsible Investment Reporting Requirements for Burma (Chevron 2017).

Box 15.1. Reputational Risk: A Practitioner's Perspective

Financial services organizations focus on two main types of risk: financial and non-financial. Financial risks include market risk, credit risk, and liquidity risk. These have been measured and managed using a multitude of tools and approaches. Non-financial risks are less readily visible, but no less relevant. Among this group, reputational risk is receiving heightened attention by risk management practitioners.

The notion underlying reputational risk is a long-standing one. Niccolo Machiavelli stressed the value of a good reputation and the adverse consequences of a poor one. That was an important theme in his now famous work of political theory, *The Prince,* written in 1513. Five hundred years later, the same principle is as relevant as ever in the today's global economic system.

Reputational risk can be broadly defined as the potential for damage to an institution's brand and reputation and the associated implications for earnings, capital, and liquidity. Reputational risk can arise in many ways and under many circumstances, including both actions and inactions. In each case, the outcome is perceived by stakeholders to be inappropriate, unethical, or inconsistent with the values and beliefs of the organization or the prevailing values and beliefs as reflected in market practice. The impact of reputational damage can be material, taking into account lost clients, lost revenue, fines, corrective action, and other costs.

The assessment of reputational risk is particularly challenging because of its intangible and evolving nature. Nevertheless, three main criteria should be considered as potential sources of reputational risk.

1. **The nature, structure, and terms of a transaction or product**
An entity can experience reputational damage by executing transactions or selling products which may be perceived as inappropriate or inconsistent with market practice. An obvious example is the crisis in the US subprime mortgage market, which in turn gave rise to the Global Financial Crisis. Financial institutions, seeking higher profits, created and sold highly complex, synthetic products which were linked to the performance of low-quality real estate loans. The sellers of these products did not fully disclose the risks to the buyers and, in some cases, did not even adequately understand the risks themselves. In the aftermath of the crisis, reputational damage was sustained by a range of market participants, including investment banks, securitization intermediaries, credit rating agencies, and investors. Ten years later, public confidence in the banking sector remains low, despite the measures to restore trust by local governments, international financial institutions, and regulators.
2. **Engaging in or affiliating with questionable or inappropriate behavior**
The Greek government, for example, consistently made misleading statements about the state of its public finances. These were knowingly tolerated by institutional investors and supranational organizations. These actions ultimately sparked the Greek crisis in 2009 and tarnished the country's reputation in the capital markets, the European Union, and the international community. Another example was the Libor scandal in 2008 in which employees at several financial institutions manipulated the Libor benchmark interest rate.
3. **Environmental and social considerations**
A company can suffer reputational damage by engaging in behavior which can have a negative environmental or social impact. One example in November of 2017 were the labor practices of Foxconn, one of Apple's main suppliers of its flagship iPhone product. Foxconn was accused of hiring under-aged workers in Zhengzhou, China in order to meet the increased demand for pre-launch of the iPhone X. This activity was clearly inconsistent with the entrepreneurial, innovative, and "social conscience" image of Apple that was carefully cultivated over many years by the company's founder Steve Jobs.

The management of reputational risk consists of two elements: preventive action and corrective action. An organization's efforts on these initiatives will be a reflection of its strategic goals as well as its fundamental cultural values. These should be aligned with broadly accepted social values, including ethical behaviors, integrity, and honesty.

After the Global Financial Crisis, global financial services firms have made progress in better understanding and managing reputational risk. Vigilance, however, remains appropriate. Losing a reputation is infinitely easier than acquiring it. This will be an important area for risk management practitioners.

Alexandre Seon, Senior Credit Risk Officer—Deutsche Bank (Switzerland)—Business Aligned Risk Management EMEA.

Other exposures may be so-called "correlated" risk. A default, for example, occurs in one country, which gives rise to defaults by other entities, which further causes financial institutions to experience vulnerability. Other exposures may be the result of scenarios that were not considered. An industrial company, for example, expands manufacturing in foreign markets in anticipation of substantial growth. The growth occurs, but commodity prices fall, reducing incentives for mining companies to bring commodities to market. Demand for heavy equipment falls. This effect offsets the benefits of growth in foreign markets, resulting in no earnings growth. As we have noted before, Country Risk arises in different forms and in different locations. So how do organizations take only the intended types and amounts of Country Risk?

15.3 Ways to Mitigate Country Risk

There are various ways to mitigate Country Risk. Some involve costs that need to be carefully assessed in relation to their intended benefits. Some give rise to new issues, such as dependency on a trading counterparty, supplier, vendor, or guarantor. Some may not be available in all markets or may address only a narrow subset of Country Risk.

One traditional way an organization can mitigate Country Risk is by being cautious about being exposed to it. However, avoiding any Country Risk is not an effective strategy either. The astute approach is for an organization to carefully assess its Country Risk and incur only those components and amounts of such risk that are wanted. This process involves extensive evaluation by an organization's risk experts and senior management, often in consultation with its board of directors. This does not, in retrospect, always result in the correct answer in that future involves uncertainty and, as we know, outcomes can never be fully known in advance. It is nonetheless preferable to try to assess Country Risk rather than to fear it and attempt to fully avoid it.

Other ways to mitigate Country Risk involve financial instruments that enable certain financial exposures to be hedged or neutralized. This is a complicated undertaking that gives rise to other serious implications that must be carefully considered, including costs, accounting treatment, and valuation of the transactions (as well as other credit, market, and operational risks). Other approaches involve guarantees by external private entities, public agencies, or multilateral organizations.

15.4 Traditional Approaches

What follows are what might be described as "traditional" approaches for the mitigation of Country Risk. In all these approaches, of course, it is important to understand and challenge all relevant assumptions.

15.4.1 Analysis and Economic Intelligence

Engage in a careful assessment of Country Risks based on rigorous research of new and resurgent challenges in countries and regions. This remains the most advisable approach that an organization can pursue (see also Chapters 4 and 5). As stressed throughout this book, access to updated and reliable information is the best tool for mitigation of Country Risk. Transforming information into economic intelligence—analyzing data with a historical perspective and cross-country context—will give country risk managers the means to prepare and implement strategies to mitigate Country Risk. This process requires an in-depth understanding of the applicable markets, countries, and regions (as well as global trends). This usually requires a combination of internal staff country risk analysts and external advisors.

15.4.2 Credit Risk Assessment

Evaluate the entities involved in transactions or activities that give rise to Country Risk. This includes an assessment of an entity's ability and willingness to fulfill its obligations. The notion of willingness is important in that ability to fulfill an obligation is not relevant if an entity does not want to fulfill its obligations under a contract.

15.4.3 Scenarios

Assess plausible scenarios, even extreme or infrequent ones. Ask, "What if?" Suppose a major power plant in a region fails? Suppose there are extreme weather conditions? What circumstances could disrupt an essential supply chain? Your existing data and models reflect the exposures you have now. You want to know what exposures you will have if the world changes quickly.

15.4.4 Risk Limits

Impose measurable limits on exposures to Country Risk. Such limits can take different forms and apply to different entities, including suppliers, vendors, and trading counterparties. Limits may differ based on the term or length of the exposure or other characteristics (or the credit rating or internal risk rating of an entity).

15.4.5 Risk Diversification

Country risk mitigation strategy involves diversifying two risks. First, the company or the fund should aim at regional and economic diversification of its country risk portfolio. Second, it also should diversify the organizations it depends upon, including banks, trading counterparties, suppliers, and vendors. Country risk managers must remember the often-used expression in the field of risk management: "Don't put all your eggs in one basket." Nobel laureate Harry Markowitz defined the rule of portfolio diversification in 1952 as a strategy that seeks to combine portfolio assets with returns that are less than perfectly positively correlated in an effort to lower portfolio risk without sacrificing return. In-country risk management, the risk of regional crisis contamination must be kept in mind as well as the spillover effect of rating agencies' downgrading.

Organizations especially need to diversify entities in their supply chain so as to reduce vulnerability to unusual but plausible circumstances such as earthquakes, industrial accidents, transit strikes, and civil unrest. Moreover, entities that enter into derivatives or foreign exchange transactions usually make use of several different counterparties or may limit the exposure based on its term (i.e., length of time outstanding). One may, for example, limit the exposure to a guarantor and diversify the number of guarantors.

15.5 Market's Risk Mitigation Devices: Credit Default Swaps, Collateral, and Master Netting Agreements

Beyond traditional approaches to country risk mitigation, one can mention several financial market instruments.

15.5.1 Credit Default Swaps (CDS)

Credit Default Swaps (CDS) have been already discussed in Chapter 13. A CDS is a form of OTC derivative transaction that enables an entity to purchase protection for a specified term against the default of any entity or portfolio of entities. One party pays a fee, either at the outset of the transaction or over its term, and is entitled to receive a payment of a predetermined amount if there is a default by the specified entity or entities. The fees for these transactions are determined by market conditions, which can change quickly. The use of these financial instruments must be carefully understood, as we have learned from the Global Financial Crisis of 2008. If not used with a full understanding of all the relevant risks, they can give rise to serious problems. If used for appropriate purposes, however, they can be effective ways to mitigate certain risks.

15.5.2 Collateral or Performance Assurance

One form of risk mitigation is a requirement by a party to provide credit support in the form of collateral or other assets to secure its performance in a transaction or group of transactions. Such collateral often involves assets that can be easily sold, such as government bonds in markets where there is ample liquidity. Such exchanges of collateral are usual in the OTC derivatives transactions. The obligation to post collateral may be for one or both parties to the transaction. The amount of collateral is based on the market value of the transactions, which can result in transfers of collateral from one party to the other on a regular basis, sometimes daily. If one party fails to make a payment on a derivatives transaction or fails to post the required collateral, the collateral holder can sell the collateral to cover any amounts due or losses incurred. Other forms of collateral may be comprised of less liquid assets such as real estate, trademarks, patents, or equity interests in businesses.

15.5.3 Master Netting Agreements

Master netting agreements are legal contracts used in foreign exchange and OTC derivatives transactions to reduce the credit exposure that the parties may have to each other. These agreements can apply to a wide range of foreign exchange or derivatives transactions which are used to manage different types of financial risk, including interest rate risk, currency risk, commodity risk, and credit risk. These agreements are designed to allow parties to transactions to determine exposures for individual contracts on a net basis, taking into account the market values of all the transactions between the parties. The standard form of agreement is the version developed by the International Swaps and Derivatives Association (ISDA). This agreement establishes a common framework that can cover all transactions between two legal entities. If a party to a transaction defaults or fails to make a payment on one transaction, then all the transactions are terminated and their current market values are determined. The amounts owing and owed are "netted" against each other to determine one single amount owed or received. The use of master netting agreements can result in significant reductions of counterparty exposure between the parties. A key assumption is that parties can enforce their rights under the master agreement in the event a party defaults and subsequently declares bankruptcy.

15.6 Cofinancing and Guarantee Operations

15.6.1 Cofinancing Operations

One can distinguish between two categories of cofinancing transactions, with private and public agencies. Public agencies can be national or multilateral organizations. Multilateral development banks play an important role in mitigating key aspects of Country Risk. First, they provide private investors with comprehensive information regarding the potential for loss or gain in emerging market countries. As we observed in Chapters 4 and 5, International Financial Institutions (IFIs) are a key source of intelligence-gathering to assess broad measures of country risk exposure, including overall external indebtedness, macroeconomic strength, liquidity, and solvency risk. Second, IFIs are a major source of balance of payments financing. In addition to providing funding, they also monitor practices relating to spending, taxation, and market-based reforms. Third, in addition to direct lending, IFIs play an important role in mobilizing sources of financing from public and private sector lenders. As such, they have a catalytic or multiplier effect.

Cofinancing is a major source of country risk mitigation, particularly in the infrastructure sector. It refers to funds committed by partners, export credit agencies (ECAs), or private sources to specific funded projects. Creditors participating in cofinancing receive benefits from the IFIs, including analysis of projects, oversight of implementation, administration of loans until their full repayment, and preferred creditor status. The four principal techniques for cofinancing include (i) direct financial participation under loan programs; (ii) guarantees of longer maturities; (iii) contingent participation in longer maturities; and (iv) sale of participation or complementary loan contracts. These techniques provide commercial banks with varying degrees of financial protection.

Box 15.2: The World Bank's Credit Enhancement and Cofinancing Program

The World Bank's Cofinancing program refers to arrangements under which the World Bank provides funding or acts as a guarantor of loans provided by third-party lenders for a particular project or program. Cofinancing—either through government agencies or multilateral financial institutions—constitutes the largest source of credit for World Bank assisted operations. The World Bank's objectives for cofinancing are to:

- Mobilize resources to help developing countries getting market access to capital in amounts and under terms that they could not obtain otherwise;
- Establish closer coordination with donors on country programs, policies, and investment priorities; and
- Provide donors with cost-effective ways to extend assistance, making use of the World Bank's experience and capacity to manage projects and programs.

Official cofinancing can be channeled in two forms—"parallel" or "joint"—each of which has distinct procurement arrangements. Under parallel cofinancing, the World Bank and the cofinance parties each provide separate financing of goods and services in agreed proportions and in conformity with other procurement guidelines set forth by the bank. Under joint cofinancing, the parties finance the same contracts in a project under agreed-upon proportions.

The International Finance Corporation (IFC), a member of the World Bank Group, has pioneered a range of innovative instruments to mobilize private sector financing toward infrastructure projects in developing countries. IFC was established in 1956 to promote private sector development as a means to reduce poverty. It is owned and governed by its member countries, although its Executive Vice-President and CEO have traditionally been selected from a European country. By joining hands into IFC-financing of such high-priority projects such as water, energy, and transportation, and telecommunications projects, investors benefit from IFC's sixty-year track record of investing in emerging markets around the world, from its global infrastructure expertise, and from IFC's local knowledge and presence in over 100 countries. Historically, the primary platform for mobilizing third-party financing into IFC loans has been through syndicated lending with commercial or public creditors. Since inception, this vehicle has mobilized over USD 50 billion, with approximately half of those funds flowing to infrastructure (Mapila et al. 2017). In 2013, IFC launched its Managed Co-Lending Portfolio Program for Infrastructure. This program is a loan-syndications initiative that enables investors to participate passively in IFC's senior loan portfolio and to benefit from IFC's senior creditor status. This initiative was launched in partnership with China's State Administration of Foreign Exchange (SAFE). The program has committed more than USD 1.6 billion in forty seven projects across thirty countries. It was extended in 2017 to address numerous infrastructure financing challenges that inhibit the flow of resources to emerging markets. The program provides combined financing from insurance companies, project origination and credit enhancement from IFC, and support from public sector donors (IFC 2016).

Several parties have raised the issue of whether financial participation of multilateral development banks does prompt private investors to inject more risky equity capital in emerging market banks. For instance, Wezel (2004) of Deutsche Bank examined cofinancing transactions that involved the IFC and the European Bank for Reconstruction and Development (EBRD). He concluded that, in the German case, financial participation of multilateral agencies in investment projects did have a positive impact on the risk exposure that investors were willing to bear. In particular, the study measures investors' equity capital that, given a country's risk profile, can be deemed "at risk." This "risk exposure"—which is called "capital-at-risk"—is a product of the absolute amount of investment multiplied with the country's probability of sovereign default, which itself is derived by linking the sovereign risk rating of the country to global historical five-year default rates on government bonds. The "umbrella" that is provided by multilateral institutions such as IFC and EBRD may lead to moral hazard on the part of investors and thus to possible misallocation of capital.

15.6.2 Guarantees

A guarantee is an agreement by a party (a guarantor) to support the obligations of another party, often a subsidiary, on terms that are usually absolute and unconditional. A common structure is that a parent agrees to support the obligations of a subsidiary for the purposes of a particular transaction or group of transactions. The type of obligations covered by a guarantee may include foreign currency transactions (i.e., spot, forward, and options), OTC derivatives, loans, payments for receivables, and other financial obligations. A subsidiary, while it may act on the basis of its own financial strength for its usual commercial activities, may have considerably less capital than a parent. It may be prudent for a lender or trading counterparty to obtain a guarantee to protect against credit exposures in the event the subsidiary defaults or fails to fulfill its obligations. The benefit of the guarantee depends on the ability and willingness of the guarantor to make payment when called upon to do so.

The IFIs, including the World Bank, have developed a dynamic guarantee program for commercial debt financing that aims at being a multiplier of financing for emerging market countries as well as an enhancer of the quality of external financing conditions. In July 1989, in parallel with the implementation of the Brady Plan, the World Bank initiated an Expanded Cofinancing Operations program. Known as ECOs, the objective was to assist borrowers in gaining or broadening their access to the international capital markets, especially through private placements and public bond offerings. Credit enhancements under the ECO program can take various forms:

- Guarantees of commercial loans in the context of financing for World Bank approved projects;
- Guarantees on medium and long-term bond issues;
- Contingent obligations such as bond issues with an option to "put" them to the World Bank under predetermined circumstances; and
- Support for limited recourse project finance.

The World Bank's guarantee program covers lenders against the risk of government non-performance of its contractual obligations to a specific project, such as the risk of nonpayment by a government or its affiliates, change in law/regulatory risk, and expropriation risk. For instance, in October 2016, Ghana issued a USD 1 billion 144A Reg S registered international bonds due 2030 ("Ghana 2030 bond"), which included a USD 400 million partial guarantee by the International Development Association ("IDA") arm of the World Bank. This credit support also represented the reintroduction by the World Bank of the application of partial guarantees to public bonds (World Bank-Rothschild 2016). Overall, World Bank guarantees have proved to be an effective instrument to mobilize commercial financing for development purposes. The multiplier and "catalytic" effects can be measured by observing that thirty four guaranteed transactions utilizing USD 4 billion in IBRD/IDA commitments supported mobilization of nearly USD 13 billion of commercial financing plus roughly USD 19 billion of public financing (World Bank 2017).

Box 15.3: The World Bank's Guarantee Program to Support Commercial Debt Financing

Through its Guarantee Program, the World Bank aims to:

- Mobilize private investment (equity and debt) for strategic projects or sector support
- Mitigate key government-related risks to enable financial viability and bankability
- Enhance the credit quality of sovereign and sub-sovereign obligors to achieve acceptable or affordable levels
- Reduce costs and improve financing terms for projects and governments
- Ensure long-term sustainability of projects

Main Features: First, World Bank Guarantees provide "AAA" risk mitigation with respect to obligations due from government, political subdivisions, or government-owned entities to private investors (e.g., equity, debt, and contractors) and to foreign public entities on cross-border projects; and second, risk mitigation is of a partial nature and aims to promote balanced risk allocation between government and private investors, or between public entities in cross-border projects

World Bank Guarantees are flexible and adaptable to multiple contractual structures; tenors may extend to up to thirty five years, and pricing is concessional

World Bank Guarantees are suitable for:

- Domestic or international investors
- Foreign or local currency obligations
- Domestic or international markets
- Project financing, corporate financing, and project, corporate or sovereign bonds

Risks Covered: Contractual risk (e.g., payment risk and performance risk); Regulatory risk (e.g., change in law, negation or cancelation of license, and tariff adjustments); Currency risk (e.g., convertibility and transferability); and political risk (e.g., expropriation and war and civil disturbance).

For Private Investors, the advantages of World Bank Guarantees include:

1. Improvement of the overall credit quality of the investment through the partial use of an "AAA" rated instrument to mitigate key risks
2. Reduction or elimination of key risk drivers which are beyond the control of private investors
3. Mitigation of counterparty risk with governments, political subdivisions, or government-owned entities
4. Strong support to maintain or open new markets despite credit downturns
5. Project bankability, sustainability, and replicability.

For Governments, the main advantages include:

1. Facilitate Public–Private Partnerships
2. Attract private sector investors to strategic sectors requiring large and long-term investments
3. Diversification of financing sources beyond development financing
4. Reduction of project costs and cost of commercial financing to affordable levels

5. Reduction of government risk exposure through sharing with private sector investors
6. Reduction of fiscal burden by reducing the need for direct government guarantees
7. Project bankability, sustainability, and replicability.

In addition, the IFIs provide guarantees for encouraging trade between developed and developing countries. As part of its mission, the IFC maintains a Global Trade Finance Program that guarantees trade payment obligations for banks in emerging markets countries. Participating in this program have been over 275 banks representing ninety countries. These guarantees are transaction specific and may relate to a range of obligations, including letters of credit, trade-related promissory notes, accepted drafts, bills of exchange, bid and performance bonds, and advance payment guarantees. The program has covered in an excess of USD 5 billion of obligations. In 2016, the organization had an average outstanding balance of USD 2.8 billion in trade finance (IFC 2017).

15.7 The Risk Mitigation Objectives of Regional Development Banks: The Role of the Asian Development Bank (ADB)

To catalyze capital flows into and within its developing member countries for eligible projects, the ADB extends guarantees for eligible projects which enable financing partners to transfer certain risks that they cannot easily absorb or manage on their own to ADB. The regional development agency guarantees infrastructure projects, financial institutions, capital market investors, and trade finance, and cover a wide variety of debt instruments. Guarantees may cover either comprehensive range of financial risk or a more limited scope, including political risk. Guarantees can be provided when ADB has a direct or indirect participation in a project or related sector, through a loan, equity investment or technical assistance. ADB offers two primary guarantee products—a political risk guarantee and a credit risk guarantee—both designed to mitigate risk exposure of financing partners:

Political risk guarantees are designed to facilitate cofinancing by providing financing partners with coverage against specifically defined political (or sovereign) risks. ADB's political risk guarantee (PRG) is primarily designed to facilitate private sector development, either through public or private sector projects. PRGs are well suited where commercial lenders are prepared to accept commercial (or credit) risks of a project, but not the political risks. Risks covered include transfer restriction, expropriation, political violence, contract disputes, and non-honoring of a sovereign obligation or guarantee (Asian Development Bank 2017).

Similarly to the World Bank's guarantee program, ADB's partial credit guarantee aims to provide credit guarantees to lenders of most forms of debt. These include commercial bank loans, loans made by shareholders, loans guaranteed by shareholders or third parties, capital market debt instruments, bonds, financial leases, letters of credit, promissory notes, and bills of exchange. Political risk guarantee covers nonpayment by the borrower or issuer on the guaranteed portion of the principal and interest due. This guarantee product is principally applied to financial services and capital markets (e.g., banking, leasing, insurance, and funds); and infrastructure (e.g., power, transportation, water supply and waste treatment, and telecommunications). Partial credit guarantees can be applied to loans or other debt instruments issued by private and public sector projects (limited recourse financings), public–private partnerships, corporates, as well as (sub) sovereign entities.

15.8 Bilateral Guarantee of OECD Countries

Developed countries provide risk mitigation devises to stimulate FDI, as well as trade flows in developing countries, with several objectives including geopolitical influence, bilateral trade and investment stimulation, and developmental support. Vietnam, for instance, has benefited from a dynamic flow of credit guarantees under the aegis of the ADB, in partnership with bilateral guarantee agencies, including from Japan and Canada. From 1970 to the end of 2016, cumulative direct value-added official cofinancing for Vietnam amounted to USD 4.6 billion for fifty four investment projects and USD 115 million for ninety one technical assistance projects. Cumulative commercial cofinancing for Vietnam amounted to USD 5.23 billion for two investment projects. Vietnam is also a good example of guarantee partnership between a multilateral institution and a national government. In 2016, Vietnam received loan cofinancing of USD 305.5 million from the Government of Japan for the Greater Mekong Subregion Ben Luc–Long Thanh Expressway–Tranche 2, as well as grant cofinancing of USD 1.8 million from the Government of Canada for the Greater Mekong Subregion Flood and Drought Risk Management and Mitigation (Asian Development Bank 2017).

Bond guarantees are also a powerful instrument for improving capital market access in that the Country Risk is transferred from the issuing country to the guarantor. Vietnam's government announced by year-end of 2017 an ambitious strategy—"2030 vision"—to stimulate the local bond market by strengthening the legal framework and providing better information to investors. To help Vietnam developing a fully functioning bond market, the ADB's Credit Guarantee and Investment Facility (CGIF) plays a critical role as an incubator of its fledgling capital market. The CGIF, which guarantees local currency debt issued by companies in several Asian countries, has already backed three Vietnamese ten-year bond sales that amount to 6.35tn VND—the equivalent of USD 280 million, with a fixed rate yield at or above 8% (Noonan 2017). ADB's risk mitigation support aims at attracting the interest of a wider range of private and institutional investors while extending the average maturities of bond issues. Beyond Vietnam, the CGIF is aiming at more bond issue guarantees, including Cambodia's nascent domestic bond market.

Elsewhere, and as discussed in Chapter 12, the commitment of official creditors vis à vis Tunisia helped the country to retain market access in the wake of the Arab Spring turmoil of 2011 thanks to a number of country risk mitigation instruments. In June of 2016, Tunisia signed a loan guarantee agreement with the United States to access up to USD 500 million from international capital markets with enhanced financial conditions. That was the third US loan guarantee to Tunisia. The earlier guarantees for USD 485 million in 2012 and USD 500 million in 2014 were successful in facilitating Tunisian access to global capital markets. Since the 2011 Arab Spring, the United States has provided more than USD 750 million in other types of foreign assistance to Tunisia. In addition, Japan has provided Tunisia with country risk mitigation support under the framework of bond guarantees, in essence shifting the Maghreb country's credit risk to Japan's Ministry of Finance. The Tunisian central bank issued three bonds in the Japanese market—USD 473 million in 2012, USD 376 million in 2013, and USD 250 million in 2014, with the Japan Bank's guarantee after the first four years. In October 2014, Tunisia issued USD 825 million ten-year bonds on the domestic Japanese market, guaranteed by the state-owned Japan Bank for International Cooperation, with an impressive low coupon of only 1.61% (Reuters 2014).

Likewise, a number of OECD countries' export guarantee agencies have provided Tunisia with official guarantees to facilitate dynamic trade flows with European trade partners. Finally, Tunisia's government coupled with bilateral and multilateral donors organized a major financial support meeting in November 2016, named "Tunisia 2020 Conference." The objective was to set up a range of risk mitigation devises and external financing commitments

	Gifts	Credits	Conditions
Saudi Arabia	220	1.800	Invest.
Koweit		1.100	5 years
Qatar		2.800	LT loans
Turkey		220	BCT deposits
Switzerland		560	7 years
Canada		50	4 year Invest.
IEB		2.500	4 years
IEB Gazoduc		380	Invest.
France AFD		3.000	4 years
FADES		3.300	30 years
EU AMF	500		M/LT
France	25	420	4 years
KFW	30	260	
AfDB		1.500	4 years
AfDB		309	
IDB		4.400	5 years
IBRD		2.200	LT loans
EBRD		650	LT loans
IMF		2.900	4 years
TOTAL	**775**	**28.349**	**29.124**

Fig. 15.1 Tunisia's expected official financing support 2016–2020 (*Source* Authors' calculation with data from national agencies and multilateral organizations)

to mobilize more than USD 15 billion in pledges and promises of investment. These investments allowed the government to kick off the first phase of the five-year development plan 2016–2020 that is targeted at priority infrastructure projects. Figure 15.1 provides a comprehensive picture of the financing commitments for Tunisia over the 2016–2020 period.

15.9 The Country Risk Mitigation Role of the Multilateral Investment Guarantee Agency (MIGA)

The Multilateral Investment Guarantee Agency (MIGA) is a member of the World Bank Group that was created in 1988. Its objective is to facilitate the flow of foreign direct investment to developing and transition economies. The agency can provide insurance coverage for up to fifteen years (in some cases twenty), which may increase the tenor of loans available to investors. In fulfilling this objective, it acts as a guarantor to investors and lenders by ensuring eligible projects against a number of losses relating to the following Country Risks:

- Currency inconvertibility and transfer restrictions (i.e., losses arising from an investor's inability to legally convert local currency payments, capital, profits, and royalties, into hard currency and/or to transfer hard currency outside the host country)
- Expropriation without due compensation
- War, terrorism, and civil disturbance
- Breach of contracts (i.e., losses arising from the government's repudiation of a contract with the investor)
- Non-honoring of financial obligations.

In a risky country such as Iraq, MIGA provided a guarantee of USD 10.4 million for an investment by Alcatel-Lucent International, involving the provision of high speed mobile broadband data and Internet service, with a coverage for a period of up to three years against the risks of transfer restriction, expropriation, and war and civil disturbance (MIGA 2015).

15.10 The Role of National Risk Guarantee Agencies: The Overseas Private Investment Corporation

The Overseas Private Investment Corporation (OPIC) is a US government agency that was established in 1971 to help US businesses invest in overseas markets. It is backed by the full faith and credit of the United States. It provides direct loans and guarantees. When private insurance is not available, it further offers political risk insurance (PRI) in amounts up to USD 250 million against losses in more than 160 developing and post-conflict countries. Coverage is offered for small and large investments that provide positive developmental benefits. The main areas of political risk covered by the guarantees are as follows:

- War, civil strife, coups, and other acts of politically motivated violence, including terrorism;
- Expropriation, including abrogation, repudiation, and/or impairment of contract and other improper host government interference; and
- Restrictions on the conversion and transfer of local currency.

OPIC can offer up to USD 400 million in total support for any one single project. OPIC can provide coverage for equity investments, guarantees from a parent company, third-party loans, technical assistance agreements, cross-border leases, and certain other forms of direct investment (https://www.opic.gov).

15.11 Export Credit Agencies (ECAs)

15.11.1 US Export Guarantee Program

The United States Department of Agriculture, through its Foreign Agricultural Service, maintains an Export Guarantee Program (GSM-102). Its purpose is to encourage commercial exports of US agricultural products. The program is available to exporters of a wide range of processed products, intermediate products, and bulk products. The guarantees for the program are issued by Commodity Credit Corporation (CCC), which is an entity owned and operated by the US government. It was created to stabilize, support, and protect farm income and prices. The guarantees support credit extended by private sector financial institutions (or, less commonly, by the exporter itself) for the sale of US food and agriculture products by foreign importers. The CCC is administered by the Farm Services Agency of the US Department of Agriculture. The amount of credit available is based on counties and regions.

15.11.2 Compagnie Française d'Assurance pour le Commerce Extérieur (Coface)

Coface provides a comprehensive line of credit insurance to protect companies against potential nonpayment by their customers. It provides coverage in approximately 200 countries. It was founded in 1946 and privatized in 1994. It is now a publicly listed company that is 44% owned by Natixis, a subsidiary of BPCE, the second-largest banking institution in France. BPCE is rated AA—by Fitch and A2 by Moody's. Coface provides protection against a wide range of Country Risks. This includes changes in legislation, contract breaches, expropriation, nationalization, armed conflict, labor unrest, and acts of terrorism. If there is an arrear in payment, Coface steps in to collect the receivable from the buyer. The company has extensive collection practices in order to maximize the potential for recovery. This "backed by Coface" protection makes use of experts that operate on a global basis to analyze the strength of companies and anticipate payment arrears.

Through its continuous review process, it provides feedback on risks relating to its extensive portfolio of customers. In 2017, Coface transferred its export credit activities on behalf of the French State to Bpifrance Assurance Export. The transfer is a "fundamental change" in the French export credit support system that aims to provide small and medium-sized companies with easier access to export credit while offering a "one-stop-shop" to respond to their growth challenges, particularly in international markets. Coface remains active as a private company offering other insurance products, credit rating and business services, debt collection, recovery solutions and receivable management services (http://www.coface-usa.com/About-Coface).

15.11.3 The Berne Union and Export Credit Agencies (ECAs)

The Berne Union is an international non-profit trade association that serves the interests of global credit export banks and investment assurance entities. Its eighty-four members include government-backed ECAs, private credit and political risk insurers and multilateral institutions across the globe who provide insurance products, guarantees, and types of direct financing in the support of cross-border trade. Members offer protection for exporting companies, investors, and financial institutions against losses as a result of commercial credit risks (buyer default) and political risks (currency inconvertibility; political violence; confiscation or expropriation of foreign assets) (https://www.berneunion.org).

Box 15.4. The Ten Major ECAs in the OECD Countries

- Austria: Oesterreichische Kontrollbank AG
- Belgium: Office National du Ducroire
- Canada: Export Development Corporation (CDC)
- France: Compagnie Française d'Assurance pour le Commerce Extérieur (COFACE)
- Germany: Hermes Kreditverischerungs AG
- Italy: Servizi Assicurativi del Commercio Estero (SACE)
- Spain: Compañia Española de Seguros de Crédito a la Exportación, SA (CESCE)
- Japan: Export-Import Insurance Department
- United Kingdom: Exports Credit Guarantee Department (ECDG)
- United States: Export-Import Bank of the United States (EXIM)

15.12 Dispute Resolution

Dispute resolution can be included in the range of risk mitigation instruments, given that it performs a role of risk reduction in the midst of a dispute with a foreign country. The International Centre for the Settlement of Investment Disputes (ICSID) was established in 1966 as an independent organization to promote dispute resolution arising from international investment. It is affiliated with the World Bank Group, although it has a separate charter established by an international treaty. The organization provides facilities for conciliation and arbitration of international investment disputes. It is the only global arbitration organization that offers a specialized forum to resolve disputed relating to international investing. It has a staff of approximately seventy professionals. It handles approximately fifty cases a year. Since its formation, over 550 cases have been registered with the organization. Figure 15.2 illustrates the steep rise in ICSID investment disputes since the Global Financial Crisis of 2008. Roughly 25% of all cases are related to the mining sector, including oil and gas business.

15.13 Brady Plan

One cannot ignore the specific country risk mitigation features of the so-called Brady debt restructuring plan that was set up in the mid-1980s to tackle the over-indebtedness of many developing countries. As discussed in Chapter 12,

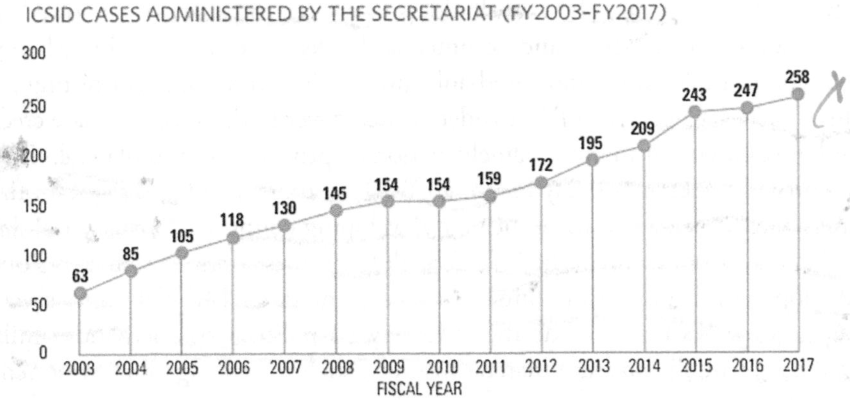

Fig. 15.2 ICSID cases (*Source* Annual Report 2017)

the debt crisis was treated by a combination of debt reduction, rescheduling, and refinancing within the framework of the "Brady Plan," between 1988 and 1993. In total, seventeen Brady debt restructuring deals were implemented on a country-by-country basis, starting with Mexico in September 1989 and ending with the last Brady type agreements in Côte d'Ivoire and Vietnam in 1997. Most Brady countries were in Latin America. The other countries included Bulgaria, Côte d'Ivoire, Jordan, Nigeria, Philippines, Poland, and Vietnam. A menu of debt restructuring options was used to match the diverse strategic and regulatory incentives of London Club banks. Substantial debt relief was obtained through the restructuring of bank loans into thirty-year discounted bonds, with a principal guarantee backed up by zero-coupon bonds and a rolling interest guarantee. In order to provide commercial banks with strong incentives to accept a voluntary debt reduction and an exchange of nonperforming bank loans for tradable bonds, several OECD governments joined the IMF and the World Bank to guarantee the newly issued bonds. To collateralize the principal on a Brady bond, developing countries purchased US Treasury, or less frequently Banque de France, zero-coupon bonds with a maturity corresponding to the maturity of underlying Brady bond. These zero-coupon bonds were held at the Basel-based BIS or in escrow at the Federal Reserve. The investor purchasing a Brady bond with a collateralized principal and partial interest guarantee knew that at maturity, the principal payment risk was canceled by the collateral, hence freeing regulatory capital. Overall, roughly USD 160 billion of Brady bonds were issued, the majority of which in US Dollars. In the mid-1990s, Brady bond trading accounted for 61% of total Emerging Markets debt trading before falling rapidly to a marginal share in 2018.

15.14 Political Risk Mitigation

PRI is being sought by bondholders, private corporations involved in cross-border investments, and commercial banks to secure their branch capital, corporate lending, and interbank funding facilities. One can distinguish three main categories of PRI providers which cover both export or trade credit and investment insurance, namely national, private and multilateral. First, national agencies are usually based in OECD countries and aim at promoting cross-border credit and investment in developing countries. Second, multilateral institutions comprise the World Bank Group's agencies as well as regional development banks. And third, the private market's PRI falls into several main categories that include the following (i) political risk activities similar to those of public and multilateral insurers, such as coverage for investments in developing countries against expropriation, political violence, and other similar risks; (ii) developing country nonpayment insurance covering contract frustration and default by governments; and (iii) corporate bond issues with collateral or PRI, that have been floated by many Latin American and Asian companies when the sovereign was a sub-investment-grade country—such as Argentina, Brazil, and Mexico—with the objective of widening the investor base and extending the payment maturity. There are numerous examples, such as Petrobras' bond issues. In May 2001, the Brazilian oil company issued USD 450 million 9.875% seven-year bonds, which carried a PRI provided by Aon. In July 2001, Petrobras issued USD 600 million 9.75% ten-year corporate bonds with PRI. The bond's rating was investment grade Baa1 awarded by Moody's on the strength of a political guarantee provided by Steadfast Insurance Company, a subsidiary of Zurich American Insurance.

PRI on bond issues typically covers convertibility, transferability, confiscation, and expropriation, thereby converting a local currency investment grade rating into the foreign currency equivalent. In essence, the bondholder takes the credit risk but the political risk is eliminated by the insurance company. Investors buy the financial guarantor's AAA risk. When bond issues are backed by securitization, the pledge assets are held offshore for investors. Overall, PRI can be considered as a useful transitory tool to enhance market access for emerging market countries that have experienced sociopolitical turmoil or that belong to a troubled regional environment.

Table 15.1 summarizes the key role of various parties in political risk protection.

15.15 Conclusion

Our discussion began with essential questions relating to the mitigation of Country Risk. From questions, we considered the various ways that Country Risk could be mitigated. The foundation for any strategy is to carefully monitor Country Risk and translate information into economic intelligence. After identifying the various types of Country Risk it has, an organization must then decide to maintain or reduce its risk, taking into account the costs and potential implications of any given path. Which outcome is the most favorable for an organization and its various stakeholders—this leaves us with additional interesting and challenging questions, but ones well worth asking. Overall, country risk managers can access a wide spectrum of risk mitigation devises, ranging from financial products to national, multi-

Table 15.1 Key role of various parties in political risk protection

Status	Entity	Members	Political risk insurance focus
National	Export credit and investment insurance agencies	Developed countries	Cross-border trade and investment for nationals
	US EXIMBANK (1934)	Independent US federal agency	War, revolution, expropriation, terrorism, currency freeze
	OPIC US (1971)	Self-sustaining US Government agency for promoting US investment in emerging markets	War, civil strife, coups, terrorism, expropriation, and transfer restrictions
	SACE (Italy) 1977	Italian joint stock company wholly owned by Cassa depositi e prestiti	Nationalization and civil disorders
	SCESE in Spain or Ducroire in Belgium	Export credit and investment guarantees	
Multinational	African Trade Insurance Agency (2001)	12 African members countries	Political risk and trade credit risk insurance products
	Asian Development Bank (1966)	67 members countries, including 48 from Asia	Loan guarantees against political risks, credit risks, and equity investments
	Inter-American Development Bank (1959)	48 member countries	Political risk guarantees for foreign debt investors
	Inter-Arab Investment Guaranty (1975)	Arab autonomous regional organization	Insurance coverage for inter-Arab investments and for export credits against non-commercial risks
	MIGA (1990)	181 member countries, including 156 developing countries	Political risk insurance to private investors and lenders Currency inconvertibility and transfer restriction expropriation, war, terrorism, civil disturbances breach of contract

(continued)

Table 15.1 (continued)

Status	Entity	Members	Political risk insurance focus
	Islamic Corp. for Insurance of Invest. and Export Credit (1994)	6 Islamic members countries	Sharia compliant risk mitigation tools
Private	Berne Union (international non-profit organization) founded 1934	84 companies from 73 countries	Association for the global export credit and investment insurance industry
	COFACE (France) 1946	Wholly-owned subsidiary of Natixis	export credit and investment insurance
	HISCOX (UK)	London-based insurer	Political risk (kidnap and ransom) and terrorism
	EULER-HERMES (Hermes-Germany: 1917)	Allianz-owned private credit agency	Transactional cover (political risk and fraud insurance)
	Sovereign Risk Insurance (1997)	Bermuda-based insurance company	Political and devaluation risks for bond issues
	Steadfast Insurance company	Subsidiary of Zurich American Insurance	Inconvertibility, transferability, and expropriation risks
	AIG (1919)	American multinational insurance corporation	Political risk turbulences (confiscation terrorism, war)
	LLOYD's (seventeenth century)	Fifty leading underwriting insurance companies	Political violence insurance
	MARSH (1871)	Insurance broking and risk management	Political risk insurance and safeguard against disputed claims

(*Source* Political risk mitigation agencies)

lateral, and private agencies whose objective is to encourage foreign lending and investment by carrying a share of Country Risk, hence reducing losses. These umbrellas are important to facilitate the return to market access of countries that have been faced with economic and sociopolitical turmoil, but they can never be substitutes for in-depth economic intelligence. This has been the guiding thread of our book on the management of Country Risk in the age of Globalization.

Appendix 15.1 Best Practices for Mitigating Risk in FX Transactions

In May of 2017, the FX Global Code was issued by a group consisting of central banks and participants in the global foreign exchange trading market. The document, which reflected feedback by individuals in sixteen jurisdictions, was intended to summarize sound practices for the foreign exchange trading market. The goal of the initiative was to "promote a robust, fair, liquid, open and appropriately transparent market in which a diverse set of Market Participants are able to confidently and effectively transact at competitive prices that reflect available market information and in a manner that conforms to acceptable standards of behavior" (https://www.globalfxc.org/fx_global_code.htm).

The Code includes fifty five principles, including Principles 24-41 devoted to risk management and compliance. The overarching theme for risk management was described as follows: "Market Participants are expected to promote and maintain a robust control and compliance environment to effectively identify, manage and report on the risks associated with their engagement in the FX Market."

The Code expressly recognizes the following "key risk types":

- Credit and Counterparty Risk
- Market Risk
- Operational Risk
- Technology Risk
- Settlement Risk
- Compliance Risk
- Legal Risk

To manage these risks, the Code calls for a range of practices, including:

- Clear ownership of the business decisions by the business unit
- Independent risk management function
- Independent compliance function
- Independent audit function to review internal control systems
- Timely reporting of understandable risk and compliance-related information to senior management
- The use of master netting agreements and collateral
- Independent reporting of the current market value of trading positions

- Adequate resources and employees with clearly specified roles, responsibility, and authority
- Appropriate processes to identify and manage operational risks
- Documented policies, procedures, and controls
- Robust risk assessment and approval processes for both new and existing products and services.

Although the Code does not explicitly contemplate Country Risk as a separate "key risk type," it must be carefully considered by regulators, market participants, and other stakeholders. It is relevant to the assessment of all applicable risks in foreign exchange trading (and any other forms of bilateral transactions, including derivatives). Particular emphasis must be given to scenarios where a problem in one country or region has the potential to give rise to problems in other countries and regions.

References

Asian Development Bank. 2017. "Viet Nam: Cofinancing." https://www.adb.org/countries/viet-nam/cofinancing.

Asian Development Bank. "Guarantees." https://www.adb.org/site/private-sector-financing/commercial-cofinancing/guarantees.

Business and Human Rights Resource Center. 2014. "Total Lawsuit in Belgium (re Myanmar)." https://business-humanrights.org/en/total-lawsuit-in-belgium-re-myanmar.

Chevron. 2017. "Human Rights Respect for Human Rights Is Rooted in Our Values and Applies Wherever We Do Business." Corporate Responsibility. https://www.chevron.com/corporate-responsibility/people/human-rights.

International Finance Corporation. 2016. "Mobilizing Large-Scale Financing for Infrastructure." Impact at IFC, October.

International Finance Corporation. 2017. "Products and Services." http://www.ifc.org/wps/wcm/connect/CORP_EXT_Content/IFC_External_Corporate_Site/Solutions/Products+and+Services.

LafargeHolcim. 2017. "LafargeHolcim Responds to Syria Review." Press Release, March 3. http://www.lafargeholcim.com/LafargeHolcim-responds-syria-review.

Mapila, Kopo, Morten Lauridsen, and Carl Chastenay 2017. "Mobilizing Institutional Investments into Emerging Market Infrastructure." Note No 36. EMCompass. IFC, April.

Masud, Faarea. 2017. "Chevron Says It Will Push for Myanmar Human Rights." *BBC News*, November 16. http://www.bbc.com/news/business-41977909.

MIGA. 2015. "MIGA's Support to the Middle East and North Africa." Brief MENA. https://www.miga.org/documents/menabrief.pdf.

Noonan, Laura. 2017. "Vietnam's Nascent Debt Markets Set for Bigger Deals." *Financial Times*, December 13.

Reuters. 2014. "Tunisia Issues $825 Million Bonds in the Domestic Japanese Market." October 10.

Walt, Vivienne. 2010. "Chevron, Total Accused of Human-Rights Abuses in Burma." *Time*, July 6.

Wezel, Torsten. 2004. Does Co-Financing by Multilateral Development Banks Increase "Risky" Direct Investment in Emerging Markets?—Evidence for German Banking FDI." Discussion Paper Series 1: Studies of the Economic Research Centre No 02/2004.

World Bank and Rothschild & C. 2016. Utilizing World Bank Partial Guarantees in Support of Sovereign or Sub—Sovereign Commercial Debt Financings, August.

World Bank. 2017. "Guarantees Program." http://www.worldbank.org/en/programs/guarantees-program.

16

Glossary: The 200 Most Important Terms and Concepts for Country Risk Management

1. **Acceleration Clause**: A clause providing that the entire principal of a note (or a loan) shall become immediately due and payable in the event of default.
2. **Accrued Interest**: Interest which has accumulated but which is not legally due before a specified payment date.
3. **Asian Development Bank (ADB)**: A Manilla-based regional development bank, focused on promoting growth in Asia. It began operations in 1966.
4. **Adverse Selection**: Consider a market in which products of varying quality are exchanged and only the sellers are aware of the quality of each unit they sell. This implies an incentive for them to market poor quality merchandise, leading to a gradual reduction in the average quality of goods and also the size of the market. It is important to underline that the asymmetry of information occurs ex-ante. George Akerlof was the first to illustrate this market inefficiency with his famous lemon problem. (See also Credit Rationing, Moral Hazard, Asymmetric Information.)
5. **African Development Bank (AfDB)**: An Abidjan-based regional development bank, focused on enhancing sustainable growth in Africa. It was founded in 1964.
6. **Agent Bank**: A commercial bank (other than a creditor bank), which collects all payments from a restructured loan or a syndicated loan, and distributes them to each participating creditor bank.

M. H. Bouchet et al., *Managing Country Risk in an Age of Globalization*,
https://doi.org/10.1007/978-3-319-89752-3_16

7. **Allocated Transfer Risk Reserves (ATRRs)**: Country-specific reserves which banks registered in the United States are required to set aside against assets which are deemed to be "value impaired" by the Interagency Exposure Review Committee (ICERC). The reserve is a charge against income and tax deductible but it is excluded from primary capital. It is calculated by multiplying the reserve percentage dictated by ICERC by the face amount of exposure classified as "value impaired," after adjustments for guarantees and previous write-downs. Generally, the provision covers all loans except performing trade credits and interbank lines. Amounts in excess of the ICERC requirement may be set aside as ATRRs at the discretion of bank management.
8. **Ambiguity**: A special case of uncertainty where we know the set of potential outcomes but do not know the probability of such outcomes. (See also Risk and Uncertainty.)
9. **Amortization**: Repayment of principal balances during a given accounting period, usually one year.
10. **Arrears**: Contractual debt service which is not paid on schedule. In practice, payments may be delayed for a few months because of administrative problems before they are classified as arrears.
11. **Asset-backed Securities**: A "fixed income" security that pays its coupon and principal from a designated portfolio of assets which serves as underlying collateral, thereby reducing or even eliminate the underlying risk of payment default. The form of collateral varies from security to security and may include government securities, corporate securities, accounts receivables, mortgages, zero-coupon bonds, and real property.
12. **Asymmetric Information**: In a world in which agents have different information about the economic environment, an agents' behavior may partially or fully reveal information it may have but which is not universally known. Hence, "neutral" variables may contain potentially valuable information in a world of asymmetrically informed agents. (See also Moral Hazard, Adverse Selection.)
13. **Average Terms of New Commitments**: The interest rate, maturity, and grace period of new commitments on public and publicly guaranteed external debt contracted with public and private creditors. Averages are weighted by the amount of the loans. (World Bank terminology.)
14. **Bailout Plan**: A plan that boils down to rescuing a troubled financial institution or a sovereign debtor to stem the risk of systemic

contagion. In 2008, the US Troubled Asset Relief Program, or TARP, helped rescue America's financial institutions (including AIG). In Greece, the European Union, the ECB, and the IMF jointly organized a lifeline of eighty six billion Euros to recapitalize Greece' struggling banks, and to make payments in arrears so as to avoid a full-fledged default.

15. **Baker Plan**: The debt strategy outlined by the US Treasury Secretary James Baker at the annual meeting of the World Bank and the International Monetary Fund (IMF) in September 1985. The focus was on fifteen heavily indebted countries, namely, Argentina, Bolivia, Brazil, Chile, Colombia, Ecuador, Ivory Coast, Mexico, Morocco, Nigeria, Peru, Philippines, Uruguay, Venezuela, and Yugoslavia. The Plan implemented London Club debt refinancing with commercial banks coupled with net disbursements by multilateral development banks for growth-oriented structural reforms (such as privatization and trade liberalization) by debtor countries. The Plan was superseded by the 1989 Brady Debt Reduction Initiative.
16. **Berne Union**: An international nonprofit trade association that serves the interest of global credit export banks and investment assurance entities. Its members include government-backed export credit agencies, private credit and political risk insurers, and multilateral institutions that provide insurance products, guarantees, and different types of direct financing in the support of cross-border trade.
17. **Bilateral Loans**: Loans from governments and their agencies (including central banks), loans from autonomous bodies, and direct loans from official export credit agencies.
18. **Bank for International Settlements (BIS)**: Based in Basle, it was set up in 1930 at the Hague Conference to manage Germany's war reparation payments. It is a key source of debt and bank cross-country credit data. The BIS is owned by sixty central banks, representing countries from around the world that together account for about 95% of world GDP. It acts as a bank for central banks.
19. **BlackRock Sovereign Risk Index (BSRI)**: An index developed by the global asset manager BlackRock that provides a framework for evaluating sovereign risk.
20. **Bond Spread**: Difference of yields between US Treasury bonds with Emerging Markets bonds of comparable maturity. Assuming the former to be a risk-free rate, the difference can be seen as a risk premium demanded by international investors for the more risky and opaque business environment in emerging markets.

21. **Bond, Zero-Coupon**: A bond that pays neither principal nor interest until maturity. It merely states the face payment that is due at maturity and is sold at a discount which reflects the timing of payments (i.e., the face value of the discounted value of the future bullet payment at maturity).
22. **Brady Bond**: Named after US Treasury Secretary Nicholas Brady, who sponsored the restructuring in 1989 of the London Club's distressed sovereign loans and interest arrears into long-term, guaranteed, and tradeable debt instruments.
23. **Brady Plan**: Describes the proposal made by US Treasury Secretary Nicholas Brady on March 10, 1989 to reduce the debt overhang of countries heavily indebted to commercial banks. Around fifteen emerging market countries have reduced their commercial bank debt through Brady-style operations, with a market-based menu of debt restructuring options including voluntary discounted debt buybacks, with funding provided by IFIs and official bilateral creditors: Mexico, Uruguay, the Philippines, Nigeria, Jordan, Ivory Coast, Costa Rica, Venezuela, Argentina, Nicaragua, Brazil, Dominican Republic, and Poland.
24. **Bridge Loan**: Used in the context of managing a country's debt profile, it is short-term financing provided to a debtor country—usually by the monetary authorities of industrial countries in conjunction with other central banks, governments, multilateral institutions, and commercial banks—to supplement the country's foreign reserves prior to finalizing adjustment programs and concerted lending packages. This short-term advance is made pending receipts of funds by the borrower.
25. **Bullet Maturity Bond**: One-time payment of principal at maturity. (See also Zero-coupon Bond.)
26. **Capital Flight**: The movement of capital from emerging markets; it is often rooted in bad governance, sociopolitical turmoil, and corruption, as well as in commodity-driven wealth concentration. It can also be explained by economic theory as a product of natural and economically rational behavior of wealthy residents of these debtor countries to diversify their portfolios in order to hedge against domestic riskiness. The calculation of the amount of capital flight is a by-product of the balance of payments and official reserve levels analysis coupled with the change in BIS banks' liabilities vis-à-vis private nonbank residents.

27. **Capitalization, Interest**: An arrangement by which interest due is added to the principal of the loan and converted into a capital liability, effectively deferring payment beyond the original schedule.
28. **Cofinancing**: A mechanism by which creditors provide project loans in parallel with loans granted by multilateral agencies such as the World Bank. Such "co-financiers" receive the benefit of the multilateral agencies' evaluation of the project and can share in certain benefits resulting from the special relationship between the debtor country and the multilateral agencies. In principle, cross-default clauses prevent debtors from defaulting on amounts owed to co-financiers without defaulting on the official institutions.
29. **Collateral**: Financial or real assets that are used to support an obligation to make a payment or to perform under the terms of a contract in some other manner. In Brady bonds, collateral consists of thirty-year US Treasury zero-coupon bonds as well as cash usually held in accounts the Federal Reserve Bank in New York. The collateral's purpose is to support the payment of the principal and/or the interest should a debtor country not honor its financial obligations.
30. **Cologne Terms**: In November 1999, the Paris Club creditor countries, in the framework of the initiative for "Heavily Indebted Poor Countries" (HIPC) and in the aftermath of the Cologne Summit, agreed to raise the level of cancellation for the poorest countries up to 90% or more if necessary in accordance with framework of the HIPC initiative. Forty-one countries are potentially eligible for the HIPC Initiative and may benefit from the Cologne terms.
31. **Commercial Credits**: (i) Credits granted by a bank or a supplier to a debtor country for importing goods and services. When these credits are guaranteed by the appropriate institution of a Paris Club creditor, they are included in the claims treated in the context of the Paris Club. (ii) Non-Official Development Assistance (ODA) credits are sometimes referred to as commercial credits.
32. **Concerted Bank Lending**: Loans made by commercial banks, coordinated by a bank advisory committee, and based on equi-proportional increases in bank exposure. (See also Free Riders.)
33. **Concessional Debt**: Loans, usually from official bilateral and multilateral creditors, that are extended on terms more generous than market-based loans. The concessionality is achieved either through interest rates below market conditions, or by long maturities, or by longer grace periods, or a combination of these three.

34. **Country Risk**: A complex set of interdependent economic, financial, and sociopolitical factors, specific to a particular country in the global economy. Country Risk can have outcomes which are either positive or negative. Country Risk is pervasive, including at times and in places that are unexpected.
35. **Credit Default Swap**: A form of OTC derivatives that enables an entity to purchase protection for a specified term against the default of an entity or group of entities. In such a transaction, one party pays a fee, either at the outset of the transaction or over its term. The other party is entitled to receive a payment of a predetermined amount if there is a default by such entity or entities. (See also OTC Derivatives.)
36. **Crony Capitalism**: A term initially developed by Paul Krugman to describe the root causes of the 1998 Asian Crisis, it focuses on bad governance, speculative and nonproductive investment, and premature financial liberalization. Lack of transparency and collusion among market players are tolerated by government officials who benefit from conflict of interest transactions.
37. **Cross-Default Provision**: A provision in a legal contract which allows one creditor to declare a default and exercise its remedies against the borrower in cases where other loans of the borrower have been suspended, terminated, accelerated, or declared in default by other creditors.
38. **Cutoff Date (Paris Club Clause)**: When a debtor country first meets with Paris Club creditors, the "cutoff date" is defined at the outset and is not changed in subsequent Paris Club treatments. Accordingly, new money credits granted after this cutoff date are not subject to future rescheduling. Thus, the cutoff date helps restore access to credit for debtor countries facing payment difficulties. When a debtor country first meets with Paris Club creditors, the "cutoff date" is defined and is not to be changed in subsequent Paris Club treatments. The cutoff date serves to protect new credits granted by Paris Club creditors after a rescheduling.
39. **Currency Redenomination**: Switching of loans denominated in one currency or currencies into another currency. The mechanism is intended to bring about a better match between the currency mix of debt service payments and the currency composition of external receipts. In cases of high levels of inflation, currency redenomination can also lead to changing the face value of a country's bank notes and coins in circulation (e.g., Turkey in 2005).

40. **Dagon Global Credit Rating**: The first non-Western credit rating agency, founded in 1994 with the joint approval of China's People's Bank and the former State Economic and Trade Commission.
41. **DBRS**: The fourth largest rating agency, based in Canada. Founded in 1976, it is privately held.
42. **Debt Buyback**: A country can be authorized by its creditors to buy-back its liabilities before maturity, sometimes at a discount, including in a menu of Brady-debt restructuring transactions.
43. **Debt Defeasance**: Extinguishing debt through the provision of a financial asset (zero-coupon or another financial instrument) to be held in a trust account as collateral against the principal of the debt. The face value and maturity of the collateral instrument are designed to match those of the debt being defeased so that the proceeds of the collateral instrument at maturity may be used to fully repay the principal in a single balloon payment. Since the principal of the debt is secured, the debt service obligations of the debtor are reduced to the payment of interest.
44. **Debt/Equity Swap**: An exchange of foreign currency debt for local currency equity in a domestic firm. This may be done by the bank holding the loan or by an investor who purchases the debt security in the secondary market. The exchange may involve a public debt and equity in a private sector company, a private debt and equity in the same company, or public debt and equity in a public enterprise that is being privatized.
45. **Debt-for-Debt Swap**: Exchange of one type of foreign debt for another with different terms and conditions. Debt exchanges involve par swaps and discount swaps.
46. **Debt-for-Export Swaps**: These swaps enable a creditor to receive export products and/or commodities of a debtor country to offset part of its outstanding claims on the concerned country.
47. **Debt-for-Nature Swap**: An exchange of a foreign currency debt for local currency that is used to finance the conservation of environmental assets such as parklands and tropical forests. A private conservation organization, for example, purchases a country's commercial bank debt (usually at a discount) or receives the debt as a donation. The debt is then canceled in exchange for the issue of local currency assets to be invested in the protection of an environmentally sensitive area like a tropical rain forest, a national park, or a biodiversity reserve.

48. **Debt Overhang**: Refers to a large burden of (foreign) debt that cannot be settled by short-term liquidity injection but rather by a combination of long-term rescheduling and write-off. (See also HIPC-Initiative, Solvency Ratios.)
49. **Derivatives Transactions**: So named because their values are derived from the performance of one or more underlying assets, commodities, currencies, interest rates, or indices. They are prevalently used by investors, corporations, and financial institutions to assume or minimize market risk, credit risk, equity price risk, or commodity price risk. Derivatives are commonly classified into two broad categories: OTC Derivatives and Exchange-traded Derivatives. They are often classified by the type of underlying financial risk they address, including interest rates, equities, commodities, and credit.
50. **Discount Bond (Brady)**: Registered thirty-year bullet amortization issued at discount, with floating market-based interest rate.
51. **Discounted Debt Buyback**: Transaction whereby the debtor country purchases all or part of its outstanding debt in the market, usually at a discount. Accordingly, the outstanding debt will decline by the nominal value of the debt that has been bought back.
52. **Debt Swaps**: These transactions may include debt for nature, debt for aid, debt for equity swaps, or other local currency debt swaps. These swaps often involve the sale of the debt by the creditor government to an investor who in turn sells the debt to the debtor government in return for shares in a local company or for local currency to be used in projects in the country. Paris Club creditors and debtors regularly provide the Paris Club Secretariat with the details of the debt swaps conducted. Debt-equity swaps involve the conversion of debt into local currency equity in a domestic firm.
53. **Delphi Technique**: A structured communication technique relying on a panel of experts. The experts answer questionnaires in several rounds. After each of them, a facilitator agent provides an anonymized summary of the experts' forecasts from the previous round. The purpose is to reduce the range of the answers and to make the group converge towards the "correct" answer. Reading previous rounds summaries, experts are encouraged to revise their earlier answers in light of the replies of other members of their panel.
54. **De minimis Provision**: A provision in Paris Club agreements that defines a "de minimis" level of claims of a Paris Club creditor. When such claims are less than this level, the creditor participates in Paris Club meeting as an observer and does not reschedule its claims. The

goal of this provision is to allow for efficient resolution of the debt relief process between creditors and debtors.

55. **Disbursements**: Drawings on loan commitments by the borrower during the year.
56. **Economic Policy Uncertainty Index**: An index which seeks to measure policy-related economic uncertainty. It is based on data relating to newspaper coverage of the economic policy. It was developed by a team of researchers at Northwestern University, Stanford University, and the University of Chicago.
57. **EBRD (European Bank for Reconstruction and Development)**: Established in 1991, it provides loans, equity investments, and guarantees for private and public sector projects, focusing on Central and Eastern Europe.
58. **Emerging Markets Bond Index (EMBI)**: An index introduced in 1999 by JP Morgan. It includes a wide range of financial instruments, including Brady Bonds, Eurobonds, traded loans, and local market debt issued by sovereign and quasi-sovereign entities. It is weighted by the market capitalization of the underlying component bonds.
59. **Emerging Market Country**: A country in transition making an effort to restructure its economy and institutions with the goal of raising its long-term performance to that of the world's more advanced nations. Emerging markets are the recipients of various international financial and technical assistance programs to boost their development. The World Bank does not maintain a list of emerging markets. The World Bank classifies economies based on their yearly Gross National Income (GNI) per capita (computed using the "Atlas" method). There are four main country classifications that are adjusted and updated from time to time.

Threshold	GNI/Capita (current US$)
Low-income	< 1,005
Lower-middle income	1,006 - 3,955
Upper-middle income	3,956 - 12,235
High-income	> 12,235

60. **Emerging Market**: The International Finance Corporation (IFC) uses income per capita and market capitalization relative to GNP for classifying emerging equity markets. If either (i) a market resides in a low- or middle-income economy (in 2018, high income was defined by the World Bank as above USD 12,235 per capita GNP) or (ii) the ratio of investable market capitalization to GNP is low, i.e., not in the top 25% of all emerging market for three consecutive years, then the IFC classifies a country as *emerging*. The IFC identified eighty-one such countries. If a country meets this latter requirement, it becomes part of the Emerging Market Data Base (EMDB) Index. Countries are "graduated" from the EMBD Index if their income rises into the high-income category for three consecutive years. In 1999, S&P acquired IFC's indices of emerging markets stock performance as part of a broad, new strategic collaboration between the two organizations.
61. **Equity-linked Bonds**: Convertible bonds or bonds with equity warrants.
62. **Escrow Account**: Special account in local or foreign currency, established on behalf of the debtor country in a domestic or in a foreign bank, in which deposits are made by the debtor periodically. Such account ensures creditors that debt payments will be made on time as a portion of the debtor's revenues are set aside for this purpose.
63. **Events of Default**: any event that allows creditors to declare the outstanding principal, as well as all accrued interest, due and payable on demand.
64. **Exceptional Financing**: A special "below the line" category in the IMF Balance of Payments used to accommodate transactions undertaken on behalf of the monetary authorities to compensate for an overall imbalance.
65. **Eurobonds**: Long-term financial instruments issued by Multinational Corporations (MNCs) or countries which are denominated in a currency other than that of the country where it is issued. Eurobonds are underwritten by a multinational syndicate of investment banks and simultaneously placed in many countries. Coupon payments are made yearly. The US Dollar accounts for a declining share of around 60% of eurobonds. Most Eurobonds are bearer bonds that are electronically traded through clearing houses, like Euroclear and Clearstream.
66. **Exchange-Traded Derivatives**: Derivatives transactions that are traded on organized exchanges. They are contrasted with OTC

Derivatives, which are entered into between parties on an individually negotiated basis. (See OTC Derivatives.)

67. **US Export-Import Bank (EXIM)**: The "official credit export agency of the United States." It was established in 1934 by President Franklin D. Roosevelt. Its mission is to create and sustain jobs in the US by promoting the exports of the country's goods and services. Its obligations are backed by the full faith and credit of the US.
68. **Exit Rescheduling**: An exit treatment is the last rescheduling a country normally receives from the Paris Club. The aim is that the debtor country will not need any further rescheduling and will thus not come back for negotiation to the Paris Club.
69. **External Debt**: External obligations in hard currency owed by public and private entities resident in a country to the nonresident public and private creditors. External indebtedness has a direct impact on the debtor country's balance of payments and liquidity position. External public debt is defined as the amount, at any given time, of disbursed and outstanding foreign currency liabilities contracted by a country or by public or private companies with a governmental guarantee. The corresponding credits are held by three categories of lenders:

    - Private Lenders (commercial banks and suppliers).
    - Bilateral Lenders (individual countries within or outside the Paris Club).
    - Multilateral Lenders (World Bank, IMF, as well as certain regional banks such as the Inter-American Development Bank and the Asian Development Bank).

70. **European Investment Bank (EIB)**: Set up in 1958, the EIB is the world's largest multilateral borrower and lender. Owned by the European Union, its mandate is to represent the interest of the EU. It finances investment projects mainly in Europe, but also in Africa, Latin America, and other countries.
71. **Face Value**: Full amount of the original debt obligation.
72. **Foreign Direct Investment (FDI) Confidence Index**: Created in 1998 by the management consulting firm A. T. Kearney, it is a qualitative ranking of countries which are perceived as the most favorable places to make long-term FDIs.
73. **Fiduciary Fund (or Trust Fund)**: Fund in which assets are safeguarded and whose stream of interest income is used to fund a specific project.

74. **Fitch**: One of the so-called "Big Three" credit rating agencies. The other two are Moody's and Standard & Poor's.
75. **Flight-to-Safety (FTS)**: Because of uncertainty or financial distress, investors move their capital away from riskier investments to the safest possible investment vehicles ("safe heaven").
76. **Force Majeure**: State of emergency or exceptional condition that permits a creditor or an investor to depart from the strict terms of a contract because of an event or effect that cannot reasonably be anticipated or controlled.
77. **Foreign Exchange Transactions**: Also known as FX Transactions, the sale or purchase of one currency in exchange for another. They generally can be classified as spot transactions (which can be settled within few days) or forward transactions (which settle at a date further into the future).
78. **Foreign Investment Risk Matrix (FIRM)**: Tool developed by B. Bhalla (1983) using political and economic risk measures to help decide on FDI. It consists of a matrix that categorizes countries based on political risk and economic risk as acceptable, unacceptable, or uncertain for investment.
79. **Fragile States Index**: An assessment of twelve social, economic, and political indicators that seek to quantify political instability. It was developed by the US think tank Fund for Peace.
80. **Free Rider**: Individual banks may refuse to participate in a bailout loan with the international banking community, thereby not matching their expected share of the concerted loan package. Similarly, small-exposure banks might refuse to join debt reduction operations while requiring full payments on their claims. Such "free riders" would then see the value of their lending portfolios rise as other banks write-down a country's debt. (See also Mandatory Repayment Clause.)
81. **Fundamental Uncertainty**: A subset of uncertainty that refers to the case where we do not even know the nature and extent of all the possible outcomes. This form of uncertainty can arise from a complex interplay of factors, including innovation and technological change as well as changes in cultural, social, and political conditions.
82. **Goodwill Clause**: A statement in Paris (or London) Club agreements that would allow the creditors in question to extend the life of a stated rescheduling arrangement, but which is not legally binding. Creditors agree to consider further debt relief after the expiration of

the consolidation period and a commitment to meet at the end of three to four years to consider the matter of the stock of debt.

83. **Grace Period**: The time period during which the debt is not amortized, i.e., no principal gets paid by the borrower, and only interest payment obligations are serviced against the total debt stock.
84. **Gross External Debt**: Amount, at any given time, of disbursed and outstanding contractual liabilities of residents of a country to nonresidents, and denominated in hard currency.
85. **Gross Financing Gap** (% of reserve assets): Current account deficit plus scheduled principal repayments on external debt plus stock of short-term liabilities as a percent of official foreign exchange reserves. An indicator of liquidity tensions.
86. **Guarantee**: A written legally binding obligation by one party to be liable for a specific obligation of a second party in the event that the second party does not fulfill such obligation on a due date. IFIs such as the World Bank and the IADB provide emerging markets countries with a financial guarantee to enhance local currency long-dated bond markets, hence offering a form of insurance with the highest possible credit rating.
87. **Hedging**: A strategy that organizations use to lessen exposure to one or more types of risk, often a market risk. Hedging often involves the exchange or transformation of one form or risk for another.
88. **Herd Behavior**: Investors "herd" when they take an action they would not have taken had they not known that other investors have taken it. Hence, investors' actions do not depend on their own private information, but only on other investors' actions. Therefore, in the presence of herding, investors' actions do not disclose any private information on market fundamentals and consequently, the social learning process stops.
89. **Highly Indebted Poor Countries (HIPC)**: See Cologne Terms.
90. **International Bank for Reconstruction and Development (IBRD)**: Also referred to the World Bank, based in Washington DC, with 189 member countries. The Bank is one of the five institutions that comprise the World Bank Group (with IFC, MIGA, ICSID, and IDA).
91. **Interagency Exposure Review Committee (ICERC)**: A committee established in 1979 by the Federal Reserve, the Office of the Comptroller of the Currency, and the Federal Deposit Insurance Corporation to evaluate transfer risks of US commercial banks.

92. **International Development Association (IDA)**: An affiliate of the World Bank, established in 1960, to promote development in the world's poorest countries. It is the largest single multilateral source of concessional lending to low-income countries. It has 173 shareholder nations. Borrowing countries typically have per capita incomes of less than USD 1,165. IDA provides interest-free loans and grants to the world's 75 poorest countries, thirty-nine of which are in Africa. In the fiscal year 2017, IDA commitments totaled nearly USD 20 billion, of which 17% was provided on grant terms. New commitments in FY17 comprised 261 new operations. Since 1960, IDA has provided USD 345 billion for investments in 113 countries.
93. **IDA Debt Reduction Facility**: A fund established by the International Development Association in June of 1989 from funding by the World Bank. The money in this fund goes to help severely indebted, low-income countries reduce their commercial debt. Since 1993, the fund has been replenished several times. Various countries have reduced their debt through the IDA Facility, namely, Bolivia, Niger, Mozambique, Guyana, Zambia, Sierra Leone, Tanzania, and Senegal.
94. **Inter-American Development Bank (IDB)**: Established in 1959, it supports economic and social development in Latin American and the Caribbean regions by lending to governments and government agencies.
95. **International Financial Institutions (IFIs)**: The so-called Bretton Woods organizations (the IMF and the World Bank Group) as well as other multilateral agencies such as regional development banks and the European Investment Bank. Abbreviation for International Financial Institutions such as the World Bank Group and the International Monetary Fund (IMF).
96. **Institute for International Finance (IIF)**: Founded in 1983 in response to the international debt crisis. The Institute has more than 450 members, including most of the world's largest commercial banks, investment banks, and multinational companies. It provides various services to its members, including analysis of emerging markets, forums for discussion among members, and the facilitation of dialogue on emerging markets issues between the private financial sector and the public sector. (i.e., IMF and Paris Club). The IIF was set up by a small number of seasoned economists on short-term loans by their respective banking institutions (e.g., BNP in France, RBC in Canada, Citicorp in the US).

97. **IMD-Lausanne World Competitiveness Ranking**: Annual ranking of county competitiveness by the Lausanne-based Institute of Management Development.
98. **Interest Rate Switching**: Selection of a new basis for interest calculations on an existing loan. The options may include LIBOR, a domestic rate, the prime rate, or a fixed rate, to which a margin is added.
99. **Interest Retiming**: Changing the frequency of interest payments, essentially allowing a debtor to defer one or more interest payments. Retiming is effectively short-term interest rescheduling in that it permits a debtor country to stretch out interest payments.
100. **International Centre for the Settlement of Investment Disputes (ICSID)**: Established in 1966 as an independent organization to promote dispute resolution arising from international investment. It is affiliated with the World Bank Group, although it has a separate charter established by an international treaty. The organization provides facilities for conciliation and arbitration of international investment disputes. It is the only global arbitration organization that offers a specialized forum to resolve disputes relating to international investing.
101. **International Monetary Fund (IMF)**: Created in 1945, the IMF is an international financial organization with 189 member countries. Its work aims at fostering global monetary cooperation and securing financial stability with short- to medium-term balance of payments support. It plays a key role in assessing countries' external borrowing requirements and in facilitating debt reduction negotiations with Paris Club member countries.
102. **Invisible balance**: Also called "Balance of trade on services," it is the part of the balance of trade that refers to services and other products that do not result in the transfer of physical objects (i.e., shipping, insurance, tourism).
103. **Irrational Exuberance**: Before being popularized by Robert J. Shiller (*Irrational Exuberance* 2000), the term was first mentioned by Alan Greenspan during a TV speech on December 5, 1996: "Clearly, sustained low inflation implies less uncertainty about the future, and lower risk premiums imply higher prices of stocks and other earning assets. We can see that in the inverse relationship exhibited by price/earnings ratios and the rate of inflation in the past. But how do we know when 'irrational exuberance' has unduly escalated asset values, which then become subject to unexpected and prolonged contractions as they have in Japan over the

past decade?" (The Challenge of Central Banking in a Democratic Society).

104. **International Swaps and Derivatives Association (ISDA)**: A trade association of derivatives dealers and other users of derivatives transactions. Among its activities, ISDA coordinates the development of standard forms of documentation for derivatives transactions, including master agreements and confirmations.

105. **ISDA Master Agreement**: The standardized form of legal contract for OTC derivatives transactions. It was developed by market participants as a way of promoting uniformity in the documentation of derivatives transactions. Among its provisions, it contains events of default that enable the non-defaulting party to terminate all transactions outstanding and to offset amounts owing and owed into one net sum.

106. **Knightian Risk**: Frank Knight (1885–1972) was an economist at the University of Chicago. In his major book *Risk, Uncertainty and Profit* (1921), he made a crucial distinction between risk and uncertainty: "Uncertainty must be taken in a sense radically distinct from the familiar notion of Risk, from which it has never been properly separated… The essential fact is that 'risk' means in some cases a quantity susceptible of measurement, while at other times it is something distinctly not of this character; and there are far-reaching and crucial differences in the bearings of the phenomena depending on which of the two is really present and operating… It will appear that a measurable uncertainty, or 'risk' proper, as we shall use the term, is so far different from an unmeasurable one that it is not in effect an uncertainty at all."

107. **Leaning Against the Wind**: Countercyclical economic policy. J.C. Trichet, former chairman of the European Central Bank described the "leaning against the wind" policy as follows: "tendency to cautiously raise interest rates even beyond the level necessary to maintain price stability over the short to medium-term when a potentially detrimental asset price boom is identified." (June 2005).

108. **Liquidity**: With respect to a financial instrument, the capacity to be converted to cash easily, quickly, and with minimum loss. Short-dated treasury bills are an example of one of the most liquid financial instruments. A liquid market is one in which there is enough activity and "depth" to meet the needs of both sellers and buyers.

109. **Liquidity Ratios**: A gauge of the ability to service debt and redeem or reschedule liabilities when they mature and the ability

to exchange other assets for cash. Examples of such ratios are debt service ratio [(Principal + Interest)/Exports], interest ratio (Interests/Exports), import coverage (Reserves/Imports), and current account/GDP.

110. **Liquidity Trap**: Describes a situation where prevailing interest rates are low and savings are high. Interest rates are expected to rise since they cannot go lower. Because a bond's value has an inverse relationship to interest rates, economic agents prefer to keep their funds in savings rather than bonds.

111. **Loan to Deposit ratio (LDR)**: A metric for assessing a bank's liquidity by dividing the bank's total loans by its total deposits. The ratio should neither be too high nor too low. If the ratio is too high, the bank may lack enough liquidity to cover any unforeseen event. Conversely, if the ratio is too low, the bank may not be earning as much as it could be.

112. **London Club**: An ad hoc association of commercial lenders to a debtor country. The association is usually led by a subgroup that represents all the creditors in negotiations. The subgroup, usually composed of the major commercial creditors, is referred to as the Steering Committee or the Advisory Committee.

113. **Mandatory Repayment Clause**: A standard clause in loan agreements between debtor countries and commercial bank creditors. It stipulates certain circumstances under which repayment is accelerated. The debtor, by being obligated to prepay any one creditor, must repay all lenders on a pro rata basis. In the context of rescheduling agreements and new money loans to rescheduling countries, the provision is intended to neutralize "free rider" banks which do not participate in debt restructuring and new money agreements. In that regard, debt conversion and debt buyback transactions amount to payment prior to contractually defined maturity. The provision applies across the universe of public sector borrowers so that a voluntary prepayment of one or more credits by one borrower would trigger mandatory prepayment not only by that borrower but also by the other public sector borrowers.

114. **Maturity**: The date on which a loan, security, or other debt instrument falls due for repayment.

115. **"Menu" Approach, Market-Based**: A series of instruments that are used voluntarily by creditors and debtors to resolve problems of external indebtedness to commercial banks. The instruments seek to change the nature of bank claims through exchange offers and

securitization, the ownership of bank claims through debt conversion mechanisms and discounted repurchases, and the financial profile of the debt obligations through interest retiming and long-term consolidation. A typical menu comprises the following instruments:

- Par Bond: An exchange of old claims for a bond with the same face value but a below-market interest rate and, generally, a bullet maturity of thirty years.
- Discount Bond: Converting old claims into a bond with a discounted face value (negotiated by debtors and creditors) and offering floating rate of interest. These bonds, too, have a bullet maturity of thirty years.
- Front Loaded Interest Reduction Bond (FLIRBs): Old claims are exchanged for a bond with the same face value with below market rate for comparable credit risk for the first few years, increasing gradually to a generally market-based rate.
- Debt Conversion Bond: Exchange old claims for a bond with an option to convert into equity in private firms or privatized.
- New Money Bonds: Purchases of new instruments with a variable rate of interest, usually a spread over LIBOR, and maturities of ten to fifteen years.

116. **Multilateral Investment Guarantee Agency (MIGA)**: Set up in 1988 with twenty-nine member states, MIGA has 181 member countries in 2018. This agency is a member of the World Bank Group. Its objective is to facilitate the flow of FDI to developing and transition economies. In fulfilling this objective, it acts as a guarantor to investors relating to currency transfers, expropriation without due compensation, war, civil unrest, and breach of contracts.
117. **Moody's**: One of the so-called “Big Three” rating agencies. The other two are Fitch and Standard & Poor's.
118. **Moratorium**: A declaration by a debtor that debt service payments will not be made for a certain period of time beyond the original maturity of the loan.
119. **The MSCI Emerging Markets Index**: A float-adjusted market capitalization index that consists of indices in twenty-four emerging economies.
120. **Minsky Moment**: In 1992, American post-Keynesian economist Hyman Minsky (1919–1996) developed his Financial Instability Hypothesis by identifying hedge, speculative, and Ponzi finance as distinct phases of mounting causes of volatility and financial crises. His theory, quite applicable to the root causes of the Global

Financial Crisis, links financial system fragility, the life cycle of an economy, deregulation, financial innovation, and speculative investment bubbles.

121. **Model**: "A quantitative method, system, or approach that applies statistical, economic, financial or mathematical theories, techniques and assumptions to process input data into quantitative estimates." (definition set forth by the Board of Governors of the Federal Reserve and the Office of the Comptroller of the Currency).

122. **Model Risk**: When analysts or investors use models, they may not completely understand their assumptions and limitations, which limit their usefulness. Worse than that, it may lead to a self-fulfilling crisis if all agents trust a wrong model, creating a deadlock.

123. **Multi-Year Rescheduling Agreement (MYRA)**: An arrangement for postponing principal repayments. It first emerged in the mid-1980s in commercial bank negotiations to "smooth" amortization profiles and reduce the administrative and other costs associated with more frequent (annual) rescheduling.

124. **Negative Pledge clause**: Granting of security interests by a debtor country over its assets to its creditors. In the case of a debt refinancing agreement, the debtor country agrees with the banks not to provide any other group of creditors with security interest on the country's reserves, exports of goods, and public sector companies' assets. The objective of such a clause is to prevent a situation where a debtor would allocate significant assets to other creditors, thereby effectively subordinating the unsecured bank credits.

125. **Net Debt/GDP (%)**: Gross external debt minus general government financial assets (cash, deposits, loans, official reserve assets, and equity holdings) as a percent of GDP.

126. **Net Flows on Debts**: Disbursements minus principal repayments, i.e., excess of new lending over amortization payments.

127. **Net Resource Flows**: Sum of net resource flows on long-term debt plus net FDI, portfolio equity flows, and official grants.

128. **Net Transfers**: New disbursement minus amortization (i.e., principal debt service) and interest payments. As such, net transfers are equivalent to net flows minus interest.

129. **New Money Bonds**: Bonds issued by debtor countries in exchange for additional financing. Such instruments are usually more senior and tradable than old claims.

130. **New Money**: Loans arranged for budgetary or balance of payments support in conjunction with debt rescheduling, usually in propor-

tion to each creditor banks' exposure, in order to enforce comparability of treatment among creditors.

131. **Net Present Value (NPV)**: The sum of all future debt service obligations (interest and principal) on existing debt, discounted at the appropriate market rate. Whenever the interest rate on a loan is lower than the market rate, the resulting NPV of debt is smaller than its face value. Also, the NPV of a project investment led abroad must integrate the Country Risk. The higher the Country Risk, the higher the discount rate and the lower the investment project NPV.

132. **Non-debt Creating Flows**: Net FDI, portfolio equity flows, and official grants (excluding technical cooperation) that finance a current account deficit without increasing external liabilities.

133. **Nonfinancial Debt**: Consists of credit instruments issued by governmental entities, households, and businesses that are not included in the financial sector (loans made to households in the form of mortgages, bank loans to corporations, or corporate bonds they have issued to raise money, etc.).

134. **Nonperforming Loans (NPLs)**: A loan in which interest and principal payments are more than ninety days overdue; or more than ninety days' worth of interest has been refinanced, capitalized, or rescheduled by agreement of the parties.

135. **Official Development Assistance (ODA)**: Disbursements of loans (net of repayments of principal) and grants made on concessional terms by official agencies of the members of the Development Assistance Committee of the OECD to promote economic development and welfare in recipient developing countries. Loans with a grant element of more than 25% are included in ODA, as are technical cooperation and assistance.

136. **Organization for Economic Co-Operation and Development (OECD)**: Based in Paris, its membership comprises thirty-five "industrialized" developed countries. It was set up in 1960 by twenty countries to promote economic growth and the expansion of world trade. Its recent members are Mexico (just before the 1994 "Tequila" crisis) and South Korea (just before the 1998 Asian crisis), and still more recently, Israel, Slovak Republic, and Estonia in 2010.

137. **Off-balance Sheet Activities**: Bank activities, often fee-based, that do not involve booking assets or taking deposits. (Examples include insurance, derivatives, LCs, and forms of advisory assistance).

138. **Official Creditor**: This includes (i) official bilateral creditors (governments or their appropriate institutions), including Paris Club

members; and (ii) multilateral creditors (international institutions such as the IMF, the World Bank, or regional development banks).

139. **Overseas Private Investment Corporation (OPIC)**: A US government agency that was established in 1971 to help US business invest in overseas markets. It is backed by the full faith and credit of the United States.

140. **Optional Prepayment Provision**: The optional prepayment provision permits the borrower to prepay all or part of the loan, provided that it prepays all lenders under the agreement on a pro rata basis.

141. **OTC Derivatives**: Privately negotiated derivatives transactions that are not traded on any organized exchange.

142. **Outstanding Amounts (Paris Club Issue)**: This amount is divided into three parts: principal, interest, and total amount. The amount of total outstanding debt must be equal to the sum of all the maturities and arrears. The amount of principal outstanding is the sum of all arrears (principal and interest) plus all future maturities in principal. The amount of interest outstanding must be equal to the sums of all the future maturities in interest.

143. **Par Bonds (Brady)**: Registered thirty-year bullet amortization issued at par, i.e., at the original face value of the sovereign loan, with fixed rate semiannual below market coupon. Usually, par bonds are backed by collateral (with zero-coupon bond) as well as a rolling interest guarantee.

144. **Paris Club**: An informal group of twenty-two official bilateral creditors whose role is to find coordinated and sustainable debt restructuring solutions to the payment difficulties experienced by debtor nations. Paris Club creditors may agree to reschedule, refinance, reduce, or restructure debts due to them, with prior macroeconomic adjustment programs under the monitoring of the IMF. The first meeting with a debtor country was held in 1956 when Argentina agreed to meet its public creditors in Paris. Since then, the Paris Club creditors have reached 433 agreements concerning ninety debtor countries. The total amount of debt covered in these agreements has been USD 590 billion. In spite of such an activity, the Paris Club has remained strictly informal. It is the voluntary gathering of creditor countries willing to provide developing countries with debt relief. It can be described as a "non-institution." Although the Paris Club is not a formal legal entity, it functions through a set of specific rules and principles.

145. **Prepayment Clause**: The prepayment clause is a standard clause in loan agreements between a debtor and a creditor bank. In its various forms, it can provide the debtor with the opportunity to accelerate repayment of the loan on a voluntary basis and/or provide for acceleration of repayment due to changes in laws affecting the creditor. In rescheduling agreements, the clause is intended to prevent the obligor to grant a preferential repayment schedule to other banks which have not signed the convention and which would be paid ahead of normal maturity terms.
146. **Primary Balance/GDP (%)**: Deficit minus interest payments on general government debt, as a percent of GDP.
147. **Principal in Arrears on Long-term Debt**: Principal repayment due but not paid, on a cumulative basis.
148. **Principal Repayments**: The amounts of principal (amortization) paid in foreign currency, goods, or services in the year specified.
149. **Private Nonguaranteed External Debt**: The external obligation of a private debtor that is not guaranteed for repayment by a public entity.
150. **Procedural Uncertainty**: A form of uncertainty that arises out of the computational and cognitive capabilities of individuals faced with decisions about the future. It comes in degrees and needs to be understood in relation to the complexity of a situation being assessed. Accordingly, it can result if either (i) there are limitations in computational or cognitive abilities of individuals in assessing their choices or (ii) a situation may be sufficiently complicated that it cannot be fully assessed even with the most robust computational and cognitive capabilities.
151. **Provisioning**: The setting aside of a financial institution's resources to cover potential losses from bad loans. Loan-loss provisions against bad claims can be tax deductible according to specific national banking regulations.
152. **Public Debt**: External obligations of a public debtor, including the direct and guaranteed debt of the central government, obligations of regional and local governments, and the nonguaranteed debt of other public sector entities, as well as autonomous public bodies.
153. **Public Sector**: Public sector is defined (unless otherwise specified) as the government of the debtor country, as well as the companies or other entities under governmental control (where the government has a direct or indirect share of 50% or more).
154. **Repudiation**: Unilateral disclaiming of a liability by a debtor.

155. **Refinancing**: Conversion of arrears and all or part of the original debt into a new loan.
156. **Rescheduling**: Formal deferment and re-timing of the principal due on a loan, with the application of new maturities to the deferred amounts. Regarding Paris Club debt agreements, they might include interest rescheduling in place of new money.
157. **Reserves**: External reserve assets that are readily available (liquid holdings, SDRs, and gold) and controlled by monetary authorities for direct financing of external payments imbalances, and for indirectly regulating the magnitudes of such imbalances through intervention in exchange markets to affect the currency exchange rate, and/or for other purposes.
158. **Reserves/Imports (in months)**: Official foreign exchange reserves (including gold at market prices) divided by monthly imports of goods and services.
159. **Risk**: A term that is often used synonymous with "uncertainty," but has also been defined in various ways for various purposes. One particularly useful definition classifies risk as a subset of uncertainty and is the set of conditions where we know both the set of potential outcomes and the probabilities of such outcomes, such as in the toss of a coin. (See also Ambiguity and Uncertainty.) But many "risk concepts" are usually associated, like the following ones:

    - **Risk appetite**: The aggregate amount of risk a company is willing to accept in pursuit of its projects and risk strategy (ex: investment of x% of the capital in illiquid assets). Risk appetite may vary across an organization.
    - **Risk Exposure**: A firm's vulnerability to some risk factors (including Country Risk).
    - **Risk Tolerance**: Specific maximum threshold applicable to each category of risk (ex: the duration of all bonds in a company's portfolio should not exceed seven years).
    - **Risk Limit**: Threshold to ensure that variation in the expected outcome will be consistent with the risk target, but will not exceed the risk appetite/tolerance.
    - **Inherent Risk**: Those fundamental exposures that are a consequence of an organization's mission. They are "part of doing business." Inherent risk can often be reduced or mitigated through controls, careful risk assessment, medium-term risk planning, or other steps.

- **Residual Risk**: The level or extent of exposure that remains after an organization introduces risk controls or other steps to mitigate the inherent risk to a lower desired level.
- **Downside Risk**: the amount of loss that could be sustained as a result of a decline. Depending on the measure used, downside risk explains a worst case scenario for an investment or indicates how much the investor stands to lose.

160. **Revolving Underwriting Facility (RUF)**: Medium-term facility on which the borrower can draw at any time of its life, usually certificates of deposits (CDs) or short-term promissory notes.
161. **Secular Stagnation**: The threat of secular stagnation has been identified in 1938 by Alvin Harvey Hansen (1887–1975), known as the "American Keynes." His conclusion comes from his observation of long-term structural headwinds, including population growth decline, technological innovation, and productivity reduction, all leading to the growth slowdown. Hansen's solution is boosting public spending. Robert Gordon argues that slow potential real GDP growth is also meaningful—both because of its direct impact on the standard of living and its indirect effect in reducing net investment, which in turn is expressed in slower productivity growth. Gordon identifies a number of underlying causes, including demography, education, and rising debt, while pointing out growing inequalities and slow productivity growth. Growth slowdown stems from the diminishing returns of the digital electronics revolution and a decline in the "dynamism" of the US economy as measured by the rate of creation of new firms.
162. **Securitization**: The process in which banks' assets become more marketable and with enhanced liquidity through the substitution of floating rate notes for syndicated lending, the introduction of transferability into international credits, the exchange of loans for collateralized bonds, and the packaging of existing assets for resale.
163. **A Self-fulfilling Crisis**: A crisis that is less triggered by weak underlying fundamentals (high debt ratios, large current account deficits, declining reserve assets) but rather by the pessimistic expectations of investors, or the snowballing effect of rating agencies downgrading. The decline in FDI, shorter credit maturities, and capital flight will precipitate and worsen the financial crisis.
164. **Set-Aside Funds**: The World Bank approved procedures to support debt reduction in May of 1989 by setting aside 25% of a country's

adjustment lending program over a three-year period (or 10% of its overall lending program) to guarantee principal reduction. An increment of up to 15% of the overall three-year program can be made available for interest support. The IMF's Executive Board approved that around 25% of a country's access to IMF resources be set aside to support operations involving debt principal reduction. The IMF may also approve additional funding up to 40% of the member's quota for interest support in connection with debt service reduction transactions.

165. **Shadow Banking**: Financial disintermediation (through "Nonbank financial institutions") outside the monitoring of central bank authorities, including wealth funds and intercompany credit lines. Nonbank financing increases leverage and transforms maturity/liquidity in financial systems while increasing the money supply. To monitor these risks, the Financial Stability Board conducts annual assessment exercises since 2011.

166. **Sharing Provisions**: A legal covenant in commercial bank agreements which specifies that debt service payments are to be made through the agent bank for allocation on a pro rata basis to all creditor banks. Further, payments received or recovered by any lender must be shared on a pro rata basis with all co-creditors under the loan agreement. Thus, no lender may be placed in a more favorable position than its co-lenders with respect to payments received and/or recovered.

167. **Short-term External Debt**: Debt that has an original maturity of one year or less. Available data permit no distinction between public and private nonguaranteed short-term debt.

168. **Short-term Credits**: Credits that have an original maturity of one year or less. Maturity is defined as the difference between the last principal repayment and the date when the credit starts (usually from the disbursement or the delivery of the goods). All other credits, having an original maturity of more than one year, are medium- and long-term credits.

169. **SKEW (CBOE Index)**: An index, developed by the Chicago Board Options Exchange, that is a measure of perceived volatility of extreme risk in the S&P 500 Index over a thirty-day period. It is similar to the VIX, except that it is based on non-normal distribution so as to capture extreme risk, often referred to as "tail risk." (See VIX index.)

170. **Solvency**: Country's ability to meet the present value of its external obligations. In theory, countries are solvent as long as the present value of net interest payments does not exceed the present value of current inflows (primarily exports) net of imported inputs. In practice, countries stop servicing their debt (long before) when the country's economic and social costs are perceived too high. Hence, the willingness to pay is more important than the theoretical ability.
171. **Solvency ratios**: Ratios assessing the stock of debt of a debtor country, for instance, Total External Debt/Export and Total External Debt/GDP (See also Debt Overhang, Reserves/Imports.)
172. **Sovereign Credit Ratings**: Quantitative assessment of a government's ability and willingness to service its foreign debt in full and on time. A rating is a forward-looking estimate of default probability.
173. **Special Data Dissemination Standard (SDDS)**: The IMF's work on data dissemination standards began in 1995 with the Fund's establishment of standards to guide member countries in the public circulation of their economic and financial data. These standards consist of two tiers: the General data dissemination system (GDDS) that applies to all Fund members, and the more demanding Special standards (SDDS), for those countries having or seeking access to international capital markets.
174. **Special Drawing Rights (SDRs)**: International reserve asset created by the IMF in 1969 to supplement countries' official reserves in case of liquidity difficulties. Roughly USD 300 billion have been issued since the inception of the program. Since 2016, the SDR value is based on a basket of five "global" currencies, including the USD (42%), the Euro (31%), the Yen (11%), the Pound Sterling (8%), and the Chinese Renminbi.
175. **Standard & Poor's (S&P)**: One of the so-called "Big Three" credit rating agencies. The other two include Moody's and Fitch.
176. **Stand-by Credit**: A commitment to lend up to a specified amount for a specific period, to be used only in a certain contingency. A commitment fee is paid on the unused portion of the credit.
177. **Stock Treatment (Paris Club Clause)**: As opposed to standard flow treatments, some Paris Club terms apply not only to the payments falling due in a particular period of time but to the whole stock of debt from which those payments fall due. The aim of the stock debt reduction is to provide a country with a final treatment by the Paris Club.

178. **Subordinated Debt**: Debt that is payable only after other debts with a higher ranking have been repaid; it is generally listed in a firm's capital structure between equity and senior debt.
179. **Subrogation Rights**: In contracts of indemnity, they allow the insurer to take over the rights of the assured against any third party who is responsible for a loss in respect of which the insurer has made a claim payment.
180. **Suppliers Credit**: Export finance that consists in installment payments (or deferred payment terms) provided by a supplier to a buyer of imported goods and services.
181. **Syndication**: Loan syndication in the Eurodollar market takes the form of a contractual arrangement by a group of banks (the "lead banks") to share a loan that is too large for one bank to make. Loan syndication is a risk mitigation tool in the banking industry.
182. **Systemic Risk**: The risk of an event affecting the whole international financial system, arising from a major spillover effect. A chain reaction-driven collapse can be triggered by regional crisis contamination and/or by the liquidity or solvency crisis of a leading financial institution. Sometimes also referred as a "domino" or "snowballing effect."
183. **TED Spread**: An acronym formed by T-Bill and ED, the ticker symbol for the Eurodollar futures contract. It measured the difference between the interest rates for three-month US government debt (T-Bill) and the three-month Eurodollars contract (through LIBOR rate). The TED spread indicates the "perceived credit risk" in the financial markets.
184. **Tombstone**: An advertisement that lists the managers, underwriters, and providers of a recently completed syndicate or bond offering.
185. **Topping-up (Paris Club Clause)**: In a subsequent debt reduction, granting more debt reduction on debt the Paris Club previously reduced to provide even further debt relief (e.g., when increasing the cancellation level from 33.33% of Toronto terms to 67% of Naples terms and to 80% under the Lyon terms).
186. **Trade Openness Ratio**: Measure of economic openness of a country in the globalized market economy by dividing the sum of exports and imports of goods and services by the country's GDP. ASEAN countries' ratios reach roughly 200%.
187. **Unallocated Loan-loss Reserves**: Value of anticipated future charge-offs on the existing loan portfolio that cannot yet be identified with any particular asset.

188. **Uncertainty**: A term that has been defined in different ways, but one useful definition is that it refers to any condition for which the particular outcome is not known. The set of potential outcomes may be known or unknown. Uncertainty can, therefore, be considered a broad concept that includes both risk and ambiguity. (See Risk and Uncertainty.)
189. **United Nations Conference on Trade and Development (UNCTAD)**: Established in 1964 as a permanent body of the UN, it deals with trade, development, and direct foreign investment issues.
190. **United Nations Program for Development (UNDP)**: The United Nations Development Program promotes a global development network "to eradicate poverty, reduce inequalities, and protect the planet". It administers the UN Capital Development Fund, which helps developing countries grow their economies by supplementing existing sources of capital assistance by means of grants and loans. The annual Human Development Index measures long-term structural inputs such as GDP per capita, wealth distribution, education, gender inequality, and demographic trends.
191. **Value Recovery Clause**: Clause included in some commercial bank debt restructuring agreements that entitle creditor banks to recover a larger portion of their loans, subject to a specific condition related with a better than expected performance of the debtor country. It is usually associated with the international price of a good or a basket of goods exported by the debtor country, or to its real GDP growth rate. This clause has been used for Mexico and Côte d'Ivoire.
192. **Variable interest Debt**: External debt with interest rates that float with movements in a key market-based rate such as the six-month London Interbank Offered Rate (LIBOR) or the US prime rate.
193. **VIX (CBOE Index)**: An index, published by the Chicago Board Options Exchange, which indicates the equity market's expectation of 30-day volatility based on the implied volatilities of the price of a wide range of S&P Index options, both calls and puts. Unlike the SKEW, this index assumes a normal distribution of prices. (See also SKEW).
194. **Waiver**: Voluntary relinquishment of a legal right as provided for in the loan agreement for the duration of a specified time period or an indefinite period.
195. **Warrant**: Options that permit the holder to buy stock for a stated price, thereby providing a capital gain if the price of the stock rises.

Bonds that are issued with warrants, like convertibles, carry lower coupon rates than straight bonds.

196. **Washington Consensus**: Initially developed by British economist John Williamson in 1989, it refers to a set of ten market-based economic policies including budget deficit reduction, trade liberalization, and privatization, in a general institutional environment of good governance.
197. **Wealth Gap**: The result of long-term income distribution distortion that can be measured by the GINI Index which is a statistical measure of distribution and a gauge of economic inequality. The coefficient ranges from 0 to 1, with 0 representing perfect equality and 1 representing perfect inequality. The Gini index is provided by several agencies, including the World Bank's Development Research Group, the OECD, the St Louis Fed, and the UNDP.
198. **World Bank Group**: Created in 1945 together with the IMF, the World Bank is composed of the IBRD, the IFC, IDA, and MIGA. World Bank Group commitments grew to more than USD 61 billion in loans, grants, equity investments, and guarantees supporting countries and private businesses in fiscal year 2016. IBRD issued a record USD 64 billion in bonds in the international capital markets to support sustainable development programs in client countries.
199. **World Economic Forum Global Competitiveness**: An annual ranking, compiled by the World Economic Forum, which assesses a country's competitive landscape, examining drivers of productivity and prosperity.
200. **Write-off Debt**: Removal from the creditor's balance sheet of obligations due from a debtor but unpaid and regarded as uncollectible. While this presents a "clean" balance sheet for the creditor bank, it need not mean that the creditor is abandoning claims against the debtor. In contrast, if a debt is forgiven, it has to be written off.
201. **Zero-coupon Bonds**: Bonds that do not pay periodic interest so that the total yield is obtained entirely as a capital gain on the final maturity date, through a "snowballing effect." Useful to collateralize long-term bullet bond repayment in debt restructuring transactions.

Country Risk: By Way of Conclusion

Our book might not deal with all the daunting economic, financial, and sociopolitical challenges that country risk managers will confront today and tomorrow. One of our objectives has been to present the changing nature of Country Risk as well as the range of approaches to reduce uncertainty and predict turmoil. Consequently, one of our conclusions is that there is no one reliable compass for assessing the multifaceted dimensions of Country Risk. The dynamics of a country's complex trajectory, as well as its interactions with the global economic system, are much too complex to be captured by mathematical formulae, econometric models, and ratings—even though all of these give the reassuring (but illusory) comfort of being "hard science." Numbers can be misleading as has been shown by the capitalist market economy's long series of sociopolitical and financial crises.

If we compare Country Risk today with the environment until the late 1990s, we must keep in mind seven new features relevant to the current global economy.

First, let us look at the useful analogy between quantum mechanics and Country Risk: both deal with uncertainty and both consider that what is true at a microlevel is not necessarily true at a macrolevel. Heisenberg's principle stipulates that the more precisely a particle's position is determined, the less precisely the momentum is known at that instant, and vice versa. Concisely, this means it is impossible to measure a particle's exact position and exact momentum at the same time. The somewhat similar "observer effect" in physics notes that measurements of certain systems cannot be made without affecting them. This relationship has important implications for such fundamental notions as causality and the determination of future behavior.

M. H. Bouchet et al., *Managing Country Risk in an Age of Globalization*,
https://doi.org/10.1007/978-3-319-89752-3

In terms of Country Risk, pinpointing the risk boils down to influencing the risk momentum. This is due to a combination of forces, including herd instinct, speculation, and the echo chamber effect of the globalized market economy. In practice, this means that rating changes generate spillover effects as well as the country reports of international organizations, but also the country risk forecasts of specialized agencies. Each of these country risk measures alters the noise/signal balance and propagates waves of risk adjustment decisions worldwide.

Second, transparency efforts and communication networks have become an essential feature of the current situation. Countries compete with each other to get market access via a regular flow of quality information. Rating agencies and international institutions monitor these efforts and assess the quality of data and economic intelligence. In turn, fund managers, investors, creditors, and bank depositors are inundated by an excess of information that requires careful discrimination and cross checking. Consequently, the globalization of information can generate rising volatility of capital flows and crisis propagation. The wide availability and instant transmission of information combine to trigger the herd instinct and self-fulfilling prophecies that result in spillover effects and crisis contamination. An excess of information and knowledge can generate uncertainty. Combining a wide range of approaches remains crucial for assessing the underlying causes of sociopolitical and financial upheaval, as well as their timing.

The third new dimension of Country Risk is that the framework itself has become volatile. Since World War II until roughly the 1970s, risk managers lived in a world of fixed exchange rates, the stalemate of the Cold War, the stabilizing role of international financial institutions, the moral promises of liberal democracy, and the social promises of technical progress—all of these functioned within the frame of undisputed US leadership. Today, liberal democracies have lost much of their legitimacy while discontent has been fueled by distorted income and wealth distribution. One of our conclusions has been that developing countries have lost the monopoly on Country Risk. Brexit—whatever its practical and institutional design—will undermine the strength of the European Union at a time when Eastern European countries adhere less to the core values of the region's integration project. Looser financial regulations in the United States might be welcomed by investors on Wall Street but such policies also create the conditions for a new round of financial crisis when rising rates will hurt overindebted corporate and private debtors. Finally, a high level of sovereign debt in most OECD countries constitutes budgetary obstacles for boosting public sector infrastructure and social investment projects.

Fourth, there seems to exist an inherent contradiction between liberal democracy and a market-based economic system. Rising wealth gaps and purchasing power stagnation lead to social polarization, generating centrifugal forces that may only be stemmed thanks to a robust and respected institution or authoritarian regimes. In the United States, as in most developed countries, there is a widening polarization between wage earners and capital owners. The spectrum of secular stagnation, with its expanding wealth gaps in most developed countries, has generated feelings of mistrust vis-à-vis political elites that seem at best unable, or at worst unwilling, to offset the brutality of the globalized market economy. In developed and developing countries, sociopolitical institutions are less and less effective in mediating social demands during the modernization process. These institutions still appear too weak in developing countries and seem less and less legitimate in developed countries. Political ineffectiveness in the age of globalization generates frustration and violence outside the traditional channels of social mobilization such as unions and political parties. Country risk analysts must ask themselves "where is the Prince?" and where are the major power circles in a country and exactly how do these interact?

The fifth new dimension is that "America First" and the strategic withdrawal from Washington-led multilateralism pave the way for competition, an additional vehicle of volatility. Retrenchment is never a source of trade openness or a level playing field for negotiations. Consequently, the condition of the global economy is named as a major threat by more than half those polled by Pew Research Center across thirty-eight countries. Practically speaking, China will fill the power vacuum wherever it can. This includes the ASEAN region, Eastern Europe (that is the end point of the "One Road-One Belt" strategy), and Africa, where large infrastructure credits flow without the conditions imposed by the IMF and the World Bank and their Western donors. We must, therefore, conclude that improvements in transparency and governance and efforts to tackle corruption will remain wishes rather than reality. This, of course, has an impact on Country Risk, with consequences on capital flight and social turmoil. The gloomy outlook of our conclusion must be strengthened by the inevitable consequences of the next recession, given that every business cycle ends and the 2009–2017 growth cycle is reaching its limits, certainly in the United States. An economic downturn can be triggered by a blend of exogenous factors (rising oil prices on the back of Middle East turmoil, bursting bubbles in China, or global trade contraction), and endogenous factors (a stock market meltdown in the OECD, a political crisis in the United States, the fragmentation of the EU). But whatever the underlying causes, the global integration of markets will make this future downturn even more dramatic than before.

The sixth dimension has to do with technological change and its impact on Country Risk. Reportedly, Peter Drucker summed up the impact of the NTIC revolution on management saying: "You can't manage what you can't measure." The goal of Big Data management is to make available a high level of data quality and variety for business intelligence with applications for investment funds, banks, corporations, government agencies, and other official organizations. Data-driven country risk assessment has developed since the late 1990s and accelerated since the outbreak of the Global Financial Crisis.

The fast emergence of Big Data technologies has already started transforming the world of risk management and it too has an impact, albeit more indirect, on the world of country risk management. Big Data provides risk managers with access to high-volume, high-velocity, and high-accuracy information inputs in the process of defining, assessing, and managing risks. The impact is overwhelming in the global financial services industry. Credit risk, market risk, and credit counterparty risk quantification have become much more complex and they require complex and numerous data, intensive calculations, including Monte Carlo scenarios. The accessibility and accuracy of Big Data enhance transparency, hence reducing uncertainty and risk.

In the field of Country Risk, where qualitative assessment is as important as quantitative measures, the impact is still more subdued. In country risk assessment, Big Data management imposes specific constraints to check the accuracy and quality of large stores of country economic, financial, and sociopolitical data whose format must be as standardized as possible. Nevertheless, given the rapidly rising level of digitized business transactions, country risk managers can use a growing volume of new data, including from social networks, to assess the magnitude and evolution of markets in remote countries. Country risk scenarios, such as financial and economic volatility, can be simulated in far greater detail by using the new technologies and their computational power. The consequence of exchange rate volatility, for instance, on official reserve assets, the balance of payments, inflation, and trade competitiveness can be calculated with much better accuracy than before, including by integrating the situation of neighbor countries. The spillover of a national and regional crisis can also be modelized with more accuracy. Demographic data, purchasing power, financial ratios, and a number of macroeconomic data can be combined across time and across countries to provide a reliable picture of the scope of a market in a number of Countries, provided these data are available. Practically, Big Data today is the world of only one-fourth of countries in the world, roughly fifty countries, including the thirty-five members that belong to the OECD.

The assessment of Country Risk thus has the potential to change in many new ways that result from rapidly evolving and promising new technological developments in the field of computer science, including artificial intelligence, machine learning, and robotics. Whereas the country risk managers once thought mainly about loans, bonds, and export finance, today they must understand complicated models and financial transactions such as credit derivatives. Once their tools were a Hewlett Packard financial calculator backed up by Excel spreadsheets; now they work with large databases, smartphones, and tablets. Whereas the prior generation of country risk managers wore tailored suits and silk ties and went out to lunch, the new generation may be inclined to wear jeans, t-shirts, and sandals. While they may look different, their minds are deeply engaged in how to understand the world, now equipped with data, software, and computing power that once seemed unimaginable.

Our final conclusion must be that the world has become a place of enhanced risk and uncertainty. Geopolitical multipolarity and the US retrenchment are paving the way for accidents in the Middle East, Iran, North Korea, Yemen, Venezuela, China, and Russia, among other places. There are also many more candidates for sociopolitical crises that might not yet have a global impact. Cyber attacks and global terrorism from state and non-state actors are also now threats for the longer term.

Overall, we will need to continue exploring the varied dimensions of Country Risk. Every day, it seems, brings us a new issue to reflect on—and then we are confronted with perhaps the most challenging question of all—namely, what do we do next? How well are we protected against adverse consequences? Are we prepared if new challenges suddenly arise? Does any new set of circumstances provide us with a new opportunity that can benefit our stakeholders? Are we prepared for the unexpected (that would require a combination of robust economic intelligence and intellectual agility) so as to be able to embrace new forms of insecurity? Do we have the programs, people, data, and systems to help imagine a future that looks very different from the present?

The authors hope that reflection on the evolving nature of Country Risk (and the appropriate methods to address it) will continue unabated. They invite private and public organizations to invest in additional resources and people to assess and respond to the volatility of Country Risk. In addition, Country Risk deserves to be better incorporated into the academic community, into the curricula of business schools, public policy programs, and universities. Currently, only a small number of schools make use of practitioners and analysts to undertake research and train future leaders in this exciting topic. Country Risk stands at the confluence of the fields of economics, finance, public policy, statistics, political science, sociology, history, and neuroscience. Its interdisciplinary nature remains today one of its most promising strengths for future progress.

Afterword by Florencio de Silanes

Country Risk in an Age of Globalization may at first appeal to those who are seeking an "answer" for the management of Country Risk—whether in the form of risk committees, top risks lists, ratios, thresholds, country ratings, and rankings. Yet upon closer reflection, the seasoned and demanding analyst will realize that simple quantitative risk assessments are often quick fixes that provide a comforting but also deceptive compass. Today, the global financial system—shaped by a complex set of spillover effects, herd instincts, and sudden rises in volatility—requires a more careful evaluation than the one provided by traditional risk yardsticks. This is the authors' first warning: quantitative risk measures are at best partial tools and at worst recipes for a simplistic outlook.

In this context, the authors stress throughout the book that gathering information and enhancing the quality of economic intelligence are key for mitigating uncertainty and improving risk management. Uncertainty is an essential aspect of Country Risk as it is deeply rooted in information deficits regarding the present and in the future, which is rapidly changing in novel and unexpected ways. As the authors argue, there is no magic formula, and any quest for a simple Holy Grail may be misleading in a world where a phenomenon similar to the "observer effect" in physics is at play. In other words, pinpointing risks may also influence risk momentum. Measures of Country Risk alter the noise/signal balance and propagate waves of risk adjustment decisions worldwide.

These useful warnings do not lead to fatalism and resignation, however. The authors recommend "scrutinizing the possible in order to anticipate the inevitable." This requires risk managers to decide which forces could stabilize or damage countries' socioeconomic systems over the medium and the

M. H. Bouchet et al., *Managing Country Risk in an Age of Globalization*,
https://doi.org/10.1007/978-3-319-89752-3

long-term horizons. This is a formidable challenge since developing countries with weak sociopolitical institutions are no longer the exclusive sources of volatility. As *Country Risk in an Age of Globalization* emphasizes, volatility risk is no longer rooted in the so-called Third World. Developed countries with mature and stable economies and apparently robust institutional frameworks are also subject to sociopolitical turbulence. The emerging risks of instability in developed nations are caused by a combination of several factors, such as wealth gaps, large debt burdens, tax evasion, and, more pervasively, a gradual dissatisfaction with established political leaders in deeply rooted democratic systems. Finally, to make risk assessment still more complex, risk does no longer exclusively affect foreign investors and creditors. Domestic residents across countries, including those in the OECD, might feel beset with Country Risk when faced with the arbitrary decisions of government that generate inflation or reduce output, inconsistent growth cycles, and political uncertainty. Indeed, the irony is that managers who deliberately choose to refocus on local markets to reduce the uncertainty of cross-border investment now face the turbulence of Country Risk in its domestic form.

Three crucial questions run throughout the chapters of this book. The first one asks: "Can one develop reliable early warning signals of Country Risk which help us avoid getting caught off guard by abrupt risk shifts?" The authors start providing an answer by analyzing and testing an interesting forward-looking measure of Country Risk: how domestic residents manage their savings, which is proxied by capital flight. The argument is that in order to understand the complexities of Country Risk, it may be useful to analyze the risks embedded in a country's matrix of social, political, and economic forces. When citizens consistently transfer their money abroad—a process which incurs both costs and risks—country risk managers should "pay attention." If citizens suddenly shift their savings in offshore banking accounts, this arbitrage may be worth the analyst's attention. In short, the authors make an argument and empirically show that expatriated private savings matter and that this variable may be a useful measure that helps capture the volatility and uncertainty in the system.

The two other questions running through the book are: "What are the root causes of socio-economic instability?" and "How can countries move from economic growth toward inclusive and sustainable development?" These two questions touch on the field of research close to my own academic interest for years. The authors do a very good job summarizing a large body of academic research that explores the relationship between economic growth and institutions. However, the book's objective is not to participate in this debate but, more prudently, to alert country risk managers of the importance of institutional buildup in emerging market countries and institutional resilience in developed countries. This issue is of high interest not only for the academic community, but also for country policymakers and officials of international financial institutions. Institutions are less volatile than economic or financial structures and they cover the fundamental rules that hold social and business systems together. Although we have made progress in showing that this is the case, there is still not much consensus regarding the order of priorities between political stability and institutional building in order to boost economic development. Should one give priority to sociopolitical order and democracy, to human capital accumulation, or to robust legal institutions? My colleagues and I have shown that empirical research fails to show that political institutions have a causal effect on economic growth and the evidence rather points to the primacy of human capital and solid legal rules to boost growth. This is bad news for those who consider that democratization yardsticks are adequate toolkits for differentiating risky from stable countries.

As emphasized in *Country Risk in an Age of Globalization*, policy choices matter. This is good news for those who strive to observe and analyze economic policies, financial regulation, investment incentives, property rights, and the evolution of sociopolitical regimes in both developed and developing countries. What is also good news is the timely publication of this book. It will certainly help risk analysts, whether academics or practitioners, to better understand the multifaceted and evolving nature of Country Risk in the globalized economic and geopolitical system where volatility is raging.

SKEMA Professor of Finance and Dean of Research.
Research Associate of the US National Bureau of Economic Research.

Index

M. H. Bouchet et al., *Managing Country Risk in an Age of Globalization*,
https://doi.org/10.1007/978-3-319-89752-3

F

G

S

9783319897516